THE MOSQUE

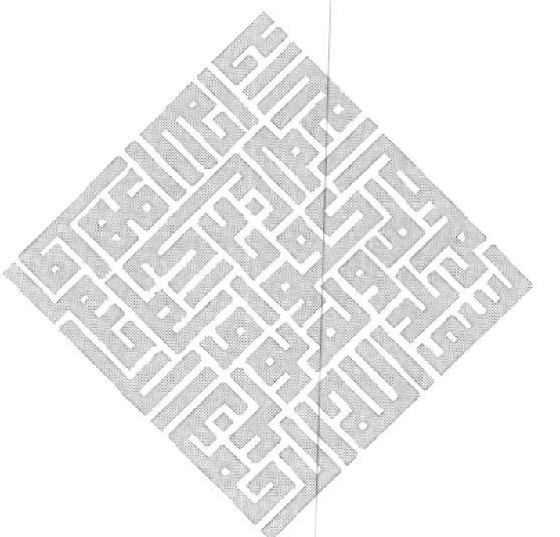

THE MOSQUE

HISTORY, ARCHITECTURAL DEVELOPMENT & REGIONAL DIVERSITY

EDITED BY MARTIN FRISHMAN AND HASAN-UDDIN KHAN

TEXTS BY

MOHAMMAD AL-ASAD ◆ MOHAMMED ARKOUN ◆ ANTONIO FERNÁNDEZ-PUERTAS

MARTIN FRISHMAN ◆ OLEG GRABAR ◆ PERWEEN HASAN ◆ MARK HORTON

HASAN-UDDIN KHAN ◆ DOĞAN KUBAN ◆ LUO XIAOWEI ◆ GÜLRU NECIPOĞLU

BERNARD O'KANE ◆ HUGH O'NEILL ◆ LABELLE PRUSSIN

ISMAIL SERAGELDIN ◆ WHEELER M. THACKSTON

with 378 illustrations, 170 in color

THAMES AND HUDSON

Page 1
llah *as part of a 'maze' designed and written in Kufic script by the Ottoman* *Ahmet Qarahisari (died 1555). The accompanying text is a quotation from* *ın (112:1–4): 'Say, He is the one God, the eternal God, He begets none, neither is He begotten, and none is equal to Him.'*

Frontispiece, page 2
The Ka'ba at Mecca as the centre of the Islamic world: frontispiece from an atlas of 1551 showing the orientation of Muslim countries in relation to Mecca, the vital determining factor in establishing the direction of prayer.

Pages 11, 71, 241
Carved ornament incorporating the name Allah within an interlaced star motif, from the north minaret of the Mosque of al-Hakim (990–1013), Cairo.

First published in the United States of America in 1994 by
Thames and Hudson Inc., 500 Fifth Avenue,
New York, New York 10110

Library of Congress Catalog Card Number 94-60347

ISBN 0-500-34133-8

Printed and bound in Singapore

CONTENTS

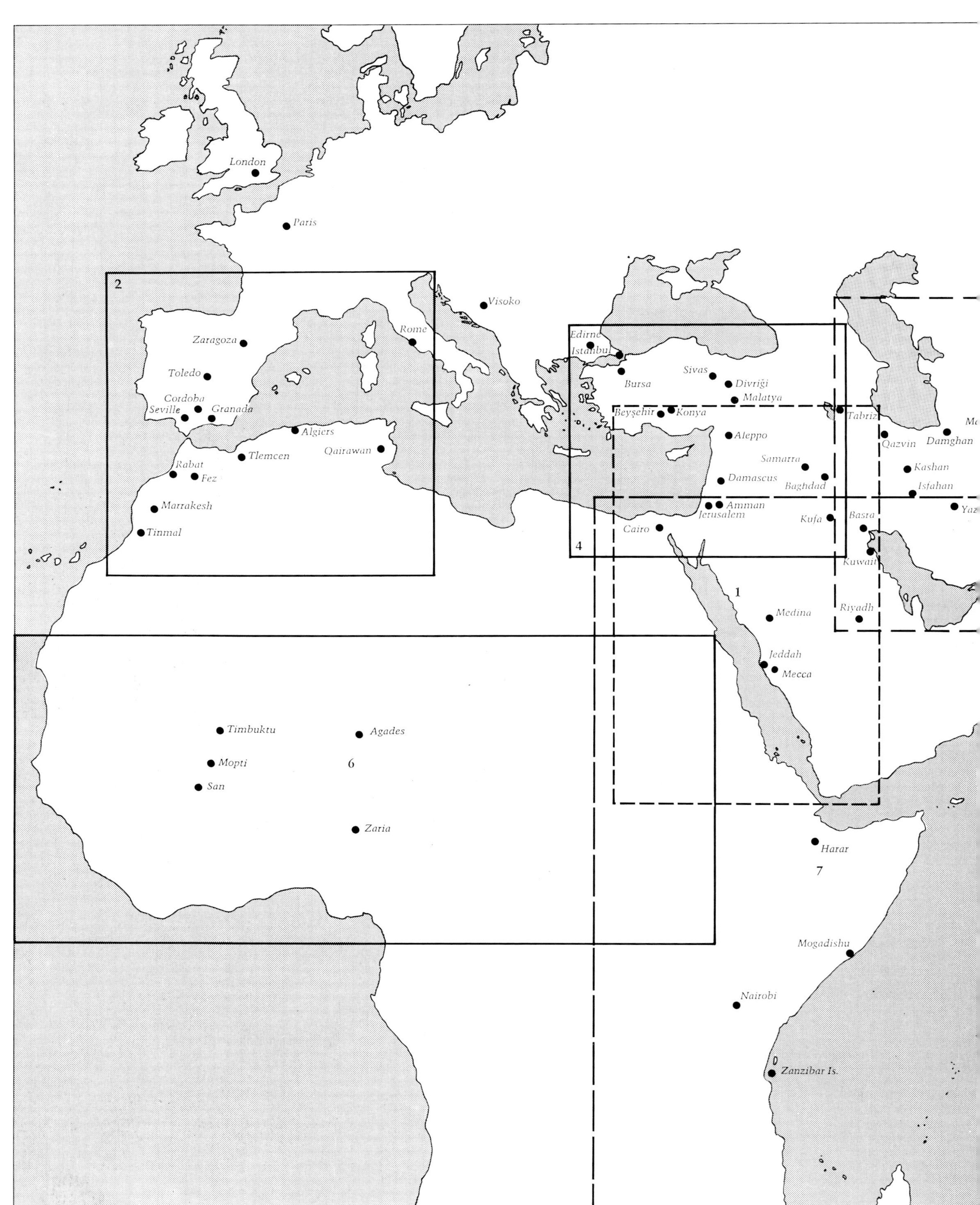

Map of the Muslim world, showing a selection of principal sites of mosques and areas of nine regional maps shown in greater detail in individual chapters.

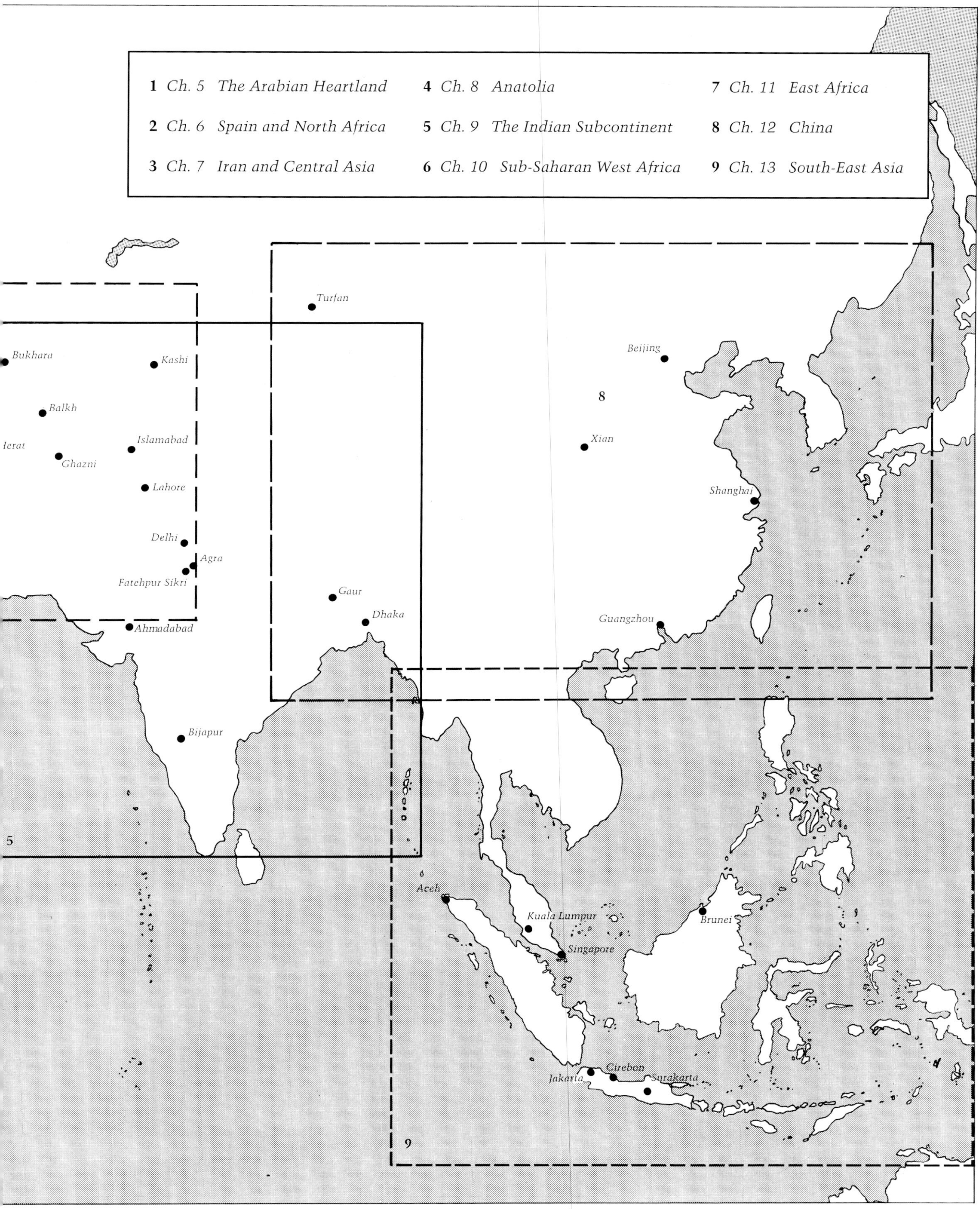

1 *Ch. 5 The Arabian Heartland*
2 *Ch. 6 Spain and North Africa*
3 *Ch. 7 Iran and Central Asia*
4 *Ch. 8 Anatolia*
5 *Ch. 9 The Indian Subcontinent*
6 *Ch. 10 Sub-Saharan West Africa*
7 *Ch. 11 East Africa*
8 *Ch. 12 China*
9 *Ch. 13 South-East Asia*

Turfan
Bukhara
Kashi
Balkh
lerat
Islamabad
Ghazni
Lahore
Delhi
Agra
Fatehpur Sikri
Ahmadabad
Gaur
Dhaka
Bijapur
5
Beijing
8
Xian
Shanghai
Guangzhou
Aceh
Kuala Lumpur
Brunei
Singapore
Jakarta
Cirebon
Surakarta
9

EDITORS' NOTE

THIS book, some four years in the making, is the result of a continuing dialogue between the individual contributors (whose familiarity with and specialized knowledge of the architecture of the mosque in different regions was a crucial factor), the publishers and ourselves. The richness and diversity of the Muslim world, embracing as it does a vast geographical and climatic range and many indigenous, historical and cultural backgrounds and architectural stylistic developments, have provided the basis for the organization of the content region by region. For the sake of simplicity, dates of buildings and historical events follow the Gregorian calendar, with only occasional reference to the Muslim calendar; because it is based on lunar months, the latter requires recourse to detailed conversion tables to calculate the slight annual shift in relation to the Christian calendar. Muslim years are expressed as 'AH' (*Anno Hijrae*), counted from the date of the *hijra*, the Prophet Muhammad's journey from Mecca to Medina (July 622).

Transliterated terms adopted from the original languages (e.g. Arabic, Persian, Urdu) are generally spelled without diacritical signs and are printed in italics, while those in more general use, such as 'caliph' or 'bazaar', are treated as normal English words. An exception to this rule concerning the use of diacriticals is made when passages of Arabic texts, e.g. from the Qur'an, are quoted verbatim. In the case of frequently used words or names which may be found in slightly varying forms in English usage, we have preferred 'Qur'an' to 'Koran', 'Muhammad' to 'Mohammed', '*madrasa*' to '*madrasah*', while a few exceptional localized usages are explained in the context in which they occur. Apart from some familiar forms of place names in general use in English, e.g. Mecca rather than Makkah, the spellings adopted are as listed in the *Times Atlas*, whether transliterated (e.g. from Arabic or Chinese) or normally written in the Roman alphabet (including Turkish).

ACKNOWLEDGMENTS

We are grateful to Oleg Grabar for his generous advice during the life of this project, to Ronald Lewcock for help in clarifying the regional organization of the content, and to Renata Holod, Karen Longeteig and William Porter for valuable comments on individual parts. We also wish to thank Mohammad Arkoun, David Castellero, Amr el-Gohary, Vimal and Gillian Khosla, Suha Özkan, Philip Rogers, Edith Sorel and Brian Taylor, for their advice and support. We are indebted to those contributors who supplied photographs and drawings for use as illustrations, as well as to several institutions. Especially helpful was the Aga Khan Program at Harvard University and the Massachusetts Institute of Technology, through its director, Barbro Ek, and the librarian/archivists Jeffrey Spurr at the Harvard Fine Arts Library and Merrill Smith at MIT's Rotch Library. The archives of the Aga Khan Trust for Culture in Geneva were an important resource, invaluable help having been provided by Farrokh Derakhshani, ably assisted by Nabil Cherouati and Hong Tang-Lam.

Advice from Mokless al-Hariri, Christiane Michaud, Labelle Prussin, Samina Quraeshi and Richard Sheppard helped us explore a wide range of photographic options, but the final choices of subjects to be illustrated were ours. A detailed listing of sources of illustrations appears on p. 284.

No acknowledgments in respect of a subject as complex and wide-ranging as the history of the mosque would be complete without mention of those who helped us with the various manuscripts – Katrina Cocks, Pascale Dufieux and Kitty Tissot – and Kimberley Mims, who undertook research on our behalf. Finally, we wish to place on record our appreciation of the efforts of all those at Thames and Hudson, without whose encouragement and support this project could not have been brought to fruition.

MF
HUK May 1994

PREFACE

THE Muslim world stretches from Spain and West Africa eastwards as far as China and South-East Asia, and the history of its architecture, of which the mosque is an outstanding example, begins in the seventh century of the Christian era. The word 'mosque' is derived from the Arabic *masjid*, meaning literally 'place of prostrations', and the building it describes serves both as a house of worship and as a symbol of Islam. Typologically, the subject of this book is confined to the mosque itself and its emblematic role in the architecture of the Muslim world, hence ancillary buildings such as mausoleums and *madrasas*, which often form part of a mosque complex, are not included.

Today, minarets punctuate the skyline of cities worldwide – a fact which is not surprising given that Muslims comprise around one-fifth of the world's population and constitute a majority in more than forty nations of the Middle East, Asia and Africa. Even though the governments of many countries in the Muslim world (where politics and religion have traditionally been inseparable) have tended to become increasingly secularized, the voice of the muezzin is still heard emanating five times daily from the tops of minarets in every city, town and village, summoning the faithful to prayer. The purpose of the call to prayer – the *adhan* – may be compared to the traditional role of church bells, the sound of which in the modern world tends to be little more than an echo of a long distant past. The *adhan*, however, is still as much a part of the culture of Muslims today as it was for past generations, for much of their world remains firmly set within an Islamic framework that often determines not only the religious practices, but also the laws and the form of government in Muslim societies. The reasons for this are complex and fall outside the scope of this book.

When considering the architecture of the mosque, it is perhaps appropriate to begin by asking why, outside the world of Islam, and even at times within it, so little is yet known about its architectural heritage. To address this question, one might cite the analogy of the muezzin's call and the sound of church bells, both devoted to the common purpose of summoning the faithful to prayer. Symbiotic the causes may indeed appear to be, yet the two sounds have for centuries – at least in the minds of Christians – induced diametrically opposite responses. Within the Western world the familiar sound of church bells may warm the hearts of Christian believers, whereas to the same ears, conditioned by the historical rivalry between Islam and Christendom, the muezzin's call may evoke a sense of strangeness, even of apprehension. This phenomenon could be said to have its roots in the defeat of the Muslim forces by the Christian army near Poitiers in 732 – a military reverse which marked the northernmost limit of the Muslim advance from Spain through France and which was to be followed by centuries of warfare in the name of religion.

Of greater relevance to the subject of the mosque is the ascent of Islamic scholarship to a position of unrivalled eminence in the fields of mathematics, science and the arts from the ninth to the sixteenth centuries – a period often referred to as the 'classical' or golden age of architecture in the Muslim world. In Spain, the period 756 to 1492, embracing the Umayyad dynasty of Cordoba and the Nasrid dynasty of Granada, witnessed the high plateau of Muslim cultural achievement in Europe, as well as an age of religious and cultural integration. The splendid and historically unique days of Judaeo-Christian-Muslim co-existence in Andalusia lasted for over four hundred years until it was brought to a close by the victory of the Christian forces of the *reconquista* and the expulsion of the Moors from Spain. Endless wars were to follow, the Christian world's fears becoming thoroughly aroused when, in 1683, the Imperial Ottoman forces reached and besieged Vienna. Subsequently, the Muslim world was for the most part gradually reduced to a collection of colonies under European rule with, notably, the British in India, the Dutch in the East Indies and the French in North Africa. Despite this expansion of Western rule, however, the Islamic world remained an important presence until the eventual collapse of the Ottoman Empire in the 1920s and with it the transformation of Turkey into a secular state under Kemal Atatürk.

Only after World War II, with the ending of the colonial era and the gradual re-establishment of Muslim sovereign states, would Islam begin to emerge from the 'cultural backwater' to which it had been relegated by its imperial masters. Had the facts of history been otherwise, architectural students throughout the world might have found that the history of architecture in what came to be known as the Third World formed part of their standard curriculum. Instead, if an image of an important Muslim building appeared anywhere, it would generally have been used simply as a decorative motif, e.g. the Taj Mahal mausoleum depicted on a postage stamp. Similarly, bookshop shelves laden with publications covering every aspect of church architecture would have only a few scholarly works on the mosque intended for a specialist readership only. The very terms used to describe the architecture of the Muslim world also stem from the colonial period, when orientalist scholars became interested in the buildings of non-Western cultures. One may cite the fact that the phrase 'Islamic architecture' continues to be used in a world where it would seem strange to speak of 'Christian architecture'. If this book serves its intended purpose, it will help to rectify this anomaly and, we hope, encourage readers to think not in terms of an inappropriate umbrella title such as 'Islamic architecture', but of specific styles like the Egyptian Mamluk, just as they might think of, say, the German Baroque in a European context.

This book, the most comprehensive of its kind, covers the architectural history of the mosque throughout the world. The story of its evolution is presented on a regional rather than a chronological basis because, generally speaking, the differences in architectural style between one geographical area and another within the Muslim world greatly outweigh those resulting from dynastic changes. In the history of Western architecture the differences between churches in the Renaissance and Baroque styles are well known and readily understood, but it takes a somewhat wider knowledge to distinguish between German Gothic and its contemporary Italian counterpart. In the case of the mosque, although there are naturally exceptions, the differences between the buildings of, say, Egypt and India are immense, while any variation resulting from historical changes within the same country are on the whole much less obvious. This holds true despite the fact that architectural elements such as the *mihrab* indicating the direction of Mecca, the courtyard and the minaret are common to most mosques everywhere, even though the architectural language in which these standard features are expressed often varies greatly from one region to another. Perhaps this diversity of forms is at least partly attributable to the relative rapidity with which Islam expanded through regions with widely differing cultures and climates during the first hundred years after the death of the Prophet Muhammad in 632.

Islam's early expansion was quite different from the spread of Christianity, which remained largely suppressed for the first three centuries of its history, and only after this period expanded steadily, but much more slowly. Islam, by contrast, quickly spread westwards across North Africa to Spain and eastwards as far as the coastal areas around the China Sea. In the areas into which it expanded indigenous populations used a wide variety of building materials, including mud brick, timber and stone, depending on the raw materials available locally. Each region thus had its own traditional and craft-related skills and building methods, and these local factors, combined with extreme differences in climate, gave rise from the beginning to highly disparate styles, many of which were of course influenced by contact with existing local cultures.

In the early days, Islam – like Christianity – borrowed features from existing buildings associated with local religions and cultures before establishing its own specific architectural identity. Initially, such borrowed styles are easily distinguishable but, with the passage of time and as and when the new style evolved, they diminish and eventually disappear. Later, as in Europe, political factors caused skilled craftsmen to venture across national frontiers: some Muslims were forced to flee westwards to escape the invading Mongols, and others southwards to escape the Christian armies in Spain; similar forced migrations occurred elsewhere, and economic factors such as the search for employment also caused skilled artisans to leave their homelands. An interesting and probably unique example of a forward and then reverse flow of special skills occurred as a consequence of the fall of Delhi to Timur in 1399. The conqueror took all the renowned Hindu stonemasons back to his native Samarqand to develop the architecture there, and the later Mughal invaders found few artisans in Hindustan capable of executing the architectural forms their emperor desired. Only after a century and a half did the original skills reappear in India as a result of the Emperor Humayun returning from Iran to Delhi, bringing with him some of the descendants of the original craftsmen who had been forcibly removed from their country by Timur. Thus to a limited extent a regional architectural language could be transferred from one place to another. Migrations certainly occurred but, possibly owing to the distances and hazards involved in travel, artisans in the Muslim world generally may have moved about far less extensively than did, for example, the medieval master-masons within Europe; such restrictions would have been a contributory factor in the retention of distinctive regional styles of architecture.

In view of the dominant role of regionalism, one must consider whether there exists any form of universal chronological evolution of mosque design by recognizable stages. One could postulate that there are three significant phases that can be regarded as common to all regions. In the early formative stage the original mosque form was a hypostyle hall with an open courtyard surrounded by colonnaded walls – a design born in the Arabian heartland and developed up to the middle Abbasid period in the tenth and eleventh centuries. The second stage saw the emergence of diverse regional styles which remained dominant in their respective geographical areas. The third stage, which overlaps with the second and does not conflict with regionalism, is what might be called the 'monumental style', characterized by the use of monumental scale (as understood from Western architecture). Only four periods truly qualify as being representative of the third stage: the Central Asian Timurid Empire of the fourteenth and fifteenth centuries; Ottoman Anatolia after 1453; Mughal India after the return of Humayun in 1555; and Iran after *c.* 1550. The architectural legacy of these imperial powers is both regional in character and grand in scale. The most recent stage of mosque architecture is that of the decades since World War II, a period in which regional traditions have had to contend with a variety of new international architectural languages; the outcome of the challenge presented by these new expressions remains in the realm of the unknown.

Over and above every other consideration, including regional factors or the use of rather subjective terminology such as 'monumental', one can say in general terms that every major mosque ever built, certainly until the arrival of the Modern Movement in the twentieth century, falls into one of five categories. These are: the hypostyle hall with a flat roof and possibly one or more small domes (as seen in Arabian and African examples); buildings with a very large central space often covered by a massive dome provided with lateral support by the weight of half-domes (such as those in the Ottoman style) or having pyramidal pitched roofs (as in Indonesia); the layout with an *iwan* (vaulted hall) placed on each side of a bi-axially divided central rectangular courtyard (as developed in Iran and Central Asia); the triple-domed mosque with large courtyard (typical of Mughal architecture in India); and, finally, the walled complex within which a number of pavilions are set in enclosed landscaped spaces (as found in China).

Both for the role they play in respect of the mosque and in their own right, there are three fields in which Islam has made a unique contribution to architecture and the architectural arts: calligraphy,

The five basic categories of mosque design occur in seven distinctive regional styles; the sketches do not show specific mosques, nor are they drawn to scale.

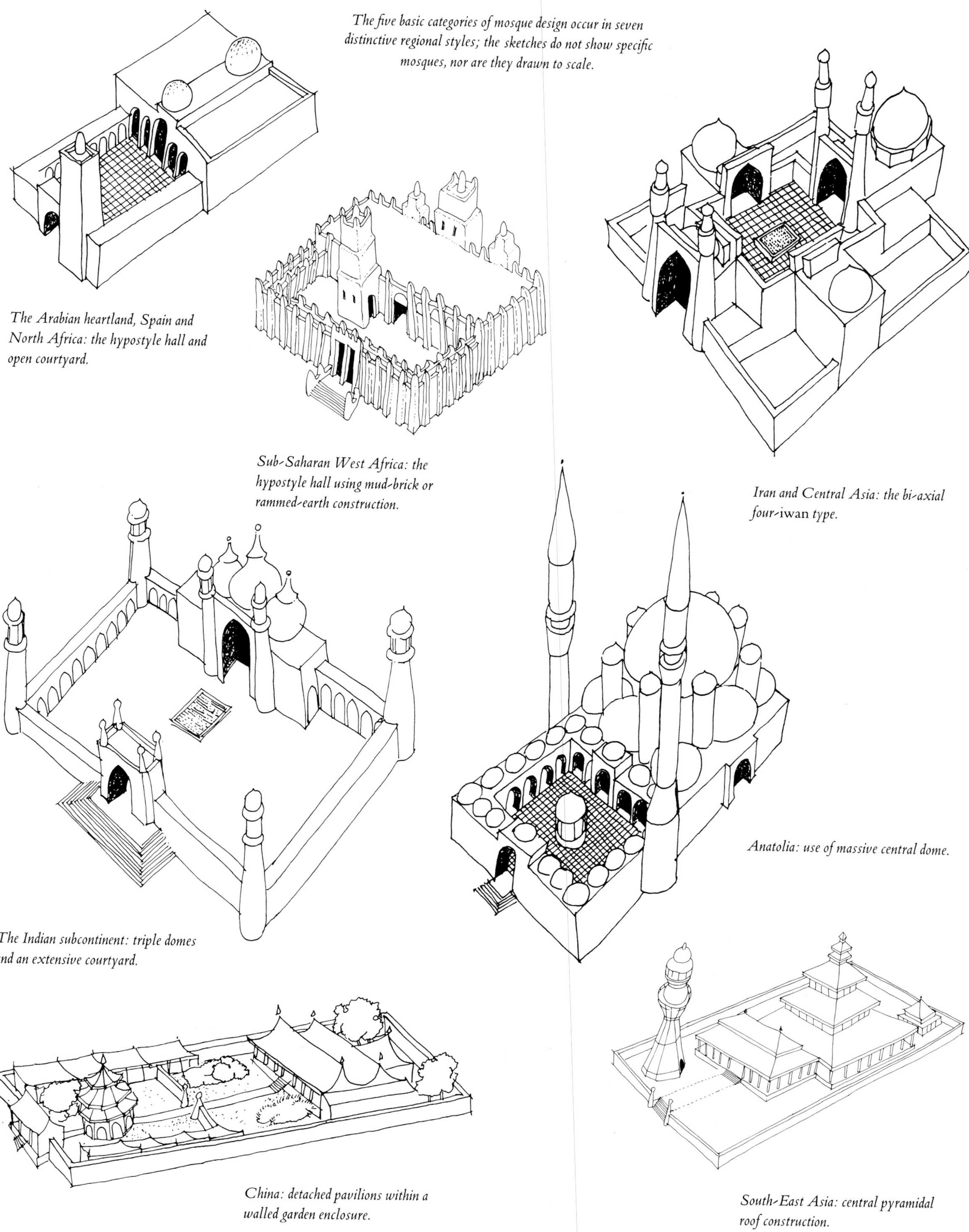

The Arabian heartland, Spain and North Africa: the hypostyle hall and open courtyard.

Sub-Saharan West Africa: the hypostyle hall using mud-brick or rammed-earth construction.

Iran and Central Asia: the bi-axial four-iwan type.

The Indian subcontinent: triple domes and an extensive courtyard.

Anatolia: use of massive central dome.

China: detached pavilions within a walled garden enclosure.

South-East Asia: central pyramidal roof construction.

geometry and garden design. The last of these is of less relevance where the mosque is concerned, except for examples in Al-Andalus featuring a courtyard with orange trees, and those in China with gardens laid out inside the walled complex. Because of its relatively minor role, garden design does not merit special treatment here; calligraphy and geometry, however, have both played major roles in the design and decoration of mosques and are therefore discussed in separate chapters.

Calligraphy demands special attention because of the unique place of the written word in Muslim architectural ornament, fulfilling a particular role which evolved for two main reasons. The prohibition of figurative ornament in Muslim art was based on the generally accepted Islamic premise that the depiction of living beings constitutes an impermissible challenge to God as sole Creator, though plant forms and occasionally animal forms were considered acceptable. The second reason is that because the Qur'an – unlike the Old and New Testaments – is held by Muslims to represent the word of God, the use of Qur'anic quotations on tiled surfaces or in stone or stucco carving assumes *ipso facto* an iconographic role and serves both to indicate that a building is considered sacred and to convey a spiritual message to passers-by and to those who come to the mosque to pray.

The use of geometry in decoration is ubiquitous and serves to cover flat, curved and convoluted surfaces in two- or three-dimensional forms. In so doing, it can be made to enrich and beautify an interior through the use of uniquely Islamic devices such as the *muqarnas*; geometry also acts in an intentionally non-tectonic capacity, diffusing the real form of a building by concealing its materials and its constructional grammar, so creating an atmosphere that may seem more conducive to meditation and prayer; finally, it throws open the door to numerology and mathematics, which have a metaphysical significance.

Two points of general relevance to the subject of the book are worth mentioning here: the question of architectural authorship and the possible meanings of the word 'Islam'. In the context of the earlier history of the mosque, architectural authorship is generally conspicuous by its absence. (This is in contrast to the history of church architecture, especially in the post-medieval period.) The work of Sinan and other architects in sixteenth-century Istanbul and some in India and Iran might be taken as important exceptions to the general rule. However, the absence of authorship of the mosque was on the whole maintained until the end of the eighteenth century. Although explanations for this can only be speculative, three possible reasons suggest themselves. First, the sponsorship of a mosque by a head of state or other eminent patron was considered an act of piety in itself, hence the resulting building would be linked to the name of the donor rather than to that of the architect. Second, within orthodox Islam innovation (whether applied to architecture or any other human endeavour) has often been equated with Creation in the divine sense and hence classified as an unacceptable form of motivation; one may therefore assume that inventiveness on the part of an architect perhaps remained unacclaimed for religious reasons. Third, the situation may be partly attributable to the fact that in the Muslim world indigenous cultural history was largely suppressed during the period of imperial domination, and earlier records have not yet received proper scholarly examination; in this context it should not be forgotten that the identity of the European master-masons responsible for the design of major Gothic cathedrals has only begun to be discovered in the last thirty to forty years.

In current historical circumstances, it is of interest to note that the word 'Islam' can have any one of four different meanings, depending on context. The most important is the literal one, 'submission to God's will' (a Muslim being a committed person who submits himself to the will of Allah). In its second meaning, Islam signifies the 'last and true divine religion' based on the holy texts – the Torah of Moses, the Psalms of David, the Gospel of Jesus and the Revelations of the Qur'an. The third meaning is the one used, mainly by historians, to describe Muslim civilization (equivalent to the term 'Christendom', as distinct from 'Christianity'). Lastly, but very common today and frequently misunderstood, the word occurs in polemical contexts, where it is imbued with a powerful politico-religious message. Thus, in many Muslim countries 'Islamic' is used to imply 'the good', while 'anti-Islamic' suggests the opposite, often being equated with ideas of 'pro-Western' and 'pro-permissiveness', whatever such terms may mean in the mind of the user. These overtones are frequently encountered due to the current ideological conflict between those Muslims who hold that religious belief and practice must be strictly interrelated with law and culture, and those who believe that the opposite should be the case, with the religious and secular spheres each enjoying an independent but symbiotic existence.

Today, Islam is the fastest growing major monotheistic religion, and consequently more mosques are being built than are new places of worship for the followers of any other faith. These new buildings are varied in style and reflect the attitudes of different clients. The role of the mosque in modern Muslim society is being re-examined: what purpose does it, or could it, or should it fulfil today, whether as a place of private or collective prayer or for other social needs in the community? The architecture of the contemporary mosque reflects the views of, on the one hand, the historicist or revivalist lobby and, on the other, the modernists, each faction being supported by its own theoreticians. Regional design models are constantly being challenged by the spirit of cultural internationalism that is transmitted worldwide by the mass-communications media and the schools. A factor that should be borne in mind is that in modern society the mosque serves as the single most important visible representation of Muslim identity and values. This may and often does take an emblematic form, as in the case of the large state-sponsored National Mosque in a Muslim country, or as a symbol offering emotional support in a Western country where Muslims are a minority.

Since Islam is a prescriptive and not a descriptive faith, we conclude these introductory remarks on an optimistic note. The almost total lack of requirement for material or symbolic features in the mosque and the absence of complex liturgical ceremonies affords the designers of tomorrow's mosques the challenging situation of an unparalleled freedom of expression.

MARTIN J. FRISHMAN
HASAN-UDDIN KHAN

May 1994

PART I

THE MOSQUE AS AN EXPRESSION OF ISLAM

- 1 -
ISLAM AND THE FORM OF THE MOSQUE

MARTIN FRISHMAN

ISLAM follows Judaism and Christianity as the third and last of the great monotheistic religions. Whereas historical events allow the inception of both Christianity and Islam to be dated quite precisely, in the case of Judaism this is more difficult. There is little historical evidence to show that monotheism was the result of a long evolutionary development, but the advent of Zoroastrianism in the sixth century BC may be taken as representing the first serious attempt to establish a universal monotheistic religion.[1] If we take monotheism to mean belief in one god to the exclusion of all others, only one pre-Judaic example is known, namely Akhenaton's action in abolishing the pantheon of ancient Egypt and substituting the concept of Aton as the 'creator of mankind'.[2] However, this phenomenon lasted for only eleven years, and after the death of Akhenaton in 1362 BC the concept of a single creative force was lost and did not reappear until the time of Moses, many centuries later.

In the third millennium BC the civilized settlements of southern Babylonia, Egypt, the middle Euphrates, Palestine and Syria were invaded by tribesmen known as the Habiru or Apiru, who can almost certainly be identified with the Arabs. (The only identifiable meaning of 'Arab' comes from *abir*, nomad.) The invaders, who were of Semitic stock, inherited and developed the ancient civilization of Sumer and Babylon. The term 'semitic' was coined from Shem, son of Noah and reputed ancestor of the inhabitants of Arabia. It is believed that Arabs from central and southern Arabia invaded the settled lands of the Fertile Crescent[3] and that the Hebrews who feature the Old Testament were Arabs and part of the population of Arabia, which also included the Israelite Hebrews under the leadership of Joshua and other tribal chieftains.

The Hebrew people were inspired by a religious belief dating back to Moses, who consolidated and unified the tribes in the conviction that they constituted a people under the special care and protection of a pastoral deity known as Yahweh, whose name appears in the English translation of the Hebrew scriptures as 'Jehovah'. To what extent Moses was the creator of this belief is difficult to establish, but certainly Yahweh was a deity familiar to the Semites. It is probable that some time before Moses a pastoral deity or '*mysterium tremendum*' called Yahweh was known among the nomadic tribes of Arabia and that Moses might not have succeeded in his mission had he been unable to invoke an already accepted Supreme Being or 'Lord God of your fathers' (Exodus, iii, 16). Moses was responsible for giving Yahweh a special place in the allegiance of the nation, but it was not till long after him and the wanderings of the Israelites that they came to accept the concept of a universal, transcendental, ethical creator of the universe – the post-exilic phenomenon which gave Judaism the distinction of becoming the first permanent monotheistic religion. The god of the Hebrew people differed from the tribal All Father in not being a remote figure uninterested in human affairs, but one who was brought into the most intimate covenant with the Hebrew clans, thereby welding them into a theocratic nation. Thus the All Father of the desert became the God of Sinai and, unlike the situation in Egypt after Akhenaton, was established permanently. The utterances of the biblical prophets from the eighth century BC onwards bear the stamp of originality, of opposition to contemporary ideas, and of the word of God finding expression through the medium of human intermediaries. Under the influence of the prophets, the monotheistic tendency and tradition were fostered and developed in Israel in a manner seen nowhere else in the ancient world.

Here we see the establishment of two phenomena that would play a fundamental role in the foundation of Islam – the concept of monotheism both as a religious belief and as a force providing the spiritual backbone of a nation, and the concept of prophethood. In the intervening centuries only one other vital contributing factor – the apostolic concept derived from Christianity – was yet to come. As the concept of prophethood was established by Moses and the tribes of Israel, so the concept of apostleship was created in the time of Christ. The title of Apostle ('messenger') was bestowed on the twelve disciples sent forth to preach the Gospel. The close similarity of the role of the Hebrew prophets such as Isaiah, Jeremiah, Ezekiel or Daniel as interpreters of God's will, and that of the New Testament evangelists Matthew, Mark, Luke and John who spread the Gospel of Christ, might account for the two frequently encountered versions of the Muslim *shahada* or creed as translated from Arabic into English. One states 'There is no God but the God and Muhammad is his Prophet' and the other that 'There is no God but the God and Muhammad is his Messenger.' The difference, if there is any, is so marginal as to be of no significance.

The life of the Prophet Muhammad

Muhammad was one of the great figures of history. He had an overwhelming conviction that there was but one God and that there should be one community of believers. The fact that he was the one

Facing page
The Ka'ba in Mecca, the focal point of the hajj *or pilgrimage; the black-draped monument is of supreme symbolic significance for all Muslims (**see p. 32**).*

chosen to receive the word of God, as embodied later in the Qur'an, is in itself testimony to his monumental spiritual status in relation to his followers, while his remarkable qualities as statesmen and political leader are demonstrated by his ability, against the greatest adversity, to inspire and lead the Arab people in a manner never achieved before or since. It is rather as though Solomon's spiritual guidance of the People of Israel coupled with Joshua's military leadership centuries later were telescoped into the life of one man. Certainly Muhammad's achievements – the establishment of a new religion, the consolidation of that faith in the form of a new nation of believers and the expansion of that nation through massive conquest within a single lifetime – are unique in history.

Born in Mecca in June 570, Muhammad was the posthumous son of a trader and camel driver named Abd' Allah. The main civilizations of the world into which he was born were Romano-Byzantine, Persian and that of Arabia Felix (Yemen). Mecca, like Petra and Palmyra before, had become prosperous thanks to its position at the centre of one of the age-old trade routes which traversed Arabia in all directions and the existence of which provides a clear indication that regular commerce was important in providing a link between the desert and the sown land.

Trading and raiding formed the basis of the economic and social life of the early Arabs, and a symbiotic relationship existed between the settled and nomadic peoples, since the latter demanded payment for facilitating safe conduct across empty desert lands, and thus trading profits were widely distributed. Trading constituted the first part of Muhammad's life. The merchants of Mecca, who had commercial links with both Persians and Byzantines, sent caravans twice yearly to both north and south, as well as having dealings with Abyssinia on the other side of the Red Sea. The Quraysh, the tribe to which Muhammad belonged, formed companies which shared in the profits of these ventures and he himself travelled to Syria with a caravan carrying wares dispatched by Khadija, a wealthy widow whom he later married and who until her death in 619 was his sole wife.

The population of Mecca consisted of pagan Arabs, Jews and Christians. The pagan Arab cared little for his religious duties. Sacrifices were popular and communal feasts and prophylactic rites were fairly widely observed. Generally speaking, the Arab believed he could get whatever he needed by his own efforts and without help from the gods. A certain prestige was nevertheless attached to those towns and villages which were centres of pilgrimage for tribesmen who gathered to mark sacred occasions and from whom the custodians of holy places, especially in Mecca, derived their income. Clearly pagan custom has left an indelible mark on Islam in the form of the *hajj*, the required pilgrimage to Mecca. The heathenism of Muhammad's day was largely animistic and very similar to most primitive forms of religion mentioned in the Old Testament and, like the prophets of the Old Testament, Muhammad took steps to extinguish practices inconsistent with monotheism. The kissing or the stroking by hand of a stone, in this case the Ka'ba in Mecca, was a pagan act of honouring the gods and bestowing holiness upon the worshipper.[4] While no such concepts were acceptable under Judaism until Isaiah, it was believed that the blood of the sacrificial goat carried away man's sins on the Day of Atonement, and to this day in the Christian sphere the sacramental bread and wine of the Eucharist reflect aspects of man's psyche which are so deeply rooted that they are difficult to remove. In the final analysis all three monotheistic religions failed to extirpate entirely practices inherited from earlier traditions.

A substantial part of the population of Arabia was Jewish, and the sixth century BC saw the founding of large Jewish settlements in Mesopotamia, and later – fleeing repression under the Romans – the Jews found asylum amongst the Arabs. Christianity and Christian domination were established by St Paul in Damascus and by St Thomas with the founding of the Church in Edessa. The Hijaz Bedouin were mainly pagan, though the surrounding tribes were Christian, their chief centres being Yemen in the south, Syria in the north, Hira in the east and Abyssinia in the west. The Christian community in Mecca belonged, like Muhammad, to the tribe of the Quraysh. Endless internal conflicts between Monophysites and Nestorian Christians led to the end of Christian Arab rule and with it the beginning of the Arab hatred of the Greeks, at whose hands they had suffered tyranny and injustice; as a result, Christianity and Byzantium came to be regarded by the Arabs as representing perfidy, and the longstanding enmity led ultimately to the capture of Constantinople by the Ottoman forces in 1453. The extraordinary rapidity of the Arab advance eastward and westward was due, at least in part, to the co-operation of local Christians disgusted with Byzantine cruelty and oppression. Although the Arabs had to defeat a number of disaffected garrison troops, this proved a comparatively easy task because in Syria the population welcomed them and joined forces with them, while in Egypt they made a separate peace stipulating that the power of Byzantium must be irrevocably destroyed. It was not until the Muslim Arabs encountered opposition further west that their expansion met with any serious check. In Egypt and the Arab world they were accepted as deliverers.

The birth of Islam

The year 610 marks the birth of Islam because it was the year of the Revelation – namely the Prophet's first encounter with the Angel Gabriel, who commanded him to 'Read in the name of thy Lord who creates man from a clot of blood. Read and thy Lord is most generous, who taught by the pen, taught man what he knew not.' (Qur'an 96:1–4). The divine messages received by Muhammad which constitute the Qur'an began when he was around the age of forty, and it is not known whether any part of them was recorded during his lifetime. However, they were passed on by remembrancers, men who, with a lifetime of training, had acquired formidable powers of memorizing texts. The Qur'an was certainly written down shortly after the death of the Prophet, in the time of the first Orthodox Caliph, Abu Bakr, and the text was later codified under Caliph Uthman between 644 and 656, thus giving the content of the Muslim Holy Book the form in which it is known today.

Inspired by the messages he received, Muhammad began to preach to the people of Mecca, exhorting them to abandon their idols and submit to the one and indivisible God. However, he gained few followers and provoked much hostility, so when invited to go to Yathrib, an oasis town 340 km (212 miles) to the north-west, he journeyed there in 622. Yathrib, which was later renamed Madinat al-Nabi or Medina, the City of the Prophet, was Muhammad's place of residence until his death in 632. The year of his journey, the *hijra*, marked the decisive moment in his prophetic mission and was proclaimed by the first generation of Muslims as the first year of the Muslim Era. While in Mecca, Muhammad had preached as a private citizen, in Medina he became a religious leader and head of a community, as well as wielding both political and military power. Muhammad's legacy included a new faith in one God and the Qur'an, as well as, through wise alliance and success in war, a new state dominating western Arabia. He also established the Muslim belief that he is the last of God's Prophets,[5] who – by founding Islam – completed the work begun in God's name by Abraham, Moses, David and Christ and established the ultimate monotheistic faith.

The Basis of Muslim Belief

The Qur'an

For the Muslim the Qur'an explains all that man needs to know in order to live a normal and spiritual life; at the same time its precepts present him with a massive spiritual challenge, because nothing stands between the individual and god and there is no one to intercede for him. Forgiveness cannot be won by merit, but flows only from God's grace, though a man may make himself worthy of forgiveness by leading a life devoted to serving God. There is always the stark choice between the path that leads to Paradise and that which leads to disaster on the Day of Judgment – a concept that comes very close to that enshrined in medieval Christian belief.

The text of the Qur'an is divided into chapters (*suras*), arranged for the most part in descending order of length; each begins with the same construct, known as the *bismillah*, which is the pronouncement 'In the name of Allah, the Merciful, the Compassionate'. The earlier Meccan *suras* are visionary in nature, devoted to proclaiming the beneficence of one God and the judgment awaiting all men, while those of the Medina period move from the purely theological to the legal and socio-political field. This change of emphasis was appropriate because of the necessity of welding together and structuring the new Muslim community resident in Medina.

The courtyard of the Badshahi Mosque, Lahore, Pakistan, filled with worshippers at the annual festival of Eid, marking the end of the period of fasting during Ramadan.

Among non-Muslims and non-Arabic-speaking people there has been a tendency to treat the Qur'an simply as a book of instruction on how Muslims should behave and what they should believe. This is perhaps largely due to a failure to appreciate that, since the Arabic *qur'an* means not simply 'reading' but 'recitation', the act of reciting the text represents a commitment to worship. The act of worship therefore serves to reaffirm the manner of the original revelation, making it the permanent well-spring of the Muslim community. Although the Qur'an contains no accounts of miracles in the New Testament sense, the book itself constitutes a miracle by virtue of its origin; in the words of the medieval scholar al-Ghazzali, 'There is no end to its miracles, it is ever fresh and new to the reciters.' With a few exceptions, translations from Arabic have been made only in recent times, perhaps because the text was formerly considered 'untranslatable', and Arabic remains the *lingua franca* of Muslim scholarship and worship.

In providing an exposition of what Muslims should believe and how they should conduct their lives, the Qur'an – like the Jewish Talmud – sets forth a compendium of duties, but unlike the Christian scriptures it formulates laws according to which believers should live. These are clearly defined in the 'five pillars' or fundamental observances which form the basis of the Muslim faith:

1 The acceptance of the *shahada*: 'There is no God but the God and Muhammad is his Messenger.' This formula comprises the irreducible minimum of Muslim belief, and it is widely accepted that anyone who utters the *shahada* may be regarded as a Muslim.

2 Prayer, or *namaz*, is prescribed to be performed five times per day; at dawn, around midday, in the afternoon, at sunset, and at night before going to bed. It may take the form of *dua* (personal and spontaneous prayer) or *salat* (ritual prayer in the company of others at home or at the mosque). It is also prescribed that every adult male join in communal prayers at midday on Friday, a practice which explains the use of the terms *masjid-i juma* (Friday mosque) and *jami masjid* (congregational mosque). The act of prayer must be preceded by self-purification through ritual ablutions and must be performed facing in the direction of Mecca. The ritual bowings and prostration accompanying the recitation of prayers clearly demonstrate the significance of the word Islam, meaning 'submission to God's will' by word of mouth and physical gesture.

3 Alms, or *zakat* (a term derived from the Arabic *zaka*, meaning 'pure'). The Qur'an stresses that the giving of alms is one of the chief virtues of the true believer, the generally accepted amount being one-fortieth of a Muslim's annual income in cash or kind. Since all revenue from alms was intended to benefit the poor and to pay for certain activities within a community, the very act of giving demonstrated the believer's sense of social responsibility, thus leaving acquired wealth free of disrepute.

4 Fasting. All believers are required to observe the ninth lunar month of the Muslim year, Ramadan, as a period of fasting in which they abstain from eating, drinking, smoking and sexual relations from sunrise to sunset (Qur'an 2:185–6). The purpose is to subjugate the body to the spirit and to fortify the will through mental discipline, thus helping the believer to come nearer to God. The difference between this practice and the Jewish observance of the annual Day of Atonement (Yom Kippur) is one of time – the requirement being limited to total fasting for a full twenty-four hours in the case of the latter – but the concept of the intensification of prayer through abstention is essentially the same.

5 Pilgrimage. The *hajj*, or pilgrimage to Mecca, birthplace of the Prophet Muhammad and the place where Muslims believe Abraham built the house of Adam, must be performed at least once in the lifetime of every Muslim, health and means permitting (Qur'an 3:97).

The 'hadith'

Next in importance after the Qur'an as a source of guidance are the *hadith*, the 'traditions' or 'sayings' relating to the life of Muhammad. Observations made during his lifetime were not recorded for posterity because writing was then an unusual accomplishment, and since they were handed down orally it is possible that, as sects and rivalries sprang up, *hadith* began to be interpreted in a manner which would support partisan interests or even to be invented for this purpose. Subsequent efforts by the theologians and jurists – the *ulama* – to distinguish the genuine from the spurious raised questions as to what tradition actually is and how powerful it should be. The problem naturally is that tradition, if slavishly followed, could keep the Muslim world permanently constrained by its past.

Orthodox theory holds that there are two kinds of revelation: that which is recited – the Qur'an; and that which is read but not recited – *hadith*. The view that both are equal in importance has been firmly rejected by those who feel that, if the Companions of the Prophet had considered them to be so, they would have written down his sayings. Hence, whereas the Qur'an was regarded as the word of God and was recorded shortly after Muhammad's death, the *hadith* remained unrecorded for two centuries. A basic consideration must be the fact that any such oral history set down so long after the event is unlikely to be fully accurate, not out of an intention to falsify, but because memory is fallible. Nevertheless, by the end of the third century of the Muslim Era, six great *hadith* collections had been compiled.[6] The problem which arises is that some orthodox Sunni opinion does place the *hadith* on the same level as the Qur'an, on the premise that the Companions learned the sayings directly from Muhammad and that the words have since been passed on in an unbroken line of succession down to any imam today; thus the *hadith* can claim to have the same authority as the

Facing page
The complex three-dimensional geometry of the muqarnas *– an architectural feature unique to Islam – is clearly displayed in a detail of the vaulting in the south-west* iwan *of the Friday Mosque in Isfahan, added during the Safavid period.*

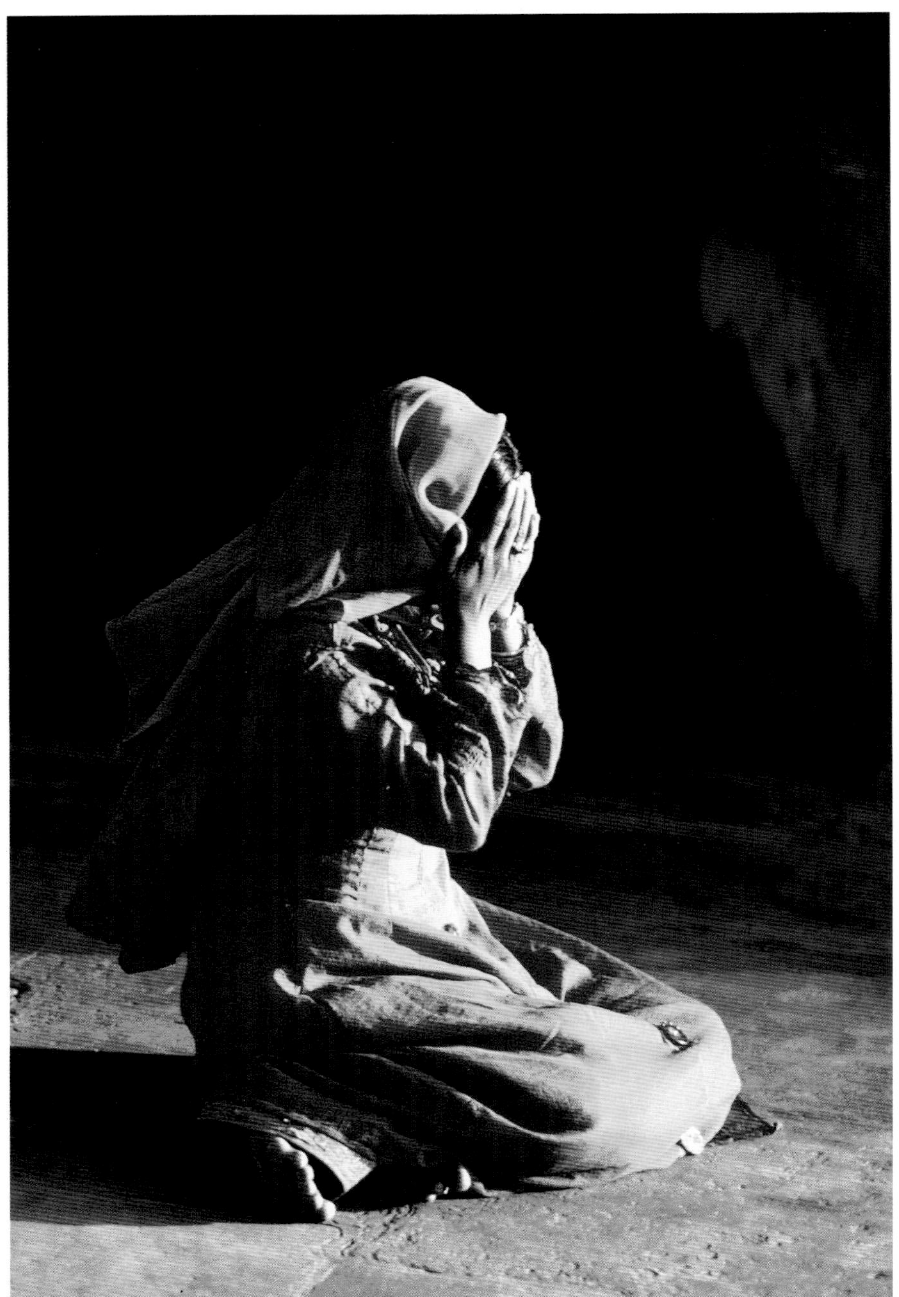

WORSHIP

The act of prayer, whether performed by an individual or collectively by a congregation, is one of the five pillars of Islam, and reciting the holy text of the Qur'an represents an act of commitment to worship.

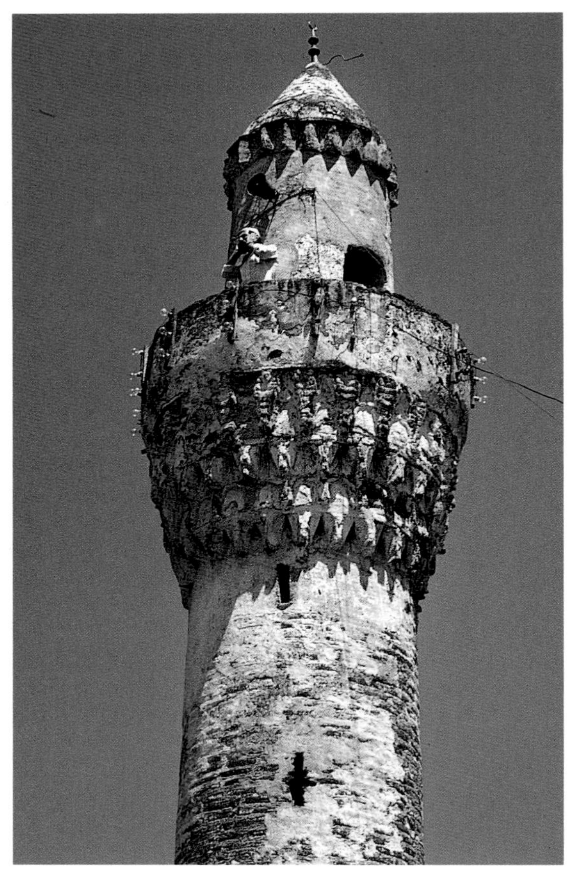

(Above) A woman at prayer in the Friday Mosque, Delhi.

(Above right) A minaret in Yemen, showing the gallery from which the muezzin is seen calling the faithful to prayer.

(Right) A group of men reading the Qur'an in the Arwa Mosque, Jiblah, Yemen.

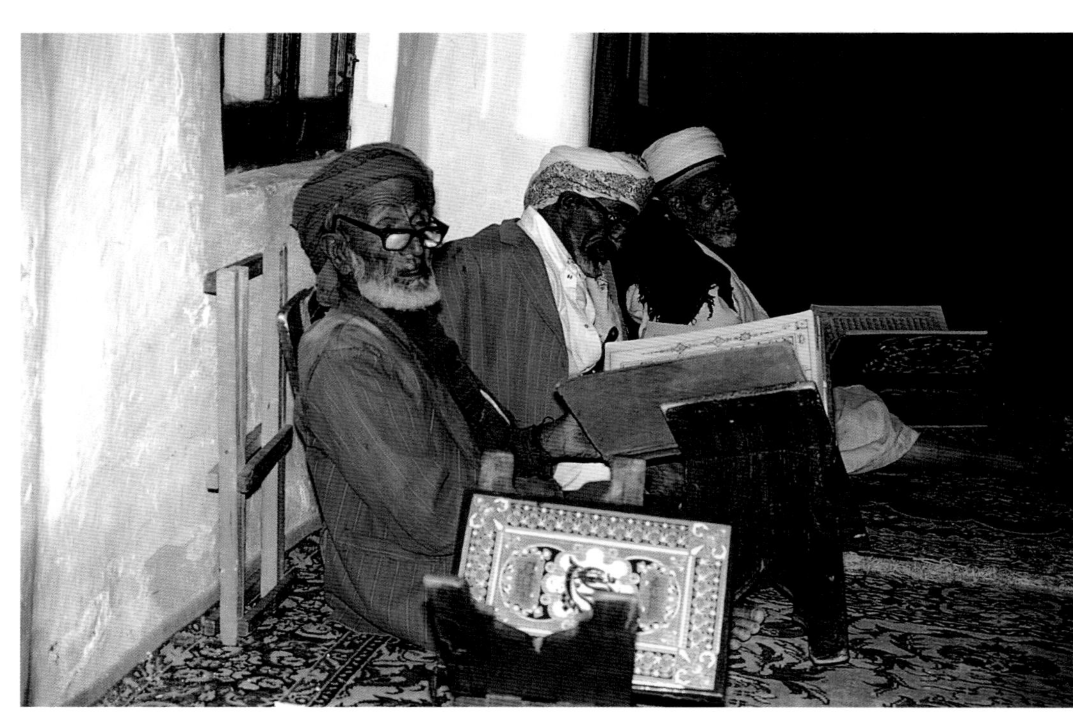

THE PORTAL

The entrance portal is a prominent architectural feature of most major mosques. Among the many variants are: (right) the Mosque of Sultan Ahmet (Blue Mosque), Istanbul, built in the early seventeenth century, with (below) a detail of the muqarnas *in the portal of the Süleymaniye complex, Istanbul, 1550–7; (bottom left) the Mosque of Barquq, Cairo, dating from the Abbasid period in the late eighth century; (bottom centre) the Buland Darwaza (Victory Gate) of the Jami Masjid, Fatehpur Sikri, 1596; and (bottom right) the Great Mosque, Seville, 1171–6.*

THE MINARET

As the principal vertical feature of most mosques, the minaret provides a local landmark as well as allowing the voice of the muezzin to carry over a considerable distance when calling the faithful to prayer. Architectural styles down the centuries have been widely different in various regions, as seen in the representative selection of regional types shown here for comparison.

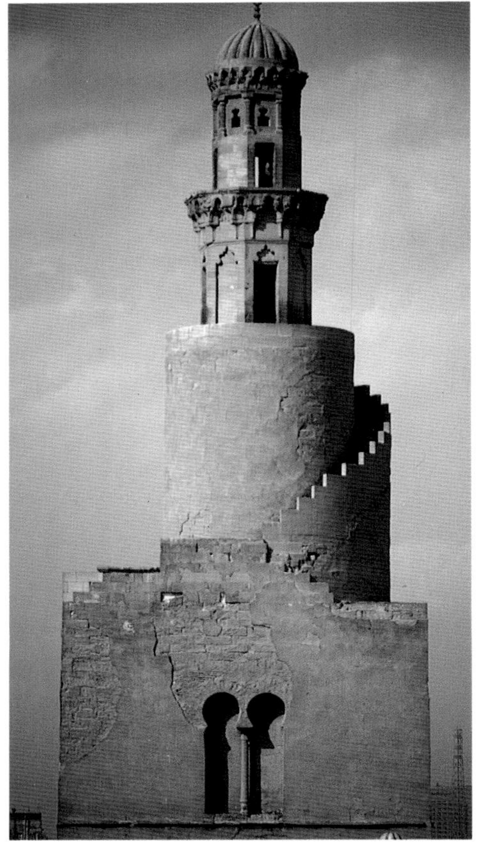

Cairo: the Mosque of Ahmad ibn Tulun, Tulunid period, 876–9.

Cairo: the Mosque of Amir Qurqumas, late Mamluk period, 1506.

Diyarbakir, Turkey: the Ayni Minare Mosque, early Ottoman period, c. 1489.

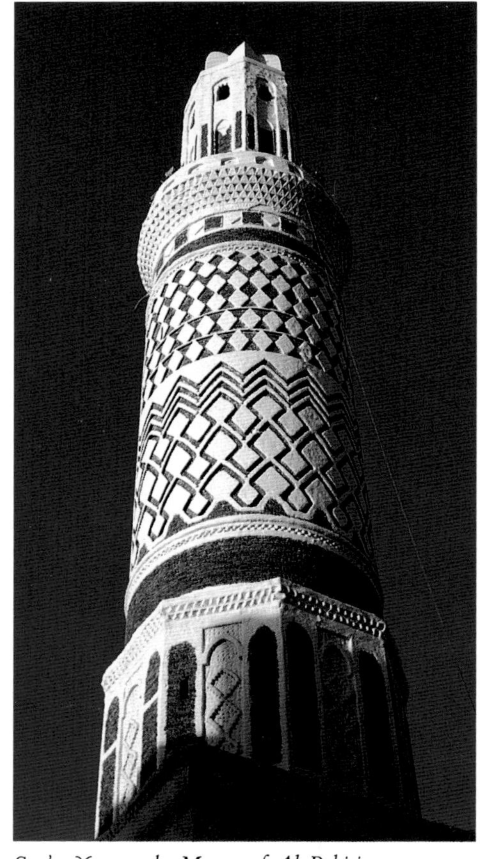

San'a, Yemen: the Mosque of Al-Bakiriyya, Ottoman period, 1598.

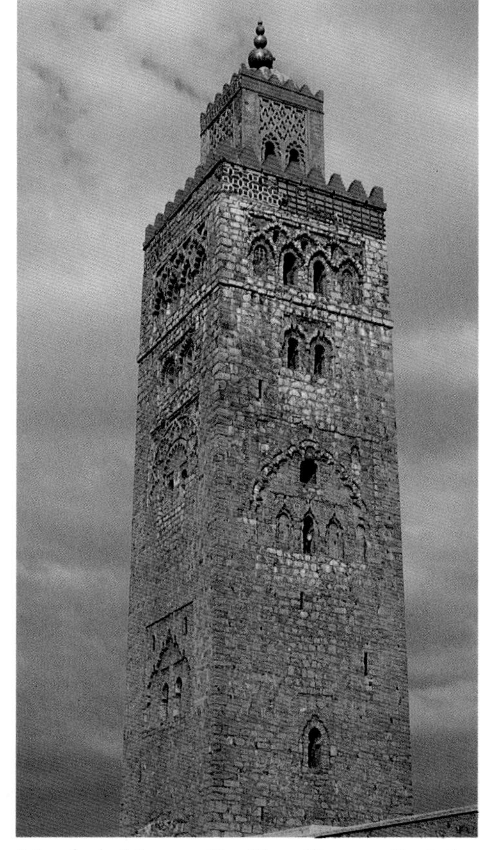

Marrakesh, Morocco: Kutubiyya Mosque, Almohad period, twelfth century.

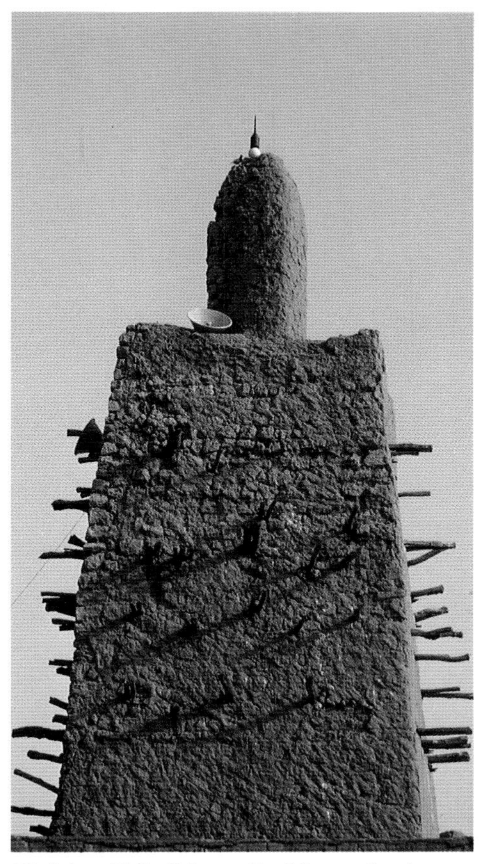

Timbuktu, Mali: DjinguereBer Mosque, Songhay period, fourteenth century.

Beni-Isguen, Algeria: a village mosque in the Mzab Saharan style.

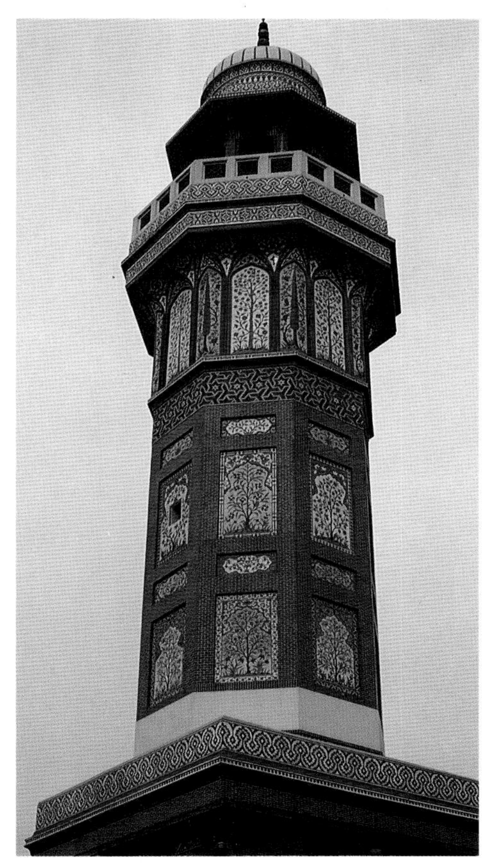

Lahore, Pakistan: Wazir Khan Mosque, Mughal period, 1634.

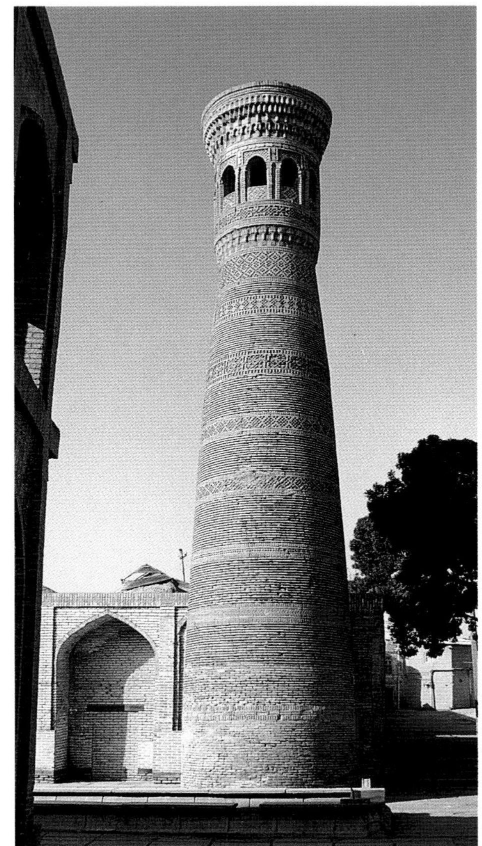

Bukhara, Uzbekistan: the Kalyan (Friday) Mosque, 1514.

Turfan, Xinjiang Province, western China: Amin Mosque, 1778.

Beijing, China: Niu Jie (Ox Street) Mosque, founded in 1362 (renovated 1978).

THE MIHRAB *AND THE* MINBAR

In mosque interiors the direction of Mecca is indicated by the qibla *wall, in which the* mihrab *niche is incorporated. As the focal point of the building, the* mihrab *is often its most elaborately decorated feature. Another important element is the* minbar, *or pulpit, from which the weekly oration (*khutba*) is delivered at Friday prayers; this is always placed to the right of the* mihrab.

(Top) The qibla iwan *in the Mosque of Sultan Hasan, Cairo, 1356–9 (with the* dikka *in the foreground). Examples of* mihrabs *in the contrasting styles are seen in the Great Mosque, Tlemcen, Algeria, completed 1136 (left), and the twentieth-century Jin Shi Fang Xie Mosque, Amoy, Beijing (above).*

(Opposite) The relationship of the mihrab *and* minbar *is clearly seen in the Great Mosque of Qairawan in Tunisia. The* mihrab *niche is decorated with marble panels featuring perforated vegetal and floral designs; these were added in 862, thirty years after the building was completed.*

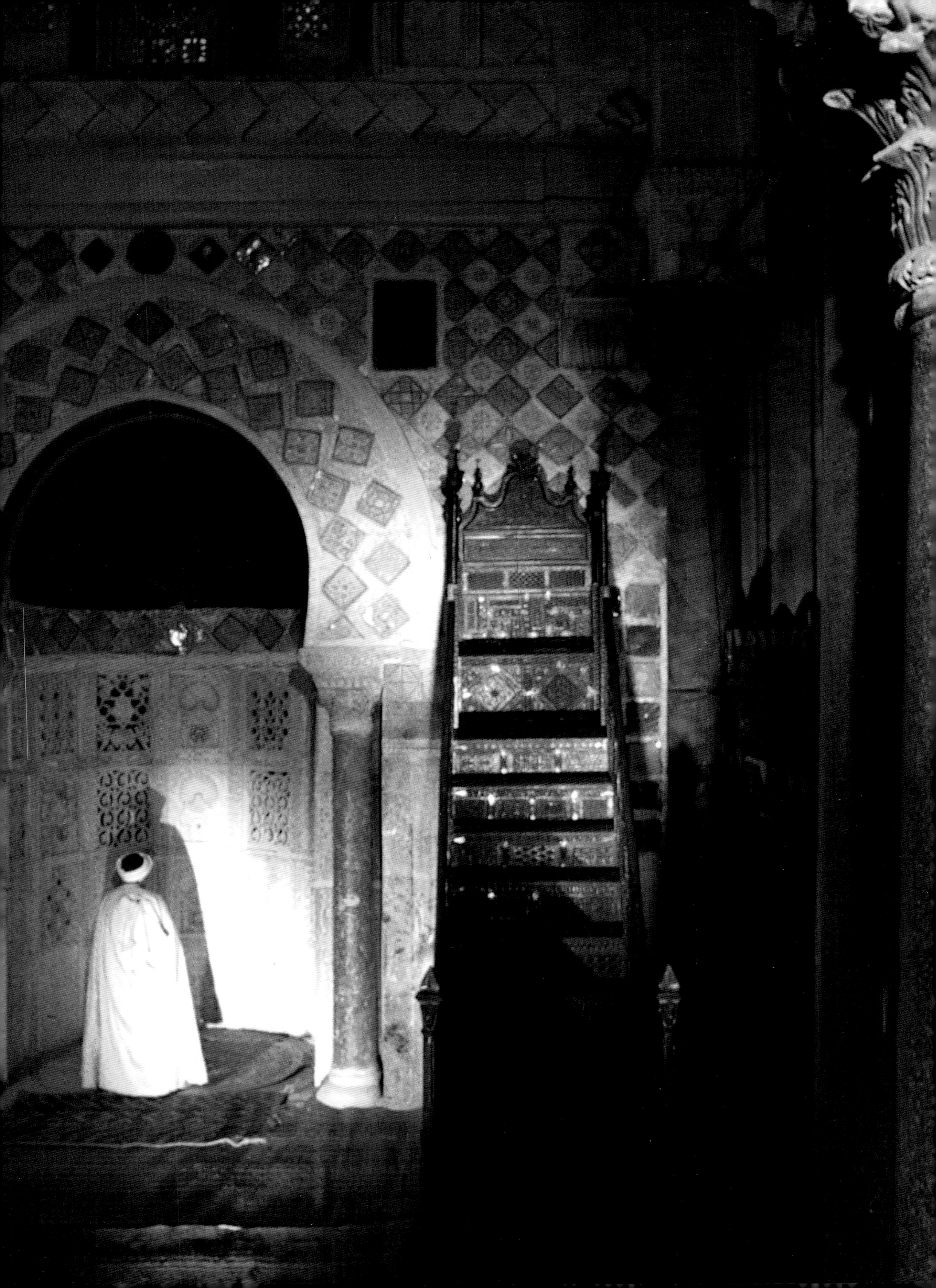

Qur'an because the texts constitute a necessary medium for a proper understanding of the Holy Book. However, if the *ulama* of today seek to enforce blind obedience to a chain of authority in which they constitute the last link, a situation arises which, according to some Muslim scholars, is little different from ancestor worship.

The 'sharia'

Third in the line of essential concepts is the *sharia* or the law. The original meaning of the Arabic word *sharia* was the 'path leading to the water', which in turn, and in its historical context, meant the 'way to the source of life'. The *sharia* grew out of the attempts made by early Muslims, as they confronted immediate social and political problems, to devise a legal system in keeping with the code of behaviour called for by the Qur'an and the *hadith*.

Scholars developed these systems by treating the Qur'an as containing the general principles by which all matters should be regulated, and where the meaning of the Qur'an was imprecise they sought clarification from the *hadith*. Thus the foundations of the *sharia* were the clear and unambiguous commands and prohibitions to be found in these sources. With the passage of time, scholars came to agree increasingly on the basic laws and the principle of *ijma*, or consensus of the community of believers, was established. Once the community's legal experts had reached agreement on a particular point, the development of new ideas on that subject was forbidden. Steadily, more and more of the law was classified as *ijma*, and the rights of individual interpretation (*ijtihad*) became confined to the decreasing areas on which general agreement had not been reached. By the mid-tenth century, many Muslim scholars had closed the gate of *ijtihad*. Thereafter, if an imam were to question the meaning of a text in such a way as to challenge the interpretation supported by *ijma*, he committed *bid'a*, an act of innovation which was not permitted.

During the first three centuries the *sharia* grew slowly into a unified system drawing on much customary practice which had become embodied in the *hadith*. Whereas Western legal systems have grown out of and been moulded by society over the centuries, for Islam it is the law which has always moulded society. The *sharia* is comprehensive, embracing all human activities, defining man's relations with God and with his fellow men; consequently it combines what in Western societies comes under the separate headings of civil and criminal law. No formal and independent legal code was created, the *sharia* being more a formula according to which Muslims ought to behave and human actions are classified, in descending order, as: obligatory, meritorious, indifferent, reprehensible and forbidden.

The 'sunna'

Unlike Christianity, classical Islam had no priestly hierarchy and no central religious authority to promulgate official doctrine. Consequently, since no religious orthodoxy existed, there could be no heresy or deviation from authorized truth. The nearest approach to clergy in Islam are the theologians and jurists known as the *ulama* (the Arabic plural of *alim*, 'one who knows or possesses knowledge'). Although these learned men may as individuals or in schools formulate rules and interpret scripture, they have never been constituted as an authority to lay down religious dogma. The *ijma* represents in reality a consensus of opinion among the learned and the powerful. As such, its formulation in a coherent fashion so as to seem tangible and constant for any one place or time appears problematical. This was certainly the case in the earliest years of Islam, but over the centuries a great body of rules for correct behaviour and belief – the basis of Islamic law and theology – came into being and gained almost universal acceptance. Its guiding principle was respect for tradition – that is for the *sunna*, a term which in ancient Arabia meant 'ancestral precedent' or the 'custom of the tribe'. *Sunna* was equated with the practice and precept of the Prophet as transmitted by the relators of authentic tradition (*hadith*), and its authority was held to override all but that of the Qur'an itself. Those who accepted this principle were and are called Sunnis; today they account for up to 85 per cent of all Muslims.

The single most important sectarian division in the history of Islam is the one which separates Sunni and Shia believers. This situation arose following the assassination in 661 of Ali, the fourth and last of the Orthodox Caliphs, over the question of the succession to the caliphate. The Sunni view has always been that the office of Caliph must be filled by election and that all candidates must be members of Muhammad's tribe, the Quraysh. The Shias (literally 'partisans'), members of the 'party of Ali' (Shiat-Ali), believed that any true successor of Muhammad must be a direct descendant of the Prophet (Ali was a cousin and, by virtue of his marriage to Muhammad's daughter Fatima, also his son-in-law) and was deemed by them to be appointed by God, not man. The resulting sectarian division persists to this day, while historically there have been a number of distinct groups among the Shias. Iran, where Shiism was introduced in 1501 under Shah Ismail I, has maintained its allegiance ever since, thus accepting the principle that only an imam who is a direct descendant of the Prophet can be an authoritative source of guidance and an incarnation of the Divine Light, and hence infallible. Adherents of this doctrine are called Twelver Shias because they recognize twelve Imams – Ali and his immediate successors – the last of whom, Muhammad, disappeared in 873 at the age of four, though his return is expected. For their part the

Facing page
Water has always played an important role in the mosque, for ritual ablutions before prayers, as a reflector of the heavens, as a temperature regulator in a courtyard, and in pools and fountains, which are often architectural features of the great beauty.

(Above) The ablutions fountain in the courtyard of the Qarawiyyin Mosque, Fez, Morocco, 859; (below left) the ablutions fountain pavilion in the courtyard of the Mosque of Sultan Hasan, Cairo, 1356–9; (below right) the marble-covered domes of the Badshahi Mosque, Lahore, 1673–4, reflected in the great pool at the centre of the courtyard.

Ismailis, whose spiritual leader is the Aga Khan, are so called because they regard Ismail as the rightful seventh Imam (rather than his younger brother, Musa, who is accepted by the Twelvers). In practical and ceremonial terms, a notable difference in Shia belief is the addition to the *shahada* of the words 'Ali is the Vice-Regent of God'.

Observance of tradition is considered good, and it is by the preservation of this observance that Sunni Islam is defined. The opposition lies in *bid'a* and is considered bad unless specifically shown to be good. This extreme traditionalist view is perhaps best illustrated by a saying attributed to Muhammad: 'The worst things are those that are novelties. Every novelty is an innovation, every innovation is an error, and every error leads to hellfire.' To condemn a doctrine as *bid'a* did not mean it was false by definition, but that it was an innovation and therefore represented a break with tradition (as distinct from the Christian concept of heresy as theological transgression).[7] Sunni officials differ on where to draw the line on matters that are social rather than theological, but a line there is and those who go beyond it are regarded as infidels. Under *sharia* law the denunciation of any doctrine as non-Islamic has meant that any Muslim professing such a doctrine was an apostate and accordingly subject to the utmost penalty of the law.[8] The sectarian on the other hand, though his beliefs might be at odds with the prevailing consensus, remained a Muslim and therefore retained his status and privileges under Muslim law.

In essence the Islamic state as conceived by orthodox Muslims is a religious polity established under divine law. This law is not limited to questions of belief and religious practice, but also deals with criminal and constitutional matters, as well as many other fields which in other societies would be regarded as the concern of the secular authorities. In an Islamic context there is no such thing as a separate secular authority and secular law, since religion and state are one.

The Mosque: Typology and Development

From their beginnings the monotheistic religions were opposed to the use of buildings specially designed to house the faithful at prayer. Paradoxically, for the true believer the very idea of such a building hinted at a concession to human vanity and, worse, to man's desire to introduce idolatrous worship of an object or edifice, rather than continue using the humble cave or shelter for communal prayer without distraction. Hence, the more impressive the building, the greater the anathema. In fact, the word 'ecclesiastical', today usually meaning 'of the church', is derived from the Greek *ekklesia*, a word meaning an assembly or gathering of people, especially in ancient Athens.

The monotheistic religions maintained their opposition until it dawned upon their leaders that any faith with no new followers would soon die out and that potential converts could be attracted by, amongst other things, some recognizable symbol such as an impressive building. Inevitably those who set foot on this path quickly came to realize that the more splendid they could make their sacred shrine, the greater would be its magnetism, and hence the deeper became the paradox.

Certainly the desire for worldly splendour in its most visible form was less a characteristic of Islam than it was of Christianity. This was due in part to the fact that the liturgical and symbolic requirements of the Church call for more symbolic objects and artefacts than are required by either Judaism or Islam, since both faiths focus on 'the Book' as the sole and essential foundation for worship. Besides its role as the place for the usual congregational offices, the church is also used for weddings, confirmations, confessions, baptisms, the veneration of holy relics and so on, none of which is associated with the mosque. In many instances, however, the mosque was the focal point of a complex of buildings associated with it; these served as hospitals, religious schools (*madrasas*), shelter for travellers etc. All these independent functions were accommodated in separate buildings and only two specific activities other than worship found their place in the mosque itself. These were religious teaching, regardless of whether there was an adjacent *madrasa*, and the weekly oration (*khutba*), delivered at Friday midday prayers, which combined religious, social and political elements, including praise of the ruler as protector of Islam.

Islam has always advocated that material things should not be considered sacred, but at a very fundamental level echoes of contradictory voices can be heard.[9] The view that buildings amounted to an extravagance seems to have been prevalent among the Arabs throughout the Orthodox Caliphate (632–661), but apart from this, in the opinion of some leading historians such as K. A. C. Creswell, Arabia at that time presented 'an almost perfect architectural vacuum, and the term "Arab" should never be used to designate the architecture of Islam.' The exception to this generalization would seem to be Yemen, although one must bear in mind that little of the architecture of that country was known in the West before 1962, because it had remained closed to outsiders.

Although there are no surviving monuments dating from the first two generations of Islam, there is abundant literary evidence to indicate the evolution of building practice – first in Medina itself and then in Basra, Kufa and al-Fustat (Cairo). Initially, owing to the nature of the Muslim faith and the minimalist nature of its liturgical requirements, a square area marked out by a line drawn in the sand was sufficient for communal prayer, provided only that one side of the square faced towards Mecca to indicate the direction of prayer. Another major consideration underlying such minimalist thinking may well have been the fact that most Muslim Arabs were nomads and consequently their lifestyle precluded the use of permanent buildings of any kind, since everything they possessed had to be demountable and portable.

At the beginning, through the Umayyad period in the seventh century and the early eighth century, the architecture of the mosque was based on the Prophet's house in Medina (see chapter 5). The phrase 'architectural vacuum' can be used to describe the environment in which both Islam and Christianity were born, in the sense that no source material could have existed to help suggest forms for their places of worship. Inventing an architectural form to provide for the worship of an invisible and non-representational deity has never been achieved, and anything that became an accepted form had to be evolved through the passage of time. Consequently, both these faiths initially had to

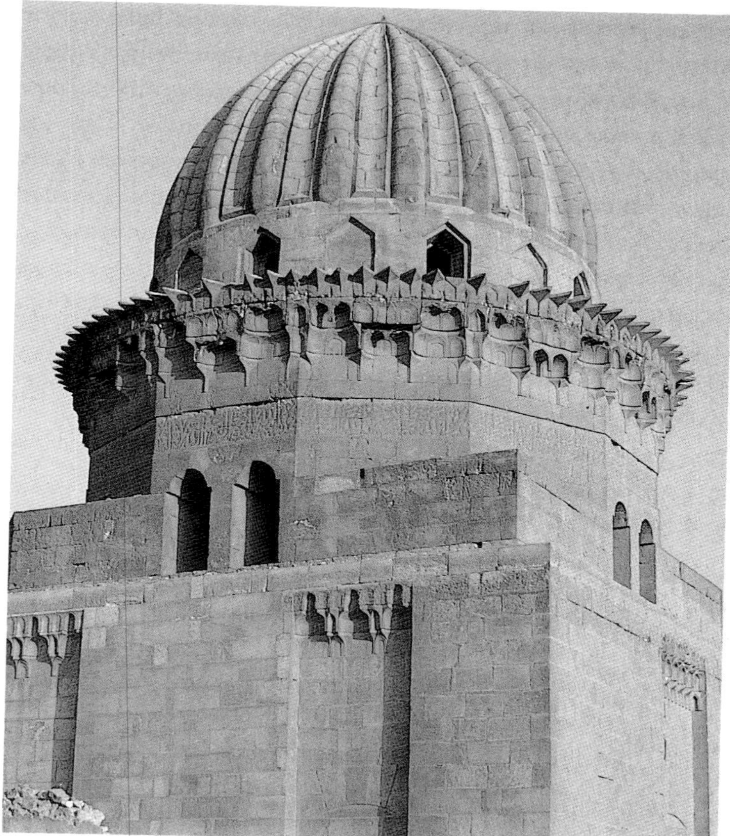

The dome as a feature of mosque architecture. On the right are two striking and unusual designs in traditional structures: the Mosque of Ibrahim Rawza (1580), Bijapur, India, featuring a rare three-quarter sphere with lotus supports; and an example of the ribbed Cairene carved stone type, dating from 1395, associated with mosques and mausoleums. A modern interpretation (top) of a traditional dome form, adopted by Hassan Fathy in the 1940s in the context of a development at New Gourna, Egypt, has since been widely used all over North Africa. The borrowing of a characteristically Indian form for use in a region with different architectural traditions is exemplified (above) by the Toa Payoh Mosque in Singapore, serving the population – mainly of Indian origin – in the first of the new towns developed in the mid-1970s.

borrow ideas from earlier societies or adapt animist temples and pagan shrines to provide the basis for the evolution of a distinct architectural language of their own. Christianity could draw on the buildings of the Romans, and Islam borrowed from Persia and Egypt, as well as from Christianity itself and thus indirectly also from Rome. There is, however, one advantage which the Church always had over Islam, namely that it could rely on powerful visual symbols to help convey its message. The crucifix is the obvious example, and the Madonna and Child falls in the same category. Both the Crucifixion and the cross symbolizing it have an extrinsic message which is universally understood, and the intensity of the emotional charge remains undiminished regardless of the background against which either is seen. The seven-armed candelabra (menorah) and the Star of David could be said to do the same thing for Judaism, although the emotional charge produced by them is less intense, at least under politically normal circumstances.

In the mosque there is no component part or object to evoke a response comparable to that associated with the symbolic cross of Christianity. The minaret, if separated from the mosque and thus divorced from its accepted function as the place from which the call to prayer is made, becomes simply another tower. The *mihrab* (see below) is the focal point of any mosque, but if it were to be removed from its position indicating the direction of Mecca and re-erected at some distance from the place of worship, it would become just another niche. Islam is virtually without symbols other than the Ka'ba at Mecca, assuming that one leaves aside mystical or allegorical motifs such as the crescent moon and star which today serve as national or political emblems, and which in any case have origins that antedate the monotheistic religions.

The Ka'ba is a black-draped, gaunt, windowless cube traditionally believed to have been built by Abraham and containing the Black Stone – probably a meteorite – said to have been given to Abraham by the Angel Gabriel. The powerful emotional impact of the Ka'ba upon devout Muslims is indisputable, but it can only be experienced in Mecca; the pictorial representations of the Ka'ba commonly found elsewhere in tile, textile or wall decoration do not evoke an emotional response comparable to that produced by a crucifix, which carries its highly charged message everywhere, regardless of the replica's size or the materials from which it is made.

The direct relationship between architectural form and function familiar from Western or Christian cultural history does not apply in the case of the mosque. Whilst the idea of communion with God is an essential part of both Judaic and Christian belief, in Islam it plays an even more direct role, since there is no intermediary such as a priest. If it should be a Muslim's wish to pray in a particular room, then that room becomes his mosque for the duration because his personal belief makes it so, and nothing more is needed to effect the transformation. (This process can also work in reverse, though in practice opposition to such a change is probably inevitable; thus, a building used for centuries as a mosque can in theory be transformed at will to serve other purposes, religious or secular.) Even without a room to pray in, a Muslim's prayer-rug or any clean surface can serve as his mosque for the purpose of prayer. Since Islam does not treat material things as sacrosanct, and since to a Muslim all things are equally subject to the will of God, the Church's differentiation between 'sacred' and 'profane' and the eternal dichotomy and conflict between body and soul do not exist. Removing one's shoes before entering a mosque and performing ritual ablutions before prayers are acts of self-purification and do not represent a crossing-over from the secular to the sacred domain. By the same token, the distinction contained in Christ's exhortation to the Pharisees, 'Render to Caesar the things that are Caesar's and to God the things that are God's', has no meaning for Muslims.

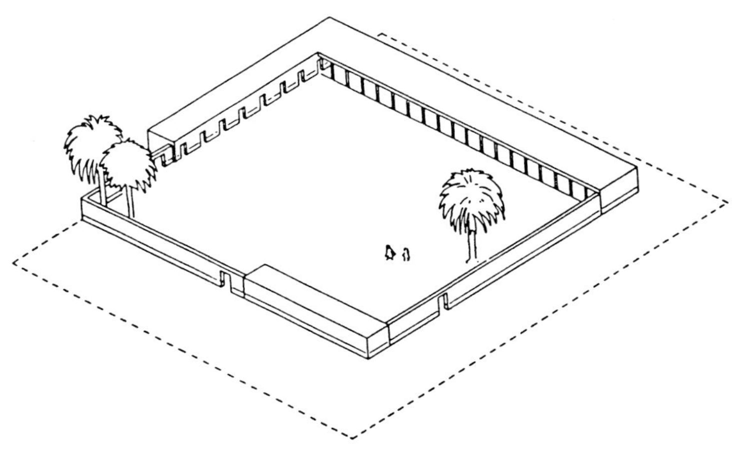

The early development of the mosque was based on the house of the Prophet at Medina with its living accommodation ranged along two sides of an enclosed courtyard (reconstruction after Creswell).

With the secular and the sacred thus welded together and expressed by means of a unified and prescribed behavioural doctrine, the role of the mosque differs from that of a church in that there is no need for some activities to be classified as 'secular' and excluded from the building for that reason. From the earliest times the mosque has always been a religious and social centre for a community, as well as – in the case of congregational mosques – providing a platform for political pronouncements at midday prayers on Fridays. In many respects, therefore, besides its religious role, the range of activities traditionally associated with the mosque was comparable to those previously associated with the Greek agora or the Roman forum.

The component parts of the mosque

In its capacity as a house of worship, the mosque has a standardized assembly of component parts, subject to minor variations depending, for example, on whether a particular building is a small village sanctuary intended largely for individual prayer, a congregational or district mosque, or the principal Friday mosque in any city or community. When women attended the mosque, they remained segregated from male worshippers, either by screens or by occupying a separate part of the building such as a gallery.

The basic elements of mosque architecture and furnishings are:

1 A demarcated space – partly roofed and partly open to the sky – to provide accommodation for the congregation at prayer. The size of the covered prayer-hall or sanctuary (*haram*) varies in relation to the area of the courtyard (*sahn*), the latter often being surrounded on three of its sides by colonnades or arcades (*riwaqs*), with the fourth side giving access to the prayer-hall; the principal factors affecting the relative proportions are the numbers of worshippers to be accommodated and the nature of the prevailing climate region by region (the beginnings of the mosque layout, derived from the house of the Prophet at Medina, are described in chapter 5). The prayer-hall – usually rectangular or square in plan – may be of the hypostyle type, i.e. having a roof supported by a large number of evenly distributed columns (sometimes with horizontal beams or systems of arches forming part of the structure). Alternatively, the hall may be covered by a single large dome on pendentives (one of the greatest contributions made by Islam to architecture)[9] or by a roof punctuated by one or more small domes.

2 The *qibla* wall and the *mihrab*. The prayer-hall must have one wall facing Mecca, i.e. perpendicular to an imaginary line pointing in the direction of Mecca. At the mid-point of this wall, known as the *qibla* wall, is placed the *mihrab*, a recess or niche which is the central and

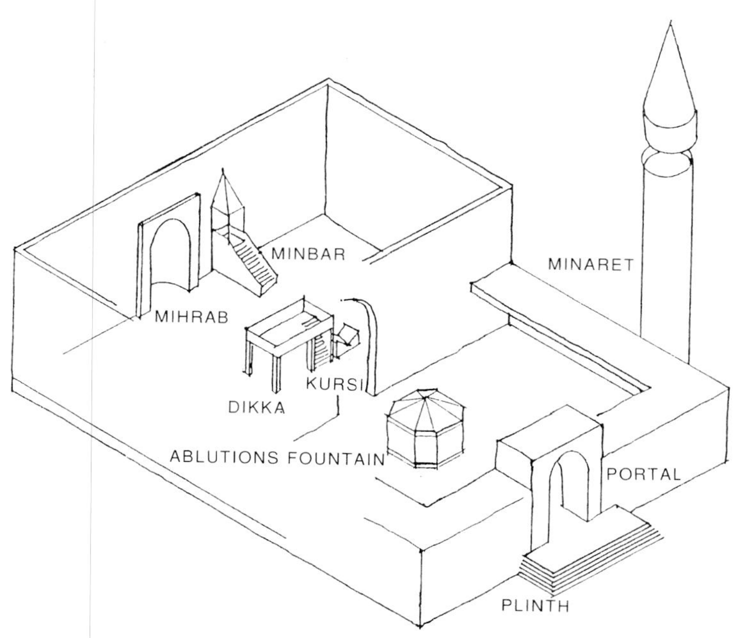

The standard components of the mosque (not drawn to scale or representing any individual mosque).

In a contemporary context, a simple representation of an open-air prayer area (below), laid out in the grounds of a hotel in Saidu Sharif, northern Pakistan, provides for the needs of individual guests; the direction of Mecca is indicated by the stone marker, serving as a mihrab.

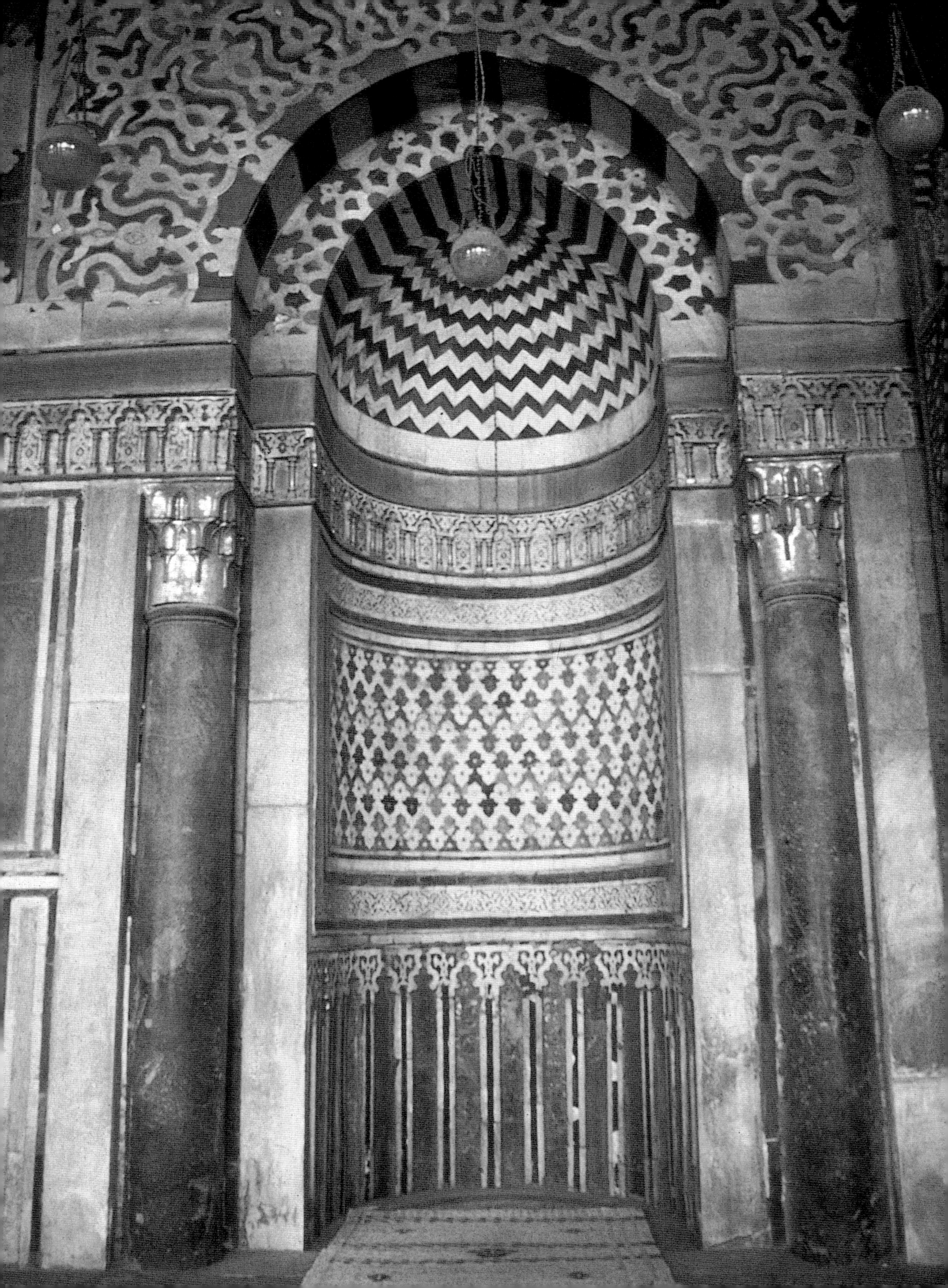

most decorated feature of any mosque. Unlike the altar in a church, however, the *mihrab* is not regarded as sacred; what is prescribed or sacred is the direction of prayer which its presence indicates. It is said that the spot by the wall where Muhammad used to stand when at prayer in his house in Medina was marked after his death by a stone (*qibla*). The form of the *mihrab* is basically that of the Roman niche – semicircular in plan and having a semicircular arched top – set in the wall. The *qibla* wall and the *mihrab* are essential components for all mosques other than the Haram Al-Sharif in Mecca itself. Since all worshippers when at prayer must face Mecca and should in theory be equidistant from the *qibla* wall, they form rows parallel to it – a practice which also explains the conventional rectangular plan of most mosques.

3 The *minbar*, or pulpit, is always positioned to the right of the *mihrab* and consists of a staircase of varying height, with or without handrails, leading to a small platform which is often crowned by a cupola-type roof, usually in some attractive shape. Its origin was the small set of steps (not unlike those made later for use in libraries) which was introduced in Muhammad's house in Medina at a time when his followers had increased in numbers, so making it advisable for him to position himself above the heads of his audience in order to make his words more easily heard. Subsequently, the *minbar* became an essential piece of equipment for use in any mosque where Muslims assembled in large numbers for Friday prayers; the imam leading the prayers would also deliver the *khutba* (oration) from it. In practice the imam reads or speaks from a step below the top platform,

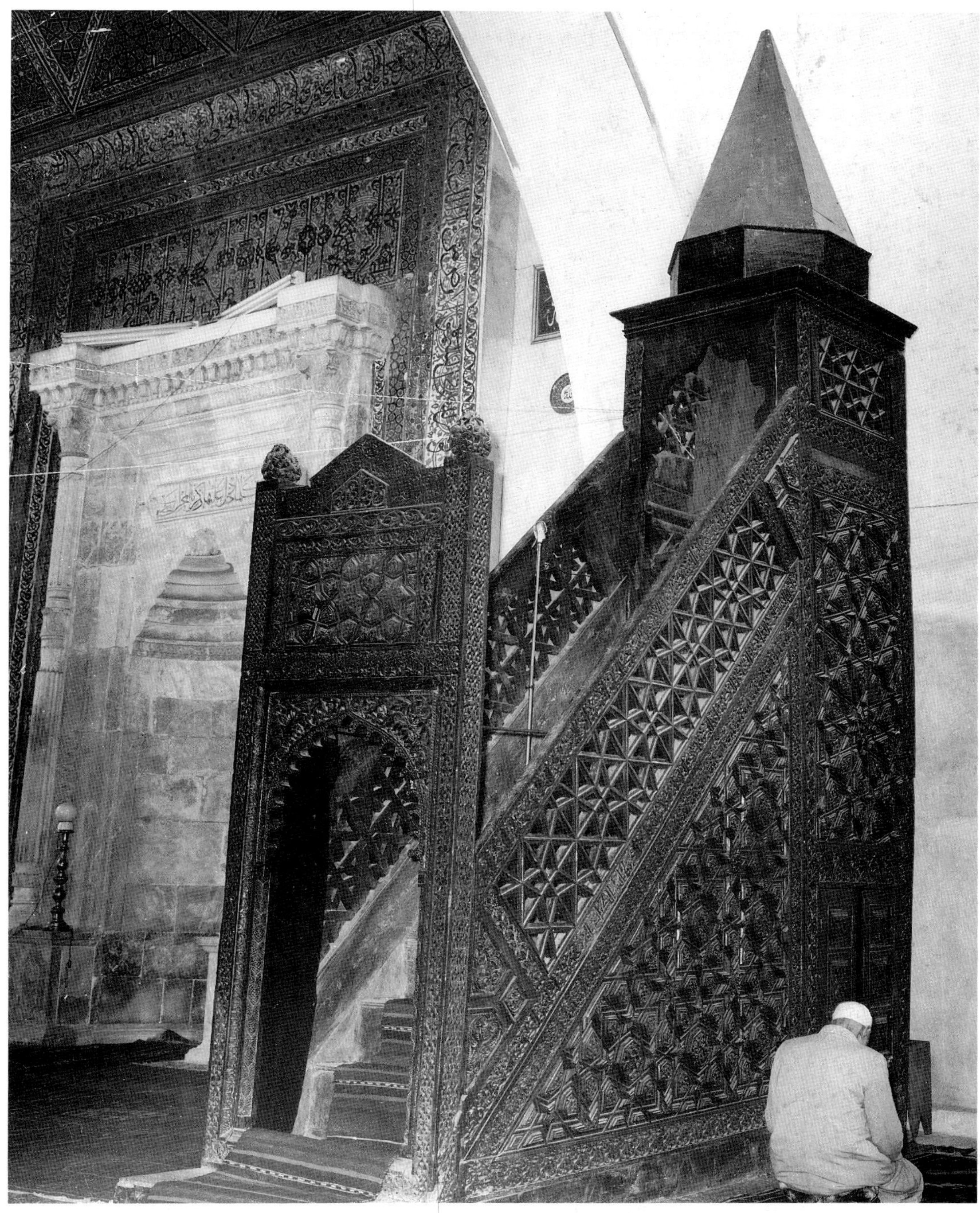

(Right) The carved ebony minbar, *standing to the right of the* mihrab, *in the Mosque of Ala ad-Din (completed 1220), Konya, Turkey.*

(Left) The lavishly decorated mihrab *of the Mosque-Madrasa of al-Muayyad Shaykh (1415–22), Cairo.*

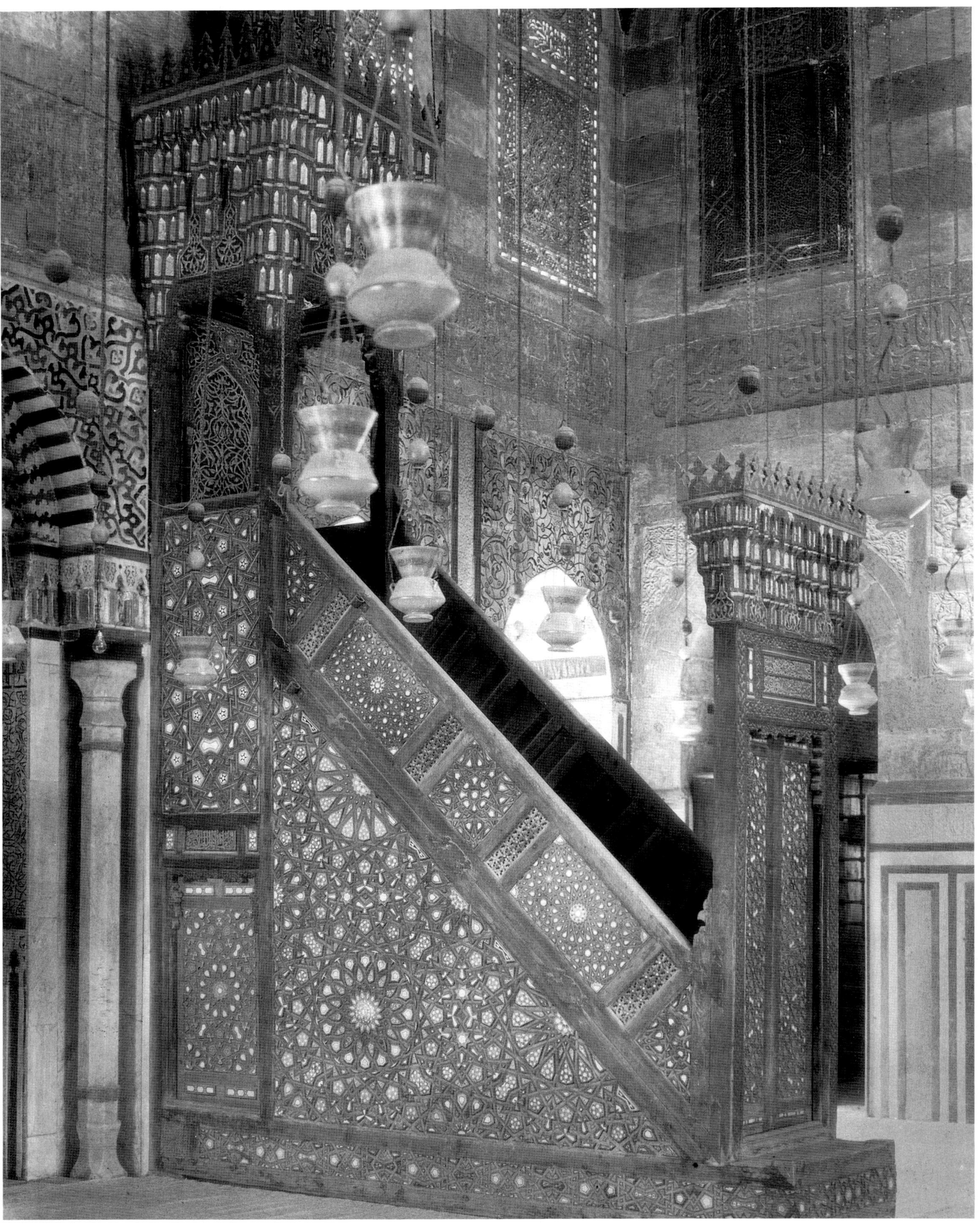

(Left) The elaborately decorated min-bar *of the Mosque of Qijmas el-Ishaky, Cairo.*

*(Right) A large wooden Qur'an stand (*kursi*) in the Mosque-Madrasa of Sultan Hasan (1356–9), Cairo.*

(Below) A finely carved wooden kursi *from Iran dated 1360; the square upper panel incorporates the name Allah, repeated in all four directions.*

which is symbolically reserved for the Prophet. Varying in size from a mere three steps to examples on a monumental scale with elaborate decoration, the *minbar* is a feature of almost all larger mosques, but is often absent from smaller buildings used for individual worship. The weekly oration in a Friday mosque may be part sermon and part political proclamation or address of state, and the *minbar* was used in former times for 'coronations' (in the sense of the inauguration of a new caliph). Whereas in Christendom the concepts of Church and State may be considered separate, in Islam the mosque can serve both as a house of worship and as a platform for official government or state pronouncements.

4 The *dikka*. A wooden platform or tribune of 'single-storey height' and positioned in line with the *mihrab*, the *dikka* is reached by its own stairs. From this raised platform the respondents (*qadi*) of the mosque repeat the ritual postures of the imam and speak the responses so that the stages of prayer can be transmitted to a large congregation (a role not unlike that of the cantor and chorus in the Greek Orthodox rite). Depending on its size and the prevailing climate, the *dikka* may also be positioned in the courtyard outside.

5 The *kursi*. This is the lectern on which the Qur'an is placed and from which the *qadi* reads and recites; it is usually placed next to the *dikka*.

6 The *maqsura*. This was originally the place set apart to safeguard the life of the imam who, in the early centuries of Islam, was also the

caliph or governor and often in danger of assassination. In the beginning the *maqsura* consisted of a raised platform with protective wooden screens. In the early period the *dar al-imara* (governor's palace) was often erected adjacent to the *qibla* wall and provided direct private access to the *mihrab* area and the *maqsura* to afford maximum security. The widened central nave – a feature introduced at an early stage – could also function as a special processional area for the complete retinue of the caliph. The introduction of a dome over the *mihrab* bay may be attributed to the fact that the presence of the caliph called for special accentuation architecturally. In addition, a separate enclosure for princely use was often shown, such as the open *iwans* of mosques in Central Asia, with side rooms reserved for local rulers. Such was the sultan's loge in Ottoman mosques, usually screened off from the prayer-hall and having its

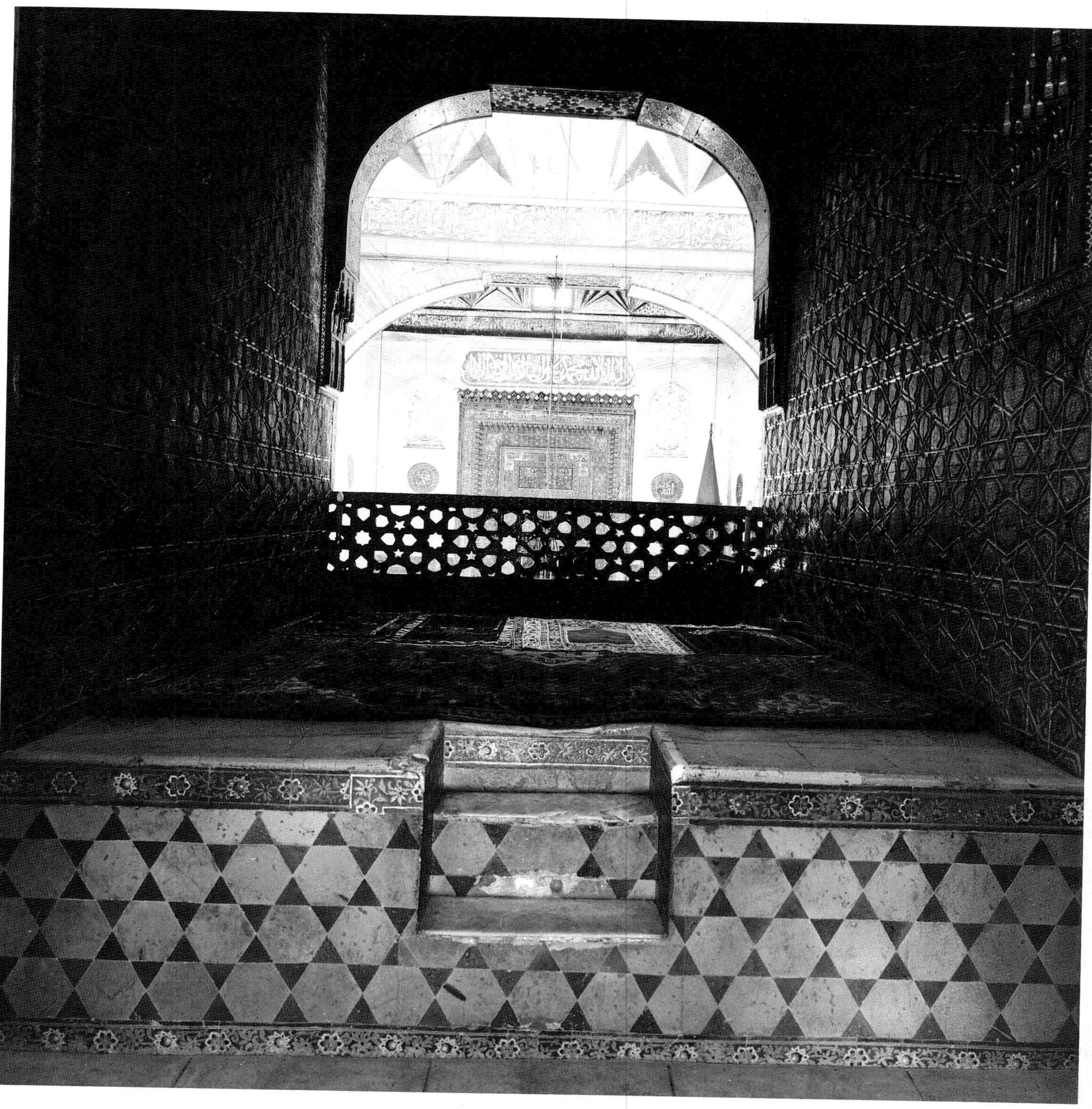

*(Opposite) The interior of the Selimiye Mosque (1569–75), Edirne, showing the raised platform (*dikka*) beneath the central dome.*

*(Above) The Sultan's loge (*maqsura*) in the Yeşil Cami (Green Mosque; 1412–19), Bursa, looking towards the* mihrab.

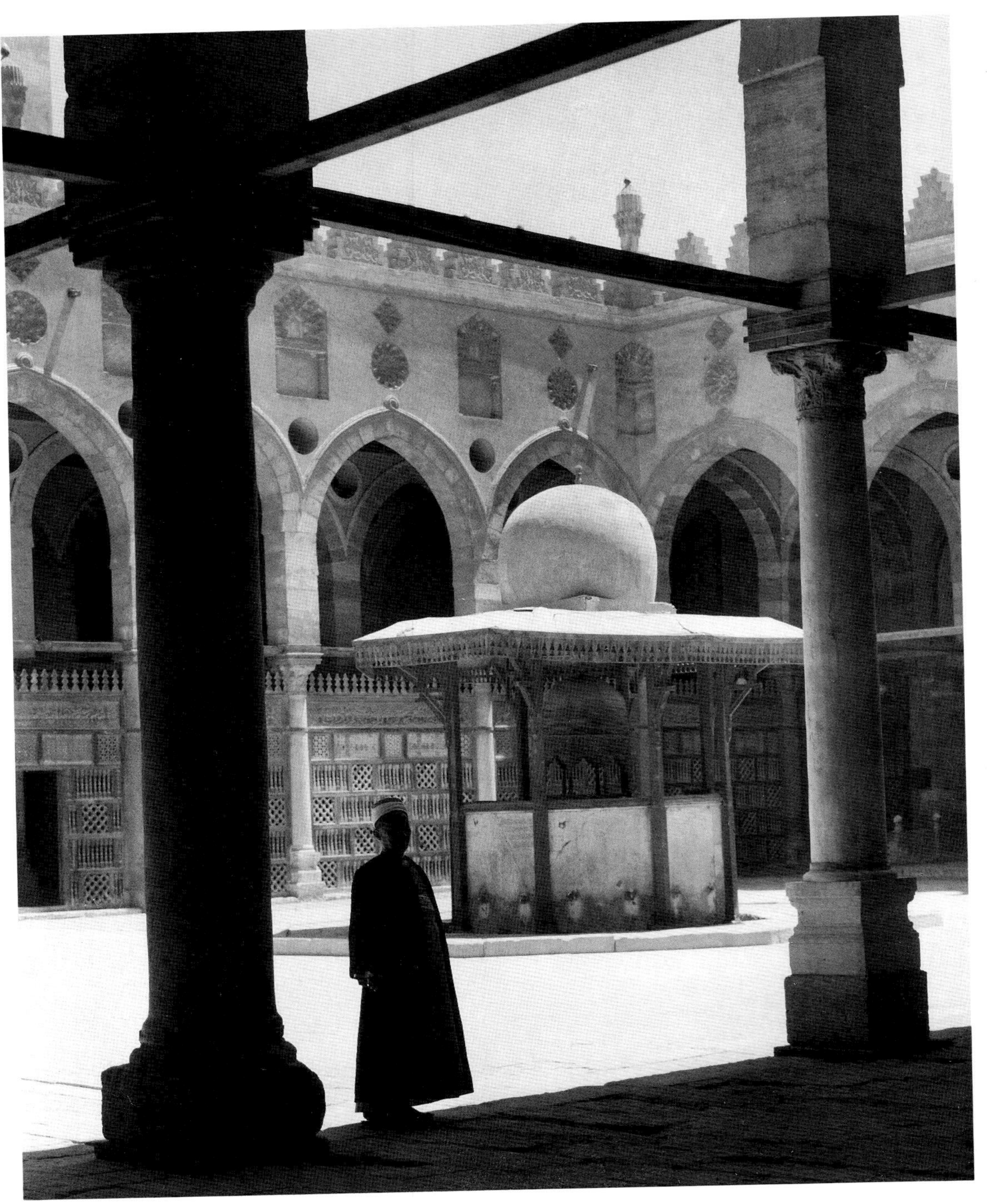

The ablutions fountain in the courtyard of the Mosque of al-Maridani (1338–40), Cairo.

own entrance. Satisfying the dual function of ensuring the ruler's safety and at the same time providing a means of surrounding his retinue with appropriate splendour often provided a special opportunity for architectural elaboration.

7 The pool. This feature may be with or without a fountain and may be intended for the prescribed ritual ablutions before prayers, but is sometimes purely decorative. When used for ablutions, it is designed to permit a number of worshippers to wash simultaneously under running water, and is placed at or near the centre of the courtyard. Fountains often display inventive designs, especially in the form of domed, small pavilion-like roofs; perhaps the most beautiful extant example is the Qubba al-Ba'adiyyin in Marrakesh (the associated mosque no longer exists). The effect of a simple square or rectangle of open water with a fountain can often be impressive in its own right, as for example at the Badshahi Mosque in Lahore. In cases where the fountain fulfils an ornamental role the obligatory washing facilities are often located in a room near the shoe-storage racks.

8 The minaret. The original purpose of this tower-like feature, apart from serving as a local landmark, was to ensure that the voice of the muezzin making the *adhan* could be heard at a maximum distance. During the lifetime of Muhammad the call to prayer was given from the roof of his house in Medina, and it was not until the fourteenth and fifteenth centuries that the building of minarets became universal. The origin of the minaret as an architectural form may be based on one of, or an amalgam of, a variety of sources

ranging from Zoroastrian symbolic fire-towers to Roman watch-towers, coastal lighthouses or church towers. A single minaret was generally provided, although under the Ottoman and Mughal Empires twin minarets (signifying royal patronage) were frequently built. Occasionally, four are found, and in the case of the Sultan Ahmet Mosque in Istanbul there are six, a figure exceeded only in Mecca, where there are seven. In modern mosques it is still usual, though not essential, for a minaret to be included, especially in the design of those built in cities. In general, however, the significance of the traditional minaret in an age when broadcasting the *adhan* via loudspeakers has become the norm, now rests in the realm of the symbolic.

9 The portal. A general characteristic of the architecture of the Muslim world is the concealment of the interior of a building from outside view, hence the mosque is almost invariably surrounded by high walls. The single impressive main portal constitutes the threshold between urban bustle and the tranquil atmosphere within; as such, the gateway to the mosque takes on a powerful psychological importance, which is often augmented by sumptuous ornamentation intended to pay homage to God's presence, as well as to emphasize the generosity of the mosque's patron. A major mosque was usually commissioned by a patron endowed with great power and wealth, such as a caliph or sultan. As the exterior – the minaret and dome often excepted – is usually plain and simple, the inclusion of a massive ornamental gateway serves to demonstrate the underlying paradox suggested by, on the one hand, the austere appearance of the House of God and, on the other, the flamboyant display of the patron's largesse. While the external walls must not be allowed to seduce the believer by means of ornamental frills, building a mosque represents an act of piety in itself, and wherever possible the scale of the donor's patronage should be appropriately commemorated.

A basic respect in which the architectural development of the mosque contrasts with that of church design is the relative importance of regional differentiation. Each region of the Islamic world rapidly evolved a stylistic image of its own, in part at least as a result of local climatic conditions and the availability of building materials combined with related craft skills. Secondly, in contrast to the history of the Church, sectarian divisions within Islam never affected architectural appearance or style. Thus, in the Christian context the influence of Reformation and Counter-Reformation is apparent in church architecture, whereas the division between Sunni and Shia – to take the nearest equivalent in magnitude in Islamic theology – cannot be readily observed. Only in the choice of quotations from the Qur'an used as calligraphic decoration can any clear distinction be found, and even this is not discernible to anybody who cannot read Arabic (see chapter 2). Finally, the restricted range of liturgical procedures (limited essentially to the reading of the scriptures and the act of prostration which accompanies the performance of prayers) is identical throughout the Muslim world.

Although the component parts which together constitute the mosque have never varied in either function or meaning, their architectural form did undergo a fundamental change during the late Abbasid period in the eleventh and twelfth centuries (the preceding centuries being sometimes referred to as the period of 'classical Islam'). With the dissolution of the Abbasid Empire, governed from Baghdad, power was distributed among a large number of new states around the perimeter of the Muslim world. This major political development was followed by the growth of regional architectural styles, each with its own character. Although the components of the core remained the same, the external appearance changed dramatically. A simple analogy would be a tree growing with a straight trunk until the eleventh century, when it divides to form numerous branches, each clad in its own distinctive foliage and representing a regional style. Saw through the trunk at any point and its cross-section will reveal the same components throughout its length. Saw through any of the branches and the components will still be the same as those of the trunk; only the foliage of the various branches will have developed differently. The language for the classical period is uniform, but thereafter regional vernacular language clothes the standardized interior of each 'branch' with a distinctive external appearance. Although virtually any of the mosque's essential component parts could be used to illustrate this point, a good example is the minaret, which serves the same purpose with the minimum of functional complexity throughout the Islamic world; however, no two regions employ the same language of design or ornament, as is clear from the examples illustrated.

Finally, it is worth mentioning two factors which affect mosque design and which are the subject of widespread and lively debate in the Muslim world. Although one of these – opposition to innovation – is a theological matter, this does not mean that its impact in other areas is in any way diminished, and in practice it exerts a powerful influence on the design of the mosque today and may continue to do so in the future. In this context resistance is directed against the introduction of any new feature which could be interpreted as evidence of a departure from, and possibly even opposition to orthodox tradition in mosque design. Such a phenomenon may be classified as *bid'a* and thus unacceptable. Given sufficient authority, the adoption of such a rigid attitude can effectively eliminate any creative element in design, leaving an architect with no choice but to resort to the use of historical revivalism. However, this school of thought has not been sufficiently widespread or powerful to prevent the realization of all free design concepts, as is evident from the examples of contemporary mosques illustrated in chapter 15.

The other factor is one that has become the subject of controversy everywhere, although it often acquires particular significance in Muslim countries: the question as to whether the continued use of regional or vernacular architectural language should be encouraged in a contemporary situation, perhaps being incorporated into an otherwise neutral and technologically standardized international style. The reason why this current debate may be of greater importance in the Muslim world than in 'Western' countries is that in the minds of the citizens of any one nation it will often be linked to the very vital issue of the establishment or preservation of that country's cultural identity.

- 2 -
THE ROLE OF CALLIGRAPHY
WHEELER M. THACKSTON

DEPICTION of the human form as 'graven image' has been a subject of debate throughout Islamic history. Although injunctions against any such depiction may have been honoured more in the breach than in the observance, as a mere glance at the history of Islamic – and particularly Persian – painting and manuscript illustration will show, it is apparent that within the confines of the mosque and other sacred and semi-sacred places – shrines, tombs, *madrasas* and the like – the strong prejudice against representation of animate forms, inherited not only from the Semitic (and partially the Judaeo-Christian Hellenistic) civilization of the Near East proper but also from Zoroastrian Iran, has been maintained.

Even in non-religious contexts, painters and illustrators, who have consistently represented human and animal subjects, have always felt that they were engaged in something that was at best 'suspect' and disapproved of, if not actually forbidden, and writers on the subject have resorted to unimpeachable precedent to justify such representation. A sixteenth-century writer, Dost-Muhammad of Gawashwan, justifies illumination and decoration by the precedent of Ali ibn Abi-Talib:

> It is etched on the minds of the masters of the arcane that the garden of painting and illumination is an orchard of perfect adornment; and the arrangement and embellishment of Korans, which bespeak the glorification of the Word of the Necessarily Exalted, are connected to the pen and bound to the design and drawing of the masters of this noble craft.
>
> It has been recorded that the first person to adorn with painting and illumination the writing of the Word that is necessarily welcomed was the Prince of the Faithful and Leader of the Pious, the Conquering Lion of God . . . Ali ibn Abi-Talib, and the gates of this commodity were opened to this group by the key of that majesty's pen. A few leaves (*barg*), known in the parlance of painters as *islami*, were invented by him.[1]

And in an attempt to justify portraiture and the representation of human form, Dost-Muhammad resorts to the tradition that attributes the beginning of portraiture to the prophet Daniel:

> If, by the externality of the religious law, the masters of depiction hang their head in shame, nonetheless what is gained from the writings of the great is that this craft originated with the prophet Daniel.
>
> It has been related that after the Prophet [Muhammad]'s death, some of his Companions went to Byzantium with the purpose of presenting Islam. In that realm they met an emperor named Hercule. After many strange and wonderful things happened, [the emperor] inquired after the Prophet and asked of his deeds and acts. Thereupon he had brought a chest, which he opened. In it there appeared to those present a marvellous portrait that astonished the group. Since the onlookers were so gratified and pleased by seeing the portrait, the Companions were asked, 'Do you recognize this person?'
>
> 'No,' said the Companions, 'never have our eyes feasted upon such beauty, and never has the gate of illumination from the origin of this likeness opened to us.'
>
> 'This,' said Hercule, 'is the portrait of Adam, the Father of Humanity.' And thus he continued to show portraits until he produced one with a miraculous visage as luminous as the sun, whose regal being took Adam from the dust of nonexistence and garbed him with a cloak of purity. The admiration that the former portrait had elicited from the onlookers was nullified by the sight of this blessed face, and the perplexity with which they had been struck by the first portrait's beauty ceased with the contemplation of the sun-like beauty of the latter. . . . When the Companions saw that portrait, teardrops streamed like stars from their eyes, and a longing for the Prophet was reborn in their hearts. Seeing their sadness, agitation and tears, Hercule sought the reason from them.
>
> 'This,' they said, 'is a portrait of our blessed Prophet. Where are these portraits from, for we know that they conform to the actual countenances of the prophets?'
>
> 'Adam besought the Divine Court to see the prophets among his offspring,' said Hercule. 'Therefore the Creator of All Things sent a chest containing several thousand compartments, in each of which was a piece of silk on which was a portrait of one of the prophets. Inasmuch as that chest came as a witness, it was called the Chest of Testimony. After attaining his desire Adam placed the chest in his treasure house, which was near the setting place of the sun. Dhu'l-Qarnayn[2] carried it away and gave it away and gave it to the prophet Daniel, who copied [the portraits] with his miraculous brush.'
>
> From that time forward the continuity of portraiture has continued beneath the azure dome of the sky, and the likeness that was painted by Daniel was meticulously preserved by the ruler of Byzantium in his treasury until the time of the death of the Best of Mankind [Muhammad]. Therefore, portraiture is not without justification, and the portraitist's conscience need not be pricked by the thorn of despair.[3]

Facing page
The Muslim shahada *or creed decorating the portal of the Mosque of al-Muayyad Shaykh (1415–22), Cairo.*

(Left) The interior of the Ulu Cami (Great Mosque; 1396–1400), Bursa, showing extensive use of bold calligraphic decoration on piers.

(Opposite) The entrance to the Islamic Center, Washington, D.C., decorated with a Qur'anic inscription (24:36, the Sura al-Nur). The text, in neo-Kufic script, reads: 'In houses which Allah has permitted to be raised to honour, for celebration, in them His name: in them He is glorified.'

Regardless of the source of the prejudice against figural representation, it was unmistakably there, even if early Muslim notables had little or no compunction about decorating their palaces with scenes filled with human and animal forms,[4] and medieval Muslims, particularly in the Iranian cultural sphere, certainly never shrank from the portrayal of such forms in miniature painting. However, when it came to the mosque, it was a different story altogether. From the earliest times the written word was used as the major, and sometimes the sole, type of mosque ornamentation, with a total absence of figural decoration, for the written word was never subject to prejudice of any kind; and in Islam, where the Qur'an is considered the actual, literal Word of God, copying quotations from it in the most beautiful fashion possible has always been considered meritorious.

> By the teaching of him to whom honor is incumbent, the tutor of the garden of nobility, sweet-tongued preacher in the realm of the imamate . . . guided by the inscription of the register of the city of knowledge, of which Ali is the gate, . . . everyone is commanded to strive to attain this noble and honorable craft [calligraphy] when he said, 'Have beautiful writing, for it is among the keys to sustenance.'[5]

In general, Qur'anic texts are selected for inscriptions in mosques, but quotations from the *hadith* and other pious phrases are also found, and whereas inscriptions are always in some sense appropriate to the locations in which they are found, relatively few passages consistently occur in a specific location.

The treatment of writing as decoration has varied from as simple as possible, with no extraneous ornamentation of the writing, to the indescribably ornate. A good early example of utter, stark simplicity is the Great Mosque at Sousse, Tunisia (850), which has a single unornamented band of Qur'anic Arabic in Kufic script running around the courtyard. In later times perhaps nowhere has calligraphic starkness been used to such effect as in the Eski Cami, Edirne, where an entire bay is filled by the single word *Allah* ('God'). It is as stark and striking – and as modern-looking – as anything one is likely to find. The elaborate mosque is typified by the Friday Mosque (Bibi Khanim) in Samarqand, which is completely covered inside and out with writing in brickwork and on tiled surfaces. (No surface of the Masjid-i Shah in Isfahan is left unornamented, but most of the ornamentation is intricate floral tilework, not writing.) Another, but very different, type of ornate writing can be seen on the interior walls of the Ulu Cami in Bursa (completed in 1400), which are covered with masterful, and sometimes rather playful, specimens of Ottoman calligraphy, particularly of the *aynali* ('mirror image') type which was popular in later centuries.

The Qur'an, or any part therof, in and on a mosque provides the viewer with a message and focus of meditation. It may incidentally be

ornamental or decorative, but a Qur'anic inscription has value in and of itself. Like the recitation of the Qur'an, an act of piety that has merit in and of itself and is completely divorced from any questions of understanding the lexicon and grammar of Arabic, the mere existence of a Qur'anic inscription is equivalent to a Christian icon: it serves as a visible representation of supernatural reality. In the case of quotations from the Qur'an, God's word is revealed in the guise of human speech. In view of this, it should not come as a surprise that much of the inscriptional material found in a mosque or any other religious building is not – and, from the builder's or designer's point of view, need not be – readable. Here we say 'readable' and not 'legible', for almost all inscriptions are 'legible' in the sense that they are capable of being read – or deciphered – eventually if not immediately. In no sense, however, are they all immediately readable: some are placed in obscured areas; others are too high and too far away to be read; others are so intertwined and convoluted that it is beyond the ability of the average person to puzzle them out.

For instance, on the wall of the shrine complex of Khwaja Abdullah Ansari in Herat (built *c.* 1425), the pleasing rectangular geometric patterns will, after a good deal of scrutiny, reveal themselves as saying '*Subhana 'llahi 'l'azimi wabihamdih*' ('Glory be to God, and by praise of Him'), but no one would suppose that an ordinary visitor to the shrine might stop to decipher the inscription, while the surrounding inscription, '*qul kullun ya'malu 'ala shakilatih*' (Sura 17:84: 'Say, Every one acteth after his own manner'),[6] is both legible and readable. The mosque in the Islamic Center on Massachusetts Avenue, Washington, D.C., has a neo-Kufic inscription across the front entrance that is all but indecipherable; few, if any, pay much heed to it.

Here also should be treated the question of familiarity. In the pre-modern period it would have been assumed that anyone who was literate enough to care to read what was inscribed on a mosque wall would have memorized the entire Qur'an during the course of his elementary education, and recognition of a single word or phrase would have instantly evoked the memory of the rest of the passage quoted. And even if not everyone remembered the entire Qur'an, most of the texts used as mosque inscriptions were oft-repeated passages with which almost everyone would have been familiar.

Early mosques were restricted, of course, to the angular lettering later known as Kufic, since it was the only style of Arabic script in general use during the early Muslim period. During the Abbasid caliphate, with the development of round hands and the definition of calligraphic proportions leading to the canonization of the classic round scripts in the tenth and eleventh centuries, *thuluth* became more and more the calligraphic style *par excellence* for Qur'anic inscriptions and epigraphy, particularly in monumental settings. Angular Kufic with its myriad variations was always retained, but over time it became more and more

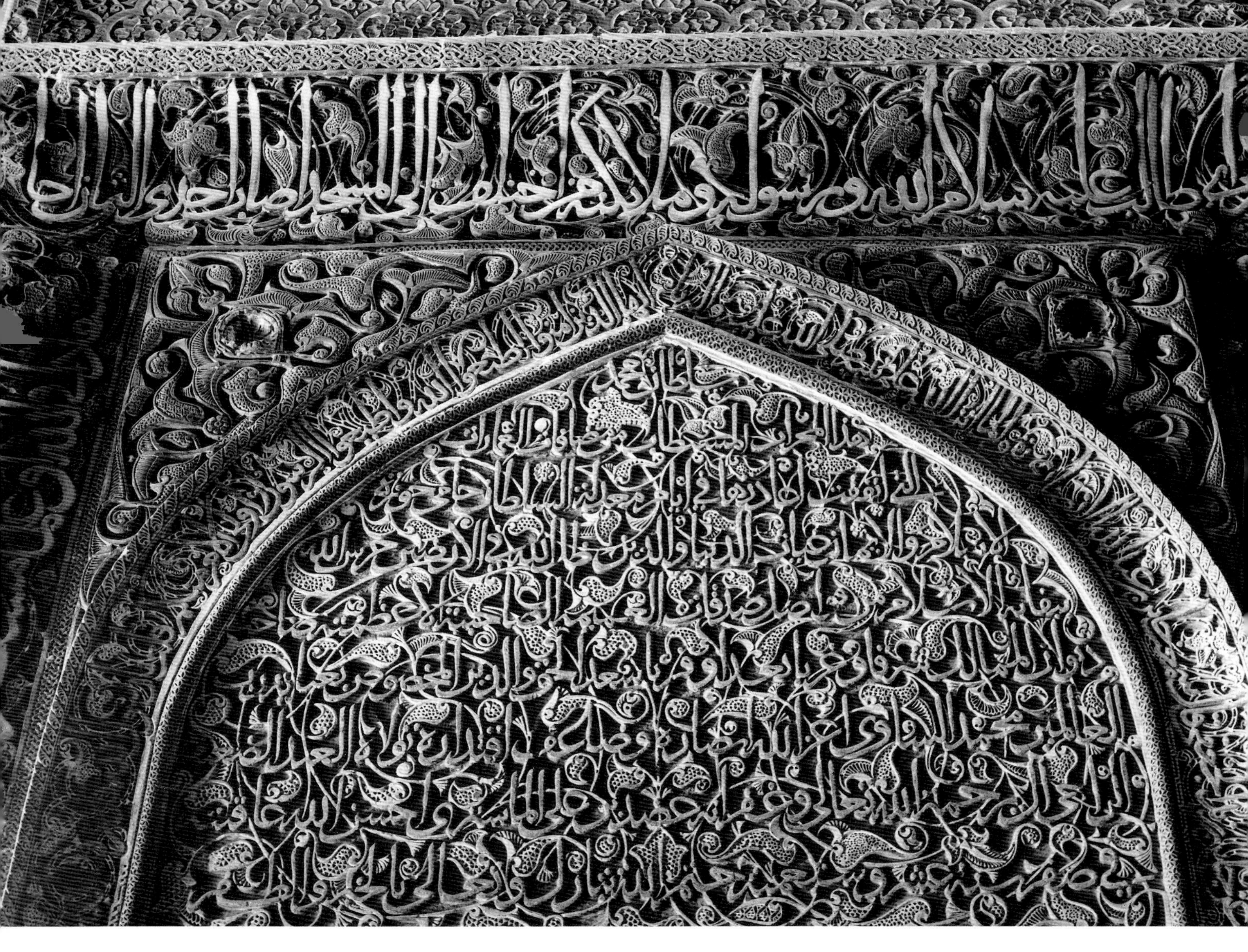

The mihrab *of Öljaytü (1310) in the Friday Mosque, Isfahan, features an ornate carved stucco panel which includes sayings of Ali.*

ornamental – and simultaneously less and less readable – with the incorporation of foliation, floriation and knotting into the letters. Of the classic scripts, *muhaqqaq* was rarely used in inscriptions and was generally reserved for copying large-scale Qur'ans; *tawqi* is the script of stucco inscriptions, occasionally being used elsewhere in epigraphy for donor's attributions etc. to contrast with monumental *thuluth. Taliq*, reserved primarily for chancery documents, and later *nastaliq* both seem to have been considered inappropriate for Qur'anic mosque inscriptions, although non-Qur'anic – and usually non-Arabic – *nastaliq* inscriptions certainly occur, as in the Masjid-i Shah in Isfahan.

Thuluth inscriptions are very often run in white letters on a dark-blue background in what appears to be a band consisting of two registers, one above the other, with a horizontal line formed from super-elongated reversed *yas* separating the two. In actuality the two 'registers' are one, with successive words, or even parts of words, moving up and down and back and forth across the horizontal line as the inscription as a whole slowly progresses from right to left.[7] Another technique, used extensively during the Timurid and Safavid periods, was to create a band of lettering in the form of a register – or multiple intertwined registers – of monumental *thuluth* with exaggerated, elongated verticals, usually in white on a dark-blue ground, while across the top of the band, and through the verticals, was run a band of small Kufic in a contrasting colour, such as ochre or umber.[8] Although the *thuluth* inscriptions are always readable, it is not seldom that the intertwining of the registers renders reading difficult, to say the least. In almost no case, however, is the Kufic band readable, for in elevated locations the lettering is always too small and obscure to be read from ground-level. Even when the Kufic can be seen, it can only be deciphered with difficulty since it lacks the diacritical apparatus necessary for easy reading. The purpose of the Kufic band is not, therefore, to convey a text, but to serve a compositional function by tying the tops of the *thuluth* verticals together and uniting it with the band as a whole. Indeed, the result was such a felicitous combination that the technique was used for centuries in Iranian mosques and religious buildings of all descriptions.

There is an enormous variety in the texts chosen for mosques, and the texts are almost always appropriate to the locations in which they occur.

A comparison of the bismillah *– 'In the name of Allah, the Merciful, the Compassionate' – written in a variety of Arabic scripts and in Taliq, a Persian script.*

Mashq

Square Kufic

بسم الله الرحمن الرحيم

Eastern Kufic

Thuluth

Naskhi

Muhaqqaq

Rihani

Taliq

Mashq – an early script, first developed at Mecca and Medina during the first century of the Muslim era.

Square Kufic – developed at Kufa, this script had by the ninth century become more ornamented and was the most influential in Islamic calligraphy generally.

Eastern Kufic – a more delicate version developed in the late tenth century, notable for extended vertical upstrokes.

Thuluth – fully developed by the ninth century, this script became the most popular for ornamental inscriptions.

Nashki – being relatively easy to read and to write, this became the most frequently used script for writing Qur'ans after it was redesigned in the tenth century.

Muhaqqaq – another popular script for writing Qur'ans, featuring shallow sub-linear curves with a pronounced flow from right to left.

Rihani – combines characteristics of Thuluth and Naskhi, the diacritical marks always being written with a finer pen than that used for characters.

Taliq – this 'hanging' script, developed by Persian calligraphers in the ninth century, continued to be used for monumental purposes even after a more refined variant – Nastaliq – was introduced in the fifteenth century and became the most generally used script for Persian documents.

There seems, however, to have been little marked preference for a particular text for a particular location. Yet the combination of texts chosen for any one building may well represent a programmatic selection to convey a specific agenda on the part of the patron, designer or builder. A good example of agenda in the selection of Qur'anic inscriptions is found on the Buland Darwaza, the huge ceremonial gateway into the mosque complex at Fatehpur Sikri built by the Mughal Emperor Akbar *c.* 1575. Carved in very low relief, the *thuluth* inscription consists of Suras 39:73–75, 41:53–54 and 41:30–31. The first section includes the phrases 'And the gates thereof shall be ready set open' and 'Praise be unto God, who hath . . . made us to inherit the earth'; and across the top of the gateway is 'Hereafter we will show them our signs in the regions of the earth' (41:53) – all particularly appropriate for a monumental gateway that was most likely built in celebration of a major military victory.

The selection of epigraphic texts may also represent a sectarian agenda. The inclusion of sayings by Ali in stucco on Öljaytü's *mihrab* (1310) in the Friday Mosque, Isfahan – not to mention the list of the Twelve Imams of the Shia also incorporated into the *mihrab* – marks the mosque as Shiite in sympathy if not in actual allegiance,[9] just as the roundels with the names of the first four Caliphs, often found in Ottoman mosques, mark them as Sunni.[10] The formula used on the drum of the Madrasa-i Sultani in the Chahar Bagh in Isfahan (1706–14), *Allahumma salli ʿala Muhammadin wa ali Muhammadin wa sallim* ('O God, pray for Muhammad and for the family of Muhammad and grant [them] peace'), proclaims the building as unmistakably Shiite. Inscriptions that include references to the 'people of the house' (11:73, 33:33) should generally be interpreted as Shiite in sentiment. On the other hand, the ubiquitous formula *la ilaha illa 'llah, muhammadun rasulu 'llah* ('There is no god but God, Muhammad is the messenger of God') is by its very nature entirely neutral and is found on Sunni and Shiite mosques alike.

An exception to the general lack of preference for a specific text to suit a specific location is the *mihrab*. Many *mihrabs* contain one of two Qur'anic quotations containing the word *mihrab*, either 3:37 ('whenever Zacharias went into the *mihrab*')[11] or 3:39 ('while he stood praying in the *mihrab*'). Other popular inscriptions for *mihrabs* are the Qur'anic imperatives to perform prayer, e.g. 11:114 ('Pray regularly morning and evening; and in the former part of the night'), as in the Congregational Mosque at Bistam, Iran (1302).

Mosque lamps with inscriptions other than the donor attribution almost always have the 'Light Verse' (24:35) or some part thereof:[12]

> God is the light of heaven and earth: the similitude of his light is as a niche in a wall, wherein a lamp is placed, and the lamp enclosed in a case of glass; the glass appears as it were a shining star. It is lighted with the oil of a blessed tree, an olive neither of the east, nor of the west; it wanteth little but that the oil thereof would give light, although no fire touched it. This is light added unto light: God will direct unto his light whom he pleaseth. God propoundeth parables unto men; for God knoweth all things.

Phrases from the same verse are also appropriately inscribed on the stained-glass windows on the *qibla* wall of the Süleymaniye Mosque in Istanbul.

Passages appropriate to domes abound in the Qur'an, one such being 35:41 ('God sustaineth the heavens and the earth, lest they fail'), which is inscribed, to name but one example, on the main dome of the Süleymaniye.

Examples of mosque lamps incorporating calligraphic ornament: (above) a bronze lamp, probably dating from the tenth–eleventh century, with pierced decoration; (right) a glass lamp of the late thirteenth century, from Syria, bearing bold decoration on the neck (including text from the Sura al-Nur) and body (in praise of the Sultan).

Calligraphy is considered one of the greatest Islamic art forms and inscriptions are used extensively in mosques, especially to glorify the name of God and quote passages from the Qur'an. This tile panel, intended for installation in a mosque, was produced in Fez, Morocco; it proclaims the name Allah in bold decorative Arabic script.

(Left) Hagia Sophia, Istanbul, Turkey, was originally a Byzantine church built in the sixth century; after the Ottoman conquest in 1453 it served as a mosque for over four centuries. A series of large calligraphic discs, installed in 1847–9, decorate the interior; they incorporate the names of the Prophet and other early leaders.

(Below) Tile panel above a window in the portico of the Fatih Mosque (1463–70), Istanbul; the Kufic inscription includes part of the 'Throne Verse' (Qur'an 2:255).

(Above) The use of cursive nastaliq *script is found in many Mughal buildings. An inscription, written in Persian in a wall panel below one of a pair of windows in the Mosque of Wazir Khan, Lahore, Pakistan, 1634, extols belief in the Prophet Muhammad and warns of the terrible fate that awaits non-believers.*

(Centre) The decorative band around the mihrab *of the Mosque of Al-Bakiriyya, San'a, Yemen (1598), contains passages quoted from the Qur'an.*

(Right) Detail of Kufic inscription carved in stone in the portal of the Masjid-i Juma, Herat, Afghanistan (built 1201–3, with later additions until 1500).

清真寺

Another extremely popular verse, the 'Throne Verse' (2:255), also a favourite as a talismanic text, is found ubiquitously:

God! there is no god but he; the living, the self-subsisting: neither slumber nor sleep seizeth him; to him belongeth whatsoever is in heaven, and on earth. Who is he that can intercede with him, but through his good pleasure? He knoweth that which is past, and that which is to come unto them, and they shall not comprehend any thing of his knowledge, but so far as he pleaseth. His throne is extended over heaven and earth, and the preservation of both is no burden unto him. He is the high, the mighty.

Other Qur'anic texts of great popularity for inscriptions include: 3:18 ('God hath borne witness that there is no God but he; and the angels, and those who are endowed with wisdom profess the same'); 9:18 ('But he only shall visit the temples of God, who believeth in God and the last day, and is constant at prayer, and payeth the legal alms, and feareth God alone. These perhaps may become of the number of those who are rightly directed'); 9:33 ('It is he who hath sent his apostle with the direction, and true religion; that he may cause it to appear superior to every other religion; although the idolaters be averse thereto'); 11:7 ('And that the hour of judgment will surely come – there is no doubt thereof – and that God will raise again those who are in the graves'); 55:26–27 ('Every creature which liveth on the earth is subject to decay: But the glorious and honourable countenance of thy Lord shall remain for ever');[13] and 112 ('Say, God is one God; The eternal God: He begetteth not, neither is he begotten: And there is not any one like unto him').[14]

Texts from the *hadith* also feature in mosque inscriptions, and those used almost always have to do with mosques. For instance, the text in stucco on the *mihrab* of the Friday Mosque in Urmiya, Iran (1277), is in translation 'The Prophet said, "Come forward to the prayer, and do not be among the negligent." And the Prophet said, "Be visitors in this world, and adopt mosques as your abodes"', which is entirely appropriate to its location. Another *hadith* often seen particularly on mausoleums states 'The Prophet said, "Hasten to pray before [the time] passes, and hasten to repent before death".'. It is found, for example, on the Tümän Äkä mausoleum at Shah-i Zinda in Samarqand (1405) and on a dome drum of the Bibi Khanim Mosque in Samarqand. The famous *mihrab* of Ölyaytü in Isfahan has the prophetic *hadith* which states that 'God builds a house in paradise for him who builds a mosque', as well as a quotation from Ali ibn Abi-Talib, *mani 'khtalafa ila 'lmasjidi* ('he who resorts to the mosque, ...').

Tomb mosques often have Sura 36 (*Ya Sin*), a favourite for funerals. An example is the Taj Mahal: across the four arches of the main building extends Sura 36 in its entirety. On the crypt cenotaph of Mumtaz Mahal is inscribed verse 3:185, so markedly appropriate for graves: 'Every soul shall taste of death, and ye shall have your reward on the day of resurrection; and he who shall be far removed from hell fire, and shall be admitted into paradise, shall be happy: but the present life is only a deceitful provision.'

In the iconography of painting, inscriptions are often used to identify a setting. A doorway with the inscription *Allahu wala sawah* ('God and none but him') and a portico with the Qur'anic inscription *wa'anna 'lmasajida lillahi fala tad u ma a 'llahi ahadan* (72:18: 'Verily the places of worship are set apart unto God: wherefore invoke not any other therein together with God') immediately identify to the viewer that the building depicted is a mosque – even before the eye has been able to take in the action of the picture, all of which is entirely appropriate to a mosque setting.

Interestingly, two phrases found ubiquitously in painting, as well as in and on mosques, *almulku lillah* ('the kingdom is God's') and *ya mufattiha 'l-abwab* ('O opener of gates'), are not strictly speaking Qur'anic at all and do not even necessarily identify a building as religious. *Almulku lillah* is derived from a host of instances in the Qur'an where the phrase *lillahi mulku 'ssamawati wal'ard* ('God's is the kingdom of the heavens and earth') occurs. Another common variant, *almulku lillahi 'lwahidi 'lqahhar* ('the kingdom belongs to God, the One, the Almighty'), derives from Sura 40:16 ('Unto whom will the kingdom belong on that day? Unto the only, the almighty God'). *Ya mufattiha 'l-abwab* ('O opener of gates'), which is found, of course, over doors and gateways,[15] is derived from an amalgamation of 7:40 ('Verily they who shall charge our signs with falsehood, ... the gates of heaven shall not be opened unto them [*la tufattahu lahum abwabu 'ssama*], neither shall they enter into paradise until a camel pass through the eye of a needle'), 38:50 (Gardens of perpetual abode, the gates whereof shall stand open unto them [*mufattahatan lahumu 'l'abwab*]'), and 78:19 ('And the heaven shall be opened, and shall be full of gates [*wafuttihati 'ssama'u fakanat abwaban*]').

Throughout the vast extent of the Islamic world the written word as mosque ornament has traversed the full spectrum from the utterly simple to the unbelievably complex, but the written word has always remained, along with floral and geometric design, the only form of ornamentation considered appropriate for mosques, and the readability of an inscription is often, and justifiably, seen to be sacrificed to ornamentality.

Facing page
Calligraphic inscriptions in mosques occur not only in Arabic, Persian and Urdu, but also sometimes in the local vernacular.

(Top) Fragment of the restored tile mosaic work dating from the Umayyad period in the prayer-hall of the Al Aqsa Mosque, Jerusalem, 715.

(Centre left) A panel below the ceiling of the Masjid Jami Ayn Al Yagin'guri, Gresik, Java, Indonesia, repeats the names Allah and Muhammad around a central point; in this mosque, dating from 1556 (rebuilt in 1860), there are a number of such panels, in which the patterning was possibly influenced by the form of the Hindu mandala.

(Centre right) The name of God (Allah) in brick relief in the Al-Ghadir Mosque (1977–87), Tehran, Iran.

(Bottom left) Broad bands of Qur'anic text in thuluth *script surround the* mihrab *of the Shrine of Qutham ibn Abbas (1370–1405), a cousin of the Prophet Muhammad, in the Shah-i Zindah mausoleum complex, Samarqand, Uzbekistan.*

(Bottom right) A modern inscription in the prayer-hall of the Great Mosque, Xian, China (thirteenth–seventeenth century), identifies the building as Qing Jin Si (Mosque of True Purity).

- 3 -
APPLICATIONS OF GEOMETRY

MOHAMMAD AL-ASAD

Any act of architectural design is inherently an exercise in geometry. Both are concerned with the properties of lines, surfaces and forms arranged in space, hence any analysis of a work of architecture is partially an inquiry into its geometry. Principles of geometry have been applied differently in various architectural traditions. In the Western world from the Renaissance onwards, the influence exercised by geometry in the conception of architectural form has generally been regulated and clearly articulated by leading architects and writers on architecture. In the architectural traditions of the Islamic world, rules of geometry were applied in a more flexible manner and were used to provide general guidelines rather than lay down specific canons of design.

The role of geometry in the evolution of Western architecture since the Renaissance has been elaborated upon in the writings and drawings of architects such as Leone Battista Alberti and Andrea Palladio in the fifteenth and sixteenth centuries, Etienne-Louis Boullée and Claude-Nicolas Ledoux in the eighteenth century, and Le Corbusier in the twentieth century. Theoreticians of Western architectural traditions have generally expressed an exclusive attitude towards the use of geometry, as is evident in their preference for elementary and pure shapes such as the square and circle and for specific proportional systems such as that of the golden section. Alberti, for example, recommended nine basic geometric shapes for the design of churches, six of which are derived from the circle, and the remaining three from the square. To Alberti, good architecture depended on the rational integration of proportions and the use of absolute geometry.[1]

The exact role assigned to geometry in the architectural traditions of the Islamic world is more difficult to assess. Surviving original drawings from the pre-modern Islamic world which could help us better understand the design process are very few in number. None of the surviving drawings belong to the formative years of Islamic architecture, but date to the post-Mongol era.[2] Although other forms of artistic expression, such as music and poetry, are adequately discussed in surviving texts from the pre-modern Islamic world, there is general silence concerning architecture, and we are not aware of treatises devoted to explaining how an original work of architecture was conceived and realized by architects and craftsmen, or perceived by users and viewers.

Facing page
A window grille in the west iwan *of the Mosque of Ibn Tulun (876–9), Cairo.*

Our knowledge of geometry as an independent discipline is more substantial, however, for Muslims viewed geometry as an important field of knowledge and continued the classical tradition of placing it at the same level as mathematics, astronomy and music. The development of geometry and other scientific fields of inquiry in the Islamic world was initiated during the eighth and ninth centuries by translations of ancient texts from languages such as Greek and Sanskrit into Arabic. By the tenth century, original Muslim contributions to the sciences became significant; in this context important developments in the field of geometry resulted from the work of, among others, Umar al-Khayyam, Abu'l Wafa al-Buzjani, Abu Mansur al-Khwarazmi and ibn al-Haytham.[3]

Although our knowledge of the development of the science of geometry in the pre-modern Islamic world is considerable, we do not know enough about the processes and intermediaries through which theoretical geometric knowledge was transferred to an applied field such as architecture. This is in contrast to the situation encountered in the European Renaissance, where information on the transfer of information is more substantial, and evidence indicates that it was partly aimed at raising architecture from the status of a manual art to that of a liberal mathematical art. Relations between geometricians and architects in the pre-modern Islamic world did exist, however, and a linguistic expression of the connection is found in the Arabic word *handasa*, which means both geometry and architecture-engineering. It has been suggested that the mathematician Umar al-Khayyam may have participated in the design of the north dome of the Great Mosque of Isfahan. He had been living in Isfahan at the time of the construction of the dome and was working on the properties of irrational numbers, which were also used for determining the proportions of its design. In the absence of supporting evidence, however, the connection remains conjectural.[4] Muslim mathematicians such as al-Buzjani (d. 998) and Giyath al-Din Jamshid al-Kashi (d. 1429) wrote manuals aimed at explaining basic geometric principles and their applications in architecture. These manuals, intended for architects, craftsmen and building supervisors, discussed issues including the composition of two-dimensional decorative geometric patterns, the outlines of domes and arches, and the characteristics of the *muqarnas* vaulting system. They were not aimed at communicating advanced mathematical knowledge, propagating geometrically derived principles of architectural theory, or exploring the symbolism of specific geometric shapes or proportional systems; they were instead technical manuals aimed at simplifying and popularizing mathematical principles for the mathematically uninitiated.[5] Hence, our knowledge of possible symbolic associations of certain geometric shapes in the context of architecture and the degree to

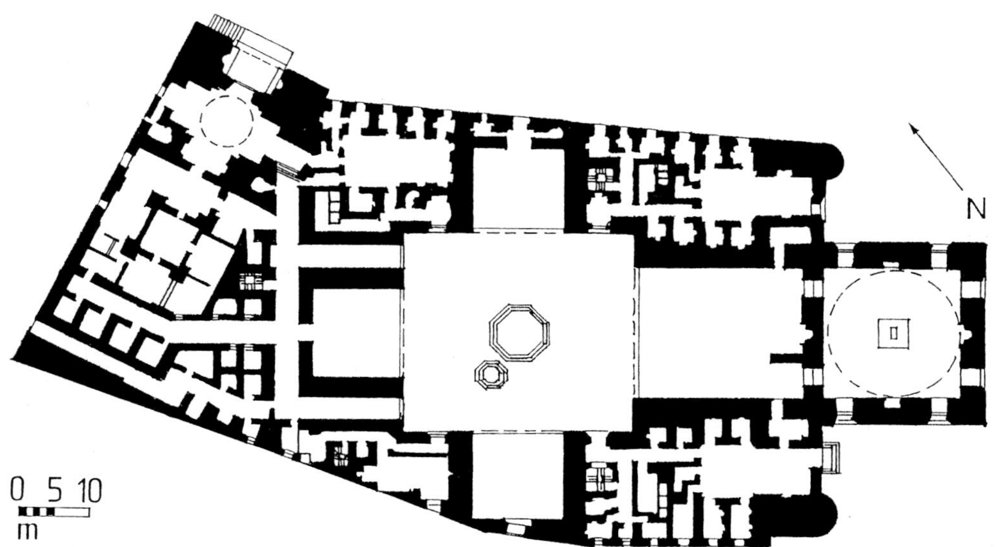

(Left) Plan of the Mosque-Madrasa of Sultan Hasan (1356–9), Cairo, showing the deviation from a rectangular layout caused by the congested urban surroundings.

(Right) View of the King Abdallah Mosque (1989), Amman, Jordan, showing the regular octagonal layout.

which architects were informed of theoretical developments in mathematics and geometry remains incomplete.

Any discussion of a topic such as the application of geometry in mosque architecture will encompass a variety of architectural traditions and will inevitably include a juxtapositioning of monuments as diverse as the eighth-century Umayyad Great Mosque of Damascus and the seventeenth-century Friday Mosque of Delhi. When dealing with such a diversity of architectural traditions, generalizations cannot and should not be made, and no conclusion can claim any sense of universality. At best, one can only aim at identifying common themes which connect groups of mosques.

The application of geometric principles to the architectural production of the Islamic world shows an inclusive and flexible approach, in contrast to the situation encountered in the European Renaissance, and this difference can be observed by comparing statements made by Alberti and al-Kashi. Alberti mentions that for the design of round churches the height of the wall up to the vaulting should be one-half, two-thirds or three-quarters of the diameter of the plan. In his *Miftah al-Hisab* (The Key to Arithmetic), a manual devoted to explaining basic principles of geometry, al-Kashi includes chapters dealing with the design of arches, domes and *muqarnas* vaults, and devotes a section to clarifying how elevational outlines of *muqarnas* units can be determined. He recommends that the height of the unit should equal twice its depth, but treats the issue of height as a flexible one and adds that the height can be increased or shortened according to the judgment of the craftsman.[6]

The same principles of flexibility generally prevailed for the design of mosques. The use of centralized plans derived from the square or circle as advocated by Alberti for the design of churches was not common. Because of the utilitarian consideration peculiar to Islam, that of accommodating large numbers of worshippers arranged in rows, mosques instead followed rectangular outlines. In urban centres such as Cairo, mosque plans might be dictated by the irregular boundaries of their sites, as in the case of the Mosque of Sultan Hasan (1356–9).[7] Of course, exceptions exist. These include lesser-known monuments such as the octagonal Timurid Mosque of Abu-Nasr Parsa in Balkh (*c.* 1460). Better known are examples including Sinan's Selimiye Mosque in Edirne (1569), whose prayer-hall contains an octagonal arrangement of piers which are nonetheless made to fit within a rectangular outline. The most important exceptions, however, are the Ka'ba in Mecca and the Dome of the Rock in Jerusalem (691). The Ka'ba, which approximates the form of a cube, measures about 11 × 12 × 15 m (36 × 39 × 49 ft). The octagonal plan of the Dome of the Rock is based

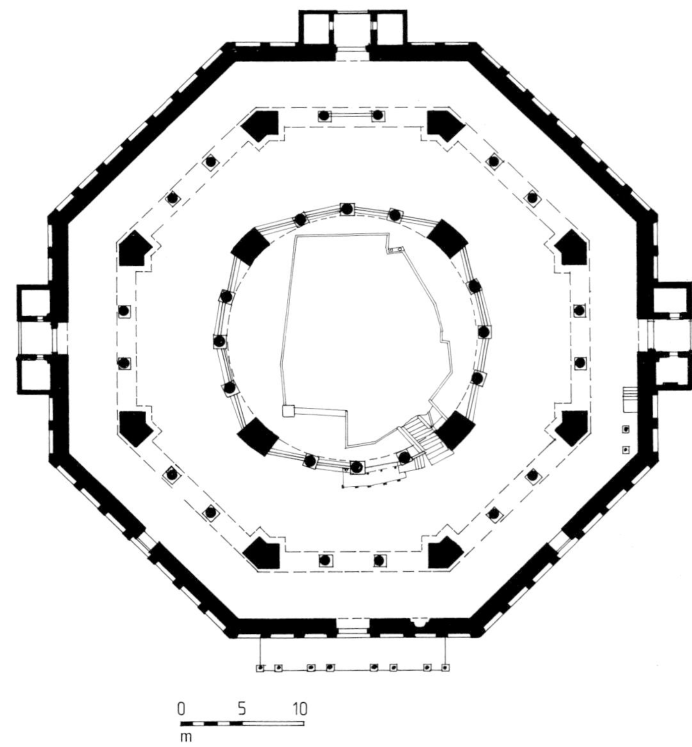

Plan of the Dome of the Rock (690–2), Jerusalem; the hexagonal scheme adopted for this building reflects the influence of contemporary Byzantine church architecture (see p. 79 for a view of the exterior).

on two identical squares sharing a common centre, one being rotated through 45°; the result is a double octagonal ambulatory surrounding a circular arrangement of columns and piers. Both monuments, however, are highly exceptional on the functional and architectural levels: although both structures have connections with the act of prayer, neither is a mosque in the true sense of the word, and each has its own unique symbolic associations. Also, both have connections with pre-Islamic architectural traditions. The Ka'ba, although rebuilt during the Islamic era, has retained its pre-Islamic cubic form. The Dome of the Rock, Islam's earliest surviving monument, was built at a time when dependence on Byzantine architectural traditions was still considerable. This influence is evident in the similarities between the plan of the Dome of the Rock and those of a number of centralized Byzantine structures, among them the sixth-century church of S. Vitale in Ravenna.

Two of the most important components of many mosques, the dome and minaret, were designed according to centralized plans. Domes rest on circular or octagonal bases, and – as discussed below – considerable geometric experimentation took place in the design of the dome. In plan, minarets have circular or polygonal outlines, and in some cases a combination of both: thus, for example, some Mamluk minarets have a square base, an octagonal shaft and a circular top; the spiral form was also used for some minarets, as at Samarra in the Great Mosque and the Abu-Dalaf Mosque, both belonging to the ninth century.

Although the centralized plan was not common in the design of mosques, it was ubiquitous in the design of mausoleums. Centralized plans, especially octagonal ones, can be found in funerary structures belonging to a number of architectural traditions, including those of the Abbasids, Timurids, Ottomans and Mughals. Beginning in the twelfth century, mausoleums were often connected to mosques or mosque-*madrasa* complexes. The first known example of this arrangement, dating from the early twelfth century, is the mosque and mausoleum of Sultan Sanjar in Merv. The massive square tomb was connected to a now destroyed mosque from its western side. In the architecture of the Mamluks, tombs were often located within a mosque-*madrasa* complex, but were differentiated from the rest of the complex by the use of a centralized plan and the incorporation of a dome. A most impressive example of this arrangement is found in the complex containing the mausoleum, mosque-*madrasa* and hospital of Sultan Qala'un in Cairo (1284–5): within the irregular outline of the complex, the mausoleum is distinguished by its highly regular plan consisting of a square surrounding an octagonal arrangement of alternating piers and columns which support a dome.

In recent years, the use of a centralized plan has become more widespread in mosque designs. Examples include the circular al-Tooba Mosque in Karachi (1969), the hexagonal King Khaled International Airport Mosque in Riyadh (1983) and the octagonal King Abdallah Mosque in Amman (1989). While the designs of these

The Friday Mosque (1644), Delhi. The large open courtyard allows the symmetrically organized façade, including paired minarets, to be seen in its entirety.

(Opposite) The Selimiye Mosque (1569–75), Edirne, by Sinan reveals the symmetry of its square plan and central dome through the presence of a minaret at each corner.

mosques hark back to the Dome of the Rock or to centralized funerary structures, the use of such plans is also linked to the modern fascination with the two-dimensional geometric patterns of the Islamic world. These patterns, many of them based on the circle and its polygonal derivatives, have at times been used as outlines for architectural plans.

Instead of using elementary geometric shapes and fixed systems of proportions, the pre-modern architects of the Islamic world relied on different geometric principles such as modularity, a system whose use can be traced back to the early hypostyle mosques. The hypostyle mosque is planned according to the basic unit or module of a rectangular bay defined by four columns or piers, and the covered spaces of the hypostyle mosque consist of multiples of the basic module. The result is usually a regular composition of covered areas placed within a rectangular outline and surrounding a rectangular court, as seen in the ninth-century Great Mosque of Samarra. However, because of site irregularities, or as the result of later additions which many mosques have experienced, the multiplication of the rectangular hypostyle unit may produce an irregular composition; this is evident in the Great (Friday) Mosque of Isfahan, which has undergone numerous additions and restorations since the eighth century.

The use of the module as a design tool in the pre-modern Islamic world is supported by a group of architectural drawings, attributed to a sixteenth-century architect practising in Bukhara, which includes plans drafted on grid paper. Here the grids not only functioned as a drawing aid, but also provided a modular system which determined the measurements of building elements.[8]

Ernst Gombrich has stated that 'the appeal of symmetry is so universal that architects have submitted to its demands in most styles of buildings all over the world'.[9] In the religious architecture of the Islamic world symmetry has played a prominent role. Among the many examples of mosques symmetrically planned along their longitudinal axis are the Great Mosque of Samarra, the Bibi Khanim Mosque in Samarqand (1399) and the Friday Mosque of Delhi (1644–58). In the prayer-halls of a number of imperial Ottoman mosques, the symmetry is extended to include both the longitudinal and the horizontal axes. The earliest example of this arrangement occurs in the mid-sixteenth century in the Şehzade Mehmet Mosque in Istanbul, which contains a central dome flanked by four half-domes.

Often, the symmetry of the plan does not extend along a whole axis of the structure, but is localized to specific parts of it, as in the case of mosques which have undergone additions and changes, e.g. the Great Mosque of Isfahan. Although the parts of the mosque containing the courtyard and four *iwans* are symmetrically arranged along the longitudinal axis, the symmetry breaks up as one moves away from the centre. The use of overall symmetry was in some instances also prevented by site irregularities, especially – as noted above – in a congested city such as Cairo. Although the courtyard and surrounding four *iwans* of the Mosque of Sultan Hasan are symmetrically arranged along the longitudinal axis, the outer areas of the structure had to follow the existing site boundaries.

The idea of frontal axiality which allows for complete views of façades is not widespread in the architectural traditions of the Islamic world, since it demands the often unavailable luxury of ample surrounding space, but significant exceptions do exist. The *ziyadas* surrounding a number of mosques built during the Abbasid era, such as the Great Mosque of Samarra and the Mosque of Ibn Tulun in Cairo (879), were partly planned to provide empty spaces around the mosque itself. In later traditions of Islamic architecture, such as those of the Timurids, Mughals and Ottomans, structures with open vistas and a frontal axial approach are not uncommon; examples include the Bibi Khanim Mosque in Samarqand, the Friday Mosque of Delhi and the Selimiye in Edirne.

In most cases, however, such spaces are not available. Because of various urban and legal factors (which extend beyond the scope of this study) most structures in pre-modern Islamic cities were at best surrounded by narrow streets, hence only fragmented, rather than complete, views of façades could be achieved. Direct frontal approaches were usually not possible, and buildings had to be approached from an acute angle. In some cases, as with the Great Mosque of Isfahan, the mosque is not even kept separate from the surrounding urban fabric but merges with it. In the modern era attempts have been made to separate some historic mosques from surrounding accretions and later constructions, so transforming the original buildings into isolated monuments; one notable example of such treatment is the Mosque of Sultan Hasan in Cairo, which was cleared of adjoining structures in the late nineteenth century.

Mosques located in heavily urbanized areas have usually had to accommodate two distinct directional requirements, that of the *qibla* and that of the adjacent streets. Most architects practising today have unfortunately decided to satisfy only the first requirement and to ignore the second, thus compromising, if not sacrificing, any sense of continuity which may have existed between their mosques and the surrounding urban fabric. In contrast, medieval designers responded to these requirements with creativity and ingenuity, transforming a potential restriction into an asset. The earliest surviving example in which these two requirements were satisfied is the Mosque of al-Aqmar in Cairo (1125). Here the differing orientations of the *qibla* and the adjacent street were overcome by inserting a triangular segment containing an entrance passageway with a bent axis between the street and the mosque's courtyard. The use of the broken axis was later elaborated into a series of shifting axes which transformed the entry process into a dynamic architectural experience: examples of this elaborate entry process range from the Mosque of Sultan Hasan in Cairo to the Mosque of Shaykh Lutfallah in Isfahan (1618).

The same inclusive and flexible approach to the use of geometry in designing mosque plans was also applied to the third dimension. Unfortunately, however, we know even less about the principles governing the design of elevations, for although a few plan drawings have survived from the pre-modern Islamic world, almost no elevation drawings are known. However, available data indicate that the proportions governing the plan of a structure were usually extended to include its three-dimensional projections. The main dome of Sinan's Süleymaniye Mosque in Istanbul rises to a height of 53 m (174 ft) above ground level, or twice its diameter.[10] The proportional system of the golden section was used in the design of both the plan and elevation of the north dome of the Great Mosque of Isfahan.[11] Similar conclusions concerning the use of unified proportional systems for plans and elevations have been reached as a result of extensive geometric analysis of the Islamic monuments of Central Asia.[12]

In designing the third dimension, architects had considerable freedom in determining which proportions and outlines to use. This is evident in al-Kashi's *Miftah al-Hisab*. In the chapter on arches, al-Kashi enumerates the variety of outlines available for one-, two-, three- or four-centred arches. He did not favour any one outline over the others, but simply informed the reader of the existing variety, leaving it up to him to make a final choice. The same applied to the design of vaults and domes, both of which are three-dimensional variations on the arch.[13]

The decision to use overall symmetry for the design of building façades would depend on the character of the plan. A symmetrically organized plan, such as that of the Friday Mosque of Delhi, has symmetrically organized façades. For mosques occupying irregular sites, the use of symmetry may be neither possible nor suitable. This is evident in the Mosque of Sultan Hasan, where only the segments of the façades containing the entrance portal and tomb chamber are symmetrically arranged.

Minarets also played a role in articulating the composition of mosque façades and forms. Twin minarets were often used to define a rectangular plane framing a façade, examples of such an arrangement being found in the Masjid-i Shah in Isfahan (1612–37) and the Friday Mosque of Delhi. In Ottoman sultanic examples such as the Selimiye four minarets serve to define a cube enclosing the three-dimensional composition of the prayer-hall. In the Mosque of Sultan Ahmet in Istanbul (1609–17) the number of minarets is increased to six to mark the corners of both the prayer-hall and the courtyard.

In spite of the sophisticated use of geometric principles for determining the spatial and formal characteristics of mosques throughout the Islamic world, authors and architects of the modern era have been primarily fascinated by another application of geometry in architecture, that of two-dimensional surface patterns. These patterns have captured the attention of modern architects and artists including Owen Jones, Louis Sullivan, E. M. Escher, and even a German mathematician, Edith Müller, who devoted a monograph to the decorative designs of the Alhambra. Architects practising in the Islamic world today use two-dimensional geometric patterns as a primary means of providing their designs with an 'Islamic character', and, as mentioned, some have even used these patterns for the generation of floor-plans.

The fact that modern authors have given two-dimensional geometric surface designs more emphasis than other uses of geometry in the architecture of the Islamic world should not be surprising, for no other major tradition of architecture accorded geometry such a central importance in the organization of its decorative schemes. Geometric patterns, which were carried out in materials including mosaics, stone, stucco, ceramics and wood, were the object of considerable effort and expense, and required the employment of highly skilled craftsmen for their execution. They can totally transform the architectonic qualities of a structure, and in contrast to their use in a Western tradition such as that of the Renaissance, two-dimensional patterns were often employed in the Islamic world to dematerialize surfaces and spaces rather than to accentuate them. The aesthetic experiences of numerous monuments of Islamic architecture are heavily, and often primarily, influenced by the characteristics of their two-dimensional decorative patterns.

In the Islamic world the preference for providing monuments with a decorative surface is almost as old as the formation of its earliest architectural traditions. Much of the Dome of the Rock was sheathed with mosaics on both the exterior and interior, and the Umayyad Great Mosque of Damascus contains the largest areas of mosaic-covered surfaces ever put together. The decorative schemes used for these early monuments consisted primarily of vegetal designs showing Mediterranean influences, with geometric patterns playing only a limited role in their compositions. The ubiquity of geometric designs was a later development, generally dated to the tenth century. It is believed to have had its origins in Baghdad, the primary cultural centre of the Islamic

Facing page
The use of geometrically arranged corbelled units in vault decoration is clearly seen in two magnificent examples of the muqarnas*: (above) in the* mihrab *niche of the Tilakari Mosque, Samarqand (mid-seventeenth century); (below) in the domed chamber behind the north-east* iwan *of the Friday Mosque, Isfahan.*

Carved and sculptural geometric decoration on domes: intricate relief patterning on the dome of the Mausoleum of Qaitbay, Cairo, 1472–4; although not in a mosque, the striking mocárabes *dome in the Hall of the Two Sisters in the Alhambra, Granada, built in the fourteenth century, is one of the finest examples of the technique in plasterwork.*

Sinan, the celebrated chief architect of Ottoman rulers from 1538 to 1588, perfected the technique of achieving a transition from a regular octagonal or hexagonal base to a circular dome supported by squinch arches; an outstanding example of this architect's work is seen above in the principal dome of the Mosque of Sokollu Mehmet Paşa, Istanbul, 1572.

Two-dimensional geometry appears in innumerable designs employing many different materials. Such decoration was encouraged, especially in mosques, by the generally perceived prohibition of the representation of human and animal forms: (top) tilework in the Madrasa of Ben Youssef, Marrakesh, Morocco (1564–5); (centre right) brick patterning in the later of two Seljuq mausoleums (1093) near Hisar-i Armani in the Qarraqan region of western Iran; and inlay work at the Masjid-i Jami of Timur, popularly called Bibi Khamum (1399–1404), Samarqand, Uzbekistan.

world at the time, and to have been disseminated from there to surrounding regions. Chronologically, it corresponds to the remarkable developments which Muslims achieved in the disciplines of mathematics and geometry. The domination of geometric decorative patterns in many of the artistic and architectural traditions of the Islamic world came to an end with the rise of new aesthetic standards under the Mughal, Safavid and Ottoman dynasties during the sixteenth century, when they were superseded by the use of more realistic and freer vegetal patterns.[14]

These geometrically organized two-dimensional decorative patterns consisted not only of abstract geometric shapes, but included inscriptions and vegetal designs organized according to rules of regular geometry, and the relatively ambiguous term 'arabesque' can be used to describe the various forms of two-dimensional geometric designs. These patterns reflect one of the most regularized applications of geometry in the architecture of the Islamic world. They are organized according to rectilinear or radial grids, in which the circle and its polygonal and star-shaped derivatives play a prominent role. Although modular units are highly regularized, considerable flexibility exists in organizing whole compositions, since the arabesque consists of multi-directional repetitions of basic units. In this regard, a correspondence exists between the basic unit of a geometric design and a single bay of a hypostyle mosque serving as a module.

These patterns could be structurally and constructionally integrated with or divorced from the buildings they sheath. Examples of the former include structures decorated in what is identified as the 'brick style', among them the Great Mosque of Isfahan, where brick was used not only as a construction material, but also for the surface articulation of the building. The same is true of the stone monuments of Seljuq Turkey and Mamluk Egypt, where stone was used both as a primary construction material and for surface decoration. In cases where decorative patterns are divorced from a structure, a comparison between architectural surface decoration and textiles is not unfounded.[15] The primary monument of Islam, the Ka'ba, is provided with a textile cover, the *kiswa*, which is ceremonially changed on an annual basis. Although the Ka'ba is a unique case, a number of other monuments of Islamic architecture have had their surface decoration changed. The original exterior mosaic covering of the Dome of the Rock had deteriorated by the sixteenth century and was replaced by ceramic tiles during the reign of the Ottoman Sultan Süleyman II. Inscriptions articulating the surfaces of the Great Mosque of Isfahan were also changed by the Safavid rulers Tahmasp I (1524–75) and Abbas II (1642–66) for ideological reasons such as the ascendancy of Shiism as the state religion, or for self-glorification. In the twentieth century, the distinction between structure and surface decoration is clearly shown in the division of major mosque competitions into two independent segments, one for the design of the structure, the other for the building's decorative programme.

Geometric principles were also used for the generation of various three-dimensional architectural elements, many of them associated with the dome. One such element is the rib, which was most strikingly used in the Islamic architecture of Spain and North Africa. Although ribbing can be used as a structural device supporting a dome, it can also have a decorative value, for ribs can be arranged to provide a variety of geometric patterns articulating its surface. In the tenth-century domes of the Great Mosque of Cordoba, ribbing was used for both structural and decorative purposes. Each of the mosque's three squinch domes located in front of the *mihrab* incorporates eight intersecting ribs which create intricate geometric patterns of eight-pointed stars and polygons, including squares and octagons. In the Mosque of Bab al-Mardum in Toledo (1000) ribbing is used purely as a decorative element; this small building, about 7.50 m (24 ft) square, is divided into nine square bays, each covered by a ribbed dome displaying a different geometric pattern. Considering the small size of the domes, the ribs could not have had a structural role and only served a decorative purpose.

Considerable experimentation in three-dimensional applications of geometry also took place in the transitional zone of the dome. The use of the traditional devices of squinch and pendentive, as inherited from pre-Islamic architectural traditions, was continued and also elaborated upon by the Muslims. Instead of using the squinch only to transform the square into an octagon on which the dome could be placed, the architect Sinan employed it to transform the rectangular domed prayer-hall of the Sokollu Mehmet Paşa Mosque in Istanbul (1572) into a hexagon. In the north and south domes of the Great Mosque of Isfahan (late eleventh century) the area containing the squinch was divided into two horizontal tiers. The upper tier was maintained as a single vault, but the lower one was divided vertically into a tripartite arrangement of a central arch flanked by two *muqarnas*-like arched units. This two-tiered composition, also called the 'one over three' arrangement, eventually evolved into multi-tiered *muqarnas* vaults, e.g. in the Madrasa of al-Malik al-Salih Najm al-Din in Cairo (1244).[16]

The *muqarnas* was an invention of the Islamic world. Although its origins can be traced to the tenth century, it was not until the twelfth century that it became a common feature of Islamic architecture in areas as far apart as Morocco and Iran. It represents a highly sophisticated three-dimensional application of geometric principles, a *muqarnas* composition being based on the replication of units arranged in rows corbelled one on top of another. These units, which can be made of wood, stone, stucco or ceramics, provide a flexible system of articulating surfaces, and can be made to fit within any configuration and to visually dematerialize and divide surfaces. The formal organization of the *muqarnas* is closely linked to that of two-dimensional geometric patterns, and a *muqarnas* composition can be viewed as a stereometric projection of these patterns. In plan, *muqarnas* configurations are also arranged according to rectilinear or radial grids in which the circle and its polygonal and star-shaped derivatives are basic features. As a stereometric formation the *muqarnas* can be understood as the result of a process of projecting the elements of a plan and carving the curvilinear or angular *muqarnas* units out of the projected blocks. *Muqarnas* compositions may be found in numerous parts of a structure, including column capitals, minaret balconies, cornices and entrance portals. Although it can be of structural value, as when associated with the transitional zone of a dome, more often it is a purely decorative feature connected to, or suspended from, a structural member.

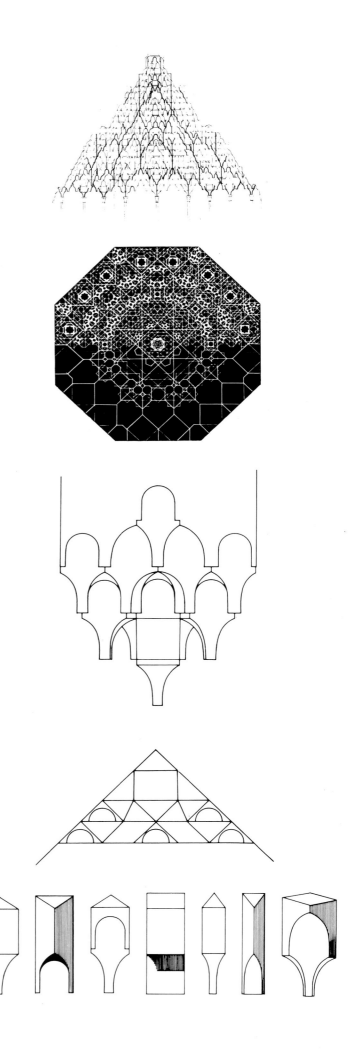

In mosque architecture, the use of the *muqarnas* is sometimes general, as in the Mosque of Sultan Hasan, where a *muqarnas* half-dome covers the monumental entrance portal, while *muqarnas* compositions articulate the minaret balconies and provide a cornice which wraps around the building, as well as defining the transitional zone of the dome. Even in Ottoman mosques, where the *muqarnas* was used more sparingly, it was an almost standard feature in elements such as the portal, *mihrab*, column capitals and minaret balconies. In Ottoman capitals the *muqarnas* was often used to achieve a transition from a circular base to a square. *Muqarnas* compositions could also be the result of later renovations and additions, as in the Qarawiyyin Mosque in Fez, where vaults were placed over a number of its bays during the twelfth century.

Considerable ambiguity surrounds the issue of meanings and associations which can be connected to two- and three-dimensional geometric constructs. This is attributable in part to the general silence of authors in the pre-modern Islamic world concerning the built environment. In spite of this absence of contemporary data, there has emerged since the beginning of the twentieth century a considerable literature attempting to explore the significance of geometry within the context of Islamic architecture. These works have concentrated primarily on two-dimensional patterns and, to a lesser degree, on the *muqarnas*. Since the use of figural representation has been discouraged for the decoration of buildings in the Islamic world, abstract decorative patterns have traditionally received added emphasis as the main components of an alternative decorative system and in their role as carriers of meanings.

One of the first art historians to address the issue of possible meanings which can be connected to the decorative patterns of Islamic art and

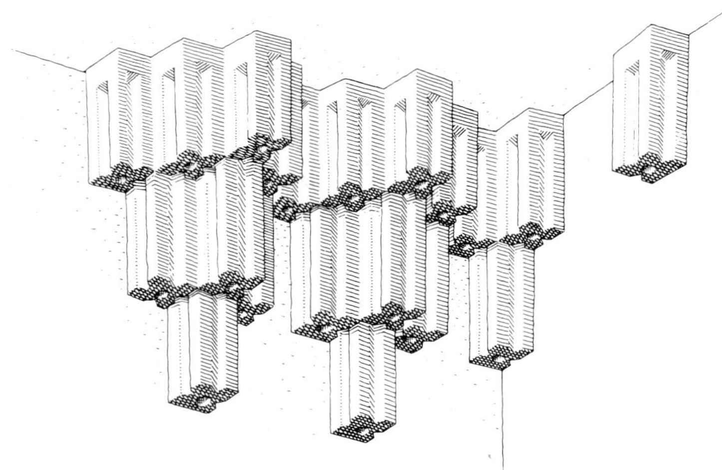

One of the earliest known examples of the use of the muqarnas *is found in the Qal'ah of the Beni Hammad (eleventh century); a reconstruction based on fragments found on the site in present-day Algeria is shown above. Most* muqarnas *volumes are made up of combinations of seven shapes (bottom right), which in section are rectangular or triangular (the latter either right-angled or isosceles), as shown in the example and plan immediately above; from a small number of basic units with at least one surface area in common, many different interlocking arrangements could be developed. A highly intricate design is seen in the Hall of the Two Sisters, in the Alhambra, Granada, with its central* muqarnas *cupola (shown top right in section and plan).*

The semicircular muqarnas *vaulting over the entrance portal of the Sultan Hasan Mosque (1356–9), Cairo.*

architecture was Alois Riegl, who dealt with it in his *Stilfragen* (first published in 1893). Riegl, who viewed decoration as 'one of the most elementary needs of man', considered the arabesque to be a manifestation of an 'oriental spirit' unique to the peoples of the Islamic world, but provided no evidence to support his claim. Similar approaches to the analysis of geometric patterns are found in the writings of later historians of Islamic art and architecture such as Richard Ettinghausen, who viewed Islamic decorative patterns as a reflection of a 'special state of mind' and of certain social conditions pertaining to the Islamic world. He connected the ubiquity of abstract decorative patterns to the 'tendency in the Islamic world toward exaggeration and lavishness' and to the preference among its peoples for the compactness and closeness of urban life over the emptiness and insecurity of uninhabited areas.[17]

An independent development of Riegl's approach, i.e. attributing Islamic art to a particularly Islamic world view, is found in a group of writings published since the 1960s by authors belonging to both the Islamic world and the West. These authors have favoured a mystical interpretation of Islamic decorative designs, presenting them as a visual manifestation of certain Islamic doctrines.[18] Accordingly, a shape such as the circle is connected to the Islamic doctrine of *tawhid*, or unity of God. Such interpretations, as with those of earlier art historians, have been criticized for their lack of methodological rigour, but most importantly they are not supported by contextual evidence found in contemporary historical texts or building inscriptions. A different approach has advocated viewing geometric patterns as symbolically neutral systems of aesthetic expression having no specific iconographic

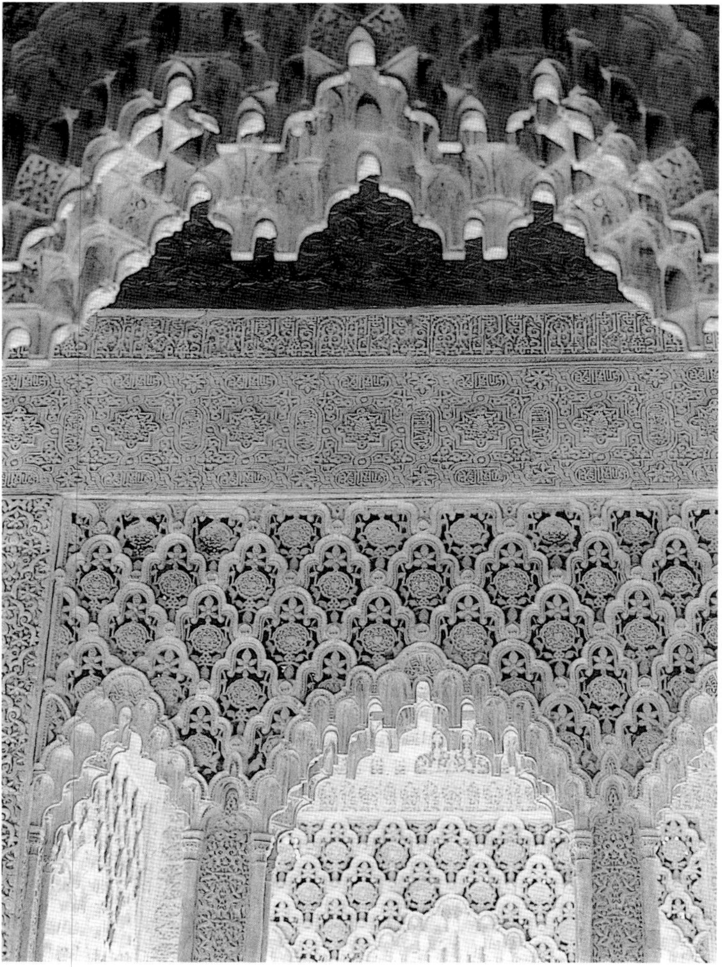

A highly developed fourteenth-century muqarnas (mocárabes) *scheme in the Court of the Lions, Alhambra, Granada; though not in a religious building, this outstanding example reprewents one of the highpoints of the technique in western Islam.*

(Above) Muqarnas *in one of the pendentives below the central dome of the Süleymaniye Mosque (1550–7), Istanbul.*

(Left) Interior of a brick-built dome in the Friday Mosque, Isfahan, showing hexagonal opening and six-pointed star.

Muqarnas *vault in the entrance portal of the Masjid-i Shaykh Lutfallah (1603–18), Isfahan.*

significances; they function instead as intermediaries which can be charged with meanings in certain circumstances. Such specific meanings usually fade away with time and need to be recharged if they are to be maintained.[19]

The same general conclusions and remarks relating to two-dimensional geometric patterns apply equally to the *muqarnas*. A number of specific *muqarnas* vaults are accompanied by inscriptions explaining them as representations of domes of heaven, but these inscriptions are generally associated with secular monuments, the best-known example being the Alhambra in Granada. It is not certain whether such meanings can be extended to include other secular monuments, let alone religious ones. As in the case of two-dimensional geometric patterns, one opinion holds that the *muqarnas* is symbolically neutral but can be charged with significances through a medium such as that of accompanying inscriptions; on the other hand, the *muqarnas* has been presented as a manifestation of Islamic theological doctrines such as that of Atomism.[20]

Our understanding of possible associations which can be linked to the use of geometry in the architecture of the Islamic world remains incomplete, and the available evidence does not support the endowment of geometric constructs with any special iconographic significances. Isolated exceptions do exist, however. These include a number of Mughal gardens, such as those of Akbar's tomb in Sikandra (1613) and the Taj Mahal in Agra (1632). Accompanying inscriptions support the conclusion that the use of two perpendicularly arranged water channels to divide the rectangular area of the garden into four quadrants was intended as a reference to the four rivers of Paradise.[21]

An equally ambiguous issue is that of the psychological effects of geometric patterns. It has been argued that within the context of mosque architecture such patterns can create a contemplative and meditative atmosphere conducive to worship. In contrast, Muslim groups advocating a more puritanical approach to religion argue that they can be distracting and instead prescribe the use of bare surfaces. Also, whereas geometric patterns may strike the modern eye as an emotionally neutral artistic medium which communicates with the viewer in an intellectual manner, it is impossible to ascertain retrospectively the extent to which this would have been true of the pre-modern period, for according to the principles of Jungian psychology, certain traditional geometric patterns such as mandalas can have strong emotional and symbolic significances.[22]

A final question which can be raised is whether rules of geometry were selectively applied to religious structures to differentiate them from their secular counterparts, in the same manner that Alberti advocated the use of specific geometric shapes and proportions for the design of churches. Utilitarian requirements influence the geometry of any building. For the mosque, they primarily consist of accommodating rows of worshippers facing the direction of Mecca and involved in a ritual sequence of standing and prostrating, and because circular and other centralized plans would not meet this basic need, mosques are better served by a rectangular plan outline. Beyond satisfying these utilitarian prescriptions, available architectural and literary evidence does not indicate that specific geometric shapes were reserved for mosques. In certain architectural traditions, such as those of the Ottomans and the Mughals, relatively strict geometric principles were followed in the design of mosques; and in many mosques of the modern era the hypostyle and four-*iwan* arrangement has been replaced by the less flexible dome-square. Otherwise, it is observed that the use of pure and elementary geometric shapes was far more common in funerary structures than in mosques. Moreover, mosques have often functioned as living entities in the urban centres they serve. In order to accommodate growing numbers of worshippers, many had their dimensions and overall outlines modified. Despite these enlargements, the rectangular outline was often maintained, though with different proportions; this is evident in the Great Mosque of Cordoba (begun in 786), which was enlarged on a number of occasions (see chapter 6). In other examples, most notably the Great Mosque of Isfahan, the growth process has resulted in an irregular outline. In all cases, however, the traditional hypostyle rectangular unit remained the primary module of expansion.

In his *Complexity and Contradiction in Architecture*, Robert Venturi remarked that 'a good deal of clutter has not managed to destroy the space of Grand Central Station but the introduction of one foreign element casts into doubt the entire effect of some modern buildings. Our buildings must survive the cigarette machine.'[23] Venturi's book deals not with geometry or the architecture of the Islamic world, but with the shortcomings of twentieth-century modernism. This spirit of versatility and inclusiveness advocated by Venturi is what characterized the application of geometry in the religious monuments of the Islamic world, and what made possible the creation of such masterpieces as the Great Mosque of Cordoba, the Mosque of Sultan Hasan and the Great Mosque of Isfahan.

PART II

THE REGIONS AND THEIR STYLES

- 4 -
INTRODUCTION: REGIONALISM

ISMAIL SERAGELDIN

THE metaphor of a tree has been used in chapter 1 of this volume in connection with the organization of the wealth of materials that are encompassed in a subject as vast as the architecture of the mosque. In keeping with this metaphor, the present chapter deals with the branches and foliage, referring to the regional diversity which produces changes in the visible form of buildings having a common ancestry, represented by the trunk. This idea is worth elaborating in order to provide a framework for the regional chapters that follow. This elaboration can be achieved by introducing two concepts: *societal specificities* and *overlay*. Societal specificities are defined by local geographic, climatic and morphological features and social practices that give a 'sense of place' to particular locations and 'character' to an environment. Overlay refers to a process by which the cultural manifestation of Islamic principles in any Muslim society interact with, enrich and create new syntheses with the existing cultures – Muslim and non-Muslim alike – with which they have extended contact. Emphasizing societal specificities underlines the importance of looking at context in interpreting individual buildings. While context is taken for granted in discussions concerning the architecture of housing or the built form of cities, it tends to be relegated to the background when individual, frequently landmark, buildings such as mosques are considered. To disregard it here would be a serious omission.

Context, for any work of architecture, exists at two levels: (1) an immediate physical context that determines the style, and (2) a wider social, cultural and economic frame of reference that gives it meaning. It is a particularly useful basis for addressing regional variations in the mosque as a building type. Meaning developed within a specific context can be transmitted to a broader context, whether intra-regionally or to a new situation like that of the modern state. For example, the architecture of Sudan has strong links to that of Sub-Saharan Africa – and in order to understand it one has to recognize the cultural cross-fertilization that took place between the two regions. A clear understanding of contexts must precede a proper interpretation of the full meaning of the content of the architecture of Muslim societies, within which that of the mosque is such an important feature.

Any architectural work has both a functional and an artistic dimension. In the case of a mosque the prayer-hall must be suitable for its purpose in accordance with the liturgy of Islam, but the building itself must also 'speak' to the local community, providing both spiritual uplift and an anchor for the community's identity. The manner in which a building communicates its message to the community is dependent on the particular *code* forged by the evolution of societies in a specific region. The differentiation of codes by region does not deny the existence of a common core, but recognizes that regional variations have provided distinct architectural languages. Like dialects that may have a common ancestry, these architectural languages have evolved to the point that they are natural contributive determinants to the culture of a particular society, yet may not be immediately recognizable by, or even accessible to, members of another society.

The recognition of societal specificities is enshrined in the work of distinguished Muslim jurists. Al-Shafei (767–820), arguably the most influential of all jurists, was known to have ruled differently when in Iraq and when he resided in Egypt; he acknowledged these differences and defended them on the basis of societal specificities.[1] If this was the accepted view on dealing with *sharia* law, in which rulings are arrived at with great care and precision, it is clear that, given the range of Islam over a very wide area, and in the absence of any prescribed form in mosque design, tremendous variety was permitted and existed in architectural expression. Traditionally, the mosque has had the common grounding of liturgy, visibility and history to make it more accessible than other types of building. Nevertheless, this common grounding did not limit expressions of regional diversity in mosque architecture, as is clear from the very wide variations illustrated in the chapters that follow.

The idea of overlay is useful in understanding the manifestations of Islamic culture as reflected in the creations of Muslim societies. Historically, the Muslim experience was very different from, say, that of Roman civilization, with its strictly defined architectural language which resulted in identically designed forts being planted in the deserts of Libya and the snows of northern Europe, regardless of climate – a situation akin to someone using a giant rubber stamp to define the boundaries of the cultural identity of the empire. Muslim civilization, on the other hand, exported no clearly defined architectural language from Arabia to the vast and varied regions that it ultimately encompassed. It spread a more subtle, yet ultimately much more powerful presence through a way of defining self and society in a non-physical sense by the 'codes of conduct' outlined in the Qur'an and the *hadith*. From Morocco in the west to Indonesia in the east, with the sole exception of the Iberian peninsula, Muslim societies, once established, have retained their Muslim identity, even after long periods of colonization.[2]

Indeed, this process transpired largely because Islam's contribution to civilization functioned as an overlay that interacted with existing realities and cultural specificities, changing them in subtle ways (see diagram) and creating a new synthesis with what existed before (i.e. an Islamicized version), and allowing it an extended period in which to evolve and find new expressions in response to interactions with different currents and cultures. For example, the exchange between the

Muslim empires of Central Asia and India led to a synthesis of form that belonged to both cultures. However, once well established, the expanding Muslim society is best understood as comprising several 'empires' functioning as states with all the power relationships and commercial transactions that are embodied in such an organization of human affairs. Then one finds architectural expression being affected by stylistic borrowings and transfers. These are, however, the manifestations of specific Muslim societies and their interactions, not the assertion of some universal specifically Muslim identity that spread from one geographic centre. For example, although Timurid architecture was known in Egypt (indeed there are two well-preserved fifteenth-century Timurid domes in Cairo), Mamluk architecture pursued its own stylistic development.

On Regionalism

In architectural literature the value of regionalism, like most other 'isms', is a much-debated topic. Simply stated, it embraces the notion that any architectural work reflects the specificities of the region in which it is located. It accepts contextualism in the broader sense of including the physical aspects (site, climate, materials) as well as the socio-cultural context, stylistically and functionally.[3] The Turkish architect Suha Özkan has contributed a useful differentiation between what he terms 'vernacularism' and 'modern regionalism' in understanding contemporary architectural work that seeks to speak to a specific identity. To paraphrase: 'vernacularism' refers to architecture evolved over time in any region and is therefore limited to existing building types and scales, whereas 'modern regionalism' refers to a contemporary interpretation of local architectures and is not limited by scale, building types or technology.[4] Özkan stresses that regionalism does not exclude modernism; rather it presents another view of architecture that rejects the idea of internationalism, a tendency largely fomented by the power of example and by wide media coverage and shifting fashions in a world that grows ever smaller through technological advances in communications.[5]

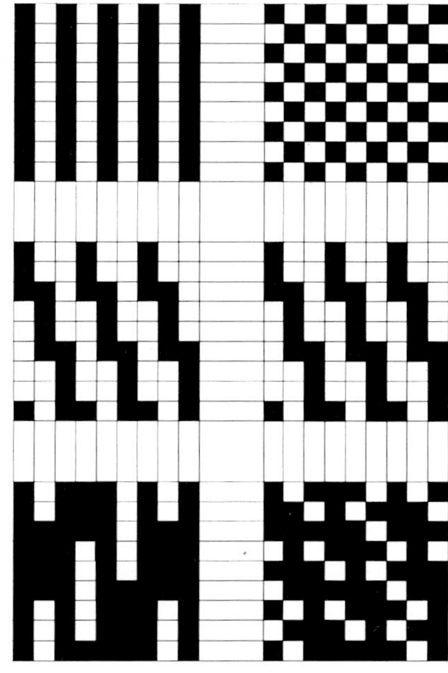

Local non-Islamic architectural characteristics attributable to climatic, geographic, traditional or other reasons can be very diverse, as symbolized by the two top diagrams. Combining the subtle overlay that Islam brings (symbolized by the common middle diagram) with the originals produces two very different results (illustrated by the two bottom diagrams). Those who try to compare only the two final appearances may find nothing in common between them – as do many observers who limit their review of the architecture of Muslim societies solely to the physical manifestations of buildings. However, the common thread (middle diagram) is certainly there and contributes much to the final outcomes.

In different parts of the Muslim world today, many practising architects are grappling with the issue of regionalism. One leading exponent, the Malaysian architect Ken Yeang, has stated that 'the emergent Regionalist architecture seeks its architectural significance through relating its built configuration, aesthetics, organisation and technical assembly and materials to a certain place and time'.[6] This view clearly defines regionalism as bridging both technology and culture. Thus, the architectural debate on regionalism has a direct link to the recognition of societal specificities, as defined above. Furthermore, the specificities of Muslim societies can be better appreciated by understanding the interaction that occurs between universalist Islamic principles and local realities as an enriching overlay which, although frequently subtle in its physical manifestation, was nonetheless pervasive and durable.

The cultural evolution of these societies, however, has for the most part been subjected to a historic rupture that permeates much of the present debate about cultural identity in Muslim societies. This has been the subject of recent critical writings, especially by Mohammed Arkoun, and is discussed here in the concluding chapter of this work.[7] His scholarly enquiry traces – in large measure – the malaise that grips contemporary Muslim societies to a 'rupture' in the evolution of the integrated and integrating framework within which individuals view self and society. An ossification of intellectual enquiry accompanied the imposition of central dogma by Muslim empires of the later Middle Ages. The European Renaissance and its subsequent intellectual ferment thus coincided with a time of intellectual stagnation in the Muslim world. This situation was exacerbated by the Industrial Revolution and the colonial experience. Attempts at modernizing Islamic thought – from Al-Afghani and Abduh in the late nineteenth century to the philosopher Mohammad Iqbal and others in the twentieth century – sought to remedy this rupture in the evolution of Muslim intellectual development. Contemporary fundamentalist currents, with their emphasis on reinstating the past, are also manifestations of this arrested development. Each region of the Muslim world, however, retains its specificity and its distinct socio-political as well as its architectural character.

The consideration of mosque architecture can be broadened by reference to this view of regionalism in the world of Muslim societies. (The typology of mosque architecture has already been discussed, the constituent elements have been analyzed, and linkages have been made with two of the most important and characteristic elements of Islamic art and architecture, namely calligraphy and geometry.) The question to be addressed then is the extent to which the regional experience of various Muslim societies redefined this typology and used these characteristic elements to produce the distinctive mosque architecture contributed by each region to the rich mosaic of this vast heritage.

Interpreting the regional perspective

In the heartland of Islam, *Al-Haramain*, as the Great Mosques at Mecca and Medina are known, owe more to their pre-eminence as Islam's holiest places than to the vernacular architecture of the Arabian peninsula. Although the architectural model of the mosque originated with the Prophet's Mosque in Medina, subsequent structures were generally built in the prevailing style of the lands of their sponsors, for example, Qaitbay's construction in Cairo (1472–4). This situation has now changed. The recent oil wealth of Saudi Arabia has contributed much to a revival of mosque building in the Arabian heartland, as well as elsewhere in the Muslim world. Indeed, one can see the emergence of a dominant style in the many state-sponsored projects in Saudi Arabia, one that continues to reflect the influence of the heritage of Egypt, the Indian subcontinent and Turkey. In recent architecture around the world one can see the *influences*, but no regional style, emerging – except perhaps for some kind of pan-Islamic manifestations, such as crenellated arch treatment.

It is noteworthy that traditional Andalusian architectural elements have been revived in the mosque architecture of twentieth-century Egypt and in many other mosques further afield, sponsored by Muslim governments, as for example in the Islamic Center (1950–7) on Massachusetts Avenue in Washington, D.C., which is a clear mix of Mamluk and North African mosque styles. Here and elsewhere the style of Maghrebi mosques, with their distinctive square minarets and green-glazed tiles, has been used as a model.

Turkey provides arguably the most powerful image that many people have of mosque architecture: the Ottoman archetype, from Sinan's masterpieces of the second half of the sixteenth century to the present-day Kolçatepe Mosque in Istanbul, feature characteristic pencil-point minarets and huge domes, now a familiar feature of many city skylines, as far apart as Cairo, Islamabad and Jakarta.

Although historically and linguistically differentiated, Central Asia and Iran produced brilliant and opulent examples of grandiose mosques with exceptional gateways and resplendent exteriors decorated with glazed ceramic tiles. The mosques and *madrasas* of Samarqand, as well as the unique legacy of Isfahan, bear witness to that grandeur. One can also see echoes of these characteristics in the architectural expression of regions reaching as far as western China and indeed down to India, where its Mughal heritage drew upon Central Asian and Hindu design traditions and craftsmanship.

Three important regions of the Muslim world are as yet relatively unfamiliar. The mosques of East Africa reflect Indian influence, while those of Sub-Saharan regions show the evolution of an endogenous vernacular in Sahelian and Western Africa, although state-sponsored mosques financed by Arab states are now transplanting a different architectural vocabulary. Eastern and southern China are remarkable in their degree of utilization of traditional Chinese elements to provide a unique mosque architecture. On the other hand, in South-East Asia Malaysia shows a self-conscious regionalism and Indonesia exhibits a totally relaxed overlay. Indeed, the orientation of the mosque structure in Indonesia was until relatively recently allowed to follow the cardinal orientations of pre-Islamic temples, with the result that worshippers had to align themselves at an angle to the *qibla* wall in order to face Mecca.

Selective by necessity, the regional surveys in the individual chapters that follow provide a sense of the immense richness of the tapestry woven by the diverse fabric of Muslim societies stretching from Morocco to Indonesia and from Anatolia to Tanzania. Each region may have a distinct personality, but each is an integral part of the same

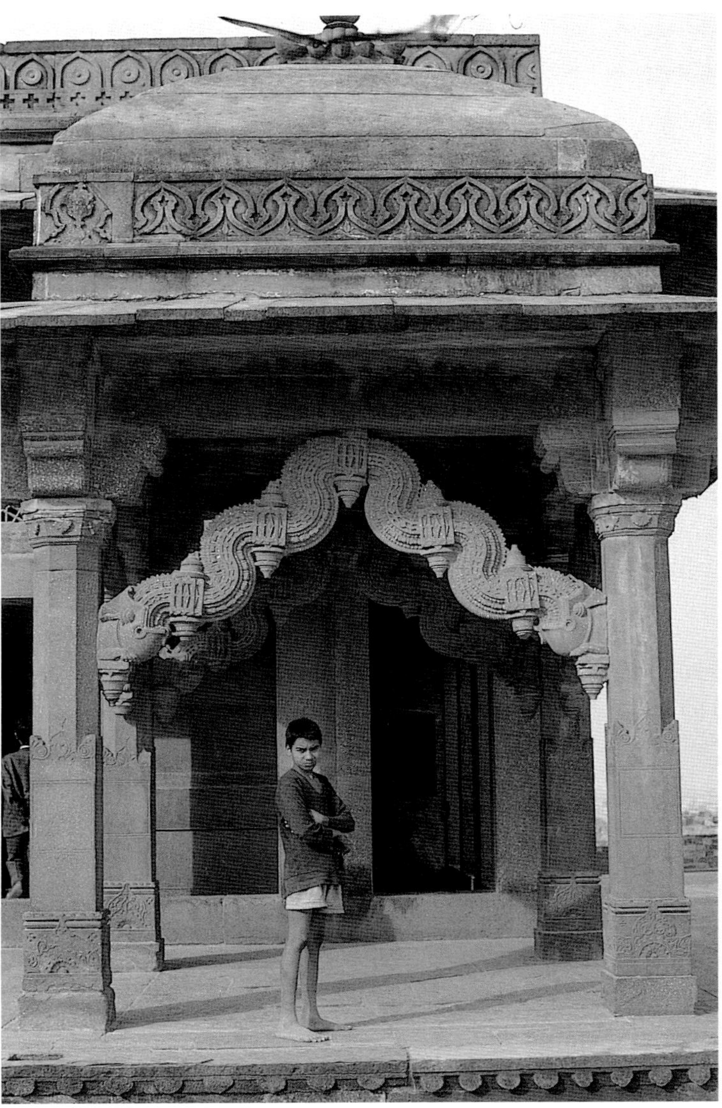

In the Friday Mosque (c. 1568–78), Fatehpur Sikri, a domed portal also featuring the prominent use of brackets shows evidence of the combination of Hindu and Muslim influences in India.

whole. The diversity of the regional experience is characterized by a range embracing the grandeur of the Great Mosque of Cordoba, the mud-brick elegance of Djenne, the opulence of Isfahan, the splendour of Ottoman Turkey and the uniquely Chinese and Javanese characteristics of examples in South-East Asia. The common thread running through all these diverse examples can be teased out only by keeping in mind the subtle overlay and reviewing how the typology of the mosque and its constituent architectural elements have been interpreted in the various regional and cultural contexts. It is precisely the typology of the mosque that remains immutable – only the styles, materials, technologies and contexts change.

Regional styles can be quite distinctive where the contrasts with adjacent regions are very abrupt, as in Anatolia and Iran, but usually they are more subtle, reflecting a gradual process of assimilation of external styles into an existing regional architecture, as in the case of Iran and Central Asia where there is a similarity between the buildings of Samarqand and Isfahan. Each of the regional contexts is itself the product of unique societal specificities that are due to historical and socio-cultural factors as well as geography, climate and materials. And, within each of these regions, much variability exists.

This is true not only for the past but also for the present. In the case of Saudi Arabia, for example, one can speak of the recent emergence of a distinct 'neo-classical' style of mosque architecture, the prime exponent of which is the Egyptian architect Abdel-Wahed El-Wakil. (Here the term 'neo-classical' relates to the period considered 'classical' in terms of Muslim architecture, i.e. the ninth to the sixteenth century.) The work of El-Wakil has been internationally acclaimed and is the subject of scholarly study. Like the present Great Mosques of Mecca and Medina, El-Wakil's architecture derives much from the Egyptian tradition, especially the Mamluk period as manifested in his Corniche Mosque (1986) in Jeddah. It is different from the Nadji Arabian architecture, which influenced the design in Ali Shuaiby's award-winning project for the Hayy Al-Sifarat Centre in Riyadh.[8] Conversely, examples in other regions demonstrate unique eclecticism. Thus one can consider that contemporary efforts to define the architecture of the Malay mosque are particularly relevant, given the history of different and frequently conflicting influences in the past, as exemplified by the incorporation of Doric columns and French windows in the Masjid Jamek at Muar, dating from 1925.

The unique characteristics of each region or sub-region should not be taken to imply that local styles evolved in isolation. For large parts in their history, these distinctive parts of the overall tapestry enjoyed close contact with one another, and this is even more the case today. The bonds of commerce and a common cultural overlay enriched them by exposing them to a wider international framework, just as connections over time and space forged a common heritage. This duality, between what is regional in character or particular to a place and what is universal to Islam, is one with which present-day Muslim societies are contending.

The meaning of regionalism and not just its form in a rapidly modernizing and changing world needs to be examined. As countries become increasingly interconnected by trade and technology transfer, as well as by global communications media and *shared* images, will a universal Islamic architectural expression take over in Muslim societies? Will the specificities that define the character of a particular regional architecture remain the wellsprings of architectural inspiration, or will they become anachronistic, serving as quaint reminders of an increasingly irrelevant past? At present these are still choices that are open to interpretation and implementation. It is possible that a dominant model will emerge, as is signalled in Arkoun's concluding chapter, through a combination of ideological, political and professional decisions, though it is too early to tell which model will prevail for mosque architecture.

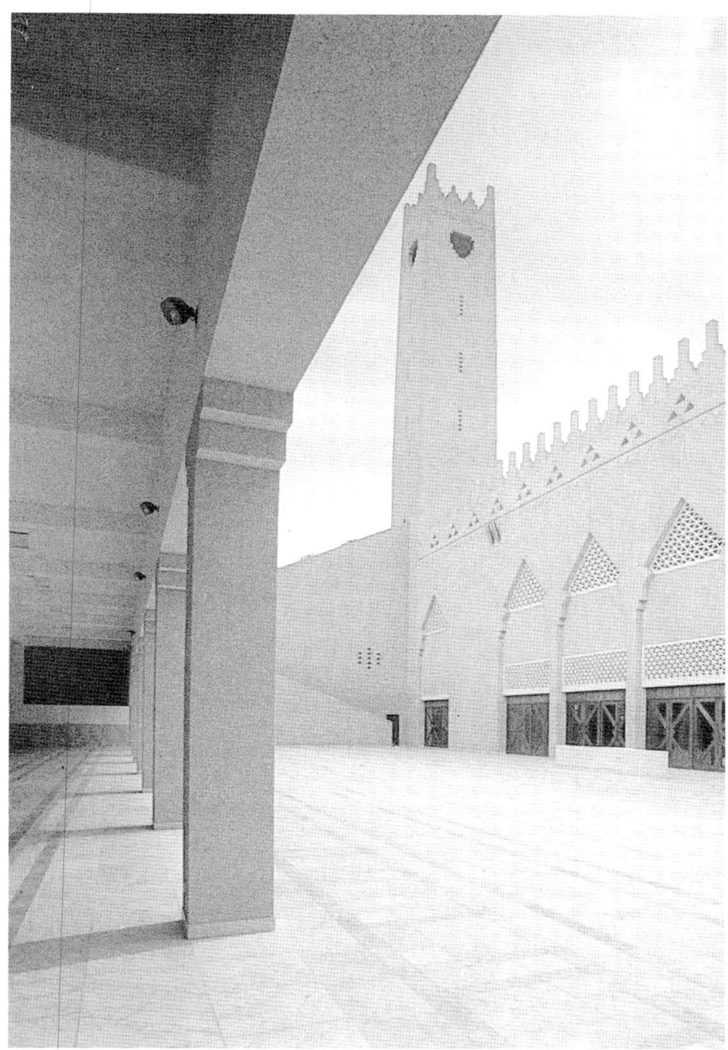

The Friday Mosque (1986) in the Diplomatic Quarter of Riyadh, Saudi Arabia, in which concrete is used to imitate the appearance of traditional mud-brick architecture of this region.

While in Islamic nations in many parts of the world the homogenizing influence of consumer-oriented societies which rely on technology-based industries will undoubtedly affect many facets of the built environment, it also reinforces the psychological need to reaffirm the identity of Islamic self and society and to reassert the uniqueness that makes them special.[9] Nowhere will this be more manifest than in mosque architecture.

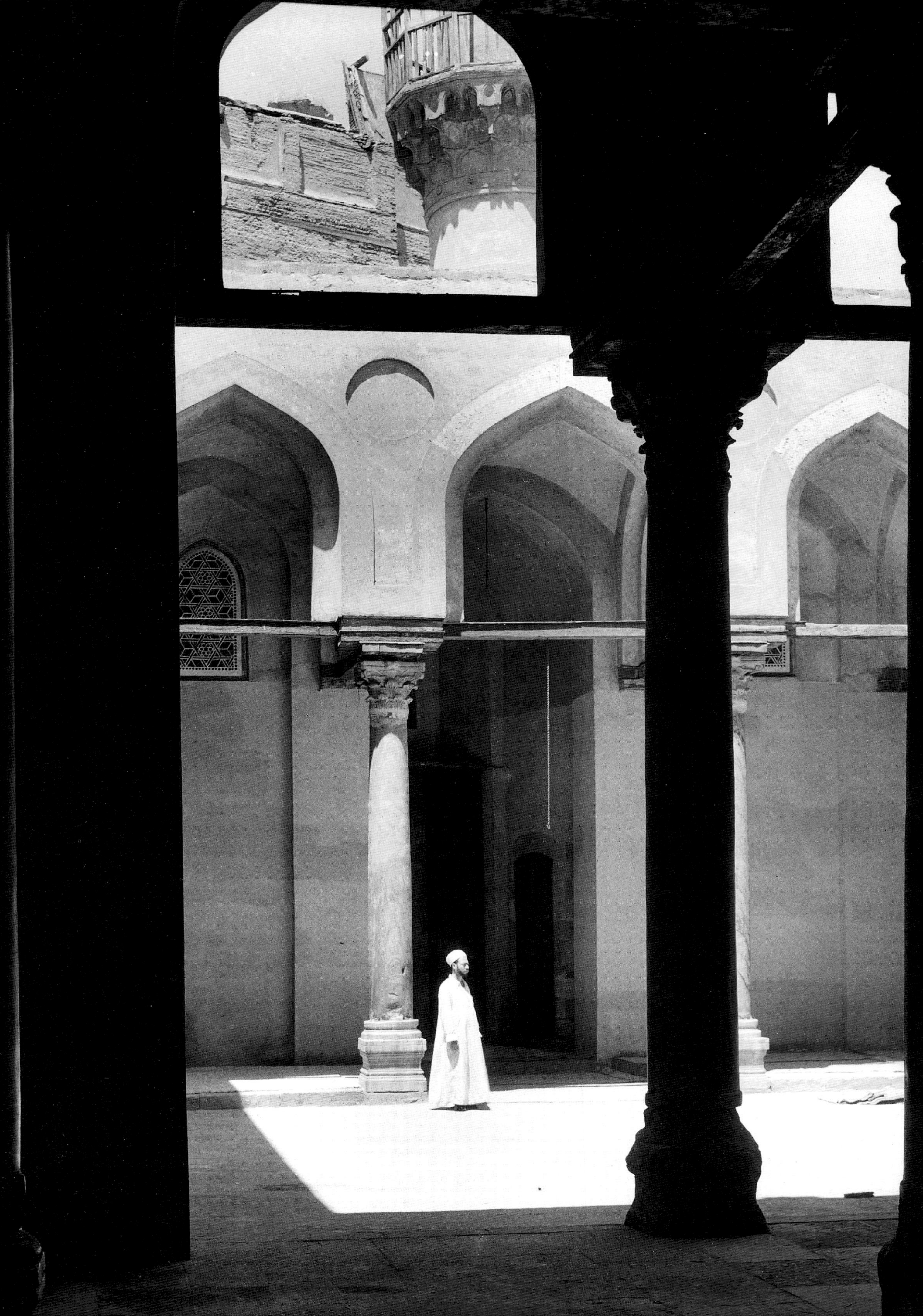

- 5 -
THE CENTRAL ARAB LANDS
DOĞAN KUBAN

THE form of the earliest mosques did not have its origins either in the pre-Islamic Ka'ba at Mecca or in any specific building known to us. It is also still a debatable question as to whether there was any codified prayer system before the Medina period, i.e. before AD 622. The first gathering place for communal prayer in Islam was the house of the Prophet at Medina, to which Muhammad immediately transferred his family once the new building was completed in 623. Like many mud-brick houses in the Middle East, Muhammad's house (see p. 32) consisted of a square courtyard with two rooms (later increased to nine to accommodate his wives) in the south-east. The first communal prayers were held in this courtyard. For the comfort of the worshippers a portico (*zulla*) made of palm-trunks and branches was built on the north side of the courtyard, together with a smaller one (*suffa* or shed roof) which gave shelter to visitors who sometimes spent the night there.[1] The *zulla* also served as a place for deliberations on community affairs, hence to this day the mosque has retained its multivalent role as the place of prayer, social activities and political debate. Practical needs thus contributed to the house of the Prophet becoming the first mosque of Islam.

From this modest and unplanned beginning has developed the basic iconography of the mosque. While formal elaboration of mosque design in Muslim history has created totally different concepts of architecture and regional styles, the image of the archetype remained unchanged: the concept of a courtyard (*sahn*) and a sanctuary (*haram*) which essentially consisted of a hypostyle hall (i.e. an interior space with multiple supports for the roof) has survived to this day. This continuity can be compared to the ubiquitous basilical scheme found in church architecture, and it represents an example of architectural symbolism that retains its validity in a practical sense.

In 624, when the Prophet changed the direction of the *qibla* from Jerusalem to Mecca, the *zulla* and the *suffa* changed places. Before it was totally taken down and replaced by a new mosque during the Umayyad period, the Prophet's house (now called 'Masjid') had been enlarged on two occasions: first by Umar (638), then by Uthman (644). Although the house did not have a *mihrab* or a minaret, the history of the *minbar* is directly connected with the Prophet's life, for he used to address the congregation while leaning on a pillar of the Masjid. Eventually, after many years, a wooden pulpit (*minbar*) with three steps was provided, and he would sit on the third step, so establishing the practice of using the *minbar* for delivering the Friday orations. In the time of the Prophet the direction of prayer, first towards Jerusalem, later towards Mecca, was indicated by a stone block (Arabic, *qibla*). Thus the word *qibla* was not the direction but the object indicating it. Eventually, however, through a semantic change, the term *qibla* came to be identified with the direction of the Ka'ba in Mecca.

In the Qur'an the word *masjid*, although used many times, is only applied to three specific buildings: the Masjid al-Haram (Ka'ba), the Masjid al-Aqsa (Jerusalem) and the mosque built specifically as a *masjid* at the oasis site called Quba, south-east of Medina. As Creswell has remarked, the first two *masjids* mentioned were not, at the time of the Prophet, in the hands of the Muslims: the Ka'ba was the Temple of Quraysh (the Prophet's own tribe, who held Mecca); and the temple site in Jerusalem was in the hands of the Christians. Thus, the word *masjid* was used to denote a holy place, a place of worship, not only for Muslims but for everybody. The Masjid at Quba shows that the word was also adopted to describe the Muslim place of worship.[2] Although they are more important in terms of the history of religious iconography than that of mosque architecture, the two most holy places to which the term *masjid* is applied in the Qur'an should be briefly recorded here.

The area around the Ka'ba in Mecca (and sometimes the city of Mecca itself) is called Masjid al-Haram. The first simple building for prayer was built by the Prophet himself, but the area has been subjected to change in almost every period of history and has a number of buildings which are extremely important for the liturgy concerning the Ka'ba and the *hajj* (pilgrimage). The grand architectural composition of large porticos surrounding the Ka'ba was first conceived under the Ottomans in the sixteenth century.

The Masjid al-Aqsa is the great temple area in Jerusalem (Al-Quds) where the legendary Temple of Solomon was built. It is also called Haram ash-Sharif ('noble sanctuary') and Bait al-Muqaddes (or al-Maqdis), meaning 'sacred house'. On this platform there are two important Islamic buildings: the Masjid al-Aqsa (literally, 'faraway sanctuary') and the Qubbat as-Sakhra. The name Masjid al-Aqsa is today associated with the mosque built on the southern end of the old enclosure. During the Caliph Umar's visit to Jerusalem in 638 it seems that a simple building was erected for the Muslims. In 668, when Bishop Arnulf visited the city, he saw an architectually insignificant timber building which could, however, accommodate 3,000 worshippers.[3] This mosque, begun under the Umayyads, has been rebuilt many times and its form dates from the reconstruction by the Fatimid Sultan az-Zahir in 1035, which followed the essential lines of the Abbasid reconstruction by Al-Mahdi in 780. Further alterations by the Mamluks are also visible.[4]

Facing page
The courtyard of the Mosque of al-Aqmar (1125), Cairo.

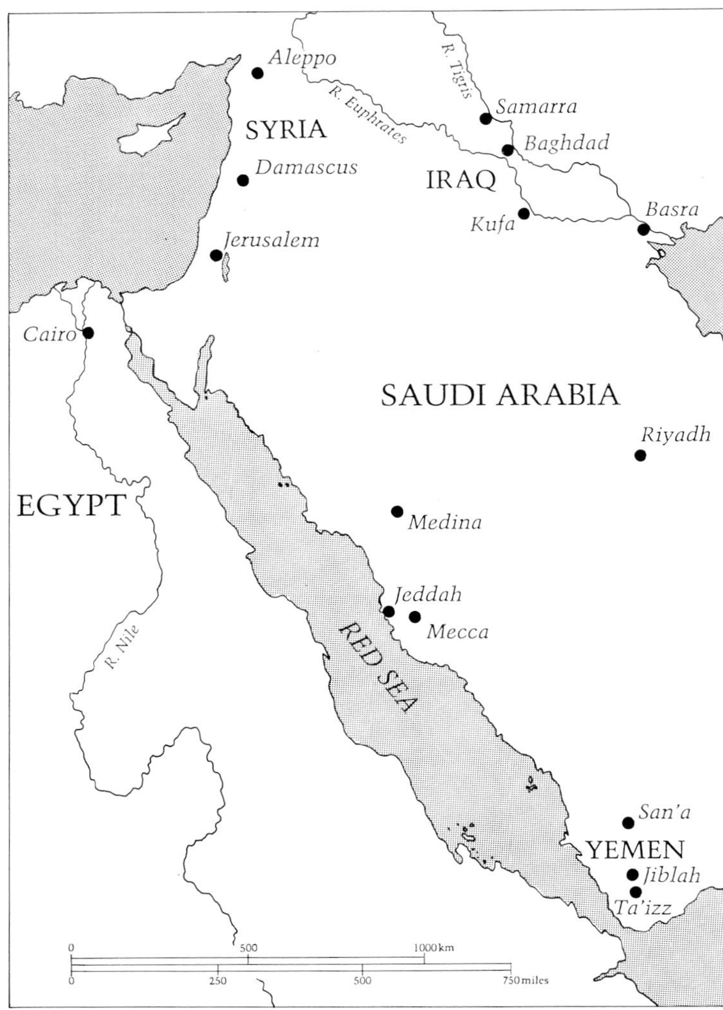

Map 1: the Arabian heartland, showing principal sites.

In the sacred enclosure Umar was shown the rock (*sakhra*) from which the Prophet made his ascent to heaven (*miraj*), and it was on this rock that the Umayyad Caliph al-Marwan built in 695 the most venerable of Muslim shrines after the Ka'ba, the Qubbat as-Sakhra. Although called a *masjid*, this is a memorial building and architecturally may be considered a direct product of the Late Antique-Early Christian style in Syria.

Dating from the time of the Prophet, the Mosque of Quba should be considered the first mosque specifically built as such. In the Qur'an (Sura 9:108) there is a mention of the first public mosque built at the place called Quba. Situated about 5 km (3 miles) south-east of Medina, this oasis was the first place where Muhammad rested before entering Medina. It was already considered a holy place with a sacred spring, where there were, according to rather hazy traditions, tribal oratories, some of them belonging to Jewish communities. Creswell considers that this was an open space enclosed within a shallow stone wall. Possibly this was a structure dating from before Muhammad's arrival. The mosque was a rectangular covered space measuring 54 × 63 cubits (approximately 26 × 30 m or 85 × 100 ft), built of mud brick and with date-palm trunks supporting the roof. It was in this mosque, in the seventeenth month of the Hijra, that the Prophet changed the direction of the *qibla* to face Mecca rather than Jerusalem. According to legend, the Angel Gabriel is supposed to have descended and miraculously opened up, through the hills and wilds, a view of the Ka'ba, so that there should be no difficulty in ascertaining its true position. Thus it came to be known as Masjid al-Qiblatayn (i.e. with two *qiblas*), the *qibla* being described as a large stone.[5] This mosque was later rebuilt in 7 AH/AD 629 by the Prophet himself.

A third place of worship for large congregations is called a *musalla*, a term which originally meant a small mat; by extension it came to mean a large open place for public prayer. Muhammad celebrated the Festival prayers in the so-called Musalla of the tribe of Bani Salima.[6] Thus, in the lifetime of the Prophet three forms of *masjid* were initiated: covered hypostyle hall; a courtyard mosque with a sheltered *haram* and a *sahn*; and a marked out open area. The *qibla* serving to indicate the direction of the Ka'ba and a *minbar* as a raised pulpit from which to address the congregation were also part of the new image of Islamic places of worship. Before the introduction of the minaret in 673, the call to prayer was made from an elevated platform or a nearby rooftop.[7] Until after the death of the Prophet, therefore, the formal aspects of a mosque were no more than the simple expression of the local vernacular architecture. Formal symbolism was not a feature of mosque design. This pattern was not followed by Muhammad's successors, except perhaps by the first four Caliphs.

As Muslim conquests outside Arabia brought the knowledge of the great cultures of the Middle East to Arab nomads, a new vision of architecture eventually replaced the simple vernacular of the Arabian peninsula. In the six years from the accession to the Caliphate of Abu Bakr (632) to the complete fall of Mesopotamia and Syria, and the defeat of Byzantine and Persian armies (638), the Arabs founded the cities of Basra and Kufa and built mosques there. They also converted a number of churches and Persian buildings to mosques, a practice which was followed in all regions newly conquered by Islam. At Hama, Damascus and Aleppo parts of churches were used for Muslim prayers, while in other parts the Christians continued to celebrate Mass. In Syria and Mesopotomia the *qibla* direction was to the south. Thus, simply by facing south the Muslims used church interiors, but whereas churches had the usual east-west orientation, mosques required a north-south arrangement. This simple practical change indicates that the early Muslims did not regard the mosque as a specially sacred and specific place. Rather, the important thing was that prayer could be performed anywhere. While the idea that the whole world is a *masjid* in which to prostrate oneself before God is well known in Muslim thinking, the importance attached to congregational prayers on Fridays eventually influenced mosque design by underlining its social and political role.

The Mosques at Kufa and Basra

In the first mosques built at Basra and Kufa the basic iconography of the mosque as defined in the Prophet's time was implemented on a larger scale. At Basra an open *musalla* was marked out, possibly by a reed fence.[8] The mosque at Kufa, however, is of special importance because it was the first building to incorporate the early features associated with the Islamic house of worship, and about which some relevant facts are known.

According to the historian and theologian Tabari (838–923), the first mosque at Kufa had a square plan, the size of which was established by a man throwing an arrow from the centre towards each of the four cardinal points of the compass, south being accepted as the *qibla*.[9] Although this romantic notion may be seen as a primitive device, it is as good as any other theory in that it determined a visualized space. The area thus designated was surrounded by a ditch (*khandaq*) and on the *qibla* side a portico (*zulla*), 200 cubits in length, was built. Marble columns taken from the buildings of al-Hira, the capital of Lakhmid princes, 4 km (2½ miles) distant, supported a wooden roof similar to those of Byzantine churches. No walls are indicated, nor was there a *mihrab* since the whole *zulla* faced the *qibla*. This simple shed merely protected the worshippers when the sun was at its zenith. Entrances to the mosque area were located on all sides, including the *qibla* side, a disposition which shows that the idea of organized space had not yet been developed.

Another important feature associated with the mosque at Kufa was the building of a governor's palace directly connected to it. According to Tabari, thieves stole part of the public treasury kept in the governor's residence and Umar then ordered the building of a Dar al-Imara adjacent to the mosque. The new Qasr al-Kufa was in brick, with the *qibla* wall facing the governor's residence.[10] This combination of

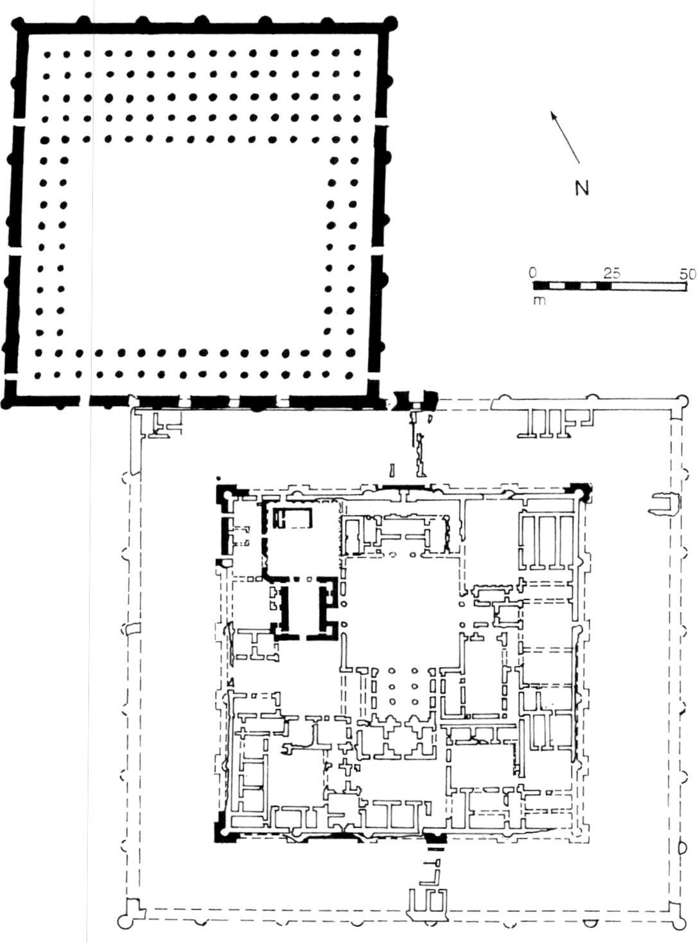

(Above) Plan of the mosque and adjacent Dar al-Imara (governor's palace), Kufa (rebuilt 670).

(Below) The Dome of the Rock (Qubbat as-Sakhra), Jerusalem, one of the holiest Muslim shrines (see plan, p. 56).

congregational mosque and governor's palace remained in favour during the early centuries of Islam. The Kufa Mosque was built by Ziyad ibn Abihi, the Umayyad governor, in 50 AH/AD 670. From the size of these early mosques outside Arabia, it is clear that the whole male population assembled for congregational prayers.

The Mosque of Amr at Fustat

After capturing Alexandria in 641, the Arab commander Amr ibn al-As built the first mosque in Egypt in his capital, Fustat. This was a rectangular, mud-brick structure measuring 17.50 × 29 m (57 × 95 ft), with six doors on all sides except the *qibla* side.[11] It was covered by a flat roof made of palm-trunks and branches, supported by columns. The model seems to have been the Quba Mosque near Medina. Although this was a congregational mosque, Amr's demand to have a *minbar* was refused by the Caliph Umar. Arabic sources mention that at that time there were also small *masjids* in the various quarters of Fustat. Thus, even after the Muslim conquest of Iraq, Syria, Palestine and Egypt, the form of the mosques remained no more than a simple shelter.

The Umayyad period (661–750)

When the struggle between Ali and Mu'awiya ended with the triumph of the latter, the Umayyad Caliphate opened a new era in the development of Muslim culture. The time of the Prophet and the four Orthodox Caliphs had been dominated by the simple culture of the nomadic tribes of the Arabian peninsula. From now on the ancient cultures of the Middle East – Roman, Early Christian, Byzantine and Persian – would become the essential sources for cultural progress.

A change from the pattern of conquest based on religious fervour to the Umayyad idea of worldly dominion was accompanied by a change in architectural expression: simple gathering places, open or sheltered, made of basic materials, were succeeded by a post-Roman version of Near Eastern architecture, following and transforming the Early Christian architectural tradition of the region. Yet the essence of this transformation was more complex. Historically, the architecture of the Umayyad period had a broader geographical basis than the Christian, the territorial extent now reaching from Central Asia in the east to Spain in the west. For all practical purposes, however, Umayyad architecture in Syria retained a post-Roman style in its major monuments. Despite Islam's advocacy of restraint, a new architectural magnificence developed and began to deplete the wealth of believers, as the Prophet had anticipated.

Before considering the oldest extant mosque, the Great Mosque of Damascus (709–15), several innovations in mosque architecture introduced in the preceding period should be recalled. In seventh-century Arab society, in which tribal affinities were a predominant feature of political life, and each tribe settled a definite quarter in a city with its own *masjid*, the role of the congregational mosque became more and more important in respect of political solidarity. For rulers and governors of the vast provinces, urban Great Mosques provided the forums for socio-political life; not only at Friday prayers, but on every occasion, political messages and orders of the government were delivered from the pulpit of each main mosque. Metaphorically, the congregational mosque rather than the governor's palace could be regarded as the effective seat of government. In fact, until the tenth century Arab governors kept their residence adjacent to the central mosque, following the precedent set by Umar.

The two Great Mosques of the period, no longer extant, were those at Basra and Kufa, rebuilt by the governor Ziyad ibn Abihi. According to written documents, the new Basra mosque was built in 670 in brick. On the *qibla* side there were five rows of stone columns supporting a roof made of teak. Pebbles were spread on the ground to counteract dust in the interior (this method was later widely used). The governor's residence stood behind the *qibla* wall, and Ziyad had a *maqsura* built for himself. This separate or screened place for private prayer was an innovation of the early Umayyad period; according to Ibn Khaldun, it was introduced by Mu'awiya to provide protection against possible attempts at assassination.[12] (Two of the Orthodox Caliphs – Umar and Uthman – had earlier met violent deaths.) This seemingly unimportant addition to safeguard the head of the community would eventually become the major factor affecting spatial change in mosque design. Its precise form in the early period is not known, but it may have been a simple screened area rather than a separate room, since the governors were also the imams officiating at congregational prayers.

The mosque at Kufa, also rebuilt by Ziyad ibn Abihi in 670, was at the time the richest mosque built by the Arabs. It stood on the site of the original mosque, and a Dar al-Imara of great architectural quality was added, having part of the *qibla* wall in common. Excavations have shown that the building was a direct descendant of Sasanian palace architecture, thus confirming the account by Tabari, who wrote that it was designed by a court architect of the Persian King Khusrau. The mosque, built in brick, was square, with each side measuring about 100 m (330 ft). Internally there were five rows of stone columns on the *qibla* side, and two rows along each of the other sides surrounding the central open courtyard, the *sahn*. The columns, which were of extraordinary height (about 15 m or 50 ft), supported a teak ceiling. The *apadanas* (throne rooms) of Achaemenian kings had similar proportions and roof constructions. Thus the Arabs, while following Roman and Early Christian traditions in Syria, adapted the original functional and primitive scheme of the earlier mosques in Iraq, and gave it a new architectural expression. From now on, the plan consisting of a central courtyard surrounded by porticos (*riwaqs*) was to become a universal pattern for monumental mosque architecture in all Muslim countries.

Facing page
The Great Mosque, Samarra, Iraq, completed in 847: (above) the freestanding spiral minaret on its square base and the bastion at the north-west corner of the enclosure wall; (below) a section of the perimeter wall showing the decorative frieze and a doorway leading to the inner courtyard.

The Al Aqsa Mosque (below) in Jerusalem, first built in 715, was reconstructed and enlarged at least six times before acquiring its present form in 1345–50, when the Mamluk architect Aybak al-Mushrif extended the east side. On the south side the mihrab *is preceded by a domed bay (opposite).*

Part of the courtyard of the Umayyad Great Mosque, Damascus, the oldest extant monumental mosque; the domed treasury (the Bait al-Mal) is seen in the background. The mosque, dating from 709–15, encompasses the former church of St John, itself built on the site of a Roman temple. The sacred enclosure was taken over by the Caliph al-Walid, who erected a great triple-arcaded prayer-hall (right).

The design of the Mosque of Ahmad ibn Tulun (876–9) in Cairo was influenced by the mosques of Samarra, Iraq (see p. 81). The complex has an unusual ziyadas *or walled entrance corridor area (above left), and arcades supported by massive piers (left and above) around a large courtyard with an ablutions fountain in the centre. The spiral minaret – a unique feature in Egypt – is illustrated on p. 24.*

The style of the arcades (right) in the Mosque of Al-Hakim, Cairo, 990–1013, is based mainly on that of the Mosque of Ibn Tulun. This building of the Fatimid period has two extraordinary stone minarets, one round and one square; the latter anticipates the form associated with minarets of the Mamluk period.

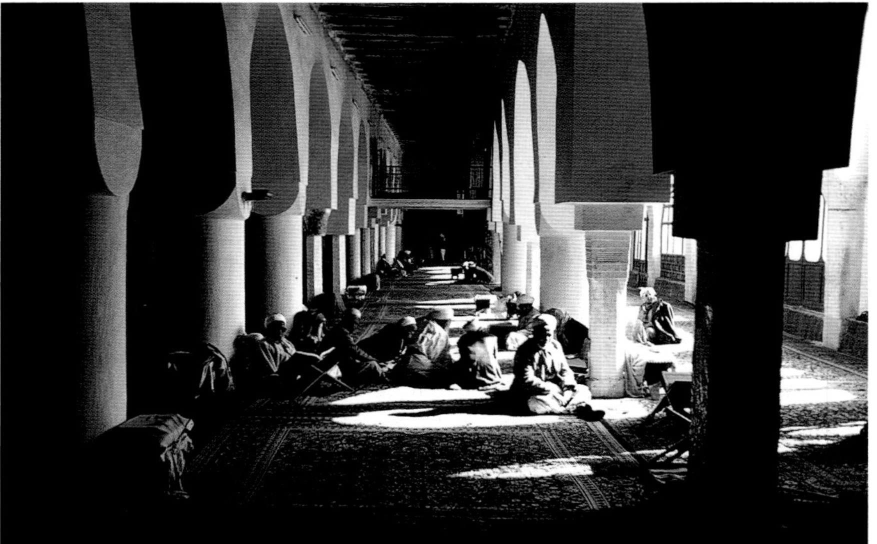

(Above) The courtyard of the mud-brick Friday Mosque at Ibb, Yemen.

(Left) One of the arcades in the Great Mosque, San'a, in which antique columns were re-used in the original seventh-century construction.

The main domes of major mosques in Yemen are usually ornately decorated. Examples in Ta'izz include (top and centre right) the Ashrafiyya Mosque (thirteenth–fourteenth centuries), and (right) the Muzaffariyya Mosque. A ceiling in the Friday Mosque, Zafar, also displays a geometric decorative scheme (above), here related to the square.

The introduction of the minaret

In 673 the Umayyad governor of Egypt, Maslama, demolished the first Mosque of Amr at Fustat, which could no longer accommodate the growing number of worshippers. Although few details are known about the new mosque which replaced it, this was the first occasion when minarets were added. The four minarets were built according to the wishes of Mu'awiya, and today the almost universal consensus is that their form was influenced by Syrian church towers. In Damascus, in the old pagan *temenos* where Muslims used to gather for prayers, there were four corner towers dating from the Christian period. In the case of the new Amr Mosque the Arabic word used to describe the minarets was *sauma'a*, which means a tower. The four minarets of Amr Mosque were built one at each of its four corners, and most probably were independent towers. Although the minaret with a square plan remained the most characteristic form in Arabic-speaking lands, in the later history of Muslim countries cylindrical towers of eastern origin were introduced in areas subject to domination by dynasties of Turkish origin. The terms *ma'dhana* (the place for *adhan*, the call to prayer) and *manar* (a place where fire burns, generally referring to the Pharos of Alexandria in the form of a tower) are both suggestive of function rather than form. With this addition of a tower, the Islamic place of worship now had all the liturgical elements, as well as the iconography of its basic form.

Al-Walid's demolition of the Prophet's Mosque

On the orders of the Caliph al-Walid I (705–15), the governor of Medina demolished the remains of the Prophet's house and the mosque, to the great consternation of the people of Medina, and built a new mosque in 707–9. Although the building has been completely lost due to later reconstructions, substantial information about it is known from Muslim historians.[13] Although some of the statements made by the historians are contradictory, it is clear that the new mosque was built by Copts and Syrian architects and artists. The Byzantine emperor sent a considerable amount of mosaic material, as well as artisans to decorate the mosque. The walls were built of cut stone and the building had a marble revetment and mosaic decoration and a timber roof. While this technical assistance from outside undoubtedly gave the building a Byzantine appearance, its general form – as reconstructed by Creswell – followed the already established pattern of the Arabian mosque: an open *sahn* surrounded by *riwaqs*, the deepest being on the *qibla* side. Arab authors have claimed that the *mihrab* niche was first introduced in this building, while Creswell asserted that the *mihrab* niche was of Christian (Coptic) origin and was 'adopted with some reluctance by Islam'.[14] If we consider that workmanship of Christian origin was a dominant feature – a fact related by all Muslim writers – this introduction from a Christian source may seem probable, as noted in the case of the minaret. The new Mosque of the Prophet was given four corner minarets.

Facing page
The dome and distinctive crenellated parapet of the Great Mosque, Jiblah, Yemen; one of the country's best-preserved medieval mosques, the building dates from 1088–9.

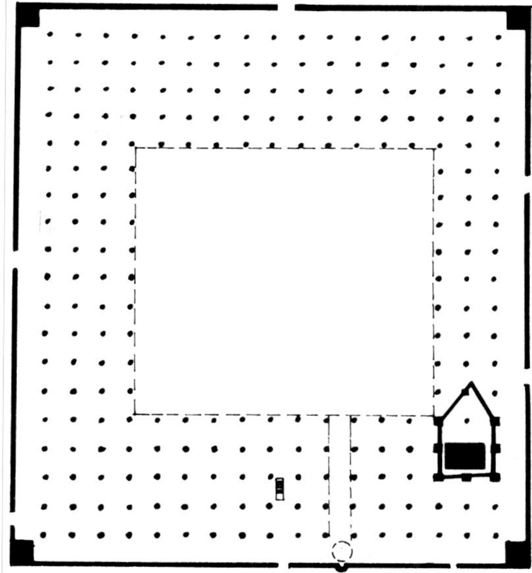

Plan of the Mosque of the Prophet, Medina. The original building on the site was replaced in 707–9.

The decoration of the mosque was extremely rich. A marble dado, decorated windows, mosaics, gilded paintings and Qur'anic inscriptions (short suras) in gold on a blue background must have greatly impressed visitors, especially the people of Medina, who were accustomed to the modesty of earlier buildings. In this highly important architectural statement the notion of modesty associated with the Prophet was entirely forgotten, and in its place world dominion by the new faith was forcefully expressed. Unfortunately, however, the building was completely destroyed by fire in 1256.

The oldest extant mosque: the Great Mosque of Damascus

As was usual with Muslim rulers, the Caliph al-Walid assembled a great workforce drawn from every corner of the known world – Persians, Indians, Greeks, etc. He also imported luxuries such as mosaics, gold and silver. Ibn al-Fakih says (903) that the cost of building the mosque absorbed seven years' land tax (*kharaj*) of the Empire.[15] The Damascus Mosque was a Muslim structure executed by Syrian craftsmanship, with certain spatial alterations and changes in proportion. Here the architectural elements are more articulated, the *sahn* being transversal rather than square or longitudinal, so creating a different directional emphasis. The *haram* has only three transverse aisles, perhaps reflecting the influence of three-aisled churches. The clerestory with windows on the façade and the double-tiered arcades in the *haram* add to the spatial associations between al-Walid's mosque and the Syrian tradition. The central nave perpendicular to the *qibla* wall and dividing the *haram* into two parts is the first spatial elaboration of the idea of the *maqsura*. The rectangular plan of the mosque, different

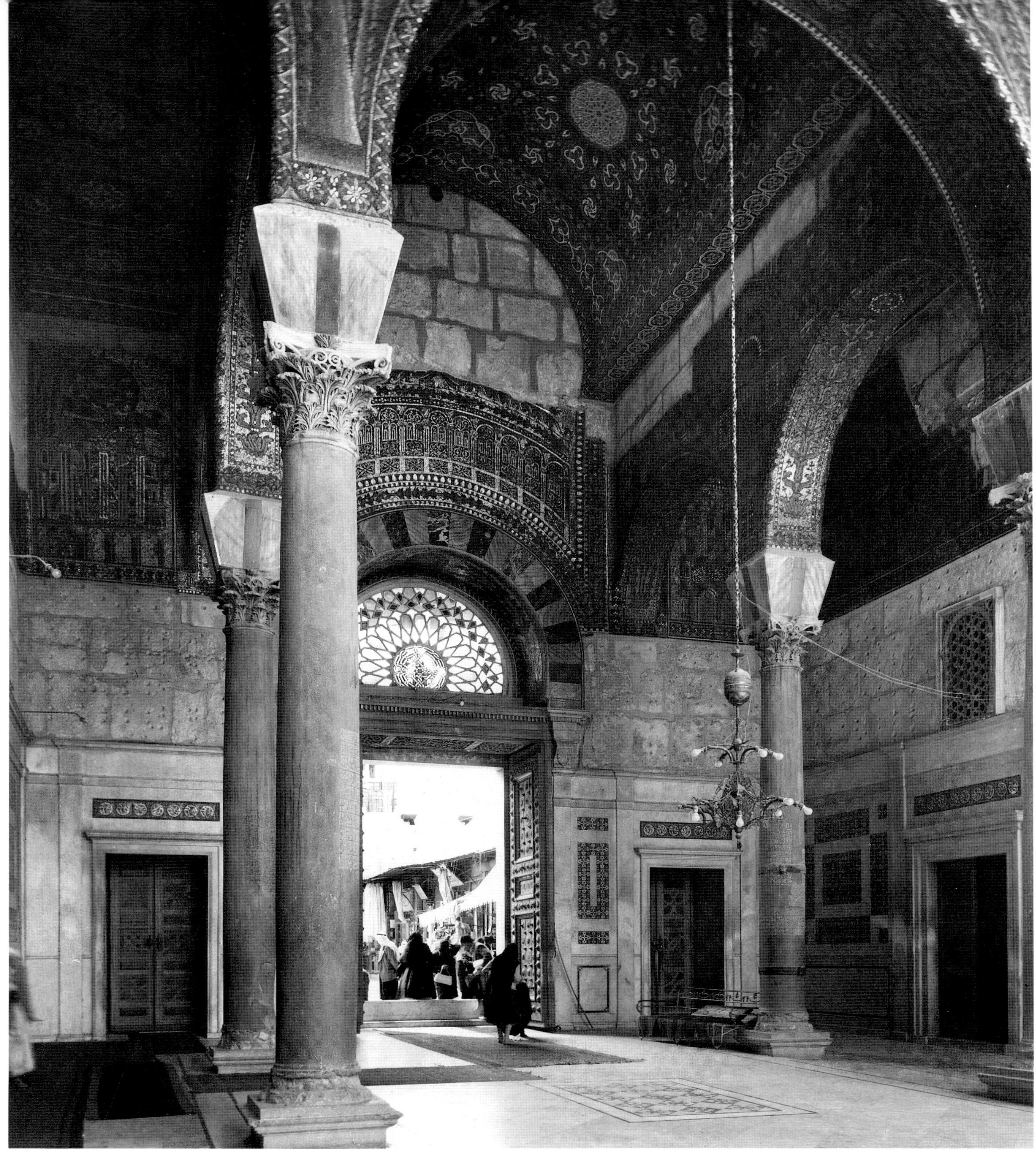

from all previous mosques with a square plan, was perhaps dictated by the site, corresponding to the shape of the old *temenos*.

The *haram* was covered by three parallel gabled roofs resting on double-tiered arcades. The central nave, also covered by a gabled roof, was higher. In its present form the central nave dates from the Seljuq period; thus both the actual dome and the courtyard façade are of eleventh-century date. In the tenth century there was probably an older wooden dome, but whether al-Walid's mosque had a domed roof is unknown. Originally the mosque had three *mihrab* niches, possibly corresponding to the triple division of the interior. Although the existing pre-Muslim corner towers of the *temenos* served originally as minarets, they were rebuilt, and today only the lower register of the south-west minaret remains from the original towers.

The octagonal domed building on columns in the courtyard is contemporary with the mosque and, according to medieval authors, was the Bayt al-Mal (public treasury). The idea of a separate structure in the centre of the courtyard seems to have been an Umayyad invention. Umar's order to place it in close proximity with the mosque so as to be under the surveillance of the worshippers may be the reason for adopting this practice, which – according to Muqaddasi – was customary in every main town, so confirming the thesis that the Bayt al-Mal of the Great Mosque was the original. The integration of this central building with a fountain for ablutions must have been an afterthought.

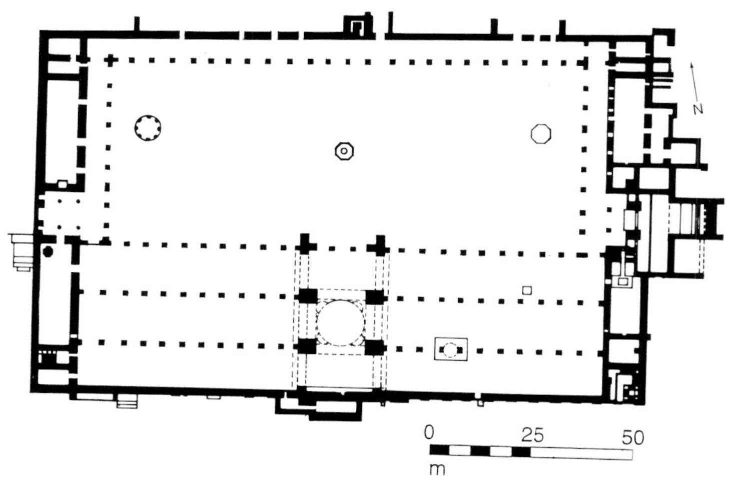

In the context of the history of mosque design the shaping of the central part is of particular interest. The simple enlarged central aisle perpendicular to the *qibla* wall is similar to the nave of a church, which also served ceremonial purposes. Its façade with arcade open to the courtyard seems to follow the pattern of early churches such as those at R'safa or Qalb Louzeh in Western Syria. In order to outdo all churches in magnificence, the mosque of al-Walid was decorated overall using every known technique: marble revetment for the lower registers of the walls, mosaic revetment for the upper registers, in both the *haram* and the *sahn*; stucco grilles in window openings. The main *mihrab* was cut from a monolithic block of rock crystal.

The geometric tracery of the window grilles and the mosaic decoration call for further examination. The subjects of decoration were real and imaginary landscapes, representations of famous cities. Above the central *mihrab* the Ka'ba was depicted; the *maqsura* walls bore a representation of the city of Medina. The historical significance of this elaborate pictorial decoration (which included no animate subjects) may be summarized as follows: this was the late phase of Syrian Christian art, as Marguerite Van Berchem concluded in her study of the mosaics of the Dome of the Rock and the Great Mosque at Damascus. Its vocabulary was both Oriental (i.e. Sasanian) and Classical (i.e. post-Roman), the latter being the dominant style. As M.

The Great Mosque of Damascus (709–15): (left) view of the main entrance seen from within; (above) plan of the mosque; (right) one of the decorative mosaic panels, sometimes called the 'Barada panel', so named after the river Barada, which flows through the city.

Van Berchem says: 'The combination of these two traditions, still very distinct here, makes this decorative scheme a monument unique of its kind.'[16] Her analysis and conclusions may also be partly applied to the architecture itself: this was essentially Syrian architecture, but built with a new spirit and imagination, with a new programme and iconography.

While the original and universal character of Islamic decoration has to be recognized, the modest and almost bare beginnings of Islamic religious architecture should not be overlooked. Only Umayyad Caliphs and governors, influenced by the recently conquered imperial domains of Iran and the Late Roman Empire, took an interest in architectural ornamentation. And as historical documents attest, they wanted – for political reasons – to show that the new religion was as great as those that preceded it. The decorative splendour attained in Medina, Damascus, Jerusalem and other places was the expression of a politically defined religious zeal, but it was not inherent in the religious culture of Islam.

Before the advent of Abbasid rule, most of the Umayyad mosques, such as the congregational mosque at Aleppo built by Caliph Sulayman (715–17), followed the model of Damascus. That this building remained as a prestigious example is attested by the twelfth-century mosque at Diyarbakir and the fourteenth-century Isa Beg Mosque at Ephesus in Turkey, both having almost identical plans. But Iraqi influence continued to be felt. One of the latest Umayyad mosques, the Great Mosque at Harran, probably built 744–50, had a square enclosure and a square minaret, a mixture of two traditions.

The Umayyad period saw the beginning of monumental Islamic architecture. In each country local building traditions prevailed, but the new image was diffused from the centre with well-established norms, especially concerning mosque design: the mosque with a courtyard, the original pattern, remained unchallenged. The principal features were the *haram* as a hypostyle hall; the *sahn* surrounded by colonnades or arcades (*riwaqs* in Arabic), minaret towers, *mihrabs*, *minbars* and *maqsuras* (possibly with symbolic domes), and decorative patterns based on geometry. The basic constructs of a universal mosque design were thus established.

The Abbasid period (749–1258)

With the geographical shift of the centre of power from Damascus to Baghdad came a change in architectural expression. The Abbasid Caliphate inherited a vast domain and, when compared to the rather provincial attitude of most of the Umayyad rulers, the Abbasids acted like emperors of the world. Under al-Mansur the circular city of Baghdad, with its palace and Great Mosque at the centre, was symbolic of this idea of world domination. Next to al-Mansur's Golden Palace (Qasr al-Dahab), crowned by a green dome (al-Qubba al-Hadra), stood the Great Mosque. Nothing now remains of the old circular city; the Great Mosque survived the sack of the city by Mongols in 1258, but gradually deteriorated and perished in the eighteenth century.

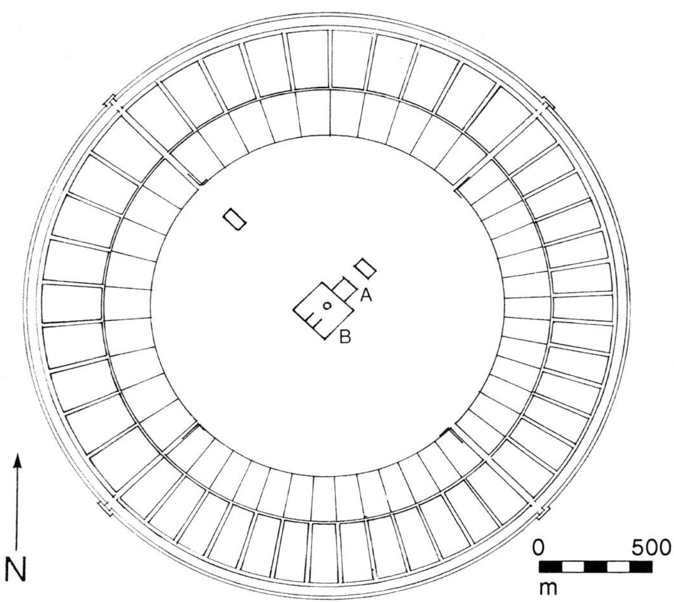

According to al-Khatib al-Baghdadi, the historian of the city, the Great Mosque was again square in plan, measuring 200 × 200 cubits (approximately 102 × 102 m or 335 × 335 ft). Its plan was similar to that of the Mosque of the Prophet at Medina, with five aisles on the *qibla* side and two rows of columns around the *sahn*. The walls were built of mud brick and the columns and roof structure were of timber. This first mosque was later rebuilt and enlarged by Harun ar-Rashid in 805–9; during this renewal the mud-brick walls were replaced by baked-brick walls (perhaps only as a revetment). The mosque had a square minaret, a *minbar*, and a *maqsura* as a screened area to the left of the *mihrab*.[17]

The Mosques of Samarra

The second wave of Abbasid Great Mosques followed the Arabian pattern, but with Iranian technical and stylistic undertones. They are part of the great urban scheme of Samarra dating from the reign of al-Mutawakkil (847–61). Situated on the Tigris, Samarra was built as an administrative capital and as the base for the Caliph's Turkish guards. A vast urban complex with monumental dimensions, symmetrical layout and grandiose perspectives, it was one of the most magnificent imperial schemes ever undertaken. However, because it was inhabited for only a short period and built hastily using earthen material, it did not survive well, though the remains of the outer enclosure are sufficiently impressive to convey an idea of the massive effort involved in the creation of the city. The Great Mosque, al-Mutawakkiliya, was built in 848/49–852. The colossal dimensions – 156 × 240 m (170 × 262 yds) overall – included an open courtyard measuring 110 m × 130 m (120 × 142 yds), the tradition of a square enclosure being abandoned. Consonant with the size of the enclosure, the *haram* was nine bays deep, and on the long sides of the courtyard the *riwaqs* consisted of four rows, while the entrance side had only three. The enclosure had thirteen doors, five on each of the long sides and three on the entrance side. The

(Left) Reconstruction plan (based on literary evidence) of the circular city of Baghdad, founded by al-Mansur in 762: (A) mosque; (B) palace.

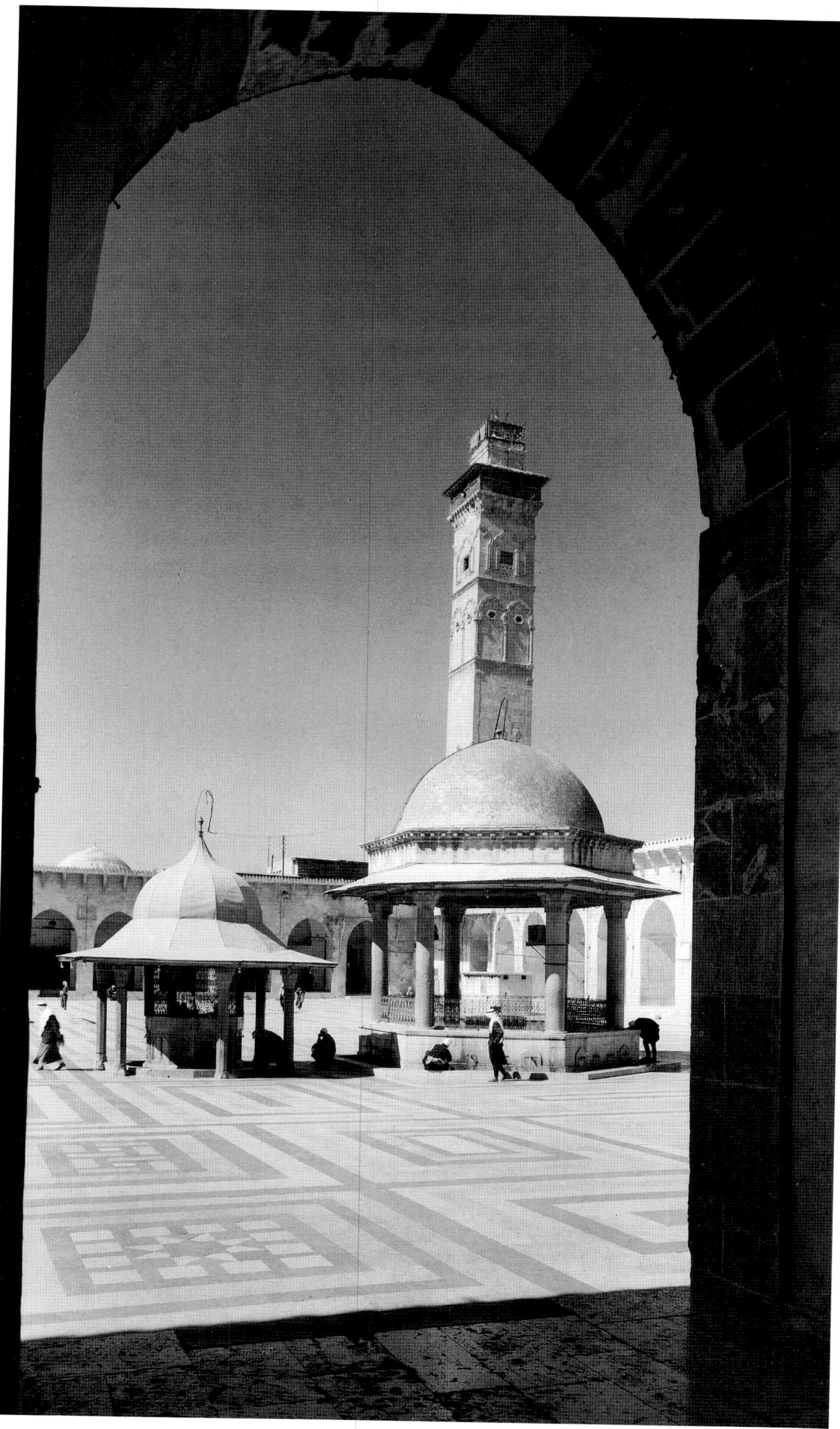

(Right) View of the courtyard and minaret in the Great Mosque (715–17), Aleppo, a building originally modelled on the slightly earlier Damascus Mosque. The spacious courtyard, paved with marble, is surrounded by a heavy masonry arcade dating from the thirteenth century, and contains pavilions and a fountain; the minaret dates from 1090.

interior had a ceiling height of about 11 m (36 ft) and was illuminated by a single row of windows.[18] The large piers in baked brick supporting the flat roof were rectangular with engaged colonnettes. The roof was covered with earthen material. Although it is no longer possible to visualize the internal appearance, the regular columnar interspacing does not suggest any imaginative change in plan, but various features – the rectangular instead of square layout, a deeper *haram*, the form of the piers, the windows, the form of the minaret and the construction method (the foundations of the walls rest on solid rock and the walls are buttressed), and an original style of decoration – are all evidence of architectural taste based on experience, as well as the existence of a new spirit of experimentation.

An unusual feature of the mosque was the minaret, standing on a square base, with its exterior spiral ramp. It was placed on the central axis of the mosque, a short distance from the north wall. With the exception of a few examples in the following centuries, this minaret type did not find favour in Islamic architecture. The minaret was surrounded on three sides by a walled enclosure (*ziyada*), the total overall dimensions being 376 × 444 m (412 × 485 yds). Here, for the first time in Islamic history, a new style reflecting the contribution of external influences was created.

The decorative art of Samarra also reveals, for the first time in Muslim history, a new style, again with the contribution of foreign sources, and no longer the continuation of a purely local tradition. The new decorative style – executed in stucco or carved wood – was, however, rather sparsely applied in the mosque, by comparison with its profuse application in residential buildings. Stucco decoration was used in the *mihrab* niche and on the exterior façades. The wall sections between the semicircular buttresses have a large frieze consisting of recessed square frames, each with a shallow saucer-shaped medallion. These were originally covered with stucco and possibly had more elaborate detailing. The use of mosaic has been confirmed by archaeological excavations.

A second mosque at Samarra was that of Abu Dulaf, also built by al-Mutawakkil, in this case for his private palace (or city), al-Ja'fariya. In spatial terms, this was a more articulate building with a number of innovations. The mosque, which also featured a minaret with spiral ramp, had a large rectangular enclosure measuring 135 × 213 m (148 × 233 yds) with *riwaqs* of different widths surrounding the *sahn*. The *haram*, for the first time in this type of building, was planned with two aisles, separated from each other and from the other arcades by very large rectangular piers running parallel to the *qibla* wall. This part of the mosque was almost completely separate and was given a special status: from the plan one can infer that some groups of worshippers had a privileged place, evidently intended for the Caliph's retinue and bodyguards, and that private ceremonial needs were fulfilled. Other aisles in the *haram* were perpendicular to the *qibla* wall, the central aisle being slightly larger than the others. This arrangement became, with some refinement, common in North African mosques.[19]

The city of al-Ja'fariya was built in the space of two years (and remained uncompleted). Today the mud-brick walls of the mosque are totally ruined but, unlike the Great Mosque, the internal piers and their arches are still standing. The Mosque of Abu Dulaf was surrounded by a large *ziyadah*; its minaret was a smaller version of that of the Great Mosque, and the stucco decor was on similar lines.

Plan of the Great Mosque (completed in 852), Samarra, showing the freestanding spiral minaret on the north side.

The rebuilding of al-Aqsa Mosque

The mosque in Jerusalem was rebuilt several times, first under Caliph Umar, then by al-Walid and al-Mansur, and again in 780 during the Caliphate of al-Mahdi. Although it was destroyed and replaced in later periods, information concerning this most important eighth-century mosque is available. According to the reconstruction by Creswell, the central aisle was slightly higher than the others and culminated in a dome over the bay in front of the *mihrab*.[20] The emphasis thus given to the central space, combined with the dome over the *mihrab*, became a general pattern for later mosques. With this rebuilding the heroic period of early Islamic architecture ended, but the Abbasid mosques in the heart of the Islamic empire would have a lasting influence on the Arabic-speaking peoples in Western Islam. The Mosque of Ibn Tulun in Cairo and the Great Mosque of Qairawan represent the two most prestigious monuments of the ninth century.

The Mosque of Ibn Tulun (876–9)

Ahmad ibn Tulun, the son of a Turkish slave of the Caliph al-Ma'mun, became governor of Egypt. He eventually became the independent ruler of Egypt and founder of the Tulunid dynasty (868–905). He founded the settlement called al-Qata'i (between Fustat and the later Fatimid city of Cairo), in which the mosque is the most conspicuous building, reflecting all the characteristic features of Abbasid art as applied to architecture. One of the mosque's original inscriptions, in ninth-century Kufic script, provides a clear statement of the aims of Muslim rulers in building mosques for the glory of religion in perpetuity: 'The Amir ... has ordered the construction of this blessed and happy mosque, using the revenues from a pure and legitimate source that God has granted him ...', followed by injunctions from the Qur'an (Sura al-Nur, 24:36–8) and the date of completion.

The rectangular enclosure measuring 118 × 138 m (129 × 151 yds) has the traditional transversal five aisles on the *mihrab* side separated by the heavy piers of the arcades. The *sahn* is surrounded by double arcades on three sides. The great rectangular piers of baked brick with engaged corner columns recall the Great Mosque of Samarra. The mosque had a flat timber roof and the bay in front of the *mihrab* was accentuated by a wooden dome. The fountain in the courtyard is a later structure which replaced the original fountain. On three sides of the mosque there are narrow enclosed arms (*ziyadas*) and within the northern *ziyada* there is a minaret with an external spiral ramp, similar to those at Samarra. The minaret was connected to the mosque by a passageway. The minaret's square base is the only original part still surviving; the second storey is cylindrical and is surmounted by later additions.

Here it is necessary to emphasize two different approaches to the *maqsura*. The Umayyads introduced an architectural approach – indeed, the most characteristic example of later Umayyad design, the Great Mosque of Cordoba, has a beautiful *mihrab* (see chapter 6) separated from the *haram*. The special case of Abu Dulaf apart, however, the Abbasids preferred screened enclosures for the Caliphs or governors. In Umayyad mosques the local influence of existing Christian architecture is indicated. The Abbasid solution was the one preferred by the Arabs, but in the later Middle Ages, with the ascendancy of the Turks, a separate *maqsura* became the most emphasized spatial element of mosque interiors.

The Mosque of Ibn Tulun had, as its forerunner in Egypt, the additions made to the Amr Mosque, but the walls do not have the heavy external buttressing seen at Samarra. However, the single row of large windows with circular openings on the upper registers of the walls, the frieze of simple square frames and the decorative terminal crenellation are probably of Samarran inspiration.

The original decorations of the Ibn Tulun Mosque are of great art-historical importance. They present, in both stucco and wood, the most valuable and best-preserved examples of the so-called Samarra style. Stucco ornaments were applied both internally and externally. The soffits of the arches were decorated with bands of stucco ornament; although these have been extensively repaired, a number of them have survived in their original state, revealing a geometric band with floral filling. On the inner arcades a frieze of floral ornament runs around the arches, and above the arches Kufic inscriptions extending to over 2 km (2,200 yds) overall set forth verses quoted from the Qur'an. The window grilles, also executed in stucco, feature various intricate geometric patterns.

Plan of al-Aqsa Mosque, Jerusalem. After many alterations and extensions, the building acquired its present form in the mid-fourteenth century.

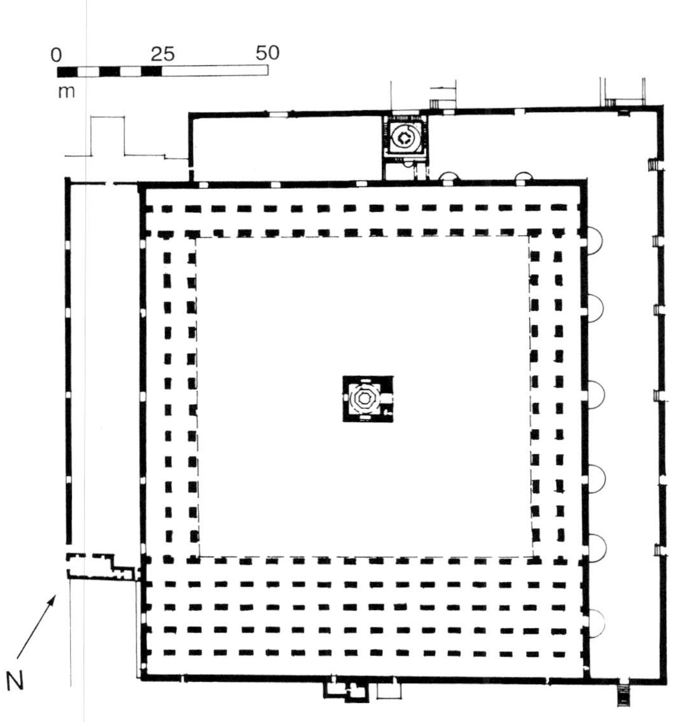

Plan of the Mosque of Ibn Tulun (876–9), Cairo. The original spiral minaret, unique in Egypt, was substantially rebuilt in the early fourteenth century.

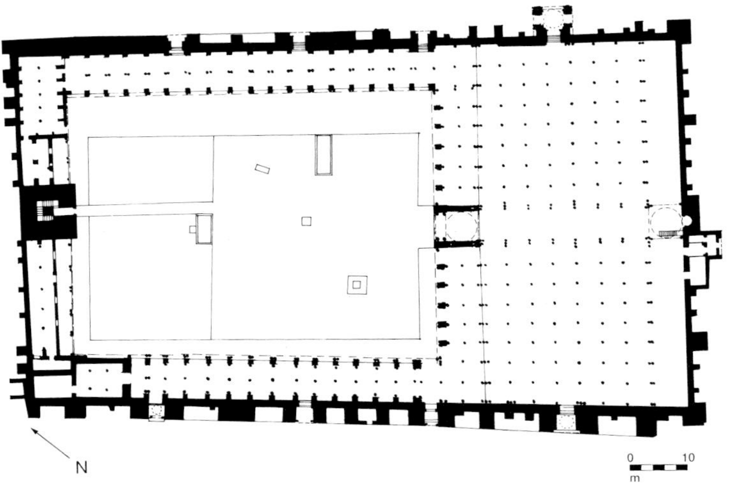

The Great Mosque (836), Qairawan: view of the minaret and part of the courtyard arcade, and plan of the mosque and courtyard.

The Great Mosque, Qairawan (rebuilt 836)

In the early history of mosque design the Great Mosque of Qairawan in Tunisia is of the greatest importance, for it possesses the oldest dated minaret, *mihrab* and *minbar*. Originally built by Uqba ibn Nafi, the Abbasid general who conquered North Africa, the mosque was reconstructed by the Aghlabid ruler Ziyadat Allah in 836. The main characteristics of later North African mosques are found here as a clear architectural statement. The large *haram*, eight bays deep, consists of seventeen arcaded aisles perpendicular to the *qibla* wall, with marble columns supporting the flat wooden ceiling. The central aisle, wider and higher than the rest, is crowned by two domes, one over the entrance bay, the other over the *mihrab* bay. The larger transverse aisle next to the *qibla* wall forms, with the central aisle, the T-shaped central axis of the interior space. The minaret is a square tower consisting of three storeys independent of, but connected with, the north wall of the mosque, as in the Abbasid examples. The *mihrab* has a horseshoe plan and two decorative columns flanking the niche; it is decorated with lustre tiles. The wooden *minbar* is contemporary with the *mihrab*.

The Outreach of the Arabian mosque design

In conquered lands the Arabs built mosques based on models in their home territories. The concept of the hypostyle hall remained constant throughout North Africa. In rural areas of Islamic countries it constitutes the common form for smaller *masjids*. In eastern Islam and later in the Ottoman domains the development of mosque architecture with a totally different emphasis given to the *haram* was the outcome of the ever-growing importance of the *maqsura*. The eastern and western development of mosque architecture is covered in other chapters, but the architecture of the Fatimid, Ayyubid and Mamluk periods needs to be discussed within the central core of Islamic architectural history.

Cairene transformations in mosque design

In Syria, Iraq and Egypt until the end of the Mamluk period mosque design followed the vicissitudes of political and dynastic history, the cultural allegiance of successive ruling houses and the influence of local building traditions. In this chapter, only the mosque architecture of Cairo, from the Fatimids to the early Mamluks, will be considered.

The Fatimids, who established a Shiite caliphate (909–1171), may be regarded as the founders of a specifically Egyptian architectural style, although existing typology remained unchallenged. The first Fatimid mosque after the founding of Cairo was al-Azhar, built in 970–2. Its plan followed the classical pattern: a *haram* five bays deep, a central nave perpendicular to the *qibla* wall, a dome over the *mihrab* bay, three aisled arcades on the long sides of the *sahn*, but none on the north side. Because al-Azhar became one of the greatest centres of religious education, the structure underwent alterations and enlargements, even in recent periods. G. Wiet has called it 'A museum of all Egyptian styles'.[21]

Another important Fatimid mosque was al-Hakim Mosque (990–1013), which followed the scheme of the Ibn Tulun and al-Azhar Mosques. Its main contribution to mosque design lay in the introduction of a gateway protruding from the main façade, at each end of which was a minaret. This disposition of the façade was the beginning of a new concept which would develop, in the Mamluk period, into a rich and articulated design.

The Fatimids introduced the smaller *masjid* type, such as al-Guyushi Mosque, in which the mausoleum of the founder was integrated into the mosque proper. Contradictory to the tradition of the Prophet, this practice gave rise to the most important building type of the Mamluk period (1250–1517), the *madrasa*-tombs of the sultans, which also served as mosques.

The outstanding era of architectural innovation was that of the Mamluks. In terms of mosque architecture this period started with the Great Mosque of Sultan Baybars I, built in 1267–9. It illustrates the

Detail of relief decoration over one of the projecting stone gateways of the Great Mosque of the Mamluk Sultan Baybars I (1267–9), Cairo.

existence of various influences at work in Cairo at this period. The mosque was conceived as a large enclosure in the classical manner, with a central *sahn* surrounded by hypostyle halls. However, it had a domed *mihrab* area covering nine bays, which was a unique feature in the Arab context. It was evidently borrowed from the Seljuq architecture of Iran, since the Sultan himself had been educated in this tradition. In this instance the Egyptian architect designed a three-aisled hall (the origin of which is Syrian), instead of including a lofty *iwan* leading to the Sultan's *maqsura*. The use of gates projecting from the façade was a Fatimid practice, and the corner towers and crenellations were similar to those of the al-Hakim Mosque. Certain decorative features of the mosque, such as the geometric ornament on the spandrels of the arched panels of the gates, or striped masonry, are of Syrian origin. Creswell even detects the influence of Crusaders in some details of the stonework. Such transferral of form is typical of all medieval buildings.

The account by Maqrizi is extremely illuminating with regard to the role of the Sultan in the building of his mosque: he selected the site and ordered that the rest of the ground should be put in trust (*waqf*) for the mosque, with a provision that it should be left unoccupied. The plan of the mosque was drawn up in his presence. He intimated that its doors should be like those of the Madrasa az-Zahiriya, and that a dome the same size as the dome of ash-Shafi, which was 15.50 m (51 ft) in diameter,[22] should be built over the *mihrab*. The Sultan sent for marble columns, good timber for the doors and ceilings, and for iron. He said 'This is a place I have dedicated to God . . . so when I die do not bury me here or change any of the characteristics of the place.' Baybars also sent building materials (columns, capitals etc.) from Jaffa, after he had captured the city from the Crusaders and destroyed it.

No trace remains of the minaret of Baybars' mosque, but it was located over the north entrance, as indicated by an engraving made at the time of Napoleon's Egyptian expedition in 1797. The nature of the interior decoration is known only from a few remains, including geometric tracery, floral bands and Kufic inscriptions.

Although only little remains of the decorative stucco of the Great Mosque of Baybars (due to the nature of the material, most stucco work of that period has been lost), some early Mamluk buildings such as the Mausoleum of Sultan Qala'un (1284–5) or that of Ahmad ibn Sulayman al-Rifai (1291) still preserve fine examples of stucco decoration. *Muqarnas* consisting of rows of pointed Fatimid arches, large bands of Kufic inscription, and geometric and floral motifs covering the entire surface of domes were common elements of decorative vocabulary.

Until the first half of the fourteenth century Cairene domes were built in brick, often on squinches. They had elongated and pointed profiles and were raised on relatively high drums, some of them profusely decorated with a row of arches embellished on their surface with geometric and floral motifs. The domes were decorated on the inside and outside with stucco work. From the late Fatimid period on, fluted exteriors were typical. After the mid-fourteenth century domes were generally built in stone, evidently under the influence of Syrian stonemasons. Late Mamluk domes might have fluted, striped decoration on their exterior, or sometimes a flat geometric network pattern on the surface, often filled with floral ornament. One of the best examples of this type of decorative treatment is to be found in the Mausoleum-Madrasa of Qaitbay (1472–4). Stone domes were often painted on the inside with similar designs. The general profile of Mamluk domes reflects unmistakably the influence of Timurid architecture in Iran and Central Asia.

The Mamluk Sultans preferred to build memorials consisting of a *madrasa* and a personal mausoleum, rather than mosques. In these compounds the main *iwan* also served as a *masjid* and was therefore correctly oriented. The *madrasa*-mausoleum composition of the Turkish Mamluks was initiated by Sultan Qala'un (1284–5). The importance accorded to the tomb of the Sultan was, however, evidently a clear transgression of tradition. The mosque-*madrasa*-mausoleum of Sultan Hasan (1356–9) is the most monumental example of this type of religious complex, in which the dome of the Sultan's mausoleum is the dominant external feature. In this group of buildings individual *masjids* took different forms, being designed as *iwans* or as basilical or transversal halls, exemplified in the latter case by the *khanaqah* of Sultan Baybars II al-Gashangir (1309). In the late Mamluk period traditional hypostyle halls were also built, such as al-Maridani (1338–40) and al-Muayyad Shaykh (1415–22).

Egyptian minarets in general retained a very decorative and multi-layered appearance, demonstrating in a conspicuous manner the originality of the builders. Square at the base and circular in the upper registers, the shafts were interrupted at intervals by very richly ornamented balconies over *muqarnas* cornices. Surface patterns consisted of niches, arches and decorative panels.

The architecture of the mosque in Yemen

As a result of its geographical position, Yemen – Arabia Felix of antiquity – had a rather independent history. In antiquity the Yemenis

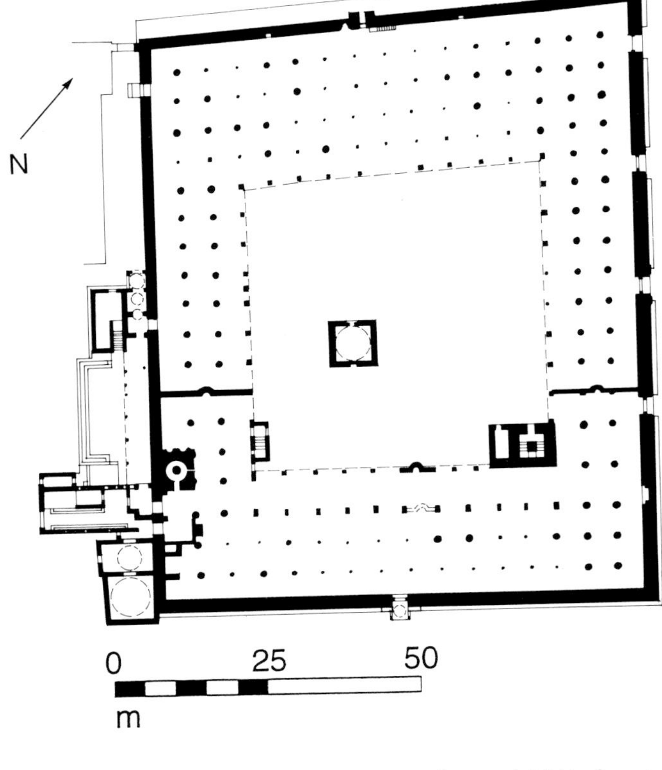

(Above) Plan of the Great Mosque, San'a, showing the Dar al-Mal in the centre of the courtyard and the twin minarets on square bases.

(Left) The Bakiliya (Bakiriyya) Mosque, San'a (1597): external view showing the principal dome and minaret.

controlled maritime trade in the Red Sea and the Gulf of Aden, and the country was the main source of incense and spices for the Roman Empire. In the history of Southern Arabia the Sabaeans, one of the tribes of Yemen, played an important role in the Near East, as attested by the biblical Sheba and its queen (I Kings 10:1–10) and in the Qur'an (27:22 and 34:15–21). Sabaean and, later, Himyarite cultures had their own original and relatively advanced building traditions. The well-known Dam of Maarib in Eastern Yemen, a great feat of engineering, being 3 km (2 miles) long and 40 m (130 ft) high, dated from the Sabaean period.

Architecture in Yemen, while adopting freely the influences of other regions – Abyssinia, Egypt, Iran, India, Arabia proper, Turkey – had developed one of the most picturesque and original styles. Both in its vernacular traditions and in religious buildings, the results were highly imaginative, using a variety of materials: stone, brick, layered mud and mud brick and wood. Perhaps due to continuous tribal warfare, tall stone buildings became, as on the Red Sea coast of Saudi Arabia, a common feature of settlements. In the tenth year of Hijra, through the mediation of Ali, Muhammad's son-in-law, the Yemenis accepted Islam by consent, although in no period of history have foreigners ever had complete control over the country.

According to Islamic tradition, the first mosque in Yemen was built in San'a following specific instructions from the Prophet. The Masjid al-Kabir, although greatly transformed over the centuries, was originally a square enclosure measuring about 55 × 55 m (180 × 180 ft) with a classical plan as seen in early Arabian courtyard mosques. Today there are no visible remains of the original building, which was enlarged in 707 during the reign of Caliph al-Walid and underwent reconstructions in subsequent periods. The first indication of the existence of a minaret occurs in the ninth century, but the present minarets date from the Ayyubid period (1169–1252). Raised on high square bases, these minarets feature a series of cylindrical and polygonal registers, but lack the picturesque quality of most Yemeni examples (the style of the minaret being the most original element of the country's mosque architecture). The present building has two separate *harams*. The one on the north side, partly corresponding to the area of the original mosque, is a hypostyle hall with five aisles; the corresponding *sahn* is surrounded by triple arcades on the east and west sides. The second *haram*, on the south side, has four aisles with a central *mihrab* and two side *mihrabs*. It shows a matter-of-fact approach to design, consonant with the spirit of early Arabian mosques. The same is also true of the siting of the minarets, which stand in the southern corners of the *sahn*. The Dar al-Mal (treasury) is a seventeenth-century Ottoman reconstruction which possibly replaced the original treasury building. Various tombs and libraries were added on the side of the mosque enclosure in later periods.

Although historically difficult to confirm, there are other mosques in Yemen which are claimed to have been erected in the first years of Islam.

One, at Janad in South Yemen, is in the early Arabian style. The arcades consist of alternating square and circular piers, while the octagonal minaret and the exterior are almost bare of decoration. Another early mosque with the same scheme is at Shibam near San'a.[23] Founded in the ninth century, it evidently underwent a number of transformations in later periods. Like the Masjid al-Kabir in San'a, it has two *harams* connected by a courtyard, each having its own *mihrab*. The stone building is fairly small, measuring about 28 × 39 m (92 × 128 ft) including the second *haram*. Internally, there are stone piers supporting a wooden ceiling which features a remarkable painted carving. The original minaret was replaced by a brick structure in the sixteenth century.

The Great Mosque at Jiblah, a small city in the south of the central high plateau, was built in 1088–9, replacing an earlier mosque; this is one of the best-preserved mosques of the medieval period. Situated in the centre of the city, surrounded by souks, the main enclosure measures about 36 × 40 m (118 × 131 ft); the layout follows the traditional Arabian scheme, with four aisles parallel to the *qibla* wall and a central nave with higher ceilings. An interesting aspect of this plan is the fifth transversal aisle, which forms part of the *sahn* rather than the *haram*, and the entrance bay of the *haram* is emphasized by a dome above – a feature usually associated with the *mihrab* bay. This disposition, which is not typical of Arabian-style *sahns*, had a direct formal relationship with Ottoman architecture, hence an intervention during the Turkish period might be suggested. Entrances are on all sides of the mosque. The wooden *mihrab* is a simple niche with carved decoration, framed by a larger pointed arch, and on the *mihrab* and *minbar* there are Kufic inscriptions. The columns of the interior are also decorated with low reliefs. The two minarets are situated at the ends of the southern arcade, the one on the east having very interesting ornamentation, almost the same as the decoration found on house façades. In its proportions and forms the minaret has an affinity with Fatimid façade design; the crenellations are debased forms of the Samarra style, most probably introduced via Egypt.

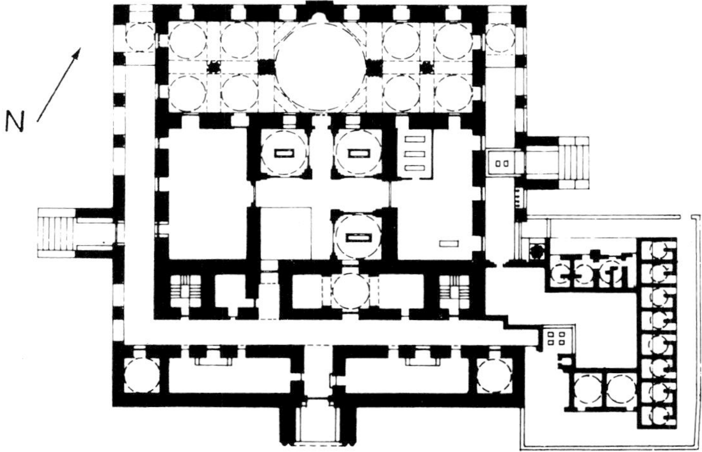

Plan of the Ashrafiyya Mosque (thirteenth–fourteenth centuries), Ta'izz, built in two separate stages by al-Ashraf I and al-Ashraf II. This mosque features twin minarets on the south side; the original courtyard at the centre is partially occupied by three royal tombs added later.

A feature peculiar to Yemeni mosques is a large pool (*sabil*) for ablutions. The Jiblah Mosque has one of the finest examples, measuring 9 × 13 m (30 × 43 ft). A large ablutions area next to the pool has galleries on three sides; there are two channels for washing the feet before using the pool itself and small rooms for private use. The whole scheme, completed by an adjacent group of latrines, is functionally the most sophisticated example of an ablutions area to be found in mosque architecture anywhere. In rural areas these pools also serve as water-tanks for irrigation. On open land large water-tanks for communal use had small *musallas* adjacent to them with a simple indication of the Ka'ba.[24]

Mosques in the classical tradition include small flat-roofed buildings with interior supports and with a very low minaret or none at all. Their form may be primitive and simple but very expressive, as in the case of the small *masjid* at Al-Magraba. They are almost always built of stone, even in areas with a mud-brick tradition.

The second type is the monumental domed mosque, most examples of which date from the Ottoman period. The dome as a roofing system had certainly been introduced to Yemen in the early Middle Ages, under the Abbasids. Ayyubid and Mamluk influence is also evident in dome design. On the shores of the Red Sea there are examples of direct importation of Indian-style domed buildings, such as al-Mansuriya, evidently the work of Indian master-builders, but perhaps due to later rebuilding Turkish influence is more preponderant. As in Egypt, Yemeni builders adapted and reinterpreted the form of Turkish domes, creating a sober and massive volumetry of great power. One of the best-preserved and most impressive mosques of the Ottoman period is the so-called Bakiliya (Bakiriyya) Mosque in San'a, built in 1597 by the Ottoman governor Hasan Pasha. The single-domed building with a triple-domed entrance porch represents the commonest type of Ottoman provincial mosque, but apart from its plan, and the corner towers placed around the drum, very little was adopted from the classical vocabulary of Ottoman architecture. The marble *mihrab* and *minbar* were, however, imported from Istanbul,[25] while the minaret was a local interpretation of the Egyptian type. Additions such as the governor's *maqsura* (here called a *diwan*) and are of much later dates.

The cities in the region of Ta'izz, centre of a medieval kingdom in the south, have picturesque skylines dominated by whitewashed domes and minarets. Their architectural style is a free interpretation of Ayyubid and Mamluk styles: typical features are massive domes resting on blind drums and the polygonal multi-layered minaret towers, richly articulated with niches and topped with small domes.

Accustomed to the idea of high buildings and having a strong tradition of façade ornamentation, Yemeni builders appear to have followed their own taste with confidence in designing minarets, generally in the form of a multi-layered tower on a square base. Those built in brick are sometimes constructed on the walls of the mosque enclosure. The frequently striking surface ornament is essentially geometric. On the high balcony a whitewashed terracotta decoration is found, while ornamentation is in the regional style. A remarkable example of an Indian-style minaret with local decoration occurs in Mocha, a port on the Red Sea coast.

- 6 -
SPAIN AND NORTH AFRICA
ANTONIO FERNÁNDEZ-PUERTAS

ISLAMIC religious architecture dating from the eighth to the fourteenth centuries in the Iberian Peninsula and present-day Morocco, Algeria and Tunisia[1] covers various artistic and political epochs: first, the Umayyad Emirate and Caliphate (756–1031) in al-Andalus, the Islamic part of Spain, which at this period extended to the north of the peninsula; then its breakdown into separate, petty kingdoms (*taifas*; 1031–86); then the Almoravid (1086–1147) and Almohad (1147–1264) empires which reunited al-Andalus under North African rule. Finally there were three independent sultanates: the Nasrid sultanate in Granada (until 1492), the Marinid sultanate in the north of Morocco, and the Abd al-Wadid sultanate in Algeria.

The two major periods of artistic development were the Umayyad era and the Almoravid and Almohad empires. Under the later sultanates the *madrasa*, a religious school with its own oratory – a building type which originated in the Near East – made its appearance.

The Umayyad Emirate

When the ruling Umayyads of Damascus were overthrown in 750 by the rising Abbasids, the young prince Abd ar-Rahman managed to escape the general massacre; he made his way to southern Spain, where he established a seat of power at Cordoba, taking the title of Abd ar-Rahman I ad-Dakhil ('the Immigrant'). During his long reign (756–88) he was thus able to sustain both the Umayyad dynasty and its art in the West. At Cordoba he built a mosque which, with progressive enlargements, was to become one of the glories of Islamic architecture. It featured the traditional geometric system of proportion, inherited from classical antiquity, that was to dominate Western Islamic art.

A site was acquired to the east of the early Christian-Visigothic palace (now the episcopal residence), and the mosque built on it had three very distinctive features: (1) Its ground-plan and elevations were given proportional dimensions, following a traditional system.[2] (2) Roman columns and capitals were re-used, and together constitute a veritable museum of classical elements dating from the first to the seventh centuries. (3) In order to create a majestic prayer-hall of sufficient height to enable the faithful to gather in large numbers for regular prayers, a brilliant system of double-tiered arcades was devised; in this the lower tier provides stability for the columns, while the upper one supports the roof and houses the gutters. This idea was probably taken from the arcades of the Great Mosque at Damascus,[3] though the upper tier there has two arches, of reduced height, above each single arch of the lower tier. Structurally, however, the Cordoba arcades followed the basic system of double-tiered arcades seen in Roman aqueducts in the Iberian Peninsula, which however feature massive pillars rather than columns in the lower tier.

The ground-plan was laid out in 785 as an almost perfect square, the perimeter wall having a thickness of 2 *rashshashid codos*, equal to 114 cm (45 in.). The brilliant architect of the original mosque divided this square into two equal areas, leaving the northern half as an open courtyard, and utilizing the southern half for the prayer-hall; the latter had eleven aisles, each twelve bays in depth, the central nave being broader than the side-aisles. The two outer aisles are narrower than the rest due to the perimeter wall being included within their width – a stratagem used in order to maintain the strict proportional system that governs the dimensions of every aspect of the mosque.

This proportional system is empirical, simple and easy to use. It is based on a square and its diagonal. If the sides of a square are given the conventional value of 1, the diagonal will always have the value of $\sqrt{2}$ (= 1.4142 etc. to infinity). To develop the system pragmatically, one simply extends one side of the original square to the point where it intersects an arc of radius $\sqrt{2}$. A rectangle can then be drawn with sides in the proportions of $1{:}\sqrt{2}$, and this rectangle will in turn have a diagonal which is $\sqrt{3}$ (1.73205 etc.). By repeating the same operation using the $\sqrt{3}$ diagonal while maintaining the length of the side of the original square (= 1), one obtains a $\sqrt{3}$ rectangle; and so on progressively. This simple proportional system was to govern all Hispano-Muslim architecture. The mosque at Cordoba was enlarged, first from a square to a $\sqrt{2}$ rectangle, and then by further $\sqrt{3}$ rectangles; these stages can be traced historically and archaeologically.

The mosque's ground-plan was basilical, like that of the Umayyad Mosque of al-Aqsa at Jerusalem, in that all the aisles extended to the *qibla* wall. The *mihrab*, recessed in the *qibla* wall, was given a scallop-shell ceiling (using a classical traditional symbol, inherited directly from pagan and Roman art, associated with the birth of Venus and transmitted through early Christian art into Muslim art).

Four external buttresses divided the east and west sides of the prayer-hall into three equal segments. The central segment on the west, facing the palace, was given a full tripartite façade, and called *bab al-Uzara* ('door of the Ministers') – probably because the Emir and his retinue passed through it to enter the mosque. The width of this door and that of the whole façade were in the ratio of 1:7, and the height of the door was double its width. The composition of this doorway and its decoration were based on a series of squares and $\sqrt{2}$ rectangles.

Facing page
The minaret of the twelfth-century Kutubiyya Mosque, Marrakesh, over 60 m (190 ft) in height.

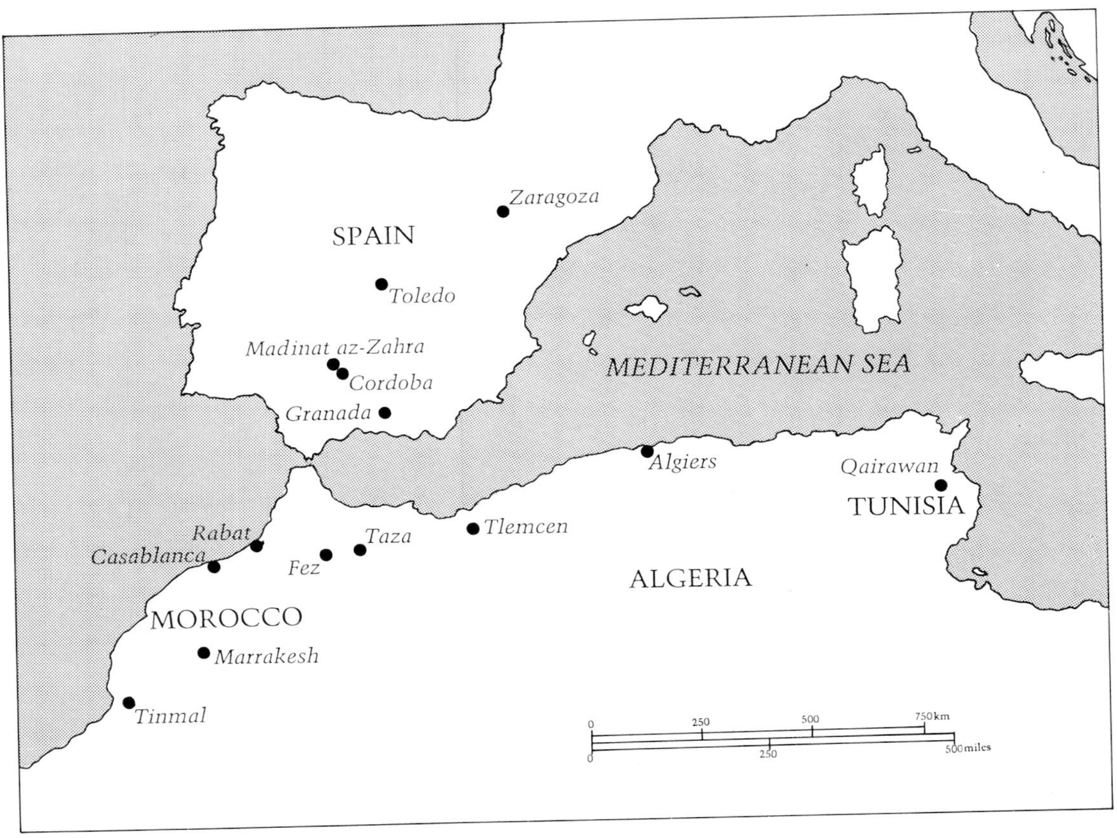

Map 2: Spain and North Africa, showing principal sites.

Internally, the prayer-hall was divided by parallel rows of two-tiered arcades. The architect's genius lay in making the arches bear down delicately on columns and capitals re-used from pre-Islamic buildings, and in giving each column its own separate foundation. The variously coloured columns resemble a shining marble forest. However, because the classical capitals were of different shapes and sizes, the level of the lower arcading had to be adjusted by inserting cruciform stones, from which the pillars of the upper arcades are also made to spring. The arches themselves are unusual in that they are of white stone alternating with red brick, a combination which gives the Cordoba mosque its unique decorative effect. The drainage channels of the roof run above each row of arches, and every aisle had its own painted ceiling. The overall effect is of an architecture that appears to be suspended from the ceiling, a style invented by the architect of the Cordoba mosque.

The mosque of Abd ar-Rahman I was completed by his son Hisham I (788–96), who also built a cubic minaret by the north gate of the courtyard. However, the population of Cordoba grew rapidly during the ninth century, while vigorous cultural links were maintained with the eastern Abbasid Caliphate in Baghdad. Abd ar-Rahman II (822–52) began the first enlargement of the mosque (see diagram, p. 104). The women, who had been using the outer (first and eleventh) aisles on either side of the prayer-hall, were now transferred to an external gallery in the courtyard, so increasing the space for the men within the hall. Even with this arrangement, however, the mosque was proving too small, so the aisles were extended southwards. The overall ground-plan, which had been a square, was converted into a $\sqrt{2}$ rectangle, leaving the area of the courtyard unchanged but enlarging the prayer-hall, which now had five external segments. This process involved piercing the existing *qibla* wall and adding eight further bays similar in depth to those of the original prayer-hall, with columns and pillars projecting from the new *qibla* wall.

Because the greater depth of the building now made access harder, a new doorway was inserted in the third segment on the east side. The ninth-century arcades essentially repeat the original arcading system, but the columns have no base, seventeen new capitals had to be carved, and the pillars of the upper tiers of arches spring from quarter-round mouldings. The positioning of the new columns was determined by the adjustment of the bays to fit within the proportional enlargement of the ground-plan. Four small columns, surmounted by finely carved new capitals which might well be mistaken for Roman, were grouped in pairs on either side of the new *mihrab*, which projected southward beyond the *qibla* wall.

The moment when the ruler left his palace to enter the mosque was always a hazardous one, exposing him to assassination attempts. For this reason the Emir Abd Allah built a narrow covered corridor bridging the street; this connected the palace with the fifth segment of the mosque's west wall. Called the *sabat*, this was similar to one that already existed in the Mosque of al-Aqsa at Jerusalem. It increased the separation of the ruler from his subjects in the interests of security.

Ninth-century minarets in the Iberian Peninsula have square ground-plans, and house inner cylindrical spiral staircases. They tend to be rather small in size and are built of ashlar blocks, their proportional dimensions being expressed in terms of *codos*. Three sides have blind windows, and the fourth has real windows to admit light to the staircase. The upper part of the minaret sometimes has dwarf arcading. The minarets of San Juan and Santiago (Cordoba), El

Salvador (Seville) and one at Niebla (province of Huelva) are examples that follow this pattern.

The minaret of Ibn Tulun in Cairo (see p. 24), a work of the late ninth or early tenth century, has the following stylistic features in common with those of the Andalusian Emirate: (1) it is built of ashlars measured in *codos*; (2) its height is twice its width; (3) it has horseshoe arches with or without frame; (4) it has double blind arches divided by a central column on its façades; (5) it stands free of the mosque, attached to the courtyard. However, it features an external staircase around a cylindrical shaft in the Abbasid manner, and the mosque itself, built in 879, has Abbasid characteristics. The Ibn Tulun minaret, which antedates the Cordoba minaret of Abd ar-Rahman III (951), provides evidence of artistic influence moving from west to east.

The Umayyad Caliphate

The establishment of a Fatimid Caliphate in Egypt induced Abd ar-Rahman III (912–61) to proclaim himself Caliph in 929. This elevation to Caliph for politico-religious reasons is reflected in the new enlargements of the Cordoba mosque. It encouraged greater grandeur and an emphasis on the Caliph's religious authority.

Abd ar-Rahman III built a magnificent royal complex at Madinat az-Zahra', some 8 km (5 miles) from Cordoba, for himself, his court and his servants, well away from the bustle of the city. It is a vast palace with dependencies. In 942 he built its mosque, correctly oriented towards Mecca. Excavations show that the Caliph descended from his palace terrace by way of a vaulted passage, similar to the system at Cordoba, crossed the road by the bridging *sabat*, and entered the mosque between two buttressed walls: the real internal *qibla* wall, and – not quite parallel to it – an external wall having the appearance of a *qibla* wall. By using the space between the two walls, the Caliph could gain access to the mosque through a door adjacent to the *mihrab*. The *maqsura* area for the Caliph, his family and his court, was formed by three bays: one in front of the *mihrab* and the two on either side of it. Its floor was paved with clay tiles and the area was enclosed by a screen of latticed or perforated wood, to separate and protect the Caliph from his subjects during prayers and religious ceremonies, as at Cordoba. The minaret at Madinat az-Zahra' is interesting because of its square ground-plan combined with an inner octagonal staircase. This may have been the model for later polygonal Mudéjar towers.

Ornate two-tiered arches of the transverse arcade in the Great Mosque, Cordoba, dating from the reign of al-Hakam II (961–6).

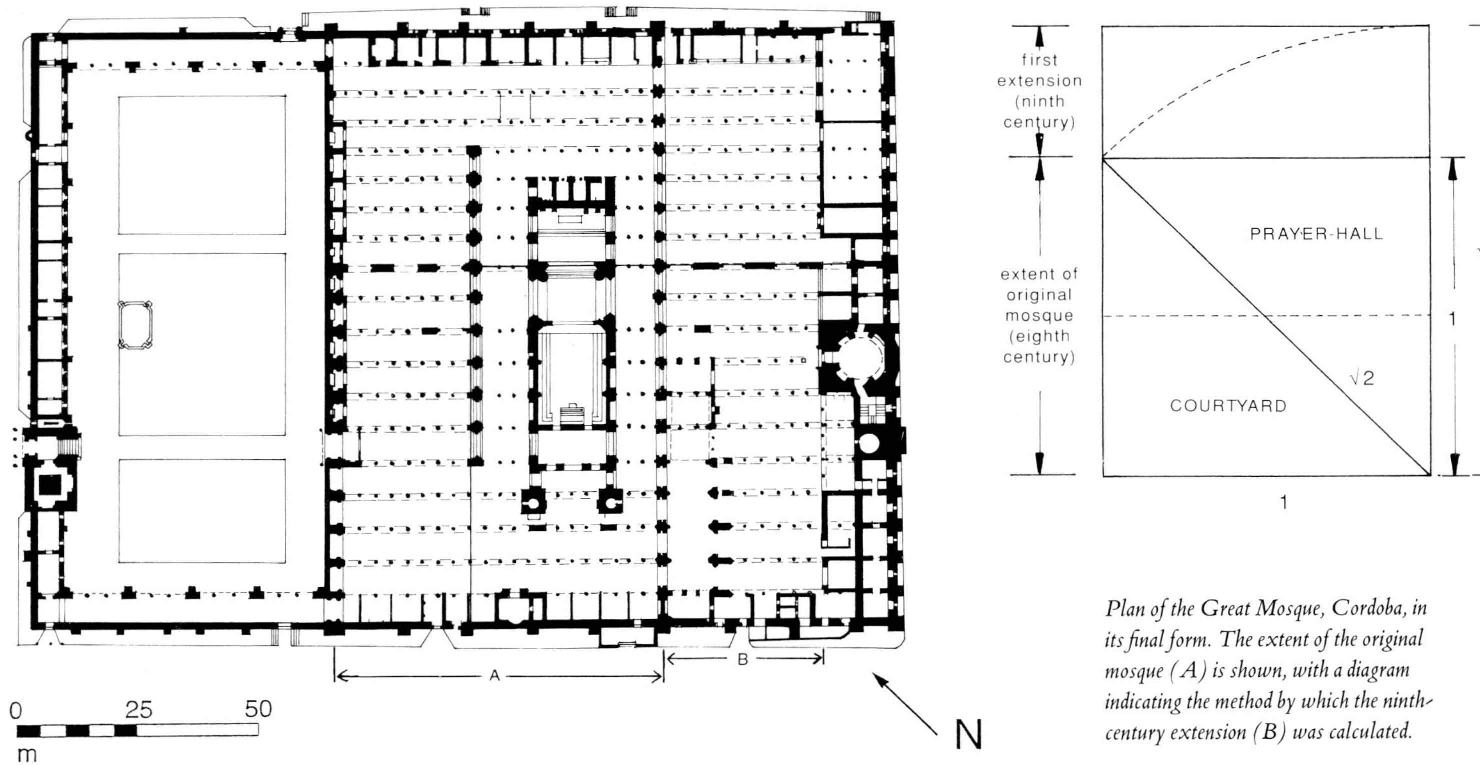

Plan of the Great Mosque, Cordoba, in its final form. The extent of the original mosque (A) is shown, with a diagram indicating the method by which the ninth-century extension (B) was calculated.

As the population of Cordoba grew, the Great Mosque had to be enlarged once again. This was done by Abd ar-Rahman III and by his son al-Hakam II (961–76). The courtyard was first lengthened northwards to make the overall mosque area a $\sqrt{3}$ rectangle, using the method already described. The new courtyard porticos were supported by groups of three arches, separated by pillar-buttresses. In 951 Abd ar-Rahman III built a great new minaret within the porticos on the new north side of the courtyard. This monumental structure, together with the new courtyard itself, transformed the provincial appearance of this whole area. In this huge minaret, square in plan, the width of the exterior wall in relation to its height was in the ratio of 1:5. Internally there were separate rectangular staircases for the *muezzin*, one of whom would climb up from the courtyard to call the faithful and to direct the prayers across the courtyard and to the south-east of the city, while the other would climb up from the street to call out over the north-west part of the city. Externally, the opposite sides of this minaret are in matching pairs: the north and south sides each have two storeys of double-arched windows that give light to the staircases; the east and west sides each have two storeys of tripartite blind arcades with stucco decoration. This minaret became the model for later Almohad and Sultanate structures.

In 958 Abd ar-Rahman III also strengthened the unstable leaning façade of the prayer-hall. The idea of further enlarging the hall itself towards the south must also be attributed to this Caliph. However, a study of the proportions suggests that this next project followed the completion of the great new minaret and courtyard, as a result of which it became apparent that the prayer-hall needed a similar grandeur.

For this second enlargement of the prayer-hall, done under al-Hakam II, the architect could not continue with a simple increasing proportional progression of rectangles, as this would have created a space that was too deep, and also risked bringing the mosque too close to the river Guadalquivir. The architect therefore reversed and reduced the proportional system. This next enlargement of the prayer-hall was built as a $\sqrt{3}$ rectangle, but based on the length of the ninth-century *qibla* wall which until then had had the value of unity (the side of the original square). By giving it the value of $\sqrt{3}$, he reduced the value of unity to a smaller scale.

Al-Hakam II assumed the Caliphate on 15 October 961, and next day gave orders for the enlargement of the mosque to begin. Given the slope of the land towards the south, very substantial foundations were built first for the new arcades and perimeter wall, in order to provide a firm level floor. The new mosque was given a double *qibla* wall, with both of the perfectly parallel walls compensating the thrust of the arcades. The massive foundations of the double *qibla* wall were made to extend round to the east and west sides, to counter the thrust of the new extension. The octagonal chamber of the new *mihrab* projects beyond the outer *qibla* wall. The double *qibla* walls provide an inner space that was divided into two storeys with separate rectangular chambers. Those on the east side housed the public treasury, while those on the west led to the *sabat* (crossing the road by way of a bridge to the palace, as in the ninth-century mosque, and altogether more perfectly built than the one at Madinat az-Zahra'). The Caliph and his court could thus reach the enclosed *maqsura* in front of the *mihrab* privately and at any time without being observed. The *minbar*, Qu'rans, lamps, candlesticks, mats, carpets and other liturgical objects for the month of Ramadan and other religious festivals were also housed in these chambers between the two *qibla* walls.

The system of two-tiered arches used in the earlier mosque was maintained, with certain variations, though al-Hakam's enlargement

The Great Mosque, Cordoba (784–6, 961–6, 987–90 and other restorations), with its remarkable structure of arcades, is among the best-known monuments of Islam. The full extent of the mosque complex is clearly seen from the air (above), with the campanile of the cathedral providing the principal vertical feature. Notable aspects of the interior include: ornate domes supported by complex rib-systems (top left); the double horseshoe arcades of the prayer-hall (above right); and the deeply recessed polygonal chamber of the central mihrab *(right).*

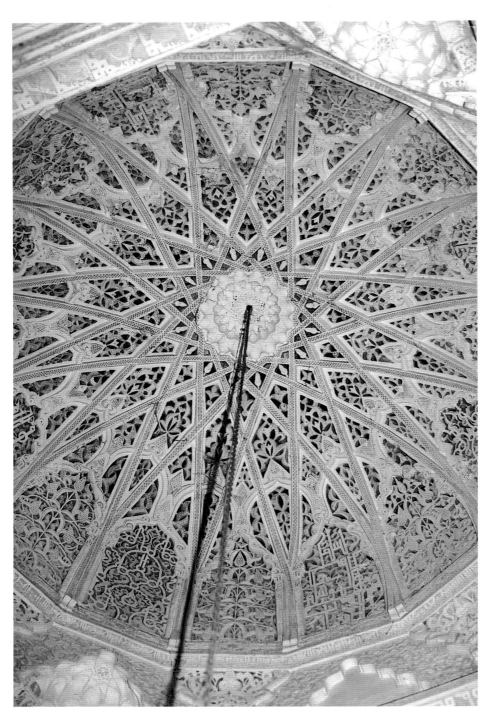

(Left) The dome over the mihrab *of the Great Mosque, Taza, Morocco, with its intricate ribbed vault.*

(Opposite) In the Great Mosque, Tlemcen, Algeria, completed in 1136, the dome over the mihrab *bay has pierced stucco decoration with vegetal motifs in the spaces between the brick ribs. This dome and a second similar one are both protected by an outer dome with windows.*

(Below) The Qubba al-Ba'adiyyin, Marrakesh, c. *1120. The exterior of the dome features a lower frieze consisting of interlaced pointed arches with a chevron pattern above, while the interior is boldly decorated with carved fluted ornament.*

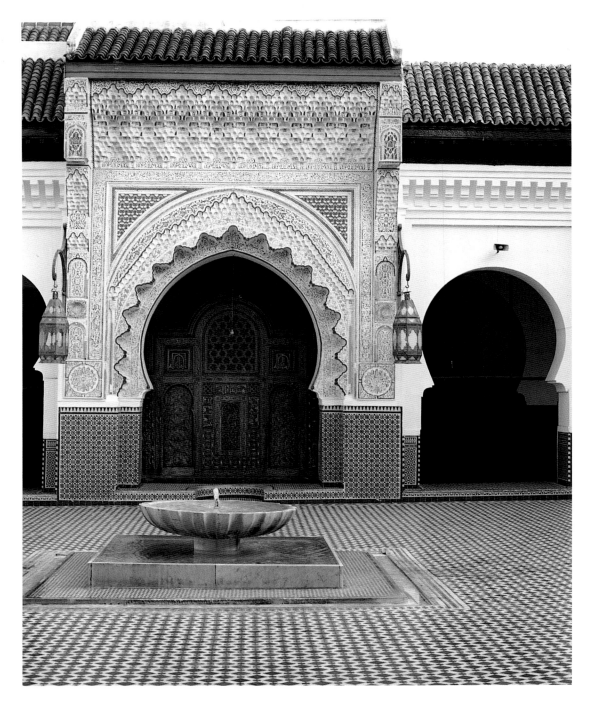

The Qarawiyyin Mosque, Fez, Morocco, was begun in 859, during the Almoravid period; the original building, which was altered and extended in 956, 1135 and subsequently until the seventeenth century, was inserted into the existing urban fabric and was surrounded by a celebrated university. This mosque is notable for its green-tiled roof. Adjacent to the large prayer-hall is a narrow rectangular colonnaded courtyard with two pavilions connected by a water channel (similar to those at Granada), added in the sixteenth century. *See also p. 28.*

contains more profuse decorative and symbolic elements. The shafts of the newly carved columns are alternately in dark-blue and pink marble conglomerate, creating a beautiful floating effect combining solidity and weightlessness. The upper semi-circular arches are of stone, and have alternating stone and red brick only on their fronts. The inside of the upper arches was decorated with stucco and painted with floral motifs. The central nave has pilasters decorated by Corinthian capitals with acanthus and other decoration in relief.

This enlargement also introduced very successfully some important new architectural features: (1) Vaults made of transverse arches which leave the centre part free, thus producing an astonishingly beautiful effect of lightness and majesty; this technique was adopted in Romanesque, Mudéjar, Gothic, Renaissance and Baroque architecture. (2) The whole plan shows the beginning of a new concept in mosque architecture: the original basilical plan with parallel aisles running from north to south starts to give way to a T-plan in which the central nave and the transverse arcade that runs along the *qibla* wall are increasingly emphasized. This T-plan did not reach its final form until Almohad times, but al-Hakam II's enlargement shows the first steps towards change in al-Andalus and its area of artistic influence. The new vaults are thus arranged over the central nave, and along the transverse arcade, which extends the full width of the prayer-hall from east to west and takes up two bays in depth. This transverse arcade has horseshoe arches and, in the five bays of the *maqsura*, pillars and richly interlaced lobed arches. The columns at the corners of the vaults appear to be grouped to help carry the weight, each having double capitals carved from a single block. (3) In this area there is a flowering of profuse decoration executed in plaster, stone, marble, stucco and mosaic. The mosaics on the façade of the *sabat* and around the area of the *mihrab* are astonishingly rich. The wooden ceilings are embellished with carved or applied patterned decoration.

Externally, each segment of the eastern and western walls was given its own tripartite façade, repeating the general pattern of the *bab al-Uzara* of 785. Since the enlargement involved incorporating the ninth-century mosque's *qibla*-wall buttresses, these were transformed into a transverse arcade, with two lobed and nine horseshoe arches, running across the middle of the mosque – an arrangement later adopted by the Almoravids and Almohads. The simple and double-layered lobed blind arches which already decorated the windows of the *bab al-Uzara* were now used structurally to brilliant effect in the four new clerestory vaults. Each of the three clerestory vaults in the *maqsura* in front of the *mihrab* has eight structural crossing arches, forming the octagonal body, and leaving small spaces in the four corners, which are closed by lobed or horseshoe arches. These arches have only windows above them, and the corner spaces are covered by little scallop-shell and lobed vaults.[4] Between the springs of the main structural arches forming these vaults, there are small arches that give light to the vaults and bays, as a clerestory. In the dimly lit interior of the mosque, these clerestory windows of the four vaults helped direct the faithful along the nave towards the *mihrab*. Later, this use of a clerestory above decorative perforated vaults would be exploited in *ta'ifa*, Almoravid and Marinid architecture.

The enlargement by al-Hakam II has been regarded almost as a mosque in its own right. The four new clerestory vaults placed in an incipient T-plan vary in shape; the three in front of the *mihrab* are square, and are built on the proportional system of $\sqrt{2}$. They provide the germ of the T-plan. However, the essentially basilical scheme of the Mosque of al-Aqsa (Jerusalem) is maintained, since all the north-south rows of aisles extend to the *qibla* wall. The T-plan was fully developed in Cairo in Fatimid mosques, a little after those of al-Azhar (970–2) and al-Hakim (990–1013). In Western Islam it culminated in Almohad architecture, in which the longitudinal aisles are made to extend only as far as the broad transverse nave that runs parallel to the *qibla* wall.

The freestanding *minbar* was a large movable wooden structure consisting of a long flight of stairs leading up to the platform of the pulpit. In the Cordoba mosque a slot was made next to the *mihrab* bay, to allow the *minbar* to be slid into the space between the double *qibla* walls and so remove it from the *maqsura* floor area when not needed.

The *mihrab* of al-Hakam II is a unique feature, and one of the glories of Islamic architecture. It is formed by an octagonal chamber having its axis on a diagonal to give it greater depth. Its marble dado, carved cornice and upper zone of tri-lobed blind arches give it internal grandeur. Its curved ceiling is in the form of an enormous scallop-shell, the motif used in the original *mihrab* of Abd ar-Rahman I.

Al-Hakam II took a personal interest in the new building. According to Ibn Idhari, about four months after the completion of the vault in front of the new *mihrab*, between 9 and 19 October 965, he rode over from Madinat az-Zahra' to inspect the works. It was on an occasion such as this that he gave orders for the four exceptionally fine small columns attached to the jambs of the old *mihrab* of Abd ar-Rahman II to be removed and repositioned in the new *mihrab*. This, together with other anecdotal evidence, shows the admiration this Caliph felt for the work of his predecessors.

The new *maqsura* enclosure in front of the *mihrab*, intended for the Caliph and his court, now extended transversally through five of the eleven perpendicular aisles, and was richly decorated in stone, marble, plaster, mosaic, wood and paint. The range of styles here shows that the various workshops involved were both Eastern and Western in origin and had already been brought together at Madinat az-Zahra', thereby mingling the Iberian Peninsula's traditions with other artistic movements from Baghdad and Byzantium – though Hispano-Muslim elements always predominate.

The other great novelty of al-Hakam II's extension is the heightened grandeur of its decoration, together with a new emphasis on the Caliph's religious functions and authority. The strict exclusion of images in mosques encouraged symbolic abstract decoration, most notably in the vault in front of the *mihrab*. The decoration of this vault is on a golden background. In Byzantine religious mosaics such golden backgrounds decorated with abstract flora symbolize heavenly paradise. Here the middle part of the vault contains a smaller vault and central hemisphere, from where golden rays seem to radiate light. Is this an indirect abstract symbol of divinity in the centre of paradise? The inner hemisphere is clearly separated from the rest of the decoration by the golden rays. In the radiating shafts or gadroons there are four trees-of-life with pomegranates, pine-cones, flowers and leaves. Each of the two gadroons on the axis with the *mihrab* has a symbolic crown set with precious stones and features floral crenellation. Although – unlike the Fatimids – the Andalusian Caliphs did not wear a crown, these two floral crowns, symbolizing majesty, were in effect 'suspended' above the Caliph when he was present in the *maqsura*, in a manner analagous to the crown of a Christian king, and seem to represent both the Caliph's religious authority as imam and his temporal authority as sovereign. Classical vaults decorated as canopies with curving borders were the source of this Islamic concept of the vault representing the 'canopy [*zillu*] of Allah on earth'. Here it is expressed as an eightfold radiance, in gadroons, angled surfaces, structural arches, spandrels, vault sections, windows, etc.

This symbolic Islamic scheme was thus fully developed in Caliphate art as early as the tenth century. A simpler symbolic scheme already existed in earlier Umayyad art in the Near East: in the mosaics of the Qubbat as-Sakhra (Jerusalem) and those in the Damascus Mosque. And in the palace at Qusayr Amra' there are representations of the zodiac, deriving from classical antiquity and from Etrusco-Roman, early Christian and Byzantine art.[5] The abstract symbolism built into al-Hakam's extension of the Great Mosque at Cordoba would culminate in the symbolic timber ceiling of the Comares throne-room at the Alhambra (1350–4), with its throne of God and four trees-of-life – having made its way from religious into palace art.

The Umayyad dynasty declined at Cordoba and, under the weak Caliph Hisham II, a military dictator, al-Mansur, came to dominate the last period of the Caliphate. Faced with a continuous growth in Cordoba's population, al-Mansur undertook the fourth and last enlargement of the mosque, by extending it to the east on a colossal scale, broadening instead of lengthening the building. Al-Mansur's scheme is simple, shows great respect for the work of al-Hakam, and follows the same proportional system based on an elongation with two $\sqrt{3}$ rectangles: The architect divided the full length of the mosque area on the east side into two equal parts, each of which was given the conventional value of the long side of a $\sqrt{3}$ rectangle. The resulting rectangular extensions gave him the complete area of his enlargement, using exactly the same proportional method as in the enlargement of al-Hakam II.

The new arcades, however, do not align properly with the earlier enlargements because there are no reinforcing buttresses alongside the courtyard and the pillars that correspond to the eighth-century buttresses are not aligned in the same way. Furthermore, there is no internal *qibla* wall in the al-Mansur extension. His was a simple extension or copy, but adjusting the new arcades to fit the older scheme required the introduction of some lobed and pointed horseshoe arches. The architect linked the new enlargement to the prayer-hall by means of eleven great lobed and horseshoe arches, destroying and demolishing and adapting the wall of the east façade of the original mosque.

So ended the construction of the Cordoba mosque. Religious building was not restricted to the capital city, however. The small mosque of Bab al-Mardum (known as the Cristo de la Luz) was built in 999–1000 in Toledo by a local citizen 'at his own expense', and although it has been interpreted by one scholar as a small-scale copy of al-Hakam's enlargement at Cordoba, with an apparent T-form at the upper level, I incline to the view that it has a central plan system similar to that of the mosques of Balkh, Abu Tabataba (Cairo), Bu Fatata (Sousse) and Las Torneras (Toledo), since it has eight square bays surrounding a square central one that rises above them. Its square plan is reflected in its elevation, which is constructed on the proportional system of $\sqrt{2}$.

The Bab al-Mardum, Toledo (now used as a church), showing the raised roof over the central internal dome.

The petty kingdoms or ta'ifas

After the death of al-Mansur's son al-Muzaffar in 1008, the Caliphate disintegrated, and by 1031 al-Andalus was divided into several petty kingdoms. When the Christian King Alfonso VI finally reconquered Toledo in 1085, the rulers of the *ta'ifas* sought help from the Berber Almoravid Emir Yusuf ibn Tashufin, who crossed the Straits of Gibraltar and put an end to their kingdoms instead, reuniting al-Andalus and annexing it to his North African Empire. The short *ta'ifa* period was therefore only transitional.

By far the best-preserved building of this period is the palace called the Aljafería, near Zaragoza. Within its nucleus lies one of the most richly decorated oratories in Western Islam. It has an irregular square plan, and arches of mixed form which interweave constantly, displaying a convex-concave 'S'-shaped springer motif. At the corners, the arcade cuts across to form an octagon. Following the caliphal model, its *mihrab* niche has a horseshoe arch on pairs of columns, polygonal walls, and a scallop-shell ceiling: a miniature version of the *mihrab* of al-Hakam II at Cordoba.

The background and spandrels of its baroque mixed-form arches are decorated with paradisial trees, alternating with pine-cones and pomegranates. Such motifs had already appeared in the Caliphal decorations at Madinat az-Zahra' and in al-Hakam II's enlargement of the Cordoba mosque. Above the arches of the Aljafería oratory runs a row of interlaced lobed arches, two on each face, with windows behind them. The oratory was covered by a vault of decorated plaster arches which apparently intersected off-centre in the caliphal manner, and had sections of perforated floral plasterwork through which rays of light would filter in from upper windows – the whole being covered by a higher tiled roof. This elevating but mysterious effect of lighting from above was adopted in later Hispano-Maghrebi vaults: in the Almoravid vault at Tlemcen (1136), and the Marinid vault of Taza (1291–2). It is an example of the Muslim tendency to convert architectonic structures into a decorative form, with a feeling of apparent weightlessness hiding the real structure.

The Almoravid Emirate (1086–1147)

The African Almoravid Emirate that conquered and reunited al-Andalus was governed by Yusuf ibn Tashufin. It was during the long reign of his refined son, Ali ibn Yusuf, that the art and culture of al-Andalus gradually came to dominate the nomadic conquerors themselves, as they in their turn were conquered by the intellectual-artistic creativity of Muslim Spain.

The fundamental new stylistic feature of this period was a greater architectural simplicity. Bricks are used in pillars, and then plastered white, together with extensive areas of plain wall. These solid right-angled pillars and white surfaces produced a new effect of gravity, space and luminosity. Columns only appear with the second ruler, Ali, as enriching elements around the *mihrab*.

Almoravid mosques are very wide and have marked transverse arcades, with a variety of mixed-form, rounded, pointed and lobed horseshoe arches, and a serpent-like motif that appears in the springs of the arches. An independent roof still covers each aisle, as at Cordoba. Porticos are built only on the east and west sides of the courtyard. The chamber or slot for the movable *minbar* is placed to the right of the *mihrab*, as at Cordoba, while to the left there is a doorway leading to the imam's room. The bay immediately in front of the *mihrab* is emphasized by a transverse arch that spans the normally wider central nave. And the vault in front of the *mihrab* is perforated to admit light, as in the Aljafería; or has crossed arches with *mocárabes* (the Western version of *muqarnas*), which were an Almoravid innovation. Developed fully in the decoration of vaults, *mocárabes* consist of a geometrical combination of hanging interlocking triangular and rectangular prisms, cut in quarter-cylinder surfaces, and were to become one of the hallmarks of Western Islamic architecture. The eastern *muqarnas* have their prisms cut to form two angular curved faces. The resulting visual effect is quite different in terms of both their form and their luminosity. The Almoravids maintained the use of a polygonal *mihrab* as at Cordoba, decorated either with gadroons derived from the Cordoba scallop-shell, or with *mocárabes* in the new manner. For floral decorations – in plaster, wood, cabinetwork, marquetry and bronze – the workshops of al-Andalus continued to be used, and the style was closer to the caliphal than to the *ta'ifa* manner.

The mosques of Nedroma and Algiers belong to the early Almoravid period under Yusuf ibn Tashufin and feature mostly square pillars. The basilical plan featuring rows of aisles leading towards the *qibla* is maintained. The small rectangular courtyard at Nedroma lacks a north gallery, and has plastered horseshoe arches that are low in relation to their width.

The Great Mosque of Algiers has eleven aisles, and the prayer-hall's three exterior aisles on either side are extended to form the side galleries of the courtyard. The prayer-hall is only five bays deep, with three distinct transverse arcades cutting across the basilical plan: an outer arcade separates the prayer-hall from the courtyard; a middle one runs across the centre of the hall; and the innermost one runs alongside the *qibla*. The wider central nave has five compartmented bays. All of this starts to break down the basilical rows of longitudinal aisles.

The Mosque of Tlemcen (Algeria), built 1135–6, belongs to the period of the Emir Ali ibn Yusuf, as do the reshaping of the Qarawiyyin Mosque in Fez and the construction of the Qubba al-Ba'adiyyin (Barudiyyin) at Marrakesh.

The Tlemcen Mosque has an irregular ground-plan because its site was adjacent to the existing cemetery of the old palace. It has thirteen longitudinal aisles and is six bays deep, with a middle transverse arcade separating the prayer-hall from the courtyard and galleries. The roof of the wide central nave rises above those of the aisles.

The arches of the two bays preceding the bay in front of the *mihrab* rest on columns. The bay immediately in front of the *mihrab* has a

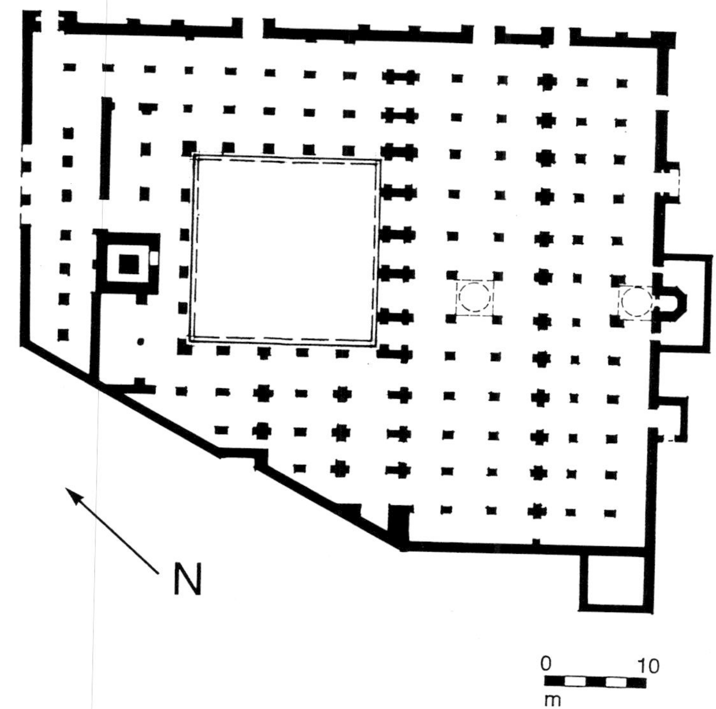

Plan of the Great Mosque (1136), Tlemcen, including the thirteenth-century extension on the north-west side. The polygonal mihrab *chamber extends beyond the* qibla *wall.*

Facing page
The mihrab *(reminiscent of the one in Cordoba, p. 105) and adjacent* minbar *of the Great Mosque, Tlemcen.*

(Right) Plan of the Qubba Ba'adyyin (c. 1120), Marrakesh, the only surviving part of the Mosque of Ali. For the dome see p. 106.

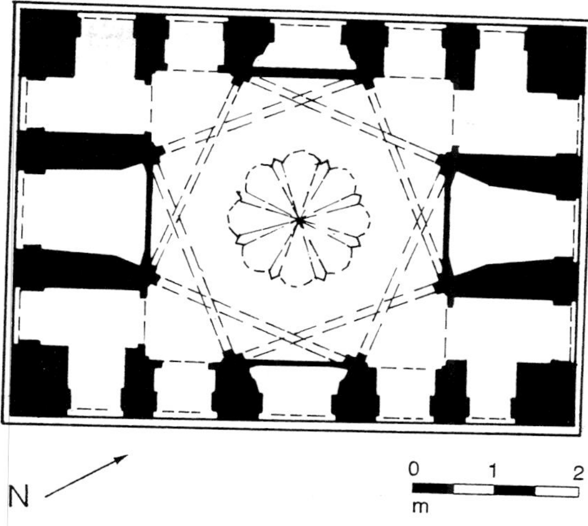

perforated vault through which light filters in mysteriously from above, creating areas of light and shade on the floor. With off-centre crossing arches, this vault supports a miniature central *mocárabes* vault, rather like a crown, from which there radiates a triple twelve-pointed star, expanding in three successive stages. The vault follows the proportional system of $\sqrt{2}$, as in the Cordoba *maqsura* vaults. Its four corner-squinches have miniature *mocárabes* vaults and arches of mixed-line profile that are repeated around the frieze.

This vault might be considered to be a dome on account of its hemispherical internal profile. However, its structure consists of inter-crossing arches with minute decorative corner-squinches, hence it is technically a vault. Its main arches are interlaced with other decorative lobed plaster arches with palm-leaf outlines. A field of branching flowers carved with perforations filters the light from the high clerestory windows above the ornamental vault. The decorated *mihrab* derives from the one at Cordoba, in its polygonal structure, its lobed shell and the decoration of its façade.

The ninth-century Qarawiyyin Mosque at Fez had seven transverse aisles running parallel to the *qibla*. The innovation of Ali (in 1136–7) was to demolish the *qibla* wall and construct three further aisles parallel to it. His most important change, however, was to build a central longitudinal nave leading from the courtyard to the *mihrab*, cutting across the aisles. Its bays contain various *mocárabes* vaults, crossed-arch vaults and wooden framework ceilings. The six bays of the nave nearest the *mihrab* rise above the others, admitting light to the interior. Rich *mocárabes* decorate the polygonal chamber of the *mihrab*. Behind the *qibla* wall there is a unique feature: a separate funerary mosque, al-Jana'iz, where the coffin was deposited while the mourners prayed for the deceased in the Qarawiyyin.

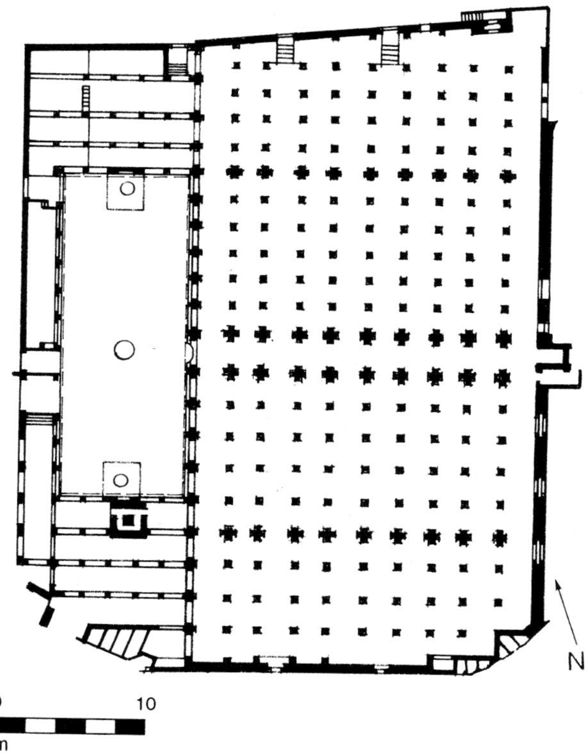

Plan of the Qarawiyyin Mosque (begun in 859), Fez. The new qibla *wall and additional arcades built in 1136 are seen on the right. For the courtyard see p. 108.*

All that remains of the Mosque of Ali at Marrakesh is its Qubba al-Ba'adiyyin (1120?), which sheltered the *mida'a* fountain used by worshippers for ablutions. The Qubba was surrounded by its privies and rooms. Its vault is unique in the Maghreb and al-Andalus. From a rectangular ground-plan, the Qubba ascends to a square which supports a vault of interlaced horseshoe arches crowned by zig-zag fluted ribs in relief. Hispano-Maghrebi influences mingle here with those from the Near East. The vault is decorated internally with a *mocárabes* frieze. The flying arches create from miniature *mocárabes* vaults in the corners, and the spandrels support acanthus foliage and large carved palmettes.

The Almohad Caliphate

The Almohads, Masmuda Berbers from the mountains of southern Morocco, rose up against the Almoravids, who were Sanhaja Berbers from the central Maghreb. The Almohads preached a new doctrine of austerity and divine unity, hence the name Almohad ('unitarian'). Ibn Tumart, who began this movement *c.* 1120, was followed by Abd al-Mu'min, who finally overthrew the Almoravids and captured their capital, Marrakesh, in 1147. Al-Andalus remained for a short time divided into small kingdoms.

Almohad mosques are immensely impressive for the grandeur of their spaces and the monumentality of their minarets. Their decoration derives from architectural elements, and linear geometric design predominates over floral patterns. In Almohad architecture the interlacing vault arches are of mixed-line form and the vault sections are filled with *mocárabes*. The exposed structural timber-framed ceilings are covered with geometric designs. The decorative inscriptions are Qu'ranic, while the floral ornament is in the Andalusian manner.

The Hispano-Muslim architectural tradition is evident in the use of the proportional system, in the arrangement of a wider central nave and a more highly decorated *mihrab* and surroundings, and in the elegant slender pointed horseshoe arches that are lobed or of mixed form, with a general predominance of rhomboid compositions (*sebcas*) of various types. The major novelty lies in the full development of the T- or U-shaped ground-plans, which eventually replaced the simpler Umayyad basilical system.

Abd al-Mu'min, the first Almohad Caliph, built the mosque at Tinmal (1153–4) in the High Atlas in memory of Ibn Tumart. The building has a T-shaped plan, i.e. it has a wider central nave which extends to the *qibla* wall, and a transverse nave, parallel to the *qibla* wall, which receives the thrust of the longitudinal aisles while separating them from the *qibla* wall. The side-aisles are extended out through the courtyard's galleries and together form a wide U-shaped ambulatory around the prayer-hall and courtyard. The transverse nave along the *qibla* wall is enriched with *mocárabes* vaulting where it meets the central nave and the outer side-aisles. A similar arrangement had already appeared in Fatimid art in the Mosque of al-Hakim, Cairo (990–1013). Recent excavations have shown that a gallery was also planned for the north side of the courtyard, but never executed. It has been thought that this ambulatory system of three arms enveloping the central area was already present in earlier Umayyad palace-halls such as Madinat az-Zahra', but there it is fully compartmented, and this suggests a completely different concept of space for palaces and for religious architecture.

The polygonal *mihrab* at Tinmal with its *mocárabes* vault is ingeniously housed within the minaret, which was built on the natural

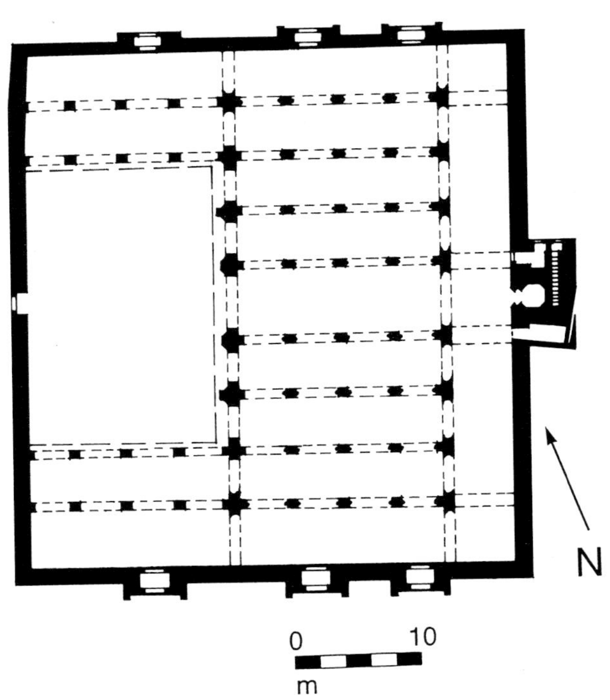

Plan of the Friday Mosque (1153–4), Tinmal.

(Right) The twelfth-century Giralda, formerly the minaret of the Great Mosque, Seville; the upper lantern was added in the sixteenth century after the tower had been incorporated into the cathedral.

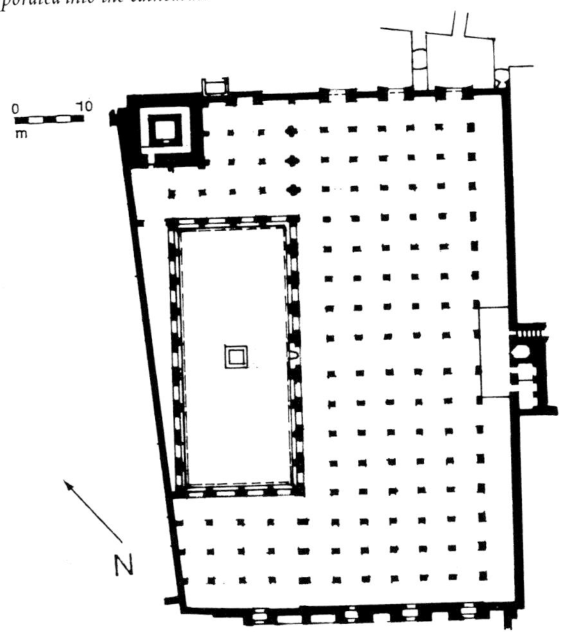

Plan of the second Kutubiyya Mosque, Marrakesh. The massive minaret *(see p. 100)**, is sited at the north-east corner of the present building.*

slope of the site, buttressing both the *mihrab* and the *qibla* wall. This minaret also contains the slot chamber for the *minbar*, the imam's entrance and stairs. The proportional system is maintained: the long side of the minaret is one-fifth of the length of the *qibla* wall and, because the minaret was conveniently placed in the middle, the result is an overall ratio of 2:1:2.

The first Kutubiyya in Marrakesh, begun in 1147, was incorrectly oriented and was demolished. The second mosque was erected backing onto the old *qibla* wall, which now served as a courtyard boundary. The minaret is sited on the side façades between the two mosques, and once again its proportional ratio to each façade is 1:5. Since the two façades overlapped by the width of this minaret, the overall rhythmic ratio of the façade was 4:1:4.

The prayer-hall of the second Kutubiyya forms a T-shape, clearly defined by the broad nave and its collateral aisles, and by the transverse aisle running along the *qibla* wall, which has five *mocárabes* vaults that alternate with rectangular sections of timber-framed ceiling. This creates alternate stretches of light and shade, producing a beautiful mirror effect – a feature copied by the Nasrids in the 'Kings' hall' at the Alhambra in Granada.

The four outer aisles on either side are extended beyond the others to form galleries. The mosque's rectangular, cruciform and T-shaped pillars and half-columns are adorned with the richest and most varied collection of twelfth-century Hispano-Maghreb capitals in existence. The slender, elegant, well-proportioned arches, with their richly varied horseshoe outlines, stand out from plain white plaster surfaces, to give this mosque a majesty exceeded only at Cordoba.

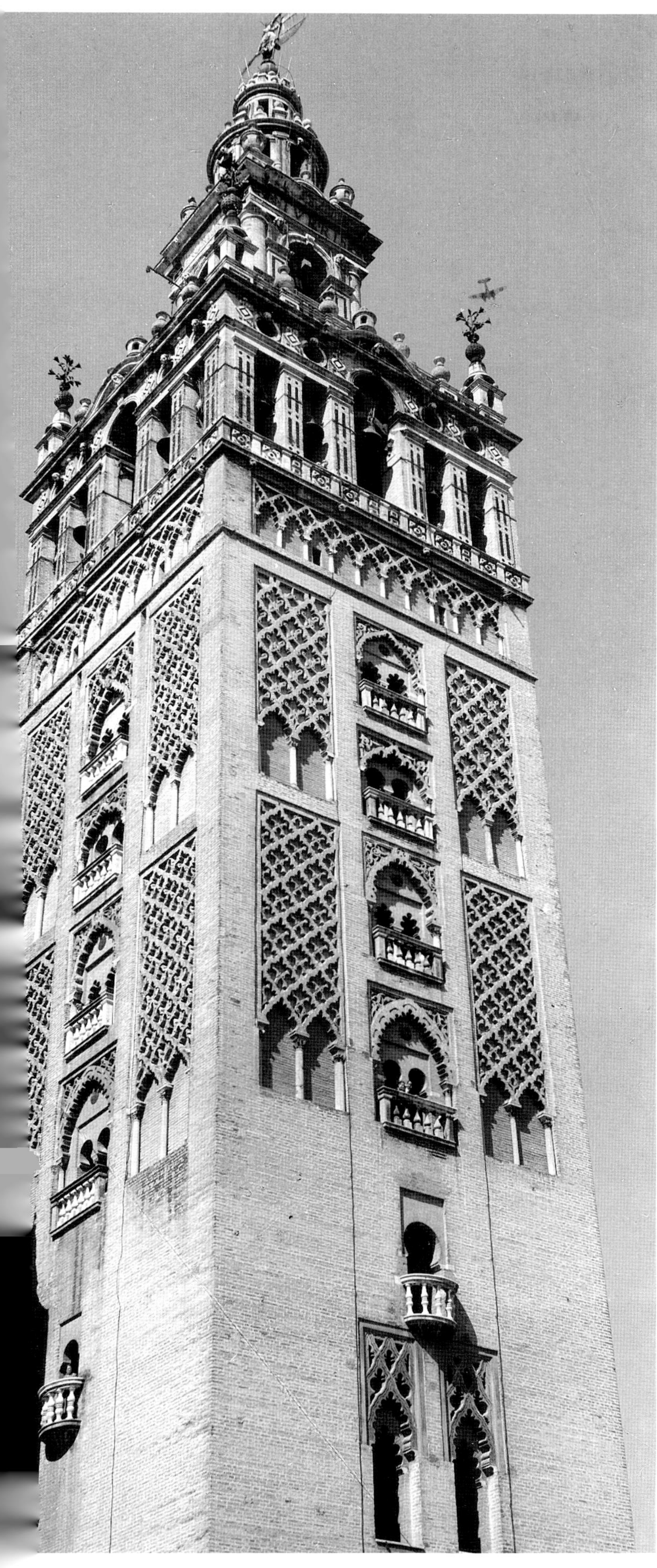

Much of the mosque of Seville, built 1156–98, was demolished to make way for the present Gothic cathedral. However, its great Almohad minaret (the Giralda) survives, as do two elegant courtyard double galleries with pointed horseshoe arches, and the enormous main gateway with its geometrically decorated metal-plated door and large knockers with floral-epigraphic decoration.

The Mosque of the Qasba at Marrakesh is Almohad in its ground-plan, and shows an astonishing reversal of the balance between inner and outer spaces. It has no fewer than five linked courtyards, and the prayer-hall aisles are reduced to a minimum. The transept is extended around the sides to form an ambulatory, with the portico on the north side completing the circuit. This radical reversal of volumes – with little covered space and enormous areas open to the sky – is unique in Hispano-Maghreb architecture. Four great arches, oversize in height and width, give onto the central courtyard area from all four sides, recalling the concept of the four *iwans* found in the East.

During the twelfth century the Christian armies in the northern part of the Iberian Peninsula continued to threaten al-Andalus. So in 1195 the third Almohad Caliph, Ya'qub al-Mansur, assembled a large army at Ribat al-Fath (Rabat), crossed the Straits of Gibraltar, and won a resounding victory over Castile at Alarcos. In honour of this victory, and financing his project with the spoils, he planned a Friday mosque at Rabat, intended to be even more extensive than the one at Cordoba. It remained unfinished, but anyone visiting Rabat today can wander over the impressive platform of this Hasan Mosque.

Work began with the minaret sited on the slope of the hill. Its positioning on the ground-plan recalls previous systems, since the width of the mosque is based on two sets of five units, which overlap at the centre, and the common central section is occupied by the minaret, giving a ratio of 4:1:4, as occurred in the façades of the two Kutubiyya mosques. The prayer-hall has 21 aisles, including a wide central nave, and a transept three bays deep parallel to the *qibla* wall. One of the transverse aisles was to be extended round the outer east and west aisles to form the U-shape. This mosque is the only Almohad example in which columns in the aisles were to be given drums varying in height. It was this attempted innovation that finally prevented progress on the work. Three inner courtyards were planned to admit light to the prayer-hall, one sited transversally, the other two placed lengthwise.

The three magnificent twelfth-century Almohad minarets – Kutubiyya, Giralda and Hasan – are modelled on the minaret built by Abd ar-Rahman III at Cordoba (951). The materials used were rubble, brick and ashlar blocks, respectively; all three had a number of superimposed vaulted chambers terminating in a lantern – a feature which in the Kutubiyya is still preserved. Internal ramps ascend around this central core. The decorated façades of the Kutubiyya and the Giralda are stepped to match the internal ramps and provide light. However, in the minaret of Hasan the external decoration of arches and panels of rhomboid *sebca* patterning begins at the same level on all four façades. The façades of the Kutubiyya also preserve remains of coloured floral-epigraphic stucco-work, and a frieze of glazed tiles above, but the Giralda, with its patterned brick façades, lost its plaster decoration in the course of a modern restoration.

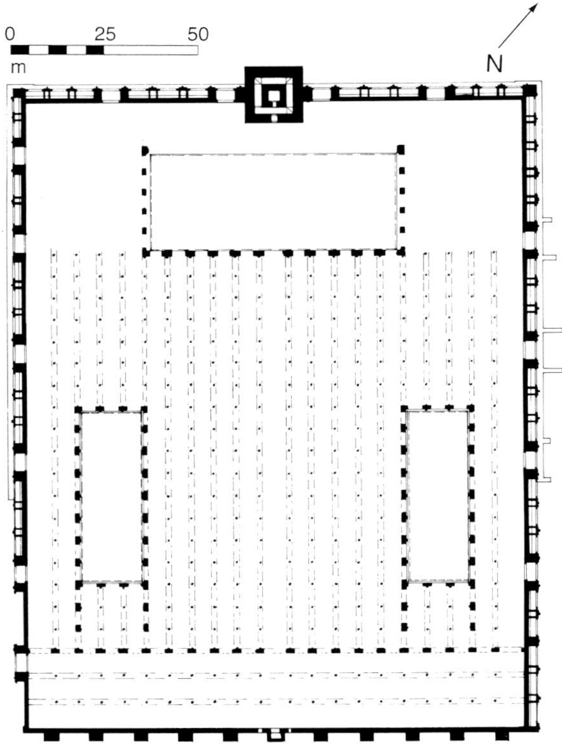

The Hasan Mosque, Rabat: general view of the platform and minaret dating from the late twelfth century, and ground-plan.

The Sultanates

After the dismembering of the Almohad Empire, Muslim rule in the Iberian Peninsula was reduced to the relatively small Nasrid Sultanate at Granada, under which the masterpiece of the Alhambra was built. A Marinid Sultanate governed in Morocco, and the Abd al-Wadid Sultanate mainly in present-day Algeria.

The al-Mansur Mosque (1303/1336) was built by two Marinid Sultans, Abu Ya'cub (1303) and his nephew Abu'l-Hasan (1336), when each was besieging Tlemcen, the capital of the Abd al-Wadid Sultanate. It had thirteen aisles with a transept three naves deep parallel to the *qibla* wall, and a square space three aisles wide directly in front of the *mihrab*, a trait reflecting Irano-Mamluk influence. At ground level the wall of the projecting minaret was pierced by the main entrance. Given its military character and purpose, the mosque has a surrounding *musalla* or terrace, originally intended to be used for communal prayers by the massed army, and behind the *mihrab* there is a funerary sanctuary. The minaret now standing is a later copy of the Almohad prototype.

The Mosque of Sidi Bu Madyan in Tlemcen was built by Abu'l-Hasan (1336) as a place of pilgrimage adjacent to the mystic's tomb; a chamber was built around the minaret to provide lodging for the pilgrims. A staircase on one side of the entrance provides access to the *mida'a* for ablutions below and to a Qu'ranic school above – an arrangement imported from Mamluk Egypt. The courtyard has porticos around its sides. The prayer-hall, with five longitudinal aisles and a transept with a restored vault, has relief plaster ceilings imitating timberwork.

During the thirteenth and fourteenth centuries a new form of religious school – the *madrasa* – spread through North Africa from the East. *Madrasas* were boarding schools, a number of which have survived; two Marinid examples and the remains of a Nasrid one are discussed below. *Madrasas* are mostly built around a central courtyard, and a notable feature of the Marinid *madrasas* is that the gallery arches facing the courtyard are of carved wood – either a central arch on its own or a central arch with side-arches; furthermore they have a broad wooden frieze and eaves. The organization sometimes shows oriental influences.

The *madrasa* al-Attarin at Fez, built under Abu Sa'id, is rich in ornament and well proportioned, with a curving entrance into its courtyard. A staircase on the right of the vestibule leads to the students' quarters; another on the left leads to the *mida'a* or washrooms. At the far side of the courtyard, the quadrangular oratory has its *mihrab* on one wall and a gallery running along the facing wall. It was used mostly by students and teachers.

The *madrasa* Bu Inaniyya (1345), also at Fez, is the most complete *madrasa* in the West and has a public mosque, with *minbar* and minaret. A time-piece (horologe) is situated across the street to mark the times of religious observance. The building's proportions are harmonious, rhythmic and balanced. There are two square classrooms placed in the middle of the long sides of the courtyard, with entrances giving onto it – an arrangement of Irano-Mamluk origin. The courtyard gallery runs around behind these classrooms. Other entrances lead to the minaret, *mida'a* and mosque. The courtyard arcades have giant arches which embrace both the upper and lower storeys. The courtyard has a central pool for ablutions, as well as a canal, with two side-bridges, running along the façade of the prayer-hall – as though to emphasize that he who is about to enter the prayer-hall must first perform his ritual ablution in its waters. The hall has two transverse naves, and the *mihrab* stands on its shorter axis, thus giving the hall a squat rather than an elongated appearance. Access to the building from the street is via a corridor, which has several bends.

Most of the surviving buildings of the Nasrid Sultanate are to be found in the city of Granada. The early minaret of San Juan and the mosque courtyard of the Albaycin (now church of El Salvador) both dating from the thirteenth century, show clear Almohad influence. A magnificent, though incomplete, bronze lamp has survived from the Alhambra mosque built in 1305 by Muhammad III. It is of the finest craftsmanship, much finer than the surviving Almohad and Marinid stepped-level lamps. All that remains of the *madrasa* Yusufiyya, built in 1349 by Yusuf I (1333–54) next to the main mosque of Granada, is its restored oratory. It has a square ground-plan adapted at the upper level to an octagon by pivoting the semi-diagonals on all four sides (as was done with the Cordoba *maqsura* vaults, in keeping with the proportional $\sqrt{2}$ system), and its timber-framed ceiling is covered with inclined panels. The side-windows originally opened onto garden

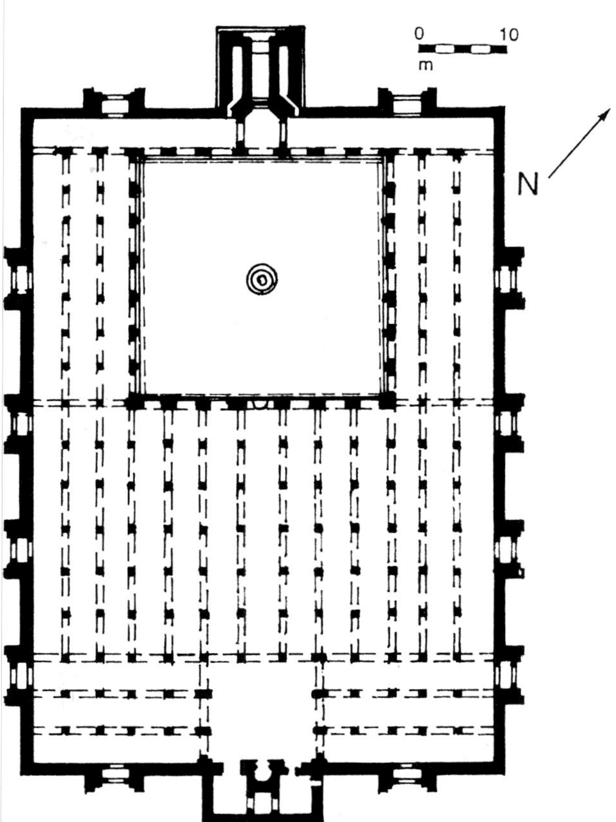

Plan of the al-Mansur Mosque (1303/1336), showing entrance and the projecting minaret at the north-west and directly opposite the mihrab.

areas. Yusuf I also built the Partal Oratory in the Alhambra, its ground-plan being a $\sqrt{2}$ rectangle. Its diagonal, equal to $\sqrt{3}$, is also the internal height. The oratory is correctly aligned towards Mecca, and is separated from its antechamber by an arch that was originally closed by a dividing curtain.

The Alhambra also has a small single-person oratory built by Yusuf I at the entrance to the great hall of Comares, and another oratory built by Muhammad V (1362), now connected to the Mexuar. Its seven arches on the north side provide magnificent views of the landscape. The *mihrab*'s polygonal ceiling is made of decorated plaster in imitation of a timber framework.

Conclusion

The large Almoravid-Almohad mosques introduced innovations in the use of columns, arches, vaults and ravishing *mocárabes* vaulting. The Almohads also developed the full T- and U-shaped ground-plans which were of major importance in the Islamic West. However, the earlier Umayyad mosque of Cordoba, with its simple double-tiered arches, interlaced arcades, vaults with arches that do not cross at the centre, decoration and symbolism, has held its unique position since the tenth century as one of the pinnacles of artistic achievement in the architecture of the Islamic world.

- 7 -
IRAN AND CENTRAL ASIA
BERNARD O'KANE

THE territory covered in this chapter ranges from Iran to western China, including the mountain fastnesses of Badakhshan and central Afghanistan, the vast deserts of eastern Iran and Transoxiana, the dry plateau of central and western Iran, and the rainy shores of the Caspian Sea. However, because most of these lands are high plateau regions, their climate is similar, with hot dry summers and cold, often snowy, winters. This was an important factor in mosque design because in some areas, a closed winter prayer-hall (*zimistan* or *shabistan*) was needed, and it influenced the design of large dome-chambers in which fenestration was kept to a minimum to reduce direct sunlight, in contrast to the light-filled interiors of Ottoman mosques, notably in Istanbul, with its predominantly overcast skies.

The natural resources available for building also vary considerably across the region. Wooden construction is found in limited areas, principally on the Caspian littoral, and in some mountain villages. The toll of deforestation should be borne in mind, however. Although the larger towns are no longer surrounded by forests or orchards, historical reports of early wooden hypostyle mosques indicate that timber was more plentiful than it is today. Good stone quarries were also rare: only in Azerbaijan do we find whole complexes constructed of ashlar masonry. Although the Sasanian technique of rubble masonry was used in a few mosques, the major alternative was baked brick, which perforce became the building material of choice. This had important consequences for architectural decoration, for although decorative brickwork is a medium with great expressive potential, it cannot be worked into the seamless flowing lines which are possible in carved stone. To produce an arabesque, a plaster coating had to be applied, which could then be either painted or worked into elaborate three-dimensional designs in stucco. Despite the monochrome of most stucco today, enough painted fragments remain to show that surfaces were originally highly coloured. Because it is fragile, however, stucco was usually confined to interiors. For exteriors, a revetment of glazed tiles later became popular, as it offered the added attractions of a surface sheen of colour, freedom of design, and relative permanence.

Iran and Central Asia were rarely under one ruler. Their unity in the Abbasid period was first challenged by a Persian dynasty, the Tahirids, in the second quarter of the ninth century, and the region was subsequently fought over by other claimants, principally the Samanids, Ghaznavids and Buyids, until the late eleventh century, when the Seljuqs were able to bring most of modern Iran within their power. Transoxiana remained largely outside the control of both the Seljuqs and the Il-Khanids who followed them. Only in the last quarter of the fourteenth century did Timur conquer and rule virtually all the lands discussed in this chapter, the exception being western China. After his death, it was never to be so again. Most of Iran was taken from his successors by Turkmen dynasties (the Karakoyunlu and Akkoyunlu), who in turn were vanquished by the Safavids at the beginning of the sixteenth century. At the same time the Uzbeks assumed control of Transoxiana, which remained permanently independent of Iran.

As in so much of Islamic art, royal patronage was the spur for the greatest monuments discussed here, although with the passing of time the power and patronage of viziers and later of the *ulama* made their own significant contribution to the arts. Even though much of the population in this region was Turkish-speaking, Persian remained, for the most part, the language of the chancery and of literature. It was also, at least from Timur's time onwards, the only language other than Arabic to be found in inscriptions on buildings.

Early Mosques

When Muslim armies conquered new territories, they first used existing buildings for prayer. In Syria these were frequently churches, but in Iran a greater variety of structures seems to have served this purpose. The majetic *iwan* of the Sasanian Palace at Taq-i Kisra (Ctesiphon) was the scene of prayers of thanksgiving after the first conquest, and the name of the early Bull Mosque in Qazvin suggests that it was converted from an Achaemenid hypostyle audience-hall like that at Persepolis, which had bull-headed capitals. A major question remains concerning the extent to which Sasanian buildings for religious worship, fire-temples, were converted to mosques. If this occurred on a large scale, it would help to explain the important role which the dome subsequently played in Persian architecture. Two caveats are: first, when the larger towns surrendered by treaty at the time of the Muslim conquest, guarantees were given that their places of worship would remain undisturbed; and second, the *chahartaq* (square dome-chamber supported on four arches) which stood at the centre of the fire-temple was reserved for the initiated and could not have accommodated the large crowds which assembled for Friday prayers. Not surprisingly, then, evidence of converted *chahartaqs* is found only in small towns. The most archaeologically convincing example is that of Yazd-i Khvast, but similar pasts have been posited for mosques in Qurva near Qazvin, and in Kuhpaya, Harand and Qihi in the Isfahan area. Evidence that this process of

Facing page
The ornate façade of the north-west iwan *in the Masjid-i Shah, Isfahan (1611–37), surmounted by a small pavilion formerly used for the call to prayer.*

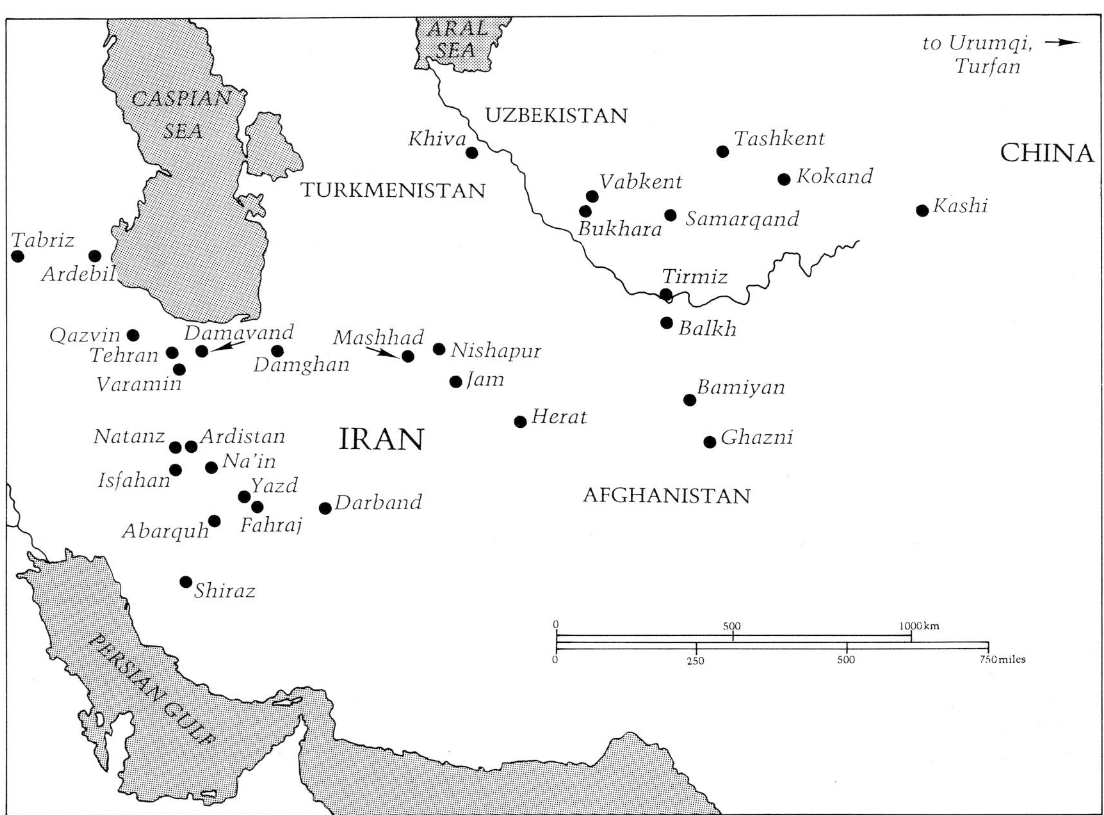

Map 3: Iran and Central Asia, showing principal sites.

transformation continued until a relatively late date is provided by the Masjid-i Birun in Abarquh and the Aqda Jami, both in areas which had long remained strongholds of Zoroastrianism and hence possibly not converted to mosques until the fifteenth century.[1] The extent to which Sasanian *chahartaqs* may have inspired imitations is problematical; a possible candidate is the Ali Gindi dome-chamber in Fahraj, although whether it was part of a mosque or a mausoleum is uncertain. The Masjid-i Sar-i Kucha in Muhammadiyya (early twelfth century), with a central dome-chamber flanked by small barrel-vaulted halls, may be seen as a natural extension of the type.

The majority of plans which have been recovered from excavations of pre-Seljuq mosques, or from those still standing, are hypostyle, like those of the central Islamic lands. This situation is not unexpected, as these trabeate structures could cover a large area without using unfamiliar, and technologically advanced, vaulting, and permitted the re-use of earlier columns, as was done for example in the hypostyle Friday Mosque of Istakhr.

A word of caution must be given here, for out of all the major cities of Iran and Central Asia, only in Isfahan has the plan of an early mosque been recovered archaeologically. Our information on the others is limited to historical sources which are often tantalisingly brief or bombastic. However, their occasional references to wooden columns (at Bardha'a, al-Ribat, Nishapur and Marv al-Rud), or to fires which destroyed presumably wooden roofs (at Bukhara), are likely indications of a hypostyle plan. Some idea of the buildings' appearance may be gained not only from mosques of this type in Turkey, but also from the Friday Mosque of Khiva, a structure which – although restored many times, most recently in the eighteenth century – retains a number of wooden columns that may date back to the eleventh and twelfth centuries. Its forest of 212 columns is broken only by two relatively small roof apertures, a characteristic of large wooden-columned mosques, whose fabric was not strong enough to withstand the stresses that would bear on long courtyard façades.

The sources occasionally refer to brick walls or columns (e.g. at Nishapur, replacing earlier wooden ones), and of course all of the excavated or surviving early hypostyle mosques have supports of either brick or rubble masonry. Many of these have a similar plan, with arcades perpendicular to the *qibla* (Tarikhana Mosque, Damghan; Friday Mosques at Fahraj, Yazd and Na'in) and a wider central nave (the former examples plus the Friday Mosque in Isfahan). At Na'in the wider central nave is emphasized by its height projecting slightly above the rest of the roofline, and although absent at Fahraj, this rudimentary version of the monumental portal (*pishtaq*) may have been present in the other examples, given its later importance in mosque façades. The Sasanian legacy of Iran is apparent in a number of these hypostyle mosques, not only in the preference shown for vaults over flat roofs (Fahraj, Damghan, Na'in), but also in the use of round piers and the elliptical profile of their arches.

At Nishapur, and particularly at Siraf, excavations have also uncovered the remains of a number of district mosques. These, which were frequently rebuilt, range from the simplest form – a single chamber – to buildings with one, two, or several piers supporting transverse arcades. The latter could be seen either as elaborations of the single square room or as reductions of the hypostyle plan, a classification that would also apply to those which they most recall, the small mosques of the Darb Zubaida way-stations.[2]

What may have been a more spacious solution to designing district mosques is seen in three Central Asian examples with related plans: the Hajji Piyada Mosque in Balkh, the Char Sutun at Tirmiz and the Masjid-i Diggaran at Hazara, north of Bukhara. All are based on a nine-bay plan, each bay having a dome, although at Hazara the central bay is enlarged at the expense of the others. The decoration at Balkh is derived directly from the stucco of Samarra, and the nine-bay plan, like Samarran stucco styles, was diffused widely throughout the Abbasid realm. However, there is no need to posit a direct connection between these various contemporary, but widely distributed manifestations. The scheme is one of such simplicity and symmetry that it could be seen as simply a domed variation of one of many pre-Islamic versions (e.g. the Parthian temple at Nysa) featuring a flat roof supported by four piers.

Another plan type is one with courtyard and an *iwan* providing the focus on the *qibla*. This has been posited in three cases, Nairiz (possibly 973), Bamiyan and Nishapur (Tepe Madrasa), although in most such cases further archaeological work is needed to render the chronology or even the facts of this beyond doubt. Nevertheless, such a plan establishes a probability that the *iwan* was already part of the vocabulary of the mosque in pre-Seljuq times. The major elements which characterize the classical Iranian mosque – hypostyle hall, courtyard, dome and *iwan* – were thus available for experimentation before their synthesis in the Seljuq period.

Although historical sources of the period mention numerous mosques with a minaret, or even two minarets in some cases, very few examples have survived. Siraf had a square minaret opposite the *qibla*,

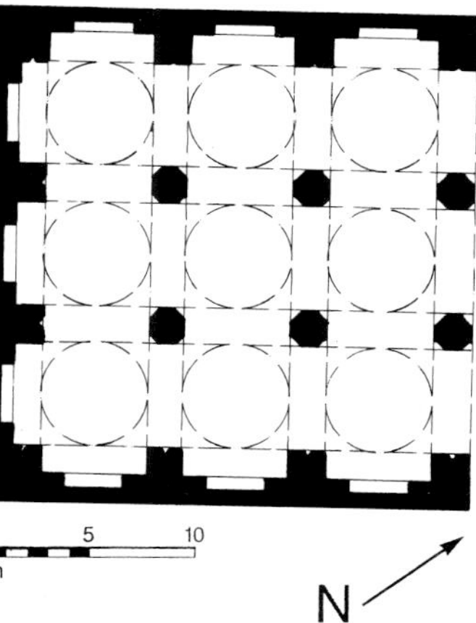

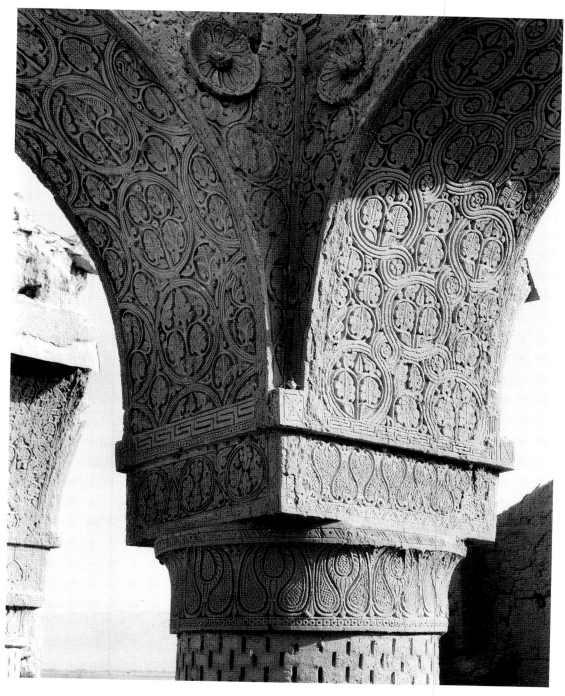

The Hajji Piyada Mosque (ninth century), Balkh: (above) plan showing the nine-bay arrangement, and (left) stucco decoration on a column capital and arches.

like several of its Abbasid forerunners. That of Fahraj is nearly circular, but undecorated, while the minaret of the Na'in Friday Mosque is a tapering octagon at its upper level, merging into a circle below a balcony. The stucco which covers the concave area below the balcony of the Na'in minaret is relatively well preserved, but the more durable qualities of brick soon became standard for decoration. A new minaret erected for the Tarikhana at Damghan *c.* 1028 presages the Seljuq style: this tall tapering tower of baked brick has bands of deep-set geometric strapwork interspersed by an inscription. The same team probably built the minaret of the Friday Mosque at nearby Simnan.

Although Khurasan and Transoxiana have provided the majority of new building types discussed so far, the finest decoration which survives belongs to mosques in the Isfahan region. The stucco of the *qibla* area at Na'in is evidence of former riches that have been lost in other monuments. Although based on the varieties of vegetal forms which characterized the Samarran style found at Balkh, it has been liberated from the constricting geometric framework of Samarra, allowing it to spread luxuriantly over soffits, spandrels, piers and the *qibla* wall. The undulating borders framing the vines on the piers are subject to a design which enables them to be read as a combination of octagons and quatrefoils, but the borders also deconstruct themselves by weaving over and under their neighbours in parallel directions so that from any one viewpoint their extremities are lost from view behind a pier – a wonderful example of the visual ambiguity which characterizes much of the finest Islamic decoration. Above the *mihrab* is a *muqarnas* vault, the form of which is usually considered to be Seljuq; however, it bears painting of a simplicity which might be contemporaneous with the stucco, which is normally assigned to the late tenth century.

The courtyard façades at Na'in are also decorated with patterns in recessed brickwork, and the style was taken further in Isfahan in the Buyid restoration of the Masjid-i Jami, where the piers added to the courtyard, some of a complicated quadrilobate plan, display a great variety of crosses and lozenges. Even greater variety is achieved in the portal of the Jurjir Mosque in Isfahan, *c.* 976–85 – the only example so far in the present survey which has been identified as the work of a major patron, the Buyid vizier Ibn Abbad. The range of forms in this portal, a complicated series of engaged columns combined with alternately recessed and protruding vertical panels, shows a mastery of design enhanced by the decoration in which terracotta and lightly incised stucco are used to increase both the number and the definition of the patterns.[3]

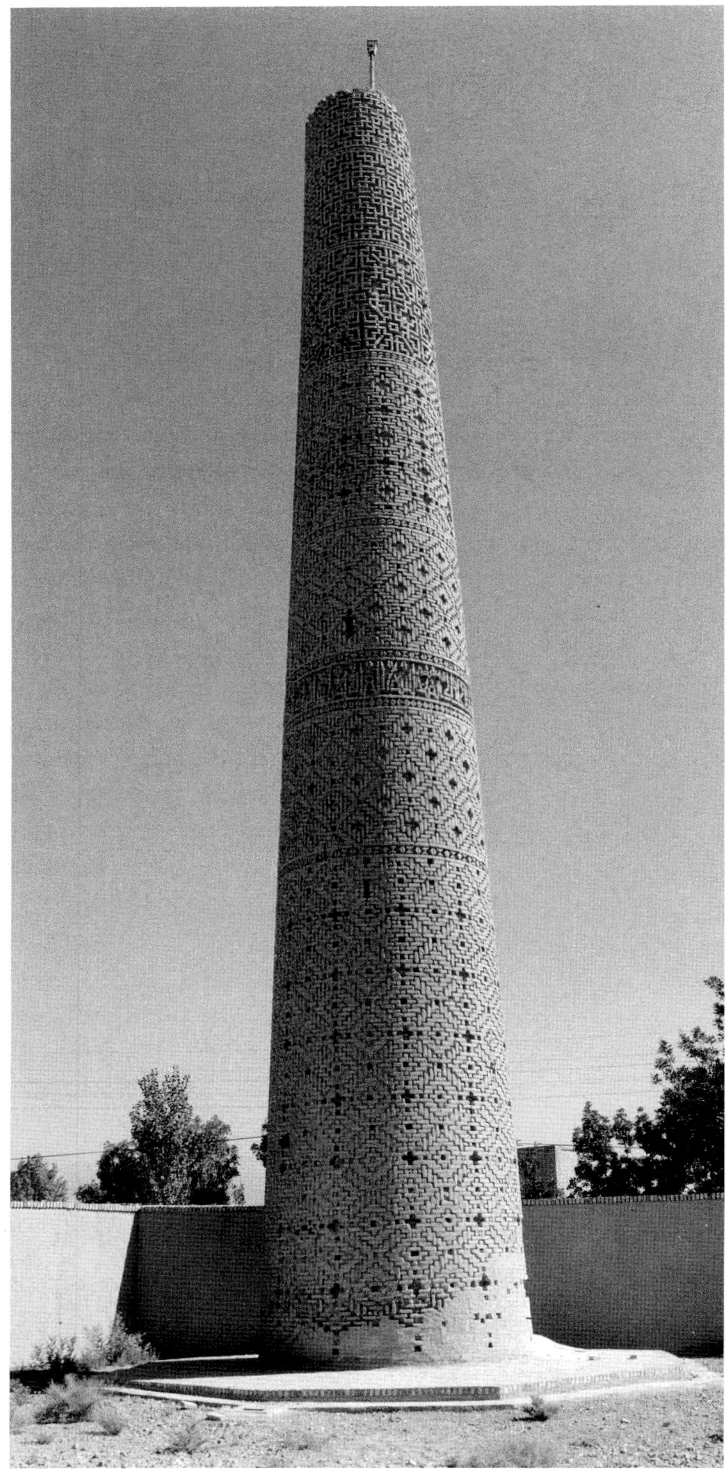

The circular brick minaret of c. *1028 associated with the Tarikhana Mosque, Damghan, founded in the eighth century.*

*(Opposite) Plan of the Friday Mosque, Isfahan, showing the four-*iwan *arrangement around the central courtyard.*

The Seljuq period (eleventh–twelfth centuries)

The much greater survival rate of buildings dating from the Seljuq period makes matters of interpretation somewhat easier, although a new problem arises in deciding whether a specific dome-chamber was part of a mosque, a mausoleum (a building type found in greater than usual numbers in the Iranian world, and one which normally incorporated a *mihrab*), or a blend of the two, a commemorative funerary mosque (e.g. at Mashhad-i Misriyyan).

The large number of Seljuq dome-chambers which form the earliest parts of surviving mosques has led to the theory that these were originally freestanding; however, in the case of the two mosques where excavations have taken place (Isfahan and Ardistan), the chambers can be shown to have been inserted into earlier hypostyle plans. Small mosques in the form of freestanding dome-chambers do survive in several Khurasanian villages (Sangan-i Pa'in [1136], Barabad, Nuk, Abdallahabad), and the limited capacity of a small dome-chamber would have suited the role of a district or village mosque.

The dome-chamber inserted in the name of Malik-Shah I and his vizier Nizam al-Mulk in 1086–7 in the Isfahan Friday Mosque marks the beginning of a new relationship between mosque and dome. While domes had been common enough in previous plans (Medina, Damascus, Jerusalem), they had not exceeded the size of one bay in the hypostyle plan. The Isfahan dome occupies twenty bays, a figure which makes it easier to comprehend the impact that the then largest dome chamber in the Islamic world must have had on viewers. There is little doubt that it functioned as a *maqsura*, an enclosure designed to protect and glorify the patron. Its visual impact led, however, to its being copied – even down to the details of its *muqarnas* squinch – in numerous smaller mosques (Zavara, Ardistan, Barsiyan) where royal patrons were not involved. It also provided the inspiration for the dome-chamber erected by Nizam al-Mulk's rival, the vizier Taj al-Mulk, on the north side of the mosque in 1088. In terms of mosque layouts this was a dead end, inspiring no imitations, for while the chamber was on the *qibla* axis, it originally stood outside the mosque and its function remains unknown; it is, however, justly famous as a consummate refinement of the architecture of the original south dome-chamber. The new verticality of the proportions is emphasized by the columns which link the eight arches of the zone of transition to the dado, and by the multiple openings and reveals of the lower square – a measure of new-found confidence in dome building.

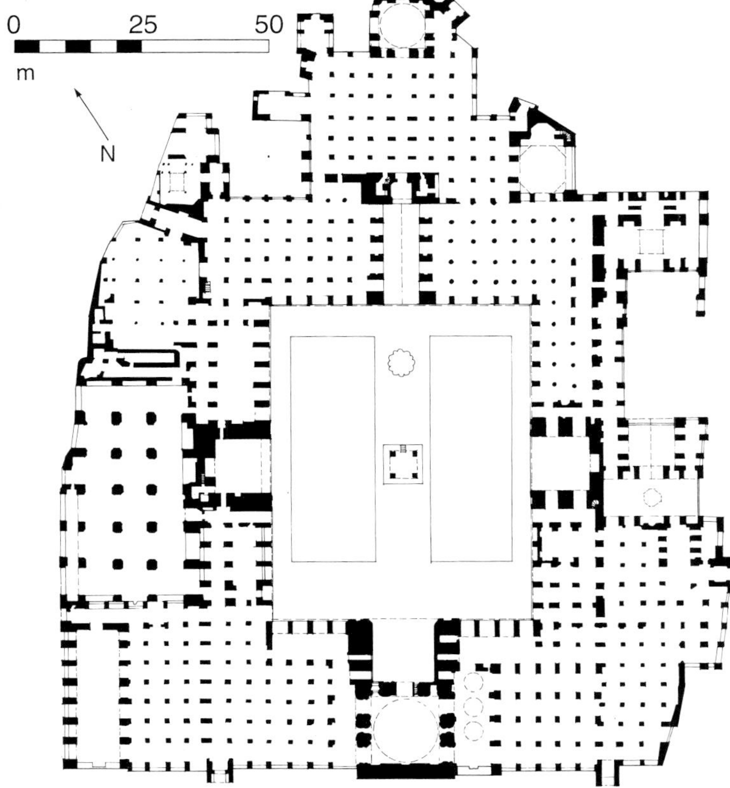

The Friday Mosque in Isfahan was also perhaps the catalyst for another revolutionary development in mosque design, the insertion into the hypostyle plan of four *iwans* facing the courtyard.[4] The most puzzling feature of this four-*iwan* plan is why it was thought desirable. The idea of a four-*iwan* courtyard is one of some antiquity – it is known from Parthian and Ghaznavid palaces – but there is a big difference in spatial qualities between the enclosed rooms adjacent to *iwans* in palaces and the open arcades of a hypostyle mosque. Mosques aspire to a space with as few impediments as possible, so that the faithful can line up in rows parallel to the *qibla*, a criterion shamelessly violated by the presence of *iwans*. Were the *iwans* on the *qibla* side and the side opposite inserted to provide a suitable processional axis to the domed *maqsura*, or were they merely its visual counterparts? Could the four *iwans* have provided more private spaces for activities such as teaching which would certainly have taken place in the mosque? We are unlikely to find definitive answers to these questions, but for contemporaries the reasons may have been of little importance, since the form appeared in numerous mosques where these considerations would not have applied. Perhaps the *iwan*'s aesthetic qualities were paramount, revealing new possibilities for varying the rhythms of large and small masses and voids, or for decorative schemes on the portal screen and the vaults of the *iwans*. At any rate the advantages were seen to outweigh any disadvantages, since the form was to remain the classic model for large mosques right up to modern times.

Just when this transformation happened at Isfahan is unknown. The earliest dated example of a mosque with a four-*iwan* courtyard and a *qibla* dome-chamber is the Masjid-i Jami (1135) in Zavara, and while it could be argued that the prestige of the Isfahan Friday Mosque provided the model, both could have been independent responses to the factors outlined above.

In addition to the single dome-chamber and the four-*iwan* courtyard with a *qibla* dome-chamber, discussed above, almost every possible permutation between these extremes of plan types can also be found in Seljuq mosques. A single *iwan* on the *qibla* side of a courtyard occurs at Firdaus, Sangan-i Pa'in and Bashan (the last in Turkmenistan). The Friday Mosques of Faryumad and Gunabad are examples of courtyard mosques with two axial *iwans*, a form which remained especially popular in Khurasan. The dome-chamber and *iwan* may occur alone or together, as at Ardebil, or a compromise between the two can be effected, as in the *qibla* prayer-hall of Sin (1133), where a rectangular space is covered by a *muqarnas* vault. The hypostyle plan is represented in its classic courtyard form at Damavand. Covered hypostyle layouts occur in vaulted form in the mosque at Nushabad and with wooden columns and flat roof in the Masjid-i Maidan at Abyana (1073).

Few mosques dating from the eleventh-twelfth centuries remain in Afghanistan and Central Asia. The single dome-chamber is seen in the Ghurid Masjid-i Sangi at Larwand, and the covered hypostyle in the palace Mosque of Mas'ud III at Ghazna (1099–1115). The Talkhatan Baba Mosque in Turkmenistan is a version of the Sar-i Kucha in Muhammadiyya: a central dome-chamber with a small extension on either side. This could also be seen as a variation of what was to become a type characteristic of Central Asia, the dome-chamber

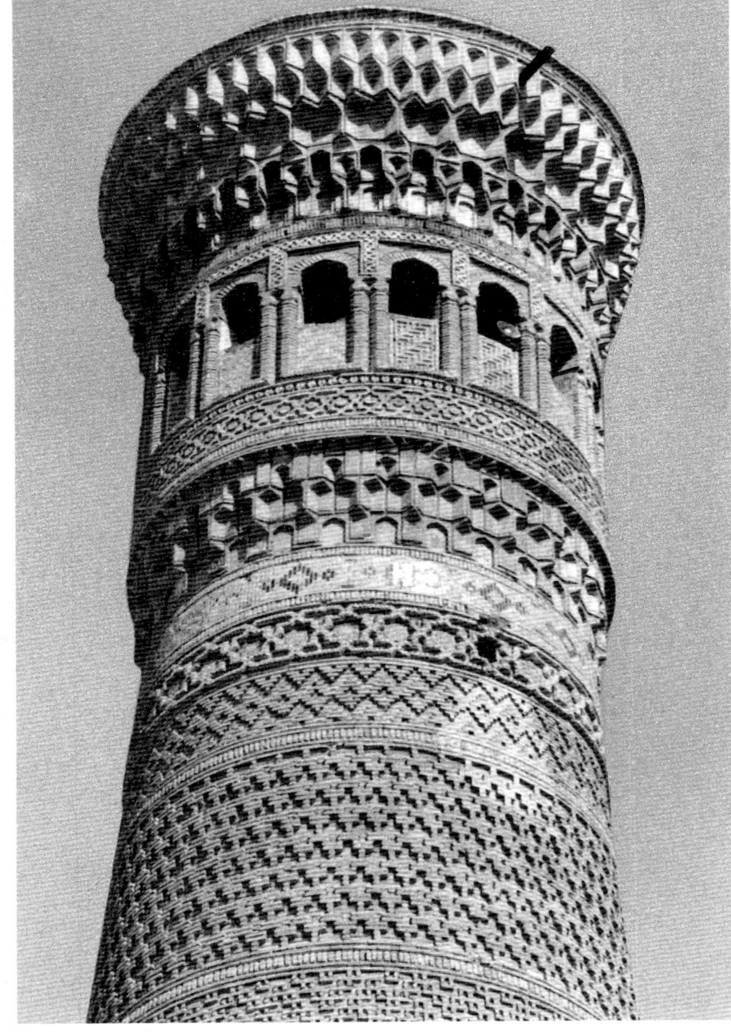

The upper part and lantern of the minaret (1127) of the original Kalyan Mosque (no longer extant), Bukhara.

flanked by hypostyle halls. These are found in Laskar-i Bazar (without courtyard) and Mashhad-i Misriyyan (with courtyard).

Some sixty minarets from this period have been preserved in Iran, Afghanistan and the former Soviet republics in Central Asia – a much larger number than in any other region; this suggests that doctrinal disputes which may have limited the erection of minarets elsewhere had little effect here. Many examples now stand alone (e.g. Jam [1194]; Ghazna), a fact which has led to their being identified erroneously as victory towers. A more likely explanation is that, being built of baked brick, they have survived the less durable mud-brick mosques to which they were attached, or were considered too dangerous to demolish or to rob for their bricks, unlike the adjoining mosques. All are circular in plan, the most spectacular being the tapering three-tiered examples of Ziyar and Jam, the latter being 65 m (213 ft) high. Both have inscriptions in turquoise tiles, a feature rarely absent from minarets since the first known dated example at the mosque of Sin (1133). Whether proclaiming the word of God or the name of the patron, the glazed inscription was conspicuous thanks to the vivid contrast it made with the brick shaft. The earliest paired minarets to survive are found in widely separated areas (Nakhchivan, Masjid-i Imam Hasan, Ardistan [1143]; a *madrasa* at Tabas). All of them occur on portals, which were gradually acquiring the repertory of decorative materials that had earlier been exploited more fully on the *pishtaqs* of mausoleums.

The minarets of Central Asia form a separate school. Those of Bukhara (1127) and Vabkent (1196–8) are typical, each with a tapering shaft topped by an arcaded lantern. In the case of Bukhara, the brick minaret – 46 m (150 ft) high – replaced an earlier wooden one (it gained notoriety in the nineteenth century as the place from which condemned criminals were thrown to their deaths).

The *mihrab* continued to be the decorative highlight in most mosques, and the increased area of wall space available in a *qibla* dome-chamber meant that decorated surfaces could now occupy a much larger area, in many cases reaching as far as the zone of transition (Zavara, Masjid-i Haidariyya, Qazvin). Most *mihrabs* were decorated in stucco, no longer only on two planes, but exploiting to the full the potential of the medium for multi-layered compositions in which a foreground motif is set above, or is even threaded into and around, an intermediate plane. Inscriptions in general, and *naskhi* inscriptions in particular, were a special feature of stucco work and became increasingly common. It was also possible to over-extend the potential of the medium: the stucco arabesque which covered the whole vault of the *iwan* on the *qibla* side of the Friday Mosque in Ardistan contrasts uncomfortably with the underlying brickwork visible through its interstices; it is therefore not surprising that the experiment was never repeated. Traces of colour have been found on many stucco panels. The visual impact of all this decoration, and the terracotta to which colour was also applied, must have been striking in its pristine state, with vivid reds, yellows and greens contrasting with a blue ground. Although great strides were made in the employment of tilework on the exterior of contemporary mausoleums, in mosques such surface decoration was largely absent, except on minarets.

Despite the attractions which stucco, terracotta and glazed tiles offered, it could be argued that the most important decorative medium of Seljuq mosques was that of their basic structural material – baked brick. It could be used in large elements such as domes and *iwans*, in the revetment of the interiors with small bricks, in a myriad of patterns in vaults (as exemplified in the Friday Mosque in Isfahan). These varied uses marked the beginnings of a tension between structure and decoration which was to give rise to their divorce in later periods.

The Il-Khanid period (1256–1353)

The horrendous scale of the Mongol destruction in the thirteenth century left Iran and Central Asia in ruins from which recovery was slow. Only after Ghazan Khan's conversion to Islam in 1295 did the pace of building accelerate. Just before this the Polo brothers had passed through Iran, confirming a resurgence in trade with China via the Silk Route, as a result of which a new taste for *chinoiserie* had been established in the Middle East, influencing contemporary Persian painting and manifested in the appearance on glazed tiles of Chinese motifs such as the dragon, phoenix and lotus, the last occurring in Il-Khanid mosque decoration. Despite the centrality of the area as a conduit for trade between the Mediterranean and China, evidence of architectural influence from either direction is lacking. Movement in the opposite direction was to be found in the 1320s, however, when a craftsman who had earlier built a mosque in Tabriz for the Iranian vizier Ali Shah travelled with a Mamluk embassy to Cairo, where he introduced the art of tile mosaic, though in practice the technique never became fashionable there.

The mosque, built for Ali Shah, the so-called Arg, or citadel, was in reality a Friday Mosque (*c.* 1320–30), the ruined *iwan* on the *qibla* side of which remained standing until the 1980s. Its outer walls, which were plain except for the curves of the *mihrab* recess and the corners of its *qibla* façade, were the finest expression of the sheer power of massive brickwork since the engaged columns of the façade of the Ribat-i Malik, a caravanserai between Bukhara and Samarqand, dating from 1078–9. Unfortunately, as an expression of power the mosque proved a poor advertisement, as the vault of the *iwan* partially collapsed soon after it was erected. It was the secretary of the same Mamluk embassy to Cairo who recorded the only contemporary description of the mosque, an invaluable aid in conjuring up the riches which were once present in so many medieval mosques. He wrote of the gold and silver *mihrab*, probably an indication that it was decorated with lustre tiles, and of the glass windows and lamps decorated with gold and silver. He also mentioned an enormous marble-lined pool in the courtyard, at the centre of which was a platform with, on each side, a lion with water pouring from its mouth, and in the middle an octagonal fountain with two jets. The fourteenth-century traveller Ibn Battuta described a stream lined with jasmine, vines and trees running through the courtyard of the mosque, a fitting transformation in a region where the garden is equated with paradise. This was not the only Mongol example, as Ibn Battuta also refers a stream which ran through the Friday Mosque of Ashtarjan.

Ibn Battuta refers to a *madrasa* and *khanaqah* which were attached to the *iwan* on the *qibla* side of the Mosque of Ali Shah. It was thus a multi-functional complex, a building type patronized with increasing frequency by the Mongols. Their destructive invasion and the subsequent displacement of local populations perhaps accounts for the variety of charitable complexes dating from this period, many of which included mosques (Bastam, Natanz, Turbat-i Jam).

The Mosque of Ali Shah may well originally have had a four-*iwan* courtyard. The size of the *iwan* on the *qibla* side was – at the order of Ali Shah – bigger than that of the Sasanian Taq-i Kisra, so enabling it to stand alone without a dome-chamber. The classic plan of the four-*iwan* courtyard with a *qibla* dome-chamber is found at Varamin. At Abarquh it was modified by substituting a transverse-vaulted hall for the dome-chamber. Virtually all of the rarer mosque plans of the Seljuq period can also be found in this period. The kiosk mosque is represented by the Masjid-i Gunbad, Azadan; the dome-chamber preceded by an *iwan* occurs in three mosques of the Isfahan region (Dashti, Kaj, Iziran); the covered hypostyle is found in the mountain villages of Asnaq and Barzuk near Kashan. The Friday Mosque of Darband (1368) has a wide hypostyle hall fronting a small *qibla* dome-chamber; across a tree-shaded courtyard are the cells of a *madrasa* which was added in the fifteenth century, a measure of the persistent popularity of these complexes.

The Friday Mosque (1364), Yazd, a building notable for its exceptionally narrow pishtaq, *surmounted by twin minarets.*

Although some of Iran's finest stucco *mihrabs* were executed at this time (e.g. the one added to the Friday Mosque of Isfahan in 1310 by Öljaytü), tile mosaic gradually became the main, and in some cases the only, form of decoration on mosques. This is most clearly seen on buildings erected by the Muzaffarids, rulers of southern Iran in the second half of the fourteenth century. The interior of the dome-chamber of the Friday Mosque in Yazd (1364) has almost complete tile revetment, and the elimination of the rear wall of the *iwan* on the *qibla* side ensured for the first time that the congregation in the courtyard could see it. This was the prototype for numerous mosques in the Yazd area which included upper galleries. The purpose of these galleries is not clear (areas for women has been one suggestion), but this feature produces a considerable lightening of the dome-chamber, both visually and structurally, and a more complex succession of solids and voids. The same considerations are found in the transverse vaulting of the prayer-hall of the Muzaffarid *madrasa* added to the Isfahan Friday Mosque, where only a fraction of the piers supporting the dome of the central lantern are visible inside.

The Timurid period (1370–1506)

All the major mosques of the Timurid period feature the classical four-*iwan* plan. What is new is the assured handling of the major components. The Timurids loved symmetry and sought a regular and unencumbered exterior; the ubiquitous tile revetment imposed unity on the design.

Timur's Friday Mosque in Samarqand (1398–1405) best exemplifies this; its colossal size was made possible by the booty and slaves which he had garnered from his Indian campaign. As in the Mosque of Ali Shah, this emphasis on sheer size proved self-defeating, for it rendered the *qibla* dome-chamber unstable. Both the entrance *pishtaq* and the *iwan* on the *qibla* side have minarets whose bases now reach down to the ground, a feature which may have been adapted from the now vanished Friday Mosque of Sultaniyya (early fourteenth century). The side *iwans* of the courtyard have been replaced by shallow *pishtaqs* leading into dome-chambers. These dome-chambers and the larger one on the *qibla* side each have double domes mounted on tall drums, a device which makes them more conspicuous on the exterior, but which underlines the character of Timurid architecture as one which emphasizes display at the expense of structure. The least satisfactory part of the mosque must have been the linking hypostyle halls, supported on stone pillars carved by craftsmen imported from India, Azerbaijan and Fars. These would have been dwarfed by the surrounding *pishtaqs* and dome-chambers, and it was to combat this tendency that a false upper gallery linking the *iwans* was introduced in the next major Timurid mosques, those of Gauhar Shad in Mashhad (1418) and Herat (1417–38). Gauhar Shad was the wife of the successor to Timur, Shah Rukh, and the monuments which she erected were the finest of the age – a clear reflection of the unusual extent of her direct participation in affairs of state.

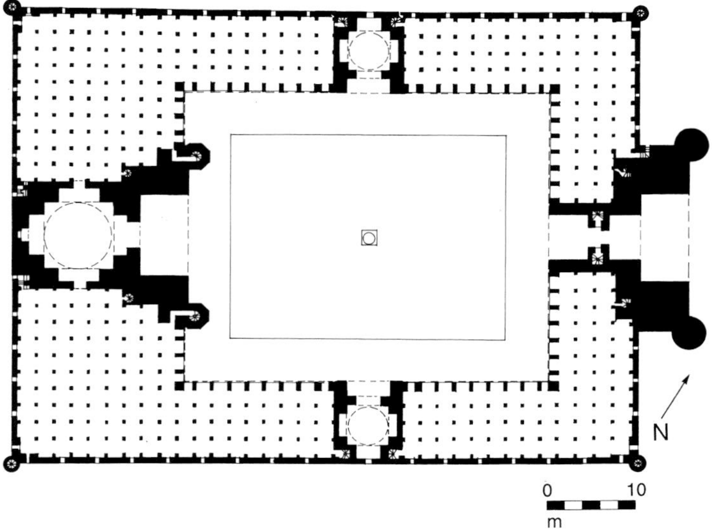

*Plan of the Friday Mosque (Bibi Khanim; 1398–1405), Samarqand, showing the characteristic four-*iwan *arrangement.*

The outstanding mosque of western Iran in the fifteenth century, the Blue Mosque of Tabriz (1465), was also built as part of a complex by a female patron, Jan Begum, wife of the Karakoyunlu ruler Jahanshah. Its unusual plan, with a domed courtyard leading to a smaller *qibla* dome-chamber, may be related to earlier Ottoman mosques in Bursa. The quality of the tilework on this building is outstanding generally, but the effect of the *qibla* dome-chamber must have been extraordinarily intense, with the entire surface above the dado consisting of dark-blue hexagonal tiles covered by gilded stencilling.

A large number of mosques dating from this period have been preserved in the Yazd area. They form a well-defined regional school which derives several features from the earlier Friday Mosque of Yazd. One feature unique to this region is a new type of platform used for the call to prayer; this is reached via a staircase which ascends the *qibla* dome-chamber (Haftador, Ashkizar, Taft).[5]

Central Asia and Western China, post-sixteenth century

With the rise of the Safavids and Uzbeks in the sixteenth century, we reach a period in which the major towns already had substantial numbers of mosques. Pious individuals who wanted to sponsor a religious building were as likely to erect a *madrasa* as a mosque. This was especially true of Transoxiana, where, after the rebuilding of Bukhara's Friday Mosque in 1514, new buildings were most often in the form of a *madrasa*, or occasionally a *khanaqah*, with nearby *khans* being built as endowments for the religious buildings. The necropolis of Char Bakr (1559–69), just outside Bukhara, contains a *khanaqah*, a *madrasa* and a mosque in a linked complex where the mosque, like the *khanaqah*, consists of a dome-chamber preceded by an *iwan*.

Another solution, found in the Tilakari *madrasa* in Samarqand (1646–59), was to devote the whole of the *qibla* side to a prayer-hall having a central dome-chamber flanked by hypostyle halls. This arrangement could also be seen as a more compact version of the plan of the Darband mosque, a hypostyle structure which later acquired a *madrasa* across the courtyard. An expanded version of this is found in the seventeenth-century Atika Mosque at Kashi in western China. Around an irregular courtyard there is a large wooden-columned hypostyle hall, 38 bays wide on the *qibla* side, the central area being

The Atika Mosque, Kashi, showing the asymmetrical façade arrangement and the adjacent bazaar.

walled off and decorated with tilework. On two sides of the court there are cells, which could have been occupied by students. The tree-lined court is divided into four irregular sections, and includes two pools, one ornamental, the other for ablutions. The main entrance *iwan*, on the side opposite the *qibla*, is flanked asymmetrically by two minarets crowned by diminutive versions of the brick lantern of the Bukhara minaret of 1127. Finally, the north-west exterior wall forms part of a bazaar lined with small booths. In its combination of monumental gateway, prayer-hall, *madrasa*, bazaar and paradisial garden plan, it provides a brilliant illustration of the flexibility of later mosques.

The Aba Khvaja complex, also in Kashi, is an interesting combination of several prayer-halls with an even greater variety of associated buildings. The largest building on the site is the usual wooden-columned hypostyle mosque. There are three other areas for prayer, together with a *madrasa*, a domed mausoleum surrounded by a walled cemetery, living quarters, a bath and kitchen, all situated loosely around a spacious tree-lined courtyard. The agglomerative nature of the complex is to be explained by several building campaigns from the early eighteenth century onwards.

(Below) Plan of the Amin Mosque (1778), Turfan; for the massive brick-built minaret, see p. 25.

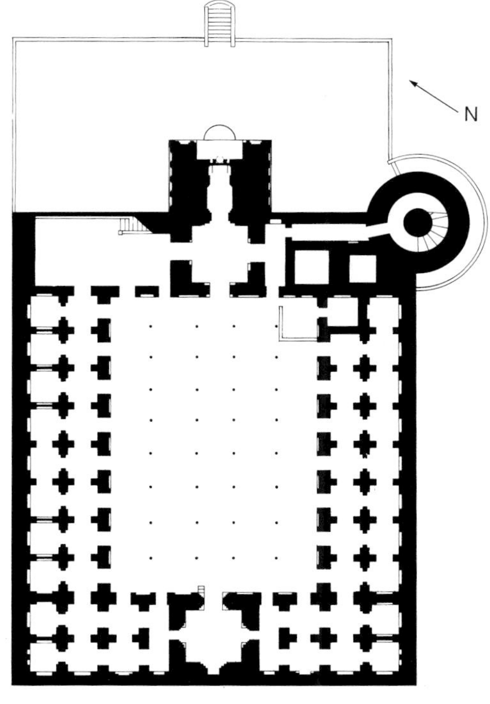

The superposed niches of the entrance portal of the Amin Mosque in Turfan (1778) are related to those of the Atika Mosque, but the resemblance to the examples in Kashi ends there. The monumental undecorated exterior walls have an inward batter, giving them a fortified appearance reminiscent of a caravanserai. This is partially offset by the massive minaret, 44 m (144 ft) high, although the extreme bulk of the base of the tower is more like that of a military bastion than the Manar-i Kalyan in Bukhara, which may have inspired its decoration of baked brick. The interior has an unusual combination of a central wooden-columned hypostyle area, without a courtyard, surrounded on three sides by domed bays. Light reaches the gloomy interior principally from one open bay in the central hypostyle area, and from the windows of the large *qibla* dome-chamber. The almost total lack of inscriptions in the Amin Mosque carries to an extreme a tendency already found in the mosques of Kashi. This is in contrast to examples in eastern China, and may reflect its geographic isolation. However, unlike the architectural form of mosques situated further east in China (see chapter 12), those of the Turfan and Kashi mosques are derived from buildings in Uzbekistan.[6]

The majority of Central Asian mosques from the sixteenth century onwards are varieties of the wooden-columned hypostyle hall or porch surrounding or fronting a central chamber which could be either flat-roofed or, more rarely, domed. The first category includes the Masjid-i Buland, Bukhara, sixteenth century; Ura-Tyube, from the eighteenth-nineteenth centuries; Friday Mosque, Kokand, 1815; Bala Hauz Mosque, Bukhara, early twentieth century. Domed examples are the Tatarguzar Mosque, Yakkabag, early nineteenth century, and Aq Masjid, Khiva, nineteenth century. A wooden-columned porch was also sometimes added to earlier structures, e.g. at the Masjid-i Diggaran, Hazara (removed in a twentieth-century restoration). As a result of the increasing popularity of these flat-roofed structures, painted wood surpassed tilework in importance as an element in the decorative repertory.

The musalla

Before considering the later mosques of Iran, it is as well to consider here a related group of *musallas*, places for communal prayer usually known locally as *idgahs* or *namazgahs*, from Khurasan and Central Asia. The earliest, at Bukhara and Merv (twelfth century?), may have consisted of simple retaining walls. That at Nysa, variously dated from the tenth to the fourteenth centuries, has been reconstructed as an *iwan* flanked by two chambers. This form was adopted in the well-preserved examples at Turbat-i Jam (late fifteenth century) and Mashhad (1676), the latter being one of the few to have extensive decoration, in this case in tile mosaic. Later examples have a central dome-chamber flanked by up to eight domed bays (two: Bukhara, sixteenth century; Kasby, sixteenth century; four: Karshi, sixteenth century; Kasan, nineteenth century; six: Samarqand, seventeenth century; eight: Tashkent, nineteenth century). These *musallas* are the most numerous extant examples of a type that has survived only rarely elsewhere in the Islamic world.[7]

The Safavid period (sixteenth–eighteenth centuries)

Safavid architecture was extremely conservative. The major mosques of this period feature the classical Iranian four-*iwan* plan, but some of Iran's finest wooden hypostyle mosques were erected in smaller towns (Masjid-i Mulla Rustam, Maragha; Masjid-i Maidan and Masjid-i Mihrabad, Bunab).[8]

Although economic development in Central Asia at this time was provided for by architectural complexes composed chiefly of *madrasas* and bazaars, Shah Abbas I's redevelopment of Isfahan begun in the late sixteenth century incorporated a new congregational mosque (the Masjid-i Shah) as a magnet to encourage the population to use the adjacent bazaars on his *maidan*. The mosque (begun in 1611) incorporates numerous features of earlier Timurid examples, such as a multiplicity of paired minarets, false upper courtyard galleries and side dome-chambers, but it is justly celebrated for its sense of scale and proportion, and for the ingenious way in which the plan accommodates the 45° angle shift from entrance to *qibla* axis. Although the person entering has a view over a waist-high wall into the *iwan* opposite the *qibla*, the wall prevents direct access and channels him to a smaller passage leading either to the ablutions area or to the courtyard. The entrance *iwan* is decorated with peacocks; as in Seljuq Anatolia, the Safavids had no compunction about depicting figural images on religious buildings. The north-west *iwan* is crowned by a small pyramidal-topped wooden pavilion (*guldasta*) which was used for the call to prayer; minarets may have played more of a decorative than a functional role by this time.[9] The formal incorporation of teaching within mosques, noted above in contemporary Central Asia, is found in the Masjid-i Shah in two *madrasa* courtyards on the *qibla* side, although only one of them has residential cells. The main criticism of the mosque has concerned the quality of its *cuerda seca* tilework, which here, unlike earlier Timurid examples, was adopted as a cheap substitute for tile mosaic. Seen from afar, however, as in the multi-level arabesques on the dome, the result is equally impressive.

Also erected by Shah Abbas beside his *maidan* was the Masjid-i Shaykh Lutfallah (1603–18), perhaps the ultimate expression of the kiosk mosque. It is situated opposite the secular pavilion (Ali Qapu) which led into the royal gardens, and, perhaps in order to stress the building's religious character, the architect chose to underline the divergence between *maidan* and *qibla* by placing the centre of the dome off-axis from the entrance *pishtaq*. However, by the time one has penetrated the *pishtaq* and the three subsequent turns of the entrance corridor, the spectator is unaware of any imbalance. A sense of harmony in simplicity is achieved by a new method of integrating the different stages of square, zone of transition and dome. A turquoise twisted-cable moulding frames both the squinches and the four identical arches in between, reaching all the way down to ground level. Within the corner arches, the tilework pattern makes no distinction between squinch and lower square; the two now blend into one continuous zone.

The fast-burgeoning population of Isfahan may have been responsible for the large number of mosques erected there in the Safavid

The Masjid-i Shah, Isfahan, built by Shah Abbas, 1612–37, has a four-iwan courtyard with a large central pool (right); tile mosaic and glazed-tile decoration is here brought to a peak of perfection both in the iwans and in the great dome (above).

*The Masjid-i Jami or Friday Mosque, Isfahan, begun in the eighth century, acquired its final form in the seventeenth century. The mosque complex is integrated into the urban surroundings, and can be approached from the adjacent bazaar or from the streets around it (above). The central courtyard (opposite) with its four-*iwan *configuration is a textbook example of Iranian architectural styles and the building is renowned for its* muqarnas *vaulting, the two great domed chambers and Seljuq brickwork patterns. In the prayer-hall there are, unusually, two* minbars *(top right); the* mihrab *niche (top left) dates from the Mongol period.*

(Top left) The mihrab *vault of the Friday Mosqu Nain, tenth century.*

(Top right) The Mosque of Gauhar Shad, Mashhe built during the Timurid period in 1419, is outstandir for its decorative tile-mosaic work (left).

(Above) Two examples of intricate tilework in the Blue Mosque, Tabriz, built in 1465.

(Opposite) The shrine of Hadrat-e Masumeh (died 816), Qom, was built in the sixteenth century, the brilliant gold-tiled dome being a nineteenth-century addition made by Ali Shah. This building, honourin the tomb of the sister of Imam Reza, presents an almost theatrical appearance of great splendour.

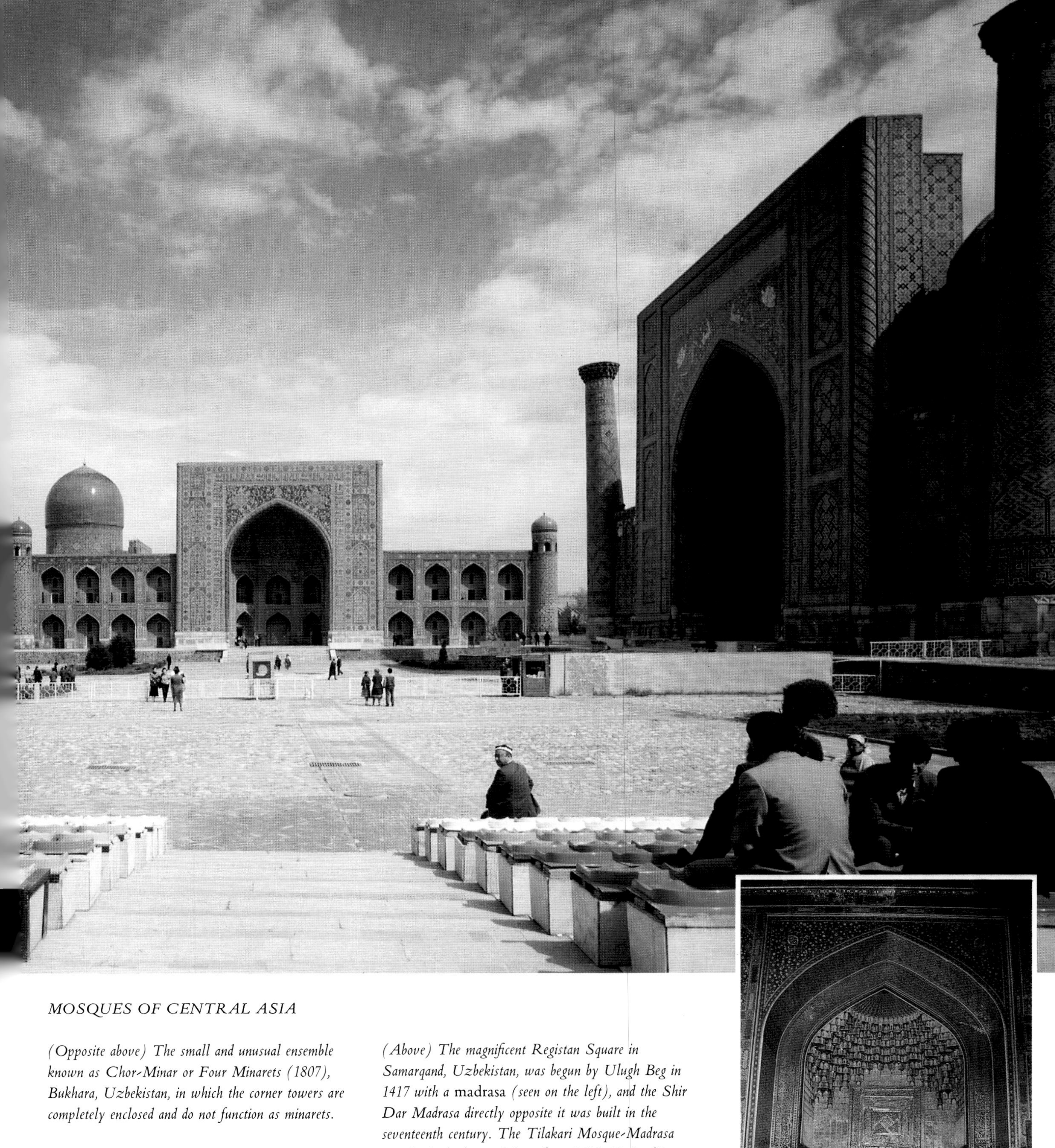

MOSQUES OF CENTRAL ASIA

(Opposite above) The small and unusual ensemble known as Chor-Minar or Four Minarets (1807), Bukhara, Uzbekistan, in which the corner towers are completely enclosed and do not function as minarets.

(Opposite below) Intricate ceiling decoration and the ornate mihrab *of the Hoja Ahrar Mosque, Samarqand, Uzbekistan, built in the seventeenth century.*

(Above) The magnificent Registan Square in Samarqand, Uzbekistan, was begun by Ulugh Beg in 1417 with a madrasa *(seen on the left), and the Shir Dar Madrasa directly opposite it was built in the seventeenth century. The Tilakari Mosque-Madrasa seen in the background dates from 1646–60. In this mosque (*tila kari *means literally 'gold work') the ornately decorated* mihrab, *in a* muqarnas *niche (right), received a new covering of gold leaf during the restoration carried out in the 1980s.*

WESTERN CHINA (XINJIANG PROVINCE)

The eighteenth-century Aba Khvaja Mosque and Mausoleum complex in Kashi (top and above left) has an open prayer-hall with tall painted wooden columns, muqarnas *capitals and painted ceilings in a decorative style that occurs widely in this region.*

The Amin Mosque (1778), Turfan, is built of mud brick, while the striking minaret, 44 m (144 ft) high, with distinctive patterning, is in load-bearing brick; an internal spiral staircase leads to the top of the minaret, which dominates its surroundings.

The Maidan-i Shah, Isfahan (1597–1611). Plan of the urban redevelopment by Shah Abbas I, an outstanding and rare example of city planning within which mosques are fully integrated. The Masjid-i Shah (A) is at 45° to the Maidan (B) in order to achieve the correct orientation with the qibla *wall facing Mecca. The Masjid-i Shaykh Lutfallah (C), similarly oriented towards Mecca, stands opposite the Ali Qapu pavilion (D), overlooking the square, which afforded access to the royal gardens. The gateway (E) at the north end of the Maidan leads to the bazaar, which provides the link between the new development and the earlier Friday Mosque (not shown).*

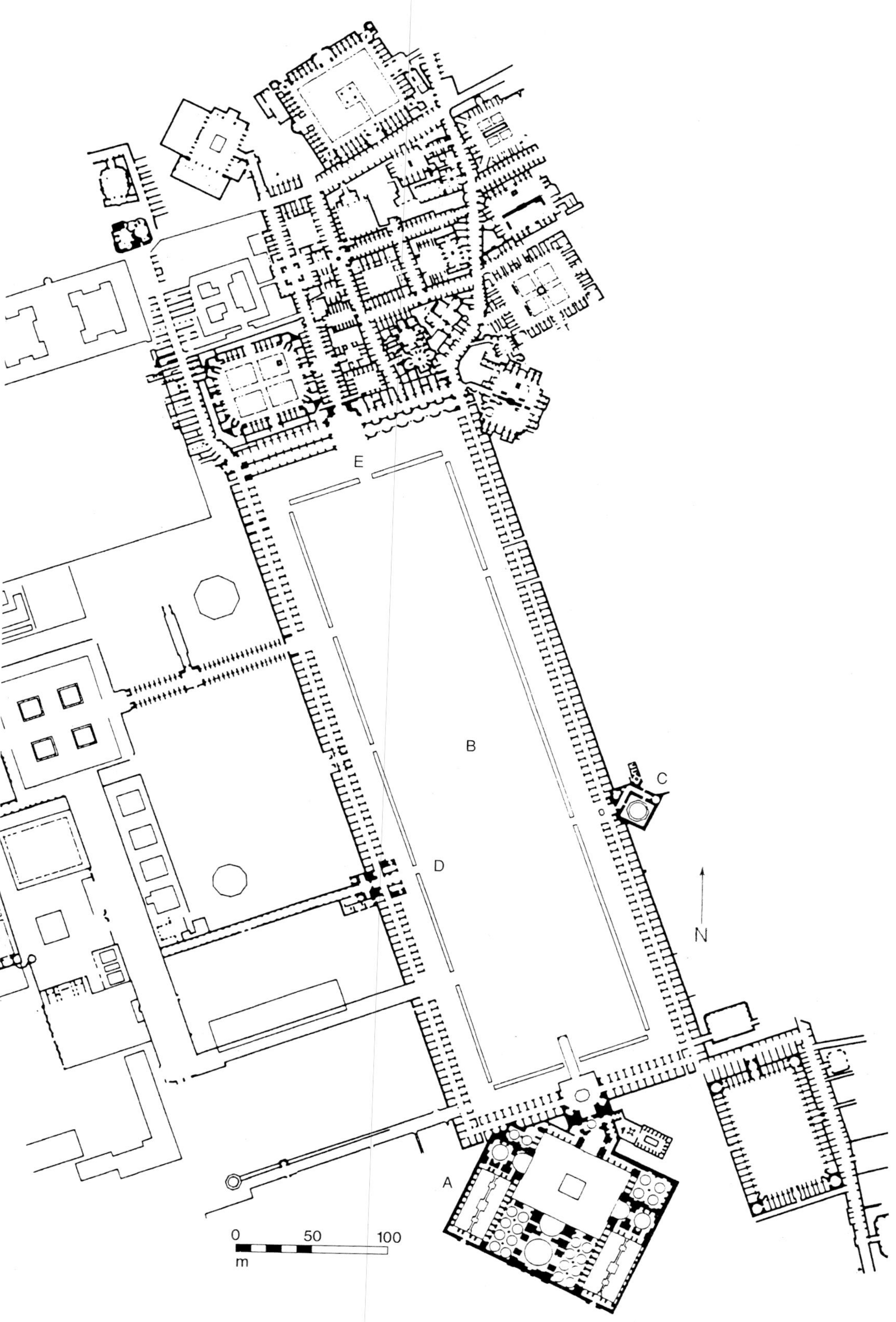

period. The Masjid-i Hakim (1656–62) displays novel rhythms in its courtyard façades. That on the main axis reads ABACABA, where C stands for the main *iwan*, B for the two smaller *iwans* and A for the two-storey niches. The number of *iwans* therefore, with the two side *iwans*, totals eight. The side façades read ABBBACABBBA, where C is again the central *iwan*, A the two-storey niches, and B is a unit of a lower niche under two gallery arches. These arches are open-backed, flaunting their status as space-fillers, unlike the disguised screens of their Timurid prototypes. The stridency of the geometric patterns of the tilework around the court is unfortunate, but as compensation the tympanum at the rear of each of the side *iwans* encloses the finest openwork tiled arabesque in Iranian architecture.[10]

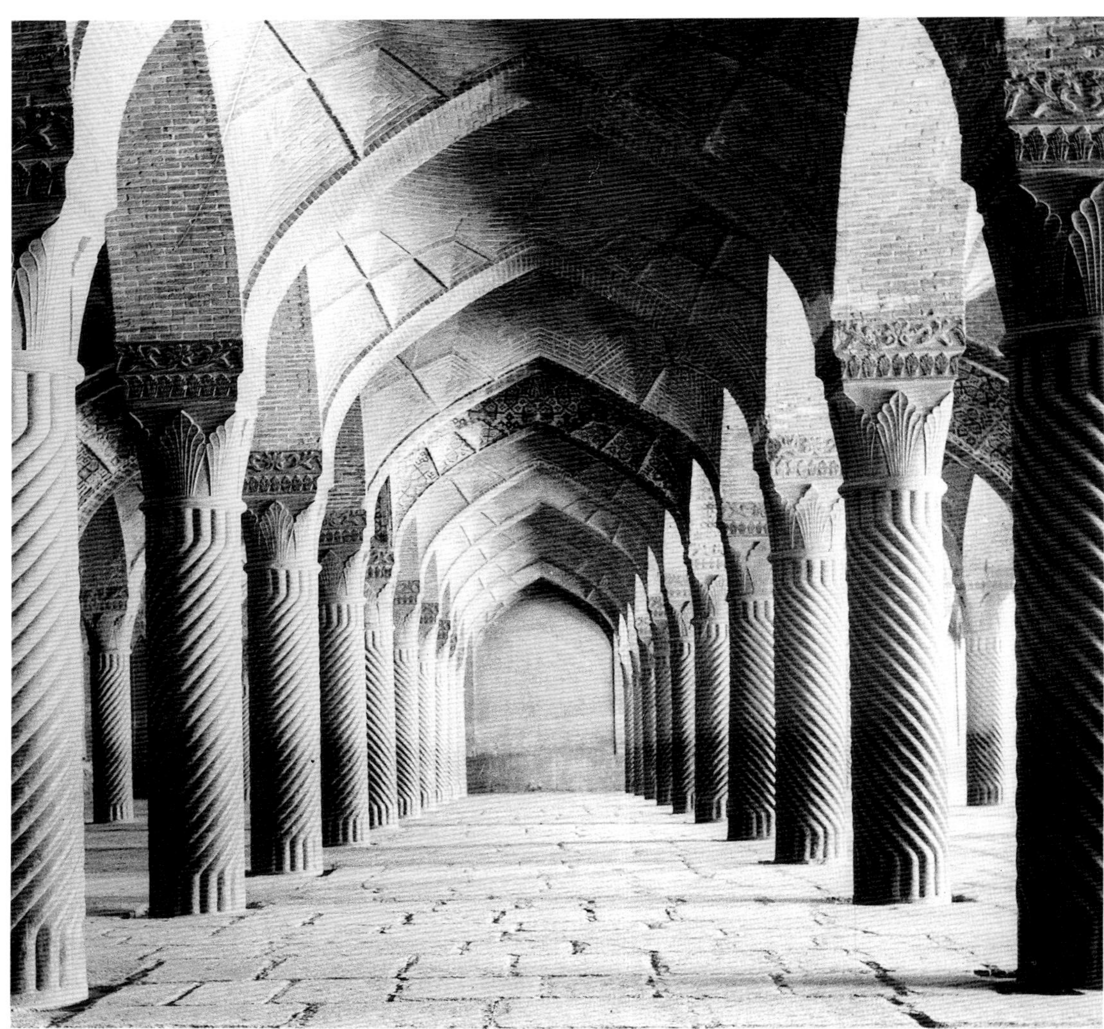

(Left) Interior of the prayer-hall in the Masjid-i Vakil (1773), Shiraz.

(Opposite) The sunken courtyard of the Masjid-i Aqa Buzurg, Kashan, as seen from the north.

In the second half of the eighteenth century, the Iranian ruler Karim Khan Zand (1750–79) was responsible for one notable mosque, the eponymous Masjid-i Vakil in Shiraz (1773). Although the tile decoration was largely added later by the Qajars, the spacious prayer-hall, with its forty-eight twisted columns, makes a powerful impression through its simplicity of form.

The Qajar period (1779–1924)

Qajar architecture continued the general conservatism of the Safavids, the courtyard of the mosque remaining the focus of invention.[11] Any attempt at making *qibla* dome-chambers compete with *iwans* placed in front of them was now abandoned, so that for the first time since the Seljuq period the exposed brick style would be enjoyed in many sanctuaries.

The most novel courtyard arrangements are those which incorporate cells for students, either by recessing the cells behind the side *iwans* (Masjid-i Sayyid, Isfahan; Masjid-i Shah, Simnan) or by placing them around a sunken courtyard (Masjid-i Aqa Buzurg, Kashan). The Masjid-i Sayyid was nothing if not versatile; it also incorporated the domed tomb of the founder (a member of the *ulama*), a tall clock-tower above the *iwan* on the *qibla* side and a unique teaching space – a lofty *talar*, just like that of the Ali Qapu, behind one of the side *iwans*.[12] This ability of architects to bring disparate elements into mosque design is also shown at the Masjid-i Aqa Buzurg, where two minaret-like wind-towers frame the ensemble.

Tilework continued to be the main decorative medium in this period, though the bright-pink shade added to the *cuerda seca* palette harmonizes poorly with the other colours.

Modern mosques

The twentieth century in Iran and Central Asia has not been a period of distinction for mosque building, which was virtually prohibited in Central Asia or at least rendered unnecessary by Soviet anti-religious policies. In Iran efforts to combine elements of traditional forms with the use of modern materials and styles, though few in number, have produced some interesting results. Variety and originality were the hallmarks of mosques in Iran and Central Asia for many centuries; some of the simple but imaginative contemporary reinterpretations of mosque design display the same characteristics (see chapter 15)[13] and give hope that its future is in secure hands.

- 8 -

ANATOLIA AND THE OTTOMAN LEGACY

GÜLRU NECIPOĞLU

WHILE the local Romano-Byzantine and Armeno-Georgian traditions undoubtedly played a part in the adaptation of mosque design to the predominantly Christian setting of Anatolia, as it existed in the eleventh century, any regional synthesis involves the selection and rejection of elements from pre-existing traditions, their merging with new ones, and their reinterpretation in changing contexts by patrons and architects with specific needs in mind. The ideological aspirations and collective cultural-religious memories of the new Muslim rulers, expressed through the patronage of monumental religious architecture, therefore played a central role in determining the development of the form of the mosque in Anatolia.

Although the mosque underwent relatively few formal changes in the central zones of the Islamic world after the Seljuq period, its history in the Anatolian-Balkan region was one of lively adaptation and creative innovation. This unusual dynamism recalled the spirit of early Islamic architecture, suggesting that the melting-pot culture of the outlying frontier territory continued to incorporate elements from other traditions. The changing identities and competing ambitions of the various Muslim principalities that ruled Anatolia were reflected in a dynamic search for form, particularly for the Friday mosque which throughout early Islamic history had remained the religious symbol of sovereignty and political legitimacy. The history of the mosque in this region cannot be adequately charted by simply combining geographical and regional factors with a diachronic sequence of ruling dynasties. Synchronic parallels between the Anatolian mosque and monuments in neighbouring regions attest to a cross-fertilization of architectural concepts across traditional boundaries. The history of the mosque in Anatolia can be divided into relatively distinct chronological periods corresponding to different cultural-political systems and patronage structures concentrated in the respective capitals of the Seljuq Sultanate of Rum (1077–1308), the Turkmen principalities or emirates (1308–1453), and the Ottoman Empire (until 1923). Each represents a paradigmatic shift rather than a continuous evolution within a single regional idiom.

The Seljuq Sultanate of Rum (1077–1308)

The Great Seljuqs, a Turkish dynasty which ruled in Iran and Iraq, seized Anatolia (*Bilad al-Rum*, or the land of Romans) from the Byzantines after their victory at the battle of Manzikert in 1071. The conquered frontier territory was immediately overrun by bands of unruly Turkmen warriors who roamed the countryside at will until the Seljuq ruler Malik-Shah banished a rebellious cousin to take control of Anatolia in 1077. The Seljuqs of Rum, with Konya as their capital, found it difficult to exercise authority over the independent dynasties in the area, such as the Danishmendids (1071–1177), the Mengüceqids (1118–1252), and the Saltuqids (1092–1202). Neither were they able to expand towards upper Mesopotamia and Syria, a highly Arabicized and politically distinct region ruled first by a branch of the Great Seljuqs and then by their atabegs, the Artuqids and Zangids (who were eventually succeeded by the Ayyubids and the Mamluks). In a land characterized by its fascinating ethnic-religious diversity, the Seljuqs of Rum were surrounded by Byzantine territories to the west and all along the coastline, the principality of Little Armenia in Cilicia, and the Crusader states of Antioch-Edessa. From the north-east their territories were geographically linked to Caucasia, Iran, and Central Asia through Azerbaijan. For over a century their power centred on Konya, remained limited to the central Anatolian plateau, a steppe region ringed by high mountains.[1]

The Seljuqs, following the Great Seljuqs and the Ghaznevids, regarded themselves as heirs of the Persian royal tradition. Their enthusiastic patronage of a Persian-type court culture was reflected in their names – Kaykhusraw, Kayqubad, Kayka'us – which set them apart from the Turkic names of their Anatolian rivals. They reached the peak of their power in the reign of Ala ad-Din Kayqubad I (1219–37), soon after the Latin conquest of Constantinople in 1204, when the weakened Byzantines had moved their capital to western Anatolia and Kayqubad was able to unify the land by pacifying Turkmen principalities. The capture of major port cities had given his landlocked state access to the sea, a factor which contributed to a considerable transit trade. It is to this period of prosperity, which was cut short by the Mongol invasion of Anatolia in 1243, that the major mosques of the Anatolian Seljuqs belong.

These mosques included Friday mosques, varying in plan, built for members or vassals of the Seljuq royal family, and small district *masjids*. However, as Bateş has noted, they were 'not the dominating element in Anatolian cities and remained unimaginative, rather somber in construction, overshadowed by such undertakings as *medreses* and caravansarays'.[2] The latter (also sponsored by the Great Seljuqs) do appear stylistically more unified and less subject to inherited tradition, while mosques remained more conservative and closely bound to the prototypes of the Islamic heartland.

Mosques dating from the zenith of Rum Seljuq power (earlier surviving examples sponsored by various principalities go back to the

Facing page
The Mosque of Sultan Ahmet (1609–17), Istanbul: principal dome and roof.

Map 4: Anatolia, showing principal mosque sites, including those of the Ottoman era on the European side of the Bosphorus.

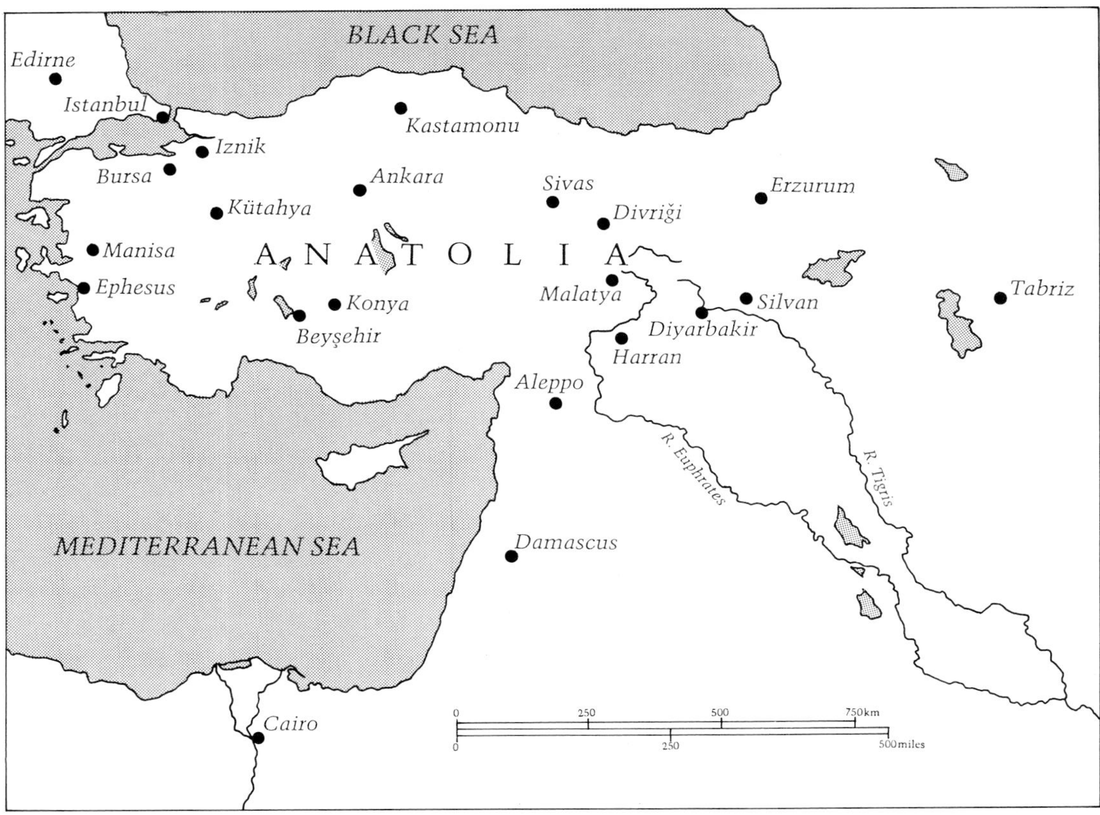

twelfth century) demonstrate how standard mosque types were reinterpreted in the Anatolian milieu. The Ala ad-Din Mosque, built next to the Seljuq palace inside the Konya citadel, was begun *c.* 1155 and completed, in the reign of Ala ad-Din Kayqubad I, *c.* 1220. It is not a single coherent project, but an irregular trapezoidal hypostyle mosque featuring a rebuilt cylindrical minaret and dynastic tomb towers, reflecting alterations dating from the period between the twelfth and the fourteenth centuries. Its striking feature is a domed *mihrab* chamber with mosaic-tile decoration, preceded by an *iwan*-like rectangular bay. The insertion of this brick dome-*iwan* unit, with Persian overtones, separated by corridor-like spaces from the lateral aisles of an ashlar-masonry hypostyle mosque, evokes distant memories of the domed *maqsura* of the Great Mosque in Isfahan and of other Iranian Seljuq mosques. The Seljuqs of Rum no doubt intended it as a means of proclaiming themselves as legitimate heirs to their cousins in Iran, as did Ravendi's early thirteenth-century history, which refers to the Sultan of Rum as the fruit of the Great Seljuq family tree.[3]

The prominent dome over the *mihrab* bay was also a typical feature of the stone-masonry mosques built by the atabegs of the Great Seljuqs, in south-east Anatolia, Syria and the Jazira. It appears, for example, in Artuqid Great Mosques (Silvan 1152–7; Mardin, 1176–86; Dunaysir, 1204), and later in Ayyubid mosques that culminated with the Mosque of Sultan Baybars in Mamluk Cairo (see pp. 96f.). As Herzfeld noted, those domed mosques with wide courtyards and aisles parallel to the *qibla* wall were largely inspired by the Umayyad Great Mosque in Damascus, but also represented parallel solutions to the problem of the domed *maqsura* introduced in Seljuq Iran: 'the occasion was given by the expansion of the Seljuq empire over the whole of Syria, and the exchange of ideas it entailed'. The idea of inserting a domed *maqsura* over the *mihrab* of the Great Mosque of Isfahan in 1086–7 was itself perhaps inspired by the fire-damaged Umayyad dome in Damascus that Malik-Shah's vizier had rebuilt in 1082–3. Combining the *qibla* dome of the Isfahan Mosque with the palatial element of the *iwan* projected the royal image of the Great Seljuq sultanate allied with the Sunni Abbasid caliphate in Baghdad.[4]

This emphasis on the domed *maqsura* can be seen as a resurgence of royal symbolism at a time when princely successor states associated with the Sunni revival of the Great Seljuqs were establishing themselves in the Middle East.[5] The Ala ad-Din Mosque was a regional interpretation of those built for the Great Seljuqs and their atabegs. It alludes to Iranian prototypes through its *mihrab* dome-chamber preceded by an *iwan*-like bay, but omits the four-*iwan* courtyard, and instead of the tripartite squinch characteristic of the zone of transition to the dome in Iranian mosques, it features the local flattened pendentives known as 'Turkish triangles'. Its ashlar-masonry hypostyle halls, with flat wooden roofs supported by arcades resting on re-used Hellenistic and Byzantine marble columns, are very different from the vaulted halls with heavy brick piers seen in Iran.

The diversity of architectural sources is also reflected in the north façade, with its two prominent portals, which has an upper blind arcade reminiscent of the one in the Artuqid Great Mosque of Silvan. Completed *c.* 1220 under the supervision of Atabeg Ayas (who had moved to Konya from the Artuqid court), this limestone façade is decorated with typically Syrian interlaced knot patterns in bichrome marble. An inscription referring to the Damascene architect Muhammad bin Hawlan al-Dimashki testifies to the impact of the Syrian stone-masonry tradition. References to Iranian Seljuq models based on the use of brick and tile are thus complemented by the cut-stone masonry tradition of Syria, with its closer affinity to the native Anatolian limestone. This eclectic mixing of traditions can be attributed in part to artisans from different regions – Anatolia, Syria, Ahlat (the *minbar* is signed by an Ahlati artist) and Iran (mosaic-tile work is believed to have been executed by craftsmen fleeing from the Mongols) – working on the building, but it also reflects the syncretism of Anatolian Seljuq frontier culture.

The Great Mosque of Malatya, built for Ala ad-Din Kayqubad I in 1224, and remodelled throughout the thirteenth century, comes closest to the Iranian Seljuq models the sultan was emulating. Quotations from Iran, however, once again remain selective and appear side by side with local elements. Here the dome-*iwan* unit in brick and tile in front of the *mihrab* is a close copy of Iranian Seljuq models, but on a reduced scale. The four-*iwan* courtyard is again omitted, however, being replaced by a shrunken court out of proportion with the monumental *iwan* on the *qibla* side. Except for the dome-*iwan* unit and the courtyard walls faced with glazed bricks and mosaic tilework in the Iranian manner, the rest of the hypostyle building is of local stone masonry, as in Konya. The unarticulated outer walls are accentuated by the decorative treatment of the monumental portals and by a cylindrical brick minaret in the Great Seljuq tradition, but their stark simplicity contrasts sharply with the playful use of patterned brickwork and coloured tiles inside. The duality of interior and exterior, already encountered in Konya, signals the somewhat schizophrenic identity of Anatolian Seljuq royal mosques where stone is juxtaposed with brick- and tilework. This hybrid combination emphasized the links with Iran that the Sultans of Rum were cultivating, despite their rapid assimilation of local Anatolian traditions. In that respect the Konya and Malatya mosques are comparable to the Great Mosque of Cordoba, begun in the ninth century by a branch of the Umayyad dynasty exiled to a distant Christian frontier, from where it emulated certain features of the ancestral Great Mosque of Damascus in a local idiom to emphasize its glorious lineage.

Aspects of the Konya and Malatya mosques were reinterpreted in the local material of cut stone at the Huand Hatun complex (1238) in Kayseri, built for the widow of Ala ad-Din Kayqubad I during the reign of their son. Like its royal prototypes, the rectangular mosque in Kayseri features a domed *mihrab* bay preceded by an *iwan* opening into a square court even smaller than the one in Malatya. The use of plain stone walls, however, creates a totally different aesthetic effect – severe, restrained, but more unified. Internally, the only carved decoration occurs on the stone *mihrab*. Blind exterior walls featuring crenellations and turret-like buttresses add to the fortress-like appearance of this stern, inward-looking building. The horizontality of its rectilinear mass is broken by tall *muqarnas* portals decorated with restrained geometric interlaced carving, by the conical cap of Huand's attached mausoleum and by the *mihrab* dome. Juxtaposed with a *madrasa*, the mosque's block-like mass exemplifies an introverted conception of architecture recalling fortified royal caravanserais of ashlar masonry that feature similar *muqarnas* portals; in it elements encountered at Konya and Malatya are rendered thoroughly Anatolian through the unifying medium of stone.

Besides royal mosques featuring the dome-*iwan* combination associated with the Great Seljuqs and their successors, a perhaps less symbolically charged, but typically Anatolian form developed, from the twelfth century on, to become the most widely encountered mosque type. The basilica-type plan without a courtyard featured three or more aisles perpendicular to the *qibla* wall, often with a wider and higher central nave culminating in a domed *mihrab* bay that was accentuated externally by a pyramidal shell, and an oculus above the central bay (provided with a pool to preserve the memory of the omitted courtyard). Although the development of this mosque type, not so far removed in conception from the al-Aqsa Mosque in Jerusalem, has been linked to the cold Anatolian climate, its inspiration can be found in local basilical churches. The theory that climate dictated the form is weakened by the consistent inclusion of courtyards in Anatolian Seljuq *madrasas* and in post-Seljuq mosques.

A celebrated example of the basilica-type mosque is the Great Mosque of Divriği, built in 1228–9 by the reigning Mengüceqid ruler and his wife who acknowledge in their foundation inscription the suzerainty of Ala ad-Din Kayqubad I. This mosque, with its rebuilt cylindrical minaret (famous for the exuberance of its unusual carved

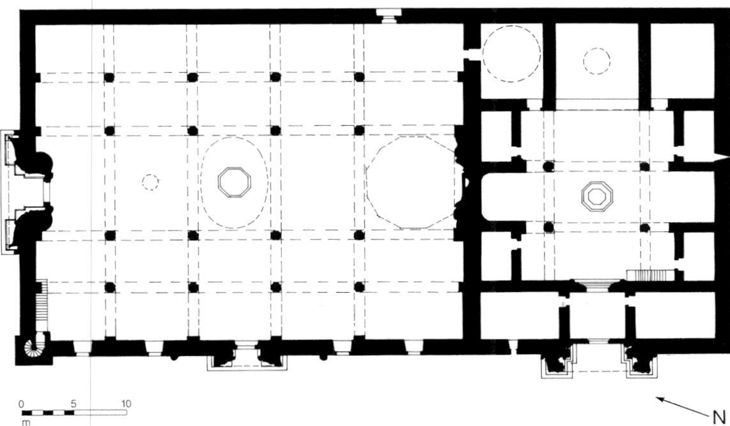

The Great Mosque-hospital (1228–9) at Divriği: general view from the south-west, and plan showing the decorated portals, corner minaret and dome over the mausoleum of the founders.

stone decoration and the variegated ribbed stone vaults covering its bays) forms a charitable complex with an adjoining hospital containing the conical capped mausoleum of its founders. Otherwise its rectangular ground-plan with the longitudinal north-south axis defined by a wider and higher nave flanked by narrower side-aisles is a relatively common feature, as is the presence, in front of the *mihrab*, of a large dome surmounted by a prominent pyramidal outer shell. The surviving decorative stone vaults of each bay can be seen as regional interpretations of Iranian and Iraqi brick vaulting; similar stone vaults appear in the Armenian churches of the region, along with stone *muqarnas* domes. The dim, windowless interior of the mosque, with pointed arches carried by rows of stone pillars forming aisles perpendicular to the *qibla* wall, culminates in an ornate *mihrab* area which contrasts with the plainness of the remaining walls. The vigorous vegetal decoration of the stone *mihrab* has been compared to the 'baroque' carved stucco ornaments of such late Seljuq monuments as the Gunbad-i Aleviyan in Hamadan; in the process of translating stucco (and other materials, such as wood) to stone the artists magnified the motifs almost beyond recognition.

The unusual variegated portals which project above the low façades of the Divriği complex are also carved with extravagant designs deriving from a wide range of sources. Boldly enlarged fantastic vegetal motifs sprout beyond the narrow vertical strips that frame the portals, as if defying confinement within linear boundaries. They are carved in high relief to create surfaces pulsating with an energy that is absent in the restrained, and predominantly geometric, low-relief carvings of Seljuq portals in central Anatolia. The mosque, signed by masons from Ahlat, seems to have been the work of a mixed group of Muslim and non-Muslim builders; its *minbar* was signed by an artist who came from Tiflis in Georgia. Of whatever background they may have been, the masons were apparently unaccustomed to the decorative vocabulary that had by then developed in central Anatolia. The impressive, but somewhat incoherent, Divriği complex should therefore be evaluated as a provincial version of a common Anatolian type. It reflects the rich diversity of Seljuq Anatolia, which never became unified under a central authority until the Ottoman period.

Following the Mongol defeat of the Seljuqs in 1243, the few congregational mosques that were built bear the names of influential governors and the viziers they appointed. The puppet Seljuq sultans, though nominally independent, had lost their royal prerogative to build Great Mosques. These later structures often elaborate earlier models; among them are several examples of wooden buildings with rows of colourfully painted pillars supporting flat ceilings. The largest and best-known example is the Eşrefoğlu Mosque (1297–9) in Beyşehir, built for Süleyman Beg, the ruler of an independent Turkmen principality; a typical basilical mosque with a *mihrab* dome, it has a single cylindrical minaret and an attached conical-capped mausoleum for its founder. Another mosque type common in Seljuq Anatolia was the small district *masjid*. Those that have survived in Konya are either flat-roofed or single-domed cubic structures built of stone or brick, with a narthex-like space at their entrance, a regional development possibly inspired by local Byzantine churches.

Anatolian Seljuq mosques can be grouped into two geographic zones with differing approaches, in addition to south-east Anatolia, which merged with upper Mesopotamia and Syria. The first is east and north-east Anatolia, connected through Azerbaijan to artistic currents arriving from Iran and Central Asia, which assimilated a living Armeno-Georgian tradition of stone construction that had already been permeated with Islamic influences under Arab suzerainty. This zone was never completely integrated into the Seljuq sultanate, whose power-base remained concentrated in central Anatolia. It came to play a considerable role in the transmission of new tastes, especially after the establishment of the Mongol Il-Khanid capitals in Azerbaijan. In the late thirteenth century an unprecedented monumentalization of architectural forms took place there: the *madrasas* of Erzurum and Sivas, featuring colossal stone portals with high-relief carving flanked by pairs of cylindrical brick minarets, became signs of Mongol domination. The second zone is central Anatolia, briefly unified under the Seljuqs. This region developed closer contacts with Byzantium and became more intimately linked with the Syro-Jaziran stone-masonry tradition; here a relatively homogeneous Anatolian Seljuq architectural idiom developed in the first half of the thirteenth century.

Since Roman times stone had been the traditional building material for monumental architecture in central, south-east and north-east Anatolia, as well as in Azerbaijan. Brick construction, common in the Balkans, west Anatolia, Iran and Central Asia, is rarely encountered in the mosques of north-east Anatolia, which were built almost entirely of stone, including their superstructures. Their decorative stone vaults and conical outer shells, also encountered in local churches, can be seen as regional interpretations of patterned brick vaults and conical domes typical of Iran and Iraq. In this region the basilical church plan without a courtyard was freely adapted to the needs of the mosque, but transformed into a symbol of the new faith through the use of a distinctive superstructure emphasizing the *mihrab*, cylindrical minarets in the Great Seljuq tradition and monumental portals with Arabic inscriptions accompanied by abstract decorative motifs.

Rum Seljuq mosques in central Anatolia more readily combined brick and glazed-tile decoration with the local limestone. Their curvilinear domes differed from the conical stone shells more common in eastern mosques and in other typical Seljuq building types such as the mausoleum or caravanserai. They featured rubble-masonry walls with stone revetments and columnar supports for the generally flat wooden roofs which were punctuated by brick or stone domes. One can sense in the royal mosques of central Anatolia an attempt to preserve the high Islamic canons developed in Iran and Syria. After all, the Seljuqs of Rum were a branch of the Great Seljuq family, which could be likened to a tripod with its legs centred on Anatolia, Iran-Iraq and Syria respectively.[6] The cultural hegemony of the Great Seljuqs had endowed these lands with a shared architectural ethos that was perpetuated in the Syro-Jaziran region by the smaller states of the atabegs and their successors. In Anatolia that heritage continued to be cultivated by a dynasty which could claim descent from the Seljuq royal family, and which synthesized elements from Iranian, Mesopotamian, Syrian and local Anatolian building traditions.

The Sultan Ahmet Mosque (Blue Mosque), Istanbul, built in the early seventeenth century by the architect Sedefkar Mehmet Agha, is exceptional in having six minarets; its alternative name is derived from the extensive blue-stencilled interior decoration (right).

Three major examples of Ottoman mosques in Istanbul designed by the great architect Sinan.

(Top left) The Şehzade Mosque (1544–8), the architect's first major work.

(Left) An Iznik tile panel in the Rüstem Paşa Mosque (1561), one of many splendid examples of floral tilework in this building.

Perhaps Sinan's most ambitious work was the extensive Süleymaniye complex (above and opposite): the mosque, built 1550–7, has a spacious courtyard with fountain and the interior is covered by a massive dome which rises to a height of 53 m (174 ft).

The sultans of Rum were faced with the same problem of translating a brick-based mosque architecture developed in the Iranian world into stone as were the Muslim rulers of India, who did it by introducing the arch and vault into a local post-and-lintel system of construction. Anatolia had the advantage of a pre-existing arcuated tradition. When one compares the Great Mosques of the early thirteenth century in Delhi and Ajmer with those built around the same time in Anatolia, the latter show a closer affinity to the mainland traditions of Seljuq architecture, though neither group used the four-*iwan* plan. While a large proportion of non-Muslim stonemasons must have been employed in both cases, Anatolian mosques acquired true domes, pointed arches, geometric ornament, *muqarnas* vaults and glazed-tile decoration more rapidly than did their Indian counterparts.

Compared to contemporary buildings in Syria and the Jazira, where colourful tile revetments alien to the indigenous stone-masonry tradition were not adopted, those in Anatolia again exhibit a stronger affiliation with Iran. It was only in the remote eastern fringes of Syria that direct quotations from Iran manifested themselves in geometric brick patterning and cylindrical brick minarets highlighted by glazed elements.[7] In south-east Anatolia, Syria and the Jazira the impact of the Umayyad architectural heritage (exemplified by a renewed interest in the Great Mosque of Damascus) was far from negligible. By evoking the Umayyad imperial heritage, the post-Seljuq successor states of the region could link themselves to a prestigious local architectural tradition that allowed them to cultivate their separate identity. The rulers of Anatolia, which did not boast any previous accumulation of Islamic architecture (except in its south-east region), had no such option. Neither did the twelfth-century classical revival of Syria and the Jazira find its parallel in Seljuq Anatolia, also a land rich in classical ruins.[8] The quotation of classicizing motifs in carved stone in the mosques of Aleppo, Diyarbakir and Harran (recalling the selective citation of late antique motifs by the Umayyads) had no echo in Seljuq Anatolia, where such motifs may have been too closely associated with the neighbouring Byzantine Empire.

Compared to the minimally decorated, austere stone architecture of Syria that followed the short-lived classical revival, Anatolian mosques exhibited a less restrained tendency in terms of decoration, as well as the greater dynamism of a recently conquered multicultural frontier region deriving inspiration from a variety of traditions to assert a distinctive identity, not unlike that of other Islamic-Christian frontiers, Sicily and Spain, which developed a similar synthesis of diverse architectural traditions. Despite their differences, however, the mosques of the Rum Seljuqs and of other Seljuq successor states represented regional expressions of a shared cultural ethos. They were all built by independent régimes constituting the branches of the same family tree, provincial in scale, and far from the imperial pretensions of earlier universal Islamic empires.

Facing page
The north portal of the Mosque at Divriği (1229), in Anatolia; this remote building is famous for the profusion of carved stonework, found on the three portals on the north and west sides.

The Turkmen principalities or emirates (1308–1453)

In the post-Mongol era, the Seljuq domains were divided up among petty Turkmen principalities – the outcome in part of the migration into Anatolia of several waves of nomadic Turkmens driven from their homelands by the Mongols. As Mongol Il-Khanid control over Anatolia diminished, these Turkmens seized the Byzantine territories in west and north-west Anatolia, and filled the vacuum created by the transfer of the Byzantine capital back to Constantinople in 1261.

Two of the numerous Anatolian emirates (*beylik*) that had proliferated *c.* 1300 emerged as the most powerful by the mid-fourteenth century. They were the Karamanids, who saw themselves as heirs to the Rum Seljuq dynasty after capturing Konya, and the Ottomans, who rapidly conquered the remaining Byzantine strongholds of north-west Anatolia and started to expand into the Balkans.[9] The Ottoman ruler Bayazid I (1389–1402), who received the ambitious title 'Sultan of Rum' from the Abbasid Caliph in Mamluk Cairo, had subjugated nearly all the Anatolian principalities, including Karaman, and had begun to challenge Constantinople, but his fortunes were reversed after an embarrassing defeat by Timur in 1402. The deposed Anatolian principalities were reinstated and the Ottomans had to wait until the second half of the fifteenth century to impose centralized rule over Anatolia with the Balkans.

The most interesting innovations of this period appear in west and north-west Anatolia. The Karamanids, who dominated central Anatolia, remained bound to the Seljuq architectural idiom as it had been transformed through Il-Khanid tastes. The Karakoyunlu and Akkoyunlu Turkmen dynasties who ruled in east Anatolia, Azerbaijan, Iraq and west Iran after the decline of Il-Khanid power merged new influences from Timurid Iran and Central Asia with local stone-masonry traditions. After Timur's victory over the Ottomans, the rest of Anatolia also became closely linked with the Turco-Iranian international culture of the Timurid world. Unlike the Arab world where the Mamluks, based in Syria and Egypt, maintained a relatively separate cultural identity after stopping the expansion of the Mongols and Timurids, the destiny of Anatolia was once again closely bound to Iran.

Besides Great Mosques that continued to be built in the Anatolian emirates, an increasing number of small-scale domed mosques incorporating multiple functions that fulfilled the needs of the new social order became typical of the age. Commissioned by rulers, viziers or local notables, the buildings reflected the more modest patronage base of a fragmented political milieu no longer subsumed under a sultanate. They included single-domed cubic mosques, often preceded by a two- or three-bay porch, a type with well-established Seljuq precedents that spread throughout Anatolia and the Balkans.

Undoubtedly the most original small-scale mosque type, more often seen in the Ottoman domains, was a multifunctional structure with an inverted-T plan. Usually featuring two central domed cubes flanked by smaller auxiliary side-spaces constituting the arms of a T, such buildings were fronted by five-bay porticos with domes, and occasionally an attached minaret, sometimes two (added later in some cases). Although their origin has been traced to Anatolian Seljuq domed cruciform *madrasas*, there is no prototype that has quite the same arrangement. This inverted-T plan may well have originated from that of convents (*khanaqah, zawiya*), given the fact that their lateral spaces (provided with chimneys and storage niches) functioned as charitable hospices or as hostels providing food and lodging for travellers and dervishes.

Multifunctional T-type mosques became the centre of urban life at a time when the semi-nomadic Turkmen population with its unorthodox religious leanings had gathered around charismatic shaykhs who played an important spiritual role in colonizing newly conquered areas. Starting with Orkhan I (1324–60), each Ottoman sultan built in the capital cities of Iznik, Bursa and Edirne at least one such mosque (entrusted to a shaykh and supported by *waqf* endowments) as part of a colonizing policy that encouraged urbanization. Often sited on hilltops, removed from the city centre with its standard features that included a Great Mosque and bazaars, these modest mosques surrounded by loosely grouped dependencies formed the nuclei of new Muslim neighbourhoods.

The earliest examples of T-type mosques have composite masonry with alternating courses of stone and brick in the Byzantine manner, spoliated columns and decorative details that point to the employment of Greek masons. After all, in terms of scale and general conception these mosques were not so far removed from multi-domed middle- or late-Byzantine monastic churches, many of which had been converted to mosques. However, their distinctive ground-plan with clearly delineated square and rectangular units so unlike the curvilinear, blending spaces of Byzantine churches, their novel arrangement of domes in varying sizes to accentuate the *mihrab* axis, and their distinctive five-bay porches, often with attached minarets, signalled their unmistakably separate identity.

The ashlar-masonry complex of Bayazid I (1390–5) on a hill in Bursa, featuring a T-type mosque surrounded by loosely grouped dependencies, marks a turning-point. After this building the use of composite masonry in brick and stone ceased for Ottoman royal mosques. The sudden switch to the luxury of cut stone and marble reflected growing Ottoman imperial ambitions fuelled by the subjugation of rival principalities. Bayazid I's mosque has two large square halls which together form a projecting rectangular space along the *qibla* axis; the first of these (covered by a higher dome) acts as an anteroom to the second, an *iwan*-shaped raised prayer-hall reached by steps. The first hall is laterally flanked by two smaller square *iwans*, also raised and dome-covered, and having, in each corner, a vaulted square convent room featuring a fireplace and niche-shaped cupboards. A combination of Byzantine pendentives, Turkish triangles and squinches is used in the zones of transition to the hemispherical brick domes. The mosque's main façade has an imposing five-bay porch with, at each end, a cylindrical minaret (both now ruined).

In the Mosque of Bayazid I ornament is reduced while emphasis is placed on the cubical massing of walls and the contrasting hemispherical domes. Familiar elements are adapted to a new idiom, different from that of the Karamanids, in which the Seljuq emphasis on

elaborately decorated flat surfaces prevailed. The building is conceived as a balanced freestanding monument meant to be seen from all sides, in contrast to Seljuq mosques, in which the main façade was emphasized and the remaining walls left largely unarticulated. Here, the façades are no longer treated merely as low, horizontal supports to which are appended, as symbols of Islam, overbearing portals, unintegrated minarets and domes; these elements are now integrated into a sculptural whole with an exteriorized vertical emphasis that signals a departure from the introverted architecture of the Seljuqs.

The most spectacular representative of the T-type mosque, the incomplete Yeşil Mosque in Bursa (1412–19) built for Mehmet I, also forms the nucleus of a hilltop complex. While its ground-plan is quite similar to that of Bayazid I's mosque, its decorative scheme, inspired by Timurid models, sets it apart. The work was co-ordinated by a court designer, Naqqash Ali ibn Ilyas Ali, who had earlier been carried off by Timur from Bursa to Samarqand and there trained in the Timurid decorative vocabulary. Built of ashlar masonry, the mosque is richly decorated inside with polychrome tile revetments signed by a workshop of artists from the Karakoyunlu capital, Tabriz. The mosque's domes are believed to have been faced with turquoise glazed tiles, an unusual feature at a time when Ottoman domes were generally covered by ordinary brick tiles (lead, commonly used in Byzantine monuments, did not become standard as a covering for Ottoman domes until around the second half of the fifteenth century). The outer walls are of cut limestone and marble, more suited than tile revetments to a rainy climate; their mature articulation and elegant carving are evidence of a development in the stone-cutting industry which, at the time of Bayazid I, had been somewhat basic.

The Yeşil Mosque demonstrates how misleading it would be to study Anatolian architecture as an isolated regional phenomenon without reference to the rest of the Islamic world. The only surviving Karakoyunlu mosque in Tabriz, the Masjid-i Muzaffariya (1465), exhibits a curious affinity to the Anatolian T-type plan, which suggests that it may originally have been more widespread. The few known T-type structures beyond the Ottoman domains include: the Ayni Minare Mosque (*c.* 1489) in the Akkoyunlu capital, Diyarbakir; the Yakub

(Opposite) The Isa Beg Mosque (1374), near Ephesus: general view of exterior showing the use of ashlar masonry.

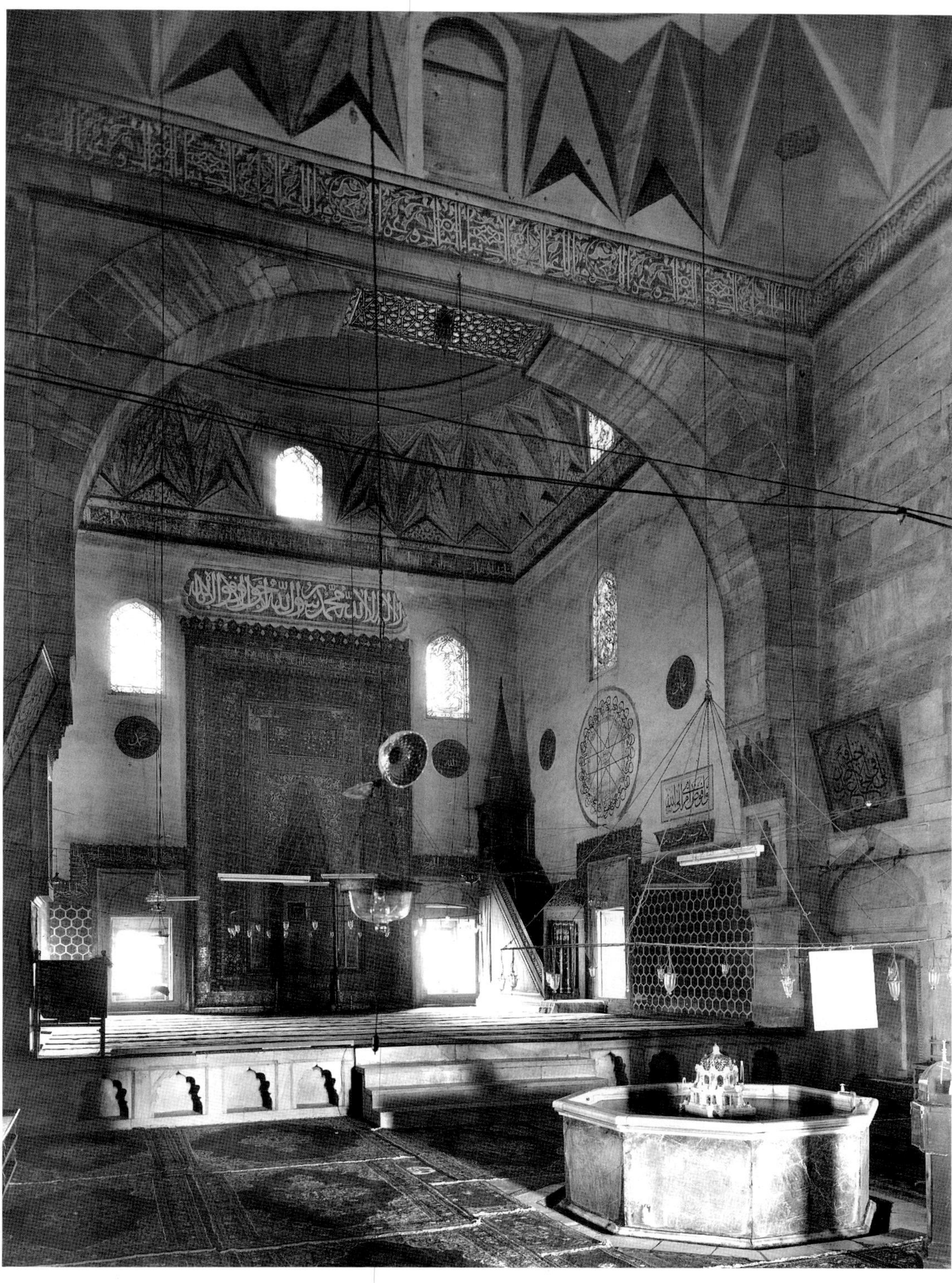

(Right) Interior of the Yeşil Mosque (1412–19), Bursa: view towards the mihrab *and* minbar, *with an unusual octagonal fountain (formerly used for ablutions) in the foreground; the niches to the left and right of the steps served as shoe racks.*

Beg Imaret (1411) in the Gemiyanid capital, Kütahya; and the Ismail Beg Mosque (1454) in the Candar capital, Kastamonu. These examples may have been built under the influence of the Ottomans, who had temporarily unified Anatolia before Timur's conquest. No matter which way the influences travelled, however, the modestly scaled domed mosques of the Anatolian emirates, closely linked through political alliances and marriage ties, reflected a shared architectural ethos. Whether built by ruler, viziers, governors or other notables, all were still roughly comparable in scale and conception, but from the mid-fifteenth century on the unrivalled status of the Ottoman sultans would be reflected in their gigantic mosque complexes that dwarfed those of other patrons.

During the emirate period, while ground-plans typical of the Seljuq era were still being used in Great Mosques, new ones made their appearance, especially in the west and north-west. These included the Great Mosques with double minarets in the Ottoman capitals of Bursa (1396–1400) and Edirne (1402–13), composed of repeated modular units of square bays with domes supported by arched piers. Among original experiments in west Anatolia is the Isa Beg Mosque (1374) near Ephesus, commissioned by the ruler of the Aydinoğlu emirate. In

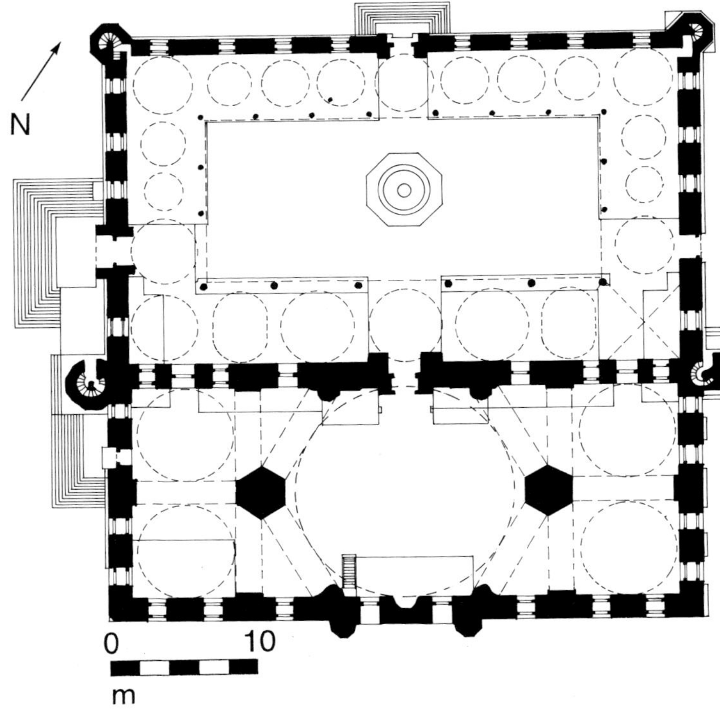

this ambitious domed mosque with two minarets and columns (the latter readily available in the neighbouring classical ruins), the plan of the Umayyad Great Mosque in Damascus (which had already influenced the Artuqid mosques of south-east Anatolia) is reinterpreted. Signed by a Damascene architect, the ashlar-masonry mosque with multiple tiers of windows sees the introduction of the large arcaded courtyard with three gates, which are placed in the same positions as those of the Damascus Mosque. The Isa Beg Mosque can be seen as a revival in Anatolia of an eastern Mediterranean type with well-established royal associations. It is an important forerunner of the Ottoman sultanic mosques in Edirne and Istanbul which, through their grand colonnaded courtyards and colossal domed baldachins, express the same royal message. The presence of a Damascene architect in Ephesus establishes a connection with the Mamluk world, whose monumental stone architecture must also have had an impact on the Ottomans (for whom building in ashlar masonry was a recent innovation).

The Great Mosque of Manisa (1376), built for the Saruhanid ruler Ishak Beg, is another innovative example from west Anatolia. Here,

(Above) Plan of the Uç Şerefili Mosque (1437–47), Edirne, showing the monumental dome over the prayer-hall.

(Below) Interior of the arcaded courtyard with its central pool in the Great Mosque (1376), Manisa.

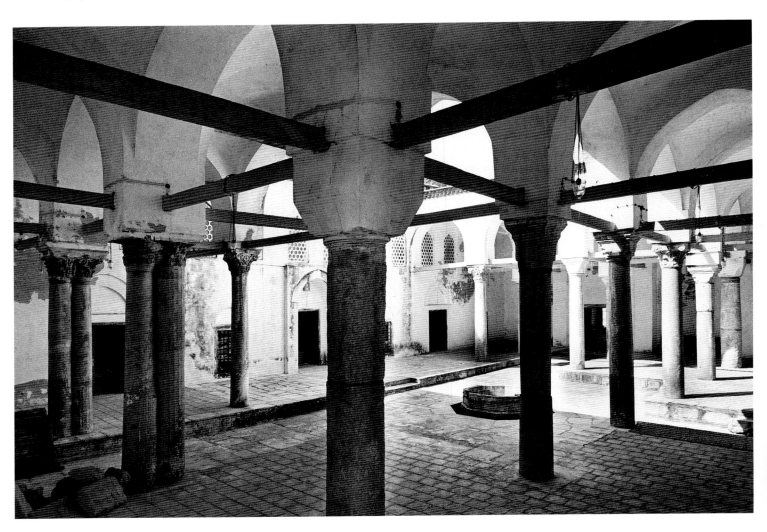

two roughly equal rectangles define a covered sanctuary with a domed *maqsura* (the *minbar* being signed by an artist from Antioch) and an arcaded courtyard with three gates and a central pool. This mosque, too, can be seen as a freely interpreted version of the Umayyad Great Mosque in Damascus. Together with the Isa Beg Mosque, it has been regarded as a precursor of the Üç Şerefeli Mosque (1437–47) in Edirne – the first Ottoman sultanic mosque to feature a monumental dome and courtyard – built for Murad II after he had incorporated the west Anatolian principalities into his kingdom.

The background of the Üç Şerefeli Mosque's architect, identified by the historian Ruhi Edrenevi as Usta Muslih al-Din, remains a mystery.[10] This mosque is composed of an oblong domed prayer-hall and a courtyard with three entrances, again carrying the distant memory of the Great Mosque in Damascus with its multiple minarets. The marble-paved courtyard which has a central fountain and is surrounded by arcades covered by small hemispherical domes, becomes a standard feature in later Ottoman sultanic mosques, just as the use of a central domed baldachin opening onto lateral spaces foreshadows future experiments with the unification of internal space under a monumental dome. The prominent central dome over the *mihrab*, flanked on each side by two smaller domed units, inaugurates the new image of Ottoman imperial mosques, with their colossal royal domes rising above constellations of smaller ones. In an environment that witnessed similar experiments with domed spaces, the unprecedented size of the Üç Şerefeli Mosque's dome and four minarets boldly announced the augmented power of the Ottoman sultans shortly before the capture of Constantinople by Mehmet II. Its monumentality recalls the grandiose domed mosques of the Timurids that also feature multiple minarets; the Ottomans who had already emulated Timurid decorative models in Bursa might still have been looking in that direction.

Although it is tempting to regard earlier architectural experiments in Anatolia as steps leading to the classical Ottoman style, the foundations of which were laid in the second half of the fifteenth century, it is more accurate to describe them as independent expressions of a shared ethos. The mosques of the Anatolian principalities showed a common concern for the dome, coupled with an emphasis on exterior articulation. Their windows and arcades signalled the emergence in the fourteenth century of a new Mediterranean spirit in west and north-west Anatolia, very different from the fortress-like introverted mosques of the central Anatolian steppe built by the Seljuqs of Rum – mosques that often translated brick prototypes with elaborately decorated flat surfaces into stone without exploiting its sculptural massing possibilities. Whereas tile revetments, attributed to a new generation of itinerant Iranian workshops, continued to be used inside, a general reduction of external ornament, subordinated to architectonic outlines, became the rule. After earlier experiments with Byzantine brick masonry, stone reasserted itself as the prestigious material of monumental mosque architecture, implying a shift in taste and identity that transcended material factors. The sudden appearance of the arcaded courtyard – a feature imported from Syria, but possibly inspired by the local Aegean tradition of classical atriums – once again demonstrated the powerful role of innovation.

The Ottoman Empire (1453–1923)

Istanbul, with its strategic site and imperial past, was the natural capital for an empire that united Anatolia and the Balkans. Here the Ottomans would create mosques on a grand scale, clearly differentiated from the modest-sized Friday mosques of the ruling élite and small urban *masjids*. Hierarchies of social status determined the mosque forms appropriate for various levels of patronage, from sultanic to royal (princes, princesses, sultanas), grand vizirial, vizirial and so on down the social ladder. Such hierarchies became even more clearly pronounced under Ottoman rule, reaching a peak in the time of the celebrated architect Koca Sinan, who served as Chief Royal Architect from 1538 to 1588. The unprecedented centralization of building construction associated with the establishment of the Hassa Mimarları (Corps of Royal Architects) meant that the earlier pattern of decentralized patronage was at an end. Architects trained in the capital spread the Ottoman imperial style across the empire, which by then extended from central Europe to western Iran and dominated the whole eastern Mediterranean basin. This style no longer represented the regionalism of a frontier principality absorbing rather than generating influences, but a trans-regional idiom expressing the hegemony of a world empire.

The imperial court's attention was largely fixed on Istanbul and to a lesser extent on Edirne, which remained a secondary capital. The hierarchy reflected in mosques of different patronage levels was also seen in the gap that separated the centre of the empire from its periphery. Smaller and less experimental mosques with standardized ground-plans were typical of the provinces, where local building traditions informed the treatment of elevations, especially in the Arab lands (Syria, Egypt, North Africa) that had a pre-existing Islamic architectural tradition. In the Balkans, Ottoman mosques of stone, often consisting of a single domed unit with three or five domed porticos and a minaret, were clearly distinct from Byzantine brick churches painted with figural murals. Their lead-covered hemispherical domes and pencil-like minarets with conical lead caps became distinctive signs of Ottoman-Islamic rule. In the recently conquered Balkans, where the ringing of church bells was banned, the minaret used for the call to prayer continued to be a visible symbol of the victory of Islam.

Among the numerous Ottoman mosques that have survived, those built for the sultans best exemplify the bold structural and aesthetic innovations of the classical period. The earliest sultanic mosque complex (1463–70), built in Istanbul for Mehmet II by the architect Atik Sinan, represents a revolutionary architectural statement, the first in a series of such complexes to crown the hills of Istanbul. Unlike his forebears, who built both Great Mosques and charitable complexes grouped around smaller T-type mosques, Mehmet merged the functions of these two building types in his monumental scheme, the nucleus of which was a Great Mosque, the Fatih Cami. The Great Mosque was now personalized by association with the sultan's mausoleum, a novel combination that would be repeated in other mosque complexes named after individual Ottoman sultans. Built on the symbolically charged hilltop site of Constantine's Church of the

Holy Apostles (burial place of the Byzantine emperors), the funerary mosque complex of Mehmet II was the largest Ottoman imperial foundation up to that point. With its symmetrically organized dependencies, this rationally planned socio-religious complex departed from the loose organization of its predecessors. Its unprecedented composition recalled the ideal city plans proposed in Renaissance architectural treatises, and these must have been available to Mehmet II through the Italian architects he had invited to his court. Noting a possible Italian connection, the late Spiro Kostof wrote: 'Nothing so early in the Western Renaissance has this grandeur.'[11]

Standing on an immense piazza-like terrace raised on vaulted substructures, the complex is composed along a grand axis of bilateral symmetry, passing through the monumental portals of the marble forecourt and the mosque and culminating in the *mihrab*, behind which were the tombs of the sultan and his wife in a garden. The axial alignment of *muqarnas*-hooded marble portals with a marble *mihrab* echoing the same shape strengthens the interpretation of the latter as a symbolic gate to paradise, represented by the funerary garden. Contemporary sources emphasize the paradisal allusions of the garden, the marble forecourt with four cypresses around a *kauthar*-like fountain and the eight *madrasas* recalling the 'eight paradises', in the midst of which rose the mosque's 'dome of heaven'.[12]

The majestic horizontal axis is counterbalanced by the vertical emphasis of the mosque's domed baldachin flanked by two slender minarets with conical caps. The bubbling silhouette of the much lower dependencies, featuring serial combinations of the domed cube, were completely dominated by the large dome of the mosque. The reconstructed plan of the original mosque (which was rebuilt with alterations after suffering severe damage in the earthquake of 1766) shows that it expanded the scheme of Üç Şerefeli by adding a half-dome over the *mihrab*. The new elements incorporated into its design included, on the left of the *mihrab*, a royal tribune raised on columns to highlight the secluded monarch's majesty, and selective forms inspired

Hagia Sophia, Istanbul, the imperial Byzantine church which was converted to a mosque after the conquest of the city by the Ottomans in 1453, and which inspired the design of major imperial mosques.

by Hagia Sophia (the ultimate imperial symbol, by then converted into a Great Mosque), such as the half-dome and the colossal arched tympana pierced with windows used to raise the central dome to an unprecedented height.

The mosque marked the beginning of an imperial age that had to develop its own architectural idiom. Writing in the late fifteenth century, the historian Tursun Beg recorded: 'And he [Mehmet II] built a Great Mosque based on the design of Hagia Sophia, which not only encompassed all the arts of Hagia Sophia, but moreover incorporated modern features constituting a fresh new idiom unequalled in beauty.'[13] His ashlar-masonry building synthesized selected elements quoted from Hagia Sophia's brick architecture with a well-established tradition of Ottoman architectural forms, here monumentalized in an unprecedented manner. With its blending of Italian, Byzantine and Ottoman elements, the mosque reflected an experimental search for an appropriate architectural iconography expressive of a universal Islamic empire ruled from Constantinople, the New Rome, by a sultan who styled himself *Kayser-i Rum* – the Roman Caesar.

The search for an imperial architectural idiom ended when Sinan became Chief Royal Architect to Süleyman I (the Magnificent; reigned 1520–66). His series of royal mosques, beginning with the Şehzade Mehmet complex, assert the confident self-image of an empire by then at the peak of its power. The sultan's vast funerary mosque complex – the Süleymaniye (1550–7) – on the third hill of Istanbul reinterpreted Mehmet II's scheme in the classical style. Like its model, the Süleymaniye complex is defined by a strong processional axis culminating in the *mihrab* and passing through the sultan's tomb in a funerary garden behind it. Its numerous small-domed dependencies, skilfully layered on stepped platforms, again emphasize the primacy of the mosque's colossal dome, flanked by two half-domes that obviously allude to Hagia Sophia. The mosque's central theme has been defined as a 'structural criticism' and 'rationalization' of Hagia Sophia's scheme with a new spatial definition.[14] Its side-aisles, each covered by five domes of alternating sizes, are blended with the central domed baldachin, whereas in Hagia Sophia they are screened off. In contrast to Hagia Sophia's dim, mysteriously lit interior covered with glittering mosaics, decoration in Süleymaniye's light-filled white interior is subordinated to a rigorous geometrization and articulation of architectonic structure. The white ground of the underglaze-painted Iznik tiles accentuating the *qibla* wall matches the whiteness of the marble revetments and the limestone masonry, and marks the invention of a new decorative canon characteristic of Sinan's mosques.

Externally, Süleymaniye's harmoniously stratified superstructure, constituting a pyramidal cascade of smaller domes around the mighty central baldachin, blended stepped buttresses, lateral arcades and multi-tiered windows, differs considerably from the heavily buttressed massive appearance of Hagia Sophia. While the dome resting on four piers and the four minarets were associated by contemporary writers with the Prophet (the 'dome of Islam') surrounded by the first four Caliphs (the pillars of Sunni theology), these forms also had dynastic resonances: the domed baldachin continued to evoke royal associations

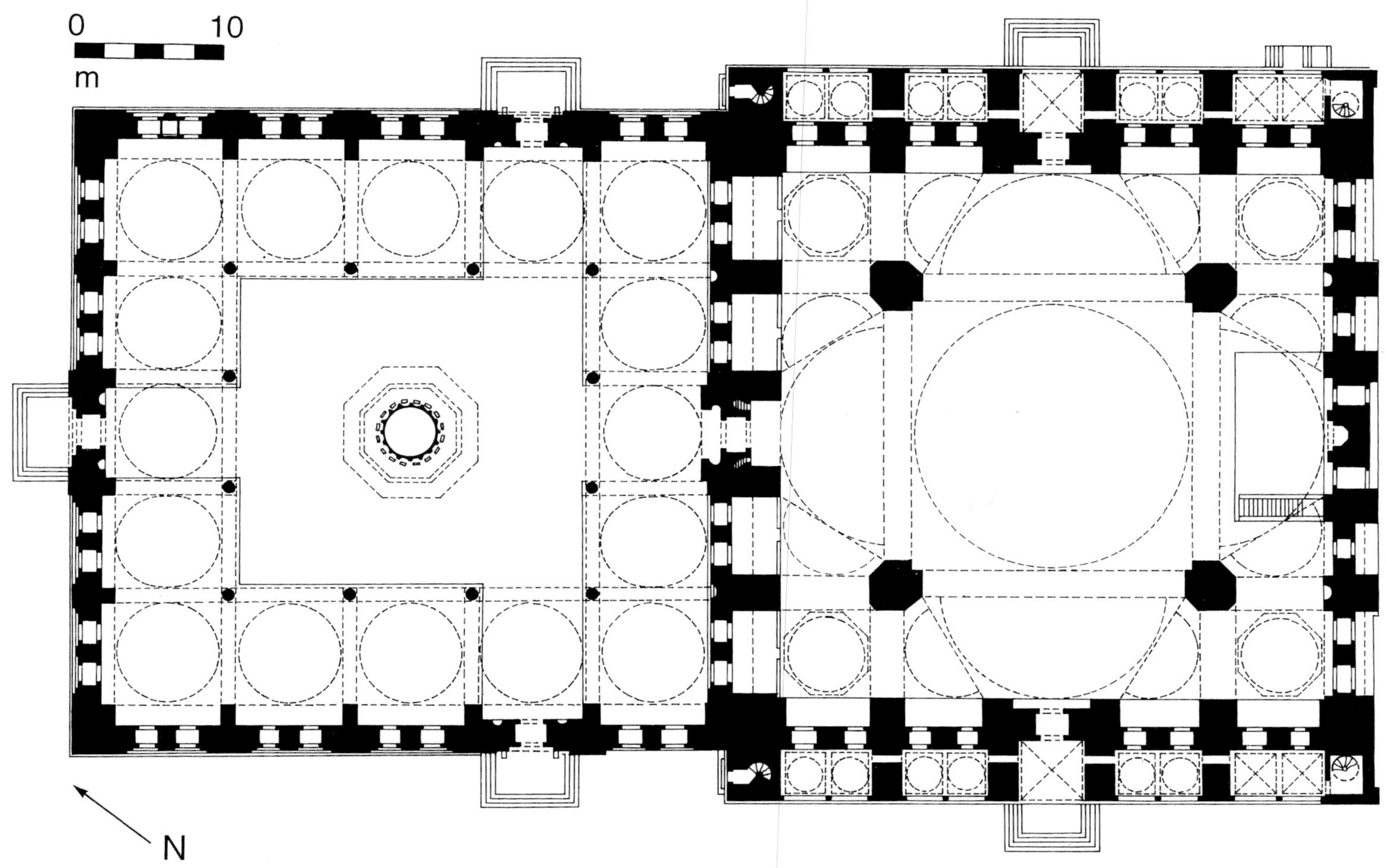

Plan of the Şehzade Mehmet Mosque (mid-sixteenth century), Istanbul; the first major work by Sinan, this building was a memorial to a much-lamented son of Sultan Süleyman I. The courtyard and mosque are both symmetrically arranged and are equal in area.

and the ten minaret balconies (3 + 3 + 2 + 2) were recognized by contemporaries as referring to Süleyman's position as tenth Ottoman ruler since the foundation of the dynasty.[15]

In the Süleymaniye regal and sacred layers of meaning were inextricably enmeshed to communicate the unification of the sultanate and the caliphate. The colossal domed space that dwarfed the visitor signalled the new identity of the Ottoman sultan as protector of Sunni Islam. Gone was the modest frontier principality with its lack of concern for religious orthodoxy reflected in the patronage of small-scale multi-functional T-type mosques. The Süleymaniye's exclusively Qur'anic inscriptions stressed the prescriptions of the *sharia* concerning the observance of ritual duties which would ensure orthodox Muslims a place in paradise and aptly expressed the official Sunni ideology of the Ottoman state.[16]

Sinan's other great imperial commission was the Selimiye Mosque (1569–75) in Edirne, built for Selim II. It too is raised on a vaulted platform, but has only a few dependencies. Its grand dome framed by four slender minarets can be seen from almost any vantage point in the city. In Sinan's autobiography (which he dictated in his old age) the architect criticizes the 'tower-like' triple-balconied minaret, with its three spiralling staircases, of the earlier Üç Şerefeli Mosque. That minaret had until then been the tallest in the Ottoman sphere, and Sinan boasts of having improved on it in the taller and narrower minarets of the Selimiye, two of which also feature three separate staircases.[17]

If the Süleymaniye was Sinan's reformulation of Hagia Sophia's overall scheme in an Ottoman idiom, the Selimiye – judging from the architect's autobiography – was his response to the challenge of its dome, the size of which had not been equalled in the Muslim era. The Selimiye's colossal dome does equal the diameter of Hagia Sophia's elliptical dome[18] and Sinan stressed that achievement by eliminating the dependencies, cascading smaller domes and half-domes which might have competed with it. He further accentuated the central domed baldachin by eight short pointed turrets, the whole mosque being framed by four perfectly symmetrical fluted minarets which provide a vertical emphasis (at the Üç Şerefeli and Süleymaniye, the varied heights of the minarets placed around the courtyard had accentuated a pyramidal silhouette). Sinan thus focused attention on the closely integrated dome and minarets (once again likened in his autobiography to the Prophet Muhammad surrounded by the first four Caliphs) and singled these features out as being symbols of Islam's victory under Ottoman rule.[19]

The mosque's soaring dome supported by eight piers achieves a breathtaking unity of interior space, at the centre of which is placed a tribune (*dikka*) – a feature that interrupts the longitudinal axis which

culminates in the *mihrab* – in order to accentuate the vertical emphasis of the dome. The floating impression created by the dome (compared in Sinan's autobiography to the dome of heaven hanging with no support) recalls that of Hagia Sophia, also likened in Byzantine sources to the suspended heavenly sphere hovering above a sea of light.[20] This parallel draws attention to the microcosmic structure of the mosque, recalling the reproduction of the image of the cosmos in Byzantine churches. The walls around the domed baldachin have now come to resemble the diaphanous screens of a crystal pavilion; the unprecedented number of windows form rhythmic patches of light that have become the main decorative elements of Sinan's architecture. Glistening Iznik tile panels with floral patterns on a white ground are mainly concentrated along the *qibla* wall and the royal tribune, contributing further to the feeling of luminous transparency with their window-like arched frames suggestive of illusionistic gardens echoing the real gardens outside.

The Selimiye Mosque (1569–75), Edirne: Iznik-tile decoration in the imperial loge (left), and the interior of the courtyard.

The unity of interior space is reflected on the mosque's harmoniously articulated exterior configuration. Multi-tiered walls delineated with elaborate mouldings have supplanted the simple cubic bases of earlier mosques; rhythmically ordered tympana, arcades and varied windows with alternating red voussoirs endow the façades with a monumental palatial quality. This represents an eloquent reversal of the traditional interiorized fabric of mosque architecture, so strongly felt in the Anatolian Seljuq monuments. The Selimiye is, however, inextricably bound to the Islamic tradition; its appended courtyard gives the whole a traditional rectilinear layout, and this inevitably detracts from the perfect centralization achieved in the domed sanctuary.

Sinan's numerous small mosques, commissioned by members of the royal family and leading dignitaries, were also ingenious experiments with domed spaces, often exploiting the structural possibilities of square, hexagonal and octagonal baldachins within the confines of strictly rectilinear walls. Except for mosques with two minarets – a privilege reserved for those commissioned by members of the royal family (only sultanic mosques could have more than two) – they all feature a single minaret. None has a marble-paved courtyard surrounded by domical arcades, for this too was the sultan's prerogative. Instead, they have porches with one or two rows of columns, and sometimes a functional forecourt surrounded by domed *madrasa* rooms on three sides. Most of them feature ashlar masonry and lead-covered hemispherical domes that are smaller in diameter than their sultanic counterparts. Those of lesser patronage levels feature alternating layers of stone and brick or cheaper materials such as wood; they are either crowned by tile-covered domes or have simpler pitched roofs. These hierarchies, combined with such factors as prestige of site, originality of plan, scale, size of domes, decorative elaboration and access to talented builders or decorators, endowed a highly standardized formal vocabulary with specific messages.

In Sinan's major complexes the primacy of the mosque over its dependent structures is stressed in programmes that reflect the ethos of a ruling élite deriving its legitimacy from defending Islam and its charitable institutions on the doorstep of Europe. The majority of this élite had only recently been converted to Islam to serve as the sultan's loyal household slaves. Unlike the Mamluks, who had mostly supported charitable funerary complexes dominated by *madrasas* or *khanaqahs*, the Ottoman élite chose to build mosque complexes (miniature versions of sultanic establishments) as signs of piety. Usually financed by spoils from the holy war, these complexes supported by rich *waqfs* contributed to the Islamicization of territories with a predominantly Christian or recently converted population, unlike the Mamluk lands long since incorporated into the Muslim world.[21]

In the post-classical age mosques continued to outnumber other religious buildings, but grand royal complexes became rare after the construction of the Sultan Ahmet I (1609–17) and Yeni Valide (1598–1663)[22] Mosques in Istanbul. The latter, which reinterpret the quatrefoil scheme of Sinan's first major work, the Şehzade Mehmet Mosque, with a new theatrical emphasis, are generally dismissed as somewhat unimaginative paraphrases of the classical idiom. Their 'baroque' flair, however, did appeal to a new aesthetic sensibility.

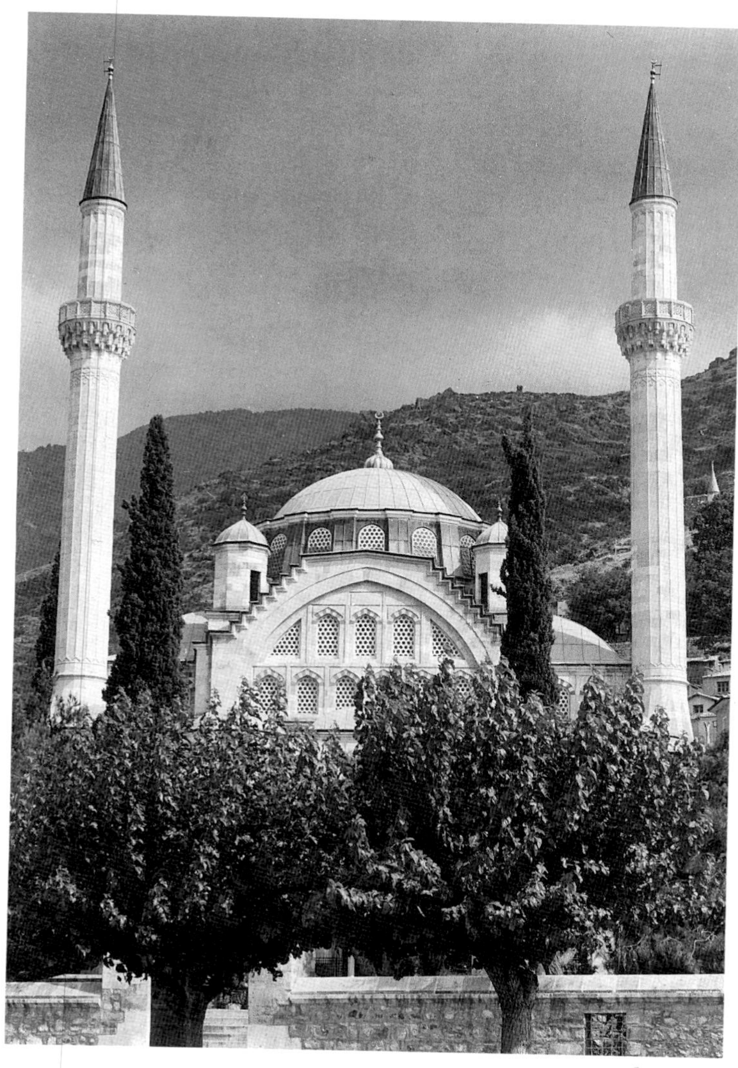

The Muradiye Mosque (1586), Manisa: this example of an Ottoman royal foundation with twin minarets was designed by Sinan but completed only after his death.

Thus, Evliya Çelebi, writing in the mid-seventeenth century, singled out the Sultan Ahmet Mosque as the most beautiful of Istanbul's sultanic mosques, so suggesting that different aesthetic criteria were at work. Not only the tastes but also the strict observance of hierarchies of status codified in the classical age began to be eroded with the changing social order. For example, the Yeni Valide Mosque, with its monumental domed baldachin and arcaded marble courtyard, exemplifies the unprecedented power of the Queen Mother, who could now adopt symbols once restricted to sultanic mosques. Aside from a few exceptions like the Nurosmaniye (1755) and Laleli (1759–63) mosque complexes in Istanbul, small-scale mosques with one or two minarets became the rule as architects turned their attention to reinvigorating the traditional Ottoman idiom with fresh new European decorative elements. The legacy of the classical Ottoman synthesis, however, remained potent. It is now felt once again in the modern Turkish outburst of mosque-building activity which takes as its model Sinan's domed structures, even in the once modest district mosques that now boast such former sultanic prerogatives as twin minarets and monumental domes.

- 9 -
THE INDIAN SUBCONTINENT

PERWEEN HASAN

When the British Raj in India ended in 1947, the country was partitioned, and the eastern and western provinces with a Muslim majority formed a new country, Pakistan. In 1971, after a bloody civil war, the eastern wing broke away and became the independent state of Bangladesh.

From time immemorial invaders entered India through the north-western mountain passes and joined the ranks of the culturally and ethnically diverse people of the subcontinent. Although Muslim invasions began in the eighth century, supremacy was established only in the eleventh, twelfth and thirteenth centuries, first in Lahore, then in Delhi, and later in most of northern India. Even at this time, India could boast of a rich artistic tradition going back almost two thousand years. Inevitably, over such a vast area, with such great variety of terrain and climate – ranging from monsoon jungles to arid deserts and in the Himalayas the highest mountain peaks in the world – there already existed distinct regional techniques and forms in architecture. As the cradle of two great religions – Hinduism and Buddhism – the land was far from being a cultural or artistic *tabula rasa*, for the fame of India's temples had spread well beyond her frontiers.

To the newly arrived Muslims the temples, which differed from region to region, and the multiplicity of deities resembled nothing that they had ever encountered before. Built mostly of stone, the temples had dark mysterious interiors with attention focused on the central shrine, the womb-like chamber housing the icon, from which all but the Brahmin priests who performed the rituals were excluded. It was in the treatment of the walls that the native craftsmen excelled, the total effect of the temple being, in most cases, more sculptural than architectural. Often, the walls and ceiling were so heavily encrusted with sculpture that they resembled rugged mountains or caves which were believed to be the natural habitats of the divinities. This concept of space was in total contrast to the Muslim idea that the mosque must be open, functional, large enough to facilitate congregational prayer, and of course bereft of imagery.

In spite of such fundamental differences, Muslim architecture capitalized on the ancient traditions of the Indian masons. As Islam took root in India by developing many syncretistic ideas, the new architecture became eclectic. In every region that was conquered, building activity passed through three different stages before the Indo-Islamic style could begin to crystallize. The first was short-lived and violent, as new Muslim rulers committed the political act of destroying the temples. The second stage followed quickly, as destroyed sites became quarries for cut stone which was re-used to build mosques and tombs. Carved figures were sometimes defaced, or the sculpted surfaces turned inwards, but hardly any effort was made to hide the source of the building material. The third stage commenced when the Muslims had become established and felt settled; during this time, building materials were prepared specially for individual structures, salvaged material being used only rarely.

Following a rough chronological scheme, the Muslim architecture of India may be divided into three main styles. First there is the Delhi or Imperial Style, from the close of the twelfth century to the middle of the sixteenth, at which point another distinctive imperial style, the Mughal, takes over (see below). Politically, right from the advent of Muslim rule, there was a tendency among the governors of far-flung provinces to break away from the central authority of Delhi. The resulting perpetual tension and interaction is well reflected in the architecture of both Delhi and the provinces, for while many features of the Imperial style were reproduced in the provinces, several regional characteristics found their way into the capital. Thus, in the fourteenth century the provincial style of the Punjab, centred in Lahore and Multan, exerted a powerful influence on the architecture of the Tughluqs in Delhi.

The second style, labelled 'Provincial', refers to buildings in the more self-contained areas after governors had declared local independence. In these areas a more effective coalescence with the local culture was manifest than in Delhi, and the style was truly formulated during the fifteenth century. At that time the independent kingdoms became powerful, and their capitals were centres of Muslim learning and culture. This was achieved at the expense of the Delhi Sultanate, which disintegrated after the collapse of the Tughluq dynasty in the wake of Timur's sack of Delhi in 1398. The flowering of the provinces was contemporary partly with the Delhi Sultanate, and partly with the beginning of Mughal rule in 1526.

The sources of the distinctive provincial styles were both Imperial and regional vernacular, the decisive factor being the latter. Consequently, the most elegant styles developed in areas where indigenous art traditions were strong and local artisans were highly skilled. Thus regional or provincial styles of mosque architecture grew out of local temple and domestic styles, which were conditioned in their turn by terrain, climate and materials, hence the enormous difference between the mosques of Bengal and Kashmir or Gujarat. The traditional hypostyle plan with enclosed courtyard, imported from western Asia and generally associated with the introduction of Islam into new areas, was in many cases abandoned in favour of schemes more suited to local

Facing page
The prayer-hall of the Moti Masjid (Pearl Mosque) in the Red Fort, Delhi (see p. 170).

Map 5: the Indian subcontinent, showing principal sites.

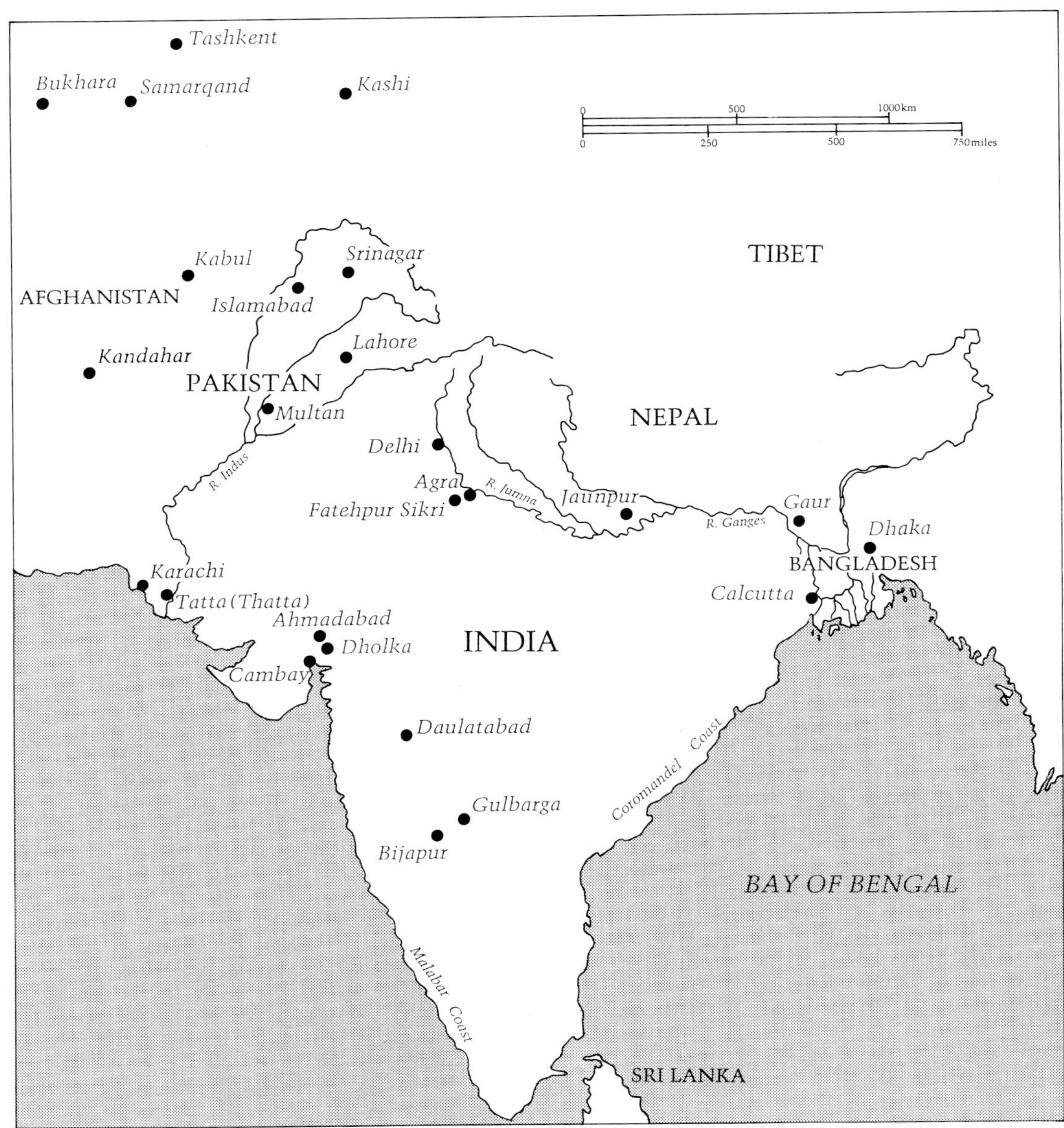

climate and needs. On rare occasions, experienced foreign craftsmen would come to a court, bringing with them a different architectural style which, depending on preference of the local ruler, might be accepted or rejected.

The Mughal style – the last and most mature of the Indo-Islamic architectural styles – started in the imperial capitals of Delhi, Agra and Fatehpur Sikri in the sixteenth century, and appeared in the provinces as, one by one, they were brought under the Mughal aegis. Although there were special features in every provincial context which were rooted in the vernacular tradition, the Mughal style has a universality by which it can be recognized anywhere. All mosques are oriented in an east-west direction, with the *qibla* on the west side and main entrances generally on the east.

The sites chosen for discussion represent the main provincial styles within the subcontinent. Delhi stands at the centre, while to the east in Bengal lies Gaur, the medieval city now divided by the international border between India and Bangladesh; and to the north, the cities of Srinagar and Lahore; to the west Tatta and Ahmadabad; and to the south, Bijapur. Key monuments have been chosen either as representing a particular mosque type, or on account of their regional or other unique qualities.

Gaur

The long, narrow city, now ruined, ran from north to south between the Ganges and Mahananda rivers; the walled portion of the city and the inner citadel to the north are in Malda district of West Bengal, India, while the southern suburb known as Chhota Sona Masjid, after the most important monument in the area, is in Nawabganj district, Bangladesh.

Geographically, the whole of Bengal (West Bengal, India, and East Bengal, now Bangladesh) is a delta formed by two great river systems, the Ganges and the Brahmaputra. The low-lying land, shifting river channels, heavy rainfall and recurrent floods have for centuries had a profound effect on the lives of Bengalis and on their art and architecture.

Before the twelfth century, when Gaur became the capital of the Sena dynasty of Bengal and was named Lakshmanavati after King Lakshmansena, Gauda was the name of a kingdom comprising the city and surrounding areas. The city remained the capital after the Muslims captured parts of Bengal in the early thirteenth century, and was known to Muslim historians as Lakhnawti. Lakhnawti became one of the three administrative units established by Sultan Ghiyath-ud-Din Tughluq (1320–5), who divided the region to facilitate control from Delhi; the two other units, Satgaon and Sonargaon, were placed under separate governorships.

From 1338 Bengal was ruled by successive dynasties of independent sultans, the first of which, the Ilyas Shahis, moved the capital to nearby Pandua, where it remained for about a century. In the middle of the fifteenth century, the capital was moved back to Gaur by restored Ilyas Shahi rulers and until the end of the sixteenth century it remained for most of the time the seat of power. It became a thriving urban centre which the Mughal Emperor Humayun renamed Jannatabad or 'Abode of Paradise' in the early sixteenth century, but decline set in after its sack by the Afghan Sher Shah Sur in 1539. By the time Bengal was consolidated into the Mughal Empire in the early seventeenth century, the capital had been shifted to Rajmahal, and the golden era of Gaur had passed. It was finally abandoned when the rivers changed course. No buildings remain from the earliest periods of Muslim occupation. All the extant structures date from the restored Ilyas Shahi (1437–87), Husayn Shahi (1494–1539) and Mughal periods, hence they do not represent the formative stages of the Bengal style. Most of the monuments originally bore inscriptions, but the tablets found among the rubble were sometimes fixed quite arbitrarily to old or new buildings, and others have been removed to museums in Calcutta, Malda, Dhaka, London, and even Philadelphia. The buildings of Gaur illustrate how mosque architecture was combined with adapted elements found mostly in the indigenous tradition. This was possible thanks to the liberal attitude of the Ilyas and Husayn Shahi dynasties, who allowed a local Muslim culture to flourish.

From ancient times brick has been the primary building material in the Bengal delta. When used occasionally as a facing or as pillars for structural support, stone had to be transported from the Rajmahal Hills of Bihar – some 250 km (150 miles) to the west – or re-used from older buildings. Generally, only the two faces of the thick brick walls were of dressed masonry and lime mortar, the core being less carefully constructed from brick and mud. The heavy monsoon rains made it essential that buildings should be entirely covered. Mosques are either large and rectangular in plan or small and square, sometimes with a veranda in front. There were no enclosed courtyards, but a grassy court was laid out in front and often there was a large tank (dug so that the earth excavated from it could be used to build up the foundation and raise the building above flood levels). During the entire Muslim period in Bengal, the Adina Mosque of Hazrat Pandua, built in 1375 by Sultan Sikandar Shah, was the only one in which the traditional courtyard plan was used. The square single-domed building, modelled on the thatched bamboo huts of the vernacular tradition, was a ubiquitous type used for mosques as well as for gateways and tombs.

The earliest building of this type with features which became standardized in the Bengal style was the Eklakhi Tomb in Pandua, traditionally considered to be the mausoleum of Sultan Jalal-ud-Din (d. 1431), the converted son of the Bengali Hindu ruler, Raja Ganesh. The typical mosque of the Sultanate period was a ponderous looking building of brick with engaged corner-towers (but no minarets), low façades, and a single dome or multiple shallow domes to cover a small square, or larger hypostyle, interior. The cornice is curved in the manner of the eaves of the bamboo-and-thatch huts of the countryside. The shape of the entire thatched roof, whether consisting of two segments (*do-chala*) or four (*chau-chala*), was sometimes reproduced as vaults for ornamental purposes.

The buildings reflect the absence of any need for monumental symbols and fit in very well with local culture, which even in pre-Islamic times generally lacked structures on a monumental scale, the Buddhist monasteries of Paharpur and Mainamati being rare exceptions. The sultans no longer had the air of foreign rulers whose buildings must symbolize political power or the majesty of religion. These mosques of modest size suggest that the Muslims had begun to feel accepted in Bengal. Instead of trying to impress people with imposing architecture, they concentrated on their own ritual needs by building small, practical mosques which fitted in with the local building tradition.

There are multiple *mihrabs* in the *qibla* wall, one corresponding to each doorway; this recalls the convention of a doorway corresponding to a niche for an image in a temple. In contrast to the plastered and otherwise plain surfaces of the later Sultanate buildings of North India, their counterparts in Bengal featured fancy brickwork and terracotta decoration; this convention goes back to the richly decorated terracotta plaques of Paharpur and Mainamati, which speak for the existence of a lively folk tradition.

In the pre-Islamic period any sculptor who made religious images of imported stone had enjoyed a higher status than a maker of terracotta. The Muslims, who had no use for stone images, reversed that artistic judgment by commissioning lavishly decorated mosques. By making terracotta decoration a medium in which excellence was sought, they accorded it a status that it had hitherto not enjoyed. The larger mosques have, situated in the north-west corner, a raised platform (*takht*) which served both as an enclosure for use by women worshippers and as a *maqsura* for royalty.

The Darasbari Mosque, now ruined, is in the southern suburb of the walled city of Gaur, on the Bangladeshi side of the border; its name, which literally means 'school', is derived from the *madrasa* which once adjoined the mosque. The building is associated with an inscription recording the construction of a Friday mosque by Yusuf Shah in 1479. The prayer-hall has a wide central bay once covered by three *chau-chala* vaults, with a multi-domed wing on either side. The veranda in front also has a *chau-chala* vaulted central bay flanked by domed side bays. There was a *maqsura* platform in the north-west corner, approached by a flight of steps on the exterior. The terracotta decoration that fills the tympana of the *mihrabs* in the interior is remarkable for its liveliness and deep relief.

The Chhota Sona Mosque, another Friday mosque, was constructed during the reign of Husayn Shah (1493–1519) by a noble, Wali Muhammad. The name, meaning 'little golden mosque', refers to the former gilding on its domes. It is a rectangular mosque of three transverse aisles each with five bays, the wider central nave being covered by *chau-chala* vaults. The exterior of the brick walls is faced with grey basalt, the surface of which is carved to emulate contemporary terracotta designs. The stone platform in the north-west corner has an entrance on that side.

The Lattan Mosque on the Indian side, datable to the late fifteenth or early sixteenth century, is composed of a single-domed square prayer-hall preceded by a veranda, which has a central *chau-chala* vault flanked by small domes. The exterior is articulated by recessed arched panels imitating *mihrabs*, and the entire surface was once covered with multi-coloured glazed tiles (of which substantial traces remain only in the interior). A more modest version is the Rajbibi Mosque located in the suburb of the walled city, in Bangladesh. Small and without any tile decoration, it represents the most common type of Sultanate mosque, which in its simplest form did not even have a veranda in front.

In contrast to the buildings of the Sultanate period, which have a marked regional character, Mughal buildings are constructed within the imperial tradition, but are more subdued than contemporary architecture elsewhere in the subcontinent. Like the Sultanate

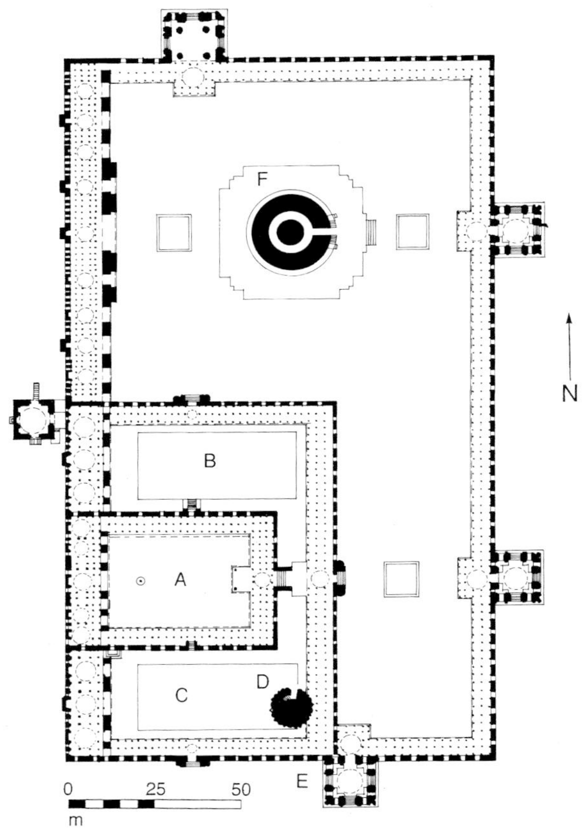

Site plan showing the original Quwwat al-Islam (A), Delhi, flanked by later extensions (B, C). The south-eastern extension embraced the massive minaret known as the Qutb Minar (D; shown on the right), completed in 1199. The entrance pavilion, Alai Darwaza (E), was added in 1311 as part of a project to double the mosque's area, including a second minaret (F) which was never completed.

prototypes, they consist only of a prayer-hall, but are single-aisled with three or five bays. The exterior surfaces are plastered and panelled, the cornices are straight, and the buildings look less ponderous because of their higher domes.

The Mosque of Shah Nimat Allah, on the south-western side of the tomb of the saint, near the Chhota Sona Mosque, is a typical Mughal mosque of the three-domed type. The interior is divided into three bays by lateral arches. The building is datable to the seventeenth century on the basis of stylistic similarities with contemporary mosques in Rajmahal, India. It features a plastered exterior articulated with recessed arches, straight cornice with merlon decoration and high domes with lotus finials, all in marked contrast to the earlier architecture of Gaur.

Delhi

Strategically situated between the Aravalli Hills and the River Jumna, in the province of Uttar Pradesh, the capital of India was mentioned by the Alexandrian geographer Ptolemy, who visited India in the second century. Traditionally, however, its history goes back 3,000 years to the age of the Mahabharata. The fact that eight major cities, including New Delhi of more recent times, have stood on this site is evidence of its continuous importance. Unfortunately, little is known of its history prior to the Muslim conquest. The first city is believed to have been founded by the Tomara Rajputs in the early eighth century.

Qutb-ud-Din Aibak, a slave of Muhammad bin Sam of Ghor in Afghanistan and Viceroy over his master's territories in India, captured Delhi from the Chauhans in 1193.[1] Almost immediately he started to build a mosque in Qila Rai Pithora, the stronghold of Rai Pithora Prithviraj Chauhan. This mosque, known as Quwwat al-Islam (Might of Islam), was built on the platform of a demolished temple; its plan was the classic hypostyle hall with courtyard, generally associated with the introduction of Islam into new areas. Representing the initial stages of activity prior to the formation of a proper Indo-Islamic style, it was built using material salvaged from the ruins of twenty-seven Hindu and Jain temples, the fourth-century iron pillar from a Vishnu temple being left *in situ* in the courtyard. The central courtyard was surrounded by arcades of lavishly carved Hindu columns superimposed to increase the height of the re-used ceilings. Many of the icons are still intact. The 'domes' over the *mihrab* and entrance bays are the shallow corbelled vaults of lantern ceilings, plastered over on the exterior to create a smooth profile.

Although the plan and the Muslim architectural forms were new, the Hindu masons followed their own trabeated structural and decorative traditions. The excellence of their craftsmanship is noticeable in the vegetal scrolls and lotus patterns, and in the execution of the unfamiliar Qur'anic script in *naskhi* on the freestanding screen of 1191. Built of red sandstone, and made up of five corbelled arches, the screen was set up in front of the western arcade to emphasize the direction of the *qibla*. Simultaneously, Qutb-ud-Din laid the foundation of the enormous minaret known as Qutb Minar to the south-east of the mosque. The minaret, 72.50 m (238 ft) high, was built not only for use by the muezzin when delivering the call to prayer, but as a victory tower and symbol of the new religion.

Detail of the entrance portico of the Alai Darwaza, the first building to reflect the introduction of an Indo-Islamic style.

In 1206, after the death of Muhammad Ghori, Qutb-ud-Din enthroned himself as the first Sultan of Hindustan, and both Lahore and Delhi functioned as military headquarters. The rise of Delhi and the consequent decline of Lahore set in with the reign of Iltutmish (1211–36), Qutb-ud-Din's son-in-law and successor, who was invested with the powers of an Islamic king by emissaries of the Abbasid caliph. Soon Delhi became the greatest centre of Islamic learning and culture in the east, and with brief intervals remained the focal point of politics till 1857. Using similar building materials and techniques, Iltutmish enlarged Qutb-ud-Din's mosque symmetrically on the north and south sides so that the minaret was incorporated into the southern court.

Ala-ud-Din (1296–1316), the third ruler of the Khalji dynasty of Afghan Turks, built the second city, Siri, but died before his project to double the size of the Quwwat al-Islam could be completed. He did, however, build the Alai Darwaza (1311), the monumental entrance pavilion on the south side, which marks a milestone in the development of Muslim architecture in India. The break-up of the Seljuq empire in western Asia and resulting migration of professionals to neighbouring lands was perhaps responsible for the novelties of Persian origin first noticed here. The earliest building in India to be conceived on Islamic principles of construction, it illustrates how Hindu masons were taking to imported forms and embarking on an Indo-Islamic style.

The Jamaat Khana Mosque (1325), located to the west of the tomb of Hazrat Nizam-ud-Din Awliya, repeats several features of the Alai Darwaza. Faced with red sandstone, it has similar horseshoe-shaped arches with keystone, voussoir, and spearhead fringe, nook-shafts, recessed planes and elaborate calligraphic ornament. (Its side compartments are so ill-related to the central square chamber that they are considered to be later additions.)

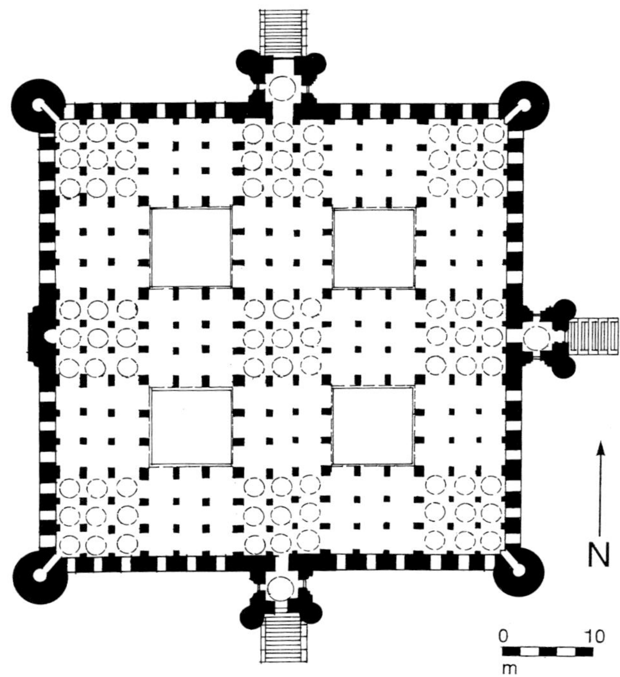

Plan of the Khirki Mosque (c. 1375), Delhi, a striking example of a cross-axial scheme, with projecting gateways on three sides creating a fortress-like appearance.

Tughluq rule from the early fourteenth century is marked by great creativity, eclecticism and experimentation in architecture. Its founder, Ghiyath-ud-Din, had been governor of the Punjab, and the brick tradition of that region influenced the style of the battered walls associated with Tughluq stone architecture. Three successive capitals – Tughluqabad, Jahanpanah and Firuzabad – were built in this period. The sponsor of the last of these was Firuz Shah (1351–88), who is famous as a prolific builder. During his reign four distinct types of mosque plans were developed: the standard hypostyle hall with courtyard; the two-storied plinth mosque; the cross-axial mosque; and simple prayer-halls. All are made of rubble masonry, and have plastered surfaces, battered walls and piers and low domes. Lintels placed above the opening of four-centred arches illustrate the Indian masons' lack of faith in the load-bearing capacities of the arch.

The Begumpur Friday Mosque (*c.* 1343) in Jahanpanah has a standard hypostyle plan, but is unique in that the four-*iwan* Iranian plan occurs here for the first time in India; an *iwan* and dome were placed in the middle of each of the arcades enclosing the courtyard. The arcades are protected by long stone eaves (*chhajjas*). The façade of the prayer-hall *iwan*, framed by a pair of non-functional, three-storied engaged minarets, as well as the royal *maqsura* chamber appended to the north-west side, are notable features, found also in Muslim architecture in eastern India.

Firuz Shah's Friday Mosque in the citadel of Firuzabad (*c.* 1354), now in a ruined state, is a two-storied plinth mosque, and the Khirki Mosque in Jahanpanah is of the cross-axial type. Also raised on a high plinth of vaulted cells, the latter has, on three sides, a projecting domed gateway flanked by tapering engaged minarets. Cross-axial, domed corridors divide the space into four, each quadrant enclosing a square court. The *mihrab* is revealed on the exterior by a projecting domed chamber with engaged towers. As seen from the roof, the composition of open spaces alternating with clusters of domes and flat ceiling areas is unique in Sultanate architecture.

The mosque at the tomb of Makhdum Shah Alam (*c.* 1375) at Wazirabad, which comprises a simple prayer-hall with two bays and five aisles, surmounted by three domes, is important because it was the precursor of the immensely popular five-bay, single-aisle mosque plan of a century later.

The Afghan Lodhis gained power in the middle of the fifteenth century, but the preoccupation of the rulers with combating insurgencies prevented them from launching major architectural projects. In 1504 the capital was transferred to Agra and for the next 150 years the court alternated between Agra and Delhi. Two mosques, the Bara Gumbad of 1494 in Lodhi Garden and the Moth-ki Masjid of *c.* 1500, began a series, being followed by the Jamali-Kamali Mosque (1535) and culminating in the Qila-i-Kuhna Mosque (*c.* 1540) of Sher Shah, who seized the throne from the Mughal emperor Humayun for twelve years. He built the mosque in the Purana Qila, around which the sixth city, Shergarh, was developed. The mosques, which continued the tradition of the simple prayer-hall, have features which were later developed in Mughal architecture, e.g. the five-bay plan, use of plaster and contrasting stones for surface decoration, special treatment of the central *pishtaq*, merlons, the projecting *chhajja*, and squinches and *muqarnas* in the zone of transition. Elegant four-centred arches set in well-defined rectangular frames appear with spearhead fringe, without any additional support.

Babur, a Mughal descended from both Genghis Khan and Timur, conquered Delhi in 1526 after overthrowing the Lodhi Sultan Ibrahim II; although he was critical of his new surroundings, his reign was too short and that of his son Humayun too disturbed for any serious change to be made in the architectural scene during their lifetimes. Humayun's contribution to the formation of the Mughal style was significant because, on his return from exile in Persia, he brought with him the craftsmen who would be responsible for a fusion of the Persian and Indian styles, best illustrated in the Emperor's tomb (built after his death in 1556).

Mughal architecture from the mid-sixteenth to the eighteenth century marks the most mature form of the Indo-Islamic style. Akbar (1556–1605), the third ruler of the Mughal dynasty, consolidated his

Facing page
Part of the east front of the Moti Masjid or Pearl Mosque (1662) in the Red Fort, Delhi. The small building faced with polished white marble was intended for the private worship of the Mughal Emperor Aurangzeb. Its interior was turned slightly to the south-west in order to face Mecca, while the external alignment conforms with that of the Fort, following the cardinal points of the compass. The prominent onion-shaped domes are crowned with lotus mouldings and finials. This Pearl Mosque was the last of three compact buildings of the Mughal period which owe their elegance and simplicity of style to the use of white marble. The first, in Lahore, dates from 1627–57, and the second, in the Red Fort, Agra, from 1646–53.

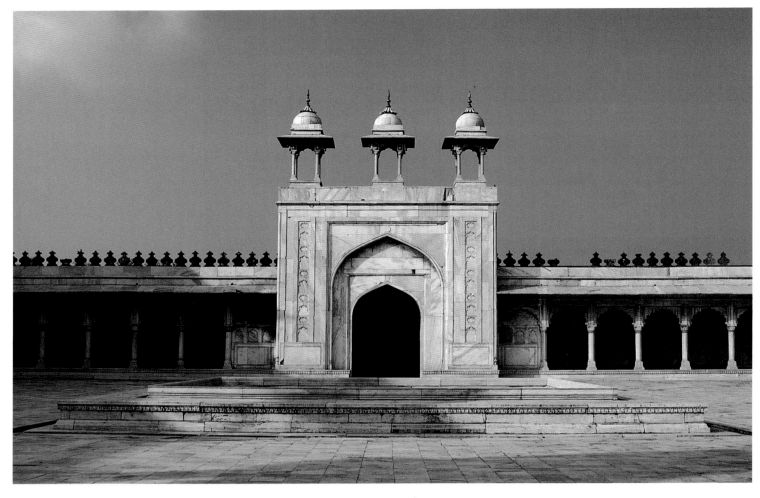

(Above) View across the courtyard of the Moti Masjid (Pearl Mosque) in the Red Fort, Agra, built 1646–53 for Shah Jehan. Beyond the central pool is the imposing entrance gateway of red sandstone.

(Below) The entrance gateway to the tomb and mosque of Ibrahim II (1615) in Bijapur is in the distinctive style of the Adil Shahi rulers, featuring slender minarets and finials topped with small domes.

(Opposite) The Jami Masjid (1571) at Fatehpur Sikri forms part of the ceremonial capital built by the Mughal emperor Akbar. Its architecture demonstrates the skilful blend of Mughal style with features of earlier indigenous Hindu and Buddhist traditions so characteristic of Akbar's reign.

Although comparatively small in scale, the red-sandstone Taj Mahal Mosque (1632–64), Agra, is representative of the classical triple-domed Mughal style; however, it has no courtyard because the building is an integral part of the mausoleum complex built by Shah Jehan in memory of his wife.

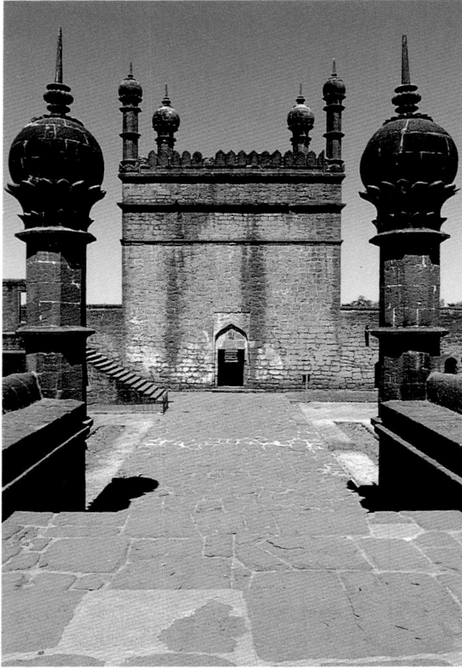

(Above) The Friday Mosque in Srinagar reflects the style of the wooden architecture typical of the mountains of Kashmir. The present mosque in brick and timber, dating from 1674, closely follows the form of the original all-timber building (1398) and two subsequent replacements, all destroyed by fire.

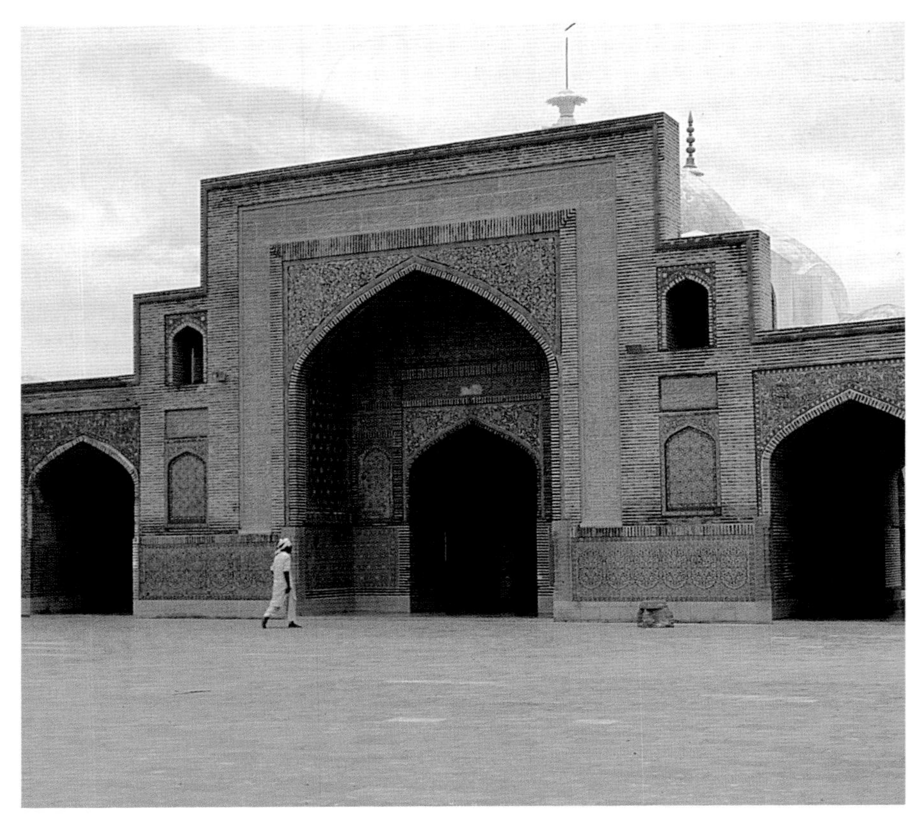

empire by conquering Malwa, Gujarat, Bengal, Khandesh, Kabul and Kandahar, and once again architecture was used as a symbol of Muslim power over people who for the most part belonged to a different creed and culture. His wide conquests were reflected in the projects sponsored by him, combining elements from earlier Timurid, Transoxanian, Persian and Indian styles. In spite of personalization by each monarch, as well as the flexibility shown towards regional characteristics and building conditions, Mughal architecture was endowed from now on with a universal quality which makes it easily recognizable in any part of the subcontinent.

In his patronage of architecture Akbar surpassed even the Tughluqs, though he did not sponsor any notable mosques in Delhi. The Khayr-al-Manazil (Best of Houses) of 1561–2, built opposite the Purana Qila by the infant Akbar's wet-nurse Maham Anga, was in the tradition of the Qila-i-Kuhna Mosque, but there were novelties such as the double-storey wings enclosing the courtyard and the imposing *pishtaq* on the east.

The Akbari style, which developed in the Sultan's secular architecture, is best illustrated in the palaces and related buildings of Fatehpur Sikri, the new capital. It is notable for a syncretism that became the hallmark of the period. Buildings were executed in red sandstone, often with marble inlays, and trabeate construction was used alongside the arcuate. Domes followed the heavy Lodhi forms, and the multi-faceted pillars had bracket supports. *Chhatris* (kiosks) were used more generously and the inner domes frequently had arch-netting in the transition zone. Interior walls and ceilings were sometimes painted with brightly coloured patterns. The workmanship of the provincial school of Gujarat is particularly noticeable. In Fatehpur Sikri's Friday Mosque (*c.* 1568–78) – the first of the great courtyard mosques of Mughal cities – the deep three-domed, trabeate prayer-hall with central *pishtaq* is reminiscent of the fifteenth-century Sultanate architecture of Jaunpur. The Buland Darwaza (1596) – a victory gate replacing one of the original entrances – featured an *iwan* of unparalleled magnificence.

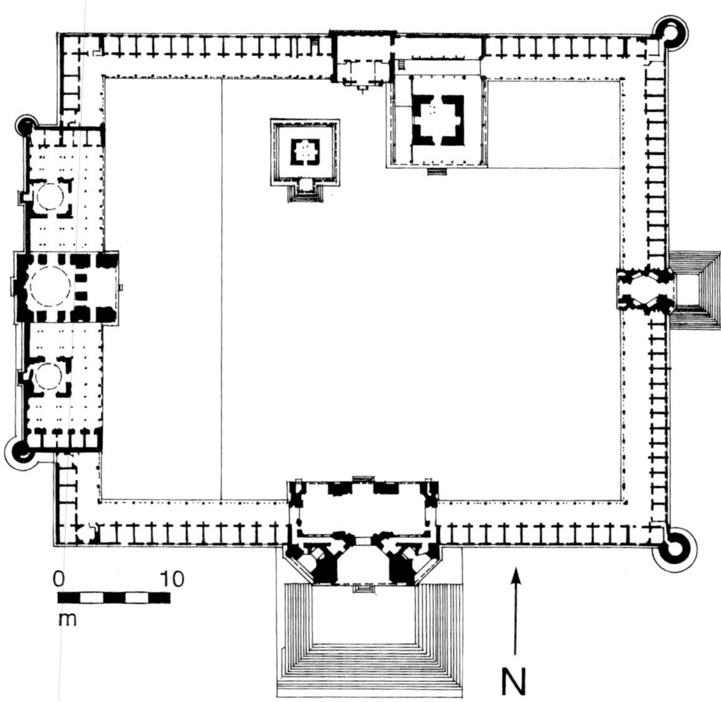

*Plan of the Friday Mosque, Fatehpur Sikri (*c. *1568–78). The colossal Buland Darwaza (victory gate) on the south side of the courtyard replaced one of the original entrances.*

The reign of Jahangir (1605–27) is considered to have been a phase of transition before the classical period of Shah Jahan. The surfaces of buildings became highly decorated, often using a variety of materials which, apart from carved sandstone, included white marble, stone intarsia, painted stucco and tilework. Stucco vaults and *muqarnas* were intricately patterned and the earlier arch-netting attained new complexities.

The classical phase of Shah Jahan's reign (1628–58), marked by symmetry and uniformity of shapes, attained new aesthetic ideals. White marble and highly polished white stucco from Gujarat replaced red sandstone, and the architectural vocabulary was reduced to a few favoured forms. The typical 'Shahjahani column' was multi-faceted and tapering, with cusped-arch or foliated base, and *muqarnas* or vegetal capital. Arches were multi-cusped, and the dome achieved a full bulbous form with constricted neck. The typical curved Bengali roof (*bangla*) with sloping lines was used to adorn palaces and throne chambers. Plaster vaults with decorative network occurred widely, as did coved ceilings used to cover rectangular halls. Naturalistic flowering plants were popular as decorative motifs, and *pietra dura* inlay replaced the earlier stone intarsia patterns. The skyline was broken by multiple minarets, of cylindrical or octagonal plan, with one or more balconies and topped by a *chhatri*.

Shah Jahan's orthodox character is revealed in his sponsorship of numerous mosques. There were two main types: the Friday mosque with massive *pishtaq* and multiple minarets, and the smaller-scale mosque in which these forms were eliminated.

Of the large city mosques the most important is the Friday Mosque (1650–6) of Shahjahanabad, the seventh city of Delhi which the

Facing page

Among the most notable mosques in modern Pakistan, one of the finest and largest examples of Mughal architecture (above) is the Badshahi Mosque (1673–4) adjacent to the Lahore Fort. It was commissioned by Shah Jahan, builder of the Taj Mahal. The prayer-hall has a prominent central portal and three white marble-covered domes contrasting with the red-sandstone façade and four corner minarets; these features, combined with a very large arcaded courtyard, produce a building characteristic of Friday mosques in the Indian subcontinent.

The Wazir Khan Mosque (below left), also in Lahore, was built in 1634, and displays a distinctly Punjabi Mughal style that reflects the influence of Safavid Iran. The walls feature rectangular decorative panels, framed by brickwork, with mosaic tilework forming floral and geometric patterns.

The Friday Mosque in Tatta (below right), in the province of Sind, was built by Shah Jehan in 1644–7. The courtyard, which has four iwans, *as well as the building's brick construction and glazed-tile decoration, as seen on the main east entrance, reflect the cultural links which existed between Sind and Iran.*

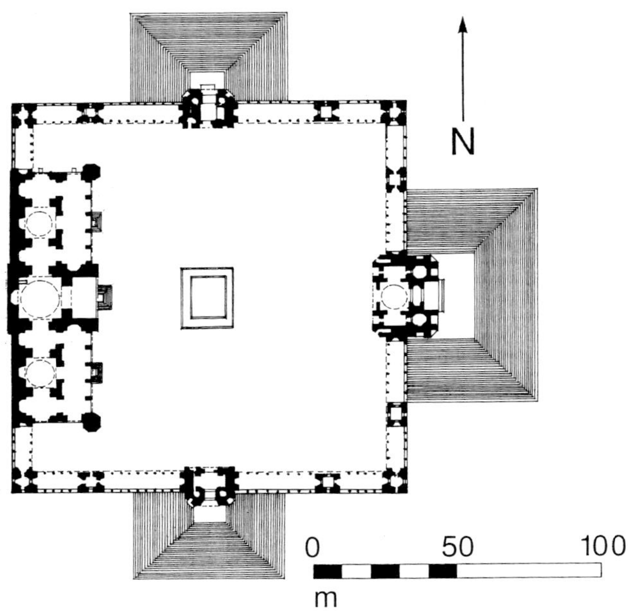

Plan of the Friday Mosque (1650–6), Delhi, showing the spacious courtyard approached by flights of steps leading to entrances on three of its sides.

Emperor had founded as a new capital. It is located across the road on the west side of the Red Fort, in the area now known as Old Delhi, and is one of the largest examples of the courtyard-style, four-*iwan* mosque in India. Strikingly faced with strips of white marble alternating with red sandstone, the building is raised on a plinth with broad flights of stairs on three sides. The central entrance salient is three storeys high with small attached minarets. The seven-bay prayer-hall is independent of the arcades surrounding the courtyard on three sides and is framed by four-stage circular minarets each surmounted by a *chhatri* matching those of the smaller minarets flanking the *pishtaq*. The rectangular halls which precede the three-bay wings of the prayer-chamber, the bulbous domes, multiple minarets with *chhatri* and the multi-cusped arches are typical features of the Shah Jahan period.

In Agra Fort the famous Moti Masjid (Pearl Mosque) was built by Shah Jahan over a seven-year period, from 1646 to 1653. Its exterior is faced with red sandstone, while the interior features veined white marble, also used for the *riwaq* around three sides of the courtyard, in the centre of which there is a large marble tank for ablutions. The prayer-hall, seven bays wide and three deep, is surmounted by three domes (symmetrically placed over the second, fourth and sixth bays of the middle row). This mosque is renowned for its simplicity and purity, both in terms of its proportions and of the use of white marble. On the east side an inlaid inscription in black marble records the dates of construction and the resemblance of the mosque to a precious pearl.

The small-scale imperial mosque intended for private use is represented by the Nagina Masjid (Gem Mosque) in Agra Fort, built by Shah Jahan for the ladies of his court; this three-domed white-marble building served as the model for the Moti Masjid (Pearl Mosque) added to the Red Fort in Delhi in 1662 by Shah Jahan's son and successor, Aurangzeb, whose architectural patronage was directed almost entirely to religious and public works. The Delhi Moti Masjid is a three-aisle, two-bay mosque of polished white marble, with a curved *bangla* vault in the central bay. The exaggeration of forms, evident in the ribbed domes with constricted necks, and the exuberance of surface decoration in marble relief were characteristic features of later Mughal architecture, which at this point was well on the road to decline.

Srinagar

The capital of the Indian province of Kashmir, Srinagar – meaning 'beautiful city' – stands on the Dal Lake and the River Jhelum; the presence of ruins of Hindu/Buddhist temples and stupas indicates that this was an important site in the pre-Muslim era. The unique wooden architecture of the region dates from the fourteenth century, when Muslim rule in the area began, and continued for 200 years until the time of Akbar, when Kashmir was consolidated into the Mughal Empire. Thanks to the readily available supply of timber in this part of the Himalayan valleys, building in wood – both domestic and monumental – became an established practice and spread even to areas such as Gilgit, Hunza and Baltistan.

Although no wooden temple of the pre-Islamic era survives, the close relationship of the typical Kashmir temple style to timber architectural forms is illustrated in the sloping and gabled roof of the stone-built Shiva Temple at Pandrethan, 5 km (3 miles) south-east of Srinagar, a structure probably dating from the ninth or tenth century. The earliest extant specimens of wooden mosques date from the fourteenth and fifteenth centuries. The form of their tiered sloping roofs resembles that of temples and points to a common source. Their architectural forms are virtually interchangeable with the tombs of saints, known locally as *ziarats*. Square in plan, these buildings are cubic in form with a tiered pyramidal roof crowned by a slender spire.[2] In mosques, a square, open pavilion is interposed at the base of the spire for the muezzin to give the call to prayer.

The building technique is unusual: instead of depending on expert joinery, as would be expected, the builders relied on gravity for the walls – just as in the ancient stone temples. The total disregard shown for economy indicates the superabundant supply of building material. Logs were laid in horizontal courses, usually cross-wise in the form of headers and stretchers, as in brickwork. Single tree-trunks of deodar, a kind of cedar available locally, were used for pillars supporting the ceilings. The inflammability of the material, resulting in frequent fires, accounts for the fact that many mosques have undergone several reconstructions.

The Mosque of Shah Hamadan, on the right bank of the River Jhelum, is a typical example of the wooden style. Originally built in 1395, it was destroyed by fire in 1479 and 1731. The two-storied building, square in plan, stands on the irregular masonry foundation of an ancient temple, and has veranda extensions with carved woodwork on the sides. Corbelled logs are used for the heavy eaves cornice. The pyramidal roof, in three tiers, is composed of rafters on which planks are laid; birch-bark is used to form a waterproof layer under the top covering of turf. Roof gardens on gates, walls and houses, and

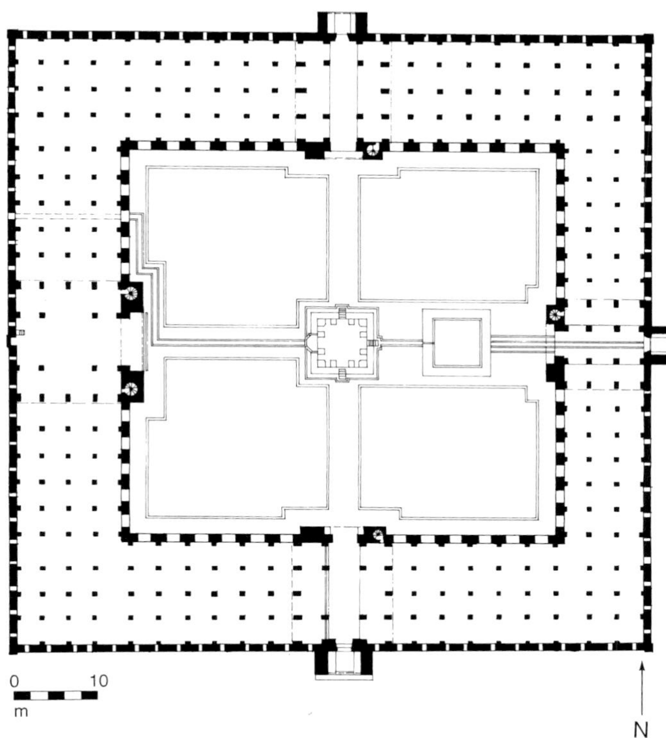

Plan of the Friday Mosque (1385; rebuilt to the original design 1674), Srinagar; the layout includes a large landscaped courtyard.

particularly the 'roof of the chief mosque' with tulips flowering in spring, fascinated the Emperor Jahangir when he visited Srinagar with his queen, Nur Jahan, in 1619. They were praised by him in his Memoirs (*Tuzuk*).[3] In the interior, the width of the originally square hall has been curtailed by small chambers on the north and south sides. The tapering pillars are eight-sided, with foliated bases and capitals, and the ceiling is painted.

The Friday Mosque is in the centre of the city, beneath Hari Parbat. Originally built in 1385 by Sultan Sikandar Butshikan, it was enlarged by his son Zainul Abedin in 1402, and subsequently destroyed by fire and rebuilt more than once. The present mosque dates from 1674, when it was rebuilt to the original design, its plan being an adaptation of the Kashmir style to the traditional enclosed courtyard type. The main entrance on the south side consists of a recessed portico which leads into the inner courtyard. The beautifully landscaped courtyard is enclosed by arched *liwans* (cloisters) covered by two-tiered sloping roofs with clerestory, supported by a total of 370 wooden pillars. Facing the courtyard in the middle of each side is a large structure with an entrance archway, surmounted by a pyramidal roof pavilion (for muezzins), and a flèche spire. Like the *iwans* of Persian mosques, one marks the central bay of the prayer-hall on the *qibla* side, while the other three function as entrance halls. Although the roofs, ceilings and much of the interior are of wood, there is also a considerable amount of brickwork in this building.

After Kashmir's absorption into the Mughal Empire, the distinctive Mughal style which flourished all over northern India was introduced there. Although the use of stone for building was revived, it was not in its ancient form, but according to the architectural ideals of the Mughals. The 'Patthar' or Stone Mosque, of local grey sandstone, is said to have been sponsored by Empress Nur Jahan in the 1620s. Totally unaffected by the indigenous wooden tradition, it is a rectangular building composed of three transverse aisles parallel to the *qibla* wall, each aisle having nine bays demarcated by arches supported by massive cruciform piers; at the west end every bay terminates in a *mihrab*, with the central one – the largest – projecting on the exterior. Such arched halls soon became popular in the mosque and palace designs of Shah Jahan in the capital.

Lahore

Located on the right bank of the Ravi, Lahore has been a provincial capital for centuries. When Mahmud of Ghazni annexed the city in the early eleventh century, it was known only for its fort, but became famous in the late eleventh and the twelfth centuries as the principal city of the Ghaznevids. Its geographical location made it vulnerable to invaders approaching from the north-west, and as a result Muslim occupation of the city antedates that of Delhi by almost a century. Even Babur, founder of the Mughal dynasty in 1526, settled first in the Punjab before setting out for Delhi. Although the area remained under Muslim control until the very end of the eighteenth century, when Sikh rule was established, few surviving buildings can be identified as pre-Mughal, and these too have undergone repairs and reconstructions at various times.

The two Niwin or 'low' mosques, one located between the Lahori and Shah Alami Gates, the other near the Yakki Gate, and the Qasabban Mosque near the Delhi Gate are all below the ground level of the surrounding area. Their solid masonry construction and low domes have been read as indications of a pre-Mughal date, but from the architectural point of view Lahore remains an entirely Mughal city. It is ironical that when distinctive provincial styles developed everywhere during Sultanate rule, there should be such a paucity of earlier remains in a city with a long history of Muslim occupation.

The early Muslim architecture of Multan, another important ancient city in Punjab, as well as the later Mughal buildings of Lahore, indicate that baked brick reinforced with wooden beams had been used in earlier times; wood was also used for brackets, doors, windows and overhanging balconies, while painted plaster or glazed tiles were used as decoration.

The Provincial Mughal or Lahore style was rooted in the indigenous tradition. Here the unique situation of a Provincial Mughal style co-existing with an Imperial one is evidence of the fact that a pre-Mughal architectural style, well entrenched in the vernacular tradition, had prevailed in the area, even though no physical trace of it now remains.

The earliest dated mosque, popularly known as Begum Shahi Masjid, was built in the Lahore style in 1611–14 by Maryam al-Zamani, mother of Emperor Jahangir. Standing opposite the Masjidi Gate of Lahore Fort, it is a massive structure in brick and plaster. The prayer-hall, at the west end of an enclosed courtyard, has a single transverse aisle consisting of five bays, an arrangement that was subsequently used for most major mosques of the city. Its massiveness is specially noticeable in the piers of the front façade. There is elaborate painted decoration in fresco, and the double dome – the first example in Lahore – has an interconnecting timber frame. The inner central dome and the half-dome of the *pishtaq* have network ornamentation in stucco. Each of the four corners of the prayer-hall is surmounted by a small pavilion with cupola.

In contrast to the elegant lines of contemporary Imperial Mughal architecture of Delhi and Agra, a general weightiness is evident, conveyed for example by the piers and the flatter contours of the domes. It seems that only the emperors built in the imported Imperial Mughal style using stone, marble and polished plaster; others, including members of the royal family and high officials, followed the local customs and were more inclined to build in brick, using tiles and painting for decoration.

The finest example of the latter style is the Mosque of Wazir Khan, built within the walled city in 1634–5 by Hakim Ilm-ud-Din Ansari, a native of Chiniot and Viceroy of Punjab under Emperor Shah Jahan, with the title of Nawab Wazir Khan. Following the orthodox or traditional plan, it has a five-bay prayer-hall at the west end, and a rectangular courtyard surrounded by *liwans* with non-communicating cells. The elongated courtyard and additional bazaar forecourt at the

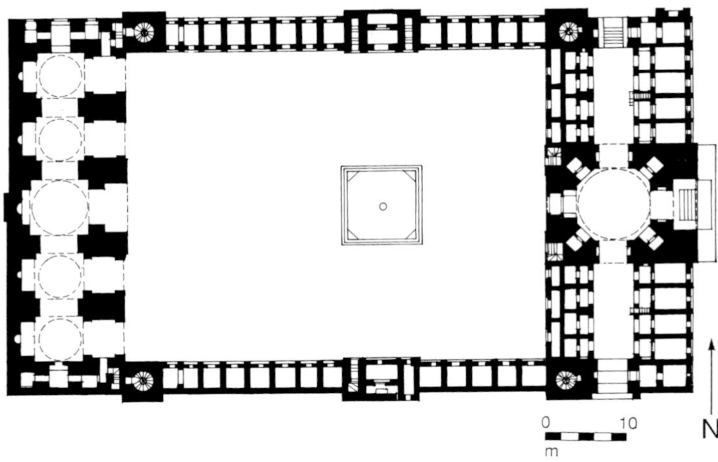

The Mosque of Wazir Khan (1634–5), Lahore: plan showing the five-bayed prayer-hall on the west side, and (below) a view across the courtyard looking west towards the prayer-hall, with two of the four symmetrically placed minarets which mark the corners of the courtyard.

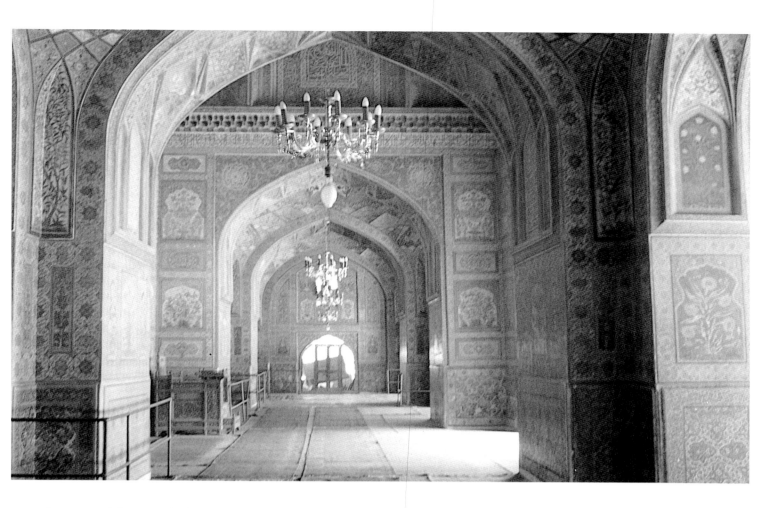

east end are unusual features. The domes, flatter than the contemporary Mughal form, and the four octagonal minarets, non-tapering and with projecting platforms, sited in the corners of the courtyard contribute to the ponderous appearance. The *chhatris* and oriel windows are typical Mughal features.

The entire exterior surface, including that of gateways and minarets, is divided into rectangular panels framed by bands of plain brickwork which are filled with calligraphic and floral and geometric designs in glazed-tile mosaic known as 'Kashi' (probably referring to Kashan in Persia, well known for its faience), using shades of vivid blue, green, orange and brown. It is believed that the technique was imported to Lahore from Tatta (see below) in the sixteenth century. Inside, the walls and ceilings are entirely covered with richly painted designs.

The Badshahi Mosque (1673–4), adjacent to Lahore Fort, built by Emperor Aurangzeb in the Imperial Mughal style using red sandstone and marble, is the most impressive building of his reign, and occupies the largest area of any mosque in the subcontinent. Elevated on a high platform and approached by a flight of steps, it echoes the Friday Mosque of Shahjahanabad in Delhi, but is on a grander scale. The gateway is two-storied with a high central arch. A tall, tapering minaret with projecting platform marks each corner of the courtyard, while octagonal turrets with kiosks frame the prayer-hall almost like a freestanding structure. The three domes covered with white marble are raised on cylindrical drums and constricted at the necks. There are rectangular bays between the domes. The red sandstone of the buildings

Interior of the Mosque of Wazir Khan, Lahore, showing some of the painted decoration, including floral designs.

(Below) Plan of the Badshahi Mosque (1673–4), Lahore; for a view of the mosque and its extensive courtyard see p. 19.

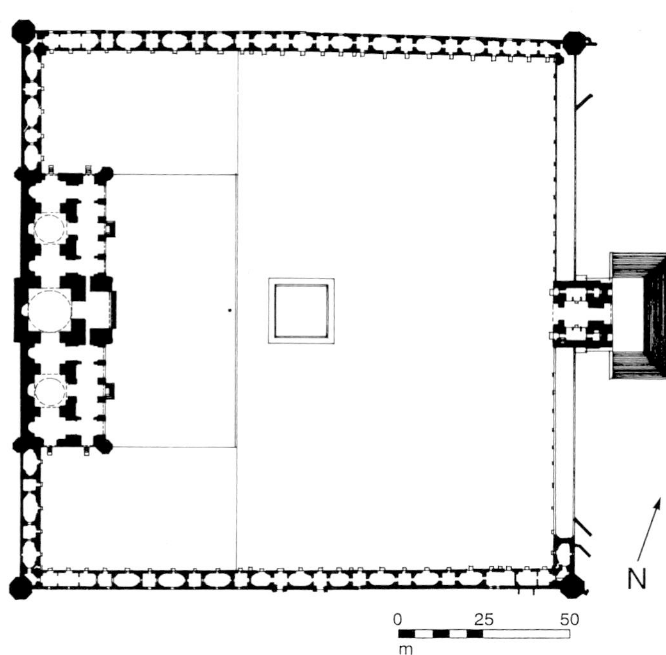

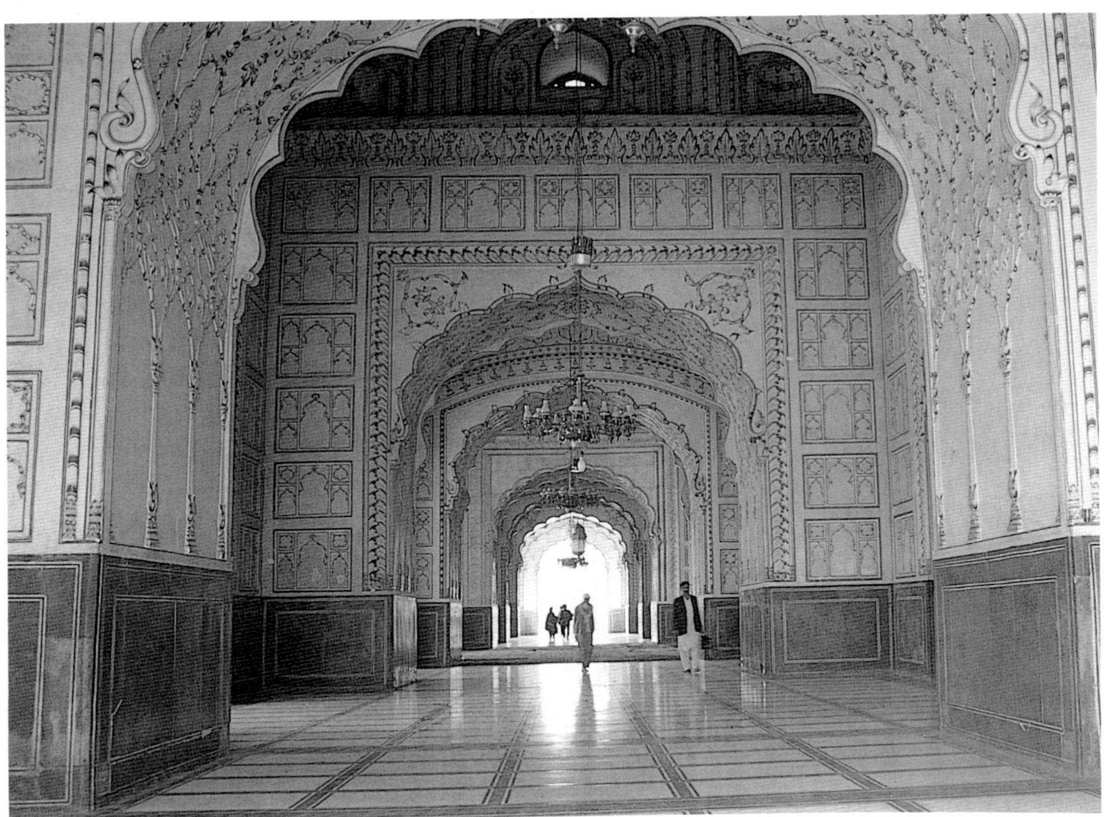

(Left) Interior of the Badshahi Mosque, (1673–4), Lahore.

(Below and opposite) Plan of the Friday Mosque (1644–7), Tatta, and interior view showing the use of massive brick construction and decorative detailing.

and minarets contrasts strikingly with the white marble used on the domes and cupolas and for inlaid decoration. The interior features elaborate relief decoration in painted plaster.

Tatta

The old city of Tatta (or Thatta – the name is derived from a Sindhi word meaning 'settlement on a river bank'), now in ruins, is located in southern Sind about 96 km (60 miles) east of Karachi, in Pakistan. The rise and fall of Tatta seems to have been linked to changes in the course of the River Indus, which now flows about 8 km (5 miles) to the east of the present town. Although the city's early history is shrouded in mystery, it was formerly – between the fourteenth and sixteenth centuries – the capital of several independent Muslim dynasties, such as the Samma, Arghun and Tarkhan rulers, and flourished as a trade and cultural centre. It was annexed into the Mughal Empire in 1593 during the reign of Akbar, but the governors sent from Delhi were not allowed to reside in Tatta, and in the seventeenth century the Mughals appointed Tarkhan governors.

The architectural remains indicate that stone was always used along with brick, the latter apparently having been the preferred material for mosques. The tilework which became a hallmark of the Tatta style was used only over brick, though not during the Samma period (1335–1520), when the rulers were believed to have been of Indian origin, for it is not seen at all on buildings of that period.

The oldest mosque in Tatta, known as the Old Mosque of Makli, is traditionally said to date from the late fourteenth century. The severe

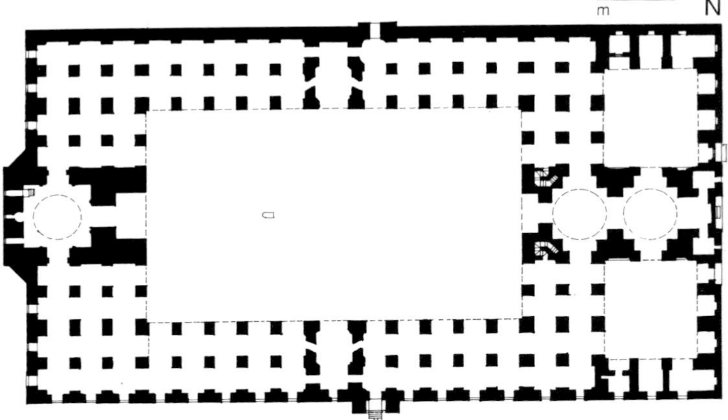

exterior and battered walls of this now ruined brick mosque are reminiscent of the stone rubble architecture of Firuz Shah Tughluq. A simple longitudinal hall was divided into three bays by lateral arches, the central bay being bigger than the others. A square projection in the south-east corner was meant for a staircase to go up to the roof.

The cultural divide between the Indian and Persian worlds, formed by the River Indus, is well manifested in the later architecture of Tatta, sponsored by the Arghun and Tarkhan tribes. Of Turkic origin and coming from Kandahar in Afghanistan, they were responsible for introducting a new Timurid taste. In the monuments built during their rule (1520–93) the most important structural change is seen in the height and shape of the domes, which are modelled on Timurid prototypes and raised on high drums. This source was common to the Mughals also, and explains the similarity of forms, especially the shape of domes and arches, in buildings of these two periods.

The new mode for decoration used glazed tiles, inspired by the Timurid school of Herat in particular, and gave the buildings a glittering look. Tilework was used on broad and simple brick surfaces with very little moulding, so permitting the maximum area to be covered. Made by local potters, the tiles were blue, white and occasionally purple and yellow; they were used to create geometric, floral or calligraphic bands, and were also cut into small pieces to create mosaic patterns. The technique became special to Tatta and was exported to other areas, such as nearby Punjab. The Tarkhan style continued even after the annexation of Sind by the Mughals.

The Dabgir Mosque, located in what used to be known as the neighbourhood of the wooden-box makers, is stated to have been built by Khusro Khan Charkas in 1588. This mosque also had a single-aisle, three-bay plan, with a staircase at either end leading to the roof; there was an open courtyard in front. It is built of brick on a stone foundation, the courtyard being paved with flagstones. In 1910 the floors of both prayer-hall and courtyard were raised to save them from the Indus floods. On the exterior, sunken-arch panels between the entrance arches have glazed-tile decoration featuring a lively floral design and stylized Chinese cloud motifs, clearly copied from Timurid originals.

The central bay – the largest – holds the stone-faced *mihrab* as well as the carved stone *minbar*. The rectangular frame of the *mihrab* is continued upwards and ends in a section covered with glazed tiles. Window openings on either side of the *mihrab* are an unusual feature of the interior. The spandrels and soffits of interior arches are also filled with glazed-tile decoration.

The Friday Mosque (1644–7), built by Shah Jahan, follows the orthodox plan and has an elongated rectangular courtyard, as seen in the Mosque of Wazir Khan in Lahore. Its eastern gateway and twin courtyards with ablution ponds were added in 1658. Unlike the Imperial Mughal mosques of Fatehpur Sikri, Agra, Delhi and Lahore, this mosque was conceived as a brick structure and the detailing follows the brick style. The use of brick construction and glazed-tile decoration continues the indigenous tradition of the Dabgir Mosque, while the four *iwans* with their *pishtaqs* facing the courtyard reflect strong cultural ties with Iran. The western prayer-hall is three bays deep, while the domed *liwans* on the north, east and south sides are two bays deep. The main dome of the prayer-hall is completely hidden by the *pishtaq* on the *qibla* side. There are no minarets.

A modified version of the window openings on either side of the *mihrab* in the Dabgir Mosque is seen here. There are screened windows in the *qibla* wall, including one which allows light to enter the centrally placed *mihrab*. The main dome of the prayer-hall and the half-domes of the *iwans* are supported on a series of intersecting arches forming squinch nets. This is another Timurid feature that was assimilated into the Mughal architecture of India.

The walls, arches and domes of the prayer-hall are totally covered in tiles, which are either painted or used for mosaic work. Although the star enclosed by geometric shapes, a motif borrowed from the Imperial Mughals, is a predominant new feature, the majority of the motifs used were derived from the Timurid sources of Samarqand, Bukhara and Herat, and worked in shades of blue, white and occasionally yellow. Those surfaces which were left bare of tiles have striking brickwork with mortar pointing of horizontal joints in a lighter colour.

Ahmadabad

The principal city of Gujarat in western India, Ahmadabad is situated on the banks of the Sabarmati River, and has become a large industrial centre. The old city, on the left bank, was annexed to the Delhi Sultanate in 1297, and ruled by governors until 1411, when Ahmad Shah, descended from a line of converted Rajputs, established himself as the founder of an independent Sultanate. During the first year of his reign, he built the new capital, Ahmadabad, on the site of the old town of Asaval, where he had resided as heir apparent.

The Muslim architecture, which is all of stone, as well as the many extant Hindu and Jain temples, bear witness to the unrivalled aesthetic resources of the province, especially stone craftsmanship, a field in which the local artisans were among the most accomplished in the whole of India. With such a rich heritage to draw upon, the architecture of Gujarat in the Muslim period included a large number of monuments which were the most indigenously Indian in style, hence the style became the most important provincial expression of Indo-Islamic architecture. It flourished for a period of over two hundred and fifty years, until the region was absorbed into the Mughal Empire by Akbar in 1572.

The architecture of Ahmadabad represents the second and third stages of the three distinct stylistic periods in the evolution of Islamic architecture of Gujarat. The first period is typified by the mosques built during the fourteenth century in Cambay, Dholka and Patan. In these, one sees the familiar process of demolition of temples and re-use of various components in building mosques; consequently, the architecture did not attain any distinctive character.

By the early fifiteenth century, in the second stage of development, a refinement and confidence in the forging of a new style is noticed. The mosques and other Ahmad Shahi monuments of Ahmadabad belong to this period. The third stage or the consummation of the Gujarat style was achieved during the second half of the century and later under the patronage of Mahmud Begarha (1458–1511) and his successors who sponsored splendid buildings in Ahmadabad and Champanir.

Ahmad Shah's Mosque within the citadel (1411) is one of the oldest in the city. Meant for the Sultan's private use, it follows the tradition of the Friday Mosque of Cambay, built in 1325. The prayer-hall is five bays wide and two deep, with an enclosure in the north-west bay, distinguished by a carved screen (*jali*) and twenty-five richly carved pillars. The hall is lit by eight perforated stone windows, and the central *mihrab* has black and white marble casing. The arched façade, with its large central entrance *pishtaq* with attached incomplete minarets, hides an interior of totally Hindu and Jain origin: stone beams are carried on slender pillars, and the domes are all corbelled.

The Friday Mosque, considered to represent the climax in mosque design in western India, reveals a logical development from earlier structures. Built by Ahmad Shah in 1423 in the centre of the city, it is connected to the royal citadel by a great thoroughfare, which passes the main entrance on the north side. The mosque is built in the traditional enclosed courtyard plan, with a vast flagged courtyard surrounded by an arcaded *liwan*. The hypostyle prayer-hall has 260 columns arranged to form fifteen square bays, five across and three deep. Its façade has a central screen of three arches, the larger central arch being framed by a pair of exquisitely carved engaged minarets, originally much taller but reduced by earthquake damage. There is a clear progression in height from the trabeated one-storied bays of the wings to the intermediate arches, and on to the great central frontispiece which corresponds to the three-storied central nave.

The architectural theme is still one of contrast. Here it is carried further and much more daringly than in earlier mosques, for beyond the screen of arches everything is of post-and-beam construction. The cusped arch carried on tall columns (flying arch), visible through the large central entrance, is a feature taken directly from the entrance gateways of temple complexes. It leads to the central bay of the nave, which is like a *mandapa* (pillared hall of a temple) transposed into a mosque sanctuary.

This area has two pillared galleries, one above the other, enclosing a central space over which there is a corbelled dome. The balconies, which have seats with sloping backs like temple *asanas* (thrones), are enclosed on the exterior and lit by clerestories of perforated stone screens. Pillars, brackets, balconies, railings, screens and interiors of domes are richly carved, but the exterior wall is plain, save for the string courses and minarets. As in the earlier mosque built by Ahmed Shah, there is a screened *maqsura* in the northern area – described by Emperor Jahangir as 'Muluk-Khana' (king's chamber)[4] – used by the ruler when he visited the mosque during festivals, but otherwise reserved for women.

The Mosque of Sidi Sayyid, in the north-eastern corner of the citadel, once formed part of the city walls. Previously thought to be of an earlier date, it is now accredited to a distinguished nobleman of the time of Sultan Muzaffar III (1561–72), and is representative of the later stage in the development of the Gujarat style. As a departure from earlier conventions, the interior is divided into fifteen bays by means of gracefully contoured true arches carried on eight pillars. For the construction of the ceiling, the squinch is used in addition to the bracket and diagonal beam, thus showing that the Gujarati builders were finally accepting this structural system. The customary minarets on the frontage are sited at the north and south extremities of the façade. The carved stone tympana of the sanctuary wall, with tracery that is unsurpassed in India, have made this small mosque world-famous. Fruit-bearing and flowering stems and branches are intertwined to produce superb specimens of stone craftsmanship.

In the mosque architecture of Ahmadabad there is little influence from the Muslim architecture of Delhi. However, in the crystallization of the Mughal style in the capital, Gujarat probably had the largest input of all the indigenous sources. The *jali* screens, trabeate constructions and bracket designs of the time of Akbar, and the white stucco (*chuna*) which was used to give a polished veneer to imperial buildings during Shah Jahan's time, all originated in Gujarat.

Bijapur

The city is in the heart of the Deccan in peninsular India, between the Bhima and Krishna rivers. In 1294, Ala-ud-Din Khalji first captured it from the Yadavas and annexed it to the Delhi Sultanate. With the shifting of the capital from Delhi to Deogir (renamed Daulatabad) in the Deccan under Muhammad bin Tughluq, a sizable population was also settled there, and many of them remained when the capital was moved back.

In 1347, one of their leaders, Ala-ud-Din Hasan Bahman Shah, rebelled and founded the first independent Deccani kingdom, which included Bijapur; he established his capital in Gulbarga, which he had held as *jagir* from Muhammad bin Tughluq. By the late fifteenth century, Bijapur was one of five independent kingdoms that had arisen out of the ruins of the Bahmani Sultanate, the others being Bidar, Berar, Ahmadnagar and Golconda. The rulers of Bijapur were known as the

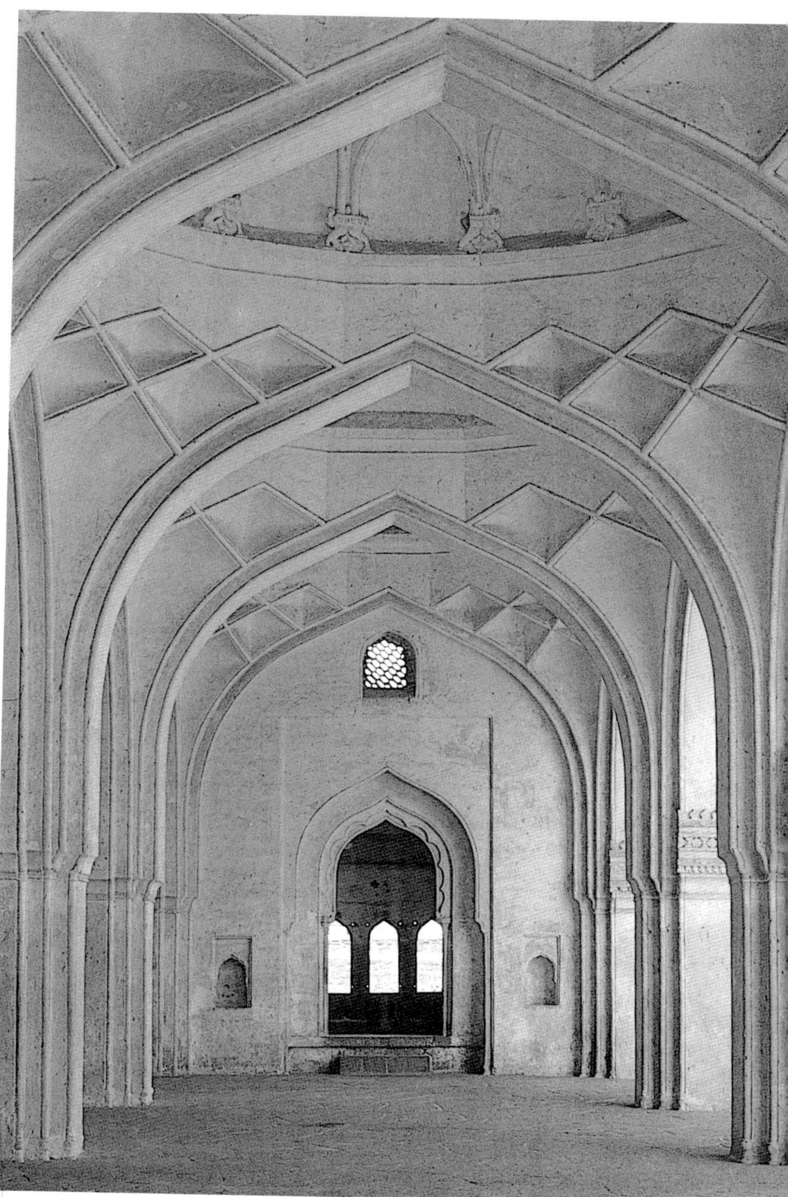

Arcade in the Friday Mosque (1565), Bijapur.

Adil Shahis and their dynasty, which ruled from 1490 to 1686, was founded by Yusuf Adil Khan, former governor of Bijapur. He was probably of Turkoman origin, and was responsible for the introduction of Shia Islam to Bijapur.

Politically and culturally, the Muslims could never entirely dominate the whole of the Deccan. Until the late sixteenth century, there was constant struggle between the Muslim kingdoms as well as with the Hindu Vijayanagar Empire in the south. During the seventeenth century, Marathas and Mughals joined the ranks of the marauders until Bijapur was absorbed into the Mughal Empire by Aurangzeb in 1686. The rural population, however, remained almost entirely Hindu.

In spite of continuous warfare, the Adil Shahi Sultans were great patrons of art, literature and especially architecture. This is evident from inscriptions which indicate that over 300 mosques were built during their rule. Among all the Deccani styles, their buildings show the greatest indebtedness to the local Hindu tradition, the other being more dependent on the development of ideas imported directly from the Islamic countries of western Asia.

The ruined Mosque of Karim-ud-Din, just inside the southern entrance of the citadel, is dated by inscription to 1320. One of the few remaining pre-Adil Shahi buildings, it was constructed entirely of Hindu and Jain pillars, and consists of a prayer-hall fronted by an enclosed courtyard. A temple *mandapa* is used as an entrance porch. The

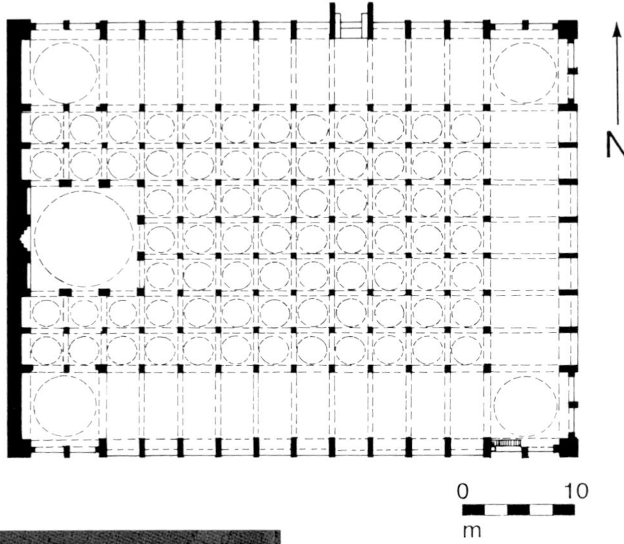

(Above and left) Plan of the Gulbarga Friday Mosque (1367) and interior view of one of the arcades enclosing the prayer-hall. There is no open courtyard, but a covered area with numerous columns supporting small domes; the principal dome occupies the area of nine bays.

(Opposite) The Mosque of Ibrahim Rawza (1580), Bijapur: exterior view and plan.

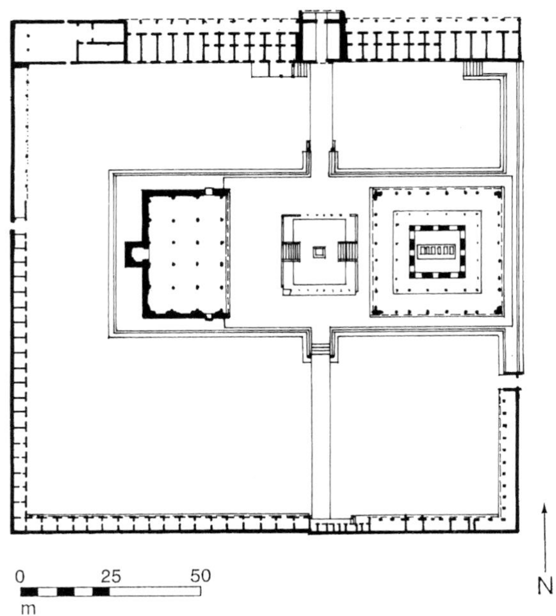

central part of the prayer-hall, raised like a clerestory on pillars, recalls the mosques of Gujarat.

Yusuf's Old Friday Mosque, actually built by Asen Beg in 1513, is the earliest firmly dated monument of the Adil Shahi period. Built using rubble and mortar, the walls are coated with plaster, as in the Tughluq buildings of Delhi. The building, which foreshadows many features of the future Bijapur style, has a three-bay prayer-hall, the central bay being wider than the others. The single hemispherical dome is mounted on a tall drum, its base surrounded by a ring of vertical foliations, which lends the whole ensemble the appearance of a bud surrounded by petals. Although minarets are absent, there are at the four corners *chhatris* with cupolas which have similar foliated bases. The *chhajja* is of wood.

The uncompleted Friday Mosque was built during the reign of Ali Adil Shah I in the late sixteenth century. The largest mosque in the Deccan, it is the only one in Bijapur built on the conventional hypostyle plan, with a courtyard enclosed by arcades on three sides. Had the mosque been completed, there would have been another arcade in the east. The square clerestory below the great dome in the centre of the prayer-hall is a more elaborate and refined version of the clerestory and dome of the Gulbarga Friday Mosque of 1367. The dome, considered the best proportioned in Bijapur, sits over a space (equal to nine bays) which is enclosed by piers. In the zone of transition, one sees the first major example of the use of intersecting pendentives. The same technique was used later in the tomb of Sultan Mohammed Adil Shah, the Gol Gumbad (1626–56), to support what was then the largest dome in the world. Decoration is restrained, the spandrels of the central arch having the typical Bijapur motif of a voluted bracket holding a medallion. The large *mihrab*, dating from 1636, has a medley of designs, and very fine calligraphy in gold and other rich colours.

The Mosque in Ibrahim Rawza, situated outside Mecca Gate to the west of the city, represents the fully matured Bijapur style. Built on a plinth, it faces the tomb of Ibrahim Adil Shah, constructed in 1626. The five-bay prayer-hall has a nearly spherical dome rising from a base of petals. The same form is repeated on top of the slender turrets at the corners of the building, and in the *guldasta* clusters over the piers of the arch openings. The merlons of the parapet have an almost filigree-like quality, and the deep eaves below have close-set stone brackets decorated with hanging chains (each cut out of a single block), though only remnants of these survive. The façade has carved bracket and medallion motifs.

The Bijapur Adil Shahi style is unique because of its consistency, and there was no noticeable decline when building activity ceased due to the fall of the dynasty at the end of the seventeenth century.

- 10 -
SUB-SAHARAN WEST AFRICA

LABELLE PRUSSIN

THE unique quality of Islam in Africa was eloquently expressed in metaphor by the eminent Africanist scholar A. Hampate Ba, who cited his mentor Tyerno Bokar, the sage of Bandiagara: 'It can happen, it will happen very often, that in becoming Islamicized a country adopts one of the many shades of colour that the huge triangular prism of Islam can offer when breaking up the white light of divine truth diffused by the Islamic faith.'[1] In Africa, Islam has no colour other than the hues of earth and stone reflected in water. Rather than being a vitiation of the faith, in Africa Islam has been rethought, rephrased, remoulded and rewoven in response to the local conditions. Nowhere is the nature of the new form and fabric more manifest, or does it find clearer expression, than in the architecture of the mosque.

Islam spread over the African continent in different ways and at different times, achieving varying degrees of integration. Sometimes militant, more often using peaceful means, its agents were various and subtle. Sometimes Islam wrought new political structures, sometimes it effected considerable economic change.

African Islam subsumes a large number of cultures and a range of economic strata and lifestyles, as well as diverse environments, building resources and technologies. Religious orientations are as diverse as the many different forms of social organization and cultural backgrounds. In some instances *sharia* based Muslim practices were adopted outright, in other cases they were integrated into more traditional local practices and beliefs.

Traditional African architecture rests on several basic principles. First, the conceptualization, the definition and the enclosure of space are organized anthropomorphically, topologically along linear paths and routes, and socially. Second, building is a continual process: there are no architectural end-products with defined completion dates; and there is never a point at which a builder or a community of builders can say 'the work is finished' because the buildings themselves require constant maintenance.[2] Both the natural and the built environment remain meaningful only so long as they continue to have relevance for people. Third, human life is perceived as a continuum from past through present to the future; and fourth, symbols in society are generated primarily through ritual.

Historically and culturally, Islam, almost from its inception, spread across sub-Saharan Africa along existing major trade routes: one extending from the Red Sea coast, the Benadir coast and the littoral of the Indian Ocean on the east through Nubia; the other overland from North Africa across the Sahara into West Africa. The presence of Islamicized Ibadite traders in the western Sudan, coming from Tahert in North Africa, was recorded in eighth-century documents.[3] These zones have expanded and merged, with the result that Islam now has its adherents spread over almost half the continent. On the east, the initial sources and inspiration for Islamic influence came primarily from Egypt, Arabia, India, China and Indonesia via maritime traders; commercial, heterogeneous, urban societies of immigrants following the Shafi'i school were established at a relatively early date. Whereas these communities were able to draw more immediately and directly upon Near Eastern skills, building concepts and traditions, in the west Islam infiltrated gradually via proselytization and trade. Malekite scholarship and doctrine, borne along long, tenuous, overland routes, were absorbed into existing political and economic structures, since they were supported by, and in turn supported, indigenous ruling élites associated with a fragmented but homogeneous rural hinterland and a minimal urban fabric.

Further, architectural styles also evolved in response to climatic conditions and the way in which available building resources were exploited. The coastal climate of East Africa (see chapter 11), with its humid sea breezes, evokes a response very different from that of the hot, dry inland desert and savannah climates of West Africa. Available natural building materials such as stone, earth and timber, as well as the indigenous technological 'styles' and skills to process and exploit them also vary considerably, despite the underlying tenets of the faith which prescribe spatial orientation and organization and a basic building concept. In considering the architecture of Islam in West Africa then, it is necessary to consider how and by whom these tenets were conveyed across such a widely diverse terrain. By what means were they originally incorporated into indigenous host societies and who were the patrons, agencies and builders responsible for making architectural decisions and choices?

In West Africa, the archaeological record often suffers as a result of the traditional use of permeable building materials, and historical reconstruction is difficult. The disintegration of architectural furnishings and wooden components, which rarely survive over time, creates a bias in the interpretation of extant evidence. The formation of Islamic societies in sub-Saharan West Africa, rather than being established by conquest and ordered by state régimes, was gradually diffused in a non-disruptive way through the migration of Muslim merchants, the proselytization of scholars and teachers, and by occasional settlers, variously interconnected via trading networks, family connections and

Facing page
Resurfacing work in progress on a pinnacle of the Great Mosque, Djenne. The projecting wooden reinforcements used in conjunction with earthen construction also serve as permanent supports for use by the men involved in the maintenance of the building, fresh mud-plaster being applied to weathered surfaces on a regular annual basis.

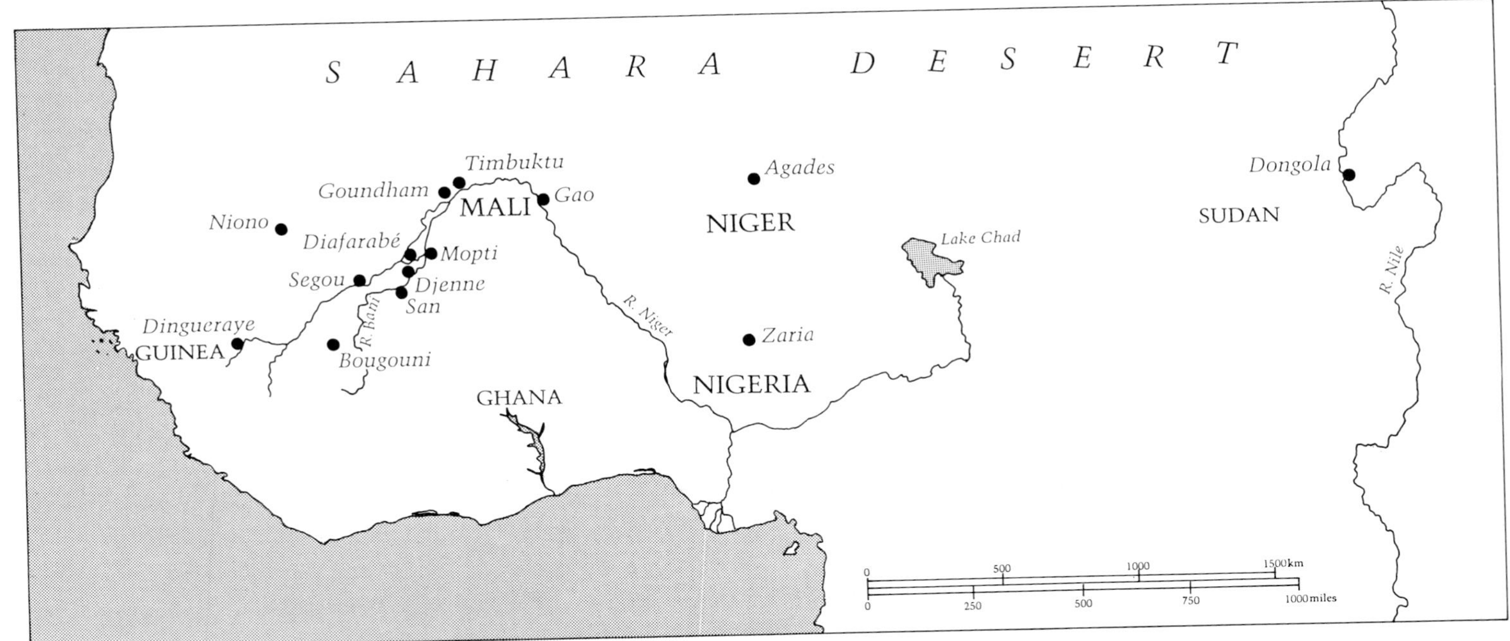

Map 6: the sub-Saharan region, showing principal sites. Many small rural mosques were built at intervals along trade routes.

teacher-student relationships. Muslim communities were often established through local marriage, within small-scale regional states or stateless societies and they often existed separately, within or adjacent to nascent urban and/or political population centres.

The Arab conquest of North African Berber civilizations in the seventh and eighth centuries intensified interest in the trans-Saharan trade routes. The earliest references to an Islamic presence in sub-Saharan Africa appeared within decades of the North African conquest. Expanding along the increasingly active routes, Sudanic states such as Takrur, KawKaw (Songhay), Ghana and Mali (Manding) acquired an Islamic identity in the wake of successive tenth- and eleventh-century conversion of their rulers, but these rulers nevertheless retained their pre-existing indigenous cultural heritage and identity. This pattern is reflected not only in the numerous historical references to 'twin-cities' and pluralist religious practices, but in regional demographic patterns where, for example, small rural mosques grew up at intervals along the pedestrian trade routes which Islamic traders, employing local transport systems (head porterage), had established.

The ephemeral seats of early West African empires such as Tegdaoust, Oualata, Timbuktu etc., evolved in conjunction with sub-Saharan termini for the caravans which plied the desert regularly. These early urban and politico-religious centres were characteristically located at the boundary between desert and savannah or along a water route which necessitated the transfer of goods from camel to either waterborne transport or head porterage. The political fortunes of empire waxed and waned with the shifting importance of these routes and their commercial nodes. It was only in the eighteenth century – and more forcefully in the nineteenth – that Islam became the religion of both ruler and ruled alike.

A feature common to all building technologies in West Africa is that primarily earthen, timber and vegetal materials are employed. Earth is used in applications ranging from tamped earth through sun-dried hand-moulded cylindrical bricks to rectangular cast bricks. Fired brick is rarely used, but architectural pottery is occasionally incorporated into the structure. The use of masonry arches was precluded until the introduction of cast bricks in the nineteenth century. Structural timber is extremely scarce. Ceiling structures consisted of palm-trunks, acacia – or tamarind – root, and woven or plaited fronds; hence structural systems were traditionally based on trabeated timber. The introduction of reinforced voussoirs in the nineteenth century in northern Nigeria and Niger evolved out of bentwood reinforcing, itself a derivative of armature frames used by nomadic tribes. Weathering, which leads to the rapid deterioration of earthen wall systems, requires constant maintenance. Earthen wall surfaces acquire a singular, plastic, fluid quality as a result of the periodic resurfacing and rerendering of the exterior. The effect of temperature changes in dry desert climates is reduced by the thick earthern walls, which in turn militate against the use of openings into enclosed spaces. Wall openings are thus rare for both structural and climatic reasons.

Traditional building technologies involved community participation and decision-making. Traditional building skills were in general not specialized, but were gender discrete: earthen construction and carpentry – functions related to tilling the soil and woodworking – were exclusively men's responsibilities; conversely, water collection, the firing of pottery and the tending of a fire, the gathering of roots and the weaving of baskets and mats – functions related to architectural pottery and fired brick, bending the frames for armatures and braiding the ceiling mats – were women's work. The gradual Islamic penetration into the West African savannah was instrumental in the introduction of specialized masonry techniques and masonry guilds and their integration into traditional technological processes.

Manding and Songhay Tradition

Indigenous Manding and Songhay beliefs rest heavily on the idea of an ancestral presence, and this presence is manifested in the form of either single-pillar shrines or a cluster of conical earthen and/or stone pillars. Ubiquitous on the savannah landscape, such shrines express the ethos and mythos of Manding and Songhay cultures, invoking the ancestors and ensuring the well-being of the habitat by means of an anthropomorphic iconography. In the course of Islamic integration into traditional society, the imagery of ancestors and elders represented on altars and shrines was transferred to the house of Islamic worship. The indigenous building expression took on a multivalent, multivocal quality, as evidenced in the countless rural mosques, each a one-day walk from the next along the network of savannah trade-routes extending from the bend of the Niger to the coastal rainforest.

Timbuktu

According to legend and oral tradition, Timbuktu was founded at the beginning of the twelfth century by Berber nomads involved in trans-Saharan traffic. In time the city became a seat of Islamic learning, but it also functioned in a commercial role – as an entrepôt, a caravanserai. The city first won renown in the fourteenth century when Mansa Musa, the converted Malian king who made the pilgrimage to Mecca in 1324–27, returned via Timbuktu and ordered the construction of the DjinguereBer Mosque. The design of the mosque has been attributed to the Andalusian poet al-Saheli, who had accompanied Mansa Musa on his return from Mecca, but what the design consisted of and how the design was translated from concept into reality by local builders remains an intriguing enigma.

Over the centuries, the DjinguereBer Mosque (from Songhay: 'great mosque') underwent many reconstructions and spatial reorganizations – the result of its low-lying site being frequently flooded, of changing Malekite religious interpretation and practice, as well as altered political and cultural alliances in the very heterogeneous city itself. The earliest references to the oldest part of the mosque suggest that it had a tower and five aisles, with tombs adjoining it on the south and west sides. It was a 'most stately temple built of limestone masonry and mortar'. Evidence of the traditional practice of burying local notables either inside the mosque courtyard (*sahn* or *musalla*) or immediately adjacent to its periphery walls can also be found in the earliest chronicles, suggesting that the indigenous tradition of incorporating the ancestral protective presence either within or adjacent to sacred shrines had been integrated into Islamic building practice.[4]

This singular practice, linked to a principle of spatial organization which continues to this day, had major architectural ramifications. Marked at the corners by four or six conical earthen pillars, these tombs are now most frequently found attached to the external, perimeter walls of a mosque or set in a surrounding terrace. The pyramidal tower-cum-minaret on the earliest (north-western) side, now completely enveloped by subsequent extensions, innumerable re-renderings and stairway access, may very well have initially been a mausoleum or tomb which was subsequently expanded into a solid built-up earthen mass. It stands in balanced contrast with the conical pillar form which marks the currently extant semi-circular *mihrab*.

In the early sixteenth century the city succumbed to Songhay conquest and to the more puritanical and enthusiastic leadership of its converted ruler, Askia Muhammed. As he expanded the realm of Songhay rule eastwards, he strongly encouraged Islam by sponsoring a number of Muslim scholars, two of whom – Al-Maghili and Sidi-Abdul-Qasem-el-Tuati – have been credited with the construction of a number of mosques during this period. Among them was the mosque at Katsina (one of the nascent Hausa states in what is now northern Nigeria), but all that remains today is its stair-minaret. The minaret's clearly articulated four faces, three levels and exterior stairway recall not only the minaret of the Great Mosque at Qairawan in Tunisia, but the form of *zawiyas* in the oasis cities north of the Sahara. There is also a close stylistic affinity between Askia Muhammed's own grand mausoleum at Gao with its peripheral stair-runs, and the tower-minarets at Timbuktu. The mathematical precision of the Islamicized Songhay architectural tradition, with its emphasis on four faces and three telescopic levels, contrasts sharply with the conical ancestral pillars of the Manding heritage.

The ambitious mosque-rebuilding programmes initiated by the Cadi el-Aquib in the late sixteenth century were particularly

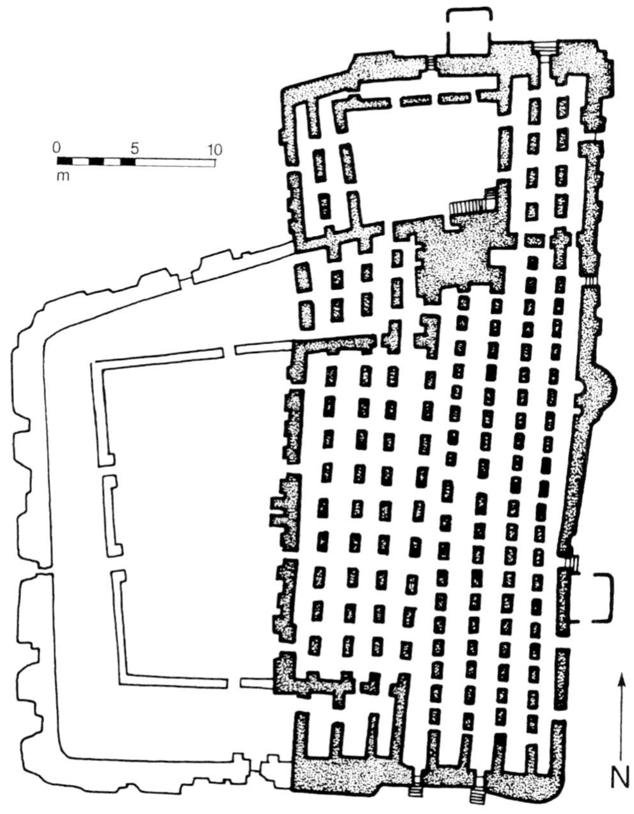

Plan of the DjinguereBer Mosque, Timbuktu, founded in the fourteenth century; extant parts are shown stippled.

noteworthy for the light they shed on another mingling of Islamic prescription and indigenous tradition: in 1581 the Cadi used his own measurements of the perimeter of the Ka'ba as a model for the perimeter of the *sahn* of the Sankore Mosque (another key monument in the city), and its size precisely matches that of the DjinguereBer Mosque. What is relevant to architectural style, however, is that the exterior faces of the Ka'ba were treated as the measure for the interior of the courtyard, thus honouring the traditional domestic African spatial emphasis on open interior courtyards as conceptual centres of the universe, as the 'stomach of the house'.

African principles of architecture as well as the building materials employed have militated against tracing the various reconstructions of the mosque throughout its subsequent history. The Moroccan conquest over the Songhay in 1591 set the stage for the establishment of a succession of Pashas who ruled, but mostly in name only, until the early nineteenth century. Between 1826 and 1865, three different Islamicized cultural entities vied for control of the city. Field documentation of the early nineteenth century suggests that the open interior courtyard which the minaret-tower now overlooks must have been rebuilt subsequent to 1828, and later information, gathered in 1863–65, provides a glimpse into the pattern of extension by means of the sequential addition of covered galleries in *sufuf* or rows.[5] The precise dating and stylistic variation of recorded constructions and reconstructions are difficult to trace, however, given the ephemeral nature of the building material. Each of the cultural entities which gained control of the city – the Fulbe, the Kunta (Hassaniya), the Toucouleur and the Tuareg – stressed and emphasized their own select doctrines and practices of Islamic belief (depending upon their choice of membership in the Qadiriyya and Tijaniyya brotherhoods) in the context of an indigenous cultural background. Furthermore, earthen construction responds more readily to the shifting architectural expression effected by such rapid political, institutional and religious changes than do more

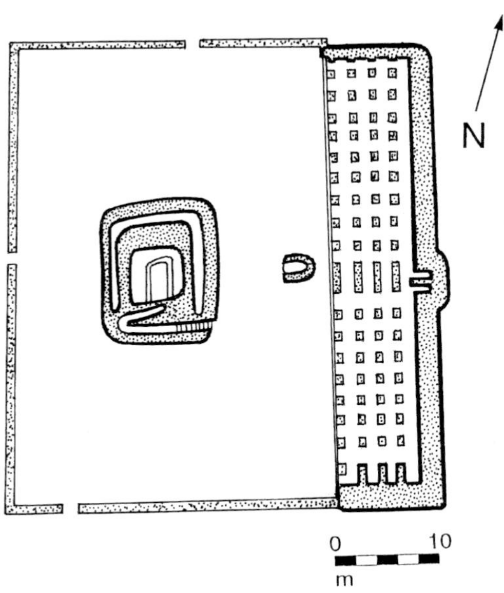

The mosque-mausoleum of Askia Muhammad, Gao: site plan and view of the massive tower-minaret (rebuilt in its present form in the nineteenth century), with external ramps and stairs.

'permanent' building materials such as stone. Earth is reused again and again: with each shift in religious and political power the walls of the old became the borrowpit for the new.

Agades

Even more than in the mosques at Timbuktu, it is in the stair-minaret – at 27.50 m (90 ft) the tallest in West Africa – of the mosque at Agades, Niger, that the Ibadite North African heritage is translated into a virtuoso achievement. Architectural verticality, the aspiration of the believer, is most difficult to achieve in earthen construction. That the great height of the minaret vividly recalls the pinnacles of the singular minarets in Algeria that rise above the city hilltops (as at Ghardaia, in the Mzab) comes as no surprise. Like Timbuktu, the city of Agades was founded by nomadic Tuareg in the distant past, but unlike Timbuktu (which always remained primarily a commercial city), Agades subsequently became the political seat of a Sultanate while continuing to serve as a major entrepôt and stopover on the eastern pilgrimage route. At the time the minaret was built (or rebuilt) in 1844, the city's most prominent merchants and the core of its spiritual leadership were Kunta who had migrated from Touat in the Mzab region. The stair-minaret measures approximately 9 m (30 ft) square at the base, tapering to 2.50 m (8 ft) square at its pinnacle. The interior spiralling stair and the four earthen walls are structurally reinforced by means of thirteen sets of split-palm ties which rhythmically project 1–1.50 m (3–4 ft) beyond the faces of the walls. These projecting wooden consoles (*toron*), which can be found on all 'sudanic' mosques in West Africa, serve not only a practical and structural purpose (as scaffolding and to reinforce the earthen mass) but also evoke human knowledge, rebirth and renewal.[6] Each face is pierced by seven openings which light the interior, and the entire structure rests on four massive earthen pillars embedded within the mosque.

Djenne

The city of Djenne developed as a sister-city to Timbuktu at a junction of the trans-Saharan and trans-savannah trade routes; its cultural roots were nourished by the Bani River, the Upper Niger Delta, and its Manding hinterland, while its commercial life was sustained by continual contact with its sister-city. The architecture of its Great Mosque, though inspired by the indigenous Manding heritage, has become the penultimate architectural symbol for Islam in West Africa, familiar to the entire community of believers and popularized abroad during the period of French colonial rule in Western Sudan.

Archaeological evidence suggests that nearly a millennium ago there was a small fishing village on an adjacent site (Djenne-Djeno). Later written documents describe how the city's first ruler (the *djenne-koi*) converted to Islam at the end of the thirteenth century, demolished his palace and replaced it with a mosque. His successor built two 'towers', and the terrace-platform which surrounded the mosque was installed by the next ruler; however, archaeological research has yet to establish the location, the precise founding date, the form and style of successors to this first mosque. During the sixteenth century the city emerged on its present site as a major convergence point for the exchange of goods between Islamicized Manding (Dyula) traders coming from its southern hinterland and North African traders coming across the Sahara to Timbuktu.

Although of questionable scholarship, the style of the mosque hypothetically reconstructed by Félix Dubois from the ruins which he recorded in 1897 may well reflect the earliest account of Djenne's Islamic history on its present site. Precisely at the centre of a large, perfectly square *sahn*, half of which was roofed over, stood a pyramidal 'tour-minaret' and at the mid-point of the east, *qibla* wall there was another tower, directly in line with it, marking the *mihrab*. Given traditional African funerary practices in which sons bury their father within the family compound and mark the ancestral presence with an earthen pillar, these two towers could well have been those built by the first successor of the *djenne-koi*. The centrally located minaret would have been a pillar-tomb and the pyramidal earthen mass at the eastern *qibla* wall would have housed, at its base, a *mihrab* stylistically similar to the conical *mihrab* in the DjinguereBer Mosque at Timbuktu. The conical earthen pillar, traditional symbol of the wisdom of the elders and ancestors, has been integrated with a key expressive component of Islamic belief – orientation towards Mecca. In the Muslim context indigenous architectural tradition became enriched with new meaning.

The ancestral earthen pillars which now represented the new wisdom introduced by Islam were also transformed into engaged columns supporting the walls of the mosque. Furthermore, these buttresses were ordered into the new spatial geometry of a three-by-three

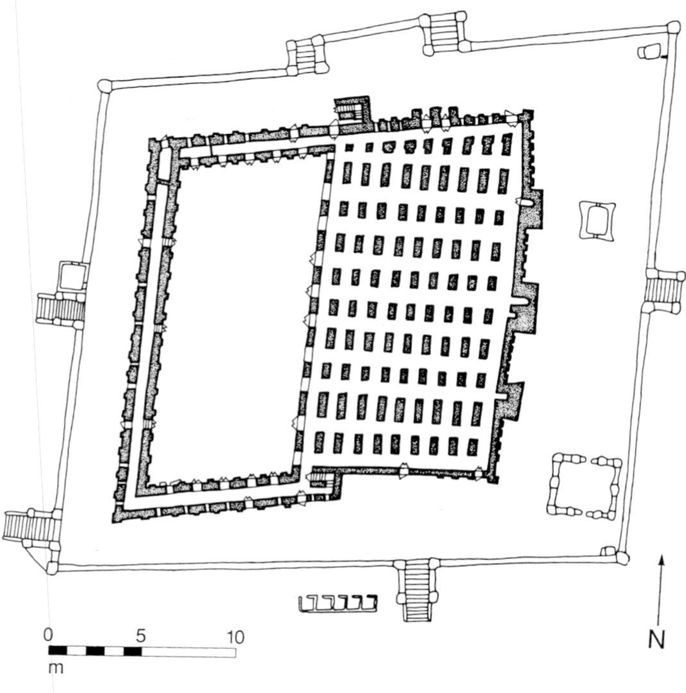

Plan of the Great Mosque, Djenne; the present building dates from 1909. The tripartite division of the qibla *wall is seen on the right.*

magic square. Integral with the platform adjacent to the eastern *qibla* wall was a cemetery which contained the tombs of the venerable marabouts, clerics and Cadis who figured in the city's Islamic history.

The present mosque was built in 1909, 'on the site and in accordance with the ruins' of its predecessor, as reconstructed on paper by Dubois. It was built, in consultation with the Manding *ulama* favoured by the new French military engineers-cum-administrators, many of whom were graduates of the Ecole Polytechnique in Paris. The design for the mosque was based on the newly-created French military *Résidence* at Segou, Mali, itself remodelled from the palace of Ahmadu, the deposed African ruler.[7]

The local builders were the *bari*, the Djenne guild-organized masons who are still famed throughout the region for their skills. The success of their achievements, however, was also the result of the unique cultural ecology in the Upper Niger Delta which produces a superb combination of clayey soils, lime, dung and chaff essential for successful earthen construction.

The tripartite arrangement on the façade of the eastern *qibla* wall was created by adding a false, flanking tower on each side of the functional central tower in which the *mihrab* is located. This façade provides a backdrop for an extensive market place, the location of which was itself dictated by the vast borrowpit created in the course of the mosque's construction. Like its predecessor, the present mosque consists of a square courtyard (in ideal if not reality), the eastern half of which is roofed over. The new roofed arcades on the north and south sides are pierced by interior stair towers, and the west side is flanked by a women's gallery. The major entrance on the north side evokes the anthropomorphic imagery of an African mask used in initiation ritual. There is a rampart around the entire mosque and the tombs of several Muslim notables are located on the terrace, following Ialamized African precedent.

Mopti

Hailed by the French colonial administration as the symbol of its great West African empire, the Djenne Mosque became a prototype for many subsequent mosques, including those at San, Segou and Mopti. When the French expeditionary forces arrived in the region in the late nineteenth century, Mopti was little more than a small encampment of Sorko fisherman at the confluence of the Bani and Niger Rivers. Its subsequent prosperity dates from the French decision to use river navigation as a means for supplying their military columns advancing to the north. The village became a French base of operations and in 1914 it replaced Djenne as a colonial regional administrative centre. By 1920 a substantial dyke had been built to link the island of Komoguel with the mainland, opening the way for European commerce and encouraging French tourism.

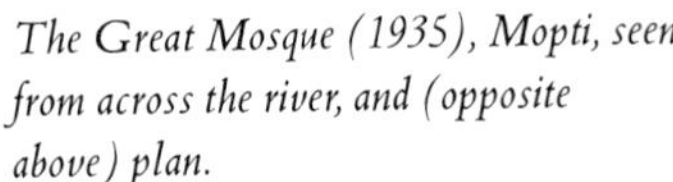

The Great Mosque (1935), Mopti, seen from across the river, and (opposite above) plan.

(Opposite, below) Interior of the Goundham Mosque, showing the use of cast brick in the construction of arches.

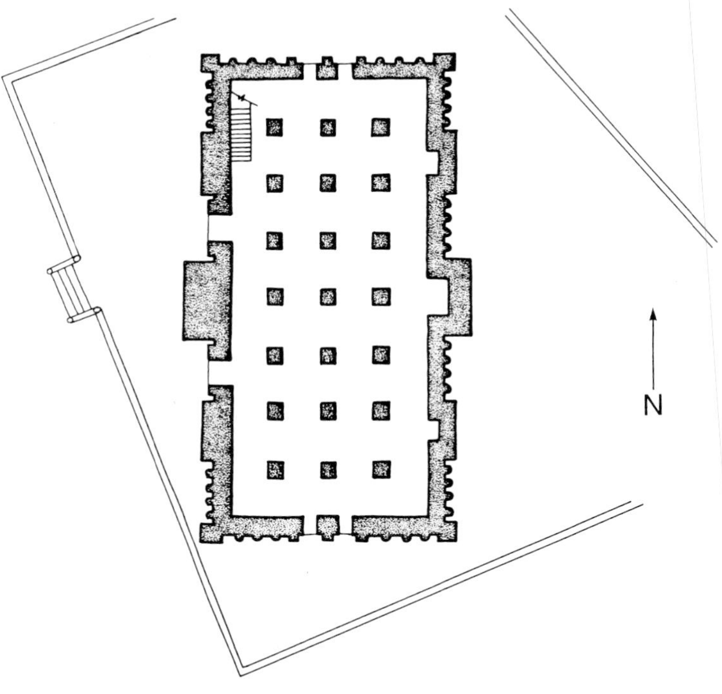

The Great Mosque, built on the island in 1935, was 'inspired by the style of the Djenne mosque' and local tradition claims that it was built by Djenne masons. M. Cocheteaux, the French Resident administrator, wrote however, that for the Imam and the local Muslim notables there were only two key requirements: an eastward orientation and a minaret. His agenda added another perspective: 'I had designed the major façade [to be] the most beautiful, but its prescribed eastern orientation made it invisible from the *digue* of Sevaré and the approach from Komoguel [by boat], both of which were essential from a tourist's point of view. In order to mitigate this inconvenience, I built two identical façades.'[8]

The plan of the mosque is perfectly symmetrical along both its axes. The interior, completely roofed, consists of four aisles defined by three ranks of seven columns from which Roman arches spring. The *mihrab* tower is matched by a false tower on the west side; the north and south entrances, recalling the traditional Djenne entrance, were symmetrically aligned and the *sahn* was eliminated. The compact plan, when executed in conjunction with the traditionally prescribed height of the engaged buttressing, wrought a proportional change in the three-dimensional form, lending its walls – not just its minaret – a sense of verticality quite unmatched elsewhere in West Africa. Although the *sahn* was lost, the ambulatory, its perimeter now corresponding to the street pattern rather than the walls of the mosque, was preserved.

Goundham

Another twentieth-century development from the traditional Sudanese style is exemplified in the Central Mosque at Goundham, about 80 km (50 miles) south-west of Timbuktu and Tendirma. Reputedly designed by a French army engineer, Commandant Renault, it was built in 1943 by local craftsmen under the aegis of the master-mason Sekou Bokari; externally, the building retains the spirit of the Sudanese style through its prominent vertical buttressing, but internally extensive use is made of sun-dried cast brick for arches (both false and true), barrel-vaults and niches. Although no stone is used, the construction is massive, partly due to the paucity of suitable building materials locally; here it is necessary to mix surface sand with the subsoil in order to achieve a workable consistency for mud bricks.

Fulbe and Hausa Traditions

Tradition suggests that Islam was introduced into northern Nigeria in the fifteenth century by merchants from Mali and that by the early sixteenth century a number of Islamic scholars present in the courts of the Hausa states were under the protection of Songhay rule (see above). Islamic law and culture were, however, peripheral to the day-to-day affairs of the greater part of Hausa society until the Fulbe-led *jihad* in the early nineteenth century. The Fulbe, a diverse pastoral population who moved freely through the savannah region of West Africa, stretching from the Futa Toro in the west to Lake Chad in the east, had been Islamicized for centuries (if only nominally) and were famed for their Islamic scholarship. The military *jihad*, begun in 1804 under the

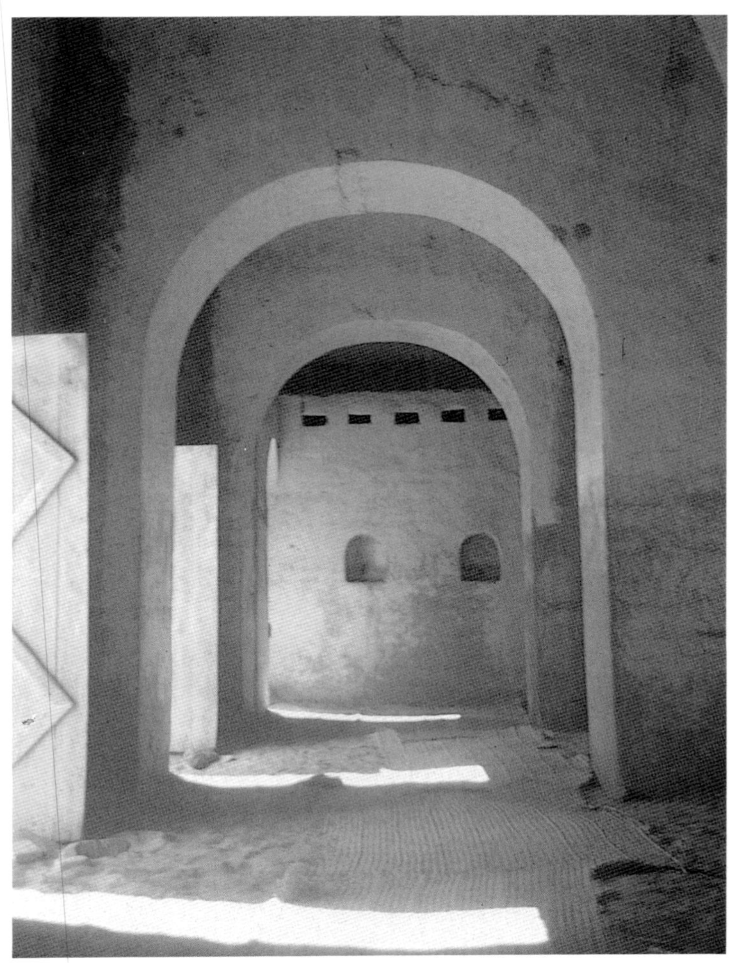

leadership of Usman dan Fodio, culminated in the establishment of a Caliphate at Sokoto which united the former Hausa states into a confederacy under Fulbe rule. Under Caliphate authority, the first decades of the nineteenth century witnessed an intensive building programme which included the reinforcement of existing city fortifications, as well as the construction of new walls, new mosques and new palaces.

The earliest of these mosques were built using traditional Hausa trabeated forms. Flat roofs were supported on a forest of pillars, and closely spaced split-palm timbers were used to create a simulated plank ceiling. This was covered with grass matting, over which an earthen roof was laid. Spaces larger than the economic span were roofed by a corbelling system used traditionally throughout the Western Sudan. By this process, shallow corbelled domes could be made to simulate true domes. The Friday Mosque at Bauchi is a good illustration of this technology. The entire interior space is roofed over and an ambulatory extends from the mosque perimeter. Entrance to the ambulatory is gained through a set of four low earthen gateway towers, recalling the classic *zaure* of domestic Hausa architecture. The tower extends above the *mihrab*, and is accessible via a stairway leading to the roof of the mosque itself.

In the later mosques, mud arches were introduced, creating more ample and expansive interior volumes. These reinforced earthen arches, which came into use for all major civic as well as religious buildings, evolved in the course of Fulbe hegemony over the Hausa states and Fulbe sedentarization in the Hausa context. They became the innovative handmaidens for a new architectural imagery. These arches are achieved in two ways: first, by plastering over the bent acacia roots (used in the Fulbe tent armature) with mud; or, second, by embedding wooden corbels in the earthen walls and or coating them with mud. A subsequent third development involved the use of radiating straight split palm-trunk members which were laid one over another in the manner of corbels, then tied back both to each other and to horizontally laid members.

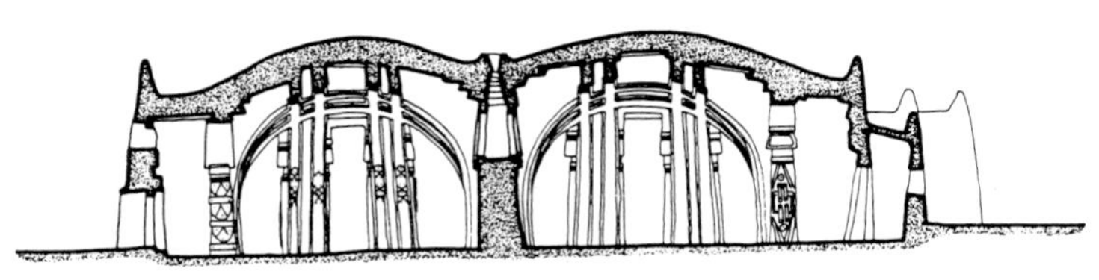

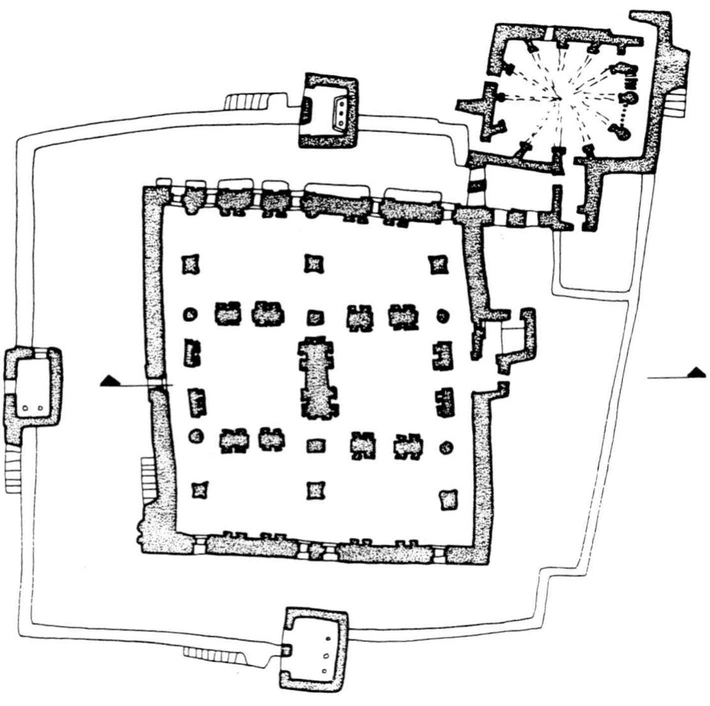

The Friday Mosque, Zaria: plan and cross-section showing the use of freestanding piers and reinforced arches.

Zaria

The Friday Mosque at Zaria probably represents the highpoint of puritanical fervour which followed on the early nineteenth-century Fulbe *jihad*. Built in the late 1830s or early 1840s by Babban Gwani, *mallam* Mikhaila, the first chief builder in Hausaland appointed by Usman dan Fodio, it is also perhaps the clearest illustration of the relationship between Fulbe client and Hausa builder. The plan and interior volumes of the mosque *sahn* are geometrically ordered by its six corbelled domes supported on reinforced-earthen arches with free-standing piers, but this structural system differs from that of the entrance or *sharia* reception court which is framed precisely like an armature tent. The key innovation is the fact that the armature ribs are enveloped in earth. The classic African ambulatory which surrounds the mosque is only accessible through the four entrances (*zaure*) which also serve as ablution rooms.

While the exterior surface decoration of these Fulbe-Hausa mosques is more restrained than the neighbouring palaces of the Emirs, equally great emphasis is placed on their interior spaces. It is on the interior surfaces that the most elaborate geometric motifs in bas-relief are to be found, very much recalling the interior richness of the nomadic heritage, where intricate tapestries and elaborately worked leather hangings of various kinds provide a vivid contrast with the plain, weatherworn tent exteriors.

Facing page
The minarets of the Diabolo Mosque, Mali, are characteristic of sub-Saharan mud-brick architecture, with projecting wooden reinforcements which also serve as ladders providing ease of access for replastering the exterior.

The Great Mosque (1909) of Djenne, Mali (opposite above), was inspired by the indigenous Manding heritage; the present mosque was built under French supervision on the site of a fourteenth-century mosque and a later Fulani building of the 1820s. Together with the Great Mosque (1935) at Mopti (top right), the Djenne Mosque represents a development of sub-Saharan building that has come to be regarded as the synthesis of local regional design. The entrance to the Djenne Mosque and the interior of the prayer-hall are also shown (opposite below). The village mosque (centre right) in Segou, Mali (rebuilt c. *1960), continues the local building traditions, featuring finials in the form of ancestral pillars.*

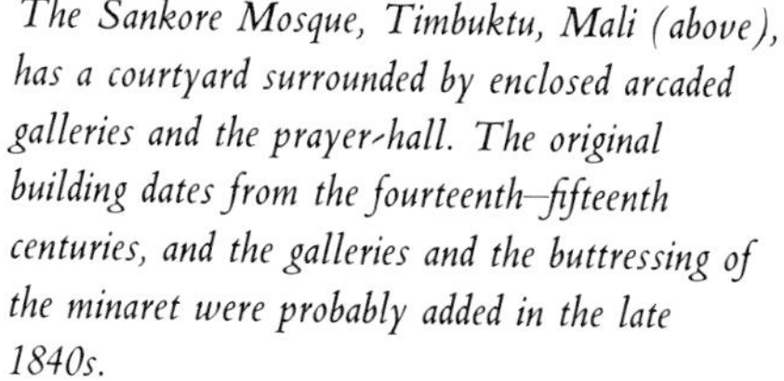

The Sankore Mosque, Timbuktu, Mali (above), has a courtyard surrounded by enclosed arcaded galleries and the prayer-hall. The original building dates from the fourteenth–fifteenth centuries, and the galleries and the buttressing of the minaret were probably added in the late 1840s.

The rural mosque at Bougouni, Mali (right), probably dates from c. *1890. The building illustrates the practice of using ostrich eggs – symbolic of purity and fertility – both as decoration and as protection against heavy rain on the most exposed points.*

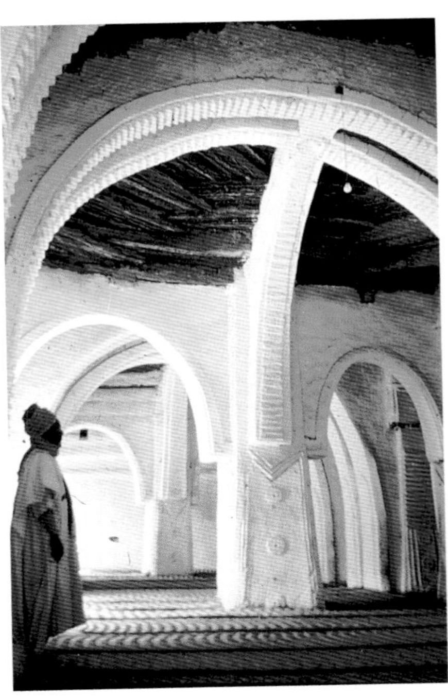

Dingueraye

The Futa Djallon region in Guinea had been witness to an early consolidation of Fulbe hegemony into an Islamicized Confederacy in 1726. Today its landscape is dotted with the local mosques – the architectural heritage of sedentarized, Islamicized Fulfulbe-speaking nomads. The plan of these mosques respects the strong Malekite prescription for a cube in emulation of the Ka'ba, but externally they are barely distinguishable from a magnified version of traditional Fulbe housing. Palace reception chambers and local mosques consisted of a low earthen wainscot wall in which was embedded a circle of wooden posts that supported a set of rafters emanating from a central apex to carry a thatched roof.

In the mid-nineteenth century, inspired by the Fulbe *jihad* in Hausaland, El-Hadj Umar organized a professional army including French-trained African builders equipped with French weapons and launched a major *jihad* from Dingueraye. Although he was killed in 1864, his family honoured his ardent wish to build a mosque in the city and in 1883 the mosque was built with the aid of one of his own drawings. The drawing, which represents a conceptual plan (a mandala-like magic square), provided the design guidelines for the earthen cube of the mosque. The seeming incongruence between concept and reality is the result of user definition: 'The mosque is not what is visible from the outside, but *only* the interior earthen walled cube within. The vast dome above is only for protection.'[9] The earthen walls are surrounded by a circular ambulatory which recalls the open ambulatories around mosques in both the Manding and Hausa tradition and, as in the case of all related West African mosques, there is a huge tree adjacent, originally planted to commemorate its founder.[10]

A second drawing found in the *Tarikh* of El Hadj Umar's family history in Dingueraye reputedly represented a mosque façade indicating what the *jihad* leader aspired to; it was evidently inspired by his memories of the *hajj*, his experiences in the Near East and the renderings of mosque façades often seen on prayer-carpets. However, the reality of what the local builders could actually conceptualize or create, even with the help of French-trained African engineers in the Futa Djallon in the late nineteenth century, was still derivative of the traditional African architectural heritage.

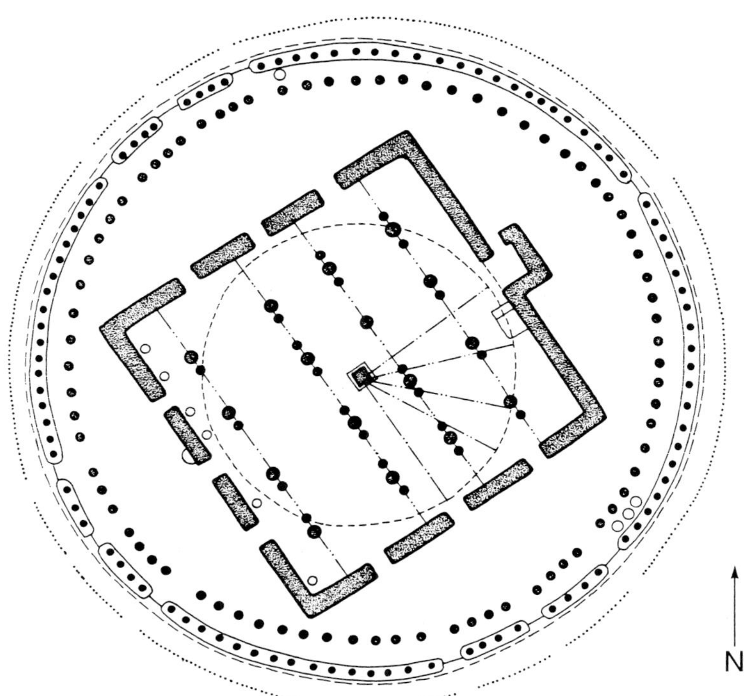

Plan of the Great Mosque, Dingueraye, showing the inner earthen cube of the mosque.

Facing page

*(Top left) The external gate leading into the courtyard of the mosque at Diafarabé (*c. *1920), Mali, south-west of Mopti.*

(Centre left) An example of a Manding rural mosque (probably built in the late eighteenth century) at Chesa, northern Ghana.

(Bottom left) The Great Mosque (1849–83; the latter date may represent a rebuilding) at Dingueraye, Guinea; founded and built by the religious leader El Hadj Umar, this remains the quintessential model of the Fulbe regional mosque type. Here, there is a reference to the mandala (the sacred cosmic diagram), in that the thatched dome covers and conceals an inner earthen cube which constitutes the prayer space.

(Top right) The interior of the dome in the mosque at Yaama, Niger (1962, with additions 1978–82); here, an intricate system of wooden ribbing covered with mud plaster is used.

(Centre right) A view across the inner courtyard of the mosque at Pana, near Sirmou, Mali (possibly built in the early nineteenth century; rebuilt in the 1960s); the entrance to the prayer-hall can be seen on the far side.

(Bottom right) Interior of the Friday Mosque (1824–62), Zaria, Nigeria, built by Babban Gwani. Here the plan is more square, reflecting the Hausa building traditions and the later zaure-sahn *circle-square relationship, in which the roof is supported by a vaulting system of arched palm-trunks plastered with mud.*

Summary

The particular examples chosen to illustrate the mosque in West Africa are intended to show a number of basic features which characterize the historical interface between indigenous cultural tradition and the universal tenets of Islam. To be sure, all the mosques include very specific features – a *mihrab*, a *qibla* wall, a minaret, the orientation of these features as dictated by the direction towards Mecca – and there is a marked threshold between the interior sacred space intended for the performance of ritually prescribed prayers and the external secular space. Beyond these basic Islamic prescriptions, however, there is little in the architectural style of the mosque as such that is recognizable by, or familiar to, the outsider, Muslim or non-Muslim. The architectural language of the West African mosque has features in common with a creole language: its underlying spatial grammar has been reconstructed to accommodate requisite Islamic behaviours and beliefs, while its vocabulary continues to be based on an amalgam of indigenous symbols and phonemes, the meaning and interpretation of which are drawn from their native soil. The architectural language of the mosque has been rephrased in West Africa by its Islamicized creators and users, but always in the context of an indigenous cultural identity.

- 11 -
EAST AFRICA

MARK HORTON

MEDIEVAL Islam extended as far south as Cape Delgado and northern Madagascar, as well as to the offshore islands such as the Comores Archipelago, Mafia, Zanzibar and Pemba Island. Thus Muslim communities of considerable antiquity have existed along the 8,000 km (5,000 mile) shoreline from Suez to Mozambique. The most important early centres were the coastal ports; only to the north in the Horn of Africa are historical Muslim settlements found inland.

The eastern seaboard was linked in with maritime trading systems providing contact with southern and western Asia from at least the first century AD, according to the *Periplus of the Erythraean Sea*.[1] Trading communities on the African coast supplied ivory, marine products such as ambergris and tortoiseshell, as well as slaves, gold and iron at certain times. Along the Red Sea, Ptolemaic expeditions from Egypt hunting for war elephants had, by the third century BC, established a network of ports which may have continued in use through the classical and early Islamic periods. Some of these ports became important as points for transhipment into caravans carrying goods to the Nile Valley, while others supplied products from Ethiopia. Along the shores of northern Somalia there were ports that may have been staging centres for the maritime route to India, as well as transfer points for supplies of incense from the interior. Pottery finds from Ras Hafun suggest that this network dates to at least the first century BC.[2]

The chronology and mechanisms for the spread of Islam into eastern Africa remain controversial in the face of contradictory documentary and archaeological evidence.[3] There are few contemporary historical sources, while indigenous chronicles and traditions that purport to give accounts of the spread of Islam into these communities are centuries later than the events they describe and must be treated with considerable caution. The only reliable indicators are physical evidence provided by the remains of mosques, tombs and inscriptions.

Indigenous traditions have contributed the unique stylistic qualities of mosques in the region and fashioned Islamic prescription to its own milieu. The absence of *madrasa*-type prayer-halls, the shallow domes, the organization of internal spaces in response to the limited span of framing members, the use of indigenous building materials such as coral or mangrove poles, the absence of keystones and the ubiquitous presence of enclosure and pillar tombs are all basic features which are tightly interwoven with various imported decorative elements such as carved Java teak, marble facings and Indian glazed ceramic plates and bowls.

Facing page
View of the mihrab *in the Mosque of Said bin Sultan* (c. *1840), Mtoni; see p. 207.*

NORTH-EAST AFRICA

There is a tradition that some of the Prophet's companions fled not to Medina but to Ethiopia during the *hijra*. If so, they may have gone to one of the ports associated with the maritime trade of Aksum. The earliest permanent Muslim communities were probably located in the Red Sea ports, in view of the close connections with the Arabian peninsula. Early towns such as Aydhab, Suakin, Badi (probably the island of Er Rih), the Dahlak archipelago and Zeyla were all established by the ninth century, if not earlier. A single inscription from Knor Nubt, near Suakin, dates to 861. Arabic inscriptions from Er Rih, Dahlak Kebir and Quiha date from the tenth to twelfth centuries, but little survives in terms of mosques or indeed of buildings in general from this early date. On Er Rih there are remains of cisterns, huge middens, cemeteries and what may have been a mosque.[4]

There is little evidence to suggest that Islam spread into the interior of north-east Africa until the fifteenth century, when small Muslim states, often involved in the trade in slaves, developed inland in the Horn of Africa on caravan routes. The best known is Harar in Ethiopia, a town that became a considerable centre of Islamic learning and in the mid-nineteenth century had at least eighty mosques.[5] In due course, the pastoralist groups further inland were converted and because of their mobility, Islam spread rapidly during the eighteenth and nineteenth centuries across what is now Somalia, southern Ethiopia and north-eastern Kenya. Often the only significant architectural remains are the tombs of well-known Sharifs.

Sudan and Ethiopia

Although the Arabs had occupied Egypt as far south as Aswan by 641, it was many centuries before Arab and Muslim peoples penetrated south into Nubia and Sudan. The spread of Islam down the Nile Valley began in the fourteenth century. From the seventh century onwards, various attempts had been made to conquer the Christian Nubian kingdoms, but the indigenous rulers were able to retain their independence, which was regulated through the *baqt* treaty with Muslim Egypt to the north. Only in 1316 was a Muslim king accepted in Dongola, but Christianity continued in Nubia until the early sixteenth century.[6] Given the wealth of Christian stone buildings in Nubia, new mosques, such as those in Dongola and Qasr Ibrim, were sited in converted churches and cathedrals.

In the twelfth and thirteenth centuries, Bedouin migrations, encouraged by the Mamluk conquest of Nubia, mixed with

Map 7: East Africa, showing principal sites; the early spread of Islam down the Swahili coast was largely attributable to settlement associated with maritime trade.

indigenous pastoral groups and exercised control over the desert trade routes, established trading communities and converted the newly emergent state rulers. The migration of Muslim scholars versed in Maleki law was encouraged and Arabic became a *lingua franca* for trade, but the court continued to speak indigenous languages.

Small Muslim states (of which the Funj are the most notable) supplanted former Christian kingdoms. Some of the nomadic groups living in the eastern desert, e.g. the Beni Kanz, were converted to Islam rather earlier than the population in the Nile Valley, but little material evidence survives.[7] Apparently Islam spread overland via established trade routes between Aswan and the Red Sea and as a result of gold-mining activity.

The northern Sudan, populated by pastoralists and nomadic cultures over millennia, became largely Islamicized in culture and outlook. Fixed Nubian settlements developed along the banks of the Nile but the still largely nomadic Funj, and a host of other nomadic groups such as the Juhanya, the Fazara, the Shukriyya, the Kababish and the Baggara, continued to populate the arid expanse beyond, whereas the southern provinces, inhabited by sedentary agriculturists, remained ethnically heterogeneous, resisting Islam and maintaining indigenous traditions of origin.

The opening of the Suez Canal in 1869 had a significant impact on the economic fortunes of the region: the Red Sea was transformed into one of the world's most important seaways. Ports such as Suakin, which in 1805 was 'nearly in ruins', became thriving centres of mercantile activity, but caravans into the interior provided the links with the contemporary Islamic world which led to the revival of the Mahdiya as a resistance to Anglo-Egyptian colonialism.[8]

Suakin

The important settlement of Suakin is on an island, at the head of a *mersha* or inlet – one of many on the Red Sea coast of Sudan. The earliest documented reference is in 969, and it had a mixed population of Muslims and Christians at least until the early thirteenth century. Suakin served as a transhipment port between the Red Sea and the caravan routes into the interior, in particular the Nile Valley. The town seems to have declined in importance during the sixteenth-nineteenth centuries while under Ottoman control, but after the opening of the Suez Canal in 1869 it revived. Many of the houses and mosques were rebuilt during the next thirty years. Between 1909 and 1922 much of the trade shifted to Port Sudan and, although the island was abandoned, the mainland settlement (*geyt*) is still occupied.[9]

The Magidi Mosque is on the mainland next to the caravanserai and, although rebuilt, is probably pre-sixteenth century in origin. Its plan consists of two rows of longitudinal aisles parallel to the *mihrab* and behind these two aisles is an open courtyard. A single octagonal stairway-minaret, located at the south-west corner, has a carved stone parapet; in the north-east corner is the Qur'anic school (*khalwa*). The Hanafi Mosque, on the island, is similar in plan; it has a plasterwork *mihrab* and a fine stone *minbar*.

The Mosque of Sayed Mohammed el Sir, the largest in Suakin, was built in the late nineteenth century. Its clearly articulated *sahn* surrounded by an aisle on three sides, its three longitudinal aisles parallel to the *qibla* wall, and its tower-minaret in the south-west corner suggest an evolution from the earlier mosques. In the north-west corner (where the *khalwa* is normally located) a domed mausoleum was built; this structure features an upper register of unusual spiral plaster patterns and elaborate wooden grilles (carved in Java teak) on each of the four sides.

Harar

Located on the edge of the Ethiopian plateau at the node for caravan routes from the ports of Zeyla and Berbera on the Gulf of Aden into the interior, Harar played an important role in the introduction and development of Islam in north-east Africa.[10] It was a walled town (1,000 × 800 m; 1,100 × 875 yds), with five gates, each of which gave its name to one of the five town quarters; within these quarters there are about sixty smaller neighbourhoods, each associated with a mosque or shrine, or linked with some form of business activity. Of the original total of 86 mosques, seven lay outside the walls and 81 were founded before 1887. Foundation dates and building dates are very difficult to estimate, given the present state of research, but most pre-date Richard Burton's visit in 1864, when he noted that the city 'abounds in mosques'.[11] However, because of the prevalence of earthquakes in this area, it is probable that little of the early fabric survives, with no wall pre-dating 1800. The foundation date of some mosques can be deduced from their name or association (five probably date to the thirteenth century, three are associated with Abadir, the traditional twelfth-century ruler, and at least two belong to the sixteenth century), but the majority seem to have been established during the late-eighteenth and the nineteenth centuries.

The traditional mosques were built of granite and limestone. The foundations, always of granite, were set in a trench, up to 1 m (3 ft) in width. The stone was bonded with a mud mortar and the tapering walls narrowed with each successive course. At ground level, granite was replaced with limestone, preferred because of its resistance to earthquakes. The walls, about 50 cm thick, were reinforced at 1 m intervals with horizontal timbers (again for earthquake protection), reaching a total height of about 4 m (13 ft). On completion, the walls were smoothed off with mortar (*guguba*) and whitewashed with lime. Roof timbers were laid on large square columns, which supported a cross-beam of juniper wood up to 5 m (16 ft) in length. The space between this beam and the side walls was spanned by rafters, and with an infill of small stones and mud mortar. A further set of secondary infill rafters were set at right-angles to the primary rafters, and on these matting was suspended, the whole surface then being smoothly plastered over. Channels on the upper surface of the roof served to collect rainwater which was allowed to flow via downspouts away from the walls. These mud-and-stone roofs were never totally waterproof and often needed a *guguba* recoating.

The Friday Mosque has an oblong prayer-hall which was extended at the *qibla* end during the period of the Amir Abdullah in the late 1880s into a 'T' plan, hence the original arrangement of the *mihrab* is not known. The present *mihrab* is a plain recess, framed with a colonnaded architrave, and adjacent to it is a wooden *minbar* dating from 1761. A particular feature of this mosque is its double minaret. Otherwise minarets were unknown in Harar until after the Italian occupation of Ethiopia in 1935.

The smaller mosques, rarely measuring more than 7 × 5 m (23 × 16 ft), have a fairly standard plan. The roof structure normally results in transverse support, creating a prayer-hall that is wider than it is long and entered through a single opening on the southern side from a veranda or courtyard which is used as an extended praying area when needed, as well as a place to grow medicinal herbs. Ablutions are performed in one corner of this courtyard, but in most mosques this is a recent innovation, the water being piped in. The prayer-hall often has a side room, sometimes reserved for women, or serving as a dormitory (*zawia*) for students and travellers; in each case it has a separate doorway from the courtyard. Virtually every mosque has a staircase-minaret on the external south-east wall of the prayer-hall, sometimes leading to a small open-sided turret (to protect the muezzin from sun and rain). The *mihrab* normally consists of a plain elliptical arch without capitals and a semi-circular recess, forming a curved rather than a square projection from the external wall.

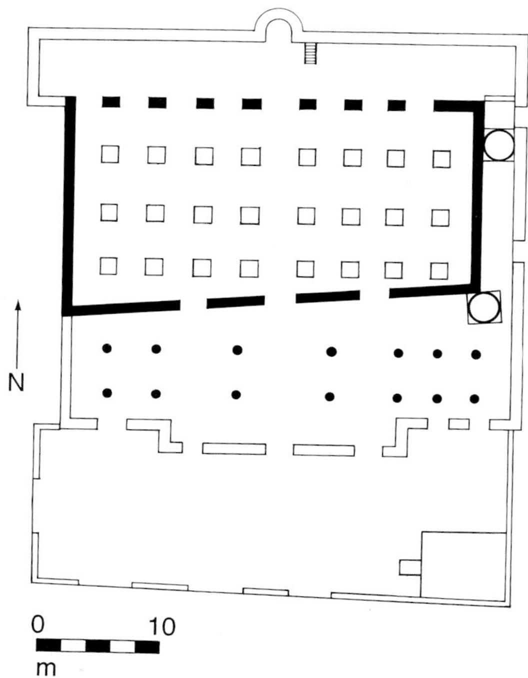

Plan of the Friday Mosque, Harar, showing the qibla *extension and the two minarets on the east side of the prayer-hall (original area shown in black).*

Dongola

In 651–2, an Egyptian Muslim expeditionary force unsuccessfully attempted to besiege christianized Dongola, the capital of the Nubian kingdom, fifty days' journey – some 600 km (375 miles) – from Aswan. Shortly after the establishment of the Fatimid Caliphate in North Africa in 969, an envoy sent to the court of Dongola to convert the Nubian king to Islam again met with no success. As elsewhere in Africa, Islam initially penetrated Christian Upper Nubia via a gradual process of infiltration. Among the nomadic groups who inhabit the region around Dongola, there is far greater consciousness of Nubian origin than is the case further south, and a Nubian dialect continues to be spoken.

In 1316, a Mamluk military expedition to Dongola succeeded in installing a converted Nubian prince as king, and al-Maqrizi, writing in the early fifteenth century, noted the inclusion of a provision that the Nubians maintain in good order the mosque which the Muslims had built in the centre of the city.

At this time the conversion of a church in Old Dongola to a mosque took place, an act commemorated by an inscription (dated 1317)

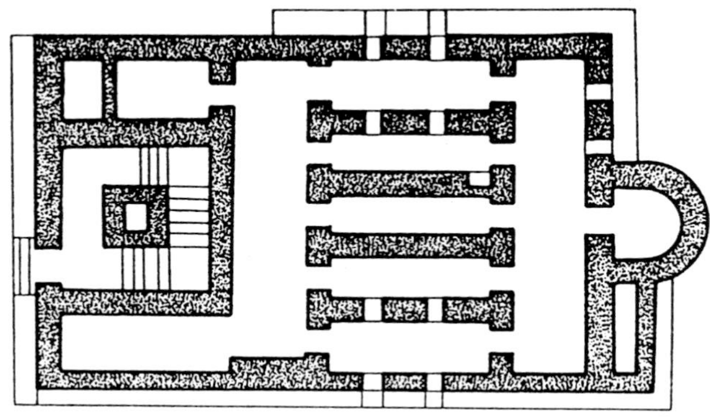

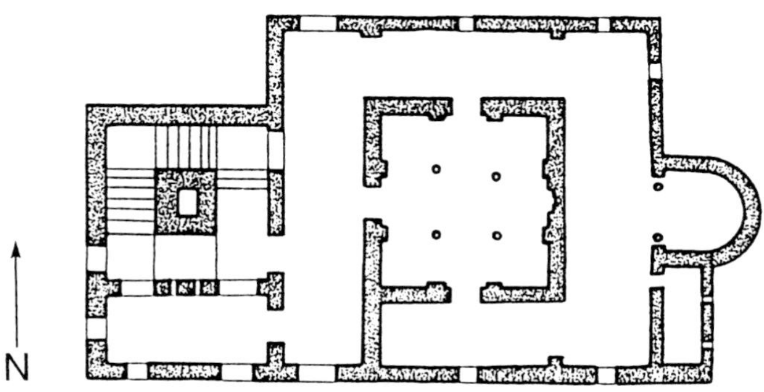

Ground-plan and upper-floor plan of the Mosque at Dongola, converted from a church in the sixteenth century.

adjacent to the upper-level *mihrab*. The result is a two-storied stone structure in which the lower floor has a pair of barrel vaults running parallel to the *qibla* and a most unusual, extremely large, semi-circular *mihrab*.[12] The upper floor has, in contrast, a central court, and the roof, built of palm-trunk rafters, is supported by four columns, one of them wooden with a trabeated cap and the other three of stone with Byzantine-like capitals.

Qasr Ibrim

The fortress of Qasr Ibrim, located on the Nile 190 km (125 miles) south of Aswan, served as a frontier post between Nubia and Islamic Egypt. Protected by the *baqt* treaty, it was the residence of both a bishop and the Eparch, a Christian official who regulated trade through Nubia. Archaeological evidence suggests that the Christians remained in control until the late fifteenth century, although much Islamic material (such as textiles, pottery, glass, metalwork and documents) has been found in levels associated with the period before *c.* 1560, when Ottoman forces took control of the fortress, where a garrison was maintained until 1811.[13] Local traditions state that the soldiers came from Bosnia. In addition to the large numbers of Ottoman houses, two mosques have been identified, both re-used churches. The impressive monumental cathedral was converted to a mosque by rotating the axis through 90°. The sanctuary area was covered with a mud-brick dome and a mud-brick *mihrab* was added.

Sennar

The defeat of the Christians at Soba in 1504 led to the establishment of the nominally Arabicized and Islamicized Funj kingdom (*al-Saltana al Zarga*, or the black Sultanate), with a population consisting primarily of nomadic pastoralists and a court constantly on the move over a region extending north to the third Cataract of the Nile, south to the foothills of Ethiopia and west to the desert of Kordofan. The Islamicization of the dynasty a century later (partly in response to northern political pressure), resulted in the permanent capital being established at Sennar and the building of its first mosque (1616–45). A five-storied palace, built shortly afterwards, is now in ruins, but as it was recorded in 1723 the building consisted primarily of rectangular keep or *donjon* with tapered walls, to which the palace apartments were attached on each floor, and European-type windows. The mosque appears to have been constructed in a similar manner: two tower-minarets with interior stairways facing the Nile, opposite them a main arched entrance, and a *qibla* wall pierced with large wooden-grille windows and featuring a rather humble projecting *mihrab*.[14]

In contrast to other religious and civic buildings in East Africa, fired-brick masonry, reinforced with horizontal wooden ties, was used for the walls of the mosque and palace at Sennar. Fired brick has been used since antiquity along the Nile, but in the Funj region historic military monuments (as well as contemporary urban housing) – often three stories high – were of massive earthen construction, the battered earthen walls (*jaous*) having no internal reinforcement (a technique similar to the building of cob walls in Europe and *pisé* walls in North Africa). Further north, undressed stone and mud mortar were the preferred materials for palaces and mosques.

The Islamicization of the peoples of the Funj Sultanate was largely the work of individual holy men (*fakis*) who settled in the countryside, taught the Qur'an, introduced a Sufi order and left reminders of their architectural heritage in the form of tombs spread across the

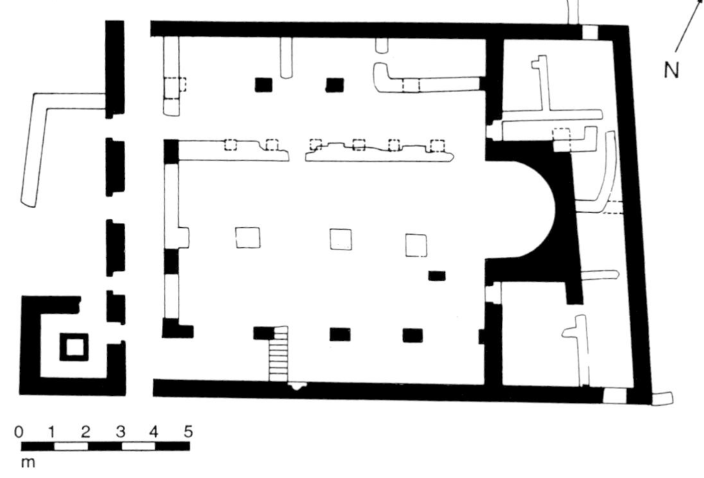

Plan of the mosque at Qasr Ibrim, converted from the seventh-century cathedral; the mihrab *and* minbar *added when the orientation of the building was altered in the early seventeenth century are seen on the south-east side, facing the direction of Mecca.*

countryside. The disintegration of the Funj kingdom in the eighteenth century facilitated the Egyptian conquest in the early nineteenth century, accelerated the process of unification and encouraged the introduction of new Islamic religious tendencies.

The Swahili Coast

The spread of Islam along the Swahili coast was via a maritime trade favoured by the seasonal monsoons. Archaeological discoveries at the site of Chibuene in southern Mozambique suggest that this trade had reached south-east Africa in the late pre-Islamic period. Burials on this site, confirming the Islamic presence, date to the ninth century. The remains of a succession of timber and stone mosques dating from the eighth to tenth centuries have been found at Shanga in the Lamu archipelago.[15]

The archaeological evidence suggests that these early settlers were indigenous, living partly off maritime resources and partly off trade with mixed populations of Muslims and those holding animist beliefs. Various mechanisms have been suggested for Islam's spread to these coastal settlements, including settlement of refugees from Arabia, the conversion of local populations and the return of captured slaves.[16]

The earliest stone architecture, dating from *c.* 900 onwards but found at only a small number of sites, includes both mosques and secular buildings. By *c.* 1100 Islam had begun spreading significantly into the Swahili coastal communities, where it became the majority religion. This turning-point is reflected in the dates of the earliest dedicatory mosque inscriptions (1104 for Barawa and 1107 for Kizimkazi, Zanzibar). Starting *c.* 1300, the use of coral instead of wood for housebuilding became widespread and the Swahili settlements took on an urban character. Towns with large numbers of houses and their own mosques grew up within a short distance of each other, supported by trade in luxury items from the interior: the most notable were Mogadishu, Barawa, Pate, Lamu, Malindi, Mombasa and Kilwa. Many of the significant mosques which have survived date to the sixteenth-eighteenth centuries, a period which was in many ways a golden age for Swahili architecture.[17]

In the early nineteenth century, the arrival of significant numbers of Arab settlers, mainly Omanis (for the first time on the African coast), in Zanzibar and Mombasa opened up new influences. They were attracted by the prosperity created by plantation slavery, the caravan trade into the interior and the political stability that was achieved by the Bu'saidi rulers. At Zanzibar, in particular, massive wealth was amassed to enable the rebuilding of the town, its mosques and royal palaces. Artisans from India as well as the Middle East were attracted and a Zanzibar style of architecture emerged out of the mingling of Swahili tradition and outside influences.[18]

Swahili settlements on the East African coast feature a most distinctive style of architecture. Houses and mosques are of stone, in contrast to earthen and mud-brick building traditions prevailing throughout the interior. Close parallels for this architecture are hard to find, however, nor can any close parallel be found across the Indian Ocean. While there was much borrowing of architectural concepts and elements from many directions, the foreign nature of this architecture has been much overstated. Foreign influences were always modified to a Swahili idiom by local, rather than foreign craftsmen.[19]

The basic building materials used were coral, plaster and wood. Coral was of two types: terrestrial and porites.[20] Solid walls at least 35 cm (14 in.) thick were constructed by bonding the hard terrestrial rock with locally prepared lime, so ensuring survival for hundreds of years. Sometimes, timber reinforcing between courses provided additional cohesion. Up till the nineteenth century (when the knowledge of porites coral carving was lost) decorated wall-surfaces were created using porites facings. *Mihrabs* were often constructed entirely in porites coral. Excavations have shown that this material was widely used in the form of neatly cut blocks for wall construction in the tenth and eleventh centuries.

Excavated fragments suggest that the use of plaster in building from the tenth century on, while a pair of stucco niches from a fourteenth-century stone house survive at Shanga. However, the finest plasterwork was developed at Lamu in the early nineteenth century, when it replaced porites coral for spectacular banks of wall-niches and door-jambs. *Mihrabs* were also decorated with fine plasterwork. The tradition of Lamu plasterwork continues to this day, though some of the fine surfaces found on ancient buildings cannot be easily replicated.

The third material used in Swahili building was timber – mangrove poles and hardwoods. Like coral, it was locally and readily available.[21] Mangrove poles, long-lived and termite resistant, were used extensively in roof construction, but the growth habit limits its span, so restricting room widths to 3 m (10 ft). Hardwoods from the coastal forests were used in high-status houses and for mosque roofs which required a greater span. Although the date for the first use of hardwoods is unknown, by the thirteenth century they were in use for roofs and columns of mosque and domestic architecture, and by the fourteenth century planks were occasionally used in ceilings. The most spectacular use of hardwoods, however, was for the intricate patterning of carved doors and lintels. Apparently no examples dating from before the late seventeenth century are known to have survived, and it is sometimes claimed that these doors feature Indian- or Omani-inspired designs executed in local wood.[22]

These same materials and technologies were used to create a local Swahili mosque style. The basic plan of the mosque is a rectangular prayer-hall, with sides in a 2:3 or 3:4 proportion, and with a roof supported on one or two rows of columns. Early mosques had wooden columns; later either round or square stone columns were used. Roofs were built of coral rock, supported on hardwood beams, with tiles of cut coral. Floors were raised above ground-level, and steps led up into the prayer-halls. An outside ablutions area, usually uncovered, with a tank and well was provided, and verandas were sometimes located on the east and west sides of the prayer-hall. In such a plan there was normally an arcade of side doorways with flat lintels or pointed arches faced in porites coral. Tower-minarets were very rare: there is a small group in southern Somalia dating to the thirteenth century and there are eighteenth-century examples from Lamu, Mombasa and Zanzibar.

The mihrab *at Kizimkazi, Zanzibar, showing floreate Kufic inscription and trefoliate inner arch.*

Staircase-minarets are more common, often located in the angle formed by the *mihrab* and the north wall.

The *mihrab*, the main decorative feature of the mosque, took a variety of forms. At its simplest it is a pointed arch with a recess, but more common is a pointed arch with several orders rising from a capital and framed with an architrave. Sometimes there is an inner trefoliate arch. Decoration is applied to the jamb blocks, the arcaded apse, the spandrels and the architrave. Finely carved roundels are placed in the architrave, herring-bone moulding frame it and inscriptions are set into the capitals.

The earliest known *mihrab*, at Kizimkazi in Zanzibar, is decorated with an inscription in floreate Kufic which dates it to 500 AH/AD 1107, and contains all these elements, but it is thought to have been largely rebuilt in the eighteenth century.[23] However, the recent discovery on Tumbatu Island of another twelfth-century *mihrab* built in the same style suggests that much may be original, including the trefoliate inner arch. One innovation was the use of an elliptical rather than a pointed opening in the *mihrab*. This feature was particularly common on Pemba Island, where there are strong traditions of settlement, from the early fifteenth century onwards, by South Arabian Sharifian families. Another feature of some of the early *mihrabs* with pointed arches is a small nick occurring as a decorative detail at the apex of the arch, in imitation of an ogee. Keystones are entirely absent, as was a clear understanding of the use of voussoirs.

Minbars were of three different types: wooden, stone and recessed. The movable wooden type was the commonest and archaeological evidence of floor-wear patterns from the thirteenth century exists at Tumbatu, but the earliest wooden *minbar* (1523) to have survived complete is at Siyu on Pate Island; others are in the mosques at Lamu, Pate, Tundwa and Matandoni. Stone *minbars* are found in a number of ruined mosques: the one at Ungwana, the grandest of all, has eleven steps and a stair-rail. The recessed *minbar* and *mihrab* are linked via steps set in the wall. All the known examples date from the eighteenth and nineteenth centuries, and this arrangement appears to have been a local invention.

There is very little evidence to show that any of the Swahili mosques were designed in a formal sense. Whilst a basic cubit was used (albeit non-standard) and proportionality was retained (at least for the prayer-hall), there is little to indicate a sophisticated layout and roofing or any rigid adherence to a surveyed plan. Precise right-angles were often lacking. It seems likely that mosques were built by local craftsmen who developed the use of local materials and adapted them to a basic esstablished form. Close examination suggests a centuries-old conservatism of style and plan. The basic plan seems to have derived from the small family mosque of the ninth-tenth centuries, then current in the Gulf, at sites such as Siraf. The earliest East African examples were generally small and similarly proportioned; hypostyle and courtyard mosques are completely absent from the region.

Over time, to accommodate growing Muslim populations, extra space was created by adding rows of columns to the basic plan. *Mihrab* design changed little and the only significant architectural innovation (dated to the late thirteenth century at Kilwa and Mogadishu) was the use of domes and barrel vaults. Domes were then employed in a number of other mosques (Mwana, Kongo, Chwaka, the Kilwa Small Domed Mosque) until the beginning of the sixteenth century, when the technique was again abandoned.

Mogadishu

The capital of modern Somalia has long been one of the most important ports on the East African coast, being the first secure harbour south of Ras Hafun. Recent excavations have failed to reveal evidence of occupation prior to the early twelfth century, and the first mention of the town was by Yakut *c.* 1210. In the thirteenth century it was certainly

Facing page
Most East African mosques built before the twentieth century are on a smaller and more intimate scale than in other regions. The Mosque of Said bin Sultan (top) at Mtoni, Zanzibar, was built c. *1840 as a private place of worship for the ruler.*

A small eighteenth-century mosque near Malindi, Zanzibar, has a plain interior whose only decorative feature is the recessed mihrab *(centre), which can be seen externally as a projection on the north wall (below, centre), while the entrance (below, right) is kept very simple.*

The Friday Mosque at Shela on Lamu Island, Kenya, dates from the early nineteenth century. The interior of the prayer-hall (above) has a series of massive square columns; the distinctive pointed minaret (opposite, below) stands at the north-west corner.

The Riadha Mosque (left) on Lamu Island, Kenya, was built in 1902–3; its style shows clear evidence of influences brought to the east coast of Africa by settlers of Indian origin.

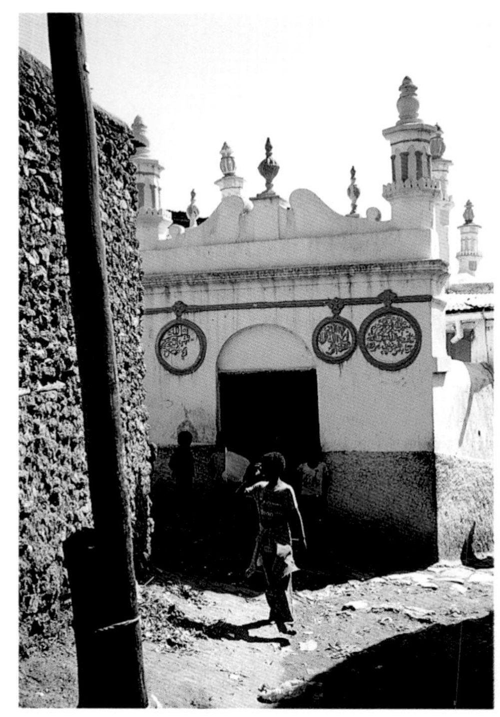

one of the most prosperous communities in the region and an exceptionally large number of inscriptions are known from the large cemeteries at Shangani and Hamar Weyne (from 1217 to 1363). Ibn Battuta, who in the course of his travels visited the city in 1329, left a full eyewitness description. Of the twenty-eight extant mosques only three have substantial early remains.[24]

The earliest surviving part of the Jamia Mosque in Hamar Weyne is the exceptional tower (1238) of porites coral, while the doorway is very narrow with a multiple-order arch and an apex nick. The present mosque is largely the product of rebuilding in the 1930s, when the previously freestanding tower was incorporated. The core of an eighteenth-century mosque survives around the *mihrab* as a rectangular prayer-hall with a central row of columns and a western side room. This was probably a rebuilding of the original thirteenth-century prayer-hall; in plan and proportion it has all the features of an early mosque, including side pilasters. The *mihrab*, with its use of plaster decoration, inset porcelain bowls and a multifloreate arch, dates largely from the eighteenth century; it does, however, incorporate a late Kufic inscription possibly contemporary with the tower and re-used from the original mosque.

The Fakr ad-Din Mosque is the only medieval example on the Swahili coast to have remained substantially unchanged, yet still in use. A unique and important survival, it is a decoratively elaborate building dated by an inscription on a marble relief to 667 AH/AD 1269 and is probably the only pre-modern building on the coast to have been designed by an architect. Its compact rectangular plan differs substantially from those of other Swahili mosques of this period. The inner courtyard is surrounded by rooms on all sides. The profiles of an eight-sided conical dome in the portico and a 'sugar-loaf' type dome centrally placed in the prayer-hall contrast sharply with those of the lower, outer domes. The portico dome is evocative of the parasol tents of the time while the 'sugar-loaf' dome not only recalls the shape of Sudanese tombs but, by being centred on the three-by-three set of nine roof bays, integrates them into the visually unified space and recalls the configuration of a magic square. The rafters are arranged octagonally around a flat roof. The outer doorways feature multiple recessed orders, with the apex nick and bosses decorating the architrave, while the main entranceway displays a superbly carved marble surround that contains floral interlace and an inscription. The inner central doorway – one of the finest surviving doorways on the entire coast – is entirely faced with imported marble slabs delicately carved with floral pattern reliefs. The construction of the conical vaults, the use of pendentives rather than squinches, the treatment of the capitals and the decorative features of the doors evoke close comparison with the nearly contemporary Husuni Kubwa at Kilwa (see below). The *mihrab*, though rebuilt in the eighteenth century in the form of an elliptical arch and a square recess, still contains the original marble plaque (with decoration almost identical to a frieze from Kilwa) and a tile bearing the name and dates of the founder.

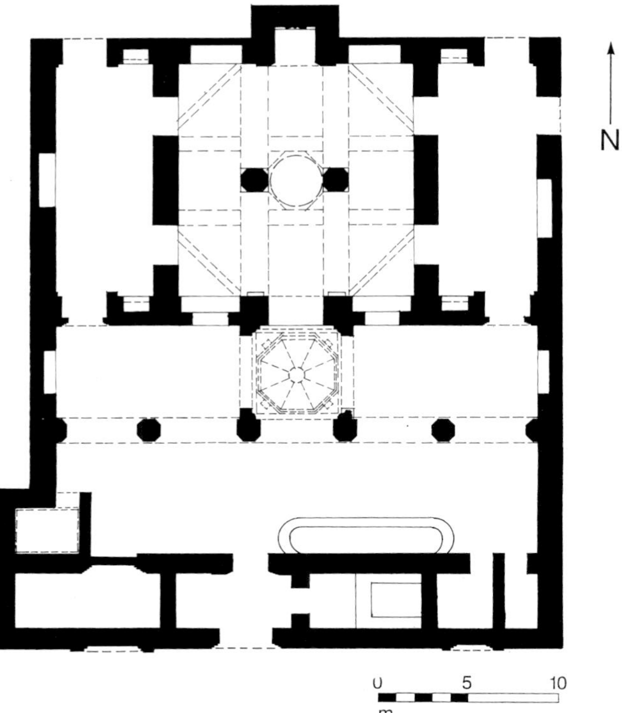

Plan of the Fakr ad-Din Mosque, Mogadishu, showing the square prayer-hall with its centrally placed dome and eight-sided conical dome over the portico.

Facing page

The Jami Masjid (above) in Nairobi, the capital of Kenya, is a major urban mosque revealing its Indian antecedents, especially in the presence of triple domes. In Harar, Ethiopia, the Friday Mosque (below), which acquired its present form in the 1880s, is noted for its twin minarets – a unique feature in East Africa until after the Italian occupation of the country in 1935.

Kilwa Kisiwani

Kilwa, now in Tanzania, is justifiably the most famous medieval site on the Swahili coast. Here are substantial remains of an exceptional group of monuments, including the Great Mosque and a wide range of domestic and palace buildings. At the height of its prosperity in the fourteenth century, Kilwa became wealthy by controlling much of the maritime trade with Mozambique and southern Africa, which included products such as gold and ivory. Excavations have revealed that occupation began in the ninth century with timber-and-daub houses. The earliest stone houses and the construction of the mosque date from the twelfth century. Around 1300 a palace complex consisting of two major buildings – Husuni Kubwa and Husuni Ndogo – was erected 3 km (nearly 2 miles) from the main town. A design with Near Eastern elements was executed in locally available coral rag and lime, and this complex represents one of the few large-scale attempts to import foreign architecture to the Swahili coast.[25]

The Great Mosque – one of the most magnificent public buildings on the Swahili coast – was compared by early Portuguese explorers to the Great Mosque of Cordoba. The prayer-hall consists of the original (northern) mosque and a later, much grander, southern extension. The northern structure (probably the second mosque on this site) was a modest rectangular prayer-hall with three rows of wooden columns. The side walls have integral pilasters and three paired entries, and there are corner doors in the south wall. Later, the walls were thickened, presumably to carry a new roof, and the ablutions area to the west was remodelled. The southern extension, which covers an area twice that of the old mosque, dates to *c.* 1300. The barrel-vaulted and domed space was arranged in five aisles, each with six bays, the domes being supported on monolithic stone columns. On the south side a large ablutions area consisting of tanks, a latrine and a well was created. On the east, a domed room with its own entrance and tank was built: this unique feature – which the Kilwa Chronicle mentions as being in existence by *c.* 1330 – was used by the Sultan for private prayer. The ambitious scheme created serious structural problems and it seems that much of the vaulted roof collapsed. The monolithic stone columns, which were cleared away and discarded, can still be seen outside. The Kilwa Chronicle recorded that the mosque was rebuilt *c.* 1421–42 and this is probably the date of the surviving vaults and west wall. The rebuilt domes were set on plain squinches along the side and end walls and on the central axis with barrel vaults over the intervening spaces. In the late eighteenth century, some of the collapsed walls were cleared and a plain *mihrab* was inserted at the north end of the southern extension; at this point the original *mihrab* in the old part of the mosque was abandoned.

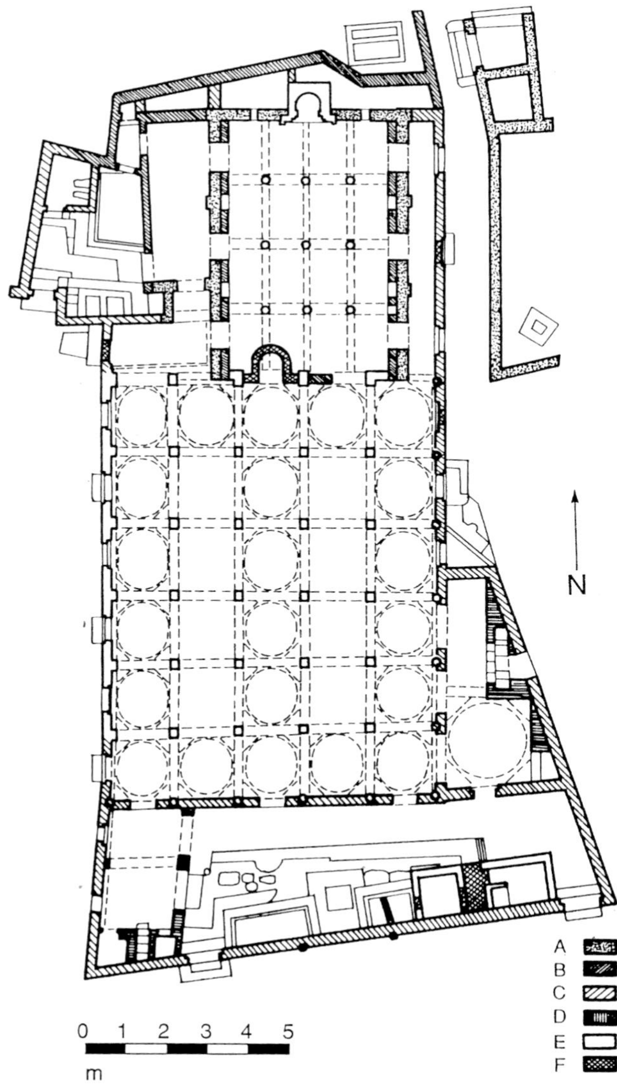

Plan of the Great Mosque, Kilwa Kisiwani, showing stages of development: (A) twelfth century; (B) late twelfth century; (C) late thirteenth century; (D) early fourteenth century; (E) mid-fifteenth century; (F) eighteenth century.

Nearby is the Small Domed Mosque, also fourteenth century, with a similar, but smaller-scale arrangement of domes and barrel vaults. Two of the six domes are fluted, while the central row of barrel vaults is decorated with inset glazed bowls of the late fourteenth century. The well-preserved *mihrab* has a capital set on four shafts with a pointed arch, spandrel bosses and a square area for an inset tile above the architrave (a fragment of a lustre tile was found nearby during excavations). These bosses are always in cut porites coral and often bear very elaborate designs and decoration. They are early (present at Kizimkazi and Tumbatu) and are a particular feature of Swahili architecture. The tanks, latrine and well are to the south-west. An unusual feature is the square column set on top of the central dome, perhaps in imitation of contemporary Swahili pillar tombs.

Excavations have also revealed the remains of a substantial stone building which may have been the late sixteenth-century royal palace, described by Portuguese explorers as located on the western outskirts of the town. It contained two courtyards, one of which was flanked by a vaulted veranda. Incorporated into this building was a barrel-vaulted mosque of unusual design: the prayer-hall consisted of a single aisle, while the *mihrab* was freestanding with a northern room beyond.

Lamu

Lamu, now in Kenya, is a well-preserved traditional Swahili town on the coast, and has attracted much research and interest. There are suggestions of tenth-century occupation at both the northern and southern ends of the town, while a description dated 1441 records how part of the town was engulfed in sand. The present town is largely of eighteenth-century date: twenty-four mosques remain in use and many contain dated dedicatory inscriptions. The Wa Pwani Mosque has the earliest (772 AH/AD 1370), though the building itself dates entirely from the late eighteenth or the early nineteenth century. The majority of Lamu's mosques belong to this later period, with dedications ranging from 1733–4 to 1880–1. During the first part of the twentieth century, a strong religious revival in Lamu, led by Comorian Sharifs, resulted in the construction of a number of mosques in a non-traditional style, and the modification of existing buildings to conform more closely to a pan-Islamic style. The earliest of these new buildings were the Riyadha and Swataa (1901–2) Mosques; the process continues, threatening the survival of traditional Swahili architecture.[26]

The Friday Mosque (originally built 1511–12) has a very large prayer-hall with five rows of chamfered columns set around a central opening, with an ablutions area to the south. Like some of the other Lamu mosques, the structure was wholly rebuilt in the nineteenth century. The *mihrab* has a trefoliate arch resting on jamb panels and adjacent to it is a wooden *minbar*, which has been largely reconstructed.

The N'nlalo Mosque (1753) is typical of the smaller mosques. It has a rectangular prayer-hall with four rows of four chamfered columns (an enlargement from the original three rows). Typical of Lamu mosques, the ablutions area lies to the south. The trefoliate *mihrab* has jamb panels and a dedicatory inscription. To the right of the *mihrab* there is a separate Imam's room.

The very fine Friday Mosque at Shela, a small settlement to the south, dates from the early nineteenth century; it remains in use and has recently been restored. The prayer-hall contains 24 square columns, eastern and western side-aisles and a southern ablutions area served by an external tank. In the north-west corner there is an unusual tapering minaret with internal spiral stairs lit by large windows. The *mihrab*, which features a dedicatory inscription dated 1829, has a trefoliate arch and an architrave supported on jamb blocks; the adjacent wooden *minbar* dates from 1820. The building style seems consistent with the date of the dedication.

Zanzibar

As the capital of the Bu'saidi Sultanate, Zanzibar experienced a period of prosperity during the nineteenth century, and much of the town, with its many fine stone houses and mosques, belongs to this period. Archaeological excavations have shown that the area has been intermittently occupied since the eleventh century, but the earliest surface remains are parts of the Fort which incorporates the Portuguese Church built in the mid-sixteenth century.

The earliest mosque is the eighteenth-century Malindi Mosque.[27] The prayer-hall itself has been rebuilt, but the minaret provides a rare example on the coast of large upper window openings and a band of double chevrons below. In style it is comparable to the minaret at Shela. The mosque, built by Mohammed Abdul Qadir el Mansabi, who is buried outside adjacent to the *mihrab*, is later.

The private mosque of Said bin Sultan lies adjacent to his palace at Mtoni, attractively sited above the beach. It has an almost square prayer-hall, with a single central column and two large windows in each of the four sides. The *mihrab*, set within the thickness of the wall, owes little to local tradition and is typically Ibadhi. Although the plan is simple, there is an ogival arch set on carved jambs, with a fluted dome, leading to an inner recess that duplicates the outer arrangement.

Indian Settlements and Mosques

The presence of small and probably short-lived communities of Indian craftsmen on the East African coast from around the tenth century is attested by archaeological discoveries made there. By 1504 Indians from Cambay were established in Mombasa, where they played an active part in the mercantile economy; the Portuguese did not record whether they were Muslims or Hindus – indeed they believed that some of them were Christians. Indians settled in the area in greater numbers from the early nineteenth century, when branches of long-established Indian firms were established in Zanzibar. Most of the new arrivals came from Gujarat, Cutch and Kathiawar. By the late nineteenth century the Indian community, acting as middlemen in the African trade, had become rich and powerful, and numerous fine Indian houses from this period survive in the Old Town of Zanzibar.

Other Indian communities grew up in Lamu, Mombasa, on Pemba Island at Chake Chake and Jambangome, and at Kilwa Kivinje; Indian mosques and houses still survive in these towns. The majority in these communities were Ismailis and Ithnasheris; other important immigrants were Bohras, often trading in ironmongery and chandlery. Other groups included a small number of Orthodox Muslims (mostly Sidhi and Maiman), as well as Hindus and Goans.

Indian mosques in East Africa, often known as *jamatkhana*, differ markedly from those of the Swahili, in that they provide a range of communal facilities including upper-floor halls, *madrasas*, kitchens and bathing areas, as well as a library and offices and at least one prayer-hall. The architecture makes little allowance for traditional forms or indeed for the use of local materials, teak often being imported from India for the purpose, while *mihrabs* are frequently decorated in an exuberant manner and owe nothing to local practice. The principal Indian mosques, associated with the merchant class, are found in the main trading towns. In Zanzibar, the Ismailis' *jamatkhana* of 1838 was rebuilt in 1905 as a mosque/community building; the Ithnasheris have three mosques there – Hujjatul Islam (1894–5), Kuwwatul Islam (1878) and Matemi (1861) – and the Bohra mosque was built before 1900.

The original Bohra mosque in Mombasa, built in 1901 at the expense of the leading Indian businessman and pioneer of Indian settlement up-country, A. M. Jivanjee, was replaced in 1982 by a concrete structure with an Arabian-style minaret. The Ismaili *jamatkhana* there is of twentieth-century date, while the Ithnasheri mosque was built after 1887. Other buildings of special interest in Mombasa are the Bhadala Mosque (rebuilt in 1950) and the Memon Mosque (1880), both of which feature ornate Indian architectural styles, retaining elements associated with Hindu temple architecture. On Pemba Island the Indian community has dwindled and the mosques are now in a ruinous state. The Bohra mosque at Chake Chake is a particularly good example of an unaltered structure of the late nineteenth century, in which extensive use was made of carved imported Indian teak.

Although the majority of the Indian workers involved in the construction of the Uganda Railway (1896–1903) eventually returned home, merchants and traders saw the opportunties that were opening up in the interior. Mostly from Mombasa and Zanzibar, they followed the railway as it progressed inland. By 1898, there were Indians in Kibwezi and Machakos. In 1903 Uganda had around five hundred Indians, and by 1911 their numbers had increased to 2,216. The construction of mosques followed the establishment of prosperous Indian communities in Nairobi, Kampala and Dar es Salaam, and also in a number of regional centres.

- 12 -
CHINA

LUO XIAOWEI

THERE are two types of mosque architecture in China: one, brought from the Near East, occurs in the north-western region, including Xinjiang Province, where there are many minorities who are predominantly Muslim; the other type is based on traditional Chinese architecture adapted to Islamic belief and ritual requirements. This chapter deals with mosques of the latter type, which are spread over a vast area of China in considerable numbers, from cities like Shengyang and Harbin in the north-east to Kunming in the south-west, from Lanzhou and Yinchuan on the upper Yellow River to the coastal cities of Shanghai, Quanzhou and Guangzhou (Canton). Most of the Muslims are of Hui nationality, one of the largest minority groups in present-day China, with a total population amounting to over 8,500,000 in 1990.

Islam was first introduced to China in the mid-seventh century via the port cities of Guangzhou and Quanzhou on the south-east coast and later by land from Central Asia. It was in the time of Kutayba ibn Muslim el-Bahili's campaign to the East in the early eighth century that the first mosques could have been built in Kashi (Kashgar) and Yecheng (Yurkan) in the Western Region.[1] Four or five centuries were to elapse before a majority among the population in Xinjiang Province belonged to the Muslim faith as a result of the gradual process of conversion to Islam.

The mosques of the Chinese type have ingeniously integrated Near Eastern Islamic influences with local architectural traditions, eventually producing a distinctive style for such buildings.

HISTORICAL AND CULTURAL BACKGROUND

The Silk Routes

Two Silk Routes linked the Orient and the Occident, one overland and the other by sea, the latter also being known as the Route of Perfume and Spice. The overland route was first explored by Zheng Qian, an envoy sent by the Han Emperor to the Western Region in 139 BC, and was later frequented and developed by caravans of traders and envoys from Central and Western Asia and even from as far away as the Roman Empire. This route, which started from Changan (now Xian), was via Urumqi and Kashi, then from Kashi it passed through Samarqand or Balkh (Afghanistan) to Merv (Turkmen), Ctesiphon (Persia) and Palmyra (Syria), and finally reached Antioch (Syria) and Tyre (Lebanon). The sea route began in the west at Siraf on the Persian Gulf; after the first stage to Mascal (Gulf of Oman), it continued around the Indian subcontinent and, after passing the Strait of Malacca, reached the ports of Guangzhou and Quanzhou. The section between China and India resulted from numerous expeditions to holy places by Buddhist pilgrims from China to the Indian Ocean from the seventh century onwards.

Once the east-west route overland was established, a succession of traders and envoys, mostly from Persia and Arabia, made their way to China, and some of them even settled down in the Middle Kingdom. It is recorded that, in the period from 651 to 798, there were thirty-seven embassies from Arabia alone. Also there were more than four thousand *se-ma-ren* ('colour-eyed people')[2] residing in Changan, the capital of the Tang Dynasty emperors. These outsiders were permitted to reside in *fan-fangs*.[3] From the end of the seventh century incessant wars were taking place in the Western Region, such as the campaign to the East by Kutayba ibn Muslim el-Bahili and later the war between the Caliphate and the Abbasids, and because the route by land was no longer safe, it was gradually abandoned. The sea route was gaining in importance and, from the ninth century on, coastal cities like Guangzhou, Quanzhou, and later Yangzhou and Hangzhou, became extremely flourishing. In Quanzhou there were streets full of shops dealing in jewelry and spices. By that time tens of thousands of 'colour-eyed people' were living in large *fan-fangs* in these cities. However, during the fifteenth century the coast of China came under serious threat from pirates, and the sea route ceased to be used.

The Muslims in China and their culture

The first Muslims to reach China were Abi Waqqas, a maternal uncle of the Prophet, and three companions. They made the journey by sea in 632, Abi Waqqas coming as an envoy from Medina. After arriving in Guangzhou, he proceeded to Changan, where he was received in audience by the Emperor. It was said that he sought permission to build three mosques, one in Changan, one in Jiangning (now Nanjing), and one in Guangzhou. There is no record of whether those mosques were ever built. After Changan, Abi Waqqas settled in Guangzhou, and after his death was buried there with one of his companions. The tomb of Abi Waqqas can be considered the oldest surviving Muslim

Facing page
Mosque in Jiuquan, Gansu Province; the roof is supported by the dou-gong *(bracket) structure used extensively in traditional Chinese architecture.*

Map 8: China, showing principal sites.

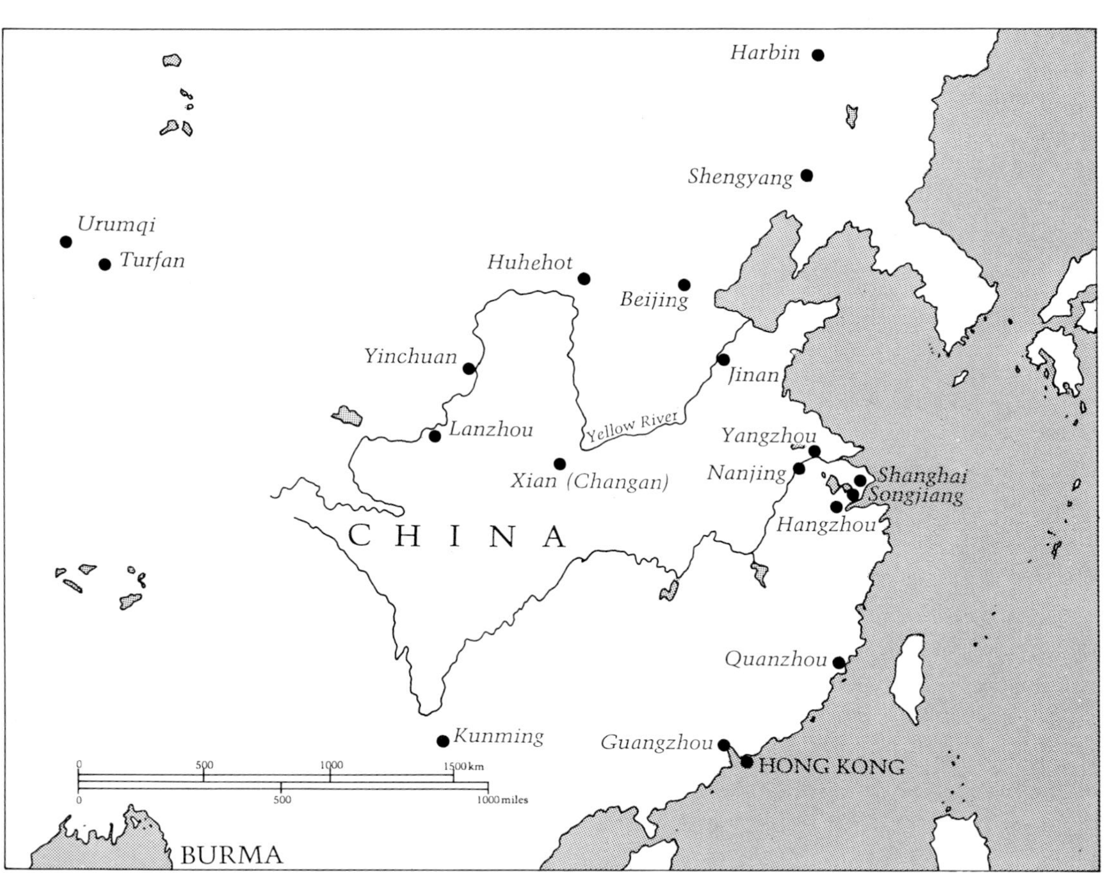

building in China. His two other companions lived in Quanzhou, and their tombs as seen there today are the result of later rebuilding.

Starting from the eighth century, when Islam was spreading into West and Central Asia, more and more Muslims travelled to China. The colour-eyed people, including Arabs, in and around Changan may have built mosques and graveyards in their *fan-fangs*, as Muslims living in the coastal cities did. Subsequently the resident Muslim population adapted themselves to Chinese ways, dressing in Chinese style, speaking Chinese and even taking Chinese names, while continuing to observe their own Islamic religious practices.

The spread of Islam in China

Shortly before and during the Yuan Dynasty (1280–1368) China witnessed a real increase in the Muslim population and Islam became one of the country's major religions. When Genghis Khan and Hülegü drove westwards with their cavalry forces (in 1219 and 1258 respectively), there were many Muslims living along the route of the invaders who had to seek refuge either by joining the troops or by escaping into China. Among those who moved eastward, most settled in Xinjiang, and quite a number penetrated as far as Gansu and Ningxia provinces. Under the Mongol Yuan Dynasty, all major cities in China had garrisons composed of soldiers of various races, most of the soldiers being Muslims. They settled down and raised families, so creating new Muslim communities throughout most of the country. In addition people of other races and nationalities were converted to Islam.

The original Muslim soldiers came from various sects within Islam. They formed communities, each occupying its own *jiao-fang*[4] with its own mosque. This *jiao-fang* principle still survives in some parts of China today.

The Evolution of Mosque Architecture in the Chinese Style

Mosque architecture in indigenous style falls into four main periods, as set out below.

The emergent period (seventh–tenth century)

No written record survives of mosques of this period, nor are there any physical remains. However, to judge from the minaret of Huai-Sheng Si in Guangzhou, built in the tenth century, and the remains of the prayer-hall of Sheng-You Si in Quanzhou, built 1009–1010, it appears that the style of earlier mosque architecture could simply have been a direct transference from the Western Region (as in the examples described), or the buildings may have been no more than simple and temporary structures which were not considered worthy of mention in documents or were unlikely to withstand the ravages of time.

Attempts at integration (eleventh–fourteenth century)

During this period the focus of interest shifted to the cities on the south and south-east coasts of China. From the mosques that were regarded as the four most important of the Song Dynasty, i.e. the Huai-Sheng Si in Guangzhou, the Sheng-You Si in Quanzhou, the Zheng-Jiao Si in Hangzhou, the Mosque in Yangzhou, as well as from the Mosque in Songjiang also dating from this period, one can see that great efforts were made to integrate functional requirements, cultural expression and building techniques from the Western Region with characteristic local architecture, producing results which would be respected by Muslim and non-Muslim alike. The 'colour-eyed' Muslims who had been naturalized and who generally had a higher social status had been adapting themselves to Chinese culture. Mosque building was no exception in their endeavour to fuse the two cultures. The physical manifestation of these efforts can be summarized as follows:

(1) A turning of the axis and a gateway preceding the prayer hall. In Chinese tradition monumental architecture usualy faces south and the main buildings were arranged along a south-north axis with open spaces in between. The mosque architecture of this period shows that in most cases the traditional orientation was adopted, with the front entrance facing south, while the prayer-hall, in order to allow worshippers to face in the direction of Mecca, must have its access from the east, hence a turning of axis was involved. In Huai-Sheng Si and Sheng You Si this turning of axis seems abrupt. The entrance hall and the prayer-hall both stand independently on their own axis; thus from a Chinese traditional point of view, each of them appears to be separate. However, in the Mosque in Yangzhou or the Mosque in Songjiang, a second portal is placed in front of the prayer-hall; this portal is one of the dominant features of the east-west axis, while blending harmoniously with other elements.

(2) Minaret – Moon Pavilion – Portal

The oldest freestanding minaret is that of Huai-Sheng Si. Its smooth masonry shaft and the treatment of internal stairways, which have no precedent in China, were unquestionably adopted from the Western Region. Later a tall, freestanding minaret in the style of Chinese pagoda developed, but very few examples are known. In Sheng-You Si there is an *iwan*-like minaret, the form of which was evidently imported. It is the only example of this type, and it serves a triple purpose: as minaret, as portal, and as a place to observe the moon, hence the name 'Moon Pavilion'. This kind of structure combining three functions was popular during this period, sometimes adjacent to the street and used as the main entrance, as in the Mosque of Na-jia Hu, in the Ningxia Hui Autonomous Region, but in most cases preceding the prayer-hall, as for example in the Mosque in Songjiang, Shanghai. The style in this period was not distinctive, but later such minarets were elaborately designed.

(3) Recess for the *mihrab* – mostly a masonry dome crowned by a wooden roof

The nature of the roof over the *mihrab* recess in Sheng-You Si is not known, but its square plan and comparison with the recesses of other mosques built in this period suggest that the roof structure was probably a dome. The recesses in Zhen-Jiao Si and the Mosque of Songjiang are masonry domes covered with timber structures. The former has a hexagonal roof, pyramidal in shape, while the latter is a hip and gable roof. This kind of roof over a dome was in part a practical response to the damp climate in this part of China, and in part a strong expression of traditional Chinese architecture, for it is accepted that one of the essential formal characteristics of indigenous Chinese architecture is the roof. In each of the two mosques mentioned above, the roof height above the dome is higher than that over the prayer-hall, thus emphasizing the symbolic importance of the *mihrab*. Mosques in the north and north-west of China, where the climate is dry, have their domes exposed; they are distinguished not by an emphasis on height but by their form.

KEY EXAMPLES

Huai-Sheng Si (Mosque in Memory of the Holy Prophet), Guangzhou (Canton), Guangdong Province; also known as Guang-ta Si (the Minaret Mosque)

Huai-Sheng Si is generally acknowledged as being the oldest surviving mosque in China. Abi Waqqas, a preacher and maternal uncle of the Prophet, came to China from Medina in 632, during the Tang Dynasty. He settled in Guangzhou, one of the busiest trading ports in south-east Asia, where numerous foreign merchants, mostly Persians and Arabs from Central and Western Asia came together; there he is said to have established the mosque of Huai-Sheng Si on the western outskirts of the city, but it is more likely that this building dates from the late Tang Dynasty or early Song period (tenth–eleventh century). Though rebuilt many times, the mosque still occupies the original site. The main entrance faces south, in accordance with Chinese tradition. On passing through the main gate from Guang-ta Road, one enters a long and fairly narrow courtyard leading to another gateway above which there is a plaque inscribed with four Chinese characters, which may be translated as 'Religion that holds in great esteem the teachings brought from the Western Region'.

Close behind the inner gateway stands a two-storied portal called the Moon Pavilion, built in the seventeenth century. The building is elegant and well-proportioned, being crowned with a gabled and hipped roof with double eaves. Its thick walls, sloping slightly outward, give a feeling of sturdiness, while the *dou-gong* (brackets) under the eaves are delicate and decorative. The pavilion opens up to a large courtyard surrounded by colonnades, at the end of which stands the prayer-hall. Thus far the layout is in typical Chinese style, with open and closed spaces planned symmetrically along a central axis running from south to north, with the dominant feature furthest from the entrance. However, due to the requirements of ritual prayer, the axis of the prayer-hall runs transversally from east to west; the main entrance to the hall faces eastward. The present prayer-hall was rebuilt in reinforced concrete in 1935.

The minaret – dating from the tenth century and the most famous feature of the mosque – is a freestanding structure to the west of the main entrance. It is a brick tower with round shaft, 36.30 m (119 ft) in height, and surmounted by an elogated pointed dome. Unlike Chinese pagodas, the tower has no external timber cladding around the masonry core. Two brick stairways, running spirally in opposite directions around the inner wall surface, were markedly different from traditional Chinese practice, for a brick stairway in a pagoda was a rare feature

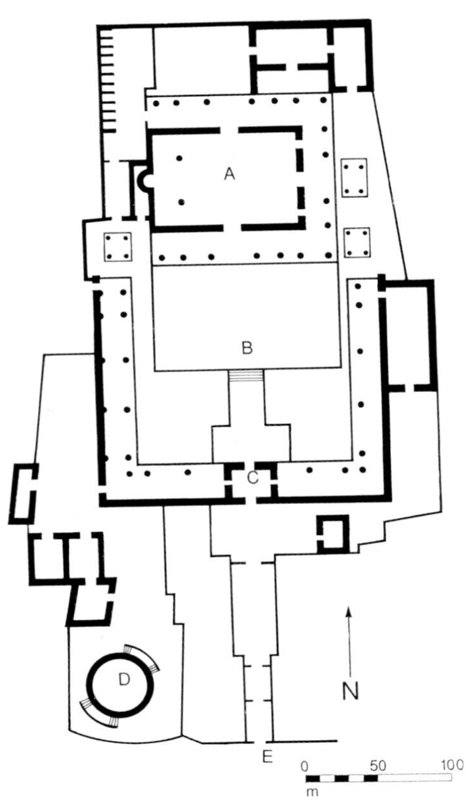

Plan of the Huai-Sheng Si (tenth–eleventh century), Guangzhou: (A) prayer-hall; (B) moon platform; (C) moon pavilion; (D) minaret; (E) main entrance.

until the Song dynasty. There is reason to believe that this idea was brought to China by Muslims. Being the tallest structure in the city until modern times, the minaret, with its metal cock atop, has long been considered the principal landmark of Guangzhou, and also served as a lighthouse for incoming ships, hence the name Guang-ta was bestowed on the mosque.

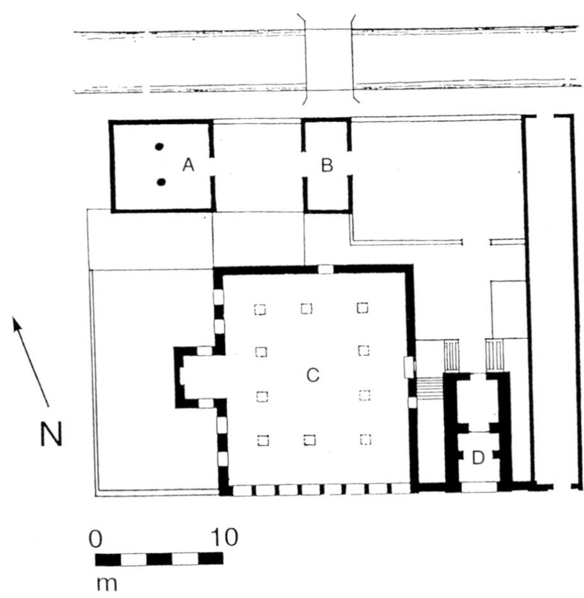

Plan of Sheng-You Si, Quanzhou, founded in 1009–10 and partially rebuilt in 1310–11: (A) prayer-hall of Ming-Shan Tang; (B) entrance portal of Ming-Shan Tang; (C) prayer-hall; (D) minaret/entrance portal.

Sheng-You Si (Mosque of the Holy Friend), Quanzhou, Fujian Province; also known as Qing-Jing Si (Mosque of Purity) and the Al-Sahaba Mosque

Sheng-You Si, now partly ruined, is an important survival of early mosques built in Central Asian style in the coastal cities of China. An inscription on the north wall of the portal records that the mosque was built in 1009–10, and renovated and partly rebuilt in 1310–11 by Ibn Muhammad al-Quds, from Shiraz. This mosque, like Huai-Sheng Si in Guangzhou, also provides valuable evidence of close links between China and Central Asia.

Unlike most mosques in Chinese cities, Sheng-You Si was located close to the city wall, and a large *fan-fang* extended to the south of it. The mosque, which stands on the north side of a main street, Tu Men Jie, has a south-facing portal. Although now in ruins, the building displays a grandness of scale and finely worked stone masonry; thanks above all to its historical value, it has always been one of the city's important monuments.

The mosque complex consists of three main elements: the original prayer-hall (built 1009–10); the portal (1310–11); and another prayer-hall, called Ming Shan Tang (Hall of Brightness and Virtue), built in 1609. For the portal, in the form of an *iwan* with crenellation, local green diabase was used, and this stone is not known in any other existing building in China. The diabase was so well dressed that, after almost seven hundred years, the ashlar masonry is still smooth and closely bonded. The portal, about 11.40 m (over 37 ft) in height and 6.60 m (nearly 22 ft) in width, served both as a minaret and as a platform for observing the moon. The outer façade has an opening in the shape of a pointed arch, 10 m (33 ft) in height and 3.80 m (12 ft 6 in.) in width, covered by a semi-dome ornamented with eight ribs. The middle section, an arched opening in the same form, but narrower, is 6.70 m (22 ft) in height; it too is covered by a semi-dome, but is ornamented with *muqarnas*. The inner section, much lower and narrower, and square in plan, is covered by a dome on squinches. All the side walls are decorated with blind arches of varying sizes. Thus, when one views the entrance from the street, layers of space are created by the use of graduated pointed arches, giving the portal a very elegant appearance.

Sheng-You Si differs from other mosques in China in that there is no formal courtyard and planning axis. The entrance to the prayer-hall was placed immediately to the left (west) of the portal. It consists of a stone arch decorated with calligraphic inscription above a rectangular opening which is in Chinese style. The hall, now roofless, is nearly square in plan, with a recess for the *mihrab* at the west end. Only a few column bases and most of the walls, made of fine beige-coloured granite, have survived. The *mihrab* is a well-proportioned arch set into the wall, and is decorated with exquisitely carved calligraphy. There are six other arches of the same kind, but smaller, three on each side of the central *mihrab* recess. The hall, although a ruin, remains very impressive. Several years ago plans were made for the restoration of the hall, but no agreement on the style of the roof could be reached and no works were undertaken.

The prayer-hall known as Ming Shan Tang is built in local Chinese style. It consists of a front yard, a portal, a prayer-hall and a

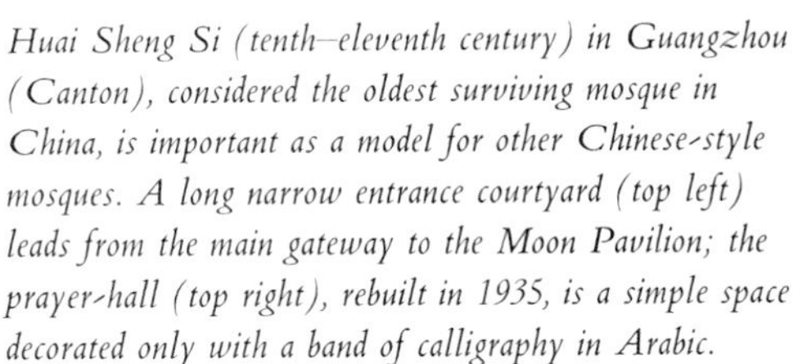

Huai Sheng Si (tenth–eleventh century) in Guangzhou (Canton), considered the oldest surviving mosque in China, is important as a model for other Chinese-style mosques. A long narrow entrance courtyard (top left) leads from the main gateway to the Moon Pavilion; the prayer-hall (top right), rebuilt in 1935, is a simple space decorated only with a band of calligraphy in Arabic.

The Bright Moon Pavilion (above) near the entrance to the prayer-hall of the so-called Mosque of the Immortal Crane in Yangzhou, probably founded in 1275, contrasts with the elaborate mihrab *(right) decorated with the* shahada *in a central medallion, flanked by smaller medallions bearing the names of the Prophet and a series of calligraphic inscriptions of Qur'anic texts arranged in parallel bands.*

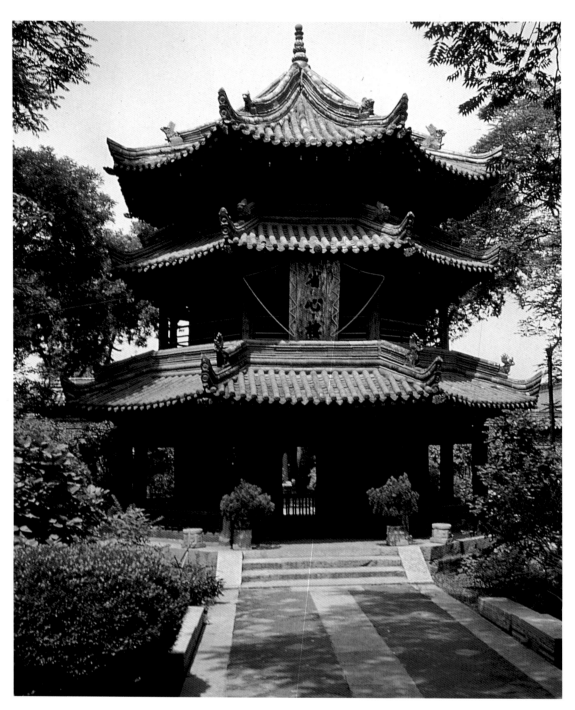

(Opposite) The ceiling of one of the pavilions, which has been restored to its former glory, features brightly painted lotus-blossom bosses.

THE GREAT MOSQUE, XIAN

Founded in 792, and much expanded in later centuries, this is one of the most important Muslim building complexes in China. The present layout, dating from 1392, consists of a series of courtyards and pavilions along an east-west axis.

The minaret (above), the tallest structure on the site, is a three-storey octagonal pagoda in the third courtyard. The roofs are decorated with traditional dragon figures (right), with their celestial and supernatural associations.

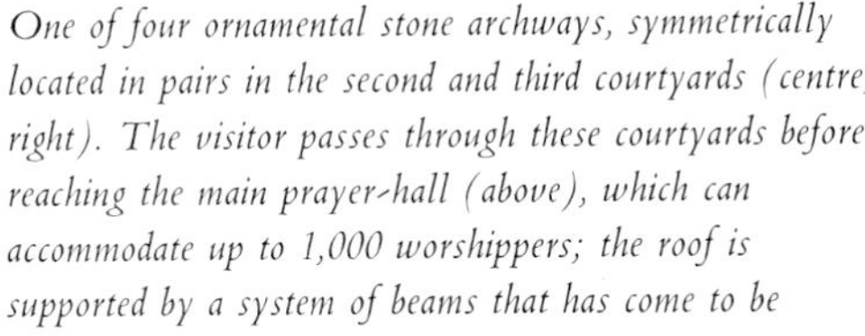

One of four ornamental stone archways, symmetrically located in pairs in the second and third courtyards (centre, right). The visitor passes through these courtyards before reaching the main prayer-hall (above), which can accommodate up to 1,000 worshippers; the roof is supported by a system of beams that has come to be associated with Hui prayer-halls generally, the height of the roof being proportional to the depth of the building. The mihrab *(right) is of wood, decorated with carved and painted motifs which are Central Asian in colour, though the floral patterns lend the design a distinctive Chinese flavour.*

The Niu Jie (Ox Street) Mosque in Beijing, built in 1362 and greatly expanded in the fifteenth century, was originally entered through the imposing portal known as the Moon Pavilion (above). At the centre of the main courtyard is the pagoda minaret (left), from which the call to prayer is still made. The interior of the prayer-hall (top) was renovated in 1978 in rich red and gold colours. The use of Arabic calligraphy combined with Chinese floral patterns featuring the chrysanthemum give the interior a unique flavour.

The qibla *wall of the partly ruined Sheng-You Si, Quanzhou; the walls of the prayer-hall, built of granite, have been largely preserved.*

courtyard in between. In one corner of the front yard there is an old well used for ablutions; this has been renovated recently and is in regular use.

As a result of a stone tablet being wrongly placed, Sheng-You Si has been mistakenly called Qing-Jing Si for over a hundred years and its dating confused; recent research has established that the inscription on the north wall of the portal is reliable.

Zhen-Jiao Si (Mosque of True Religion), Hangzhou, Zhejiang Province; also known as Feng-Huang Si (Phoenix Mosque)

Zhen-Jiao Si is situated on the west side of Zhong Shan Road, a main street near the city centre. The existing mosque is much smaller than formerly, since the widening of the road in 1929 resulted in the loss of the portal and part of the area in front of the prayer-hall. The mosque has a long history. Although it has been claimed that it was built in the Tang Dynasty, no evidence for this is known. More reliable sources suggest that it was originally built between 1131 and 1149, rebuilt and extended first in 1281 and again 1451–93, renovated in 1670, and partly rebuilt in 1953.

The key architectural features of the mosque are the three large domes and the *mihrab*. The domes, each of which is covered by a hexagonal roof in Chinese style, stand in line atop a cubical structure at the west end of the site. The middle dome, 8.84 m (29 ft) in diameter, and the *mihrab*, which is elaborately decorated with delicately carved calligraphy in Arabic, date from the Northern Song Dynasty; the other two domes, one 7.20 m (23 ft 6 in.), the other 6.80 m (22 ft 3 in.) in diameter, are later additions from the Ming Dynasty.

The original dome was over a hundred years old when it was damaged in the mid-thirteenth century. In 1281, a Muslim preacher named A-la-din (Chinese pronunciation) arrived and settled in Hangzhou. He succeeded in financing repairs and the extension of the mosque. A prayer-hall, built in wood in the Chinese manner, was added, the space under the dome became a recess for the *mihrab*, and a

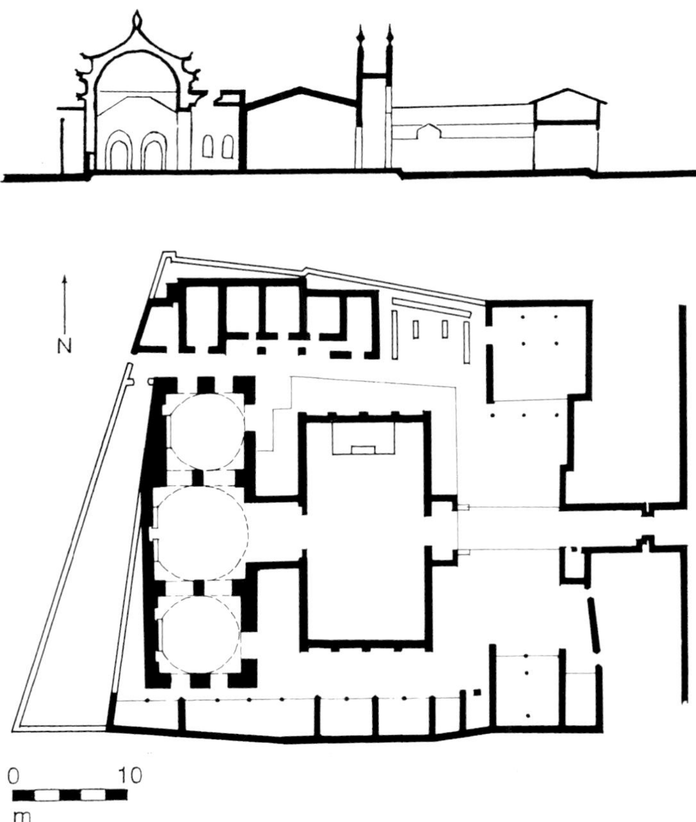

Section and plan of Zhen-Jiao Si, Hangzhou, probably founded in the first half of the twelfth century.

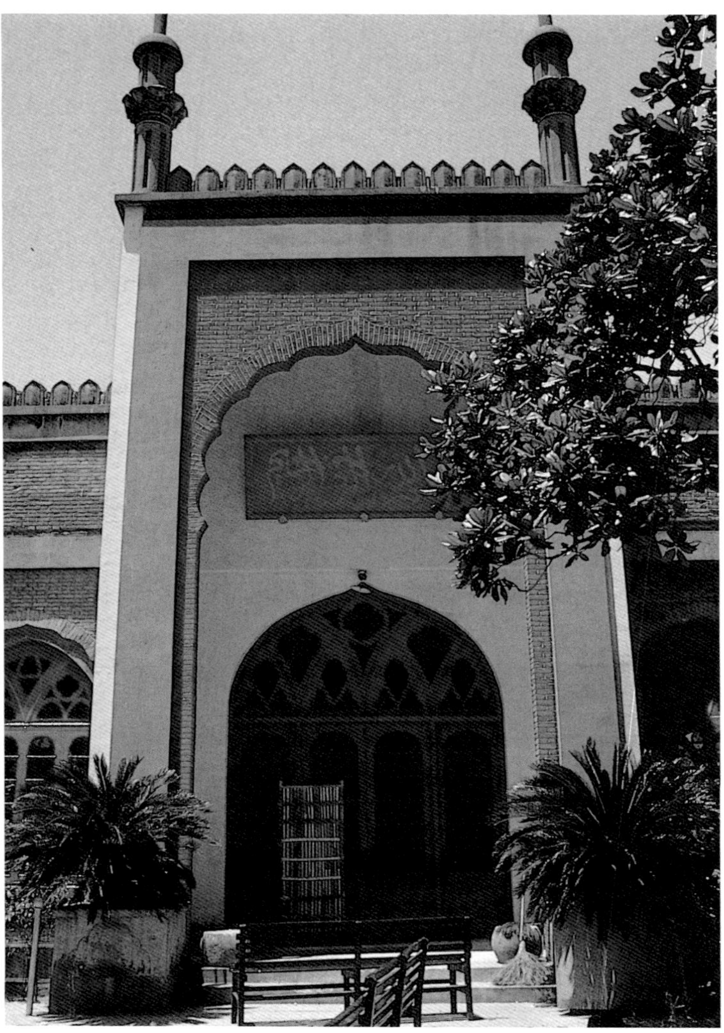

The imposing portal of Zhen-Jiao Si, Hangzhou, which also served as a minaret and as a platform for observing the moon.

new portal was built. Although there is no record of how the prayer-hall and the portal looked, the mosque as it existed after the extension in the fifteenth century is known from documents to have been grand in style. The two smaller domes were added, one on each side of the original one, the space below being made into a large lateral hall; the prayer-hall was enlarged to provide five aisles with colonnades on all sides; and the portal was rebuilt as an elaborate multi-storied structure serving as a minaret and a platform for observing the moon. The magnificent appearance of Zhen-Jiao Si, especially its portal with multiple exquisitely carved and moulded eaves, made it a centre of attraction, giving rise to mosque's alternative name, Feng-huang Si, or Phoenix Mosque.

A new hall was built in front of the domes in 1953 in a style similar to Central Asian mosques. The resulting contrast of architectural styles produces an incongruous effect; however, each part represents a unique manifestation of its period. The domes with their hipped hexagonal roofs are evidence of a combination of Chinese and Islamic architecture which evolved before the Ming Dynasty. The simplicity of geometric form of the cubical base supporting the domes and daring contrast of black and white are typical of domestic architecture in south-east China. The incorporation of Central Asian style for the recently built hall heralds a new trend in mosque design.

The Mosque, Songjiang, Shanghai

At the time when Shanghai was developing from a small village into a town during the Yuan and Ming dynasties, Songjiang was already a prosperous city in the region, famous for its cotton fabrics. It was boasted that the cloth produced in Songjiang was sufficient 'to clothe the whole world'. Historical records show that, from 1336 on, over thirty 'colour-eyed people' served as officials in various levels in the city government during an eighty-year period. The Muslim population must therefore have been significant in overall numbers.

The Mosque in Songjiang is believed to date from the middle of the fourteenth century. Near the main gateway an inscribed tablet inserted in the late seventeenth century states that a tomb was built here for Da-lu-hua-chi (Chinese pronunciation), a senior government official in the Yuan Dynasty (1280–1368), evidence which lends support to a fourteenth-century date for the original mosque, which was renovated and partly rebuilt *c.* 1522–66, in the Ming Dynasty; further renovations were carried out during the eighteenth century and in 1812, but the surviving parts date mostly from the Ming Dynasty.

The most notable features of the mosque are the recess for the *mihrab*, the portal (the second gateway) along the east-west axis, and the part linking the recess and the prayer-hall. The *mihrab*, built in the Yuan Dynasty, is square in plan; it is surmounted by a dome resting on squinches, and crowned by a gabled and hipped roof with double levels of curved eaves. The roof has ridges running at right angles in the

Plan of the Mosque, Songjiang: (A) main entrance; (B) moon pavilion; (C) moon platform; (D) prayer-hall; (E) mihrab *chamber.*

The second portal in the Songjiang Mosque, showing the dramatic double-eaved roof construction.

form of a cross, a rare and perhaps the oldest existing example of its type in Chinese architecture. The raising of the roof height gives the structure that houses the *mihrab* a magnificent appearance. The roof of the second portal is in a style similar to that over the *mihrab* recess, but is of later date, having been built in the Ming Dynasty. The portal, smaller in plan than the recess and having more elaborately decorated eaves, is a very attractive feature. The area between the recess and the prayer-hall is covered by a barrel vault, creating a dramatic contrast. The wooden *mihrab* and *minbar* are survivals from the Ming Dynasty, the former being in the same style as that in Zhen-Jiao Si, Hangzhou, but smaller.

The mosque, though not small in size, has a human scale. The entrance gateway resembles that of any large, but modest, residence, and blends comfortably with its surroundings. The use of a plain black-and-white colour-scheme is evidence that the design of the mosque was concerned more with inherent quality than with grandeur in appearance. The use of a dome and vault provide evidence of architectural features probably imported from the Islamic world far to the west.

The Mosque, Yangzhou, Jiangsu Province; also known as Xian-He-Si (Mosque of the Immortal Crane)

By the time of the Song Dynasty (960–1280), Yangzhou was already one of the busiest cities in trade and commerce. This mosque – the oldest and largest in the city – is believed to have been built in 1275 by a Muslim preacher, Pu-ha-din (Chinese pronunciation), whose lineage could be traced back through sixteen generations to the Holy Prophet, it was renovated and rebuilt twice during the Ming Dynasty (1368–1644) and again in the late eighteenth century; the present remains are mostly from the last rebuilding phase. The reason for the alternative name Xian-He-Si is obscure, but the theory most favoured is that the overall city plan of Yangzhou resembled the silhouette of a red-crowned crane in flight. (In Chinese mythology the crane was associated with longevity and immortality.)

Owing to the restricted area of the plot size and inclusion of a school for Muslim children in the building scheme, the plan of the mosque was cleverly divided into three parts, the prayer-hall on the north side, the school on the south side, with the space between them forming two courtyards. The outer, entrance courtyard has a gateway facing east, while the inner one is laid out as a garden, with a small building called the Bright Moon Pavilion standing close to the prayer-hall. The siting of the main entrance in relation to the prayer-hall is rather awkward: on entering the outer courtyard, one has to turn right, then backward, passing through a passage before reaching the second gate of the courtyard facing the prayer-hall. From the second gateway on, the layout follows the formal pattern typical of other mosques, along an east-west axis.

The prayer-hall is an imposing timber structure with five front bays built in traditional Chinese style. Timber structures of this type are

Plan of the Mosque, Yangzhou; (A) prayer-hall; (B) second portal; (C) Bright Moon Pavilion; (D) inner courtyard; (E) main entrance.

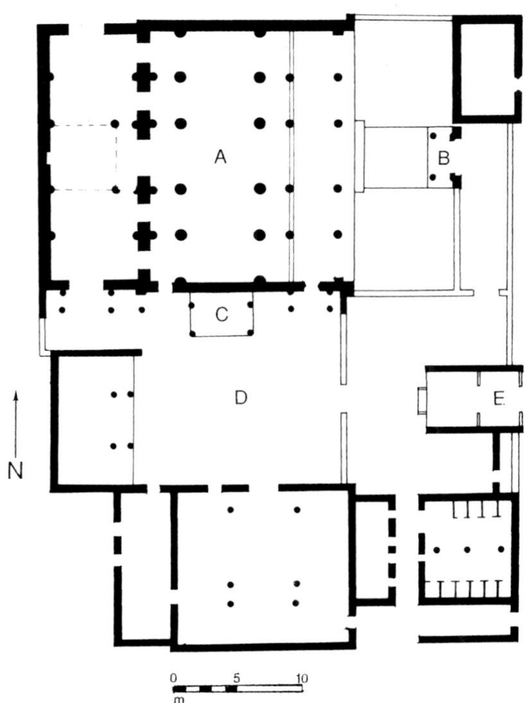

(Left) Exterior of the prayer-hall, Yangzhou, seen from the first courtyard.

(Opposite) The entrance porch of the prayer-hall in the Great Mosque, Xian, a timber structure notable for its carved decoration.

always limited in their depth. Here, in order to increase the capacity of the prayer-hall, two structures joined lengthwise accommodate a large internal space under two roofs. The wall separating the two structures is punctuated by five walk-through openings in the form of pointed arches, connecting the inner and outer spaces. Another interesting feature is the recess for the *mihrab*, which is placed in the central bay of the inner structure of the prayer-hall. The roof over the recess is higher than that over the rest of the hall. It is an individual tower-like gabled and hipped roof with a clerestory below the eaves. This treatment of the roof, which improves both the internal lighting and external appearance of the mosque, was a device developed after the Ming Dynasty. The *minbar*, an exquisitely carved wooden structure in the form of a hexagonal pavilion resting on a platform, is a rare and valuable relic dating from the Ming Dynasty.

The mature period – in search of mannerism: fourteenth–nineteenth century

Just as architecture generally in China during this period reveals a concern with artifice in design, mosque architecture can be said to be moving towards a pure Chinese style. However, distinctive features are apparent in the prominence of the east-west axis and the relationship of primary and secondary elements within the buildings. The minaret/moon pavilion/portal combined into one, and a raised roof over the *mihrab* recess are other distinguishing elements.

The use of a masonry dome had become obsolete in most of the mosques built in Chinese style in this period. The construction method used for building domes to span large halls, introduced in mosques like Zhen-Jiao Si in the previous period, had influenced architecture in the Chinese style as a whole, however, and this resulted in a type of construction for monumental architecture called the hall without beam. The characteristic feature of mosques in Chinese style built during this period was, in fact, a consolidation of earlier innovations, which could be summarized as follows:

(1) The main axis is east-west and the prayer-hall is the principal feature of the mosque, as seen in the Great Mosque of Xian and the Mosque on Niu Jie, Beijing.

(2) In order to increase the capacity of the prayer-hall to accommo-

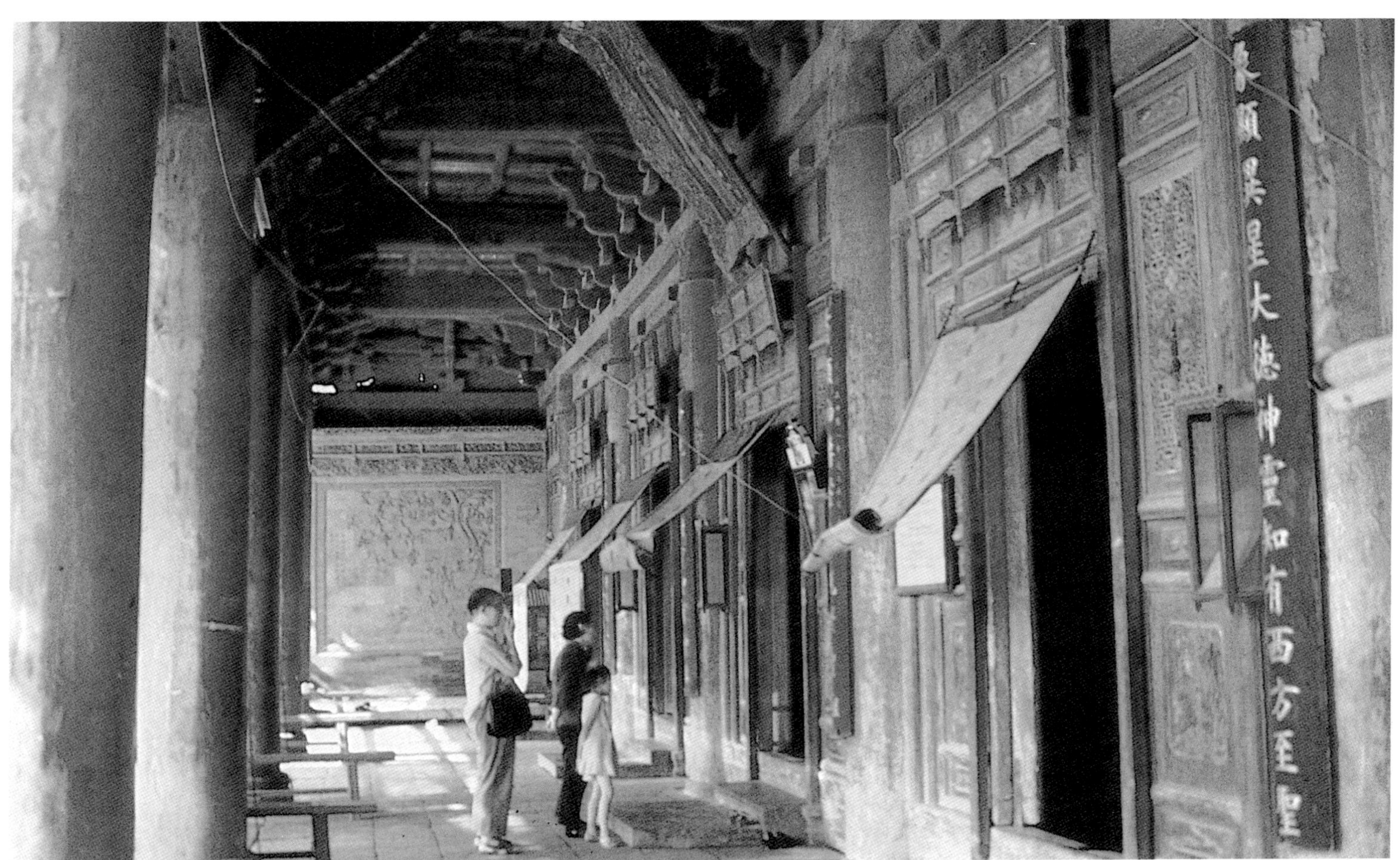

date a large congregation – a requirement not previously faced in Chinese architecture – two or three halls were built one in front of the other and joined lengthwise to create a single spacious interior. The mosque was the first building type in China in which halls built as separate structures were combined. This was a real innovation in both functional layout and building technology, since it provided a solution to roof drainage.

(3) The use of a tower-like timber structure with pointed Chinese roof and clerestory to admit light to the *mihrab* recess was prevalent. The roof over the recess in the Mosque of Yangzhou was rebuilt in this way. Other examples include those in the Great Mosque in Xian and in the Mosque on Niu Jie. In the later part of this period, more towers of this kind were erected, sometimes with dramatic results, e.g. in the mosques in Huhehot and Jinan. In the former there are four tower-like structures on the roof of the prayer-hall, one on each side of the entrance, one at the centre of the prayer-hall and finally – the highest and biggest – above the recess. In Jinan the prominent hip-roof over the recess stands out as a feature of the city's skyline. Such features can be compared with mosques in the Western Region having numerous domes varying in height.

(4) The combined minaret/moon tower/portal as a distinguishing feature in this period was mostly of elaborate construction, e.g. in the Great Mosque in Xian and the Mosque on Niu Jie. Also in mosques built before this period, some – as in Zhen-Jiao Si and the Mosque in Songjiang – were rebuilt to include this feature. The former was demolished early in this century, but the latter, which is a very spectacular example, still exists.

(5) Treatment of the *dou-gong* (brackets under the eaves) as a decorative element. In Chinese architecture the *dou-gong* is both functional and decorative. In many mosques, probably in association with the use of *muqarnas*, the *dou-gong* was emphasized both in height and in form, those in the Mosque in Jiuquan being good examples.

(6) The present pointed arch was introduced and subsequently adapted into various forms, and they were used in a decorative manner. Examples can be seen in many mosques, one notable instance being the Mosque in Jinan.

KEY EXAMPLES

The Great Mosque; Xian, Shaanxi Province; also known as the Mosque on Hua Jue Lane

The Great Mosque in Xian is the largest and the best preserved early mosque in China. It was built in 1392, early in the Ming Dynasty, then renovated and partly rebuilt successively in 1413, at the end of the fifteenth century, in the middle of the sixteenth century, and a thorough reconditioning took place in the period 1662–1772. An inscribed stone tablet in which it is stated that the mosque was built in 742 has been proved to be a fake.

The site of the mosque measures 245 m (800 ft) long, aligned from east to west, and 47 m (154 ft) in depth. It extends along a quiet street called Hua Jue Lane, only one block distant from the Drum Tower

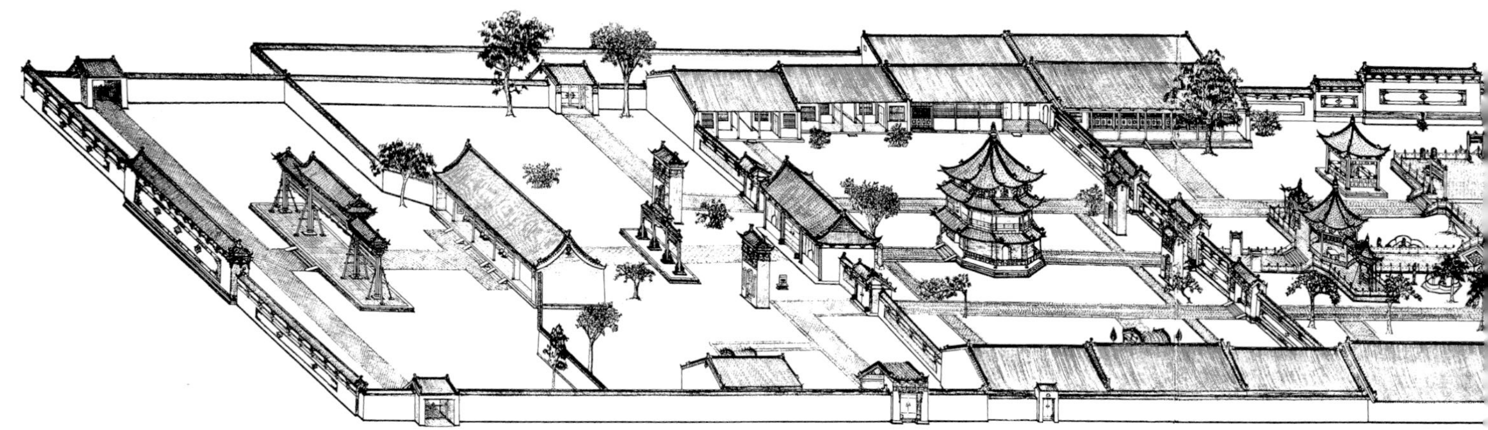

near the city centre. To the north and west of the mosque, *jiao-fangs* were concentrated. Hence this is an ideal location for a mosque building.

The layout is typical of Chinese courtyard planning, with four courtyards placed in a series along a central axis. The main entrances, which face south and north on the long side of the site, give access to the first courtyard. Each successive courtyard has its centre of attraction, either a pavilion, a *pailou*,[5] or a screen wall, each of these methodically designed, meticulously executed and strictly planned to complement the surroundings.

The principal feature of the mosque is the prayer-hall, dating from the Ming Dynasty. This is a timber structure with seven front bays preceded by a large granite-paved platform known as the Moon platform. The hall, 33 m (108 ft) in width and 38 m (125 ft) in length, occupies – with the *mihrab* – an overall area of 1,270 sq m (1,420 sq yds); it is in fact made up with two similar structures joined lengthwise. The hall, together with the platform, can accommodate nearly two thousand worshippers. The *mihrab* features an arch in Central Asian style and a canopy above in Chinese style; the entire *mihrab* is highly decorated with carvings in calligraphy and foliage exquisitely carved in wood. The roof over the recess is higher than that over the rest of the hall; it is a tower-like timber structure in gabled and hipped form, with a clerestory below the eaves.

Another major building within the complex is the so-called Pavilion for Introspection (Xing Xin Ting) in the third courtyard preceding the prayer-hall. Also dating from the Ming Dynasty, this octagonal pavilion is a spectacular structure consisting of two stories crowned with a triple-eaved pyramidal roof. It served as a minaret in former times.

This mosque is recognized as one of the most magnificent architectural monuments in China. It is at once solemn and dignified, intriguing and spectacular. In addition, the carvings in brick and wood, which are of excellent craftsmanship, are regarded as being the best surviving examples of their period.

The Mosque on Niu Jie, Beijing

Beijing, when it was the capital of the emperors of the Yuan Dynasty (1280–1368), had a large Muslim population. The Mosque on Niu Jie, at the south-east corner of the inner city, still contains two Muslim tombs, dating from 1280 and 1283 respectively. It was in 1427, in the early part of Ming Dynasty, that the mosque was elaborately developed, and at that time it was regarded as the biggest and most important of its kind. The mosque was renovated and partly rebuilt many times, for example in 1442, 1474, 1496, 1613 and in the latter half of the seventeenth century.

All the major elements of the mosque – the portal, the prayer-hall, the minaret and the *madras* – are formally arranged along one axis, following traditional Chinese practice. The main entrance faces west to Niu Jie, while the prayer-hall, in accordance with the direction of worship, requires access from the east, i.e. at the opposite end, hence the layout is somewhat unusual. After passing through the portal or the two doorways, one on either side of the portal, one has to walk around the prayer-hall to reach the main courtyard, then turn back to enter the hall itself.

The entrance portal, called the Moon Pavilion, is a two-storied structure, hexagonal in plan and crowned with a double-eaved pyramidal roof covered with yellow-glazed tiles. The colour of the tiles indicated that the Mosque had been honoured by the Emperor. The entrance portal is emphasized by a *pailou* of three bays in front and a screen wall standing opposite it.

The prayer-hall, which measures about 30 m (100 ft) in width and slightly more in depth, consists of two adjoining timber structures, each of five front bays. To emphasize its entrance, a portal, which is a smaller structure consisting of three bays, is placed directly in front of the hall. The wooden *mihrab* is decorated with delicately carved calligraphy and foliage, and the recess for it is built in the usual manner adopted during the Ming Dynasty, with the roof in the shape of a pyramid, raised to a greater height to allow a clerestory. Since the interior of the hall is rather

The Great Mosque, Xian: drawing from an undated Chinese scroll showing the series of courtyards viewed from the north. The wide prayer-hall is seen on the right.

dark, the clerestory here seems to be more successful than usual, for the light entering from above gives the *mihrab* recess a particularly strong visual emphasis.

The main courtyard at the east front of the prayer-hall is on a monumental scale. It has a minaret on its central axis, and two pavilions, one on each side of the axis. Opposite the prayer-hall stands the *madrasa* at the east end of the courtyard, all designed in accordance with the axis. Together these buildings help to emphasize the importance of the prayer-hall.

The square minaret, a two-storied structure with a gabled and hipped roof, is an echo of the Moon Pavilion but in a varied form. The minaret and the Moon Pavilion are both very impressive, the lower storey being heavy and solid in each case, the upper storey open and light, and both are lavishly decorated with brightly coloured patterns painted on railings, architrave and *dou-gongs*. Together with the raised roof over the *mihrab*, they give the roof-line of the mosque an undulating and dramatic effect.

Beijing was also the capital of the Ming emperors. The culture of Beijing at that time, after being a capital city for centuries, had unquestionably influenced mosque design. The quest for monumentality, the use of artifice in employing secondary objects to emphasize the primary features and exuberance in decoration are perfectly exemplified in the style of this mosque.

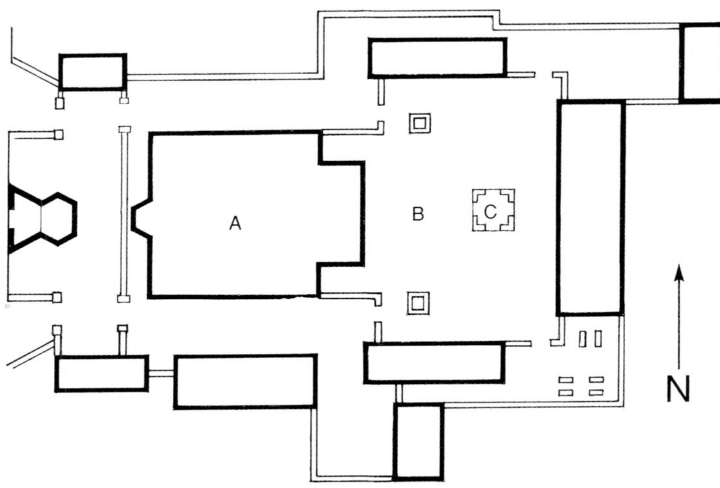

(Below) Plan of the Mosque on Niu Jie, Beijing: (A) prayer-hall; (B) courtyard; (C) minaret.

Developments in the twentieth century

From the mid-nineteenth century on, two factors – one political and financial and the other technical – had an important influence on mosque architecture. In the later years of the moribund Qing Dynasty, due to the government's closed-door policy and financial problems, many mosques were in a run-down state. After the revolution led by Sun Yat-sen, which began in October 1911, some minor improvements were made in large cities, such as the prayer-hall in Huai-Sheng Si in Guangzhou, which was rebuilt in reinforced concrete in 1935, but many problems remained.

Since 1949, when the new China was born, the official government policy has been to allow freedom of worship. As a result, mosques began to be renovated in many places, especially in regions with a significant Muslim population. Since China is a developing country, with limited resources, much still remains to be done. The decade of the Cultural Revolution, beginning in the mid-1960s, was disastrous for mosques and it was not until the late 1970s that restoration started. Since then most existing mosques have been repaired and some new ones have been built. In architectural terms these new mosques have tended to move away from traditional Chinese style and to adopt that associated with the Xinjiang Region. With the availability of new building techniques, the construction of domes and tall minarets presents no problems.

- 13 -
SOUTH-EAST ASIA
HUGH O'NEILL

ANY examination of the architecture of societies on either side of the Strait of Malacca, separating the Malay Peninsula from northern Sumatra, and beyond is inevitably concerned with one of the most complex patterns of acculturation in history. Although the Muslim religion predominates among the people of this region, large communities scattered throughout the mainland and archipelagos of South-East Asia adhere to aspects of Hinduism, Buddhism, Confucianism, Tao and Christianity, as well as celebrating autochthonous traditions and rituals. This diversity has developed from successive incursions by traders into a remarkably richly endowed region. From the beginning of recorded history the islands of gold and spices attracted adventurers from the Middle East, the Mediterranean, China and Japan, and later from northern Europe. This extraordinarily complex array of outside influences has resulted in an unusually diffuse approach to building.

The formation of the timber mosque and the variety of its interpretation throughout the region is a fascinating study of architectural evolution. It has its richest expression in the Indonesian archipelago and will be analyzed from a number of points of view: formal composition, constructional technique, deployment of imagery and its symbolic meaning. The centralized timber-columned hall must be regarded as a clearly differentiated type. Elements widely associated with Muslim architecture elsewhere, such as the dome and geometric surface ornament, do not feature in these traditions. These buildings in timber, which have their apogee in the Great Mosques (*Masjid Agung*) of the Islamic royal centres in Java from the fifteenth century, were adapted from open pavilions (*joglo*) in the palaces (*kraton*) of pre-Muslim rulers.

Chinese origins for the mosque in South-East Asia have sometimes been postulated. From pre-history, immigrants from south-western China have moved into the region and timber-framed buildings, raised above the ground, are found wherever their descendants have settled. However, the distinctive structural methods used by house-builders in the region have been refined into techniques where tensile curves and light, stressed roof-membranes are dependent upon the use of a wide range of timbers and fibres. The shipbuilding skills of these transmigrants may well have been influential in such developments. The classical monumental buildings of China and of Japan rely on other structural systems in which roofs are built up from timber blocks and brackets to support lateral and transverse beams stacked and pegged together. Diagonal struts and double rafters are used to extend the heavy tiled roofs into spreading eaves.

The traditional use of timber and fibre building materials and techniques has also been subject to the influence of ideas from the Indian subcontinent. In deciphering their genesis, there are several places in the Indic world where the processes of metamorphosis from timber buildings to more universal masonry structures can be observed. In the southern regions of the Himalayas, from the Kulu valley and Nepal as far as Burma, and in parts of southern India and Sri Lanka there remain rich traditions of construction using organic materials. Even more direct influences can be traced to the mosques of foreign trading communities along the Malabar and Coromandel coasts of south-west and south-east India, and of Sri Lanka.

It was only in the nineteenth century that mosques with domes were first built in South-East Asia. This development occurred in the Muslim states of Malaysia and North Sumatra when European trade and economic domination in much of the Islamic world had caused reactionary movements in centres of Islamic reform. One of the oldest mosques of this type in the region was built in Aceh: in 1873, as international trading companies tried to force treaties upon the Acehnese Sultan, Mahmud Syah, the Netherlands Indies government became impatient and, in attacking the city, destroyed the existing mosque. Temporary occupation of the capital allowed the Dutch to build a new mosque, begun in 1879 and completed in 1881. Its timber-framed dome was clad in fine black ironwood shingles. Although the new Masjid Baiturrachman was for many years considered by the religious leaders to be alien and inappropriate for regular use, during the twentieth century it has been extended with the addition of four more domes and two minarets. Its renown has now spread through the whole of Indonesia, much of the building's prestige being derived from the reputation of the Acehnese people as independent members of the *umma* sustaining their links with the international world of Islam.

Other mosques in these exotic styles followed as European colonial governments extended their control of world markets in the early twentieth century. Treaties were made with local rulers who were encouraged to give expression to their new-found, deputed authority by engaging in building programmes. Through the auspices of the colonial authorities and community leaders, mosques and palaces were designed using styles variously referred to as Mughal or Indo-Saracenic. Many of the buildings were inspired by contemporary construction programmes of the British Raj and of wealthy princes in India. The Masjid Ubudiah of the Sultan of Perak in Malaysia and the mosque dominating the walled city of Jolo in the Sulu archipelago of the

Facing page
*The upper part of the single central column and brackets supporting the roof over the prayer-hall of the mosque associated with the oldest palace, the Kraton Kasepuhan, in Cirebon (**see p. 234**).*

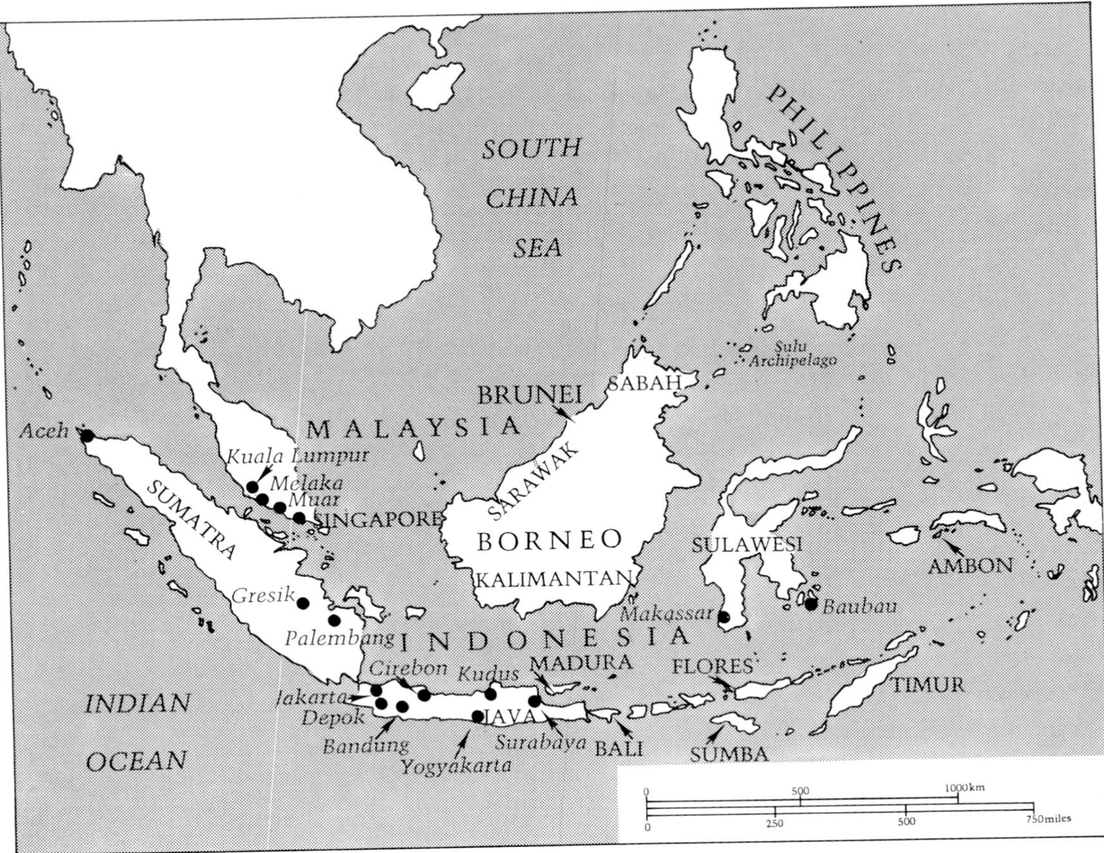

Map 9: South-East Asia, showing principal sites in the Indonesian archipelago and the Malay Peninsula.

southern Philippines are flamboyant examples, featuring bulbous domes clustered about with tall minarets.

The Coming of Islam

The teachings of Muhammad were introduced to the indigenous populations of the Malay Peninsula and the coastal communities of Sumatra, Java, the Sulu archipelago, Borneo, Kalimantan, southern Sulawesi and the Maluku during the thirteenth, fourteenth and fifteenth centuries. For at least two centuries previously, Muslims had been finding their way into the courts of rulers where surviving gravestones, particularly in North Sumatra and East Java, indicate that some members of the ruling families had already been converted to Islam. The Shafi'i school of Islamic law, which was adopted in South-East Asia from the earliest times, has since remained dominant in the region.[1]

Political centres in East Java and Thailand were expanding as Muslims arriving from Arabia, Iran and India sought new trading opportunities in the region. The descendants of these settlers have continued their links with the Middle East and southern Asia to the present day and maintain an important role within the local *umma* as they extend their enterprises, forming family connections among local producers. Well before the twelfth century, traders from Arabia and Iran had established their emporiums in India, along the coasts of Gujarat and Malabar into Tamilnadu and up to Bengal. From here they sailed south-east, following the routes which had been taken by Hindu and Buddhist travellers and merchants more than a thousand years before.

In Burma, over the isthmus of southern Thailand to the lower reaches of the Mekong river, across to the east coast of Vietnam and out into the islands of the Philippines, Malaysia and Indonesia, the ideas of Indian visitors had transformed cultural expression and religious observance for a millennium, particularly amongst the ruling élites. From early beginnings five hundred years before the birth of the Prophet, the kingdoms of Dvaravati, Funan, Chenla, Champa and Angkor in regions of mainland South-East Asia had interacted with those of Kutai in East Kalimantan, Srivijaya in Sumatra and others in Central and East Java, all under inspiration from Hindu and Buddhist doctrines about a divinely inspired ruler.

Although the Muslim religion was known in southern China within two centuries of Muhammad's death, there is no evidence that the Arab traders who frequented South-East Asia at this time had succeeded in converting many Chinese to their creed. However, it is recorded that Muslims who escaped the proscriptions of the Tang Emperor Wu-tsung (841–7) against external 'barbarian' beliefs found their way to settlements on the west coast of the Malay Peninsula. As Chinese traders had already been active in many parts of the region for almost five hundred years, it is probable that a few Chinese converts and their Arab and Indian counterparts would have been practising their faith at settlements in the estuaries along the sheltered coastlines some time before the end of the thirteenth century.

Centres of political authority on the mainland and in Sumatra and Java had become powerful entities with internal rivalries focusing on the trade routes passing between Sumatra and the Malay Peninsula. Chinese and European visitors recorded that Indian and Arab Muslims were establishing their trading presence and introducing their religion to coastal communities. During his second visit to Sumatran north-coast towns in 1292, the intrepid Venetian traveller Marco Polo noted that the ruler of Perak had adopted the teachings of Muhammad, although few of the townspeople had yet been converted by the foreign settlers. By the early fifteenth century, Malacca (Melaka), on the west coast of the Malay Peninsula, was established as an important trading port. Its founder was Paramesvara, a princely refugee from Palembang in south Sumatra, who was converted to Islam upon marrying a Muslim princess from Pasai in the north.[2] For a century, until its overthrow by a Portuguese naval force from Goa in 1511, the city was an important centre for the propagation of the teachings of Muhammad in the whole region.

A twentieth-century wantilan *(pavilion) at Kosiman, Bandung, Bali, featuring the traditional centralized hipped roof.*

The form of the South-East Asian mosque

From whichever direction elucidation of the genesis of its form is sought, the South-East Asian mosque lies within the strong Java-centred tradition of tall, multi-roofed, open halls with timber columns as structural supports. The Great Mosques of the Central Javanese principalities of Yogyakarta and Surakarta, dating from the eighteenth century, are the finest examples; modelled on the first large mosques erected at the trading ports on the north coast of Java, they reflect that island's abundance of natural resources and its economic dominance in the region.

This renewed political focus in inland Central Java emerged in the late sixteenth century as the alliance of Islamic city-states on the north coast waned under the impact of Portuguese and then Dutch and British trading interests from 1511. Their predecessor, the East Javanese capital Majapahit (founded in 1292), had succeeded to Hindu-Javanese principalities in Central and East Java from the eighth to the thirteenth centuries. Relief sculptures on a number of stone monuments, dating from the ninth and tenth centuries in Central Java and the twelfth to fourteenth centuries in East Java, show some domestic structures. Vernacular sources for these images are revealed in many details. They provide clues to architectural details and show that there were direct continuities with the buildings erected by aristocrats who, seeking to preserve their Hindu-Buddhist way of life, later fled to East Java and settled in Bali. These migrations occurred during the late fourteenth and early fifteenth centuries, as the new Muslim communities established at points along the north coast of East Java made military excursions inland.

The Mengkunegaram Palace Mosque, Surakarta, seen from the south-west.

These continuities between the buildings of pre-Islamic Java and mosque architecture in the region may still be seen at royal complexes in South Bali. The rectangular high-walled courts contain pavilions which resemble those depicted on the East Javanese reliefs. Although few habitable buildings in Bali date from before the nineteenth century, there is every reason to suppose that their forms and construction conserve much of the traditions of architectural space of the city of Majapahit. The most significant buildings are the open pavilions (known as *wantilan* or *badung*) located at the entrances to major temple compounds in South Bali. These are the most impressive structures of Balinese temples and villages today, having been built to accommodate large crowds attending ritual cockfights.

A hierarchy of building types according to use

Building codes in East and South-East Asia prescribe roof forms according to a hierarchy which indicates the purpose of a building, the activities or rituals carried on there, and the social status of its occupants. These relationships follow a natural order. It comes as no surprise that a building with an open-ended gable would be the least specific in terms of its use. On the other hand it is appropriate that a building with a centralized hipped roof would be reserved for functions associated with a ritual or an enclosure of state; the emphasis provided by a centralized roof form multiplied vertically is even more appropriate to a more elevated symbolic function.

In the sacred architecture of the Indian subcontinent such formations are universal. It is clear that if a ritual movement pauses or an object of veneration is focused in space, the moment of pause or object of special significance should be marked with a centralized superstructure. Many Hindu and Buddhist buildings have multiple forms to emphasize that symbolic role. Implicit reference to cosmic mountain, lotus or anthropomorphic physiognomy underlie their formal significance, which is frequently clarified and elaborated by design details expressing height and multiplicity. The symbol of the universal cosmic axis (*stambha*), given powerful expression in Indian architecture, finds many manifestations in the South-East Asian context: as mountain, tree, lotus stem and stamen, it appears frequently as a motif on buildings of Hindu or Buddhist inspiration. The invisible axis of the Hindu temple projecting vertically from the image contained within the *cella (gharba griha)* is made explicit in many details.

In India, outer halls (*mandapa*) for worship and preparation are usually supported on columns which have intrinsic meaning. In some cases these columns can rotate on their axes, their mundane role of providing physical support having been eclipsed by their inherent symbolism, based on the cyclical nature of cosmic existence. The interiors of square *mandapa* commonly have as their focal point four central pillars supporting the upper layers of the roof, and the ceiling is usually carved as a lotus blossom. Completing this symbolic schema, there is, at the apex of the exterior, an elaborate finial in the form of the receptacle (*mula*) of the regenerative elixir of life (*amrita*). The mosques and prayer-halls of Java clearly have origins in these buildings, although no example of a *mandapa* from the Hindu-Javanese period with the specific form described now remains in South-East Asia. However, a recently unearthed ninth-century Shiva sanctuary, Sambisari, near Yogyakarta, suggests fundamental links. Like many mosques in the region, it stands on a raised basement within a walled enclosure and is surrounded by a channel of water. The stone column – Shiva's *linga* – within its *cella* is placed centrally under the square, layered roof, and refers to the 'cosmic pillar'.

Autochthonous origins for the mosque form

Village and house forms in the region also have symbolic systems of great vitality. They can be traced from south-western China through Indo-China and Borneo to Aceh, Batak North Sumatra, Nias, Minangkabau West Sumatra, Central Java and Madura, Dyak and Banjar Kalimantan, Toraja Sulawesi, Bali, Flores, Sumba, Timor and Irian. Although many of these sub-ethnic groups have never been part of the Islamic sphere of influence, they indicate the richness of the cultural ground within which the Muslim traditions took root. This variety of house form has been sustained by the great natural abundance of the region.

In many parts of South-East Asia houses are characterized by clearly defined symbolic elements referring to the inhabitants' place in a vertically structured spiritual hierarchy of space. As well as the ubiquitous belief in the regenerative vitality of volcano and vegetation, ancestor worship is a continuing spiritual force which is made explicit in rituals of place.[3] It is possible that the Indic and South-East Asian systems have common origins in Central Asia, where both cultures have prehistoric links. In the houses of many communities where old Indonesian *adat* prevails, expression is given to the notion that life-giving forces flow from ancestral spirits above. In a tripartite system (which can be found in many traditions) these ancestral spirits occupy the upper roof space, secure and undisturbed, accompanied by heirlooms (*pusaka*). The inhabitants (*manusia*) live in the intermediate level, above the realm of unruly and unpredictable influences, misanthropic spirits and animals.

In Batak Karo communities near Lake Toba in North Sumatra there are multi-family houses with tall hipped roofs capped by small symbolic replicas incorporating motifs from the sacred charnel-houses (*geriten*). The deployment of a centralized hipped roof for buildings of ritual importance (*balai*) occurs in a number of other South-East Asian communities where autochthonous *adat* is still vital. Such a vertically oriented hierarchy is clearly manifested in the spectacular houses of west Sumba in south-eastern Indonesia. They cluster around the tops of eroded limestone sinks in the undulating landscape and face onto an open central communal area occupied by freestanding stone sarcophagi containing the remains of ancestors. Three distinct levels are created by four cylindrical timber columns, which are believed to act as channels for spiritual energy. These re-usable members, made from durable timber, give direct support to the upper high-pitched roof, the abode of

Facing page
*The Masjid Agung (top) in Demak, Central Java, Indonesia, is the oldest extant mosque in the archipelago. The original square plan of the prayer-hall, dating from 1474, has been extended over the years, but the three-tiered roof structure remains unaltered. The interior of the prayer-hall (left, centre) retains its original character, but – as with most early mosques in Indonesia – its orientation towards Mecca is only approximate. The traditional drum (*bedug*), which was formerly beaten to summon the faithful to prayer, stands on the veranda (below left) and is still used on special occasions.*

The Masjid Menara in Kudus, near Demak, has a square brick tower (below, centre) dating from the early sixteenth century (with a later pavilion above). This minaret – the oldest in Java – unusually housed the drum and served as a landmark structure signifying the presence of a mosque.

The Friday Mosque, in Singkarak, Sumatra (below, right), built in the nineteenth century, has a roof consisting of five tiers, the largest number present in South-east Asian mosques. The building is a fine example of the traditional Indonesian mosque based on a square plan.

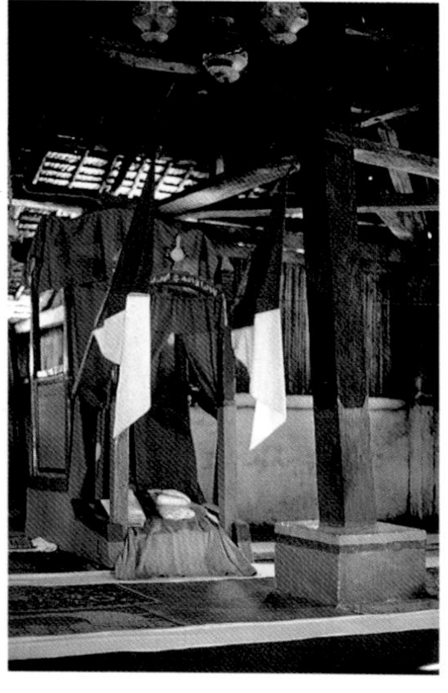

The royal Masjid Agung (1565) in Banten, West Java, Indonesia (above); this major complex is notable for its minaret resembling a lighthouse (this feature has been attributed to the Dutch architect Hendrik Lucasz), while the mosque itself has a tiered roof with a wide spreading lower part.

A view of the interior (far left) shows some of the columns supporting the superstructure. The internal appearance of this building forms a strong contrast with that of the early Masjid Wapaue (left), a small mosque removed in 1664 to its present site at Leihitu on the island of Ambon, Maluku, eastern Indonesia.

The interior of the Masjid Agung (1848) associated with the kraton *(palace) at Surakarta, Central Java, illustrates the traditional* saka guru, *the four-column structure creating a central open space with a vertical emphasis (above right) which together symbolize the five pillars of Islam. Here, as in many pavilion mosques, only the* qibla *side (defined by the* mihrab*) is enclosed.*

The Masjid Tua on the island of Ternate in the northern Maluku (right), dates from the eighteenth century; its graceful tiered roof is seen against the looming bulk of Mount Gama Lama, an active volcano.

MOSQUES OF THE MALAY PENINSULA

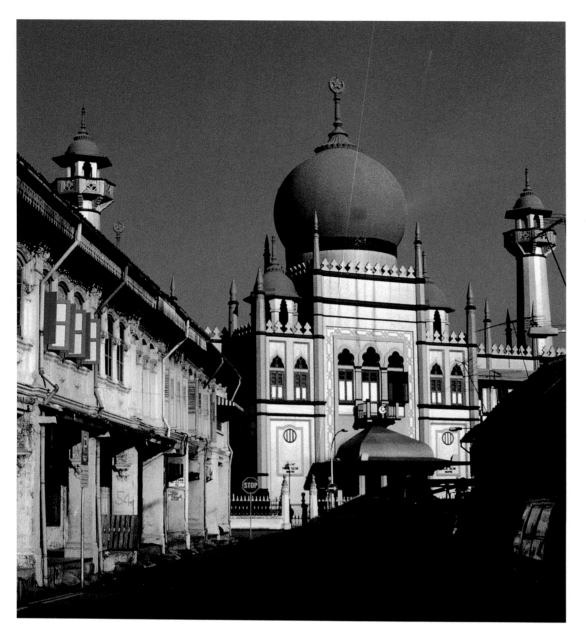

The Sultan Mosque, Singapore (left), built 1924–8, replaced the original mosque on this site dating from 1825. The style of this building is heavily influenced by late-Mughal provincial architecture in India.

The Jami Masjid, Singapore (below), which dates from 1830–55, is notable for its twin minarets of unusual design and colour, reflecting a Hindu influence brought by Indian settlers from the Coromandel Coast who built this mosque.

The Jami Masjid (1897) in Kuala Lumpur, Malaysia (left), has a traditional layout of walled courtyards and minarets; standing amid coconut palms in the city centre, the building features alternating bands of red brick and white detailing.

the protective spirit *Marapu*; at the intermediate level they penetrate the floor at the corners of an earth-filled platform containing the hearth, while the undercroft shelters horse, pig and domestic fowl which gather round the bases of the columns. The main spaces for human habitation are sheltered by hipped planes of radially structured roofing which are suspended from the extended rafters of the upper roof. In some old houses the main roof hangs out in space with no further support at its perimeter. Sumbanese lore suggests that the form of these houses, with their double-pitched, hipped roofs, is derived from a Javanese prototype. The symbolism of the form and construction, however, is so directly related to their use that it is much more likely that the traditions of Sumba and Java have common origins in an ancient antecedent now submerged by processes of cultural change.

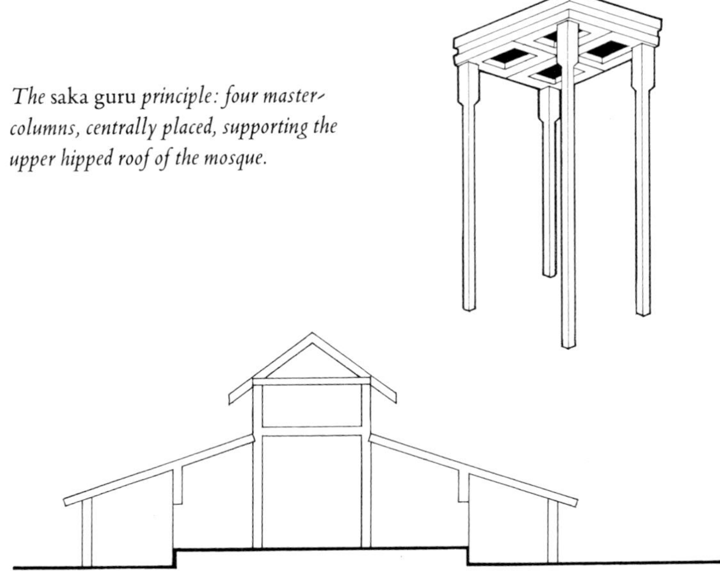

The saka guru *principle: four master-columns, centrally placed, supporting the upper hipped roof of the mosque.*

The spatial characteristics of the mosque

The master-columns (*saka guru*) of the mosque – usually four, but sometimes six and occasionally only one (*saka tunggal*) – set up a powerful vertical axiality which is in counterpoint to the direction of approach and the orientation of the *qibla* as people gather for prayer. The vertical focus of these soaring interiors is reflected and reinforced by concentric ranks of columns which provide structural support to the lower roofs. On the exterior, the upward sweep of the roofs terminates in an elaborate finial (*melolo* or *mustaka*) in place of the Hindu symbol of the flaming jewel at the summit of the cosmic tree (*brahmamula*).

This strong vertical and centralizing tendency clearly expresses continuities between the Hindu belief in the identity of self and the universal principle *atma*, and the Sufist view that an ultimate unity exists between Allah and the faithful believer. These tall interior spaces rise towards sources of subdued light filtering between the upper roofs. The multiple columns thread through the space in harmony with the upward tapering tiers. This form of centralized, layered, hipped roof is described as *tajug* (crowned).

Early mosques

The oldest mosques in South-East Asia were probably either re-used buildings within royal courts or small prayer-halls built in village communities of recent converts and modelled on existing building types used for a similar sacral purpose. At Leihitu, on the north coast of the island of Ambon in Eastern Indonesia, there is a small mosque said to have been built in 1414. The interior – 3 m (10 ft) square – probably maintains this form as originally constructed in the mountain village of Perdana Jamiku, the structure having been removed to its present site in 1664. The early provenance of this building is supported by the fact that the uplands of these eastern islands produced the cloves and nutmeg so sought after by the early Indian and Arab visitors.

Another example of a preserved provincial mosque, this one said to have been erected by Muslims arriving by sea in the seventeenth century, was at Kampung Laut, a coastal settlement near Kota Bharu, capital of the State of Kelantan in Malaysia. As the oldest surviving mosque in Malaysia, it was removed to the campus of the Centre for Higher Islamic Studies, Nilam Puri, in 1970. Its timber floor is raised about 1 m (3 ft) above the ground in the manner of typical mosques in most rural areas. The four main columns support the uppermost roof, separating it from the double-layered outer roof by timber louvres which admit light to and allow ventilation of the central space.

The large mosques built at the Javanese north-coast trading settlements of Cirebon, Demak, Jepara, and Kudus, Tuban, Gresik and Surabaya are venerated as the oldest of their kind in South-East Asia. Tradition suggests that the first of these was at Demak, begun in 1474. Although much of its fabric has been renewed in the course of a number of nineteenth- and twentieth-century reconstructions, most recently in 1975, there is little doubt that in its present form the mosque closely resembles the original building. If the ceiling inserted in 1848 were to be removed, the essential integrity of its impressive interior would be restored.

The city of Demak, founded by a Chinese Muslim named Cek Ko-po during the second half of the fifteenth century, was originally a

The oldest surviving mosque in Malaysia, originally built at Kampung Laut in the seventeenth century.

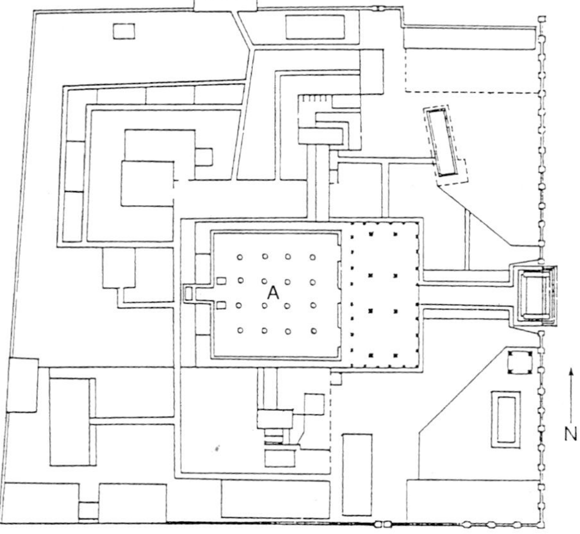

Site plan of the Masjid Agung, Demak, traditionally said to have been founded in 1474; at the centre of the square prayer-hall (A) are the four saka guru *columns.*

seaport but is now some distance from the coast through silting up of the swampy shoreline. It became the centre of political rivalry with the court of Majapahit in East Java, then in decline. Cek Ko-po's granddaughter married a Muslim from North Sumatra who, as Sunan Gunungjati, is one of the nine or ten fabled saints (*walis*) who spread the Muslim faith from the coastal cities. Legend suggests that several of these leaders were of Arab, Indian or Chinese descent. It is believed that nine *walis* co-operated in the construction of the Demak Mosque. When it was realized that insufficient large timbers were available to complete the crucial fourth massive *saka guru*, Sunan Kalijaga, with practical inspiration, used off-cuts to make up the north-eastern column. These central supports stand 22 m (72 ft) high. The laminated column (*saka tatal*) has become an object of veneration for pilgrims seeking spiritual contact with the saint.

The *walis* lived and taught over a period of more than a century, and their tombs (*keramat*), at centres along the north coast associated with their spiritual hegemony, have become places of pilgrimage. A tenth *wali*, Sunan Bayat, who converted the population of the southern parts of central Java, is buried on top of a hill at Tembayat, south of Klaten.

Mosque building during the sixteenth century

Mosques were under construction in many places on the Java coast when Portuguese adventurers arrived to set up their warehouses soon after they captured Melaka in 1511. Apart from a few drawings of simple buildings on the coastlines of the island of Flores, made by Francisco Rodrigues in 1515,[4] no contemporary records exist to suggest the nature of these projects.

Several important mosques survive from the sixteenth century. They were founded by rulers able to resist the rapid penetration of Portuguese trading interests. An early example is at Cirebon in West Java, where a chronogram[5] suggests that the mosque was founded in 1500. Its construction was directed by three of the *walis* – the local Sunan Gunung Jati of Egyptian royal descent,[6] Sunan Bonang from Tuban, who had studied at Melaka, and Sunan Kalijaga from Demak. Today, in fragile condition, it stands to the north-west of Cirebon's oldest palace (*kraton*), shored up with steel supports from a restoration carried out in the late 1930s. The rectangular plan is turned towards the *qibla* at an angle to the royal compounds which are approximately cardinally oriented. Three supplementary porches (*serambi*) and a high brick wall have been added since the sixteenth century. The uppermost of the two concentric hipped roofs features a ridge; could the reason for this unusual detail be that the prayer-hall (*Langgar Alit*) of the ruler within the *kraton* took ritual precedence, and was therefore crowned by a centralized, pyramidal roof appropriate to the status of its user? The single central column (*saka tunggal*) of the prayer-hall also emphasizes such hierarchical association.

The royal mosque at Baubau on the island of Buton in the Sulawesi Sea – some 1,500 km (950 miles) east of Cirebon – has a similar ridged-roof profile. This, the oldest mosque in Sulawesi, was built by

Cross-section of the Masjid Agung, Demak, showing the mosque and its entrance veranda. The mihrab *extension (see plan above) is shown on the left.*

The Masjid Agung, Kraton Kasepuhan (founded 1500), Cirebon, Java.

Sultan Marhum after his conversion to Islam in 1558 by Said Abdul Wahid, a prince of Johore and a descendant of the Sultan of Aden. In all probability Sultan Marhum knew the Javanese north-coast cities well. This spectacularly sited building is set on a basement within the stone ramparts of the *kraton* and commands a broad vista of neighbouring islands. The double hipped roof is supported on tall timber columns and the building is enclosed by thick stone walls rendered with lime plaster made with white of egg. Centrally placed east doors are reached by a covered axial stair in the centre of the façade. A *serambi* with suspended timber floor extending on either side of the entrance to the full width of this façade is sheltered by the projecting lower roof; a similar overhang of about 1 m (3 ft) at the west end covers the projecting *mihrab*.

Banten was the westernmost trading port on the north coast of Java when, in 1525, it was drawn into the sphere of the Javanese Islamic states. The royal *Masjid Agung* built by Sultan Maulana Hasanuddin (r. 1552–70) on the west side of the square to the north of the *kraton* is notable for its five-tiered roof; a few other five-tiered mosques in the region are discussed below.[7] The lower roof at Banten has widespread, encompassing porches on the north and south sides which shelter the graves of religious leaders and members of the families of the early rulers. Of a later date, the wide rectangular *serambi* on the east side also has a broad hipped roof extending the full length of the main building. Although this complex has been well preserved, the effect of the graceful proportions of the columned interior space has been reduced by recently fitted ceiling linings.

A Dutch adventurer visiting Java in the last years of the century recorded seeing the unique minaret (*menara*) at Banten, although tradition ascribes both it and the two-storied brick pavilion (*tiyamah*) adjacent to the south porch to a Dutch architect, Hendrik Lucasz Cardeel, who worked in the city some time during the seventeenth century. In form the tapering hectagonal *menara* resembles a European lighthouse; possibly it served as a beacon and lookout tower for this busy port which was subject to attack by rival European powers. The small eaves and large, divided sash windows of the *tiyamah* are modelled on those of contemporary buildings in Holland and make the second-floor meeting-room vulnerable to the tropical sun and hence particularly unsuitable for its intended purpose.

The only other mosque tower of the period is in the old pilgrimage town of Kudus (Arabic: *al-Quds*) near Demak. It forms part of a sacred complex, including the tomb of the *wali* Sunan Kudus, dating from the middle of the century. The structure and profile of the body of the tower closely resemble those of the brick sanctuaries and gateways of Majapahit still to be seen at Trawulan. At its top is an open, double-roofed pavilion which is reached by a steep brick stair on its west side. Standing at the entrance to one of the walled compounds, it may have been a prototype for pavilions at gateways of mosques in East Java, Madura and the northern Maluku Islands (Moluccas), but above all it recalls the *kul-kul* towers of Balinese villages.

The tower at Kudus contains a cylindrical drum made from a hollowed-out tree-trunk and hide. In South-East Asia it is common for such a drum to be beaten at times of prayer before the muezzin calls the *adhan*. The drum is usually found in the *serambi*, but at Kudus, Semenup and other East Javanese and Malukan mosques it is placed in

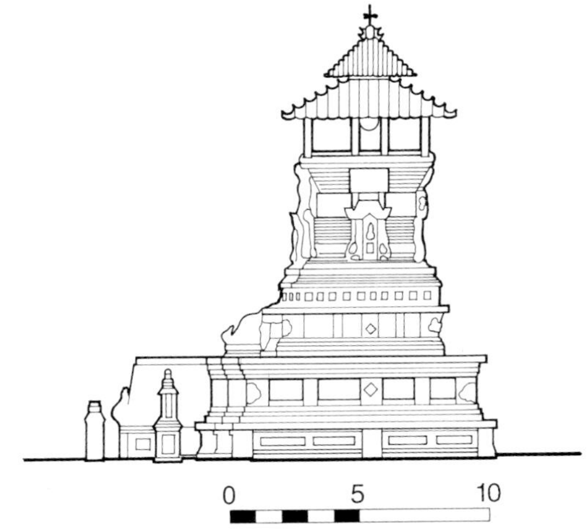

Cross-section of the tower at Kudus; the traditional bedug *(drum) is housed in the upper pavilion.*

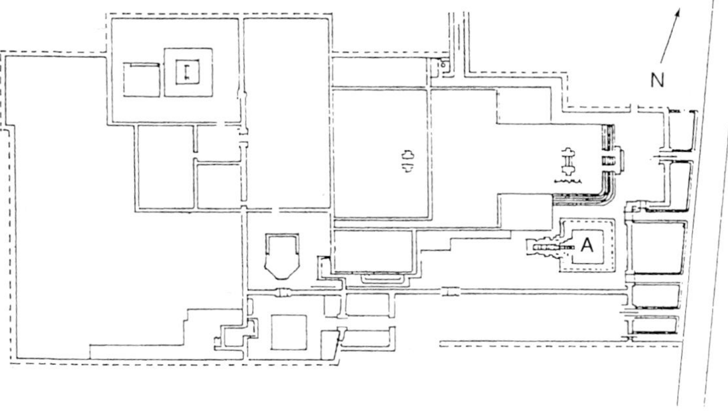

Site plan of the Kudus mosque complex, showing the location of the tower (A) within the enclosed area.

the raised gate pavilion. This complex at Kudus belongs to approximately the same period as the tomb of the tenth *wali*, Sunan Bayat, built in 1533 on Mount Jabalkat in the hinterland of Central Java and in the vicinity of other hilltop burial sites of the rulers of Mataram.

At both Kudus and Tembayat (close to the tomb of Sunan Bayat) a series of architectural elements – mosque and sequential walled courts with ceremonial gateways focusing on the tomb of a saint – are aligned from east to west. At Tembayat the ensemble stands on a hillside below the tomb, and at both sites graves of relatives and followers occupy the inner enclosures. The gateways giving access to the sequence of concealed courts are in the form of *candi bentar* and *gapura*, the traditional gateways to Javanese pre-Islamic sanctuaries, but best known from Balinese temple complexes. Pilgrims to these grave-sites anticipate that spiritual benefit will accrue from meditation, in a way similar to the outpouring of spiritual forces in the animistic setting of the traditional house. Such old Indonesian beliefs also imbue the tenth-century Hindu-Javanese Loro Jonggrang temple at Prambanan, which was the mausoleum of a spiritual leader of royal status. Mosques and tombs of saints are similarly associated in many parts of South-East Asia, and pilgrims habitually travel to these sacred sites in search of enlightenment in times of adversity.

The seventeenth century

English and Dutch ships began to explore the New World during the last decades of the sixteenth century. The defeat of the Spanish Armada in 1588 and the ebb of Portuguese maritime power encouraged English and Dutch adventurers to open trade routes to the Far East. Rivalries arose between the southern European states now in economic and political decline and the newly founded British and Dutch companies which set out to gain control of trade from Middle Eastern and Asian merchants active in South-East Asia. These new intrusions disrupted economic opportunities for Muslim rulers in centres established during the sixteenth century. From the early seventeenth century trading agreements were negotiated with or imposed upon these rulers wherever cloves, nutmeg, cinnamon and pepper, gold, benzoin and other exotic products were available. As the East India Companies of the Dutch and English gradually wrested control of international markets from the old trading ports and extended their influence into the courts of Central Java, South Sulawesi and the Maluku, armed confrontation effectively precluded the initiation of major building programmes among Muslim communities.

There is no clear record of the mosque in the important seventeenth-century North Sumatran trading city of Banda Aceh, but remnants of the royal pleasure gardens beside a stream near the centre of the modern city date from this period. They are in the form of an elevated, walled enclosure some 6 m (20 ft) square opening onto gardens dominated by the *gunungan* ('mountain-like sanctuary'), a stuccoed masonry construction approximately 8 m (26 ft) high. A small platform situated at its apex is accessible through a series of narrow tunnels and terraces. Legend suggests that the ruler meditated here, within a pavilion lined with silver.

A drawing of the royal mosque in the volumes of François Valentijn (1724–6)[7] suggests that it was similar to the seventeenth-century mosque which survives at Indrapuri, approximately 20 km (12½ miles) to the south. It is square in plan and sheltered by a triple *tajug* roof supported on multiple timber columns. Standing high within a walled, fortress-like enclosure, it has the appearance of a defensive retreat. It is said that Sultan Iskandar Muda withdrew there during the 1640s. The insertion of a timber ceiling in recent years has impaired its spatial elegance as well as reducing the comfort of its light and airy interior. Replacement of the former thatched roof, or perhaps the substitution of ironwood shingles, would allow this beautiful building to claim its important place as the oldest and most authentic extant mosque in Sumatra.

The eighteenth century

During the eighteenth century, as the Europeans tried to consolidate their position of advantage in international trade, administrative structures were set in place to regulate production in response to the demands of fluctuating markets in Europe and, eventually, in America. Local rulers were patronized by European representatives of state and trading enterprises. Brutal attempts to control production of valuable commodities such as spices, coffee and sugar resulted in the development of widespread armed resistance and piracy. Regional powers expanded their independent trading links and, in the late eighteenth century the Acehnese, Minangkabau, Banjar, Bugis and Gowanese, as well as the rulers of the islands of the Maluku, vied with each other for a role in the changing patterns of agricultural and mineral production as the rapacious policies of the Dutch failed.

Traders from many parts of the region established themselves at entrepôts such as Melaka, Palembang, Banten and Batavia (Jakarta), Surabaya and Makassar (Ujung Pandang). Muslims – Acehnese, Melayu, Minangkabau, Javanese, Banjar and Bugis – as well as

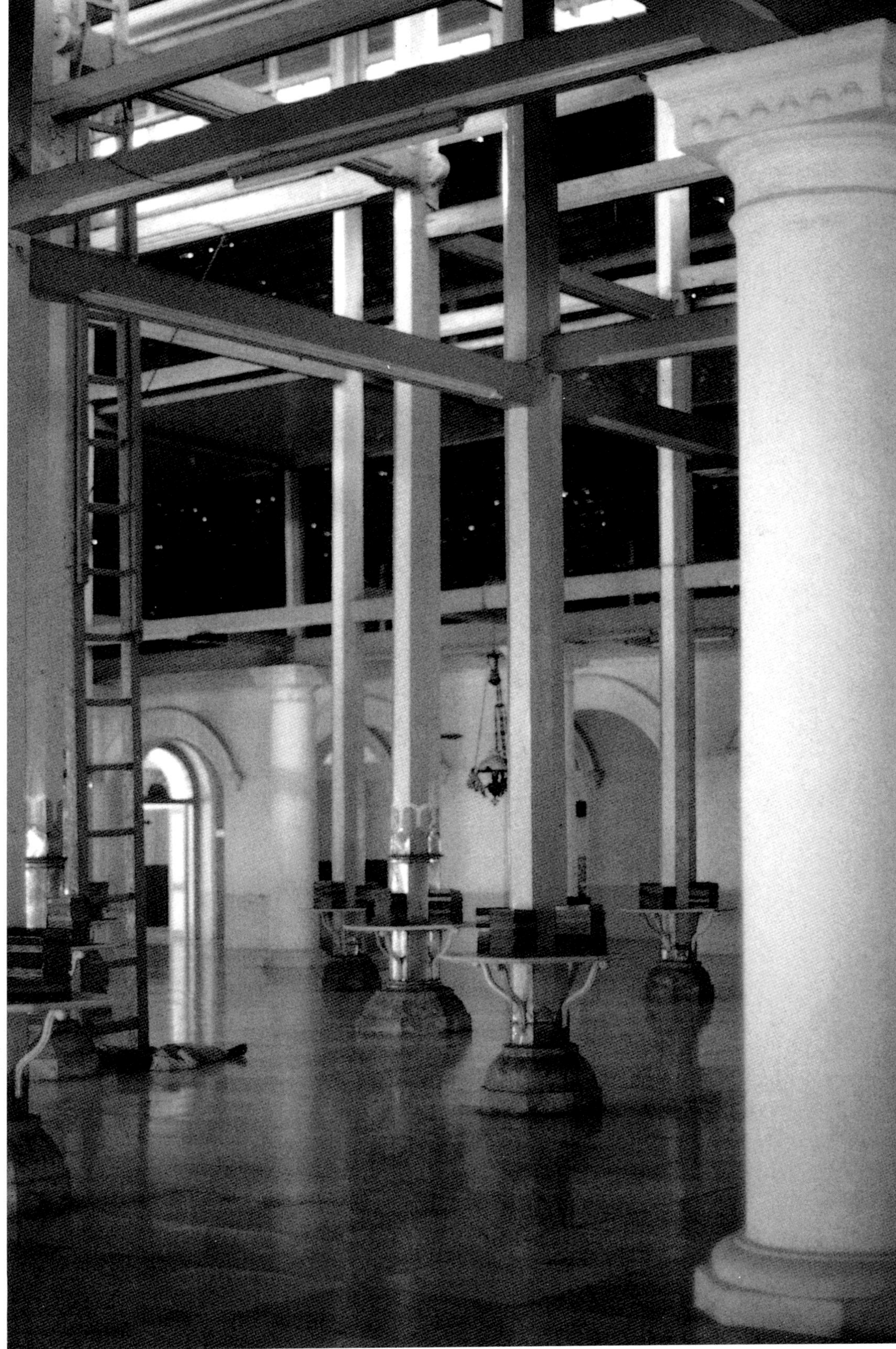

Interior of the prayer-hall of the Masjid Ngampel (1746), Surabaya; Qur'an stands are placed around the supporting columns.

Indians and Arabs, had settled in these centres, forming communities with the life of the mosque as their focus. Relatively small in scale, these complexes were based on the traditional schema of mosques of the previous two centuries, although their design was possibly also influenced by those of Islamic communities of coastal India and Sri Lanka. Masjid Kampong Kling and Kampong Hulu in Melaka, Masjid Agung in Palembang, Masjid Kebun Jeruk, Masjid Angke and the Masjid Jame (Friday Mosque) at Kampung Baru in Jakarta all

have a similar profile, in which a flared pyramidal upper roof is raised on four great columns, held clear of a single or double lower roof, with the gap between roofs as the source of subdued light and ventilation for the cool interior. A wide range of decorative motifs of Middle Eastern and Indian, sometimes of European and Chinese or even regional inspiration, were applied to the doors and windows and internal details of the rendered masonry walls. In Melaka and Palembang, and occasionally in Jakarta, a graveyard and minaret were enclosed by a high wall providing protection from the busy streets.

These buildings in major urban situations contrasted dramatically with mosques being constructed in more remote towns and villages as the teachings of the Prophet became more widely accepted. On Halmahera, Ternate, Tidore and other islands of the northern Maluku, an attenuated version of the multi-roofed mosque had emerged from traditional techniques of house construction. The five-tiered roof of Masjid Tua on Ternate, recently renovated, is supported on sixteen columns. The building is sited on the eastern coast of the island which is dominated by an active volcano, Mount Gama Lama. The direction of Mecca is indicated on the west side by the alignment of the *mihrab* with the graveyard and the mountain peak. The imagery of the tapering layers of its roof, referring to symbols of the cosmic mountain resonates in a magnificent natural setting.

At Lima Kaum near Lake Singkarak, amongst the Minangkabau communities of West Sumatra, there is another mosque which dramatically expresses this imagery. A total of 68 timber columns cluster around a massive central trunk reaching to the apex of the five-tiered roof more than 20 m (65 ft) above the ground. A spiral stair gives access to the top for the muezzin to call members of the five sub-clans to prayer. In nearby districts the old mosques at Rau Rau and Lubuk Bauk show even more directly the identification of indigenous elements with the requirements of Muslim tradition. The incorporation of motifs from Minangkabau house forms suggests that these buildings, which were originally clad in lustrous black thatch (*ijuk*) obtained from the areka palm, are derivative of older pre-Islamic sanctuaries. They bear a striking resemblance to the *geriten* of the Batak Karo communities situated to the north.

Nineteenth- and twentieth-century mosques

The collapse of the Dutch East India Company in Java at the end of the eighteenth century and the temporary British administration for seven years from 1811 was followed by even greater resistance to the Netherlands government upon its return there in 1818. Anti-European conflict until the middle of the nineteenth century and then even more direct control of export production stifled development of the life of the *ummat*. Towards the end of the century, however, opposition from liberal movements in Europe to injustices in the colonies created an

(Right) Mosque at Lubuk Bauk, West Sumatra; the roofs, originally thatched, are now covered with corrugated metal.

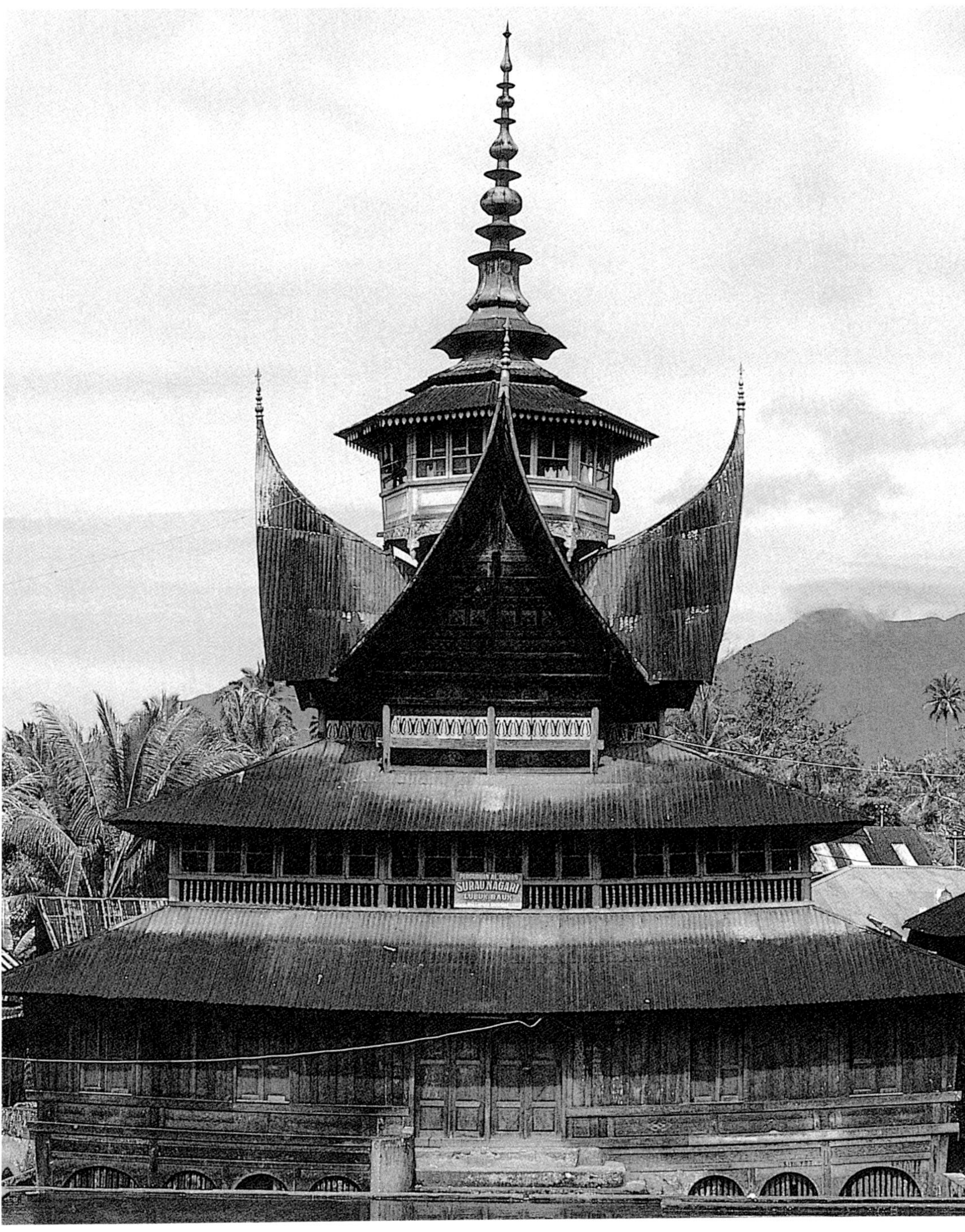

(Opposite) The Masjid Kampong Kling, Melaka.

interest in indigenous cultural and religious life. One outcome of the new Ethical Policy[8] of the Netherlands Indies in the early twentieth century was official support for the refurbishment of existing mosques, particularly in Java and Madura, in the context of expanding programmes of primary production and export. Large mosques sited on the west flank of public squares (*alun alun*) in Bandung, Sumedang, Garut, Tasikmalaya, Semarang, Pati, Jember, Malang, Pamekasan and Sumenep were worked on during the 1920s and 1930s. A departure from local tradition saw the addition of a freestanding *menara*, and sometimes two; and, as part of the programme, an iron *menara* surmounted by an Indian-style dome was built alongside the old mosque in Demak. This appendage, its retention supported by conservative opinion during the latest renovations, has been compared to 'the diving structure in a swimming bath'.[9]

From the end of the nineteenth century new directions of theological, educational and social reform throughout the Islamic world introduced alternative architectural styles which emanated from Cairo and Arabia. Although these were accepted to some extent in Malaya and North and West Sumatra, they were resisted by other more nationalistic sections of the *ummat*. In the second half of the twentieth century, after independence, this trend was reversed in a movement towards solidarity among Muslim nations and the development of a wide range of styles in the context of modern technology and idiosyncratic design. Recent additions to the mosques in Mecca and Medina have already been

The Masjid Baiturrachman (1881), Banda Aceh, Java, an example of a mosque which has been enlarged on several occasions. The form of the domes reflects Indian influence.

reflected in prayer-halls and mosque design throughout the region. Since the 1970s, however, a number of interesting mosques have been built by younger designers who are searching for an authentic architecture more responsive to their environment. These include the Masjid Al'Kautsar in South Jakarta by Zaenuddin Kartadiwiria, the Mosque at the Depok campus of the University of Indonesia, and the Said Naum Mosque at Kebun Kacang in Central Jakarta, designed by the firm Atelier Enam (see chapter 15).

There is no doubt, however, that the most extensive Islamic building programme ever undertaken in the region is that initiated in the late 1970s by President Soeharto of Indonesia; since then more than four hundred buildings have been completed throughout the country. The government-sponsored foundation *Yayasan Amal Bakti Muslim Pancasila* offers economically disadvantaged communities a building of standard design to be used as school, prayer-hall or mosque. The buildings have a basic plan and are available in three sizes – 15, 17 or 19 m (about 49, 56 or 62 ft) square – all enclosed beneath a triple *tajug* roof. Their authenticity, however, is flawed, for although the profile matches that of the old mosque at Demak, the four columns which have such an important place in the structural and symbolic schema of this ancient typology are omitted. The absence of the columns denies their metaphorical role of suggesting strands of enlightenment that link the believers gathering within, at prayer or study, to their Spiritual Source. In the great South-East Asian tradition of mosque architecture these central elements have had an inevitability intrinsic to the hovering canopies of this elegant structural system.

Today the *umma* in this region represents almost a quarter of the world's Muslims. In response to this dramatic expansion in population, large mosque complexes have been built in recent years, notably those in Kuala Lumpur, Shah Alam, Brunei and Jakarta, designed to accommodate tens of thousands at prayer. In each case local tradition has been set aside in pursuit of forms deriving from cultural developments in India, the Middle East and North Africa.

In many building traditions details revealed through the use of one material or structural method reflect those of their antecedents in another. In this gradual process of transference and osmosis, remembrances of primal elements can be contained and celebrated in the collective memory. In South-East Asia profound patterns in the transfer of symbols and natural forms have evolved through the architecture of the mosque, and in recent years planners of complexes to accommodate the faithful at prayer in this eastern extremity of Muslim Asia have begun to re-examine their rich heritage. Inevitably they will continue to work through this great tradition of mosque-building and make their architecture resonate with the grace and power of its expressive forms.

PART III

THE CONTEMPORARY SCENE

- 14 -
THE MOSQUE IN ISLAMIC SOCIETY TODAY

OLEG GRABAR

When the historian of Islamic art enters one of his favourite mosques built centuries ago or when he encounters an ancient religious building long known through publications but never actually seen, or indeed when he discovers an old Muslim sanctuary for the first time, two immediate reactions usually occur. One is to observe all those features of a building which are genuinely old and belong to the times when the mosque was built and to try to imagine the building as it would have looked at the time of its inauguration. The second reaction is to bemoan the ravages of time and man, to count the cracks in the walls and to regret – indeed to resent – repairs, later decorative schemes and accretions of any sort.

Unlike human beings, totally dependent at birth, potentially admirable and hopefully useful in their maturity, and cared for in old age, buildings are, as a rule, celebrated by historians only at the time of their construction. Everything else is mentally blotted out. At times, as for example in the preparation of drawings and plans, later additions may be wilfully omitted as if they do not exist, in fact as though they never existed. At best, they may be explained away as unfortunate modifications which ruined a presumably wonderful original. However much one admires the internal space of the Great Mosque in Cordoba, the last major extension in the tenth century is regretted for having destroyed the symmetry of the original composition, but is somehow acceptable because it too has a long history, and because it is presumed that the craftsmen and planners of old could not design something ugly. And, in the Great Mosque of Isfahan, celebrated for the harmony of its proportions and for the brilliance of its tile-covered courtyard with imposing *iwans*, a very complicated history over several centuries is obscured by the assumed existence of an original plan for a courtyard with four *iwans* which would have created the visual order of the mosque. In Isfahan a successful composition as seen today is viewed as an original creation and cannot easily be imagined as the result of slow development involving many reconstructions, while in Cordoba what was a necessary modification has been interpreted as a formal misfortune.[1]

Fascinated as he is with buildings and with works of art, the historian often tends to forget people, except perhaps the patron of a building or its architect and the craftsmen involved in its construction if their signatures are present or their names were recorded. The worshippers are absent from the holy places as presented by the historian; and the changing needs of a dynamic culture are hardly matters of great importance, whether in terms of achievements such as the adaptation of mosques to meet new requirements of space, for example in Cordoba, or of religious behaviour, as in Isafahan. There were modifications of taste, as seen in Ottoman mosques built in a very classical sixteenth-century style which often acquired a late Baroque, Rococo, or even neo-classical decoration. And certainly the advent of loudspeakers and of tape recorders, not to mention neon lights and of all sorts of other kinds of electrical fixtures, has altered our perception of both the internal and the external configurations of mosques. The Süleymaniye in Istanbul remains a place of prayer inside, but its floodlit exterior has become a spectacular element in the visual theatre of the city by night. Such developments are, for the most part, unlikely to be reversed, and even if one feels entitled to criticize their specific application in a particular context, it is hardly worthwhile to object to the technology that made them possible, any more than it is worthwhile to regret the invention of the automobile or the aeroplane.

The point of these preliminary remarks is to argue that the historian, equipped to analyze specific moments in the past, does not always possess the type of critical acumen and the psychological and emotional criteria needed to cope with the dynamics of cultural development. Difficulties are compounded when he has to deal with contemporary mosques, for two main reasons. One is that, in studying or visiting them, he cannot avoid direct involvement with either the people who commissioned, built, decorated and organized a particular mosque or with those who use it for worship. Their presence is still felt, either physically or through records and memories of living individuals. Thus the structure – unlike some historic mosques – cannot easily be divorced mentally from those who created it or who live with it. The second reason – intellectually much more interesting and much more important – is that, to a much greater extent than with the building of, say, a house or of a school, or with an evaluation of a contemporary hotel or market, to consider a modern mosque is to deal at once with the present and with the past. What are the burdens of that past which seem to affect feelings towards modern mosques? What are the expectations of the present which should somehow feature in today's mosques? These are the two broad questions to be explored here.

Presence of the past

Just as religious feelings and emotions vary from one individual to another, the contemporary religious experience begins, in part at least, with attitudes different from those of centuries past. Religious behaviour is, however, almost by definition tied to traditions hallowed for centuries, because the techniques for handling queries and issues are part and parcel of a long-established inheritance and because the pattern of behaviour required of those who profess a given faith has become established and sanctified by time. Among the requisites for worship is

The Sultan Ahmet Moque, Istanbul, by night; floodlighting has introduced a sense of visual drama not previously associated with places of worship.

a space dedicated to that purpose, and there is a sort of assumption that the space which was considered good for one's ancestors should also be good enough for oneself. I recall, for instance, how an architect as sensitive and cultivated as the late Hassan Fathy was very critical of Notre Dame du Haut, Le Corbusier's pilgrimge chapel at Ronchamp (1950–4), generally acclaimed as one of the masterpieces of twentieth-century architecture, because, he argued, its design departs from the forms traditionally associated with the Latin Church. The argument is, or so it seems, that the historical precedent is valid simply by virtue of being an inheritance, not because what is old is intrinsically good or useful. And it can well be added that religious activities – whether of the kind dictated by established liturgical practices or the more personal kind required of individuals privately seeking answers to their problems – can take place more naturally in surroundings which are familiar to the faithful and do not distract by their novelty or originality. At this level the argument is valid for almost all long-established religions. In the case of Islam, however, the legal restrictions – developed over centuries – on innovation in religious matters[2] give a particular power to an attachment to what is old – almost to a need for it.

Within a century of the Revelation, the main components which make up a mosque – large space, *mihrab*, *minbar*, frequent (but optional) courtyard occasionally with composed inner façades, a place for ablutions, as well as a central location convenient to the living areas of a community and a standard procedure for the call to prayer – had all become generally accepted by Muslims. Whether developed at the time of the Prophet in Medina or over the following decades, these components constituted the more or less fixed body of functions and of signs necessary for a gathering of any Muslim community. In these early centuries all collective activities took place in whatever space – sometimes adopted by accident at other times created for the purpose – could meet these particular requirements. This identification of the needs associated with a mosque and communal prayer was accomplished within the communities of the central Muslim lands (essentially the Fertile Crescent, Egypt, and the Arabian peninsula) within the lifetime of the immediate descendants of the Companions and Followers of the Prophet, more or less within the period of the gathering of the Traditions (*hadith*) which, after the Revelation itself, became the main regulators of the life and behaviour of the faithful. These components of the mosque became elements of the non-negotiable, untouchable and immutable ethical and behavioural corpus of principles governing the life of all Muslims.[3]

No fixed forms were prescribed for any of these components, although the *mihrab* was a niche and the *minbar* acquired a conventional system of steps. The predominant ordering of interior space was initially the so-called hypostyle system, with a large number of evenly distributed supports for the roof. As time went on, other formal systems were introduced: courtyard with one to four *iwans*, large central cupola with adjoining courtyard, and a number of variations on any of these. Forms would be modified over the centuries, usually as a reflection of the local practices and existing ideologies in different lands to which Islam spread, because forms (as opposed to functions) were not part of the early corpus of permanent obligations associated with the Muslim faith. It is only around the minaret that a slight problem does exist: all the evidence points clearly to the fact that the towers we now associate as a matter of course with the call to prayer did not appear systematically until the twelfth century and that their function was not initially restricted to a purely liturgical purpose connected with prayer, for in some instances minarets may also have served as local landmarks or as lighthouses.

In short then, at the time when, from the twelfth century onward, and in ways which are still far from clearly established, an ever larger majority within the Muslim world began to close the 'doors of innovation',[4] and a body of functions required of the mosque had been established and, so to speak, implicitly sanctified by their association with the generations which succeeded the lifetime of the Prophet. In addition, the mosque complex had become the focal point for activities involving almost all aspects of collective life, from teaching to the exchange of information, from prayer to sheltering overnight while travelling. There were, however, no canonical or obligatory forms associated with any of these activities.

This is where the second theme from the past, the sense of comfort derived from the known, the familiar, comes into play. This sense of comfort is nurtured by two entirely different aspects of contemporary Islamic culture. One characteristic of Islam since the very beginning is the absence of an institutionalized ecclesiastical system with the kind of authority accorded, almost abstractly in the Christian context, to the Church. The result for our purposes is that in Muslim society no authority exists to sponsor, accept, promote or reject changes, except the consensus of the community as a whole. For the community, for any community, maintaining the ways of the past is a safer and simpler option than introducing change, for, among other things, it avoids conflicts over matters which are secondary to the main issues of the faith, as architectural and artistic questions have come to be regarded over the past century.

A second factor contributing to the attachment to past forms is more interesting to explore. From Morocco or Senegal to Indonesia and China, the overriding concern of the post-colonial era has been the establishment of a country's national self-identity and of signs denoting that identity, as well as of symbols connoting it. There are many sides to this concern, but without doubt one of them is how to express the Islamic identity of individuals, groups or nation-states. Within this particular concern the mosque plays a central role. Inside a Muslim country or geographical area the mosque becomes a highly visible feature which authenticates its Islamic quality, while in non-Muslim lands, where many millions of Muslims now live and work, it announces a Muslim presence to non-Muslims and signifies 'home' to the faithful. Furthermore, especially arising out of the wealth of the major oil-producing states, private endowments of mosques, such as had existed throughout the Middle Ages, have reappeared not only in the native countries of the patrons, but often also in countries where they live or find their relaxation (e.g. the several 'Saudi' mosques built in what used to be the vacation areas of the Lebanese mountains). In addition to these small places of worship, Senegal, Kuwait, Iraq, Malaysia, Pakistan (in Islamabad) and Indonesia have all built or planned enormous 'national' or 'state' mosques. And, in European or American cities with a sizable Muslim population, local communities have either sponsored the construction of a new mosque of transformed some existing building to serve as a mosque.

Nearly all these examples exhibit some relationship to the past which is fascinating to a historian. With a few exceptions (most of which were not actually built, but published as projects in professional journals or as parts of the record of international competitions), to which I shall return, they reflect a hankering after old forms, a copying or imitation with varying degrees of success of the four or five traditional types. Some, especially in the Far East, where there is a less developed history of monumental Islamic architecture, can be classified as ecumenical, as they borrow from several traditions. However, the vast majority appear as modifications, sometimes simplified and at other times embellished by fancy decoration, of a small number of traditional formal arrangements. The ancient and regularly repeated rituals associated with communal prayer seem easiest to accomplish in the kind of settings in which they have been performed for centuries. It seems reasonable to assume that for most worshippers established ritual acts are best performed and most meaningful in a traditional setting.

This particular point operates at two different levels. For the faithful it is emotionally and psychologically reassuring to know that the area of prayer and of gathering has remained unaffected by changes in the outside world and that eternal truths continue to be proclaimed in a space which seems itself to symbolize the eternal. And, at a different level, as international travel and movement have become the lot of many Muslims, and as emigration, temporary or permanent, has affected many individuals and sometimes whole families, a mosque with traditional domes and minaret appears like a restful 'home' in the midst of alien surroundings.

The aspects of a physical setting or settings which help a believer to feel comfortable, both physically and emotionally, as a Muslim are probably best explained by psychologists of religious behaviour.

Expectations for the present

It is much more difficult to identify the expectations of the modern world than it is to explain the attraction of the past. The task is made all the more difficult because the future will reflect the dreams and aspirations of our contemporaries, especially of the younger generation in whose hands the destiny of tomorrow's world will lie. Here I can do no more than attempt to sketch out a few of the basic themes which, it seems to me, must be part of the expectations that the present formulates for the future.

One theme is at first glance a relatively minor matter. There has occurred a subtle, and usually not acknowledged, shift in the uses of the mosque. In most Muslim countries educational and many other social functions of the traditional mosque (except in the case of major State mosques) have been taken over by the State. Curiously, it is now in non-Muslim lands that educational facilities most frequently form part of the mosque complex, because, within generally secular state educational systems, the mosque becomes the natural focus for formal religious instruction. However, most mosques no longer function as formal educational centres,[5] except at the elementary level, and as a result of these changes the mosque has tended to become a far simpler and more functional and pious place than ever before, and this in turn has led to a new use for the mosque as a place for imparting political slogans and propaganda to the faithful assembled for Friday prayers. The practice recalls the reputed activities of al-Hajjaj, an Umayyad governor of Iraq in the eighth century, who was said to have terrorized the population when he made dramatic appearances at the mosque.[6] In reality, however, we are dealing not with a return to the past, but with a very recent phenomenon of practising mass-manipulation techniques on crowds of believers who are far more unified in their faith than were the congregations of old. Regardless of this particular use of the mosque, however, the more important point is its transformation into what is essentially a consecrated space, that is to say one which is not only, as it had always been, primarily restricted to believers, but which has an aura of holiness. One can only wonder whether this occurred as a response to the character of Christian or other sanctuaries endowed with a presence of the 'holy' that is usually absent from traditional mosques (as opposed to mausoleums or other types of sanctuary) or whether it was a logical development arising from changes within the Muslim community itself.

A larger contemporary issue is that of altered attitudes and behaviour resulting from the various technological advances which revolutionized everyday life in the second half of the twentieth century in almost totally irreversible ways. Furthermore, these recent inventions accompanied the development in the arts generally known as 'modernism' which was (and is) attractive on account of its universal applicability. Can the mosque as a form be fitted within these new trends? Nothing in Muslim theory precludes the use of the latest construction methods and modern design in the building of mosques, and any historian can demonstrate that over the centuries Islam – and especially when it was introduced into lands like Malaysia, Indonesia, China or central Africa – readily adopted local building habits. Yet it is probably not an accident that, although projects had been developed for 'modernistic' mosques, most remained on the drawing board. Apart from a few small buildings and State mosques, the most interesting exception is the Mosque at Visoko (1967–80), near Sarajevo, built by and for a Muslim community living in what was then the secular socialist state of Yugoslavia.

While the use of loudspeakers has made it possible to increase the area available for hearing sermons and prayers, air-conditioning has eliminated the need for courtyards in hot climates, recorded calls to prayer played over loudspeakers have superseded the traditional function of the muezzin, and elaborate security measures have increased the protection available to heads of state or other secular dignitaries attending mosques, very few religious buildings constructed in recent decades have been designed to take into consideration the formal consequences of any of these novelties. A comparable situation is evident in most new churches, in which modernism has also been generally shunned, and where it does exist in exceptional cases like Ronchamp, the buildings in question have come to be viewed as seminal works of art. Equally, the sponsors of new mosques seem uncertain about the degree to which they are willing to accept modern developments in the design of religious buildings, while readily adopting the latest technological advances as part of their personal and professional lives.

The last aspect of modern life likely to affect the mosque is the rapid change in patterns of living. In Kuwait City the grandiose State Mosque completed in 1984 stands totally isolated from any urban living space except the palace of the country's ruler, and resembles a monument rather than a place for worship and collective social activities. All around the mosque, however, large areas were cleared to make way for office buildings and other commercial enterprises, yet several small mosques – once the places of worship used by local communities – which reflected a traditional Muslim society centred on shared ethnic, religious or other bonds, were left standing. Even though the communities had been displaced, the mosques remained because of a law that had, quite wrongheadedly, designated them as sacred spaces. The old mosques stood empty, while even the vast new mosque could only be reached via the parking areas and as a result had become more a symbol for a faith than a place intended for liturgical occasions, for prayer and for meditation and learning. The deeper lesson of the Kuwaiti example is that aspects of modern life, such as regular travel between home and place of work, television and other communications media, and supermarkets, have contributed to an altering of traditional modes of behaviour and of the ways of thinking of many Muslims. Sooner or later, the mosque will have to adapt to these new ways, and it will be up to architects to develop appropriate forms to accommodate the outlook of the believer in the twenty-first century.

Among the modern mosques I have personally visited or studied, the very small district mosques of Bangladeshi cities, with their essentially local associations, have seemed more alive than any of the grandiose building designs for state capitals. Perhaps the future of the Muslim faith lies in local communities rather than in nation-states.

Examples of the overt use of loudspeakers to broadcast the call to prayer and of a lack of aesthetic feeling in their placing on mosques are seen in a low-cost modern building near Jakarta, Indonesia (top), and a traditional village mosque in the Hunza Valley, northern Pakistan.

- 15 -
AN OVERVIEW OF CONTEMPORARY MOSQUES

HASAN-UDDIN KHAN

IN the course of the four decades since *c.* 1950 mosques have been built throughout the world in substantial numbers, commissioned by a variety of clients ranging from national governments to private individuals. This chapter presents a preliminary overview which examines recent mosques in terms of their functional and formal aspects.[1] The buildings chosen for discussion come from countries and regions ranging from Senegal to Indonesia, and reflect the interaction between individual decision-making (the client) and practical interpretation (often by an architect) region by region. To the careful student of cultural phenomena these buildings may seem too diffuse and diverse to be reviewed in a coherent fashion. The mosque, however, is by definition a building type which transcends regional boundaries in its symbolic and functional role, though not in its formal realization. It retains its traditional role as the central public space for the men (and to a lesser extent, the women) of a neighbourhood or group. In recent years it has become the nucleus in the planning and layout of new neighbourhoods and institutions – often representing an idealized recreation of a traditional neighbourhood – in the rapidly growing cities of the Islamic world. Also, the formal interconnections are more self-aware and apparent than may have been suspected, as becomes clear when the details of the professional education and culture of individual architects are traced and the effect of these factors is assessed in relation to the periodically proclaimed regionalist ambitions of national governments.

Since most countries of the Islamic world have achieved independence only since the late 1940s as a result of rapidly changing conditions, traditional regional mosque design has been subjected to the influence of internationalism and modernism. And, as Mohammed Arkoun speculates in the concluding chapter of this volume, the uses of the mosque are being determined not only by religious practice but also by ideological considerations, which give rise to varied architectural approaches – each illustrating the particular point of view or stance of a Muslim society. Although it is perhaps too soon to be able to present the architecture of the mosque since the 1950s with the benefit of 'critical distance', changes in mosque design are an important indicator in understanding Muslim societies today.

Any study of contemporary architecture in different regions must (as Ismail Serageldin has pointed out in chapter 4) take account of the physical and visual surroundings of a building and the forms chosen for it. Ruptures in the continuity of adapting historical forms and practices – the symbolic language of architecture – can be detected in all regions of the Islamic world, most of which were transformed physically and culturally during a long period of colonial rule by European powers. The effects of this non-Muslim hegemony on the physical environments and on the symbolic systems which created them cannot be underestimated. One need only look closely at any city to ascertain the extent of the introduction of new urban forms (most often in new developments) and new building types.

Representative examples of the rupture of a symbolic language are two buildings in Cairo: the Mosque of Muhammad Ali (dating from the 1840s) and the Mausoleum of Zaghlul Pasha (built in the 1920s). Although, as Viceroy of Egypt, Muhammad Ali was independent of central Ottoman control, he nonetheless chose to build a monumental mosque in what appears at first glance to be a classical Ottoman style,[2] instead of using the prevailing Mamluk vocabulary. The Mausoleum of Zaghlul Pasha, with its neo-pharaonic references, illustrates the extent of the cultural rupture and dissonance present in Egypt at the time. This building represented an attempt to define identity in nationalist terms, and was the first in which reference to pharaonic models was even considered. These two examples are cited here merely

The Mosque of Muhammad Ali, Cairo, built by the Viceroy of Egypt in the 1840s in the Ottoman style.

Facing page
Prayer-hall of the Islamic Cultural Center Mosque (1991), New York, by Skidmore, Owings and Merrill. The glass-panelled mihrab *is surrounded by Qur'anic texts in Kufic script. The cubic space is surmounted by a central dome.*

to demonstrate the processes involved in the formation of the attitudes adopted, which were symptomatic of the distancing and the rupture that took place in the intervening decades not only in Egypt, but in all areas where Islamic cultures had taken root.

The term 'rupture' has been used increasingly by Muslim scholars when describing architectural manifestations that relate directly to a particular Muslim social system. What might be termed the 'first rupture' occurred at the time of the European Renaissance in the sixteenth century which caused 'breaks' with the historical and local contexts. Another major rupture came about as the result of colonization – what I have termed the 'recent rupture'. In the years following the granting of independence reaction to the colonial era has been a factor in determining expressions of national identity through building. The recent rupture with the symbolic and visual past was first achieved in the 1920s in the newly established Turkish Republic as it moved to define itself in purely secular terms and to treat historical precedents, as represented by the country's monuments, not as a continuous line but as relics of a distant, ideological and inaccessible past to which neither architect nor client was permitted to have recourse under Kemal Atatürk. This process of refashioning the country into a secular nation-state provided a powerful precedent for the late Shah Mohammed Reza Pahlavi in Iran when, in the 1950s, he set about building at least the trappings, if not the replication of the 'modern' state. Indeed, the modernization project for Turkey has been very influential throughout the Islamic world, in terms of the success of its secular forms and symbols, just as – in ways we have yet to fully understand – the country's Islamic monumental architecture of the sixteenth century has been a major source of inspiration elsewhere.

Mosque design and construction, regionally differentiated throughout history, have been affected in contemporary society by an overlap of important factors: the expression of place (or region); the emergence of a 'pan-Islamic' viewpoint based essentially on a political view of the world of 'us' (Muslims) and 'them' (others); the imposition from without of a form of modernity as desirable internationalism; and the individual aspirations of client-groups and designers. The manifestation of modernism and internationalism is the outcome of the views of client-groups, hence some indication of the nature of contemporary clients is of assistance in understanding the changes which mosque design is undergoing.

Responding to the clients

While individual clients can be seen to continue the tradition of patronage which led to the building of many older mosques, the appearance of new Muslim nation-states, particularly after the progressive dissolution of the Western colonial empires, has introduced a somewhat different source of funding. Since *c.* 1960 these states, whatever their political ideology, have increasingly engaged in mosque-building projects at all levels and on several scales. These ever more capital-intensive building programmes can be seen as attempts to create new expressions not only of political power, social control and piety, but also of sovereignty, national identity and modernity. These processes may be viewed against the background of popular architecture, in which artisan and contractor built mosques for a variety of individual or community clients in situations where making choices between traditional and non-traditional mosque forms was apparently a less important factor. Thus, although the *State as client* has given rise to a number of major buildings, the history of the mosque as a building type does record examples of individual buildings which would have served in their day as symbols of the power of a dynasty, and therefore of state, e.g. the Umayyad Great Mosque of Damascus, the Cami Fatih of Mehmet the Conqueror in Istanbul, or even the Great Mosque of Fatehpur Sikri in India. However, these were also the results of individual patronage by the current ruler, rather than of a corporate structure or a republic. The attempt by governments to define their state in modern and Islamic terms is a very recent phenomenon, often occasioned by the special need to develop a source of national identity. Such was the case with the new Islamic Republics of Pakistan and Malaysia, both of them post-colonial creations as political entities. In other predominantly Muslim states such as Morocco, Indonesia and Kuwait the concept of the State or National Mosque also plays a central and symbolic role.

The State Mosque symbolic of nationhood (as distinct from the mosque of a ruler) is a building funded and visualized by a committee and having a clearly recognizable visual identity which must be explicit in its regional, modern and Islamic references. As the building complex is generally intended to be seen as a symbol of national identity in the eyes of an international audience, the resulting mosques have been large, with a capacity of around 20,000 worshippers under covered space, and up to 200,000 in the courtyard during the major Muslim festivals such as Eid. The largest such project so far proposed was for Iraq through an international design competition held in 1982, in which seven firms (out of the twenty-two which entered) were invited to participate. The mosque was intended to accommodate 40,000 worshippers and was to be a national monument of a contemporary character whilst drawing on Arab-Islamic architectural and ornamental traditions.[3] The jury awarded the first prize to the Jordanian architect Rasem Badran, but the building was never realized. Interestingly, this concept of a State Mosque usually envisaged a multiple use of space, with the inclusion of a *madrasa* and sometimes an Islamic University, a library and other spaces for social activities.

The State as patron seems for the most part to have taken over the traditional role of the King or ruler in respect of commissioning mosques that express nationhood. If State mosques are an expression of political will and national identity, as symbols for the nation and the outside world alike, then mosque projects undertaken by *local authorities* can be seen as signs of the concern that the government has for neighbourhood communities. With the establishment of European colonial administrations in the nineteenth century came a shift of responsibility away from individuals and village or town committees to a more centralized authority, accompanied by the concept of physical development plans and master-plans for urban and rural settlements. In assuming this responsibility, local administrations felt obliged to

Artist's impression of the winning design by Rasem Badran for the projected State Mosque in Baghdad (competition 1982).

provide communal religious facilities, just as they provide schools and hospitals to serve the public. This was also coupled with a generally socialist outlook and organization influenced by models in Europe and the former Soviet Union. With the advent of the master-plan and zoning as an organizational device, the multiple role of the mosque complex was diminished, leading to the construction of separate buildings with more limited functions. Twentieth-century planning brought with it what might be called the secularization of space, even though the function of the mosque itself remains unchanged.

Since the mid-twentieth century, local authorities in the Islamic world have probably been responsible for building more urban mosques than have individuals or even neighbourhood communities. Local government interventions appear to take two forms: either they create a building which is individual and special, or they produce a mosque design capable of being repeated in similar contexts and situations. In the latter case, the mosque is usually related to a new settlement, as in the case of Islamabad in Pakistan (the Capital Development Authority) and Singapore (the Housing Development Board). In considering the design of mosques, it appears that they are built either because of pressure from local inhabitants or because they fit into the local authority's plan which calls for the provision of mosques on a per capita basis, the population figure being determined by the planning authority itself. In general, governments have essentially turned their attention to the Friday mosque providing space for communal worship, i.e. a building conceived on a larger scale than that of a *masjid*. In addition, the Friday mosque has a public role with symbolic and propagandistic undertones which are perforce denied to the *masjid*. The result is, in some senses, a showpiece intended to exhibit the benevolent nature of a government concerned with the spiritual well-being of its people. Not surprisingly then, experiments in architectural design have concentrated on this mosque type.

The third major client-group consists of *institutions* such as *waqfs* (religious endowments), universities, hospitals and airports. In the planning of new developments the mosque has become a standard integral feature of complexes for institutions, as a result of broader educational concerns and a recognition of the need for the provision of places for collective prayer. The historical parallel with the traditional mosque-hospital or mosque-school complex is apparent. In such situations the size of the mosque is dependent on the number of people in a particular institution, but the design is usually based on maxima in order to emphasize the importance and size of the institution. This legacy of Western planning practice, in which buildings are separated into functional typologies, is currently being questioned in the context of Muslim societies.[4] Within these new planned environments the mosque plays an ever more central role in terms of its function and of its siting. For example at Jondishapur University (1974) in Iran and the King Khaled International Airport (1983) in Riyadh, Saudi Arabia, the mosques are sited centrally and conceived in each case as a spatial connector. The place of prayer assumes a symbolic importance in

(Left) The Mosque (1981) of the National headquarters of ISNA, the Islamic Society of North America, Plainfield, Indiana: view of the entrance.

(Below) The Dar al-Islam Mosque (1980), Abiquiu, New Mexico.

(Bottom) The Taric Islamic Center (1991), Toronto, Ontario.

signalling the centrality of Islam in the institution. Mosques marking the edge of a city are often highly visible features, as in the case of the Corniche in Jeddah, where mosques have been built in various styles at intervals of about 3 km (2 miles).

In rural or village *communities*, where traditional beliefs and practices tend to be less subject to rapid change, the function and place of the mosque in relation to the community have remained much the same as in the past, when such communities were traditionally made up of different groups organized by guilds, castes or tribes, each group having a landlord or sheikh as its chief. In some cases a patron, e.g. a sultan or wealthy landowner, would finance the building of a mosque, but the decision-making process remained collective, thus allowing the community a role in shaping its environment. Participation in such decisions inevitably engendered a sense of responsibility and commitment among the community because its members were actively involved in forming, as well as maintaining, the local surroundings. Each group would build its own mosque using whatever collective resources it had, according to local traditions passed down through generations. Such was the case of the Yaama Mosque (1962–82) in Niger and the Niono Mosque (1973) in Mali. No architect, in the modern professional sense of the word, was necessary and the construction was usually undertaken by a local mason aided by members of the community. Since the *masjid* was essentially there to cater to basic religious needs, it was usually a functional structure often with few external signs distinguishing it as a mosque because everyone knew what and where it was. The design of the *jami*, on the other hand, was usually more expressive.

However, the situation since the 1960s has been considerably different, in that the decision-making process became the affair of centralized government authorities on both a local and a national scale.

The Sherefuddin Mosque, Visoko (1980), Bosnia: an uncompromisingly modernist architectural approach in an area formerly associated with the Ottoman Empire and more recently with socialist values.

The consequences of this shift of responsibility are particularly evident in urban settings. In the past, the mosque was usually integrated into the urban fabric, central to the community it served, although mosques isolated from the urban fabric and treated as major monuments intended for society at large were not uncommon. (This is still true of older urban settings and of new urban settlements where traditional models are sometimes repeated.) However, in many cases the problem of the rapid growth of cities had led to the development of new urban settlements in which governments make site decisions based mainly on zoning considerations; the result is the creation of a number of 'strategically located' Friday mosques which are not usually integrated into the community they serve. These mosques thus become separated from the neighbourhood, so leading to a breakdown in the inhabitants' relationship with their local place of prayer and gathering.

Within states and community structures, *individual patrons* have always played an important part in the building of mosques, usually as an act of piety or as a gesture towards their own community. Often a Muslim ruler would erect a mosque in a foreign land as a reminder of his dominion and the presence of another faith. This can be seen in countless examples in India and Indonesia. In recent times the international nature of the élite has led to individuals making such gestures within their own community and to others as well – for example, several Saudi Arabian princes have built mosques in Pakistan, Morocco and Spain. Such modern patrons are of necessity well-off, and the range is enormous – from a national and religious leader such as King Hassan II of Morocco to a businessman in Bangladesh. The resulting mosques usually reflect the individual taste of the patrons, as in the case of the eclectic Indian-style mosque complex built by the landowner Ghazi Mohammed Rais in Bhong, Pakistan.[5] Here, it is not important to elaborate on the question of the individual as client but to record it as a continuing and important force in mosque-building.

One other new client type (other than the State) is that of *Muslim communities in predominantly non-Muslim countries*. With the extensive movement of people around the world and the establishment of new communities, this category of client has become an important one; for example, in the USA the Dar al-Islam Mosque (1980) at Abiquiu, New Mexico, designed by the Egyptian architect Hassan Fathy (1900–89) in a traditional Nubian mud-brick idiom, functions as a landmark for a small Muslim community in a rural situation. Interesting urban examples are the Taric Islamic Centre (1991) in Toronto, Canada, designed by Azhar Loghman, and the ISNA Mosque (1983) in Plainfield, Indiana, designed by the Pakistani architect Gulzar Haider. Both make elegant contemporary architectural statements and signal the presence of increasing numbers of Muslims in North America.

In another instance, the Sherefuddin Mosque (1980) in Visoko, Bosnia, designed by Professor Zlatko Ugljen, illustrates a modernist approach by an indigenous Muslim community in the former socialist republic of Yugoslavia. Perhaps its modernist image was essential in order to avoid associating the building with the historical Ottoman

The Islamic Centre Mosque (1992), Rome: (above) detail of one of the four corners of the prayer-hall showing structural columns which also incorporate service ducts; (below) site plan.

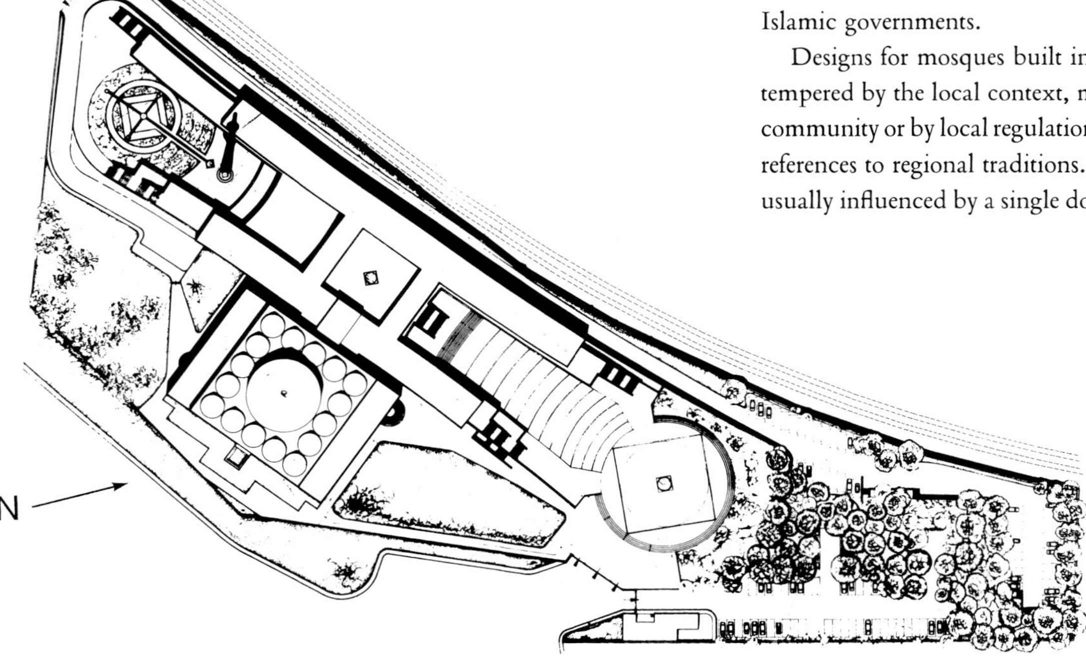

mosques of the region. Bordered on one side by an existing cemetery, the building stands on the site of an earlier mosque destroyed by fire; its design is based on the typical plan of regional mosques while making overt reference to the modern design of Le Corbusier's pilgrimage chapel Notre Dame du Haut at Ronchamp. Perhaps the most unusual feature of this mosque is its minaret, featuring abstract calligraphy in a green tubular pipe structure. Similarly, the so-called 'store-front' mosques found in North American cities with substantial black populations signal the presence there of Afro-American Muslims, and an analogous situation exists in Indonesia, with the Chinese shop-house mosques of Jakarta.[6]

Projects for mosques expressing a Muslim presence in non-Islamic countries started to take shape in the 1950s, coinciding with the rise of independent states of the Islamic world. Earlier, England's first purpose-built mosque in Woking, Surrey, had been a version of the Taj Mahal and Lahore's Badshahi Mosque; founded in 1889 by Shah Jehan Begum, the wife of the then Nawab of Bhopal, it displayed its Indian connections just as the Paris Mosque (1926) imitated Moroccan architecture. Even after the ending of colonial rule, however, links between countries or areas like Great Britain and India or France and North Africa remained strong. During the 1950s and 1960s significant numbers of Muslims began emigrating to Britain, France and other parts of Europe, as well as to North America, and the burgeoning immigrant communities began to feel the desire to express their presence by building new mosques. Projects that had been initiated in the 1950s like the Islamic Centre in Hamburg (funded jointly by the Iranian community in Germany and religious institutions in Iran and built between 1960 and 1973) were finally seeing the light of day. Like their counterparts in newly independent Muslim countries, major mosques built in the West as statements of Muslim identity have usually been financed entirely or in part by Muslim governments, notably that of Saudi Arabia. Very often, the prime movers in such projects are members of Muslim diplomatic missions who use their position and influence to obtain the necessary funds from their own and other Islamic governments.

Designs for mosques built in foreign cultural settings are generally tempered by the local context, modified by pressures from the existing community or by local regulations and planning laws, and they include references to regional traditions. In the latter case, the external form is usually influenced by a single dominant style derived from one country

Views of the Regent's Park Mosque (1977), London, and the Islamic Center Mosque (1957), Washington, D.C., two examples of major Muslim buildings in non-Muslim urban contexts.

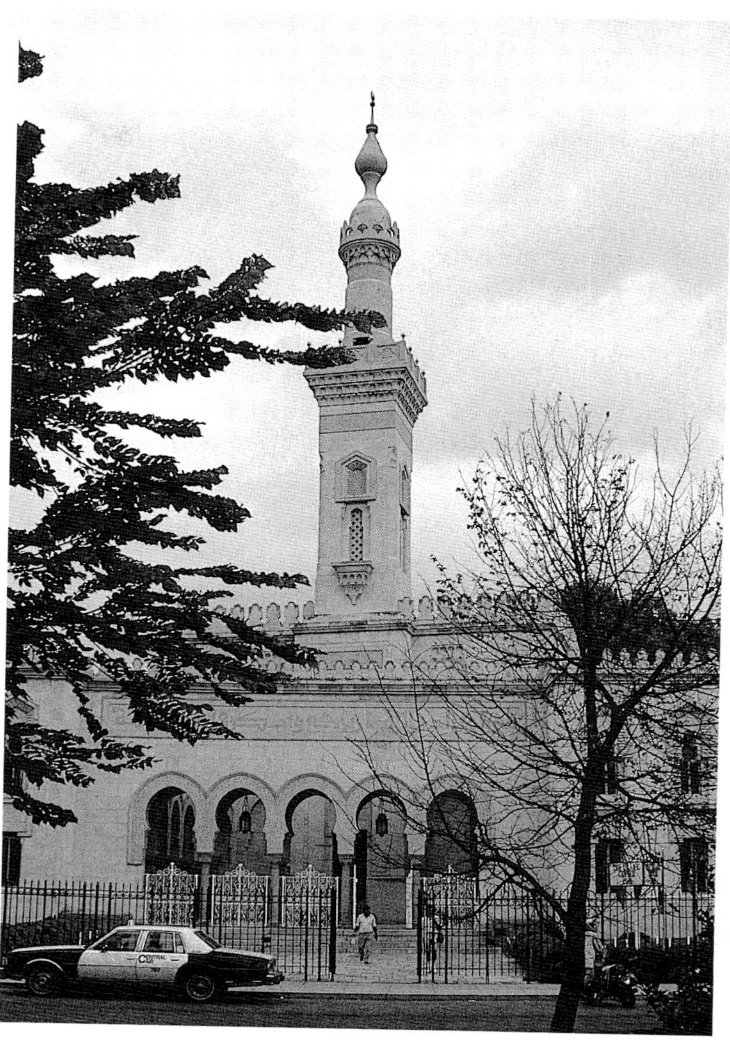

or region,[7] depending on who is financing, designing or leading the project. In this sense, the design reflects the self-identity and aspirations of the group that takes the initiative in the project. Although the internal layout or plan generally follows the style of the exterior, the interior ornamentation is quite frequently inspired by a pot-pourri of styles having no direct connection with the formal expression. While the outside must be designed to fit into a non-Muslim cultural context, the inside may be exuberantly decorated with Islamic ornamentation as if to emphasize that space as Muslim. Examples of such buildings are the Islamic Center in Washington, D.C. (1957) by Mario Rossi (1897–1961) and the Regent's Park Mosque (1977) in London by Sir Frederick Gibberd and Partners. Other recent projects, such as the one in New York (1991) by Michael McCarthy and Mustafa Abadan of Skidmore, Owings & Merrill, and the Islamic Centre Mosque in Rome (1992), by Portoghesi, Moussawi and Gigliotti, express a more restrained statement of a 'synthesis' of form and a contemporary architectural expression. In terms of its structure, the Rome Mosque draws its inspiration from Cordoba and Tlemcen. The prayer-hall (based on approximately the same plan and area as that of the Mosque of the Prophet in Medina) conveys a sense of calm and majesty more successfully than is the case in most new mosques; the hall is capped by a number of shallow Turkish-inspired domes. The design of the rest of the complex, which includes a library and social spaces, draws upon Roman buildings and colonnades. The minaret is a modern slab that rises as a place marker. Characteristically, such Islamic Centres serve not only as places for prayer, but also encourage social, educational and cultural activities among local Muslim populations.

Trends in Recent Mosque Design

Specific examples of mosques from different parts of the world help to illustrate the directions which mosque design has taken and provide an indication of the various currents present today. They range from government-sponsored and institutional mosques to individually and community funded mosques. Examples representing the mosque in the West provide an insight into Muslim perceptions of the role of Islam in the international community.

In the past regional architectures were substantially affected by local conditions – climate, available materials and technology – and tempered by cross-cultural exchanges of design ideas among builders and craftsmen brought together on a particular project by the patron or ruler. With the progressive diffusion of cultures on a world-wide scale, it is no longer possible to build within what might be called a purely regional mode. 'On the one hand there is something specific to and inseparable from a given cultural and geographical situation (which we call regionalism), whilst on the other hand there are developments that are global and for all areas of mankind. These polar forces exist within a dialectic within which architects today have to operate.'[8] And these forces are also apparent in buildings not designed by architects, as the images of tradition and modernity filter into the consciousness of local populations as a result of exposure through television and other mass media. It now appears impossible for designs for new buildings not to be influenced by international trends or for them to rely strictly on regional traditions.

Architecturally, mosques reflect several main influences that alter their regional characteristics. The *vernacular*, in which buildings are defined by a traditional indigenous architectural languages, and *historicist* models that refer back to styles generally regarding as 'classical' in Islam (i.e. the period from the ninth to the sixteenth centuries) are still being used. Both act as reminders of a glorious past and reinforce the ideas of continuity and traditional values in Islam. For instance in the 1960s and 1970s a direct association between Islam and socialism was common in countries like Algeria, Pakistan and Indonesia, and the governments of the day felt that designs which could be identified with an Islamic past would help to endow their buildings with a sense of legitimacy in the minds of the predominantly Muslim population. Using architecture to lend credence to a particular viewpoint is of course common in most fields of endeavour, be it the politics of fascism or the image of stability that a bank seeks to convey through the solid appearance of its buildings. A third trend is the reinterpretation of different models into some kind of *cross-cultural* manifestation. The borrowing of styles, methods of construction and decoration combined with a local model or one adopted from elsewhere is a growing trend. This presents a self-conscious search for the reinterpretation of difficult models, leading in most cases to eclecticism and in some to an interesting synthesis. The fourth category is that of being *modern*, the overriding concerns being originality and dealing with the twentieth century. Design, image and technology point to a break with the past so as to portray the modern Muslim in a progressive light. This is the domain of the formally trained architect (in the Western sense) and the educated client, whereas in the first three categories there is a wide range of actors. Whilst the difficulties of this kind of classification are apparent, it still serves a useful function as an analytical tool which helps in discerning the directions in which mosque design is moving. However, the broad categories need to be understood within their own regional, physical and social contexts.

It would seem logical that in the 'peripheral' Muslim countries of West Africa and South-East Asia the expressions of regional characteristics would be most evident. The absorption of Islam into these societies, physically so far removed from the heartland, in past centuries seemed to make greater allowances for local architectural expressions to persist rather than the more usual pattern of the mingling and transformation of styles that is evident in Central Asia and India. The following summary, region by region, presents some significant mosques of recent decades.

A survey of recent mosques

In the westernmost region of Islam, West Africa, vernacularism is clearly demonstrated in mosque buildings. The traditional use of earth retains its character and style and the traditions of such Great Mosques as Djenne in Mali (see chapter 10) still continue with some innovations. This regional expression is apparent in the mosques of Yaama (first built in 1962, with later additions until 1982), Niger, and Niono (1973), Mali. Both buildings are highly visible in their settings and are constructed using mud-brick techniques derived from Hausa arch and dome construction. The Niono Mosque, by the master-mason Lassine Minta, has a simple rectangular prayer-hall of the hypostyle type surrounded by secondary freestanding buildings. Its façades are in the style of the Djenne Mosque without being exact copies. 'The typical projecting bundles of palmwood sticks – as decorative as they are useful for maintenance purposes – cast slowly evolving shadows on the walls, as if they were so many sun-dials. The pilasters are treated in a way that appears singular to Minta's work. They are joined, on the level of the base of the parapet, by arches in the same shallow relief, expressing on the outside the arches of the interior. The main entrance on the west façade, facing the *mihrab*, is dominated by a fourth tower that would seem to be an element all Minta's own. One wonders if it is inspired by the church buildings that Minta must have seen while he was working for the colonial administration.'[9] The adaptation of traditional structures is visible in several such mosques, especially in the internal spaces, where the supporting columns are more slender and a generally more spacious and lighter appearance is achieved. The approach is additive where elements are not replaced but altered to provide clearly apparent improvements.

Unusual and noteworthy, because they illustrate cross-cultural interpretations of history, are the distinctive mosques of southern Nigeria and Benin, which at first glance are often mistaken for churches because they feature a front elevation composed of a central pediment flanked by two towers. These European baroque manifestations follow a Portuguese design from Bahia in Brazil. The Bahian churches, which started as austere structures in the late seventeenth century, became more elaborate, visually transformed by ornamentation added by the Muslim African slaves who provided not only the manual labour for their construction, but also worked as painters, masons and carpenters. These artisans, who were deported to Africa by the mid-nineteenth century, began to build mosques, financed by their fellow repatriates, in the Afro-Brazilian genre that is still evolving in the region.[10] This lesson in aesthetic acculturation has given the Afro-Brazilian style a vitality that enables it to continue to develop and evolve as a contemporary form of architecture.

In North Africa the continuation of traditional 'classical' styles is evident in one of the largest contemporary mosques, inaugurated in 1993 in Casablanca under the aegis of King Hassan II of Morocco. Designed by the French architect Pinseau, this mosque imitates the great architecture of the eleventh century. Importance is given to this look as being 'authentically and indigenously Islamic' in terms of form and perhaps more importantly in decoration, design and colour.[11]

Mosque façade (probably late nineteenth or early twentieth century) in Abomey, Benin, showing strong Bahian influence.

The Mosque in Yaama (1962–82), Niger, a striking example of mud-brick construction.

Al-Qiblatain Mosque (1989), Medina, one of a number of recent mosques in Saudi Arabia designed by Abdel Wahid El-Wakil.

In Algeria, however, mosques reflect a mix of traditional vernacular and modern styles. Questions of historic continuity seem to be less important here, and whilst attempts were made to express a socialist ideal using a modern language readily understood by ordinary people, only a few significant buildings resulted. The work of the Miniawi brothers who planned some of the so-called 'socialist villages' within which the mosque was centrally located, is worthy of note, however. Hanny and Abdel-Rahman Miniawi, Egyptian architects who have lived in Algeria since 1969, were influenced by the work of their compatriot Hassan Fathy: in the village of Mahder (part of the 'thousand villages programme') experiments were made with local materials for construction, namely earth stabilized with cement. In other villages greater reliance was placed on the post-and-beam aesthetic associated with concrete construction. Although socially totally different from Fathy's experiment in the 1960s in New Gourna, near Luxor, the language developed by the Miniawi brothers in Algeria referred strikingly to that of vaults and load-bearing walls that speak of some kind of North African semi-desert vernacular.

This style and use of the vernacular is perhaps the most important evoked by many countries and architects trying to reflect an indigenous Islamic architecture. Hassan Fathy's approach and philosophy of design within this manner has greatly influenced the new generation of architects practising since the 1970s. His buildings were seen as offering a serious alternative to internationalism in the vein of E.F. Schumacher's philosophy of 'small is beautiful'. In his scheme for the rural community of New Gourna, Fathy incorporated a mud-brick mosque which constituted an amalgam of several Egyptian styles and technologies; with it Fathy invented a composite 'instant vernacular' which was then adopted by designers in North Africa and in other areas where earth was a commonly used building material. This architecture quickly became associated with hot dry climates.[12]

In addition to the Miniawi brothers, Hassan Fathy's many apprentices and followers include the Egyptian architects Abdel Wahid El-Wakil and Omar El-Farouk, the Moroccan Elie Mouyal and the Jordanian Rasem Badran. This is not to suggest that most new mosques in Northern Africa necessarily reflect Fathy's visions. His ideas are counterbalanced by the use of new technologies and forms, as for example in the Nilein Mosque outside Khartoum in the Sudan. This concrete structure, with its hemispherical ribbed dome, reflects the technological vision of Islam as being modern. However, the most successful mosque buildings in North Africa do seem to hark back to older vernacular traditions, while East African mosques continue to reflect their primarily Indian antecedents.

In the traditional 'heartland' of Islamic culture, the so-regarded Arab world of the Middle and Near East, comparatively recent wealth resulting from the exploitation of oil has financed much new building, including mosques. Interestingly, whereas Cairo – always a major centre of learning in Islam – has exported designers and technical know-how to much of the Arab world in recent decades, Egyptian architects have designed significant new mosques not in their own country but in other Arab states. For example, El-Wakil has designed a number of mosques, both large and small, in Saudi Arabia, a country whose example is important for the rest of the Muslim world because of

Facing page

The imposing Al-Ghadir Mosque (1977–87) in Tehran, Iran, designed by Jahangir Mazlum; the angular monochrome exterior is enlivened by patterned brickwork and contrasting inscriptions in blue-glazed tiles. The prayer-hall is twelve-sided (reflecting the twelve Imams of Shia belief), with the recessed mihrab *forming an external projection clearly visible from the street (below). The 'dome' of the prayer-hall (above) is designed as an ascending series of regular geometric forms, reducing from dodecahedron to octagon, hexagon and finally two squares.*

Influenced by the work of Hassan Fathy, the Egyptian architect Abdel Wahid El-Wakil designed a number of small mosques, including the Island Mosque (top left) built in 1986, each standing in isolation at intervals along the corniche around Jeddah, Saudi Arabia.

The eclectic Bhong Mosque (top right), in the Punjab province of Pakistan, was financed and built (1930–82) by Ghazi Mohammad Rais; it represents a populist vernacular of the Indian subcontinent, using profuse decoration and a liberal juxtaposition of different materials and building styles.

The Qasr al-Hokm or Palace of Justice Mosque (1989) in Riyadh, Saudi Arabia, by the Jordanian architect Rasem Badran, successfully combines indigenous Nadji traditions with modern construction techniques to create a synthesis of the old and the new (centre, left and right).

The mosque at New Gourna (1948), near Luxor in Egypt (left), was designed by Hassan Fathy as an expression of traditional vernacular architectures; this building was to become one of the most influential models for North African and Middle Eastern architects.

The Sher-e-Bangla Nagar Capital Complex (1962–83), Dhaka, Bangladesh, by the American architect Louis Kahn, is an uncompromisingly modern architectural statement. The prayer-hall of the mosque (opposite above), situated above the entrance to the complex, conforms with the general style of the building, but can be distinguished by its orientation towards Mecca.

The Sherefuddin (White) Mosque in Visoko, Bosnia, designed by Zlatko Ugljen and completed in 1980, has a strongly sculptured exterior with an unusual minaret (far right), while its interior (right) with the mihrab *niche and* minbar *is kept simple; the only trace of Ottoman influence can be seen in the decorative calligraphic medallions and the* minbar *finial.*

The Mosque of the Islamic Centre for Technical and Vocational Training and Research (1986), some 30 km (18 miles) north of Dhaka, Bangladesh (bottom, centre) was designed by the Turkish firm Studio 14 (Dorük Pamir and Ercüment Gümrük) using pure geometric forms in brick.

The competition for the Shah Faisal Masjid and Islamic University in Islamabad, Pakistan, was won by the Turkish architect Vedat Dalakoy; he designed this State Mosque (1970–86) as a tented concrete complex echoing its hillside setting, while the tall pencil minarets (bottom right) betray clear Ottoman influence.

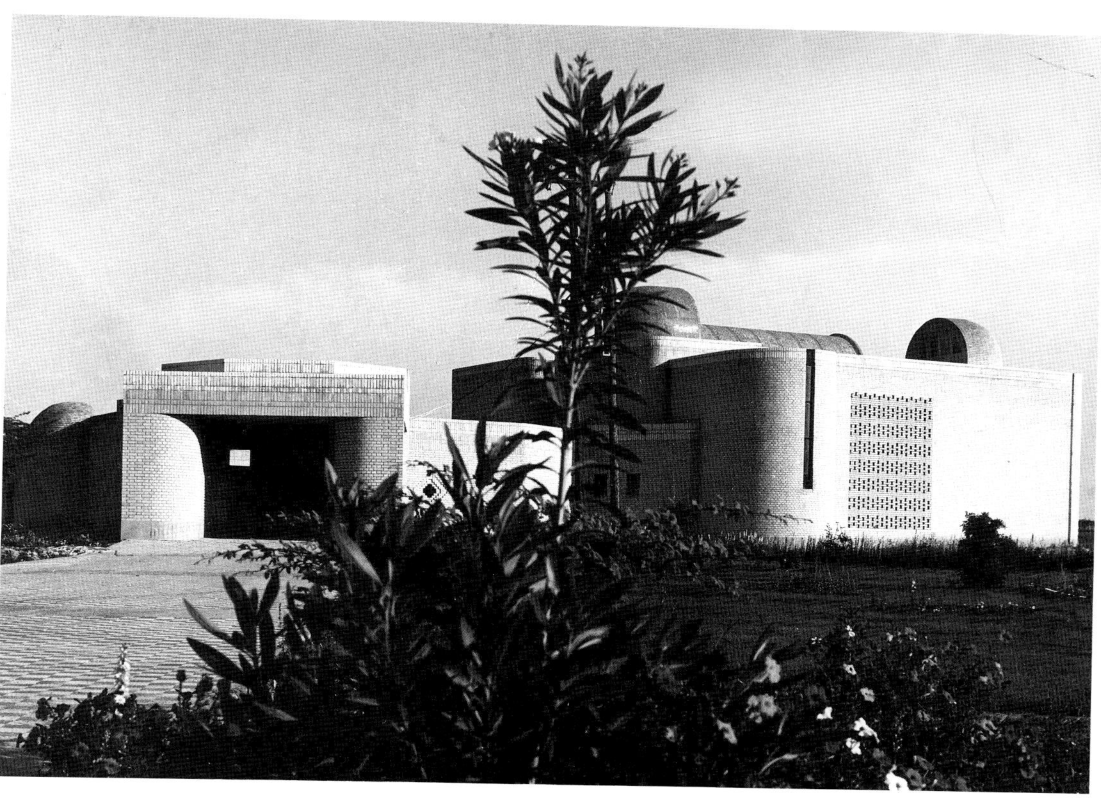

The courtyard of the Jondishapur University Mosque (1974), a building which makes an elegant statement in brick without recourse to traditional architectural forms.

its role as guardian of the Ka'ba and its image as a state that seeks to exploit the best of everything modern. Significantly, Saudi Arabia has funded the building of more mosques outside its own borders than has any other country.

In Saudi Arabia itself three trends are discernible: new mosques may reflect local Najdi architecture, or they may be based on an Arab-Egyptian Mamluk model, or they may be uncompromisingly modern. The style of the Najd region, featuring solid earthen walls, restricted openings and crenellated parapets, has been adopted in concrete in developments such as the Diplomatic Quarter of Riyadh (1986), within which the Friday Mosque (to accommodate 7,000 worshippers) was designed by Ali Shuai of the Beeah Group. Rasem Badran's project of 1989 for Qasr al-Hokm (Palace of Justice) Mosque in Riyadh combines the same vocabulary with other design motifs from desert architecture. Both examples point to the establishment of a 'new' regional style acceptable to clients in Saudi Arabia. At the historicist end of the spectrum are a number of mosques by El-Wakil, such as the elegant Corniche Mosque commissioned by the municipality of Jeddah and the larger Harithy Mosque designed for a private client (both 1986) and the dramatic Qiblatain Mosque (1989), Medina.

Facing page
The central dome of the Islamic Centre Mosque (1977) in Rome. Although inspired by the Great Mosques in Cordoba and Tlemcen, this modern design for the Italian capital (by the team of Paolo Portoghesi, Sami Moussawi and Vittorio Gigliotti) succeeds in combining the modular and circular systems inherent in these historical models. The design of the prayer-hall and the bold use of materials in the complex make a significant contribution to the architecture of Islam.

Among the most interesting modern examples is the King Khaled International Airport Mosque (1983) in Riyadh, designed by the US firm Hellmuth, Obata & Kassabaum, because of its location within a new type of building complex unknown to traditional Muslim societies. The rich interior of this mosque tries, however, to be more traditional in its use of tiles, carpets, woodwork and other crafts.

Major gestures have also been made by other central Arab lands such as Iraq and Kuwait in the form of State Mosques. The Kuwait Grand Mosque (1976–84), designed by the Iraqi architect Mohammed Makiya, is an example of historic mannerism of a high quality. Perhaps the most ambitious project of this kind was for a State Mosque in Baghdad, already noted.

In the Central Asian region, which includes Uzbekistan and the Xinjiang province of China, there are as yet no recent examples of international merit, and the first new mosques have been built only since 1990 in the former Soviet Republics. In Iran, however, new buildings still express a strong regional character while presenting a synthesis with the modern. Some good examples are seen in the work of the talented Iranian architect Kamran Diba, who has designed a number of mosques as part of campus and housing projects. His use of local materials, mainly plain brick, has produced simple and sophisticated contemporary architectural statements. The Jondishapur University Mosque (1974) is located on the principal walkway connecting the various university buildings, and acts as both a marker and a spatial connector. The brick building is determinedly modern in eschewing obvious elements such as domes; instead other devices were used to identify the building as a mosque, including rounded corners and, standing on the *mihrab* axis, a tower (reminiscent of traditional wind-towers) faced with tilework, serving as a source of diffused light.

The compact namez-khaneh *(1978) in the grounds of the Carpet Museum, Tehran, showing the internal change of axis.*

A tiny but significant place of prayer, or *namez-khaneh* (1978) – designed by Diba in collaboration with Parvin Pezeshki – is in the garden of the Carpet Museum in Tehran. Its plan consists of two squares, the outer one aligned with a visual axis through the museum grounds and the inner one rotated to achieve the necessary *qibla* axis for the prayer area. The enclosure is open to the sky and vertical slots serve to indicate the *mihrab* and direct the eye towards a standard erected on the lawn outside, further emphasizing the orientation, especially when one is inside the prayer area.

A more recent example is the Al-Ghadir Mosque (1987) – also in Tehran – designed by Jahangir Mazlum, who has managed to provide a good solution to the problem of reconciling street layout and an awkward entrance location with that of the *qibla* axis. The covered spaces lead to a twelve-sided prayer-hall roofed by a series of rotating and diminishing squares that evoke a dome. Here brick is used (in the manner of the marvellous ninth-century Samanid mausoleum in Bukhara) to produce a patterned surface of square Kufic script on both the exterior and the interior.

As has been noted above, the Ottoman Turkish mosque type has had a major impact on contemporary design the world over. However, in Turkey itself there are few examples of innovative design. One such building is the Parliament Mosque (1989) in the capital, Ankara, designed by Altug, Behruz & Can Cinçi, which is interesting as a statement of Islam in a secular republic; attached to the older government building, it was conceived to avoid all overt signs identifying it as a mosque. Conversely, in the Islamic Republic of Pakistan, which identified itself with the progressive modernism of Turkey in the 1960s, the effect of Ottoman expression can be seen in the Shah Faisal Mosque in Islamabad. The building, designed by the Turkish architect Vedat Dalakoy in 1978, was completed in 1986. It features four distinctive Ottoman-style minarets 90 m (300 ft) high, while the prayer-hall, accommodating 7,500 worshippers, is an open-plan tent-like concrete structure – the concept of a soaring central interior space was a common feature of Ottoman mosques. The covered prayer area can be extended when required by the temporary use of tents (for which permanent moorings are provided) in the adjacent open spaces, thus increasing the capacity to over 300,000 worshippers. The complex also includes an Islamic University.

Many recently built mosques in the Indian subcontinent either follow the Indian tradition, as in the case of the eclectic Bhong Mosque already noted, or attempt to be modern. There are proportionately far fewer historicist recent mosques here than in most other Muslim societies. In Bangladesh, just outside the capital Dhaka, is the mosque of the Islamic Technical Centre which serves as the focal point of the small campus. Designed in 1983 by the Turkish architect Dorük Pamir of Studio 14 and completed in 1986, it is built prinicipally of brick and recalls the ideas explored in Louis Kahn's Capitol Complex housing in Sher-e-Bangla Nagar, Dhaka.

Plan of the Al-Ghadir Mosque (1987), Tehran, showing the series of rotating and reducing squares employed to produce a dome-like effect in the prayer-hall *(see interior view, p. 257)*.

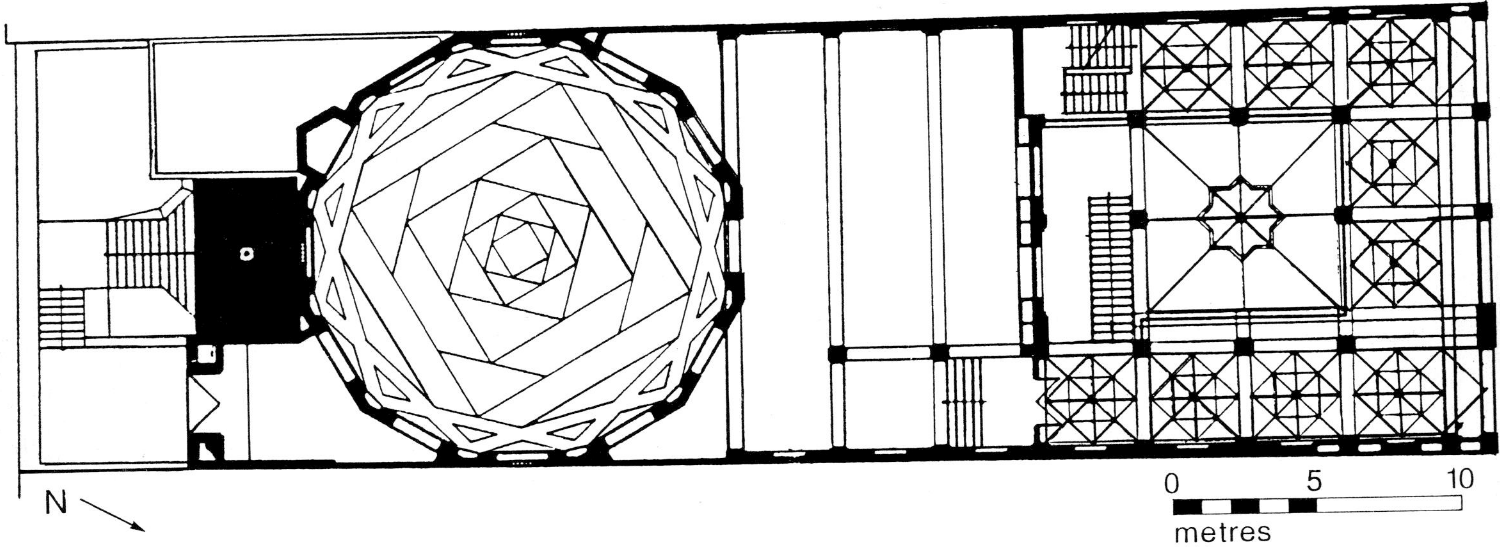

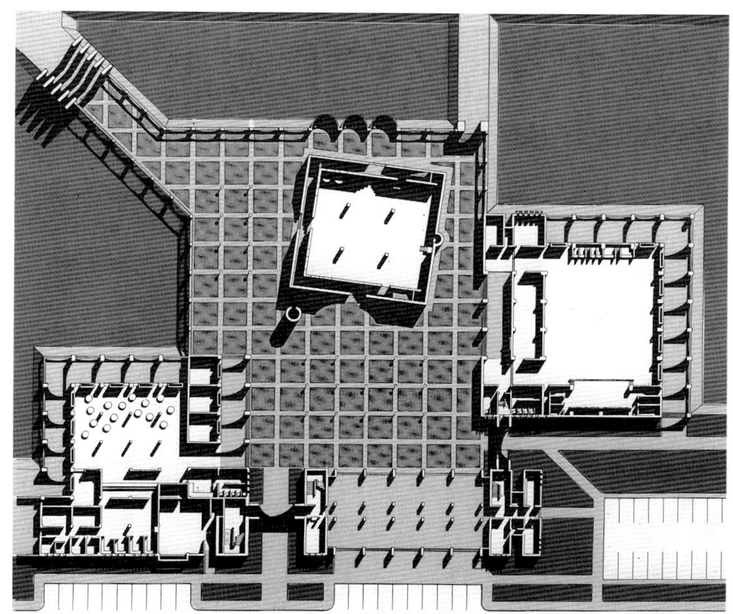

In South-East Asia, the easternmost region of the Islamic world, a number of competing images have become evident since *c.* 1970. Three trends are present: the Javanese vernacular; the Indo-Arabic cross-cultural mix; and the modern. The indigenous architecture of Indonesia and Malaysia in general has characteristics that are prevalent in all structures, ranging from individual dwellings to public buildings. Perhaps the clearest characteristic features of the mosque

(Above left) Plan of the Mosque of the Islamic Technical Centre (1986), near Dhaka, showing the modular grid within which the mosque itself is angled to face Mecca.

(Above right) The Shah (King) Faisal Mosque (1986), Islamabad: general view showing pencil-like minarets in the Ottoman style.

(Below) The Parliament Mosque, Ankara (1989): this structure in concrete and glass makes no reference to any historical model and was designed not to be readily identified as a religious building.

The Said Naum Mosque (1977), Jakarta, an example of the adaptation of forms made possible by the exploitation of new materials in place of traditional timber construction.

(Right) The prayer-hall of the Darul Aman Mosque (1986), Singapore, in which the roof form harks back to indigenous pre-Islamic structures.

(Below) The Masjid Negara (National Mosque; 1985), Kuala Lumpur; this was the first example of a State Mosque built in a Muslim country which had recently gained independence in the post-colonial era.

included the pitched (*meru*) roof combined with the four-column (*saka guru*) structure in the centre of the main interior space. This principle has been used in Said Naum Mosque (1977) in Jakarta, designed by Adhi Moersid of Atelier Enam. Here the architect used new materials to reinterpret traditional forms, rotating the *meru*-type roof and omitting the four columns to provide an uninterrupted central space, thus altering long-established meanings and structural symbolism (see chapter 13). Another similar successful building is the University of Indonesia Mosque (1986) on the campus at Depok, near Jakarta, designed by Triatno Y. Hardjoko. In the same vein is one of a number of community mosques built by the Housing Development Board of Singapore, the Darul Aman Mosque (also 1986). It too recalls indigenous Malay buildings in its tripartite pre-Islamic roof form, hypostyle prayer-hall and rhombic patterns. Taking this one step further is the earlier Masjid Negara (National Mosque) of 1965 in Kuala Lumpur: here the architect Baharuddin reinterpreted the roof form using a folded concrete slab to make a modern technological statement. This synthesis of the vernacular with modernism was the first

of its kind in a major State Mosque. The architect went on to execute a number of other major mosque projects in the country using the same design principles.

Examples of contemporary mosques following Indian and Arab forms are of no architectural significance. However, an interesting example of the breakdown in the meaning of forms is illustrated in the use of prefabricated Indian-style tin domes in new mosques, regardless of methods of construction and stylistic relationship to the building. The adoption of an Indian-style dome, imported into a region which never had such a traditional building form, raises issues not only of appropriateness but of Indonesia's apparent need of validation from the heartland of Islam. (Interestingly, although Indonesia has the largest Muslim population of any country in the world, it does not represent itself as a Muslim State.) The 'instant dome' example is not a trivial one, for it reflects both an image of Islam and a segment of Indonesian society's image of itself. A more literal copy of an Indian mosque is the Sultan Omar Ali Saifuddin Mosque (1958) in Brunei Darussalam, with its golden domes, minarets and crenellations reminiscent of the British adoption in the eighteenth century of Mughal design. Its imposing scale and location, surrounded by water, and its detailing make it a significant, though not an innovative example.

Indonesia and other South-East Asian nations also have their share of mosques in the modern idiom. The Salman Mosque on the campus of the Institut Technologi Bandung in Central Java was designed by Achmad Noe'man in 1964 and completed in 1972. The building, influenced by the International Style of the 1950s, is successfully adapted to a wet tropical climate by being well ventilated and surrounded by deep verandas. The minaret, a separate structure, rises as a slab in a manner reminiscent of that of an obelisk.

Prefabricated Indian-style 'instant domes' offered for sale at the roadside in Indonesia.

As can be seen from the diverse examples cited from different regions, the regional models prevalent in the past can no longer be comfortably grouped according to geographic area, climate or

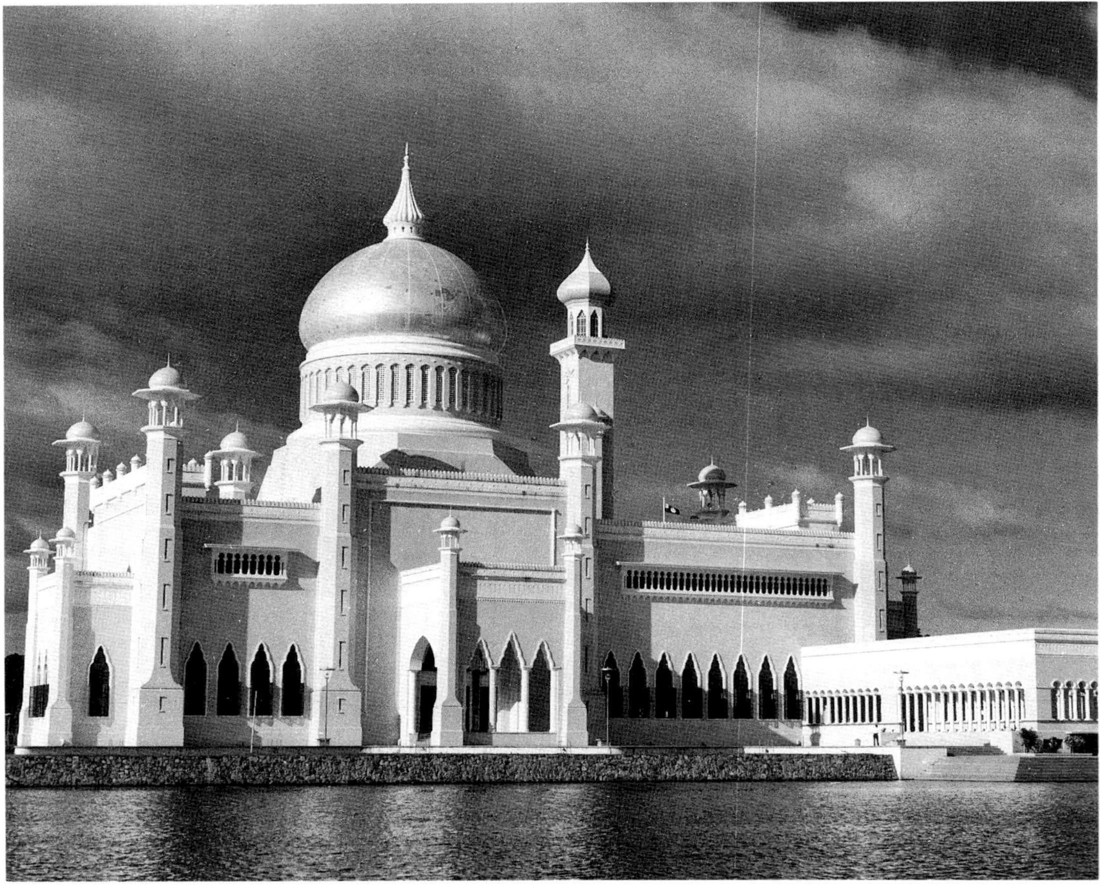

The Sultan Omar Ali Saifuddin Mosque, Bandar Seri Begawan, Negara Brunei Darussalam; completed in 1958, this large building, surrounded by water and featuring a gilded dome reaching a height of over 50 m (166 ft), makes clear reference to late-Mughal architectural elements.

materials. Mosques of the modern era are demonstrably the result of overlays and images transmitted worldwide through the mass media and cultural exchanges.

Towards a contemporary mosque architecture

The way in which Muslims relate to each other and to society in general raises issues concerning the kind of image they might wish to project. Considering relations between people and how a sense of community is articulated has a parallel in the relationship of neighbouring buildings one to another. The questions raised concern the way Muslims view their role *within* the society in which they live. The aspirations of different groups may be expressed in various ways. For instance the idea of a Arab-Islamic homeland often equated 'Muslim' with 'Arab', especially outside the Islamic nation-states. In recent times this has been extended well beyond the question of identity to that of politics – the Arab-American dichotomy being one such manifestation. This alternative system of values was equally dramatically illustrated in Iran in the 1970s and 1980s. In the 1990s Muslims in South-East Asia also seem to be confronting these issues – in what has sometimes been referred to as 'the Chinese problem' – although not in such dramatic ways. In the USA itself the minority Afro-American Muslims are struggling with the same problem.

In the architecture of mosques, confrontation within communities begins to take on the physical forms of the home base or of the predominant cultural group by expressing ethnic identity through building style. Immigrant communities seem to follow the same process. However, the situation becomes less clear when a number of different social, ethnic or national groups try to establish a collective identity through a single building complex. The often eclectic solutions are only occasionally innovative.

It is worth noting that mosque design today has to be considered in relation to such ideas as the mosque as *sacred* space, since the notion of a fixed sacred space is not inherent to Islam. The individual can pray anywhere, as can a group, and the chosen place of prayer is sacred for the duration. What is prescribed is the ritual: the need for a clean surface and the acknowledgment of a physical direction. As collective prayer was established in the time of the Prophet, performed in the courtyard of his house, the space used for this ritual became more formalized. In some *tariqas*, or ways of Islamic belief, such as Sufism and other traditions that leaned towards mysticism and meditation, the space appears to have also become defined in terms of atmosphere and use as the symbolic heart of a community. The practice of communal prayer demanded a recognizable space – a fixed location – where people could gather, and thus the space came to be perceived as sanctified. However, although progressive secularization resulted from the transfer of political functions to citadels, palaces or government houses, and of education to specially constituted buildings of *madrasas* and other schools, the memory of and the potential for these functions within the space of the mosque has remained constant to the present day. It is interesting to note that whereas in recent years mosques have tended to move towards the single function as places of prayer, churches have often acquired a multi-functional use as social centres in an attempt to attract younger people back to places of worship.

It may be extrapolated that due to the traditional integration of the sacred and the secular in Islam the place of prayer never stood alone, but was complemented by the other spaces catering for general social needs. The mosque complex thus provided spaces and functions such as hospitals, *madrasas* and even the bazaar adjacent to it. The role of the mosque as a political statement was limited to special cases until the era of the modern Islamic State, in which it has become a statement of Muslim identity isolated as a distinct building type – an identity that carries over to its presence in other cultures today. In building terms one can discern two major trends. Within a country that has a predominantly Muslim population stylistic references are very often to Ottoman sources. This may be tempered by considerations of nationalism and modern technology (taking their cue from the modern state of Turkey that came into being with Kemal Atatürk), but in general the images of recurring historical and regional stylistic references are overwhelmingly Ottoman and Mamluk, and to a lesser extent Iranian, Indian Mughal and Moroccan.

Another development which has been expressed in a shift from particularism in the built environment towards universalism is the appearance of a *Pan-Islamic style*. As a result of pressures to become more 'normative' and international, as well as of a conscious desire on the part of Muslim communities to be seen as Muslim, the use of clearly identifiable, universally 'Islamic' elements such as the minaret and dome is becoming ever more frequent in modern-day mosque architecture. The Pan-Islamic style, with its kit of standard parts, has had a significant impact throughout the Islamic world, and especially in regions such as South-East Asia where, as noted above, it is gradually supplanting traditional architectural styles in both urban and rural contexts.

Lastly, the mosque has always been the building type in which both patrons and architects have made the strongest design and technological statements – a trend which today has become even more pronounced. Mosque design takes on a *persona* reflecting the aspirations of the dominant group, which can in practice be quite small. Analysis of the case studies of a wide range of recent buildings reveals clearly just how few decision-makers and their designers have influenced so much. For example, the committees that decided on most of the State Mosques, or the juries that judged design competitions, have typically consisted of five to fifteen members. The mosques that resulted subsequently became models which were often copied (with variations) many times over. In other instances, the works of leading architects such as Hassan Fathy continue to be emulated as a result of the dissemination of images by the mass media. The diffusion of the architects' ideas and the far-reaching impact of those ideas, even in the context of remote rural situations, are significant factors.

In the modern world the mosque, more than any other building type of Islam, signals and reflects the values both of client groups and of society, and thus becomes a manifestation of changes occurring in Muslim society.

- 16 -
THE METAMORPHOSIS OF THE SACRED

MOHAMMED ARKOUN

THE title chosen for this concluding chapter is intended to introduce the idea of the changing uses and meanings of the mosque in contemporary Muslim societies. Although, when in the mosque, the believer might expect to be in direct contact with that which he regards as sacred, in practice he increasingly finds himself confronted with manifestations of altered uses of the house of worship – changes of a non-religious nature which he may find difficult to understand and to relate to. The analysis presented here is an attempt to create a better understanding of present-day Muslim societies and their relationship to the mosque. My contention is that the entire history of the mosque has to be reconsidered and reinterpreted, with particular reference to forms and designs, as well as to semiological systems (i.e. the signs and symbols used by members of any social group to convey shared values) which determine the perception of abstract concepts such as the 'sacred' and the way in which they are employed. I would also stress the idea that the very nature of what is considered sacred in any society is itself subject to change.

Just like the synagogue, the temple or the church, the mosque as a place of worship is a building enclosing a space that is regarded by believers as sacred and distinct from its secular surroundings, and that by virtue of its sanctified status it can enhance the meaning of the words and actions of the believer while he is present there. If any change is made to the traditional concept of the mosque and its sacred character, the main function of the building is distorted. It is for this reason that the design, the forms and the special features of the building, including the dome, the minaret, the *mihrab* and the *minbar*, are usually reproduced in accordance with the familiar architectural imagery which has been instilled into the minds of individuals as the result of constant repetition down the centuries.

Like monuments associated with any religion, mosques have traditionally provided a central focus for communities living in towns and villages, and such buildings have represented for believers the permanence of values guaranteed by a divine presence in their place of worship. The psychological aspect of the place of worship – involving memory, perceived ideas and emotions, both collective and individual – is often not taken fully into account by historians, even though it is a rich, complex and significant ingredient of history. In the case of the mosque, aside from the traditional and well established attitudes of believers towards what they regard as sacred, there is the modern approach to the meaning of the 'sacred' based on reason, revealing aspects and changes which remain beyond the understanding of those whose faith is founded only on unquestioning belief. The choice, then, in making a study of the place of the mosque in contemporary Muslim society is between merely accepting the tradition-bound viewpoint of believers – one which simply repeats what they regard as being 'sacred' – or attempting to analyze perceptions and beliefs by placing them in their historical, sociological, anthropological and psychological perspectives.

Within any particular socio-cultural group the concept of the sacred varies in its definitions, its limits and its role, depending on that group's response to changing historical circumstances. Thus people are 'social actors', that is to say they play different roles at the same time: for example, when the faithful go to the mosque to worship, they will be sharing the building equally with other members of society whose presence there may be motivated by political or social considerations, and on a personal level worshippers will interact with them in different ways, playing out different roles. In trying to make a study of the mosque as a sacred space in modern society, we should consider the following interrelated aspects:

(1) a historical appraisal;
(2) an anthropological approach;
(3) a semiological analysis; and
(4) an assessment of how authority gains legitimacy.

All of these, discussed in more detail below, will help to explain the metamorphosis of the sacred and its expression, providing as they do a framework for a reassessment of the whole issue of religion as a phenomenon and of its altered role and loss of meaning – a process of 'semiological deterioration' – in societies which are becoming increasingly secularized and socially fragmented.

In the context of the mosque and contemporary Muslim societies the task is made particularly difficult because current scholarship in Islamic studies tends to be more concerned with the analysis and interpretation of textual sources than with the meanings and values associated with the mosque. A critical evaluation of the latter is urgently needed because every so-called Islamic society is facing a general crisis in the interpretation of meanings inherited from Islamic tradition and past history. As a consequence, the functions and uses of mosques today for purposes other than worship reveal evidence of a breakdown in the traditionally accepted relationship between the individual believer and his place of worship.

A historical appraisal

In any attempt to define and understand the role of the mosque it is necessary to take note of the situation that prevailed in Medina in the lifetime of the Prophet Muhammad.[1] As was true of every new religion, the question of the 'sacred' and its cognitive and ritual status was a relevant issue in the earliest years of Islam; the act of building a mosque for the emerging Muslim group in Medina was seen as both a political and a religious gesture. The Qur'an makes an explicit reference to a rival group which built its own place of worship to compete with the 'true' mosque founded by the Prophet.[2] In its emergent phase any religious movement needs to establish its own places, buildings, rituals, norms and styles of dress to provide the new group with a distinctive identity, clearly differentiated from all others around it, and especially from those living in the same place and using the same symbols, textual sources and concepts – as was true of the Jews and Christians already established in Medina before AD 622. Examples of changes introduced in the earliest years of Islam include the shifting of the direction of the *qibla* from Jerusalem to Mecca and the choice of Friday as the 'day of the Lord', Sunday and Saturday having already been adopted by the Christians and Jews respectively.

Achieving the aim of winning popular acceptance of a particular concept of the sacred which acquires religious authority and political power depends more on popular perception and appeal than on its substance or its essential ideas. In other words, the early mosque form – a hypostyle hall with adjacent courtyard – acquired a 'sacred' quality not because it was built or designed in a certain style, but because in the course of time it became sanctified by virtue of the functions it fulfilled for believers. The concept of the sacred was a product of common perceptions among Muslims and of the solidarity shared by members of the group.

The traditional – theological or metaphysical – definition of the sacred as something emanating from or dedicated to God takes into account the role of those members of society who seek to establish their own permanent religious framework incorporating values which would serve as the foundations for the political and legal order. For Muslims the concept of the sacred is linked directly to the word of God, the revelation of His commands and teachings, as well as to the *hadith* of the Prophet and the interpretation of their meanings. Such a concept does not of course preclude aesthetic and architectural creativity in the design of a building, for such creativity is in the domain of the architect and thus remains quite separate from the idea of the metamorphosis of the sacred.

In historical terms mosque architecture offers a great variety of styles, resulting from the influence of such factors as cultural and geographical environment, the aims of the patron and the skills of the architect and craftsmen engaged in the building process. Each mosque thus provides a reflection of the particular cognitive system which gave rise to the individual perceptions and attitudes of those involved in its construction, resulting in a diversity of readings and meanings.

An anthropological approach

By contrast with the many and varied historical periods and styles, there are in the history of human psychology essentially only two stages of development to be considered, that of mythical knowledge with its integrated signs and meanings, and that of demythologized knowledge (i.e. knowledge based on rational thought), but with the proviso that the two are not clearly demarcated in a chronological sense and can coexist in individual societies over a period of time.

What I have termed 'mythical knowledge' is concerned with the construction of 'truth' founded on imagination rather than on critical reason and logical categorization. Myth is a kind of narrative (*qasas*, a term often occurring in the Qur'an) engendered by the marvellous, the fantastic and the supernatural, and the 'truth' which it expresses appeals directly to the emotions and the imagination. Thus, when the Qur'an states that Abraham – a prophetic figure from the distant past – visited the Ka'ba in Mecca, nobody bothers to ask why, when or how. The original purpose of such an account was to create in the minds of the early followers of Muhammad the idea of a symbolic religious figure whose direct connection with the Ka'ba would reinforce its sacred quality for Muslims, replacing its earlier pagan associations with a new 'true' religious meaning. A parallel instance of such a metamorphosis of the sacred in early times can be seen in the adoption by Muslims of pre-Islamic temples, which were converted to serve as the House of Allah. This semiological change – an alteration in the meaning of an existing physical symbol – resulted from the ritual needs and the social and political beliefs of those first Muslims. Many similar examples are recorded in the Bible, both in the Old Testament and in the Gospels.

The process of demythologization of knowledge began in Europe as early as the sixteenth century, but it was not until the great period of industrialization in the nineteenth and twentieth centuries that there was a simultaneous process which produced a cognitive system dominated by philosophers rather than theologians, by mathematics and the physical sciences instead of religious belief, and by applications of technology replacing familiar craft skills. The nineteenth century also saw the beginnings of a breakdown in the traditional values of Muslim societies, a process that was encouraged by external factors (European capitalism and colonization) and not compensated for by the substitution of alternative systems generated from *within* those societies; the effect was therefore destructive, for while in Europe secular ideas were gaining the ascendant and supplanting the traditional concept of the sacred, in the Islamic world its theological basis was simply undermined and not subsequently replaced with any constructive and meaningful alternative.

Building a mosque, cultivating the land, weaving a carpet, teaching law or theology, or practising medicine can all be regarded as praiseworthy and beneficial activities falling within the overall scope of the vision of human society set forth in the word of God and subsequently developed by man in semiological contexts in the sphere of mythical knowledge. The aesthetic of a mosque designed and built within this sphere cannot be attributed solely to patronage and the talent of the architect; other factors to be considered in the evaluation of a building include the questions as to whether the inspirational roles of religious faith and the sacred are strengthened or diminished by the building itself.

In the context of past societies based on mythical knowledge it would have been unthinkable to build mosques at some distance from

The Grand Mosque (1976–84), Kuwait City.

centres of population, for the place of worship has traditionally always been closely integrated with the daily life of each Muslim community. By contrast, some recent mosques – such as those sited at intervals along the Corniche around Jeddah – have been built as independent units. I am not making a value judgment in respect of the architecture of any of these contemporary mosques which are unrelated to local communities, but simply drawing attention to a radical change in semiological context. To be fair, the example cited may be seen as the result of a previously unimaginable phenomenon, namely the rapid mobility afforded to individuals by the widespread use of motor vehicles in many modern societies.

A political role for the mosque has always existed, but because political considerations were absorbed by the mythical perception of commonly shared knowledge, the concept of the 'sacred' could still imbue all other activities and events occurring in the mosque with its presence and efficacy. A good historical example is the Friday oration (*khutba*), in which it was standard practice to praise the name of the caliph or sultan as ruler; the purpose of this, if viewed in strictly rational and secular terms, would be regarded as merely political, but in the mythical system of the time the ruler was equally a sanctified figure by virtue of his office, his role as protector of Islam being regarded as sacred. In a study of modern 'State Mosques' Mohammad Al-Asad has shown that even in the nineteenth century it was still possible to build mosques in accordance with the paradigms of mythical knowledge.[3] A major exception was the case of Muhammad Ali, Viceroy of Egypt, who as a purely political leader in the 1830s sought to demonstrate that his rule was powerful enough to allow him to build in Cairo a mosque as prestigious as any commissioned in earlier centuries by Ottoman sultans, whose authority was both political and religious.

We may now move on to consider the altered role of mosques throughout the Muslim world since each country gained its independence from colonial rule. From the eighteenth century onwards, traditional attitudes to mythical knowledge had started to break down under the influence of the West, though Muslim society in general remained unaffected by this process; initially, only small urban élites were educated in the modern way of thinking and of perceiving and interpreting human existence and social values. In the rural and tribal areas culture – in its ethnological meaning – resisted the new forces; indeed, in some ethno-cultural groups like the Berbers and the Kurds, who stuck to their own languages and customs, mythical knowledge continued to dominate their societies until the late 1940s and the 1950s.

The phenomenon of the single-party nation-state which emerged as a new political force after independence was to bring rapid and radical change to the socio-cultural situation, resulting in a loss of deeply rooted and coherent cultural codes and creating semantic confusion. This has meant that the signs and symbols of imported cultures and the views expressed by the social élite and the *ulama* often ceased to be understood by ordinary people, so leading to a deterioration of social relationships.[4] For example, the various styles evident in the design of mosques in any one place today frequently do not relate to the local cultural traditions. As far as the concept of the 'sacred' in the mosque is concerned, it is necessary to bear in mind the fact that Muslim societies did not move from a state of mythical knowledge, with its integrated symbols, to one of rationalized scientific knowledge (modernism),[5] but to a disorganized amalgam of so-called Islamic authenticity (supposedly based on the example set and recommended by the Prophet) and decontextualized fragments of modern developments in the economic and political spheres. I stress the disorganized nature of the resulting ideological amalgam, which was developed, indeed first imposed in the 1960s by the single-party nation-state – an ideology which has, since *c.* 1979, been criticized and rejected by Islamicist (to be differentiated from Islamic)[7] political movements that have come to be regarded, especially in the West, as 'fundamentalist'.

In this confused ideological situation neither classical Islamic thought and culture nor modernity in its positive and intellectual aspects are seriously developed to produce a new synthesis of ideas. Commissioning and building new mosques, and of course the purposes for which they are used, are subject at all levels and at every stage to *conflicting ideological considerations* imposed by the governments of single-party nation-states and by the new Islamist movements. In a few countries major mosques have been built in recent years which enhance the prestige of dynastic rulers (eg. the Grand Mosque in Kuwait City and, in Morocco, the King Hassan II Mosque in Casablanca); mosques in this category are in effect symbolic statements of power rather than evidence of piety, with a subsidiary role for worship. What has happened and what is happening in the increasing secularization of such sacred spaces is a kind of defilement of their true purpose, although most believers coming to the mosque to pray do not necessarily have cause to be aware, as any objective analyst must, of a political motivation in the building of a house of worship 'founded on piety' (Qur'an 9:109).

We also encounter the psychological phenomenon of popular perception in the ideology and culture of the young, who demographically constitute the majority among worshippers in most Muslim countries today. In the case of members of the younger generation raised in the poorer districts of over-populated cities, their 'culture' is no different from that of their contemporaries in run-down urban areas throughout the world. As far as I am aware, no scientific survey has been undertaken to record the attitudes of the young towards religion, the sacred, piety, God and spirtuality. My guess is that they have to a large extent lost interest in such matters, while at the same time the mosque is being used for many other types of activity carried on in the name of religion. The young are more concerned with seeking tangible results in respect of jobs, housing and social welfare, as well as with pressing for participation in political affairs, greater fairness in the distribution of wealth and a reduction in corruption. If such demands were to be satisfied, would existing mosques cease to have a role in society, and would there still be initiatives to build new mosques? The existence of this continuing doubt about possible future trends represents another aspect of the metamorphosis of the sacred in contemporary Muslim societies.

A semiological analysis

In the mosque there is a rich cultural code which is universally accepted as such by believers. The forms, structural elements and the various spaces and facilities are in this context less essential than the historical validation derived from the initial dedication of the first mosque to the one 'true' God, its sanctification by the presence of the Prophet and, in mosques built since his time, of the *ulama*, whose members have always been respected for their deep religious knowledge and spirituality. Famous teachers have made use of mosques, and it is generally accepted that religious knowledge and personal piety are inseparable. Similarly, those saintly figures known as 'friends of God' (*awliya*) are often buried near a mosque, thus extending the concept of a sacred beyond the building itself. Even the bazaar surrounding a mosque, or the modest shops in a village, can partake of the sacred aura associated with the place of worship. To those doing business its presence provides a constant reminder of correct behaviour; Allah, the Prophet, the friends of God, verses from the Qur'an, the *hadith* – all these play a part in the regulation of everyday social affairs. Such, in essence, is the semiological context which is preserved by the mosque, which has always been a place for cultural exchanges in traditional Muslim societies, and not merely a religious building where the faithful congregate for acts of worship; in other words, as an institution the mosque has a clear social *and* spiritual basis.

A major change has already taken place in Muslim societies – one that brings into question their Islamic nature – and it is because of this that I have referred to 'so-called' Muslim societies. The change has been so fundamental that the very meaning of the partnership or relationship between the individual and God, between worshipper and worshipped, has become a new topic for theological debate. This question first arose as a result of the rupture in the eighteenth century, when the traditional balance between theologians and rulers underwent a radical change, with each usurping the others' roles. Because of the perceived inseparability of the sacred and the secular in Islam, it was then still possible to 'justify' these changes to the people, but today the situation is unfortunately very different. In many Muslim countries we are witnessing a subjugation of religious freedom following the usurpation, by those who hold political power, of religious authority. In that situation, any direct relationship between the *ulama* and the people has come to be regarded by those in authority as politically charged and therefore as something to be suppressed. Political pressures thus lead to a loss of religious freedom.

Because the mosque is a sacred space it is regarded as belonging to all members of a Muslim society. The protection which it provides for all those within its walls has been exploited by some for various overtly political ends. There are those who treat the mosque as a physical refuge from perceived oppression; others may use it as a political rallying point or as a springboard for the ambitions of a particular ruler or group. If a mosque is used for such propaganda purposes or as an instrument in retaining power, do such practices necessarily detract from the spirituality of the building as a place of worship or demean the spiritual nature of the believer's personal relationship with God? When we consider the metamorphosis of the sacred, we need to ask whether current non-religious activities in the mosque affect the very nature of what Muslims generally regard as 'sacred'.

The signs and symbols used in the past in the course of normal religious debate served to stimulate individual believers to think and to seek deeper meanings, but in much current practice they have been replaced by the general dissemination of ideological slogans which leave no room for discussion. Teaching is no longer a function associated with the mosque, and the general education offered in state-run schools and universities, which provide 'modern', pragmatic, technical training, takes no account of metaphysical or theological issues; conversely, the *ulama* maintain their own faculties of theology and law in which scientific methodologies are simply discounted. After taking into account the various ways in which the traditional multiple roles of the mosque have been stripped away, can we continue to describe it as a 'sacred' place?

An assessment of how authority gains legitimacy

The criteria by which the role of the mosque is judged are equally valid in respect of the church, synagogue or temple. In Muslim societies today there exists a crisis of meaning because the long-established roots of religious authority have been superseded by a pluralistic outlook based on post-modern ideas which no longer recognize the concept of a single reality and demand a thorough re-evaluation of existing boundaries between specialized fields of knowledge.[7] Thus, in traditional Muslim societies governmental authority was formerly rendered legitimate only by having a religious basis. In modern times, however, although the role of places of worship as dynamic sources of spiritual energy and creativity has declined, Muslims – like members of some other faiths – still feel a strong affinity with their sacred spaces, which represent for them the last vestige of the characteristic features of their religion and its collective identity. Despite this, mosques have tended to become places of political refuge, while their multiple roles as place of worship and institutional foci for debating social and religious issues have declined. As a result, mosques are no longer seen as the ultimate and universal source of confirmation of the ethical, spiritual and intellectual validity of human endeavours of all kinds. Nowadays, that role is often accorded to politicians, economists and scientists in North America and Europe, who constitute the core generating what is generally accepted as the truth. In this situation the political and economic centre is represented by the world's major financial powers,[8] whose hegemony in the creation of truth by economic and scientific means constitutes a development which I believe to be more harmful to spirituality than the often criticized identification of religion with state, as found in many Muslim countries. Although the latter may be considered to represent a threat within the Muslim sphere, the effects of the former are felt throughout the entire world and will in the longer term be a factor in determining the fate of mankind as a whole. In other words, traditional centres of authority within Islam which were also concerned with social values and spiritual matters have been given a different role or effectively disqualified as the final arbiter in deciding intellectual, social or civic issues.

The paradox surrounding the question as to what in fact constitutes legitimate authority is exemplified in the so-called Islamic nation-states by the manner in which discrimination is practised, not only towards resident foreigners, but among sections of their own populations. While these nations subscribe to the principle of tolerance enshrined in many religions, Islam among them, whereby the rights of all people shall be respected and protected, regardless of their ethnic, religious or national background, few governments have done so in practice. For this reason, among others, it is not possible to plead retrospectively that traditional systems of government founded on religion have provided better models than do modern, secular states.

Those who designed and built the early temples, synagogues, churches and mosques were, in their respective cultures, part of an integrated social environment and, because the roles and meanings of their religious buildings were well understood, architects and master-builders could express such meanings in their designs. They thus made significant contributions to the civilizations of their time. I consider that there is an urgent need today for this relationship to be re-established so that the close tie between the sacred and the socio-political in Muslim societies can be made evident. The achievement of such a fresh understanding could help restore the lost sense of order to societies that are subject to rapid change, as well as allowing new places of worship to be designed and built, utilizing modernity in a new and appropriate architecture.

NOTES ON THE TEXT

Some bibliographical citations are given in abbreviated form; for full details see the listing in the Bibliography, pp. 279–82.

CHAPTER 1

1 The prevailing view of the origin of Zoroastrianism is that the sage Zarathustra (Zoroaster) chose Ahura-mazda from the existing pantheon, attributing to him the origin of all matter and elevating him to the status of supreme deity. Nevertheless, because the Mazdeans continued to worship a dualistic godhead – Ormuz, the 'good' force of light, and Ahriman, the 'evil' force of darkness – true monotheism was not yet born. Previously, a long line of anthropomorphic and theriomorphic deities is known to have existed in various parts of the ancient world. The nomadic Aryan invaders from Central Asia who first penetrated the Indus Valley *c.* 1500 BC left four great books (Vedas) as a record of their religion and culture. Their deities included Varuna, a heavenly figure who acted as guardian of the cosmic order, but who was not regarded as a creative force.

2 The reign of the Pharaoh Amenophis IV, who changed his name to Akhenaton, was followed by that of Tutankhamum and a return to religious orthodoxy in Egypt.

3 Fertile Crescent: the phrase coined in 1916 by James Breasted, Director of the Oriental Institute of Chicago, to describe those regions in which conditions for early agriculture were favourable – a geographical area stretching from Egypt through the Levant to southern Anatolia and northern Mesopotamia, and bounded in the east by the Zagros Mountains.

4 The extent of the division of opinion on this subject is reflected in the fact that very soon after the death of Muhammad, the Caliph Umar said 'Had I not seen the Prophet kiss you [the Ka'ba at Mecca], I would not kiss you myself.' Trees, wells and springs were also regarded as sacred.

5 In all, twenty-five biblical prophets, the pious men who were entrusted with God's messages, are mentioned in the Qur'an; in the case of Jesus, stress is laid on his immaculate conception and on the miracles he performed, but any claim to his divinity as the Son of God is denied.

6 Of the six collections, that compiled by Bukhari (810–70), with 2,762 entries, is especially venerated; these collections are accepted as authoritative by Sunnis, but not by Shiites (who adopted their own collections of traditions).

7 For some Muslims *bid'a* includes any practice or, in the context of the mosque, physical feature that was not in existence in the early days of Islam and must therefore be rejected; the most obvious feature of the mosque in this respect is the minaret, introduced much later. For the majority, however, the introduction of something new is considered *bid'a* only when in their view it clearly contradicts the spirit of Islam. Since the possibilities open to Islam can never be rendered fully explicit in any one epoch, most believers may allow for the acceptance of *bid'a hasanah* ('good innovation'), though which standpoint will prevail in the context of mosque design in any particular nation is impossible to predict.

8 Charges of apostasy were not unusual, and – like accusations of heresy in the Christian sphere – were a matter of extreme seriousness; in either case the penalty for dissent was death.

9 On the one hand *hadith* states that 'Allah would build a home in paradise for those who build a *masjid*'. On the other, Ibn Sa'd (845), in his biography of Muhammad, relates a story first told by Abd'Allah ibn Yazd, who visited Medina in 707, when the house of the Prophet was still intact. There Abd'Allah met and talked to a grandson of Umm Salama, one of Muhammad's wives. She had told her grandson that when Muhammad was absent on a mission to Duma in 626, she had ordered an addition to her living quarters with walls built of burnt bricks, and that on his return Muhammad had rebuked her, saying 'Oh Umm Salama! Verily the most unprofitable thing that eateth up the wealth of a believer is building.'

10 Pendentives: convoluted triangles by means of which the circle of the dome or hemisphere is made to sit upon a supporting structure that is square, hexagonal or octagonal in plan; the spectacular originality of the methods developed and used by medieval times – due in part to the unique mastery of three-dimensional geometry and mathematics in the Islamic sphere – was never emulated subsequently in the West.

CHAPTER 2

1 Dost-Muhammad Gawashwani, Preface to the Bahram Mirza Album (Istanbul, Topkapı Sarayı Müzesi, H.2154), translated by Thackston, *A Century of Princes*, p. 343. The term *islami* is normally *islimi*, the vine-and-tendril motif of the familiar 'arabesque'. The tradition given here of the 'invention' of *islimi* by Ali ibn Abi-Talib was used to justify the use of arabesque ornament, and it is no accident that Dost-Muhammad calls it *islami* ('Islamic'), for it was considered the 'most Islamic' of all ornamentation.

2 Dhu'l-Qarnayn, the Qur'anic prophet often identified as Alexander of Macedonia. In the legend of Dhu'l-Qarnayn he is said to have reached the 'setting place of the sun' (*maghrib al-shams*; 18:86).

3 Dost-Muhammad Gawashwani, Preface to the Bahram Mirza Album (Istanbul, Topkapı Sarayı Müzesi. H.2154, translated by Thackston in *A Century of Princes*, pp. 343f.

4 E.g., the 'Bathing Woman' at the eighth-century Syrian palace of Qusayr 'Amra', with its well preserved mosaics and frescoes of Hellenistic inspiration.

5 Mir Sayyid-Ahmad Mashhadi, Preface to the Amir Ghayb Beg Album (Istanbul, Topkapı Sarayı Müzesi, H.2161), translated by Thackston in *A Century of Princes*, p. 353.

6 A quotation of which Sufis are particularly fond.

7 A good illustration is from a *madrasa* in the Congregational Mosque in Isfahan; the *madrasa* dates from 1366, but the tiles and inscriptions are much later.

8 An early example occurs in the Congregational Mosque at Abarquh, Iran (second half of the fourteenth century).

9 During the Il-Khanid period particularly, the use of formulas that would later be overtly Shiite does not necessarily convey overt Shiism; during that period a piety centred on the *ahl al-bayt* was fairly common in Sunni Islam. Strict lines of confessional demarcation were drawn during the Safavid period.

10 The most familiar examples are the huge roundels in the Hagia Sophia (Ayasofya) Mosque in Istanbul.

11 As in the *mihrab* of the Sokollu Mehmet Paşa Mosque in Istanbul (1571).

12 The doorway of a mosque was often equated with the interior *mihrab*, and as such the Light Verse was frequently inscribed on the main portal of a mosque, as in Cordoba (957) and in the great entrance to the *madrasa* of Sultan Hasan in Cairo (1356–9).

13 Also a favourite tombstone inscription. See *Islamic Calligraphy* (exhib. catalogue), Geneva, 1988, p. 165.

14 See lists in E.C. Dodd and S. Khairallah, *The Image of the Word*.

15 In a wonderful anachronism a Safavid painter has portrayed the pre-Islamic king Nushirwan passing by a ruined building, over the door of which can be read the purely Islamic *ya mufattiha 'l-abwab*.

CHAPTER 3

1 Concerning the role of geometry in Renaissance architecture, see Rudolf Wittkower, *Architectural Principles in the Age of Humanism*, New York, 1971.

2 Concerning surviving architectural drawings from the pre-modern Islamic world, see Renata Holod, 'Text, Plan, and Building: On the Transmission of Architectural Knowledge', in Margaret Ševčenko (ed.), *Theories and Principles of Design in the Architecture of Islamic Societies*, Cambridge, Mass., 1988, pp. 1–12.

3 For a brief history of the development of geometry in the Islamic world, see *Encyclopaedia of Islam* (2nd ed.): ''Ilm al-Handasa'.

4 See Oleg Grabar, *The Great Mosque of Isfahan*, New York and London, 1990.

5 For more information on such manuals, see Gülru Necipoğlu, *Geometry and Decoration in Islamic Architecture: The Evidence of a Late Timurid Design Scroll* (forthcoming); a preliminary study of the scroll appears in Lisa Golombek and Maria Subtelny (eds.), *Timurid Art and Culture*, Leiden, 1992, pp. 48–66.

6 For additional information on al-Kashi's *Miftah al-Hisab*, see Necipoğlu, op.cit.; also Lisa Golombek and Donald Wilber, *The Timurid Architecture of Iran and Turfan*, Princeton, N.J., 1990.

7 For further details of individual mosques, see John Hoag, *Islamic Architecture*; George Michell (ed.), *Architecture of the Islamic World*; and Richard Ettinghausen and Oleg Grabar, *The Art and Architecture of Islam 650–1250*.

8 See Holod, op cit., pp. 5f.

9 E. H. Gombrich, *The Sense of Order*, Ithaca, N.Y., 1979, p. 157.

10 Concerning the proportional systems used in the Süleymaniye, see Godfrey Goodwin, *A History of Ottoman Architecture*, London and New York, 1987, p. 231.
11 Grabar, *The Great Mosque of Isfahan* (op. cit.), p. 39.
12 For the geometric analyses carried out by Soviet scholars, see Golombek and Wilber, *Timurid Architecture* (op. cit.).
13 For a discussion of al-Kashi's chapters on arches and vaults, see ibid., pp. 152f.
14 For the evolution of geometric patterns, see Necipoğlu, *Geometry and Decoration in Islamic Architecture* (op. cit.).
15 See Lisa Golombek, 'The Function of Decoration in Islamic Architecture', in Margaret Ševčenko (ed.), *Theories and Principles of Design in the Architecture of Islamic Societies*, Cambridge, Mass., 1988, pp. 35–45.
16 For the construction of domes in the Islamic world, see Ronald Lewcock, 'Architects, Craftsmen and Builders: Materials and Techniques', in George Mitchell (ed.), *Architecture of the Islamic World*, pp. 141–3.
17 See Richard Ettinghausen, 'The Taming of the Horror Vacui in Islamic Art', *Proceedings of the American Philosophical Society*, 123 (February 1979), pp. 18–19.
18 Examples of such writings include Nader Ardalan and Laleh Bakhtiar, *The Sense of Unity*, Chicago, 1973; Keith Critchlow, *Islamic Patterns: An Analytical and Cosmological Approach*, London and New York, 1976; and Issam El Said and Ayse Parman, *Geometric Concepts in Islamic Art*, London, 1976.
19 See Oleg Grabar, *The Mediation of Ornament*, Princeton, N.J., 1992. For a more detailed analysis of the associations which can be attributed to the geometric patterns of the Islamic world, see Necipoğlu, *Geometry and Decoration in Islamic Architecture* (op. cit.).
20 Concerning the symbolic interpretation of the *muqarnas*, see Oleg Grabar, *The Alhambra*, Cambridge, Mass., 1978, pp. 146–7; idem, 'The Iconography of Islamic Architecture', in Priscilla P. Soucek (ed.), *Content and Context of Visual Arts in the Islamic World*, University Park, Pa, 1988, pp. 57–9; Yasser Tabbaa, 'The Muqarnas Dome: Its Origin and Meaning', *Muqarnas* 3 (1985), pp. 61–74.
21 See Wayne Begley, 'The Myth of the Taj Mahal and a new Theory of its Symbolic Meaning', *The Art Bulletin* 61 (March 1979), pp. 7–37.
22 See Aniela Jaffé, 'Symbolism in the Visual Arts', in Carl G. Jung (ed.), *Man and His Symbols*, New York, 1964, pp. 240–9.
23 Robert Venturi, *Complexity and Contradiction in Architecture*, 2nd ed., New York, 1977, p. 42.

Chapter 4

1 See Muhammad Abu Zahra, *Al-Shafei*, Cairo, 1978, pp. 158–61, for further elaboration on this aspect of the work of the great jurist.
2 It is important to distinguish between Islamicization and Arabization of societies exposed to the powerful drive of Islamic expansion from the seventh to fifteenth centuries. From the earliest days, Egypt, the Levant and Iraq were Arabized as well as Islamicized; Iran (Persia) was not. Historians such as A. A. Al-Duri have addressed this question in many works.
3 See Ismail Serageldin, *Space for Freedom: The Search for Architectural Excellence in Muslim Societies*, London, 1989, pp. 60–3; and 'Architecture as Intellectual Statement: Modernism in the Muslim World', in *Criticism in Architecture*, Singapore, 1989, pp. 16–30.
4 Suha Özkan, 'Regionalism within Modernism', in *Regionalism in Architecture*, Proceedings of a seminar held by the Aga Khan Award for Architecture, Singapore, 1985, pp. 8–16.
5 Paul Rudolph observed: 'The influence of the Architectural Press, the worship of fashion, and our desire to conform ... is still a deterrent to true Regionalism', *Regionalism in Architecture* (op. cit.), p. 43.
6 Ken Yeang, *Tropical Urban Regionalism: Building in a South-East Asian City*, Singapore, 1987, p. 12.
7 See *inter alia* M. Arkoun, *Pour une critique de la raison Islamique*, Paris, 1984, and 'Islamic Culture, Modernity and Architecture' and 'Current Islam Faces Its Tradition', both in *Architectural Education in the Islamic World*, seminar proceedings (Aga Khan Award for Architecture), Geneva, 1986, pp., 15–22 and 92–103; and 'Muslim Character: The essential and the changeable' in *The expanding Metropolis: Coping with the Urban Growth of Cairo* (AKAA), Geneva, 1985, pp. 233–5; and I. Serageldin, 'Individual Identity, Group Dynamics and Islamic Resurgence', in Ali E. H. Dessouki (ed.), *Islamic Resurgence in the Arab World*, New York, 1982, pp. 54–66. See also I. Serageldin, 'Mirrors and Windows: Redefining the Boundaries of the Mind', in *Democracy and the Middle East. Views from within and without*, London, 1993.
8 El-Wakil's Corniche Mosque (1986) in Jeddah uses Mamluk design elements and decorative features although other Egyptian and Mediterranean styles can also be discerned. This mosque won an Aga Khan Award for Architecture in 1989. See I. Serageldin, *Al-Tajdid wal Fa'sil fi 'imarat Al Muitam'at Al-Islamiyya: Dirasa li Tajribat Ja'izat Al-Aga Khan Lil'Imara* (Innovation and Authenticity in the Architecture of Muslim Societies: A Study of the Experience of the Aga Khan Award for Architecture) in Arabic (AKAA), Geneva, 1989, pp. 118–21. See also 'El-Wakil and Mosque Architecture in Saudi Arabia', *Albenaa*, vol. 6, no. 34 (April/May 1987). Also Serageldin (op. cit.), pp. 108–13 for the Hayy Al-Sifarat Centre in Riyadh.
9 Some more recent thinking on the issue of identity has brought new dimensions to the traditional constructs. For example, Alain Touraine considers contemporary identity to be defined in terms of choices, not tradition: 'Ainsi l'identité devient-elle aux yeux du sociologue non pas l'appel à un être mais la revendication d'une capacité d'action et de changement. Elle se définit en termes de choix et non pas de substance, d'essence ou de tradition'. See Alain Touraine, *Le Retour de l'Acteur*, Paris, 1984, p. 178.

Chapter 5

1 For a detailed account of the Prophet's house see K. A. C. Creswell, *Early Muslim Architecture*, I, 2nd revised edition, pp. 6–12.
2 In the Qur'ran (9:108) reference is made to the first public mosque of Islam, the *masjid* at a place called Quba.
3 Bishop Arnulf's statement quoted by Creswell, *EMA* I, p. 34, note 2.
4 For the later history of al-Aqsa Mosque see Creswell, *EMA* II, 2nd ed., pp. 373–80; and R. W. Hamilton, *The Structural History of the Aqsa Mosque*, Jerusalem, 1947.
5 See Creswell, *EMA* I, p. 12; various opinions have been offered concerning the location of the mosque in which the *qibla* direction was first altered.
6 The *musalla* was the open prayer-ground next to the *masjid* at Quba.
7 Even up to modern times there have been instances of small *masjids* without a minaret.
8 Creswell, *EMA* I, p. 15.
9 Tabari quoted by Creswell, *EMA* I, pp. 16f.
10 Tabari quoted by Creswell, *EMA* I, p. 26.
11 Maqrizi gives this description quoting Al-Himyari, an eye-witness; Creswell, *EMA* I, p. 37.
12 Ibn Khaldun, Muqaddimah, Cairo, 1322 AH, quoted by Pedersen, article 'Masjid' in *Encyclopaedia of Islam*, vol. III, p. 336.
13 See J. Sauvaget, *La Mosquée Omeyyade de Médine*, Etudes sur les origines architecturales de la Mosquée et de la Basilique, Paris, 1947.
14 Creswell, *EMA* I, p. 147.
15 For a detailed account see Creswell, *EMA* I, pp. 100–35; O. Grabar, 'La grande Mosquée de Damas et les origines architecturales de la Mosquée' in *Synthronon, Art et Archéologie de la fin de l'Antiquité et du Moyen Age, Recueil d'études*, Paris, 1968, pp. 107–14.
16 M. Van Berchem, 'The Mosaics of the Dome of the Rock and of the Great Mosque at Damascus', *EMA* I, pp. 321f.
17 Of the circular city of al-Mansur nothing has survived. The ninth-century geographer Yaqubi and the eleventh-century historian al-Khatib al-Baghdadi are the main sources. The latter's description of the Great Mosque, based on an eye-witness account dating from the early ninth century, is the only genuine description of the mosque. For a translation see *EMA* II, pp. 31f.
18 E. Herzfeld, *Geschichte der Stadt Samarra*, Berlin, 1947. Earlier observations by Herzfeld and Sarre were published in *Erster vorlaeufiger Bericht ueber die Ausgrabungen von Samarra*, Berlin, 1912; Creswell, *EMA* II, pp. 254–65.
19 Based on the discovery by Herzfeld of some column bases in the centre of the central nave, Creswell argues that the idea of a T-shaped central spine is untenable. I consider that Herzfeld's findings tend to support the contrary argument, for if there was no intention to have a larger nave, intermediary columns would not have been used to enlarge it (see *EMA* II, p. 279).
20 Creswell, *EMA* II, p. 125.
21 G. Wiet, *The Mosques of Cairo*, Paris, 1966, p. 8.
22 Maqrizi gives the Sultan's opinion from the biography of Baybars, *Sirat al-Zahiriya*: see Creswell, *Muslim Architecture in Egypt*, vol. II, p. 155.
23 R. Lewcock and G. R. Smith, 'Two Early Mosques in the Yemen: A Preliminary Report', *Art and Archaeology Research Papers*, London, December 1973, pp. 117–19.
24 These large water-tanks, sometimes connected with mosques as *sabils*, have impressive architecture. They may have a background in Indian Kund in Rajasthan and Gujarat. An interesting example is the *sabil* of the Dhi Bin Mosque and Madrasa; see F. Varanda, *The Art of Building in Yemen*, London, 1982, pp. 50–1.
25 R. Lewcock and G. King, 'Key Monuments in Islamic Architecture: Arabia', in George Michell (ed.), *Architecture of the Islamic World*, pp. 210f.

Chapter 6

1 For a discussion of the Great Mosque at Qairawan, see chapter 5.
2 Proportionality in architecture is based on the use of a scale of magnitudes whereby all dimensions – from the smallest to the largest – relate to each other as multiples of a common factor.

3 Built 709–15, the Great Mosque of Damascus is the oldest extant mosque; see chapter 5.
4 Although these arches might be thought to provide support, in practice they have no significant load-bearing function.
5 The buildings housing the palace baths at Qusayr 'Amra' (now in Jordan) date from *c.* 712–15. The original decorative scheme in mosaic and frescoes also includes hunting, domestic and palace scenes.

Chapter 7

1 For a more detrailed discussion of the role of *chahartaqs* in early mosques, see B. O'Kane, 'Čahārṭāq II. In the Islamic Period', *Encyclopaedia Iranica* IV, pp. 639–42.
2 These have not yet been published as a group; preliminary reports can be found in *Atlal* I–VI (1977–82).
3 For a detailed analysis of this portal and other early mosques, see R. Hillenbrand, 'ʿAbbāsid Mosques in Iran', *Rivista degli Studi Orientali* LIX (1985, published 1987), pp. 175–212.
4 The essential publication of this monument is E. Galdieri, *Esfahan: Masğid-i Ğum'a* I–III, Rome, 1972, 1973, 1984.
5 For this type of minaret see B. O'Kane, 'The Rise of the Minaret', *Oriental Art* xxxvii (1992), pp. 111–12, figs. 5–7.
6 The mosques of western China are inadequately published as yet. In the meantime see 'Mosques of Northern China: Beijing, Xi'an, Turfan and Kashi', *Mimar* III (1982), pp. 58–73; and Chinese Academy of Architecture, *Classical Chinese Architecture*, Hong Kong, 1986, pp. 187–9.
7 Only the *musallas* of former Soviet Central Asia have been published together in detail: see B. D. Kochnev, *Srednevekovye Zagorodnye Kul'tovye Sooruzheniya Srednei Azii*, Tashkent, 1976. For Turbat-i Jam see O'Kane, *Timurid Architecture*, cat. no. 48; for Mashhad see A. Godard, 'Khorāsān' Ā͟thār-é Īrān IV (1949), pp. 125–37.
8 For these mosques, see G. Curatola, 'Architettura religiosa lignea nella zona di Marāgha', *Rivista degli Studi Orientali* LIX (1985; published 1987), pp. 77–93.
9 See further J. Bloom, *Minaret: Symbol of Islam*, Oxford Studies in Islamic Art VIII, Oxford, 1989; also B. O'Kane, 'The Rise of the Minaret' (op. cit.), p. 111.
10 This is illustrated in *Isfahan: City of Light* (exhibition catalogue), Tehran, 1976, p. 87. Excellent drawings can be found in K. Herdeg, *Formal Structure in Islamic Architecture of Iran and Turkistan*, New York, 1990, pp. 21–4.
11 The essential study of Qajar mosques is R. Hillenbrand, 'The Role of Tradition in Qajar Religious Architecture' in C. E. Bosworth and R. Hillenbrand (eds.), *Qajar Iran. Political, Social and Cultural Change 1800–1925. Studies presented to Professor L. P. Elwell-Sutton*, Edinburgh, 1984, pp. 352–82; see also J. Scarce, 'The Arts of the Eighteenth to Twentieth Centuries' in P. Avery, G. Hambly and C. Melville (eds.), *From Nadir Shah to the Islamic Republic*, Cambridge History of Iran VII, Cambridge, 1991, pp. 895–924.
12 No plans have been published of this mosque; photographs can be found in L. Hunarfarr, *Ganjīna-yi āthār-i tārīkhī-yi Isfahān*, Isfahan, 1350/1971, pp. 764–88.
13 See, for example, M. Falamaki, 'Al-Ghadir Mosque', *Mimar* 22 (1988), pp. 24–9.

Chapter 8

1 For the history of Anatolia in this period see Claude Cahen, *La Turquie pré-ottomane*, Istanbul-Paris, 1988.
2 Bates (1980), p. 55.
3 Muhammad b. Ali b. Süleyman al-Rāvendī, *Rāhat-üs-Sudūr ve Āyet-üs-sürūr* (trans. by A. Ateş from Persian into Turkish), 2 vols., Ankara, 1957/60, vol. I, pp. 29, 65. For the most recent study of this mosque, dealing with its incorporation of the remains of a Byzantine church and its inscriptions, see Scott Redford, 'The Alaeddin Mosque in Konya Reconsidered', *Artibus Asiae* 1/2, vol. LI (1991), pp. 54–74.
4 Ernst Herzfeld, 'Damascus: Studies in Architecture, IV', *Ars Islamica* 13–14 (1948), p. 137. For the domed mosques of south-east Anatolia, Syria and the Jazira see R. Ettinghausen and O. Grabar, *The Art and Architecture of Islam 650–1250* (1987), pp. 297–313; Tom Sinclair, 'Early Artuqid Mosque Architecture', in *The Art of Syria and the Jazira 1100–1250* (Oxford Studies in Islamic Art I), Oxford, 1985, pp. 49–67. Like the domed *maqsura* of Isfahan, that of Silvan (raised on stone squinches imitating *muqarnas* elements in brick) was originally surrounded by corridor-like open spaces that separated it from the side-aisles. For the Great Mosque in Isfahan see Oleg Grabar, *The Great Mosque of Isfahan*, New York and London, 1990, and R. Ettinghausen and O. Grabar, op. cit.
5 George Maqdisi, 'The Sunni Revival', in I. A. Richards (ed.), *Islamic Civilization 950–1150*, Oxford, 1973, pp. 155–68; Carole Hillenbrand, 'The History of the Jazira, 1100–1250: A short introduction', in *The Art of Syria* ... (op. cit.), pp. 9–19.
6 The 'tripod' analogy is found in a Persian *Shahnama* of the Anatolian Seljuqs attributed to a little-known fourteenth-century author, Ünsi, a source whose authenticity has been questioned; see Mesud Koman (ed.), *Ünsi'nin Selçuk Şehnamesi*, Konya, 1942, p. 21.
7 Robert Hillenbrand, 'Eastern Islamic influences in Syria; Raqqa and Qalʿat Jaʿbar in the later 12th century', *The Art of Syria* ... (op. cit), pp. 21–48.
8 J. M. Rogers, 'A Renaissance of classical antiquity in North Syria, 11th–12th centuries', *Les Annales Archéologiques de Syrie* 25 (1975), pp. 347–56; Yasser Tabbaa, 'Propagation of Jihad under Nur al-Din (1146–1174)', in V. P. Goss (ed.), *The Meeting of Two Worlds*, Kalamazoo, Mich., 1986, pp. 223–40; Terry Allen, *A Classical Revival in Islamic Architecture*, Wiesbaden, 1986.
9 For the Emirate period see Faruk Sümer, 'Ḳarāmān-Oghulları', *Encyclopaedia of Islam* (2nd ed.), vol. 4, pp. 619–25; I. H. Konyalı (1965); Colin Imber, *The Ottoman Empire 1300–1481*, Istanbul, 1990.
10 Rūhī Edrenevī, *Tārīḫ-i āl-i ʿosmān*, Ms. Berlin Staatsbibliothek Or. Quart 821, fol. 119v. According to an anonymous source, the Üç Şerefeli Mosque and the Edirne Palace were built by the same architect, Beşir Çelebi, who was paralyzed (see 'Tarih-i Edirne, Hikâyet-i Beşir Çelebi', ed. J. H. Ertaylan, Istanbul, 1946, p. 7.
11 Spiro Kostof, *A History of Architecture. Settings and Rituals*, New York and Oxford, 1985, p. 459. For the tempting hypothesis that the Italian architect Filarete (who was planning to visit Istanbul in 1465) might have contributed to the design of Mehmet II's complex, see Restle Marcell, 'Bauplanung und Baugesinnung unter Mehmed II. Fatih', *Pantheon* 39 (1981), pp. 361–7.
12 For these paradisial associations see Tursun Beg, *The History of Mehmed the Conqueror*, ed. H. Inalcık and R. Murphy, Minneapolis and Chicago, 1978, fols. 58r–60r, and Idris-i Bidlisi, *Tercüme-i Heşt Bihişt*, Topkapı Palace Library, Ms. Baghdad 196, fols. 46r–49v. The former atrium of Hagia Sophia also had a fountain surrounded by cypresses.
13 Tursun Beg, *History* (op. cit.), fols, 58r–58v. For the Ottoman reception of Hagia Sophia and the history of its repairs, see Necipoğlu (1992).
14 Kuban (1987), p. 84.
15 Sources are cited in Necipoğlu (1985), pp. 105–6.
16 For an interpretation of Sülemaniye's programme of inscriptions see ibid., pp. 107–13.
17 M. Sözen and S. Saatçi (eds.), *Mimar Sinan and Tezkiret-ül Bünyan*, Istanbul, 1989, p. 170.
18 Ibid., pp. 170, 172. According to Kuran (1987), the diameter of Selimiye's dome measures 31.22 m (102 ft 5 in.), its height from ground level being 42.25 m (138 ft 7 in.); the elliptical dome of Hagia Sophia has a diameter of 30.90/31.80 m (101 ft 4 in./104 ft 3 in.) and a height of 55.60 m (182 ft 5 in.).
19 The central calligraphic roundel of the Selimiye dome quotes the *al-Ikhlas* Sura (112) from the Qur'an (also known as *al-Tauhid*), which stresses the oneness of God – an appropriate choice highlighting the interpretation of the all-encompassing dome as a metaphor for the victory of Islamic monotheism.
20 For Procopius's description of Hagia Sophia, see Cyril Mango, *Art of the Byzantine Empire 312–1453*, Englewood Cliffs, N.J., 1972, pp. 72–8.
21 R. Stephen Humphreys, 'The Expressive Intent of the Mamluk Architecture of Cairo', *Studia Islamica* 35 (1972), pp. 69–119. While the majority of the population in Syria, the Jazira and Egypt had been Islamicized by the fourteenth century, Anatolia became predominantly Muslim only in the late sixteenth century (the Balkans remained largely Christian).
22 The two minarets were added some sixty years after the mosque itself was built.

Chapter 9

1 Chauhans: a leading Rajput clan in Ajmer.
2 Although the origin of the spire is not known, its form is close to that of the Hindu temple *shikhara*; the latter, however, is usually curved.
3 For an English translation, see A. Rogers (ed.), *Tūzuk-i-Jahangīrī* (trans. H. Beveridge), vol. 2, pp. 144–5 (reprinted Delhi, 1989).
4 Op. cit., vol. 1, p. 425.

Chapter 10

1 'Il peut arriver, il arrivera très fréquemment, qu'en s'islamisant, un pays adopte une des couleurs multicolores que le gigantesque prisme triangulaire islamique peut offrir, en décomposant la blanche vérité divine dont l'Islam diffuse la lumière.' Cited by Vincent Monteil in *L'Islam Noir*, Paris, 1964, p. 41.
2 When enquiries were made in the course of fieldwork in West Africa, in an effort to establish construction dates for mosques, the date given by the local elders in each case referred to the original consecration of a site, not the particular building on it. More often than not, the extant mosque was not the original one.
3 Tadeusz Lewicki, 'L'Etat nord-africain de Tahert et ses relations avec le Soudan occidental à la fin du VIIIe et au IXe siècle,' *Cahiers d'Etudes Africaines* 2, 4 (1962), pp. 513–35.
4 Pre-Islamic history in West Africa rests heavily on oral tradition. With the introduction of Islam, indigenous chronicles were often recorded in local *Tarikhs*,

written in Arabic script. These sources are often rich in material relating to personages and events in a particular city or region, but they lack descriptive data on which to build an architectural history.

5 René Caillié is credited with being the first European to visit the city of Timbuktu and to document its architecture. His description and his rendering of the plan and elevation of the DjinguereBer Mosque provide a remarkable basis for comparison with subsequent building changes. In the mid-nineteenth century, the intrepid explorer Henry Barth was the second European to visit the city, and he too left a rich documentation of its architecture and morphology.

6 The term *toro* (pl. *toron*) may be a derivative of the Bambara (Manding) term *sutoro*, used in conjunction with the Bambara *komo*, the initiation society specifically associated with human knowledge. Knowledge has four parts, each of which is represented by a mother. According to Dominique Zahan, *The Bambara* (1974), pp. 2 and 6, 'the *toro* symbolizes germination, proliferation and rebirth. The name *sutoro* alludes to the funerary custom of burying a branch of this particular tree with the dead, to represent rebirth. The second mother, *sutoro*, represents enlightenment, and teaching by demonstration.'

7 Lt Underberg, the young French architect responsible for converting the palace to a French military administrative centre, had trained at the Ecole des Beaux-Arts in Paris, and, perhaps in keeping with the spirit of Viollet-le-Duc and Rational Building, had great respect for indigenous building styles and traditions.

8 M. A. Cocheteaux, personal communication to Labelle Prussin, Nice, 27 June 1968.

9 Prussin Fieldnotes. Interview with the elders and with El Hadj Umar's family at Dingueraye, February 1979.

10 The indigenous tradition of planting a tree to mark the tomb of a deceased elder or head of a family, i.e. an ancestor, either in the corral of a nomadic household or in the compound of a sedentary family, is ubiquitous throughout West Africa. By association, the same practice extends not only to the palace of a ruler, but to the founder of a mosque.

Chapter 11

1 Casson 1989; the *Periplus* reports on the coastal routes from Egypt to India and along the East African Coast. For archaeological evidence, see Mark Horton, 'The Periplus and East Africa', *Azania* 25, 1990, pp. 95–99.

2 M. C. Smith and H. T. Wright, 'The Ceramics from Ras Hafun in Somalia', *Azania* 23, 1988, pp. 115–42.

3 For general views on Islamization of the eastern seaboard, see Trimingham 1952, 1964, Pouwels 1987, Chittick 1977, Allen 1993. Freeman-Grenville 1966 contains translations of the main sources.

4 Vantini 1975 contains translations of the main Arabic sources to the Red Sea towns and Nubia. See also Crowfoot 1911. On inscriptions, Schneider 1967, 1983, Combe 1930. A plan of the possible mosque on Er Rih was published by H. E. Hibbert, 'El Rih, a Red Sea Island', *Sudan Notes and Records* 18, 1935, pp. 308–13.

5 Significant numbers of ruined mosques and tombs of this date are also known from the mountainous region of northern Somalia; for a brief account of the stone architecture of this area, see Curle 1937; Chittick 1976, p. 127.

6 For general accounts of the relations between Christian Nubia and the Islamic north, see Adams 1977, Shinnie 1978, Trimingham 1949.

7 Hrbek 1977, especially pp. 75–80. An interesting phenomenon, which has hardly been explored because of scant evidence, is the use of tents as mosques both in peripatetic capital cities and among smaller nomadic populations. For their use in a Christian context see R. Pankhurst, 'The Tents of the Ethiopian Court', *Azania* 18, 1983, pp. 181–95.

8 Holt 1970. For ethonographic evidence of Mahdism, see R. A. Bravmann, *African Islam*, Washington, D.C., and London, 1983, pp. 46–57.

9 Bloss 1936–7; for a comprehensive account of the buildings and styles at Suakin, see Greenlaw 1976; Matthews 1954.

10 Trimingham 1957; Wilding 1976; Tamrat 1977. A. Zakeria, 'The Mosques of Harar', unpublished dissertation, Institute of Ethiopian Studies, Addis Ababa, provides the most detailed account of the architecture, and I am most grateful for this information.

11 Harar is not mentioned in a single external source until the sixteenth century, even though local traditions suggest that the town was founded by refugees arriving from Mecca in the tenth century. Thirteenth-century tombstone inscriptions in Arabic are known in the area between Harar and Dire Dawa. Harar became the capital of the Adal Sultanate in 1520, when it replaced the nearby town of Dakker; the town was effectively refounded at this later date during a revival of Muslim, especially Adali power in the Horn of Africa. Richard Burton wrote: 'The city abounds in mosques, plain buildings without minarets, and in graveyards stuffed with tombs' (*First Footsteps in East Africa*, p. 216). Paulitschke 1888 shows an early view of Harar.

12 Shinnie 1957. The spatial configuration, particularly on the ground floor, distinctly recalls the apse of a church rather than the prevailing styles of *mihrabs* in the region.

13 Details on the cathedral and churches from Qasr Ibrim will be published by M. C. Horton (ed.), *The Cathedral and Churches of Qasr Ibrim*, London: Egypt Exploration society. A useful summary of the historical background to the Ottoman occupation is V. L. Menage (1988), 'The Ottomans and Nubia in the Sixteenth Century', *Annales Islamalogiques* 24, pp. 137–53.

14 Cailliaud 1823; Crawford 1951; 1953

15 For Chibuene, see P. J. Sinclair, *Space, Time and Social Formation*, Uppsala: Societas Archaeologica Upsaliensis, 1987, pp. 86–91. Horton 1987 and 1991 describes the Shanga mosques; Allen 1993 (p. 36, note 3) has taken issue with my chronology, and has suggested a tenth-century date for the earliest mosques.

16 Chittick 1977; Nurse and Spear 1985. For an excellent summary of Swahili culture, both within a contemporary and historical perspective, see Middleton 1992.

17 A feature of the Swahili coast is the linear distribution of Muslim settlements; none existed further inland than 5 km (3 miles) before the nineteenth century. The arrival of the Portuguese from the late fifteenth century onwards had little economic or religious impact, see Strandes 1971. For the architecture of the Swahili coast, see Garlake 1966; Wilson 1978, 1980; Allen and Wilson 1979; Chittick 1958–64. Kirkman 1964 provides a useful overview. Freeman-Grenville and Martin 1973 list the inscriptions.

18 It is often suggested that much of the teak employed was imported from India; there is little evidence of this, and excellent hardwoods exist in East Africa; for a discussion of the local species of timber used in architecture and doors, see Aldrick 1990, Allen 1974.

19 An important case study comes from Siyu, which was one of the most important centres of craft working on the coast. There is virtually no evidence for the settlement of Indian or foreign craftsmen or of foreign influence. Brown 1988. Allen 1979. A considerable debate has surrounded the origins of Swahili houses; Allen 1973, Allen and Wilson 1979; Donley 1982, Donley-Reid 1990.

20 Terrestrial coral is quarried from limestone reefs that make up the shore and islands which have become exposed through changes in sea-level; the coral is hard and uneven in texture and cannot be easily shaped, although with modern technology it can now be sawn into blocks. Porites coral, much lighter, is quarried from living coral reefs of *Porites solida*; when first collected, this coral is very soft and ideal for carving decorative panels and inscriptions, niches, jambs and voussoirs. There is an eighteenth-century description of how this type of coral was worked at Jeddah on the Red Sea (Arrowsmith 1991, p. 23). It seems probable that the East African technique originated in the Red Sea area; Horton 1987.

21 Ibn Hawqal (*c.* 970) reported the export of *sai* and other types of wood to build houses at Siraf; this is probably a reference to the trade in mangrove poles, which are still exported today to the Middle East. East African hardwoods may also have been exported.

22 The Portuguese, however, describe elaborate wooden doors in sixteenth-century Mombasa. Another type of lightly carved and painted door that survived in Siyu on Pate Island into the twentieth century may represent the more ancient doormaking tradition.

23 Garlake 1966, pp. 11, 70; Flury 1922.

24 Garlake 1966; Inzerillo 1988; Cerulli 1957; Chittick 1982; Monneret de Villard 1943. Yakut's description of Mogadishu is translated in Trimingham 1964, p. 5; engraved views in Révoil 1885–6.

25 Chittick 1974; Garlake 1966.

26 Lamu mosques are listed in J. de V. Allen, *Lamu Town, A Guide*, published by the author (1974); Ghaidan 1976; Siravo and Pulver 1987. For an early account of the Lamu archipelago see Stigand 1913; the role of Sharifs in Lamu, see Zein 1974 and Pouwels 1987.

27 A. Sharif, 'The Mosques of Zanzibar', *Azania* 26 (1992), M. C. Horton and C. M. Clark, 'Zanzibar Archaeological Survey 1984–5', Ministry of Information, Zanzibar 1985; *Zanzibar Guide* 1949, Zanzibar Government Printer; Pearce 1920.

Chapter 12

1 Western Region: term used since the Han Dynasty (206 BC–AD 270) to describe the area west of Yumen Guan in present-day Gansu Province and including what is now Xinjiang Province in China and part of Central Asia. For later mosques in Central Asia see chapter 7.

2 'Colour-eyed people': a literal translation of the Chinese term used since the Han Dynasty to describe people from Central and Western Asia, also applied to Arabs.

3 *Fan-fang*: a term used to describe residential quarters occupied by colour-eyed people. *Fan* means foreign or foreigner, *fang* a block in a city.

4 *Jiao-fang*: a term used to describe communities of Muslims belonging to various sects. It was derived from *fan-fang*, for since the 'colour-eyed people' had been naturalized, they were no longer foreigners, hence could

not be called *fan*, which was replaced by *jiao*, meaning religion.
5 *Pailou*: a type of monument in the form of a freestanding gateway.

Chapter 13

1 According to M. C. Ricklefs, 'The Moroccan traveller Ibn Battuta passed through Samudra [Sumatra] on his way to and from China in 1345 and 1346 and found that the ruler was a follower of the Shafi'i school of law. This confirms the presence from an early date of the school which was later to dominate Indonesia, although it is possible that the other Orthodox schools (Hanfi, Maliki and Hanbali) were also present at an early time.' (*A History of Modern Indonesia*, p. 4).
2 As a result of internecine struggles between East Java (Majapahit) and South Sumatra (Palembang), Parameswara fled *c.* 1400 to the settlement of Melaka, where he established trading with Malays, Chinese, Arabs and Indians (see Ricklefs, op. cit., p. 18). It has been suggested that late in life Parameswara married the daughter of the king of Pasai, North Sumatra, and converted to Islam, adopting the name Iskander Syah (see G. Coedes, *The Indianised States of Southeast Asia*, p. 246).
3 W. H. Rassers noted that 'When a circumcision is about to be performed and the *pendapa* [outer pavilion of the Javanese house] has to be changed into a *tarub* [circumcision pavilion] for this purpose, then it is considered necessary that the blessing of the higher power concerned should be invoked over this consecration of the house, and for this purpose they go with the boy who is to be circumcised to the grave of his father or to that of his father's ancestors.' (*Panji, the culture hero. A structural study of religion in Java*, p. 269).
4 It is probable that these illustrations of 1515 – see *The Suma Oriental of Tome Pires* (trans. A. Cortesão), London, 1944 – represent buildings with a sacred function, possibly for Muslim prayer.
5 H. H. Ambary cites the Cirebon palace tradition in which the chronogram *Waspada* (2) *Panembe* (2) *Yuganing* (4) *Ratu* (1), signifying 1422 in the Javanese calendar, represents AD 1500; see Paramita R. Abdurachman (ed.), *Cerbon*, Jakarta, 1982, p. 83).
6 Sunan Gunung Jati (Syarif Hidayat) was the son of Syarif Abdullah from Cairo and Rara Santang (Syarifah Modain), a princess of Pajajaran, a pre-Islamic kingdom of West Java (see Abdurachman, op. cit., p. 37).
7 François Valentijn, in his *Oude en nieuw Oost-Indien* (8 vols., Dordrecht and Amsterdam, 1724–6), includes a now celebrated illustration of the Mosque at Jepara, an important entrepôt near Demak in central Java; it shows a five-storey pagoda-like superstructure (since disappeared) which is not otherwise recorded.
8 Humanitarian concern in The Netherlands resulted in the emergence of this new policy which sought to balance the welfare of Indonesians against profits. Dutch 'pacification' of many regions, including Aceh and Bali, at the beginning of the twentieth century opened up even greater opportunities for exploitation. Snouk Hurgronje, an administrative adviser and student of Islam, was one amongst many Netherlanders who at this time became fascinated by Indonesian social and cultural development, and thus encouraged educational and religious reforms already stimulated by sources in the Middle East and Egypt.
9 W. F. Stutterheim, *Oudheidkundig Verslag over 1940*, p. 8.

Chapter 14

1 The most accessible depiction of the Great Mosque of Cordoba is in Georges Marçais, *L'Architecture Musulmane d'Occident*, Paris, 1954, pp. 135–50; L. Torres Balbas, *La Mezquita de Córdoba*, Madrid, 1965. Concerning Isfahan, see O, Grabar, *The Great Mosque of Isfahan*, New York and London, 1990.
2 The legal aspects of innovation in Islamic law are subsumed in the concepts of *bid'a* and *ijtihad*. For a discussion of the meaning and implications of these terms, see chapter 1, pp. 29f. and note 7.
3 These conclusions reflect the consensus view of leading historians of Islamic art and culture, as elaborated by, for example, K.A.C. Creswell, *A Short History of Early Muslim Architecture*; Oleg Grabar, *The Formation of Islamic Art*, New Haven, Conn., 1973; or D. Kuban, *Muslim Religious Architecture*, 2 parts, Leiden, 1974 and 1985.
4 Since Islam has no official religious hierarchy, agreement was apparently reached among the implementors of the legal system that the most significant issues involving the practice of the faith had been resolved. See note 2, above.
5 The al-Azhar in Cairo did introduce a curriculum in the natural and physical sciences, but it trains neither the professional cadres nor even the artisans of Egypt in the practice of their crafts.
6 Al-Hajjaj arrived at the Mosque of Kufa in Iraq, hiding his head in his cloak. When he reached the place of the preacher, he lifted his head and announced that he had come to bring order to the city and that heads would roll.

Chapter 15

1 The material included here represents the core of a major study of contemporary mosques by Professor Renata Holod of the University of Pennsylvania and myself, based on first-hand studies during numerous trips, responses to questionnaires sent to architects and clients, and work brought to our attention by colleagues and the architects themselves over a period of over seven years. The questionnaires, which were based on the documentation process we set up for the Aga Khan Award for Architecture, requested detailed information on the history and economics of each project and the evolution of the design concepts from the point of view of both architect and client. Some eighty buildings were documented in this manner, while in other cases secondary sources of information were used. Although the forthcoming publication by Renata Holod and myself provides the basis for this chapter, the views expressed here are my own, as is the choice of examples and their characterization.
2 The Mosque of Muhammad Ali, usually attributed to the architect Yusuf Boshnak, was the largest mosque built anywhere in the world in the first half of the nineteenth century. Muhammad Ali, an Albanian by birth, joined the Ottoman army and in 1805 was appointed governor of Egypt. By the 1820s, when he had firmly established his rule, Egypt had been under Ottoman suzerainty for over three centuries. As Mohammed Al-Asad has noted, such a major new building in Cairo would be expected 'to have a predominantly Mamluk vocabulary ... Ironically, it was the governor who most aggressively sought Egypt's independence from Istanbul who also provided Cairo with its most Ottomanized structure.' ('The Mosque of Muhammad Ali in Cairo', *Muqarnas* IX [1992], p. 43).
3 Had the project been realized, the Baghdad mosque would have been not only the largest contemporary mosque in the world, but second only in size to the ninth-century Great Mosque of Samarra (also in present-day Iraq).
4 Although town-planning legislation which divided urban space in accordance with functional zones and hierarchies was essentially a Western colonial legacy, local governments still adopt this approach despite its often inappropriate nature, both culturally or climatically, in much of the Islamic world.
5 The Bhong Mosque in the Punjab, completed in 1982, was built over a number of years using a variety of materials and styles. The Aga Khan Award for Architecture which it received in 1986 caused controversy in architectural circles due to the populist and mixed imagery of the building. For more about this complex see Ismail Serageldin (ed.), *Space for Freedom. The search for architectural excellence in Muslim societies*, London, 1989.
6 Store-front mosques are sometimes found in urban centres, where they are used as temporary premises for gathering and prayer. In the USA such facilities appear to be a uniquely Afro-American phenomenon and have a more permanent character with 'walk-in' access for meeting and prayer. A paper (unpublished) on this communal activity among minority Muslims, entitled 'Storefront Mosques of New York City', was presented by Susan Slyomovics at a Social Science Research Council seminar held at Harvard University in November 1990.

In 1989, while walking in Jakarta, I observed a number of quite elaborate mosques in the traditional shop-houses in the Chinese part of the city, but I am not aware of any study, sociological or architectural, devoted to these particular buildings in Indonesia.
7 The Great Mosque of Dakar, Senegal, is a case in point. Because this mosque, completed in 1976, was financed and built as a gift from the Moroccan government, it replicated the Great Mosque of Qairawan in Fez in plan, style and materials.
8 Hans Hollein, Preface to *Sedad Eldem*, Singapore and New York, 1967, p. 11.
9 Raoul Snelder, 'The Great Mosque at Djenne', *Mimar* 12 (1984), p. 73. The Niono Mosque, which is partly modelled on Djenne, received an Aga Khan Award for Architecture in 1983.
10 The transplant of the mosque style is discussed by Barry Hallen in 'Afro-Brazilian Mosques in West Africa', *Mimar* 29 (1988), pp. 16–23.
11 In the mid-1980s King Hassan of Morocco proclaimed through national newspapers the need for all major buildings in the country to be 'culturally correct' by reflecting the nation's historical arts and crafts. The effect of this pronouncement was to limit diversity of ideas about architecture and to promote stylistic conformity and regional homogeneity; it also brought about a revitalization of local crafts, and lent an easily discernible stylistic character to the country's new buildings.
12 Hassan Fathy, a member of the highly educated Egyptian élite, consciously developed an architecture for the common man. His elegant buildings had more impact outside his own country, and perhaps his most important contribution was to make other architects aware of indigenous factors. Fathy's major book *Architecture for the Poor*, Chicago, 1973, and E.F. Schumacher's *Small is Beautiful: Economics as if People Mattered*, London, 1973, both embody ideas of self-reliance and were seen by architects and others as providing answers to the predicament of development in an increasingly materialistic world.

CHAPTER 16

1 Perhaps the best example of the historical approach to the mosque is the article 'Masjid' in the *Encyclopaedia of Islam*, which provides a chronological coverage of the period from the time of the Prophet in Medina until the Ottoman era, with particular emphasis on the functions of the mosque during the classical age. The article originally written by Pedersen for the first edition has not been extended in the second to cover the modern period, nor does it address any of the issues under discussion here.

2 The Qur'an (9:108–9) refers to 'those who have built themselves a mosque for opposition, and unbelief and division among believers, and for a refuge for him who in the past fought against God and the Prophet; and they swear: we intended only good. God is witness that they are liars! Thou shalt not stand up in it for, verily, a mosque which is founded on piety from the first day of its existence has more right that thou shouldest stand in it; in it are men who desire to purify themselves.'

3 Mohammad Al-Asad, 'The Modern State Mosque in the Eastern Arab World, 1828–1923' (doctoral thesis, Harvard University, 1990). I do not agree with the concept of the 'modern state' as defined by the author, and would prefer to use the phase 'contemporary state' because in the Muslim context nation-states established since the 1950s did not integrate or lead their societies towards *intellectual* modernity.

4 A recent and accurate presentation of this complex evaluation is to be found in Olivier Roy, *L'Echec de l'Islam Politique*, Paris, 1992. I have also touched on this issue in my own book *Ouvertures sur l'Islam* (2nd ed., 1992).

5 This is not an appropriate place to elaborate a critical appraisal of modernism, but I feel it necessary to emphasize the fact that I use the term as a general concept in the context of the history of thought as it has been understood in the West since the sixteenth to eighteenth centuries, and the same is ture of post-modernism in the twentieth century. Architectural critics view the two concepts differently, and exclude other aspects relevant to philosophy, theology, literature, painting, music, linguistics, semiotics and ethics, all of which need to be taken into consideration when one considers the metamorphosis of the sacred in traditional, archaic societies as yet uninfluenced by classical modernity, not to mention post-modern trends of recent decades. The different uses of the terms 'modernism', 'modernity' and 'post-modernism' by writers in the fields of archiecture, literature, philosphy, etc. raise the problem of a fragmented way of thinking in the West; this fragmentation has far-reaching adverse effects in conservatively minded societies such as those in the contemporary Muslim world. For more detailed discussion of these issues see my *Ouvertures sur l'Islam* (op. cit.) and *L'Islam, Hier, Demain* (2nd ed., 1982).

6 It is necessary to make a clear distinction between 'Islamism' and 'Islamicist', 'Islam' and 'Islamic', just as we distinguish 'historicist' from 'historical'. The terms 'Islamism' and 'Islamicist' (Arabic, *islamawiyy*) are concerned with the ideological aspects of Islam, with particular reference to political and militant questions, changes in intellectual outlook, the search for meaning and critical reasoning in attempts to conjure up 'values' and 'models' which would have been significant and relevant in the age of 'authentic Islam'. 'Islam' and 'Islamic' continue to be used with reference to concepts and theories (both traditional and modern) associated with Muslim thinkers and scholars, as well as to the beliefs and rituals that are peculiar to Islam as a religion.

7 The term 'post-modern' and its connotations as used in this chapter have an essentially cultural/political significance in relation to Islamic civilization, although the word has been used elsewhere by sociologists and philosophers such as Gellner, Giddens, Lyotard, Baudrillard and Foucault, as well as by writers such as Barthes and architectural critics including Jencks and Portoghesi. Here, the term presupposes questions about the project of modernity and a heightened scepticism concerning traditional orthodoxies, and encourages a spirit of pluralism. In his book *La Condition Postmoderne: Rapport sur le Savoir* (1977), J.-F. Lyotard writes that post-modernism is 'the state of our culture following the transformations which, since the end of the nineteenth century have altered the game rules for science, literature and the arts', while in *Uncommon Cultures: Popular Culture and Post-modernism* (1989) J. Collins notes that it 'allows the juxtaposition of discourses (architectural, psychological, narrative, etc.) . . . as representations of experience', as well as the mixing of diverse ideas in which 'the fragmentation of the modern world may be understood', as D. Harvey states in *The Condition of Postmodernity: An Enquiry into the Origins of Cultural Change* (1989). There is much to be said about this concept, but I cannot engage in such a discussion here without reference to the general history of ideas in several cultures rather than to current practices in the field of architecture taken in isolation. Cf. E. Gellner, *Post-modernism, Reason and Religion*, London, 1992.

8 Representatives of the so-called G7 countries (the seven major industrialized nations: the U.S.A. Canada, the UK, France, Germany, Japan and Italy) hold regular meetings to consider questions relating to economic and financial affairs worldwide, and their decisions can have adverse consequences for the developing countries in terms of their cultural heritage. Such effects are seldom analyzed or taken into account: the stances adopted in the face of the policies of the G7 powers by, for example, Iraq, Iran, Saudi Arabia and Algeria are of particular interest. In all these countries, as well as others, religion has been and is being used, through the introduction of connotations such as 'sacred' or 'ethical', in attempts to combat breakdowns of a social, political and cultural nature which are seen as resulting from economic decisions and strategies adopted by the G7 powers.

BIBLIOGRAPHY

General Works

The *Encyclopaedia of Islam* (1st and 2nd editions) includes important articles on the mosque ('Masjid') and specific related subjects. Other standard works on the architecture of the mosque are:

Atasoy, Nurhan, Bahnassi, Afif, and Rogers, Michael, *The Art of Islam* (Unesco Collection of Representative Works: Art Album Series), Paris, 1990

Brend, Barbara, *Islamic Art*, Cambridge, Mass., 1991

Burckhardt, Titus, *Art of Islam: Language and Meaning*, London, 1976

Creswell, K. A. C., *Early Muslim Architecture* (2 vols.), Oxford, 1932/40 (revised ed., vol. I, Oxford, 1969); reprinted New York, 1978/9

Ettinghausen, Richard, and Grabar, Oleg, *The Art and Architecture of Islam 650–1250*, New York and Harmondsworth, 1987; paperback ed., New Haven, Conn., and London, 1992

Grabar, Oleg, *The Formation of Islamic Art*, New Haven, Conn., and London, 1973; revised ed. 1992

Hillenbrand, R., *Islamic Architecture*, Edinburgh, 1988

Hoag, John, *Islamic Architecture*, New York, 1977

Kuban, Doğan, *Muslim Religious Architecture*, parts I and II, Leiden, 1974/85

Kühnel, E., *Die Moschee: Bedeutung, Einrichtung und kunsthistorische Entwicklung der islamischen Kultstaette*, Berlin, 1949

Michell, George (ed.), *Architecture of the Islamic World*, London and New York, 1978; reprinted 1984, 1991

Papadopoulu, A., *L'Islam et l'art musulman*, Paris, 1976

Prochazka, Amjad Bohumil, *Mosques*, Zurich, 1986

Vogt-Göknil, Ulya, *Mosquées*, Paris, 1975

Chapter 1. Islam and the Form of the Mosque

Ahmad, Chaudhri Rashid, *Mosque: Its Importance in the Life of a Muslim*, London, 1982

Ardalan, Nader, 'An Inventory of the Generic Forms and Typology of Islamic Mosques', *Architecture as Symbol and Self-Identity*, Philadelphia, Pa, 1979;

——, 'The Visual Language of Symbolic Form: A preliminary study of mosque architecture', op. cit., 1980

Asad, Muhammad, *The Message of the Qur'an*, Gibraltar, 1980

Freeman-Grenville, G. S. P., *The Muslim and Christian Calendars*, 2nd ed., London, 1977

Schimmel, Annemarie, *Islam: An Introduction*, New York, 1992

Zakaria, Rafiq, *Muhammad and the Quran*, London, 1991

Chapter 2. The Role of Calligraphy

Begley, W. E., *Monumental Islamic Calligraphy from India*, Villa Park, Ill., 1985

Begley, W. E., and Desai, Z. A., *Taj Mahal: The Illuminated Tomb*. Seattle, Washington, and London, 1989

Blair, Sheila S., *The Ilkhanid Shrine Complex at Natanz, Iran*, Cambridge, Mass., 1985

Dodd, Erica Cruickshank, and Khairallah, Shereen, *The Image of the Word. A Study of Quranic Verses in Islamic Architecture* (2 vols.), Beirut, 1981

Hill, Derek, and Grabar, Oleg, *Islamic Architecture and its Decoration, A.D. 800–1500*, Chicago, 1964

Hutt, Antony, and Harrow, Leonard, *Islamic Architecture: Iran 1*, London, 1977

Islamic Calligraphy (exhibition catalogue), Musée d'Art et d'Histoire, Geneva, 1988

Koran, The (trans. George Sale), London and New York, n.d.

Lentz, Thomas W., and Lowry, Glenn D., *Timur and the Princely Vision: Persian Art and Culture in the Fifteenth Century*. (exhibition catalogue), Los Angeles County Museum of Art and the Arthur M. Sackler Gallery, Smithsonian Institution, Washington, D.C., 1989

Lowry, Glenn D., *A Jeweler's Eye: Islamic Arts of the Book from the Vever Collection*, Washington, D.C., 1988

Naji, Zain un-Din, *Atlas of Arabic Calligraphy*, Baghdad, 1969

Necipoğlu-Kafadar, Gülru, 'The Süleymaniye Complex in Istanbul: An Interpretation', *Muqarnas*, 3 (1985), pp. 92–117

Safadi, Yasin Hamid, *Islamic Calligraphy*, London and New York, 1978

Schimmel, Annemarie, 'The Art of Calligraphy', in R. W. Ferrier (ed.), *The Arts of Persia*, New Haven, Conn., and London, 1989, pp. 306–14;

——, *Islamic Calligraphy*, Leiden, 1970

Sourdel-Thomine, Janine, and Spuler, Bertold, *Die Kunst des Islam*, Berlin, 1973

Thackston, W. M., *A Century of Princes: Sources on Timurid History and Art*, Cambridge, Mass., 1989

Welch, Stuart Cary, *Wonders of the Age: Masterpieces of Early Safavid Painting, 1501–1576* (exhibition catalogue), Fogg Art Museum, Cambridge, Mass., 1979

Williams, Caroline, 'The Cult of 'Alid Saints in the Fatimid Monuments of Cairo. Part I: The Mosque of al-Aqmar', *Muqarnas*, 1 (1983), pp. 37–52; and 'Part II: The Mausolea', *Muqarnas*, 3 (1985), pp. 39–60

Chapter 3. Applications of Geometry

El-Said, I., and Parman, A., *Geometric Concepts in Islamic Art*, London, 1976

Encyclopaedia of Islam (2nd ed.): 'ʿIlm al-Handasa'

Grabar, O., *The Mediation of Ornament*, Princeton, N.J., 1992

Hill, D., and Grabar, O., *Islamic Architecture and its Decoration, A.D. 800–1500*, Chicago, 1964

Jung, C. G. (ed.), *Man and his Symbols*, New York, 1964

Kühnel, E., *Die Arabeske: Sinn und Wandlung eines Ornaments*, Wiesbaden, 1949

Soucek, P. P. (ed), *Content and Context of Visual Arts in the Islamic World*, University Park, Pa, 1988

Chapter 4. Introduction: Regionalism

Powell, R. (ed.), *Regionalism in Architecture* (Proceedings of a seminar held by the Aga Khan Award for Architecture), Singapore, 1985

Serageldin, I., *Space for Freedom. The search for architectural excellence in Muslim societies*, Singapore, 1989

Chapter 5. The Central Arab Lands

Brandenburg, D., *Islamische Baukunst in Ägypten*, Berlin, 1966

Briggs, M. S., *Muhammadan Architecture in Egypt and Palestine*, Oxford, 1924

Brisch, K., 'Observations on the Iconography of the Mosaics in the Great Mosque at Damascus' in P. P. Soucek (ed.), *Content and Context of Visual Arts in the Islamic World* (1988), pp. 13–20

Creswell, K. A. C., *Muslim Architecture of Egypt* (2 vols.), Oxford, 1952/59 (revised ed. 1969); reprinted New York, 1978/79

Esin, E., *Mecca the Blessed, Madinah the Radiant*, London, 1963

Fikry, A., *L'Art islamique en Tunisie. La grande mosquée de Kairouan*, Paris, 1936

Finster, B., 'Die Mosaiken der Umayyademoschee von Damaskus', *Kunst des Orients*, 7 (1970–71), pp. 117ff.

Hamilton, R. W., *The Structural History of the Aqsa Mosque*, Jerusalem, 1947

Hautecoeur, L., and Wiet, G., *Les Mosquées du Caire* (2 vols.), Paris, 1932

Herzfeld, E., *Geschichte der Stadt Samarra*, Hamburg, 1948

Hirsch, S. and M., *L'Architecture au Yemen du Nord*, Paris, 1983

Lambert, E., 'Les Origines de la mosquée et l'architecture religieuse des Omeyyade', *Studia Islamica*, VI (1956), pp. 5–18

Lewcock, R., and Smith, G. R., 'Two Early Mosques in the Yemen: A Preliminary Report', *Art and Archaeology Research Papers*, 4 (1973), pp. 117–30;

——, 'Three Medieval Mosques in the Yemen' (parts I and II), *Oriental Art*, XX/1 and 2 (1974)

Monneret de Villard, U., *Introduzione allo studio dell'archeologia islamica: le origini e il periodo Omeyyade*, Venice/Rome, 1966

Sarre, F., and Herzfeld, E., *Archaeologische Reise im Euphrat- und Tigris-Gebiet*, Berlin, 1912–20

Sauvaget, J., *La Mosquée Omeyyade de Médine*, Paris, 1947;

——, *Les Monuments historiques de Damas*, Beirut, 1932

Sourdel-Thomine, J., 'La mosquée et la madrasa', *Cahiers de Civilisation Mediévale*, XIII/2 (1970), pp. 97–115

Stern, H., 'Les origines de l'architecture de la mosquée Omeyyade', *Syria*, XXVIII (1951), pp. 269–79

Survey of Egypt (for the Egyptian Ministry of Waqfs): *The Mosques of Egypt* (2 vols.), Giza, 1949; revised edition (ed. M. K. Ismail), London, 1992

Varanda, F., *The Art of Building in Yemen*, London, 1982

CHAPTER 6. Spain and North Africa

Caillé, J., *La Mosquée de Hassan à Rabat* (2 vols.), Paris 1954

Ewert, C., and Wisshak, J. P., *Forschungen zur almohadischen Moschee: I Vorstufen; II Die Moschee von Tinmal*, Berlin, 1981/84

Fernández-Puertas, A., *La mezquita de Córdoba* (forthcoming; including a detailed analysis of proportional systems)

Gomez-Moreno, M., 'El arte árabe español hasta los Almohades. Arte mozárabe', *Ars Hispaniae*, III (1951);

——, *Guía de Granada* (2 vols.), Granada, 1982

Hernandez Giménez, F., *El alminar de 'Abd al-Rahman III en la Mezquita Mayor de Córdoba. Génesis y repercusiones*, Granada, 1975;

——, *El codo en la historiografía árabe de la mezquita mayor de Córdoba*, Madrid, 1961

Hill, D., Golvin, L., and Ettinghausen, R., *Islamic Architecture in North Africa*, London, 1976

Hutt, A., *Islamic Architecture: North Africa*, London, 1977

Lehmann, K., 'The dome of Heaven', *The Art Bulletin*, XXVII (1945), pp. 1–27

Marçais, G., *L'Architecture musulmane d'Occident: Tunisie, Algérie, Maroc, Espagne et Sicile*, Paris, 1954

Meunié, J., and Terrasse, H., *Recherches archéologiques à Marrakech*, Paris, 1952

—— and Deverdun, G., *Nouvelles recherches archéologiques à Marrakech*, Paris, 1957

Stern, H., *Les mosaïques de la grande mosquée de Cordoue*, Berlin, 1976

Terrasse, H., *L'Art hispano-mauresque des origines au XIIIe*, Paris, 1932;

——, 'La Mosquée al-Qaraouiyin a Fès', *Archéologie Méditerranéenne*, III (1968)

Torres-Balbas, L., 'La portada de S. Esteban en la mezquita de Córdoba', *Al-Andalus*, XII (1947), pp. 127–44;

——, 'Los alminares de las mezquitas hispanas', *Al-Andalus*, X (1945), pp. 387–92

CHAPTER 7. Iran and Central Asia

Golombek, L., and Wilber, D., *The Timurid Architecture of Iran and Turfan*, Princeton, N.J., 1988

Grabar, Oleg, *The Great Mosque of Isfahan*, New York and London, 1990;

——, 'The Visual Arts' in *Cambridge History of Iran*: vol. IV, *From the Arab Conquest to the Saljuqs* (ed. R. N. Frye), 1974, pp. 331–51; and vol. V, *The Saljuq and Mongol Periods* (ed. J. A. Boyle), 1968, pp. 629–41

Herdeg, K., *Formal Structure in Islamic Architecture of Iran and Turkistan*, New York, 1990

Hillenbrand, R., 'Safavid Architecture' in *Cambridge History of Iran*, vol. VI, *The Timurid and Safavid Periods* (ed. P. Jackson), 1986, pp. 759–842

O'Kane, B., *Timurid Architecture in Khurasan*, Costa Mesa, Cal., 1987

Pope, A. U., and Ackerman, P. (eds.), *A Survey of Persian Art from Prehistoric Times to the Present*, vols. I–VI, London and New York, 1939

Seherr-Thoss, S. P. and H. C., *Design and Color in Islamic Architecture: Afghanistan, Iran, Turkey*, Washington, D.C., 1968

Wilber, D., *The Architecture of Islamic Iran: the Il Khānid Period*, Princeton, N.J., 1955;

——, 'Builders and Craftsmen of Islamic Iran: the Early Period', *Art and Archaeology Research Papers*, 10 (1976)

CHAPTER 8. Anatolia and the Ottoman legacy

Akurgal, E. (ed.), *The Art and Architecture of Turkey*, New York 1980

Arık, Oluş, 'Turkish Architecture in Asia Minor in the Period of the Turkish Emirates' in E. Akurgal (ed.), op. cit., pp. 111–36

Bates, Ölkü, 'Architecture', in E. Atıl (ed.), *Turkish Art*, Washington, D.C.–New York, 1980, pp. 44–136

Erzen, Jale, 'Sinan as Anti-Classicist', *Muqarnas*, 5 (1988), pp. 70–86

Goodwin, Godfrey, *A History of Ottoman Architecture*, London, 1971, and Baltimore, Md, 1979; paperback ed. 1987

Kiel, Machiel, *Studies on the Ottoman Architecture of the Balkans*, 1990

Kuban, Doğan, 'The Style of Sinan's Domed Structures', *Muqarnas*, 4 (1987), pp. 72–98;

——, 'Architecture of the Ottoman Period' in E. Akurgal (ed.), op. cit., pp. 137–69;

——, 'The Mosque and Hospital at Divriği and the Origin of Anatolian Turkish Architecture', *Anatolica*, 2 (1986), pp. 122–30

Kuran, Aptullah, *Sinan, The Grand Old Man of Ottoman Architecture*, Istanbul, 1987;

——, 'Anatolian-Seljuq Architecture', in E. Akurgal (ed.), op. cit., pp. 80–110;

——, *The Mosque in Early Ottoman Architecture*, Chicago, 1968

Müller-Wiener, Wolfgang, *Bildlexikon zur Topographie Istanbuls*, Tübingen, 1977

Necipoğlu-Kafadar, Gülru, 'The Süleymaniye Complex in Istanbul: An Interpretation', *Muqarnas*, 3 (1985), pp. 92–117;

——, 'Plans and Models in 15th- and 16th-century Ottoman Architectural Practice', *Journal of the Society of Architectural Historians*, 45/3 (September 1986), pp. 224–43;

——, 'The Life of an Imperial Monument: Hagia Sophia after Byzantium' in R. Mark and Ahmet Gakmak (eds.), *Hagia Sophia from the Age of Justinian to the Present*, Cambridge, 1992, pp. 195–225

Ögel, Semra, *Der Kuppelraum in der türkischen Architektur*, Istanbul, 1972

Petruccioli, Attilio, 'Mimar Sinan: the Urban Vision', special issue of *Environmental Design*, 1–2 (1987)

Riefstahl, Rudolf, *Turkish Architecture in Southeastern Anatolia*, Cambridge, 1931

Rogers, J. M., 'The Çifte Minare Medrese at Erzurum and the Gök Medrese at Sivas, a Contribution to the History of Style in Seljuk Architecture of 13th Century Turkey', *Anatolian Studies*, 15 (1965), pp. 63–85;

——, 'Recent Work on Seljuq Anatolia', *Kunst des Orients*, 6 (1969), pp. 134–69;

——, 'The State and the Arts in Ottoman Turkey: I. The stones of Süleymaniye', *International Journal of Middle East Studies*, 14 (1982), pp. 71–86; 'II. The furnishing and decoration of Süleymaniye', op. cit., pp. 283–313

Sinclair, T. A., *Eastern Turkey: An Architectural and Archaeological Survey* (3 vols.), London, 1989

Sözen, Metin, *The Evolution of Turkish Art and Architecture*, Istanbul, 1987

Stierlin, Henri, *Soliman et l'architecture ottomane*, Fribourg, 1985

Ünsal, Behçet, *Turkish Islamic Architecture in Seljuq and Ottoman Times (1071–1923)*, London, 1959

Yenişehirlioğlu, Filiz (ed.), *Ottoman Architectural Works Outside Turkey*, Ankara, 1989

Yetkin, Suut Kemal, *Turkish Architecture* (trans. B. Ünsal), Ankara, 1965

CHAPTER 9. The Indian Subcontinent

Abid Ali Khan, M., *Memoirs of Gaur and Pandua*, Calcutta, 1931

Brown, P., *Indian Architecture (Islamic Period)*, Bombay, 1956

Burgess, J., *The Muhammedan Architecture of Ahmedabad* (Architectural Survey of Western India, vol. 7, 1900)

Burgess, J., and Cousens, H., *Mohammedan Architecture in Gujarat*, London, 1896; reprinted, Varanasi, 1971

Cousens, H., *Bijapur and its Architectural Remains*, Bombay, 1916; reprinted, Varanasi, 1976

Dani, A. H., *Muslim Architecture of Bengal*, Dacca 1961;

——, *Thatta: Islamic Architecture*, Islamabad, 1982;

——, *Islamic Architecture: The Wooden Style of Northern Pakistan*, Islamabad, 1989

Davies, P., *Monuments of India*, vol. 2, London, 1989

Grover, S., *The Architecture of India, Islamic*, New Delhi, 1981

Hasan, P., 'Sultanate Mosques and Continuity in Bengal Architecture', *Muqarnas*, 6, 1989

Koch, E., *Mughal Architecture*, Munich, 1991

Latif, S. M., *Lahore: Architectural Remains*, Lahore, 1892; reprinted 1981

Merklinger, E. S., *Indian Islamic Architecture. The Deccan 1347–1686*, Warminster, 1981

Michell, G. (ed.), *The Islamic Heritage of Bengal*, Paris, 1984;

——, *Islamic Heritage of the Deccan*, Bombay, 1986

Mumtaz, K. K., *Architecture in Pakistan*, Singapore, 1985

Nath, R., *Colour and Decoration in Mughal Architecture*, Bombay, 1970;

——, *History of Sultanate Architecture*, New Delhi, 1978

Sharma, Y. D., *Delhi and its Neighbourhood*, New Delhi, 1974

Welch, A., and Crane, H., 'The Tughluqs: Master Builders of the Delhi Sultanate', *Muqarnas*, 1, 1983

CHAPTER 10. Sub-Saharan West Africa

Ba, A. H., and Daget, J. *L'Empire peul du Macina (1818–1853)*, Paris, 1962

Barth, Henry, *Travels and Discoveries in North and Central Africa* (3 vols.), New York, 1857–9

Caillié, René, *Journal d'un voyage à Tembouctou et à Jenne* (4 vols.), Paris, 1830

Cuoq, Joseph M., *Recueil des sources arabes concernant l'Afrique Occidentale du VIIe au XVIe siècle*, Paris, 1975

Dubois, Félix, *Tombouctou la mystérieuse*, Paris, 1987

Ibn Battuta, *Travels in Asia and Africa, 1325–54*, London, 1929

Lapidus, Ira, *A History of Islamic Societies*, Cambridge, 1988

Monteil, Vincent, *L'Islam Noir*, Paris, 1964

Moughtin, J. C., *Hausa Architecture*, London, 1985

Pâcques, Viviana, *L'Arbre cosmique dans la pensée populaire et dans la vie quotidienne du nord-ouest africain*, Paris, 1964

Prussin, Labelle, *Hatumere, Islamic Design in West Africa*, Berkeley, Cal., and London, 1986
Saint-Martin, Yves-J., *L'Empire Toucouleur (1848–1897)*, Paris, 1970

Chapter 11. East Africa

Adams, W. Y., *Nubia, Corridor to Africa*, London and Princeton, N.J., 1977
Aldrick, J., 'The Nineteenth Century Carved Wooden Doors of the East African Coast', *Azania*, 25 (1990), pp. 1–18
Allen, J. de V., 'Swahili Ornament. A study of the decoration of the 18th century plasterwork and carved doors in the Lamu region', in *Art and Archaeology Research Papers* (1973): 3, pp. 1–14; 4, pp. 87–92;
——, 'Swahili Culture Reconsidered', *Azania*, 9 (1974), pp. 105–38;
——, 'Siyu in the eighteenth and nineteenth centuries', *Transafrican Journal of History*, 8 (1979), p. 2;
——, *Swahili Origins. Swahili Culture and the Shungwaya Phenomenon*, London, 1993
Allen, James de Vere, and Wilson, Thomas H., 'Swahili Houses and Tombs of the Coast of Kenya' in *Art and Archaeology Research Papers*, 12 (1979)
Arrowsmith, J. H., *Poutky's Travels to Ethiopia*, London, 1991
Bloss, J., 'The Story of Suakin', *Sudan Notes and Records*, 14 and 20 (1936–7)
Brown, H., 'Siyu: Town of Craftsmen', *Azania*, 23 (1988), pp. 101–14
Cailliaud, M. Frédéric, *Voyage à Meroé . . . à Syouah et dans cinq autres oases 1819–22* (4 volumes) Paris, 1823
Cerulli, E., *Somalia: Scritti Vari Editi ed Inediti* (2 vols.), Rome, 1957
Chittick, H. N., *Annual Reports of the Department of Antiquities*, Dar es Salaam, 1958–64;
——, *Kilwa: an Islamic Trading City on the East African Coast* (2 vols.; British Institute in Eastern Africa, Memoir 5), Nairobi, 1974;
——, 'An Archaeological reconnaissance in the Horn', *Azania*, 11 (1976), pp. 117–34;
——, 'The East Coast, Madagascar and the Indian Ocean' in R. Oliver (ed.), *Cambridge History of Africa*, III, Cambridge, 1977, pp. 183–231;
——, 'Medieval Mogadishu', *Paideuma*, 28 (1982), pp. 45–62
Combe, E., 'Four Inscriptions from the Red Sea', *Sudan Notes and Records*, 13 (1930), pp. 107–18
Crawford, O. G. S., *The Funj Kingdom of Sennar*, Gloucester, 1951;
——, 'Castles and Churches of the Middle Nile Region', Sudan Antiquities Service (occasional paper 2), Khartoum, 1953
Crowfoot, J. W., 'Some Red Sea Ports of the Anglo-Egyptian Sudan', *Geographical Journal*, 37 (1911), pp. 523–50
Curle, A. T., 'The ruined towns of Somaliland', *Antiquity*, 11 (1937), pp. 315–27
Donley, L. 'House Power: Swahili Space and Symbolic Markers' in I. Hodder (ed.), *Symbolic and Structural Archaeology*, Cambridge, 1982
Donley-Reid, L. W., 'A Structuring Structure: the Swahili House' in S. Kent (ed.), *Domestic Architecture and the Use of Space*, Cambridge, 1990, pp. 114–26
Flury, S., 'The Kufic Inscription of Kizimkazi Mosque, Zanzibar, A.D. 1107', *Journal of the Royal Asiatic Society*, 21 (1922), pp. 257–64
Freeman-Grenville, G. S. P., *The East African Coast: Select Documents from the first to the earlier 19th centuries* (2nd ed.), London, 1966
Freeman-Grenville, G. S. P., and Martin, B. G., 'A Preliminary Handlist of the Arabic Inscriptions of the East African Coast', *Journal of the Royal Asiatic Society* (1973/2), pp. 98–104
Garlake, P. S., *The Early Islamic Architecture of the East African Coast* (British Institute in Eastern Africa, Memoir 2), Nairobi, 1966
Ghaidan, U., *Lamu: A Study of Conservation*, Nairobi, 1976
Greenlaw, Jean-Pierre, *The Coral Buildings of Suakin*, Stocksfield, 1976
Holt, P. M., *The Mahdist State in Sudan*, Oxford, 1970
Horton, M. C., 'Early Muslim Trading Settlements on the East African Coast: new evidence from Shanga', *Antiquaries Journal*, LXVII (1987), pt 2, pp. 290–323;
——, 'Primitive Architecture and Islam in East Africa', *Muqarnas*, 8 (1991), pp. 103–16
Hrbek, I., 'Egypt, Nubia and the Eastern Deserts' in R. Oliver (ed.), *Cambridge History of Africa*, III, Cambridge, 1977, pp. 10–96
Inzerillo, M., *Le Moschee di Mogadiscio*, Palermo, 1980
Kirkman, J. S., *Men and Monuments on the East African Coast*, London, 1964
Matthews, D. H., 'The Red Sea Style', *Kush*, 1 (1954)
Middleton, J., *The World of the Swahili*, New Haven, Conn., and London, 1992
Monneret de Villard, U., 'I Minareti di Mogadiscio', *Studi Etiopica*, 3 (1943), pp. 127ff.
Nurse, D., and Spear, T., *The Swahili. Reconstructing the History and Language of an African Society, 800–1500*, Philadelphia, Pa, 1985
Paulitschke, Philipp, *Harar – Forschungsreise nach den Somal- und Galla-Ländern Ost Afrikas*, Leipzig, 1888
Pearce, F. B., *Zanzibar, the Island Metropolis of East Africa*, London, 1920
Pouwels, R. L., *Horn and Crescent: Cultural Change and Traditional Islam on the East African Coast, 800–1900*, Cambridge, 1987
Révoil, C., 'Voyage chez les Benadirs, les Çomalis et les Bayouns, en 1883', *Le Tour du Monde*, 56 (1885–6), pp. 385–414
Schneider, M., *Stèles funéraires musulmanes de îles Dahlak*, Cairo, 1967;
——, 'Stèles funéraires musulmanes de la région du Quiha', *Annales d'Ethiopie* (1983), pp. 107–18
Shinnie, P. L., 'Old Dongola Church', *Kush*, 3 (1956;
——, 'Christian Nubia' in J. D. Fage (ed.), *Cambridge History of Africa*, II, Cambridge, 1978, pp. 556–88
Siravo, F., and Pulver, A., *Planniong Lamu*, Nairobi, 1986
Stigand, C. H., *The Land of Zinj*, London, 1913
Strandes, J., *The Portuguese Period in East Africa* (2nd English edition, ed. J. Kirkman), Nairobi, 1971
Tamrat, T., 'Ethiopia, the Red Sea and the Horn' in R. Oliver (ed.), *Cambridge History of Africa*, III, Cambridge, 1977, pp. 98–177
Trimingham, J. S., *Islam in the Sudan*, London, 1949;
——, *Islam in Ethiopia*, London, 1952;
——, *Islam in East Africa*, London, 1964
Vantini, G., *Oriental Sources Concerning Nubia* (Field Manual for the Society for Nubian Studies), Heidelberg and Warsaw, 1975
Wilding, R. F., 'Harari Domestic Architecture', *Art and Archaeology Research Papers*, 9 (1976), pp. 31–7
Wilson, T. H., *The Monumental Architecture and Archaeology North of the Tana River*, Nairobi, 1978;
——, *The Monumental Architecture and Archaeology of the Central and Southern Kenyan Coast*, Nairobi, 1980
Zein, A. H. M. el-, *The Sacred Meadows: A Structural Analysis of Religious Symbolism in an East African Town*, Evanston, Ill., 1974

Chapter 12. China

Chinese Academy of Architecture: *Classical Chinese Architecture*, Hong Kong, 1986
'Mosques of Northern China: Beijing, Xi'an, Turfan and Kashi', *Mimar*, 3 (1982), pp. 58–73
Sickman, Laurence, and Soper, Alexander, *The Art and Architecture of China*, revised ed., Harmondsworth 1968; paperback ed., New Haven, Conn., and London, 1992

Chapter 13. South-East Asia

Abdurrachman, Paramita R. (ed.), *Cerbon*, Jakarta, 1982
Bernet-Kempers, A. J., *Ancient Indonesian Art*, Amsterdam, 1954
Bosch, F. D. K., *The Golden Germ*, The Hague, 1960
Coedes, G., *The Indianised States of Southeast Asia*, Canberra, 1975
Hall, D. G. E., *A History of Southeast Asia*, London, 1958
Heuken, Adolf, *Historical Sites of Jakarta*, Jakarta, 1982
Hooker, M. B., 'The translation of Islam into South-East Asia' in M. B. Hooker (ed.), *Islam in Southeast Asia*, Leiden, 1983
Jessup, Helen Ibbitson, *Court Arts of Indonesia*, New York, 1990
Nasir, Abdul Halim, *Mosques of Peninsular Malaysia*, Kuala Lumpur, 1984
Pijper, G. F., 'The minaret in Java', in F. D. K. Bosch *et al.* (eds.), *India Antiqua. A volume of oriental studies*, Leiden, 1947
Prijotomo, Josef, *Ideas and forms of Javanese architecture*, Yogyakarta, 1984
Raffles, Thomas Stamford, *The History of Java* (2 vols.), London, 1817; reprinted Kuala Lumpur, 1958
Rassers, W. H., *Panji, the culture hero. A structural study of religion in Java*, The Hague, 1959
Ricklefs, M. C., *A History of Modern Indonesia*, London, 1981
Stutterheim, W. F., *Oudheidkundig Verslag over 1940*, Batavia, 1941
Sumintardja, Djauhari, *Kompendium sejarah arsitektur*, Bandung, 1978

Chapter 15. An Overview of Contemporary Mosques & Design Directions

Al-Asad, Mohammad, *The Modern State Mosque in the Eastern Arab World, 1828–1985*, doctoral dissertation, Harvard University, 1990
Diba, Kamran, *Kamran Diba. Buildings and Projects*, Stuttgart, 1981
Effendi, M. Prasetiyo, *The Development of Mosques in Indonesia*, Bandung, 1990
Khan, Hasan-Uddin, 'Présence Musulmane à Rome', *Connaisance des Arts*, 483, Paris, May 1992
Imamuddin, Abu, Shamim Ara Hassan, Debashir Sarkar, 'Community Mosque – A Symbol of Society' in R. Powell (ed.), *Regionalism in Architecture* (Proceedings of a seminar held by the Aga Khan Award for Architecture), Singapore, 1985;
——, 'The Mosque Architecture of El-Wakil', *Albenaa*, 34, vol. 6, Riyadh, April–May 1987

CHAPTER 16. The Metamorphosis of the Sacred

Ahmed, Akbar S., *Postmodernism and Islam: Predicament and Promise*, London and New York, 1992;
——, *Discovering Islam: Making Sense of Muslim History and Society*, London, 1988
Arkoun, Mohammed, *Ouvertures sur l'Islam*, Paris, 1989; 2nd ed. 1992
——, *Pour une critique de la raison islamique*, Paris, 1984;
——, *L'Islam: morale et politique*, Paris, 1986;
——, *Arab Thought*, New Delhi, 1988
Barthes, Roland, *Barthes: Second Writings* (edited and with an introduction by Susan Sontag), London, 1989
Eagleton, Terry, *Ideology: An Introduction*, London, 1991
Gottdiener, M., and Lagopoulos, A. (eds.), *The City and the Sign: An Introduction to Urban Semiotics*, New York, 1986
Foster, H. (ed.), *Postmodern Culture*, London, 1985
Giddens, Anthony, *Modernity and Self-Identity: Self and Society in the Late Modern Age*, Cambridge, 1991
Lash, Scott, *Sociology of Postmodernism*, London, 1990
Nasr, Seyyed Hossein, *Knowledge and the Sacred*, Edinburgh, 1981
Tibi, Bassam, *The Crisis of Modern Islam: A Preindustrial Culture in the Scientific-Technological Age*, Salt Lake City, Utah, 1988
Watt, W. M., *The Formative Period of Islamic Thought*, Edinburgh, 1973

GLOSSARY

The terms defined below will be found in more than one chapter of this book. Other specialized words and phrases occurring only rarely are defined in the relevant textual context.

adhan – the daily call to prayer, delivered by the muezzin
badgir – wind-tower
bismillah – 'In the name of Allah, the Merciful, the Compassionate', formula used especially at the head of each chapter of the Qur'an
chahar-bagh – a structure in which four arches support a dome
chhajja – eaves of a roof
chhatri – miniature pavilion or kiosk
dikka – raised platform from which the words and actions of the *imam* are relayed to members of a congregation
hadith – a saying or action traditionally attributed to the Prophet Muhammad
hajj – pilgrimage to Mecca
haram – sanctuary within a mosque
hijra – the departure and journey of the Prophet Muhammad and his followers from Mecca to Medina in AD 622, thus marking the beginning of the Muslim Era
imam – leader; any adult male who leads prayers during congregational worship in a mosque
iwan – a chamber that is roofed or vaulted and open on one side (e.g. facing on to the courtyard of a mosque)
jami – congregation (see also *masjid-i jami*)
jihad – holy war
khanaquah – convent or monastery
khutba – oration delivered to the congregation at midday prayers each Friday
kiswa – the traditional covering of black cloth, renewed annually, on the Ka'ba, Mecca
külliye – complex of buildings associated with a mosque, including those used for medical, teaching and charitable purposes
kursi – a lectern, especially a stand used for a Qur'an
madrasa – literally, 'place of study'; a school of theology and law associated with a mosque
maidan – a large open space for ceremonial use
maqsura – an enclosed loge in a mosque (formerly used by rulers and dignitaries for privacy and self-protection)
masjid – a district or neighbourhood mosque
masjid-i jami – a congregational mosque or principal mosque
masjid-i juma – a Friday Mosque
mihrab – the recess or niche in a mosque indicating the direction of Mecca (*qibla*)
minaret – tower from which the *adhan* is delivered by the muezzin
minbar – pulpit in a mosque, used for the delivery of the *khutba*
muezzin – the official (Arabic, *mu'adhdhin*) at a mosque who delivers the *adhan* five time daily
muqarnas – ornamental vaulting composed of small concave elements, often employed to fill the zone of transition between supporting walls and a dome
musalla – an open-air place for communal prayer
namaz – prayer
pishtaq – a monumental portal forming the open side of an *iwan*
qibla – the direction of prayer towards Mecca, indicated by the presence of the *mihrab* set in the wall of a mosque
qubba – dome; the term is sometimes also applied to a mausoleum
riwaq – portico, a covered area usually along one side of a mosque courtyard (*sahn*)
sahn – courtyard of a mosque
shahada – the Muslim creed: 'There is no God but the God and Muhammad is his Messenger.'
sharia – the law of Islam
sunna – the custom of the Prophet; the majority Sunni sect within Islam derives its name from this word
sura – a chapter in the Qur'an
ulama – learned theologians and jurists qualified to interpret scripture and lay down rules of conduct for the faithful
umma – the Muslim community as a whole
waqf – a charitable endowment
zakat – alms; a tax to help the poor
ziyada – an enclosure around, or an extension of a mosque

The table opposite lists a selection of events relating to the history and spread of Islam, together with lists of major religious buildings, both Muslim and Christian (the comparative chronology is approximate due to the long construction periods of many medieval buildings).

AD	AH			
AD 600				Hagia Sophia, Constantinople (532–7)
	1 AH			
		Hijra (622); beginning of the Muslim Era		
		Death of the Prophet Muhammad (632)		
		Arab forces conquer Iraq, Syria, Egypt	Masjid al-Haram, Mecca	Baptistery of St John, Poitiers
			Dome of the Rock, Jerusalem	
700	100	Arab armies invade Spain; Al-Andalus established	Great Mosque, Damascus	
		Battle of Poitiers (732); Muslim advance halted	Al-Aqsa, Jerusalem, rebuilt	
		Abbasid capital founded in Baghdad	Great Mosque, Cordoba, begun	
800				Chapel of Charlemagne, Aachen
	200			
		Abbasid caliphs subject to Seljuq suzerainty	Great Mosque, Qairawan	
			Great Mosque, Samarra	
			Mosque of Ibn Tulun, Cairo	
900	300			
			Mosque on Niu Jie, Beijing	
			Mosque of al-Azhar, Cairo	
			Mosque of al-Hakim, Cairo	
1000	400			S. Miniato, Florence
		Persia conquered by Seljuq Turks	Great Mosque, Seville	St Mark's, Venice
				Pisa Cathedral
		First Crusade (1095)	Kalyan Mosque, Bukhara	Canterbury Cathedral
1100	500			Worms Cathedral
		Second Crusade (1144)	Great Mosque, Tlemcen	S. Ambrogio, Milan
			Kutubiyya, Marrakesh	Notre Dame, Paris
			Great Mosque, Kilwa, begun	Wells Cathedral
		Third Crusade (1189–92)	Quwwat al-Islam, Delhi	Chartres Cathedral
1200	600	Fourth Crusade (1204)		Rheims Cathedral
			Mosque of Ala ad-Din, Konya	The Sainte-Chapelle, Paris
			Mosque-hospital, Divriği	Cologne Cathedral
		Mongol invasion of Asia Minor; Baghdad sacked		Strasbourg Cathedral
		Christian states in Nubia ousted by Arab invaders	Mosque of Sultan Baybars, Cairo	Florence Cathedral
1300	700			
			Sultan Hasan Mosque, Cairo	Gloucester Cathedral
			DjinguereBer Mosque, Timbuktu	Milan Cathedral
1400	800	Sack of Delhi by Timur	Friday Mosque, Samarqand	
			Great Mosque, Xian	Pazzi Chapel, Florence
			Friday Mosque, Ahmadabad	Santo Spirito, Florence
		Capture of Constantionople by Ottoman forces		King's College Chapel, Cambridge
			Fatih Cami, Istanbul	Sta Maria Novella, Florence
1500	900	Granada falls to Christian armies (1492)	Masjid Agung, Demak	Sistine Chapel, Rome
				Westminster Abbey, London
		First siege of Vienna	Süleymaniye complex, Istanbul	St Peter's Basilica, Rome
		Battle of Panipat; Mughal Empire established	Selimiye Mosque, Edirne	S. Giorgio, Venice
		Battle of Lepanto: Turkish naval supremacy ended	Friday Mosque, Fatehpur Sikri	
			Al-Bakiriyya Mosque, San'a	
1600	1000			
			Masjid-i Shah, Isfahan	Sta Maria della Salute, Venice
			Friday Mosque, Delhi	
1700	1100	Second siege of Vienna	Badshahi Mosque, Lahore	St Paul's Cathedral, London
				St Martin's-in-the-Fields, London
				Karlskirche, Vienna
		Nadir Shah captures Delhi	Masjid Agung, Yogyakarta	Vierzehnheiligenkirche, Bamberg
			Amin Mosque, Turfan	St Sulpice, Paris
1800	1200	Napoleon's campaign in Egypt		
		Colonial expansion by European powers in the Middle East, Africa and South-East Asia	Friday Mosque, Zaria	
		British Raj established in India	Mosque of Muhammad Ali, Cairo	La Madeleine, Paris
		Suez Canal opened	Masjid Agung, Surakarta	St Patrick's Cathedral, New York
1900	1300	British occupation of Egypt and the Sudan		Unity Temple, Oak Park, Illinois
			Great Mosque, Djenne	
		Demise of the Ottoman Empire; Turkish Republic established		
			New Gourna, near Luxor	Notre-Dame-du-Haut, Ronchamp
		Partition of India (1947)	Sherefuddin Mosque, Visoko	Brasilia Cathedral
2000	1400	Former colonies gain political independence	Islamic Centre Mosque, Rome	

SOURCES OF ILLUSTRATIONS

Illustrations are identified by page numbers. The following abbreviations have been used: *a* above, *b* below, *c* centre, *l* left, *r* right.

PHOTOGRAPHIC CREDITS

Aga Khan Program, Fine Arts Library, Harvard University: (photo Fogg Fine Arts Films) 68*b*, (photo Doğan Kuban) 146
Aga Khan Program, Visual Archives, MIT: (photo J. Bloom & S. Blair, 1984) 34, 130*al*, 139 (photo Michael Brand, 1982) 52*cl*, (photo Walter Denny, 1984) 37*a*, 67*a*, (photo William Gilchrist, 1981) 202*b*, (photo Mark Horton, 1981) 25*al*, 190*a&bl&br*, 191*a*, (photo Tunney Lee, 1981) 216*a*, (photo A. Mulla, 1981) 204*a*, (photo Labelle Prussin, 1983) 180, 187*b*, 189, 191*b*, 192*al&cr*, (photo Cherie Wendelken, 1984) 26*br*, 213*br*, 218*a*, 220, (photo J. Westcott) 227*b*, 231*a*, (photo Zhu You-Xuan, 1984) 221
The Aga Khan Trust for Culture, Geneva 45, 75, 82*ar*, 98*l*, 172*b*, 264*a*, 265, (photo Kamran Adle) 192*ar*, 255*b*, 257*a&b*, 261, (photo E.M. Balcioğlu) 201*al&ar&c&bl&br*, (photo J. Bétant, 1986) 52*a*, 251, 258*ar*, 259*cl&cr*, (photo Christopher Little) 25*br*, 127*a*, 136*br*, 215*a&br*, (photo Garry Otte) 265, (photo Suha Özkan) 52*bl*, 134*bl&br*, 135*a*, (photo Rahman Ram) 61*a*, (photo I.C. Stewart) 259*br*, 263*ar*
Courtesy Altug, Behruz & Can Cinçi 263*b*
Al Araby Magazine 16
Mohammad Al-Asad 57
Courtesy R. Badran 249, 258*cl&cr*
Cradoc Baghaw, courtesy Dar al Islam Foundations 250*c*
Carla de Benedetti 255*a*
Roloff Beny 27, 61*b*, 125, 130*ar*, 131, 132*ar&bl*, 133
BOAC Photography 266*b*
Emmanuel Boudot-Lamotte 59, 156*a*
Museum of Islamic Art, Cairo 42
A. Costa 118
Direction Générale des Antiquités et des Musées, Damascus 91*b*
David Collection, Copenhagen 48*a*
Murlidhar Dawani 175
Documentation Française Photothèque, Paris 184*b*
Courtesy Abdel-Wahed El-Wakil 256
Helen Espir 136*bl*, 214*b*
Paolo Favoli 50*a*, 81*a&b*,
Martin Frishman 22*ar*, 23*al&ar&bl&bc&br*, 24*al&ar&bl&bc*, 25*ac&ar*, 28*bl&br*, 31*ar&br*, 51*a*, 62*a&b*, 67*b*, 68*a*, 74, 84*a&b*, 85*a&bl*, 88, 100, 105*cl&br*, 106*bl&br*, 108*a*, 145*b*, 146*al&bl*, 163, 166*a&bc*, 168*bl*, 177, 179*a*
Georgetown Design Group, Washington, D.C. Photo Wahbi al-Hariri Rifai 82*a*, 85*br*, 134*al*, 168*br*, 214*a*, 215*bl*, 216*bl*, 229*a&bl*
Courtesy Sir Frederick Gibberd and Partners 253*l*
R. Günay 259*a*
Courtesy Gulzar Haider 250*a*
Sonia Halliday 35, 145*a*
David Harris, Jerusalem 79
The John Hillelson Agency Ltd. Photo Roland and Sabrina Michaud 21, 22*al*, 49, 130*b*
Hirmer 154
Mark Horton 194, 200
A.F. Kersting 36, 38, 40, 54, 76, 90, 93, 151, 158, 162*r*, 165, 166*bl*
Hasan Uddin-Khan 22*b*, 24*br*, 25*bl&bc*, 31*al&bl*, 33*b*, 51*bl*, 52*br*, 63, 64*ar&b*, 105*al&ar*, 124, 135*b*, 136*a*, 215*cr*, 229*cl*, 243, 245*a&b*, 246, 258*b*, 264*b*
M.N. Khan 232*ar&b*
Courtesy Azhar Loghman 250*b*
Luo Xiaowei 208, 213*al&ar&bl*, 216*br*, 219*a*
London: Conway Library, Courtauld Institute of Art, University of London 46, 96*l*; India Office Library and Records 58
Courtesy M. Makiya 270
Pascal Maréchaux 86*a&b*
Photo Copyright © Antonio Martinelli 166*br*, 202*a*, 203*r*, 252*a*, 260
Mas, Barcelona 103, 110, 112, 115
Victoria Meinecke-Berg 247
Courtesy *Mimar* 258*al*
K. Mims 253*r*
Courtesy Adhi Moersild, Atelier Enam 264*a*
The Metropolitan Museum of Art, New York, Rogers Fund 1910 37*b*
Bernard O'Kane 26*a&bl*, 50*b*, 82*b*, 83, 87*a&cl&cr&b*, 105*bl*, 106*a*, 107, 132*al*, 121, 122, 147, 148, 167, 178*b*, 262*a*
Hugh O'Neill 224, 227*a*, 229*bc&br*, 230*a&bl&br*, 231*b*, 232*al*, 233*b*, 235*a*, 237–40
Suha Özkan 266*a*
Courtesy Department of Archaeology, Government of Pakistan 173*a*, 174*a*
Courtesy D. Pamir 259*bl*, 263*al*
Paris: Bibliothèque Nationale de France 2; Musée du Louvre 48*b*
Antonello Perissinotto, Padua 140, 157
Josephine Powell 19, 28*a*, 51*br*, 69, 108*b*, 116, 129*a&b*, 132*cr&br*, 138
Labelle Prussin 186, 191*cl&cr*, 192*cl&bl&br*
Samina Quraeshi 168*a*
Ismail Serageldin 73
Ray Silverman 204*bl&br*
T'oung Paa Archives 217*a*
Turkish Tourist Board, Paris 150
E. Widmer, Zurich 39, 143*a*, 152*b*, 156*b*
Yan 44

Sketches by Martin Frishman 13, 33*a*. Maps drawn by Robert Thorn. With the exception of the items noted below, plans and elevations were drawn by Peter Bridgewater, John Kaine, Garry Martin and Christopher Woodward, or supplied by individual contributors to this volume; those appearing in chapter 15 are reproduced by courtesy of the architects.

After K.A.C. Creswell, *Early Muslim Architecture* (Oxford, 1932/40) 32
After M. Prasetiyo Effendi, *The Development of Mosques in Indonesia* (Bandung, 1990) 233*l*, 234*al&b*, 235*b*, 236
After J. Lassner, *The Topography of Baghdad in the Early Middle Ages* (Detroit, 1970) 92
After G. Marçais, *L'Architecture Musulmane d'Occident* (Paris, 1954) 66.

INDEX

Individual mosques are listed under place names; each one is identified by its name or usual description, e.g. Friday Mosque/Great Mosque, as appropriate. Page numbers printed in italics refer to illustrations.